The European Company

The European company ('SE') is a new legal entity offering a European perspective for businesses, which became a reality on 8 October 2004. Its purpose is to allow businesses that wish to extend their activities beyond their home Member State to operate througout the European Union on the basis of a single set of rules and a unified (one-tier or two-tier) management system. This book explains how to set up and organise a European company and sets out the text of the relevant EC instruments (a regulation and a directive) that serve as its legal basis as well as the national implementing legislation.

The Regulation gives Member States 66 different options and contains 31 references to national law. It is therefore essential for businesses and their advisers to understand the implementing legislation of the relevant Member States in deciding where to establish an SE. This book provides comprehensive coverage of such legislation in all Member States of the European Economic Area which have, as at 1 July 2005, implemented the Regulation containing the SE Statutes and the Directive on employee involvement in the SE. A second volume, covering further Member States once they have brought the legislation into force, will follow.

Divided into two sections, the book first offers a critical review of the usefulness of, and the opportunities presented by, this new vehicle, analyses the Regulation and the Directive, and gives an overview of the tax aspects of the SE. The second section contains chapters on the laws of each Member State, each conforming to a common format and contributed by a practitioner from that state.

DIRK VAN GERVEN is a partner at NautaDutilh Brussels and a member of the Brussels and New York Bars. He has extensive experience in all areas of corporate law, including litigation, international arbitration, securities regulation and finance. He is head of continuing legal education for the Dutch-speaking Bar of Brussels, a research fellow at the University of Leuven, and has published widely in the fields of corporate and financial law. Since 2003 he has been a member of the Supervisory Board of Belgium's Banking, Finance and Insurance Commission.

PAUL STORM is a retired partner of NautaDutilh and an emeritus professor of law at Universiteit Nyenrode. Until 2005, he was chair of the Combined Committee on Company Law of the Royal Dutch Notarial Society and the Netherlands Bar Association. He is co-author of one of the leading Dutch textbooks on business organisations.

Law Practitioner Series

The *Law Practitioner Series* offers practical guidance in corporate and commercial law for the practitioner. It offers high-quality comment and analysis rather than simply restating the legislation, providing a critical framework as well as exploring the fundamental concepts which shape the law. Books in the series cover carefully chosen subjects of direct relevance and use to the practitioner.

The series will appeal to experienced specialists in each field, but is also accessible to more junior practitioners looking to develop their understanding of particular fields of practice.

The Consultant Editors and Editorial Board have outstanding expertise in the UK corporate and commercial arena, ensuring academic rigour with a practical approach.

Consultant editors
Charles Allen-Jones, retired senior partner of Linklaters
Mr Justice David Richards, Judge of the High Court of Justice, Chancery Division

Editors
Chris Ashworth – Ashurst Morris Crisp
Professor Eilis Ferran – University of Cambridge
Nick Gibbon – Allen & Overy
Stephen Hancock – Herbert Smith
Judith Hanratty – BP Corporate Lawyer, retired
Keith Hyman – Clifford Chance
Keith Johnston – Addleshaw Goddard
Vanessa Knapp – Freshfields
Charles Mayo – Simmons & Simmons
Andrew Peck – Linklaters
Richard Snowden QC – Erskine Chambers
Richard Sykes QC
William Underhill – Slaughter & May
Sandra Walker – Rio Tinto

Other books in the series

Stamp Duty Land Tax
Michael Thomas, with contributions from KPMG Stamp Taxes Group; Consultant Editor David Goy QC
0521606322

Accounting Principles for Lawyers
Peter Holgate
0521606322

The European Company

VOLUME I

General Editors

DIRK VAN GERVEN
PAUL STORM

CAMBRIDGE UNIVERSITY PRESS

CAMBRIDGE UNIVERSITY PRESS
Cambridge, New York, Melbourne, Madrid, Cape Town, Singapore, São Paulo

Cambridge University Press
The Edinburgh Building, Cambridge CB2 2RU, UK

Published in the United States of America by Cambridge University Press, New York

www.cambridge.org
Information on this title: www.cambridge.org/9780521859745

© Cambridge University Press 2006

This publication is in copyright. Subject to statutory exception
and to the provisions of relevant collective licensing agreements,
no reproduction of any part may take place without
the written permission of Cambridge University Press.

First published 2006

Printed in the United Kingdom at the University Press, Cambridge

A catalogue record for this publication is available from the British Library

ISBN-13 978-0-521-85974-5 hardback
ISBN-10 0-521-85974-3 hardback

Cambridge University Press has no responsibility for the persistence or accuracy of URLs for external or third-party internet websites referred to in this publication, and does not guarantee that any content on such websites is, or will remain, accurate or appropriate.

Contents

Contributors ix
Preface xi
DIRK VAN GERVEN, *NautaDutilh*

Part I The European legal framework

1. The Societas Europaea: a new opportunity?   3
   PAUL STORM, *NautaDutilh*

2. Provisions of Community law applicable to the Societas Europaea   25
   DIRK VAN GERVEN, *NautaDutilh*

3. European involvement: rights and obligations   77
   PHILIPPE FRANÇOIS AND JULIEN HICK, *NautaDutilh*

4. International tax aspects of the Societas Europaea   98
   RODERIK BOUWMAN AND JAN WERBROUCK, *NautaDutilh*

Part II Application in each Member State

National reports for EU Member States

5. Austria   119
   ANDREAS HABLE AND HORST LUKANEC, *Binder Grösswang Rechtsanwälte*

6. Belgium   146
   DIRK VAN GERVEN AND ELKE JANSSENS, *NautaDutilh*

7. Denmark   174
   VAGN THORUP, NIKOLAJ HANSEN, CLAUS JUEL HANSEN AND ARNE OTTOSEN, *Kromann Reumert*

8. Finland   203
   BERNDT HEIKEL AND JOHAN NYBERGH, *Hannes Snellman*

Contents

9   Germany   237
WILHELM HAARMANN AND CLEMENS PHILIPP SCHINDLER, *Haarmann Hemmelrath*

10   The Netherlands   263
MARIANNE DE WAARD, FRITS OLDENBURG AND PAUL STORM, *NautaDutilh*

11   Estonia   299
SVEN PAPP AND MAARJA OVIIR-NEIVELT, *Raidla & Partners*

12   Hungary   331
JACQUES DE SERVIGNY, *Gide Loyrette Nouel*

13   Lithuania   346
ZILVINAS KVIETKUS, MINDAUGAS CIVILKA, *Norcous & Partners*

14   Poland   369
AGNIESZKA SZYDLIK, JACEK BONDAREWSKI, MAGDALENA MOCZULSKA, MALGORZATA KOZAK, MICHAL BERNAT AND MORVAN LE BERRE, *Wardynski & Partners*

15   Slovak Republic   397
KATARINA ČECHOVÁ AND MICHAELA JURKOVÁ *Čechová Rakovsky*

16   Sweden   425
KLAES EDHALL, ANNE RUTBERG, HELENA REMPLER, ANNIKA ANDERSSON, ANNA-KARIN LILJEHOLM AND KERSTIN KAMP-WIGFORSS, *Mannheimer Swartling*

17   United Kingdom   456
NIGEL BOARDMAN, *Slaughter and May*

National reports for EEA Member States

18   Iceland   487
THORUNN GUDMUNDSDOTTIR, *Thorunn Gudmundsdottir Lex Law Office*

Annexes

Annex Ia   Council Regulation (EC) No 2157/2001 of
8 October 2001 on the Statute for a European Company (SE)   509

Annex Ib   Public limited-liability companies referred to in
Article 2(1) of the Regulation   527

Annex Ic   Public and private limited-liability companies
referred to on Article 2(2) of the Regulation   530

Annex II   Council Directive 2001/86/EC of 8 October
2001 supplementing the Statute for a European company
with regard to the involvement of employees   533

Annex III   List of national laws implementing the
Regulation and the Directive   547

Index   551

Contributors

AUSTRIA
Andreas Hable
Horst Lukanec
Binder Grösswang Rechtsanwälte

BELGIUM
Dirk Van Gerven
Philippe François
Elke Janssens
Jan Werbrouck
Julien Hick
NautaDutilh

DENMARK
Vagn Thorup
Nikolaj Hansen
Claus Juel Hansen
Arne Ottosen
Kromann Reumert

FINLAND
Berndt Heikel
Johan Nybergh
Hannes Snellman

GERMANY
Wilhelm Haarmann
Clemens Philipp Schindler
Haarmann Hemmelrath

THE NETHERLANDS
Marianne de Waard
Frits Oldenburg
Paul Storm
Roderik Bouwman
NautaDutilh

ESTONIA
Sven Papp
Maarja Oviir-Neivelt
Raidla & Partners

HUNGARY
Jacques de Servigny
Gide Loyrette Nouel

LITHUANIA
Zilvinas Kvietkus
Mindaugas Civilka
Norcous & Partners

POLAND
Agnieszka Szydlik
Jacek Bondarewski
Magdalena Moczulska
Malgorzata Kozak
Michal Bernat
Morvan Le Berre
Wardynski & Partners

SLOVAK REPUBLIC
Katarina Čechová
Michaela Jurková
Čechová Rakovsky

SWEDEN
Klaes Edhall
Anne Rutberg
Helena Rempler
Annika Andersson
Anna-Karin Liljeholm
Kerstin Kamp-Wigforss
Mannheimer Swartling

Contributors

UNITED KINGDOM
Nigel P. G. Boardman
Slaughter and May

ICELAND
Thorunn Gudmundsdottir
Thorunn Gudmundsdottir Lex Law Office

Preface

The European company or *Societas Europaea* ('SE') has become a reality. Since 8 October 2004, it has been possible in at least some Member States of the European Union and the European Economic Area (i.e., Iceland, Norway and Liechtenstein) to incorporate an SE. Regardless of where it is formed, and keeping in mind that some countries have yet to adapt their national legislation accordingly, the SE can operate throughout the European Union and beyond like any other company.

The SE is not the first legal entity to be introduced under Community law. In 1985, the European economic interest grouping ('EEIG') was launched. However, the unlimited and joint liability of its members, the rigidity of its management structure, and its transparency for tax purposes makes the EEIG less attractive. Last but not least, the similarity of the EEIG's name to that of the relatively unknown economic interest grouping (a specific type of legal entity under French law) has caused some national companies to shy away from this corporate form. The SE differs from the EEIG in these fundamental respects.

The SE is a company and, therefore, is in essence no different from national corporate forms. Several larger corporate groups are currently examining the possibility of creating an SE by merging some of their holding companies. Complicated employee involvement rules may be burdensome but should not prove an obstacle to the creation of an SE, as most European managers are used to dealing with employee representation issues.

Several business leaders have expressed interest in setting up an SE and practice indicates that companies throughout Europe are interested in doing so. An explanatory book is therefore a useful tool. This book provides an overview of the legal rules applicable to the SE. The first part explains the legal framework contained in the SE Regulation and the Directive supplementing the Regulation with regard to employee involvement. The second part focuses on the rules applicable to the incorporation and management of an SE in specific Member States with reports from all countries that have implemented both the Regulation and the Directive thus far (with the exception of Norway and Latvia). Volume two will cover those countries which have yet to adapt their national laws but plan to do so in the near future.

Preface

Finally, I wish to thank the contributors to this book from law firms throughout Europe, all of whom are very well positioned to discuss the rules applicable in their countries. I also wish to thank those whose names are not mentioned in the reports but whose work was essential for the success of this project, namely Katherine Raab (who carefully edited most reports), Nele de Wilde, Eva Coudyzer, Bianca Porcelli, Steven Hippe, Reem Fakhreddine Mohamed and Sandra Dixon, all of whom work at NautaDutilh.

Dirk Van Gerven
Brussels, 29 July 2005

PART I
The European legal framework

1
The Societas Europaea: a new opportunity?

PAUL STORM
NautaDutilh

I	Introduction 3	
II	The concept of the SE and shortcomings of national laws	3
	1 Cross-border mobility under national law 4	
	2 Summary 6	
III	Can the SE make up for these shortcomings? 7	
	1 Cross-border mergers 7	
	2 Transfer of an SE's registered office 11	
	3 Indirect transfer of seat 13	
	4 Summary 13	
IV	What are you in for when you have an SE? 14	
V	Employee involvement 16	
	1 Introduction 16	
	2 Background 16	
	3 Can employee participation be avoided? 18	
VI	Conclusion 24	

I   Introduction

You have just started reading a book on a subject which, for around 35 years, was largely academic, as could even be seen from its Latin name: the *Societas Europaea*. Now it is no longer academic, but will it be a real opportunity for *you*? Let me give you my answer to this question upfront: it may be, depending on your requirements and your willingness to pay a price in the form of a considerable degree of legal uncertainty.

II   The concept of the SE and shortcomings of national laws

It also depends on your expectations. If these are the same as those of the initial drafters of the Statute for a European Company, you will certainly be disappointed. The original concept of the SE was a truly European company governed by a single set of rules, irrespective of where its seat[1] was located, and having the freedom to move from one EU Member State to another without being

---

[1]   The concepts of 'seat', 'registered office' and/or 'head office', denoting the place where a company is registered or from where it conducts its business, differ widely from one country to

3

bothered by the traditional obstacles faced by companies subject to national law. I will come back to the issue of a single set of rules later. But first, I will focus on the principal benefit expected from the SE: cross-border mobility. In order to assess the value of this benefit, it is appropriate to begin by considering the situation where there was no SE.

1 Cross-border mobility under national law

On several occasions, businesspeople have expressed regret that there was no EU-wide corporate form available for a *cross-border restructuring by way of merger*. Consider a scenario in which there are two companies of similar size and economic importance, each located in a different Member State, whose businesses are already more or less integrated. They could, however, be managed more efficiently and raise capital more easily if they were a single company. So far, these types of companies have had to use rather complicated dual structures, such as those of Unilever, Royal Dutch/Shell, Reed Elsevier, Fortis, Rothmans International, Smith Kline Beecham, Eurotunnel, RTZ-CRA and, earlier, AGFA/Gevaert, Pirelli-Dunlop, VFW-Fokker and Hoogovens-Hoesch (Estel). Some of the above groups have resorted to devices such as 'stapled stock' (by which the shares of two companies are traded as a single unit) or extremely complicated corporate structures. In all cases, however, the device or structure chosen has been considered to be only second best.

Under most national company laws, it is impossible for a company in state A to *merge* with a company in state B. Even where such a move is possible from a company law point of view, the tax regimes of the countries concerned usually form insurmountable obstacles. It should be mentioned that the *tax* problems are currently being addressed by various EU directives, as will be explained in Chapter 4. However, at the time of the adoption of the SE Statute (Regulation 2157/2001[2] ('the Regulation') and Directive 2001/86/EC[3] ('the Directive')), the *legal* problems had by no means been solved. It was only after the Statute (in particular the Directive) was adopted that a basis could be found for political agreement on a directive on cross-border mergers. The main obstacle to such agreement has always been the participation of employees in the corporate structure ('employee participation'). At the time of finalising this contribution (June 2005), it is not yet certain when the relevant directive will be adopted and what its terms will be. In any event, it is not expected to be due for implementation by Member States until 2007.

another. In this chapter, the word 'seat' is used as a general term (also covering registered and/or head office). The specific meanings of 'registered office' and 'head office' will be discussed further below.

[2] Council Regulation (EC) No. 2157/2001 of 8 October 2001 on the Statute for a European Company (SE).

[3] Council Directive 2001/86/EC of 8 October 2001 supplementing the Statute for a European company with regard to the involvement of employees.

On the other hand, with increased cross-border mobility of people and other production factors and with market opportunities moving from one country to another, the demand for cross-border mobility of companies, by way of *transfer of seat*, is growing. In most EU Member States, cross-border transfer of the *registered office* of a company[4] is impossible without loss of legal personality (liquidation and dissolution in the country of incorporation ('the home Member State') and formation of a new company in the country of immigration ('the host Member State'), with often prohibitive tax consequences). In 2004 the European Commission published a consultation document on the cross-border transfer of the registered office of companies, but by June 2005 this had not yet resulted in a proposal for a directive. The consultation document does not offer a clear solution for the problem of employee participation, which has been dogging the issue of cross-border transfers for decades. The legal situation with respect to transfer of the registered office is therefore unlikely to change in the near future, but in practice this may be less of an impediment to cross-border mobility than would appear at first sight.

Until the end of the twentieth century, transfer of a company's '*head office*' (as opposed to its registered office; head office being understood to be the company's actual centre of administration) was either prohibited or penalised by liquidation in most home Member States or, in many cases, penalised in the host Member State by non-recognition or by the application of that state's company law.

However, between 1986 and the end of 2003 the Court of Justice of the EC ('the Court') delivered a string of judgments which put a different complexion on the issue of cross-border transfer of head offices within the Community.[5] These judgments lead to the conclusion that companies from one Member State are free to set up branches in other Member States and pursue activities there, even if they do not pursue any activities in the home Member State and the sole purpose of such an arrangement is to evade the application of more severe or restrictive company law rules in the host Member State. This is inherent in the exercise, in a single market, of the *freedom of establishment* guaranteed by the EC Treaty. Setting up a branch in another Member State without pursuing any activities in the home Member State amounts, of course, to transfer of the head office.

As a result of these judgments, cross-border transfer of the head office of companies governed by national law has been secured to the extent that *host* Member

---

[4] By 'registered office' I mean the place where the company's offices are located according to its official registration and/or its articles of association (called 'statutes' in the Regulation).
[5] *Commission/France*, 28 January 1986, Case 270/83, ECR 1986, p. 273; *Segers*, 10 July 1986, Case 79/85, ECR 1986, p. 2375; *Daily Mail*, 27 September 1988, ECR 1988, p. 5483; *Centros*, 9 March 1999, Case C-212/97, ECR 1999, p. I-1459; *Überseering*, 5 November 2002, Case C-208/00, ECR 2002, p. I-9919; and *Inspire Art*, 30 September 2003, Case C-167/01, ECR 2003, p. I-10155.

States cannot impede such a transfer.[6] However, this does not hold to the same extent for impediments put up by the *home* Member State. In *Daily Mail*, the Court ruled that home Member States may restrict the freedom of their 'own' companies to transfer their head office to another Member State. In *Überseering* the Court repeated this, but I see no convincing justification for this exception to 'one of the fundamental provisions of the Community' (*Segers*). The distinction made by the Court between restrictions imposed by the host Member State and restrictions having exactly the same effect but imposed by the home Member State appears to be artificial.[7] In addition, the ruling by the Court in these cases was without any reservation, rendering this submission to national law quite atypical of the Court's case law. The Court's reasoning seems to be based on the idea that companies (other than SEs) owe their existence to the company law of the Member State in which they were incorporated and that therefore the relations between the relevant company and Member State are exclusively governed by that (company) law. I agree with this in principle. However, where the effect of that law is incompatible with Community law (in particular a fundamental provision thereof), I submit that Community law prevails in case a provision of national law purports to limit the full effect of the freedom of establishment or any of the other fundamental freedoms of the EC Treaty. I would not be surprised if, in a suitable case, the Court were to change its stand on this aspect of cross-border transfers of head offices. In any event, for the time being the issue of transfer of a company's head office is surrounded by some uncertainty.

2   Summary

My conclusion from the foregoing is that, with respect to cross-border mobility, there are substantial shortcomings in domestic company law. A distinction should be made between (a) cross-border mergers and (b) the cross-border transfer of a company's seat and, as to the latter, between (b)(i) cross-border transfer of a company's registered office and (b)(ii) cross-border transfer of its head office.

(a) With regard to cross-border mergers, tax and legal obstacles continue to prevail for the time being. It is currently uncertain when and exactly to what extent the legal problems for companies under national law will be solved by the Tenth Directive.

---

[6] The only proviso being that restrictions of the freedom of establishment may be justified if four conditions are met (these are listed in para. III. 1 below). So far, the Court has refused to accept any restrictions in this context, even where a company had been formed in Member State A with the sole purpose of pursuing activities in Member State B and thereby avoiding the application of B's company law which was considered to be more severe (see *Segers*, *Centros* and *Inspire Art*).

[7] This distinction is also at odds with the other freedoms guaranteed by the EC Treaty: Arts. 23 and 25 prohibit customs duties on imports *and exports* of goods between Member States, Arts. 28 and 29 prohibit quantitative restrictions on imports *and exports* and Art. 56 prohibits *any* restrictions on the movement of capital and on payments *between* Member States (i.e. irrespective of whether capital moves, or payments are made, into or from a Member State).

(b)(i) Regarding cross-border transfers of a company's registered office, it looks as though both the tax problems and the legal problems will take quite a few years to be solved for companies under national law.

(b)(ii) For the cross-border transfer of a company's head office, a further distinction must be made between restrictions imposed by the home Member State and those imposed by the host Member State. With regard to the latter, the case law of the Court has removed virtually all restrictions. However, the home Member State appears to be free to impose restrictions (although I expect this freedom to be limited in due course).

III Can the SE make up for these shortcomings?

One of the principal aims the SE has always been intended to achieve is cross-border mobility, in particular by way of merger and by way of transfer of registered office. Under the Regulation, the following options are offered:

(a) Two or more public limited-liability companies ('public companies') from at least two different Member States can merge, resulting in an SE as the surviving or the new company.

(b) In situation (a) above, one or more of the companies participating in the merger can themselves be SEs.

(c) Once an SE has been formed it can transfer its registered office to another Member State.

(d) An SE may itself set up one or more subsidiaries in any Member State.

So why not use the SE as a vehicle for a cross-border merger or transfer of seat? Let us consider the merits and demerits of this proposition. Again, I focus only on the cross-border aspect, leaving aside for the time being a whole range of other important ones.

1 Cross-border mergers

The Statute can be used for the merger of two or more public companies provided that at least two of them are governed by the laws of different Member States. Pursuant to Article 3(1) of the Regulation, an SE may take the place of one of these companies. The limitation to public companies does not seem to pose a serious obstacle for private limited-liability companies ('private companies', see Annex II to the Regulation) because in most Member States they can easily convert into a public company.

Article 2(1) of the Regulation sets out an additional requirement: all the public companies involved in the formation of an SE must have their registered offices and head offices within the Community. However, a Member State may allow a company the head office of which is not in the Community to participate in the formation of an SE if that company is formed under the law of a Member State, has its registered office in that Member State and 'has a real and continuous link with a Member State's economy' (Art. 2(5) Reg.). According to recital 23 of the preamble to the Regulation, such a link 'exists in particular if a company has an establishment in that Member State and conducts operations therefrom'. Interestingly, the SE formed as a result of the merger may have its registered office (and head office, see below) anywhere within the Community, and not necessarily in a Member State where one of the merging companies had its registered and/or head office.

The Regulation does not give a definition of the term 'head office'. Although this is a Community concept, in the interpretation of which the Court has the final say, for the time being (and it may be a very long time before the Court is called upon to give a preliminary ruling on this issue[8]) the authorities and courts of Member States have some degree of latitude in interpreting the concept of 'head office'. The more broadly this concept is construed, the more hospitable the Member State is likely to be to SEs. The Dutch government, for example, has stated that what is important is from which country the company is run, that this requires an interpretation of the actual circumstances, and that the head office is likely to be deemed to be situated in the Netherlands when board meetings and general meetings of shareholders are held there. This condition can quite easily be met even if the day-to-day management is conducted, and/or important strategic decisions are made, outside the Netherlands.

What about an intermediate holding company? This type of company holds shares in one or more subsidiaries in a group of companies, but is itself a subsidiary of the company at the 'top' of the group. Its activities are often confined to administrative formalities, with strategic and other decisions being made at the 'top' of the group. Where is its head office? According to the Dutch point of view, it is at the place where formal meetings are held. Other Member States, however, may apply different criteria. In Germany, for example, more importance seems to be attached to the place where decisions are implemented. In all Member States, the concept of 'head office' appears to be rather vaguely defined. Ominously, Article 64(4) of the Regulation provides that '[w]here it is established on the initiative of either the authorities or any interested party that an SE has its head office within the territory of a Member State in breach of Article 7 [i.e., in a Member State other than that where its registered office is situated], the authorities of that Member State shall immediately inform the Member State in which the SE's registered office is situated'. Article 64(1) provides that the latter Member State 'shall take appropriate measures to oblige the SE to regularise its position within a specified period'. What if the two Member States disagree as to the interpretation of 'head office'? In order to protect yourself in such a

---

[8] In *Daily Mail* (see footnote 5) all the Court said was: 'the real head office, that is to say the central administration of the company.' This gives us little to go on, because it raises the question as to what the 'central administration' of a company is.

case, evidence will be of the essence, so make sure you can be seen to comply with all formalities, preferably those of the most restrictive Member State.

As will be set out in some detail in Chapter 2, the formation of an SE by means of a (cross-border) merger is by and large governed by the technical provisions of the Third Directive[9] on mergers within a Member State. The Regulation adds to the Third Directive's regime a number of provisions relating to the cross-border elements of a merger that is intended to result in the formation of an SE. The fact that the Regulation has direct effect in all Member States enables it to regulate such cross-border elements with binding force throughout the Community. I would like to draw your attention to a few of the provisions that may cause problems if you wish to form an SE by way of merger.

One such provision is Article 26, which requires the legality of the merger to be scrutinised as regards the *completion of the merger and the formation of the SE*. This must be done by the competent authority in the Member State in which it is proposed that the SE have its registered office, on the basis of certificates issued by the competent authorities in each Member State involved after these have scrutinised the *pre-merger acts and formalities*. The authority in the first Member State 'shall in particular ensure that the merging companies have approved draft terms of merger in the same terms and that arrangements for employee involvement have been determined pursuant to Directive 2001/86/EC',[10] and must also satisfy himself/itself that the SE has been formed in accordance with the requirements of the law of his/its own Member State.

This double scrutiny by authorities of at least two Member States may cost the participating companies quite a lot of effort, money and, above all, time. The exact translation of the terms of merger may be cumbersome, but the requirement that the competent authority in the Member State in which the SE is to have its registered office ensure that arrangements for employee involvement have been determined pursuant to the Directive could turn out to be an excessive burden. This could be the case if that authority considers it to be his/its duty to scrutinise the observance of all the complicated rules of the Directive (see Chapter 3) as transposed into even more complicated rules by the various relevant Member States. In several Member States this authority will be a notary. How will this poor man or woman acquit him/herself of this awful task without spending sleepless nights worrying about professional liability?

Another potentially problematic provision in the Regulation is Article 19, which permits a Member State to prohibit a company governed by its law from participating in the formation of an SE if any of that Member State's competent authorities[11] opposes that company's participation. Such opposition may only be based on grounds of public interest and must be open to review by a judicial

---

[9] Third Council Directive 78/855/EEC of 9 October 1978 based on Article 54(3)(g) (now 44(2)(g)) of the Treaty concerning mergers of public limited liability companies.
[10] I.e. the Directive.   [11] See footnote 13.

9

authority. In the single market that the EC constitutes, it is very difficult to conceive how a merger of two companies (outside areas that are subject to government supervision e.g. financial services, where specific merger control rules may apply) could be against the public interest. (This is unless the issue of employee participation is considered to be one of public interest within the meaning of Article 19, which seems unlikely given the fact that the Directive and the Regulation, in particular Article 12(2) of the latter, contain an extensive set of rules to safeguard employee participation in relation to SEs.) Also, it would seem absurd that a Member State could oppose a merger between two companies while being unable to do anything to prevent one of them acquiring all the shares of the other. In any event, opposition under Article 19 would constitute a restriction of the freedom of establishment. It is important to note that, according to the Court's case law, such a restriction may only be imposed if it fulfils four conditions: (i) it must be applied in a non-discriminatory manner; (ii) it must be justified by imperative requirements in the general interest; (iii) it must be suitable for securing the attainment of the objective it pursues; (iv) and it must not go beyond what is necessary in order to attain that objective. These conditions will not be easily fulfilled; nevertheless, a Member State may have a different view and frustrate your merger if it is perceived as threatening vital national interests. Just imagine: you have been secretly negotiating a merger for many months, you go public with the draft terms of merger, the general meeting approves the terms, there is no opposition by any creditor, the competent authorities issue their certificates attesting to the completion of the pre-merger acts and formalities, you expect to receive the certificate as to the completion of the merger any day and then one of the Member States involved notifies you that it opposes the merger.

Under Article 24 of the Regulation, 'the law of the Member State governing each merging company shall apply as in the case of a merger of public limited-liability companies, taking into account the cross-border nature of the merger, with regard to the protection of interests of creditors ... '. In addition, a Member State *may* adopt provisions designed to ensure appropriate protection for minority shareholders who have opposed the merger. It will be important to examine such provisions closely in each of the Member States involved. Bear in mind that any such protective provisions are subject to the above four conditions regarding restrictions on the freedom of establishment.

There is, however, some good news when it comes to the cross-border elements dealt with by the Regulation. Once the SE has been registered after all the scrutinising, it cannot be declared null and void (Art. 30 Reg.). In addition, Article 29 provides for *ipso jure* cross-border transfer to the SE of all the assets and liabilities of the disappearing company/companies, and for the shareholders of that company/those companies in Member State A *ipso jure* becoming shareholders of the SE in Member State B. The latter consequence, in particular, cannot be brought about by the legislation of a single Member State.

2 Transfer of an SE's registered office

Once an SE has been formed it can, pursuant to Article 8 of the Regulation, transfer its registered office to another Member State. The good news is that such a transfer will not result in the winding up of the SE or the creation of a new legal entity. The bad news is that the procedure is cumbersome.

Before I go into the issue of the procedure, I would like to draw your attention to what appears to be a major restriction on the cross-border mobility of SEs. Article 7 of the Regulation provides that the registered office of an SE shall be located in the same Member State as its head office.[12] This means that transfer of an SE's registered office must entail the transfer of the head office. It also means that an SE cannot transfer its head office while maintaining its registered office in the home Member State. Whereas every company created under national law is free to exercise its freedom of establishment, the SE appears to be denied this freedom to the same extent. Is this discrimination against the SE valid? Admittedly, it is provided for by a regulation adopted by the Council at the proposal of the Commission and in accordance with the opinion of the European Parliament. However, it follows from Article 230 of the EC Treaty that regulations may not be in violation of the Treaty. If they are, they can be annulled (either wholly or in part) by the Court at the request of a Member State. This is unlikely to happen. More realistically, any national court which is in doubt about the validity of Article 7 can request that the Court give a preliminary ruling on its validity. Such a ruling will be binding on the relevant national court as well as having the effect of a judicial precedent throughout the Community. I should reiterate that the Court has identified the Treaty provisions on freedom of establishment as 'fundamental provisions of the Community'.

One could argue that the SE, unlike companies under national law, is a creature of Community law and can therefore be made subject to any rules of that law. However, I submit that such rules must always be in accordance with the EC Treaty, which is the supreme source of Community law. Therefore, I am of the opinion that there is a valid case for an SE being free to transfer its head office to another Member State without at the same time transferring its registered office. However, I cannot deny there is quite some uncertainty on this point. It should be noted that Article 7 was one of the most controversial topics during the negotiations on the Statute. Indeed this is the first issue mentioned in the list of specific issues to be dealt with by the Commission under Article 69.

There is another major inconvenience connected with the transfer of an SE's registered office, namely that such a transfer inevitably entails a change in the company law rules applicable to that SE. This holds both for the provisions of laws adopted by the Member States in implementation of the Regulation

---

[12] Note also Art. 64 Reg., which requires Member States to take appropriate measures against, and possibly even liquidate, an SE that does not comply with Art. 7.

and the Directive, including any future additions and amendments thereto (see Art. 9(1)(c)(i) Reg.), and for provisions of national company law applicable to public companies to which the Regulation or the Directive refers either specifically (see, e.g., Arts. 5, 15, 51, 52, 53, 54, 56, 57, 61, 62 and 63 Reg. and Arts. 4(4) and 6 Dir.) or generally (see Arts. 9(1)(c)(ii) and (iii) and, probably, Art. 10 Reg.). In fact, the above two categories of provisions cover a very substantial part of the company law of each Member State. Apart from the fundamental subjects referred to in footnote 14, matters such as the following may radically change as a result of a transfer of registered office: the rules relating to groups of companies (including the right to give instructions to the board of a subsidiary and the consequences as to liability), voting agreements, validity and annulment of resolutions, enquiry into a company's affairs, compulsory acquisition of minority shares, etc. It is therefore essential to consider very carefully the possible consequences of a transfer in your particular situation. In addition, the SE's statutes (articles of association) will have to be adapted to the law of the host Member State. This is likely to involve a complete revision.

Let us now turn to the procedure for transferring the registered office of an SE. This is set out in the longest article of the Regulation: Article 8 consists of 16 paragraphs, many of which are longer than quite a few full articles of the Regulation. The procedure is similar to that for mergers: a transfer proposal, publication, a justificatory report, a waiting period of two months, a decision by the general meeting, protection of creditors and possibly minority shareholders, a certificate from a competent authority, registration in the host Member State only after submission of the certificate and production of evidence that the formalities required for registration in that country have been completed (what formalities?), and publication again. All these formalities take time and effort.

As in the case of formation of an SE by merger, Article 8(14) gives each Member State an option to provide that any of its competent authorities may oppose the transfer on grounds of public interest. Of course this provision, too, is a source of uncertainty and I cannot see any justification for it which would be acceptable under Community law.[13]

Finally, a piece of good news for the transfer of an SE's registered office is that the Directive dated 17 February 2005, amending Directive 90/434 on the common system applicable to mergers etc. (see Chapter 4 of this book), provides for special tax rules for the transfer of the registered office of an SE.

---

[13] It should be noted that there is a special sub-paragraph (the third sentence) of Art. 8(14) which gives a national financial supervisory authority the right of opposition where an SE is supervised by it. It follows from this that the 'competent authorities' referred to in the first sentence of Art. 8(14) are not just any national authority, but apparently only the authorities designated in accordance with Art. 68(2), i.e. the authorities in charge of issuing the certificate referred to in Art. 8(8). Interestingly, there is no such sub-paragraph in Art. 19 concerning formation of an SE by merger.

These rules must be implemented by 1 January 2006 and will, for the most part, have direct effect from that date, meaning that it will be possible to rely on them in court against national tax authorities even if they have not yet been transposed into national law. It should be noted, however, that these directives do not apply to Iceland, Liechtenstein and Norway.

3 Indirect transfer of seat

The Regulation's provisions on formation of an SE by merger and on the transfer of an SE's registered office are complicated and burdensome. However, there would appear to be a way to avoid most complications. Surprisingly, this would be by forming an SE by way of merger, but now with a subsidiary created for that purpose.

For example, an English public company, PLC, wishes to transfer its registered office to Belgium. It forms a Belgian public company, NV, with no activities and, of course, no employees. PLC and NV then effectuate a merger under the Regulation whereby PLC ceases to exist, NV becomes an SE, all the companies' assets and liabilities are transferred to (or remain with) the SE and PLC's shareholders become shareholders of the SE. In fact, what has essentially happened is that PLC has transferred its registered office to Belgium. From the point of view of Belgian law, the procedure is quite simple because NV has neither activities nor employees. The procedure may be more complicated from the UK point of view, depending on PLC's situation, but there may be ways to make it less so for the occasion. In addition, there may be problems with the issue of employee involvement. For this issue I refer the reader to section V below.

4 Summary

My intermediate conclusion as to the merits and demerits of using an SE for a cross-border merger or transfer of seat is as follows. Both for a merger and for a transfer of seat you will have to deal with a lot of red tape, in particular with respect to scrutinisation by the competent authorities. Secondly, if your company happens to be active in a politically sensitive industry, you may experience legal uncertainty due to the possibility that a Member State may have opted to enable a particular authority to oppose the merger or transfer. Thirdly, your legal position may be affected by uncertainty as to the definition of 'head office'. Fourthly, the rule under the Regulation that an SE's registered office and head office must be in the same Member State may be inconvenient.

On the other hand, once you have complied with all the formalities you will have accomplished an operation which, in all likelihood, you could not have accomplished under national law. In addition it looks as though the SE will benefit from a tax regime that is as favourable as, or even more so than, the regime applicable to national companies, in particular with respect to the transfer of its registered office. Lastly, the above-mentioned possibilities of indirectly transferring a 'national' company's registered office to another Member State may be attractive.

IV What are you in for when you have an SE?

So, from a cross-border mobility point of view, the SE holds interesting prospects. But what are you in for once you have formed one? Let us first dispose of a few myths.

First, there is the myth that the SE is a 'European' company governed by a single set of rules, wherever its seat is located. Over the decades of negotiation, it became increasingly clear that, given all the differences between the company laws of Member States, it was unfeasible to realise the ideal cherished at the outset. More and more of the Statute's 'own' rules were deleted and replaced with references to the laws of the Member States. The Regulation expressly provides that, for a whole range of matters,[14] an SE is to be governed by provisions of national law. These cover a significant part of any national company law. Furthermore, many of those provisions are not covered by 'harmonisation' directives. The 67 substantive articles of the Regulation (as against 282 in the first Commission draft of 1970), contain 65 references to national law and 32 options for Member States. In addition, the Directive contains five references to national law and eight options for Member States. As a result, what we have is not one SE but 28[15] 'European' companies. Of course, with little prospect of the existing differences between national company laws being eliminated in the foreseeable future, this disparity will be a source of legal uncertainty for a long time to come.

Then there is the myth created in 1995 by a group of industrialists (headed by Carlo Ciampi) and circulated by the Commission.[16] According to this myth, the SE would 'avoid the need to set up a financially costly and administratively time-consuming complex network of subsidiaries governed by different national laws'. A single SE with branches in the other Member States where it conducts business would be sufficient. It was asserted that the SE could

---

[14] Capital; maintenance of capital (which includes, *inter alia*, issuance of and payment for shares, contribution of assets for shares, distribution of profits, financial assistance, statutory reserves, and purchase and redemption of own shares); shares (including most of the rights attached thereto); formation and registration; merger; rights (if any) of minority shareholders to appoint directors; disclosure of information by directors; liability of directors; powers of the general meeting; organisation and conduct of general meetings (including convening and voting procedures); preparation and contents of annual /consolidated accounts; and winding up, liquidation, insolvency; cessation of payments and similar procedures.
[15] One for each of the 25 Member States of the EU and one for each of the EEA Member States that are not EU members: Iceland, Liechtenstein and Norway. In 2007 there will be two more 'European companies': a Bulgarian one and a Rumanian one.
[16] See the Commission's website http://europa.eu.int/comm/internal_market/company/Directives and other official acts/Regulations/The European company Statute/ Frequently Asked Questions.

save the business community up to €30,000 million per year in legal and administrative costs. It would seem that Mr Ciampi and the Commission grossly underestimated the importance attached to subsidiaries: limitation of liability, clear legal structure, clear tax position, possible facilitation of disposal of assets where these are held by a separate legal entity, and image to the outside world (especially in the case of a subsidiary in another country: 'local' company, etc.). Why would there otherwise be so many large groups of (sometimes hundreds of) companies in one and the same Member State? As to the amount of €30 billion, this seems to lack any foundation in reality. It suggests that Europe could easily beat the USA as a lawyers' paradise.

Unfortunately, as both the Regulation and the Directive show, the legal regime governing the SE is very incomplete and in many respects unclear. The numerous specific and general references to national company law have already been highlighted above. I refer in particular to Articles 9 and 10 of the Regulation, which have given rise to countless legal writings in different Member States. In many respects, it is very difficult to fit the SE into a national company law system. To mention just a few examples:

- Where the Regulation lays down certain rules about the relationship between the management and supervisory organs (Arts. 40 and 41), to what extent do stricter or more detailed rules of national company law apply to the SE?
- Article 56 of the Regulation provides that shareholders who together hold at least 10% of the SE's capital may request that additional items be put on the general meeting's agenda. Under the law of some countries, a lower percentage (e.g. 1% in the Netherlands) is required for companies under national law. What percentage applies to an SE in such a country?
- Among Dutch listed companies there is a widespread habit of using depositary receipts for shares as a protective device against hostile takeovers. These receipts carry no voting rights but entitle the holder to all the economic rights attached to the underlying shares (see the national report of the Netherlands). What if a Dutch company that has issued depositary receipts for shares merges into an SE having its registered office in a Member State where such a device is unknown? What rights will the receipt holders have?
- Can an SE divide into two or more SEs or two or more national companies?

A positive characteristic of the SE Statute is that the Regulation offers a choice between the one-tier and the two-tier system of corporate management. The parties drafting the statutes of an SE are free to choose either of the two systems. Where, in relation to public companies under national law, no provision is made for the two-tier system, a Member State may adopt 'the appropriate measures in relation to SEs' (Art. 39(5) Reg.), which means that such Member State may create rules specifically intended to apply to SEs that have adopted the two-tier system and whose registered offices are located in that Member State. The same applies, *mutatis mutandis*, to the one-tier system (Art. 43(4) Reg.). In my view, Member States where there is employee participation in a two-tier system, such as Austria, Estonia, Germany, the Netherlands and the Slovak Republic, are obliged to create rules to facilitate such participation in a one-tier system.

V   Employee involvement

1   Introduction

So far, I have been silent (perhaps suspiciously so) about this subject, which is the most delicate aspect of the SE. But you will have to face it. Or will you? Are there ways to avoid it?

On the face of it, there is no escape. First, there is Article 1(2) of the Directive, which provides that 'arrangements for the involvement of employees shall be established in every SE'. See also Article 3(1) of the Directive which is clearly based on the same principle. Then there is Article 12(3) of the Regulation, which provides that an SE may not be registered (i.e. it may not acquire legal personality) unless:

- an agreement on arrangements for employee involvement pursuant to Article 4 of the Directive has been concluded, *or*
- the special negotiating body ('SNB', about which some information below and more in Chapter 3) has by a special majority decided not to open negotiations or to terminate negotiations already opened, *or*
- the period for negotiations of six months (possibly extended to one year) has expired without an agreement having been concluded.[17]

2   Background

I shall briefly explain what this means. From the very conception of the SE one issue proved to be an obstacle to agreement: the participation of employee representatives in the board(s) of companies. In 1966, when Professor Piet Sanders prepared the first draft of a Statute for the SE (and in 1970, when the first Commission proposal was submitted to the Council), Germany was the only Member State (of the six at that time) where the law provided for employee representation (*Mitbestimmung*) on the supervisory board (and to some extent even on the management board). In the event of a cross-border merger or transfer of seat, this raised a political problem, which can be illustrated as follows. Say a German public company (an 'AG') and an Italian

---

[17] See also Arts. 26(3) and 32(6) Reg. and Arts. 1(2) and 3(1) Dir. These provisions all premise that arrangements for the involvement of employees shall be established in every SE.

public company (an 'SpA') wished to merge. One of them (or both) would have to disappear, with the remaining (or new) company being an SE. If the SE was made subject to exactly the same regime as the German *Mitbestimmung* (which, incidentally, comes in three different varieties), there would be no problem for the Germans (assuming they accepted only one variety being applicable to SEs); however, there would be for the Italians (and all other Member States not wishing to force employee participation upon their undertakings if they opted for the SE). On the other hand, if the SE Statute did not provide for employee participation in the structure of SEs, the German company would be deprived of (or, depending upon one's point of view, rescued from) its *Mitbestimmung*. This would be unacceptable to the German government. From its side, the Commission has always taken the view that employees should be able to influence the course of events through participation in the corporate structure. This problem led to continuous deadlock for over 30 years. In the meantime, a number of other Member States introduced employee participation for their companies: it now exists to a greater or lesser extent in Austria, Denmark, Finland, Germany, Luxembourg, the Netherlands and Sweden, as well as some 'new' Member States, such as Poland and the Slovak Republic.

Employee participation (termed 'participation' in the Directive) should be clearly distinguished from other forms of employee involvement. The Directive deals with three forms: information, consultation and participation, each of which has a special meaning as defined in Article 2 of the Directive. Because *participation* is by far the most important form, I give the (abridged) definition: influence of employees' representatives in the affairs of a company by way of the right to elect or appoint, or to recommend and/or oppose the appointment of, some or all of the members of the company's supervisory or administrative organ. Of the different forms of employee involvement under the Directive, only participation affects the *structure of the company*. Information and consultation are normally realised through a works council or, in rare cases, through direct contacts between management and employees or their representatives. Directive 94/45[18] ('the EWC Directive') deals with information and consultation. It is this directive which has provided one of the bases for a compromise on employee involvement in the SE. The EWC Directive obliges companies of a certain size to negotiate with a 'special negotiating body' of representatives of their employees ('SNB') with a view to concluding an agreement on the establishment of a European works council or some other procedure for informing and consulting employees. Where no agreement can be reached, the EWC Directive provides for certain standard rules laid down in an annex thereto. Exactly the same technique has been applied in the Directive.

[18] Council Directive 94/45/EC of 22 September 1994 on the establishment of a European Works Council or a procedure in Community-scale undertakings and Community-scale groups of undertakings for the purposes of informing and consulting employees.

Another element which has made adoption of the Directive less difficult is the 'before and after' principle under which, as regards involvement in company decisions, employees' rights in force before the establishment of an SE should provide the basis for such rights in the SE (see, in the Directive, recital 18 of the preamble; Arts. 4(4), 7(2), 13(3)(b) and 13(4); and Part 3(a) of the Annex). The principle also implies that where none of the companies participating in the formation of an SE was governed by employee participation rules before registration of the SE, such rules shall not apply to the SE (Part 3(b) second para. of the Annex to the Directive). The 'before and after' principle applies not only to participation, but also to the other forms of employee involvement (Arts. 13(1) and 13(3)(a) Dir.). For further details, see Chapter 3 of this book. My only comment is that, as a result of numerous political compromises, the rules of the Directive are very complicated and open to different interpretations.

3 Can employee participation be avoided?

For a proper answer to this question, each step in the series of decisions to be taken when an SE is formed must be closely examined. Please note that in this section (V.3), I am dealing *only* with *participation*, not with information or consultation.

3.1 First, Article 3(1) of the Directive requires that the management of the 'participating companies' (see Art. 2(b) Dir.: 'the companies directly participating in the establishing of an SE') take the necessary steps 'to start negotiations with the representatives of the companies' employees on arrangements for the involvement of employees in the SE'. They must do so as soon as possible after publishing the draft terms of merger or of formation of a holding SE or after agreeing a plan to form a subsidiary or to transform into an SE.[19] The most important step is to enable the employee representatives to create an SNB.

What if none of the participating companies has any employees? Then it is impossible to start negotiations and neither Article 3 nor any of the other provisions of the Directive can be applied. But what about Article 12(2) of the Regulation, which provides that an SE may not be registered unless one of the three things referred to in section V.1 above has occurred? This provision does not take into account the possibility that none of the participating companies has any employees. In my view, a sensible interpretation of the Regulation should permit an SE to be registered in that event. This means that it is possible to form an SE that does not have any arrangements for employee participation.

One might wonder whether the same applies where the participating companies have no employees but have subsidiaries that do. For example, the participating

---

[19] It is unclear what kind of 'agreement' is necessary with regard to transformation (conversion) into an SE.

companies could be holding companies without (as is often the case) any employees. It should be noted that, under the system of the Directive, the employees of a 'concerned subsidiary or establishment'[20] have a role to play in the SNB. Therefore, excluding these employees from any influence on the formation of the SE could 'smell' of abuse (about which I will say more below).

3.2 Now for the situation where at least one of the participating companies does have employees. In that event an SNB must be created. Negotiations must then be opened unless the SNB decides by a qualified majority not to open them, in which case the SE can be registered (Art. 12(2) Reg.), none of the provisions of the Annex to the Directive will apply to the SE (Art. 3(6) Dir.) and only the national rules on information and consultation of those Member States where the SE has employees will apply.[21] The negotiations may continue for six months; however, this period may be extended by the parties for up to a further six months. After negotiations have been opened, the result can be one of the following:

(a) Agreement on some form of employee involvement is reached. This need not necessarily concern employee participation; it can be any form of employee involvement, including some or all of the 'standard rules' laid down in the Annex to the Directive (see Arts. 7(1)(a) and 4(3)Dir.). The only limitation on the freedom of the negotiating parties is to be found in Article 4(4): where an SE is established by transformation (conversion), the agreement shall provide for 'at least the same level of all elements of employee involvement as the ones existing within the company to be transformed into an SE'. So, if prior to the conversion the public company in question was subject to employee participation, the SE will be subject to exactly the same regime.[22] Part 3(a) of the Annex to the Directive even says that the rules on participation that applied before registration 'shall *continue* to apply to the SE'.

(b) No agreement is concluded,
  (i) either because the SNB has by a qualified majority decided to terminate the negotiations (with the same consequences as where the SNB has decided not to open negotiations, see above),
  (ii) or because at the end of the maximum period of one year the parties could not reach agreement.

---

[20] See Art. 2(d) Dir.: 'a subsidiary or establishment of a participating company which is proposed to become a subsidiary or establishment of the SE upon its formation.'
[21] These rules will include legislation implementing the EWC Directive if the SE is a Community-scale undertaking within the meaning of that Directive (Art. 13(i) Dir.).
[22] It is not clear how this works out if the Member State in question has failed to provide for employee participation in one-tier SEs (as is the case in the Netherlands), the statutes of the SE provide for a one-tier system and the participation regime in the 'old' public company pertained to the supervisory board.

In the latter event (i.e. scenario (b) (ii)), it is not entirely clear what the consequences will be. This is because the Regulation and the Directive appear to contradict each other on this issue. According to Article 7(1)(b) of the Directive, the standard rules will apply where no agreement has been concluded within the said period *and* 'the competent organ of each of the participating companies decides to accept the application of the standard rules in relation to the SE *and so to continue with its registration of the SE*'.[23,24] The italicised words suggest that in the absence of the acceptance by each of the participating companies of the standard rules, no registration can take place. Article 12(2) of the Regulation, however, provides that the SE may be registered when the period for negotiations has expired without an agreement having been concluded, but does not contain any reference to acceptance of the standard rules. This seems to suggest that registration can take place without the standard rules being applicable. In community law there is no order of priority between regulations and directives. However, as far as involvement of employees is concerned, the Directive is the *lex specialis* compared with the Regulation. In my opinion, the express wording of the Directive (italicised above) should prevail: if, upon expiry of the period, no agreement has been concluded and the standard rules are not accepted by all participating companies, the SE cannot be registered.

3.3 What happens if the standard rules[25] are applicable? The outcome here may turn out to be better than expected. First, the standard rules may not in fact apply after all, thanks to Article 7(2) (and in some cases 7(3)) of the Directive. Article 7(2) sets out certain additional requirements for the applicability of the standard rules. Pursuant to this provision, the standard rules shall only apply:

(a) in the case of conversion: if the relevant national rules on employee participation applied to the company converted into an SE;[26]
(b) in the case of an SE established by merger: if some form of participation applied in one or more of the *participating* companies (not their subsidiaries) covering at least 25% of the total number of employees in all the *participating* companies or, if that percentage was less than 25, if the SNB so decides (i.e. in that event the merging companies are at the mercy

---

[23] Also, the SNB must not have decided to terminate or not to open the negotiations, but this is rather superfluous because Art. 3(6) Dir. already provides that in that event none of the provisions of the Annex shall apply.

[24] In the German version: 'das zuständige Organ jeder der beteiligten Gesellschaften der Anwendung der Auffangsregelung auf die SE *und damit der Fortsetzung des Verfahrens zur Eintragung der SE zugestimmt hat.*'

[25] Keep in mind that it is not the standard rules contained in the Annex to the Directive that will apply, but those standard rules as transposed into the national law of the Member State where the SE has its registered office. There may be differences between Member States in this regard.

[26] I assume that where, pursuant to its national law, that company met the criteria for employee participation but was exempted (as can be the case in e.g. the Netherlands), the rules on participation will be considered not to have applied to that company.

of the SNB even if participation applied only to a company covering, say, 3% of all the employees);

(c) in the case of a holding SE or subsidiary SE: the same as in the case of a merger, except that the applicable percentage is 50.

Note that under Article 7(3) of the Directive, Member States may provide that the standard rules will not apply at all in the case of the formation of an SE by merger. In Member States which have exercised this option, such an SE can only be registered *either*:

if an agreement has been concluded on employee involvement, *'including participation'*, *or*
if none of the participating companies was governed by participation rules. (See Art. 12(3) Reg.)

The foregoing (especially the italicised words *'including participation'*) must apparently be understood to mean that, where one of the participating companies was governed by participation rules, an SE to be registered in a Member State which has exercised the option under Article 7(3) will have to be governed by some set of agreed participation rules, even though the relevant participating company might have been free from those rules had the standard rules applied.

All the foregoing is more or less in line with the 'before and after' principle referred to in section V.2 above.

The same principle is reflected in the second paragraph of Part 3(b) of the Annex to the Directive which contains the standard rules and reads as follows:

'If none of the participating companies was governed by participation rules before registration of the SE, the latter shall not be required to establish provisions for employee participation.'

3.4 However, in all other cases the standard rules provide for the application of participation rules to the SE. It is even provided (in the first paragraph of Part 3(b)) that the employees 'shall have the right to elect, appoint, recommend or oppose the appointment of a number of members of the administrative or supervisory body of the SE equal to the highest proportion in force in the participating companies concerned before registration of the SE'. This purely numeric criterion completely ignores the content of the participation rights. It is self-evident that the right to *recommend* (in a non-binding manner) a candidate for *any* vacancy on the supervisory board is of much less consequence than the right to *appoint* one-third of the members of that board. Also, the powers of the supervisory board may differ greatly from one Member State to the other.

3.5 My conclusion from the foregoing is that, with respect to employee participation, the 'before and after' principle is generally observed in the Directive and the Regulation. Even where participation rules apply to one or more of the participating companies, it would be possible for them to set up one or more subsidiaries or independent special entities without any employees, or with a few employees who are prepared to agree to forgo any participation rights. It would even be possible for the resulting SE subsequently to acquire companies with a large number of employees, or the assets, liabilities and employees of such companies.

3.6 Here, however, I must sound a note of caution. The drafters of the Regulation and the Directive were aware of the possibility of companies attempting to dodge the provisions on employee participation. Several statements in the preambles and provisions of these instruments bear witness to this, the strongest being Article 11 of the Directive, which reads as follows:

> 'Member States shall take appropriate measures in conformity with Community law with a view to preventing the misuse of an SE for the purpose of depriving employees of rights to employee involvement or withholding such rights'.

The reader may recall that Articles 12(2) and 12(3) of the Regulation prevent an SE from being registered unless the provisions of the Directive have been complied with. The same goes for Article 26(3) of the Regulation.

Article 12 of the Directive obliges each Member State to ensure that all parties involved abide by the obligations laid down in the Directive, 'regardless of whether or not the SE has its registered office within its territory'[27]. Member States are also obliged to provide for appropriate measures in the event of failure to comply with the Directive.

All the same, close examination of the Directive brings to light an enormous gap: the rules on employee involvement are limited to the stage of formation of the SE. What happens thereafter is not covered by either the Directive or the Regulation. The only indication that the drafters have thought about this problem is to be found in recital 18 of the preamble to the Directive which, after stating that it is 'a fundamental principle and stated aim' of the Directive to secure employees' *'acquired rights'* as regards involvement in company decisions and that those rights should provide the basis for employee rights of involvement in the SE, goes on as follows:

> 'Consequently, that approach should apply not only to the initial establishment of an SE but also to structural changes in an existing SE and to the companies affected by structural change processes.'

However, the Directive does not contain a single provision that, with regard to this issue, is intended to be applicable after an SE has been formed. This was recognised at the consultations held in Brussels among officials of the Member

---

[27] However, at consultations held in Brussels for the purpose of co-ordinating the implementation of the Directive (see, the text below), it was concluded that Art. 12(1) does not require the Member States to supervise SEs.

States and the Commission for the purpose of co-ordinating the implementation of the Directive. The Member States concluded that Article 11 of the Directive was not suitable for implementation because it is insufficiently specific or concrete as to enable Member States to assess the question of when there is misuse and how, in light of this, any changes occurring after the SE has been formed should be considered. No agreement was reached on a joint approach or a uniform system of implementation, and it was concluded that the matter should be left to each individual Member State. As a result, there is a wide variety of 'anti-misuse' provisions (in some cases none) in the implementing laws of the Member States. I refer to the national reports in this book, e.g., the report from Finland (item 69). The Dutch legislation implementing the Directive requires the agreement between the participating companies and the SNB to lay down rules about renegotiation of the agreement. In the absence of such rules, the parties are in certain cases required to negotiate a new agreement if a certain number of employees so request. However, these requirements relate to information and consultation and not to participation, although they may result in the application of the standard rules, including those on participation.

Apparently, the employee participation game has continued on another chessboard: that of the tax directives. As a result, an utterly foreign ingredient has been stirred into the tax soup. As from 17 February 2005, Directive 90/434 on the common system of taxation applicable to mergers (see Chapter 4 of this book) provides in Article 11 that a Member State may refuse to apply or withdraw the benefits of that directive where it appears that a merger (etc.):

> 'results in a company, whether participating in the operation or not, no longer fulfilling the necessary conditions for the representation of employees on company organs according to the arrangements which were in force prior to that operation.'

This 'shall apply as long as and to the extent that no Community law provisions containing equivalent rules on representation of employees on company organs are applicable to the companies covered by this Directive'.

With these very vaguely worded provisions, it looks as though a very large bomb has been planted in the luggage compartment of the SE just as it is about to take off.

Compare this with the much more balanced wording, also in Article 11 of the same directive, on the issue of tax evasion or tax avoidance, and the vicious nature of this provision will be apparent. Just imagine that the tax authorities (with all their special powers of assessment and collection) should be the authority to judge whether you have complied with the extremely complicated rules implementing the (SE) Directive.

The consequences of a bona fide restructuring of a group to which an SE belongs or from which an SE emerges may be so draconian that businesspeople may well decide to avoid that risk by bypassing the SE. Fortunately, Member States are not obliged to apply Article 11 of Directive 90/434. It will therefore be essential to see which Member States implement this part of the directive and how they do so.

My conclusion about the potential for using the SE in a creative manner without undue employee participation is that there are many such possibilities, both at the stage of formation and thereafter. However, it is essential to obtain both legal and tax advice in order to make sure you do not fall into an 'anti-misuse' trap, even if your intentions are totally innocent.

VI Conclusion

My overall conclusion is that the SE may be attractive in cases where there is a need for cross-border mobility. This will to a great extent depend on your particular situation. There will be a major difference between, for example, the formation of an SE by two large independent companies with many employees, and the use of an SE solely for the purpose of carrying out a cross-border restructuring of a group of companies.

In certain small-scale scenarios, the formation of an SE by participating companies which have been set up specifically for that purpose may be quite simple. However, in most of the situations where the need for an SE may be felt, the Regulation and the Directive are fraught with cumbersome procedures, legal uncertainty and, sometimes, tax risks. In some cases, it will be possible to reduce these negative aspects to an acceptable minimum, but this will require extensive advice and careful planning.

2

Provisions of Community law applicable to the Societas Europaea

DIRK VAN GERVEN
NautaDutilh

I	Introduction 26
II	Application 28
III	Definition and characteristics 28
	1 Definition 28
	2 Legal personality 29
	3 Public company 30
	4 Comparison with the European economic interest grouping 30
IV	Identity 32
	1 Name and corporate form 32
	2 Registered office 33
V	Capital 34
VI	Formation 35
	1 General remarks 35
	2 Different means of formation 37
	A Formation by merger 37
	B Formation by merger through acquisition by a parent company holding at least 90% of the share capital of a subsidiary 45
	C Formation by merger through the acquisition of a wholly owned subsidiary 46
	D Formation by incorporation as a holding company 46
	E Formation by incorporation as a subsidiary 50
	F Formation by conversion 52
	3 Registration and publication 54
	A Registration 54
	B Publication 55
	C Effects of publication 56
	4 Acts committed on behalf of an SE in formation 57
	5 Subsidiaries 57
VII	Articles of an SE 58
VIII	Organisation and management 59
	1 General remarks 59
	2 General meeting of shareholders 59
	A Powers 59
	B Organisation 60

C   Quorum and voting   61
            D   Amendments to the articles of an SE   61
        3   Management (two-tier system/one-tier system)   62
            A   Powers and functioning   62
            B   Appointment, removal and liability   63
            C   Two-tier system   64
            D   One-tier system   67
IX   Annual accounts and consolidated accounts   68
X   Transfer of registered office   68
XI   Dissolution   73
XII Conversion into a national company   73
XIII Applicable law   75
XIII Conclusion   77

I   **Introduction**

1. Council Regulation No 2157/2001 of 8 October 2001 (the 'Regulation') introduced a new legal entity under Community law, the European company[1] or *Societas Europaea*, abbreviated 'SE' (Art. 1(1) Reg.).

The rules governing the SE were developed over the course of many years. The first proposal for a regulation on a European company dates from 1970. This proposal was based on one prepared by a group of experts in 1967. The provisions intended to establish a supervisory board with worker participation appeared in particular to be a step in the wrong direction. After years of discussion in various working groups, the European Commission issued a new proposal in 1989.[2] An amended proposal was prepared by the Commission in 1991[3] which, after much negotiation between the Member States and numerous amendments, finally resulted in the Regulation of 8 October 2001. In total, it took 30 years for Community lawmakers to develop a complete set of rules, which appears to regulate the SE only in part and refers to national law (of the Member State where the SE's registered office is located) on many key issues. This delay is deplorable considering the common market's need for swift regulation.

2. The European company is the second legal entity introduced by Community law. An SE can be established in any Member State of the European Union or the European Economic Area, provided the law of that Member State so permits. The first legal entity created under Community law was the European economic

---

[1] *Official Journal*, L 294 of 10 November 2001.
[2] *Ibid.*, C 263 of 16 October 1989.
[3] *Ibid.*, C 138 of 29 May 1991. See also the opinion of the Economic and Social Committee (*OJ*, C 124 of 21 May 1990) and of the European Parliament (*OJ*, C 342 of 20 December 1993).

interest grouping ('EEIG'), introduced by Council Regulation No. 2137/85 of 25 July 1985.[4] Recently a third legal entity, the European cooperative society ('SCE'), was introduced by Council Regulation No. 1435/2003 of 22 July 2003.[5] The Member States must adapt their legislation to make the incorporation of an SCE possible as from 18 August 2006. The three legal entities differ from those governed solely by national law in that they are (partially)[6] regulated by a uniform set of rules adopted at the Community level, which apply throughout the European Union and the European Economic Area (see below).

Employee involvement in an SE is governed by Council Directive 2001/86/EC of 8 October 2001 (the 'Directive').[7] A directive contains the general framework of the rules it intends to implement[8] and must be transposed into national law by each Member State.

Both the Regulation and the Directive apply not only in the European Union, but also throughout the European Economic Area ('EEA').[9] The EEA comprises the European Union and the three EFTA countries that entered into the EEA Agreement, i.e., Norway, Iceland and Liechtenstein. Consequently, any reference to the European Union in the Regulation and the Directive should be construed to refer to the European Economic Area. All references in this report to the European Union or to its Member States should be construed to include Norway, Iceland and Lichtenstein.

3. It is an established policy of the European Commission to create vehicles of Community law, in addition to harmonising company law throughout the Member States.

The SE is intended to offer a company with a European dimension *'free from the obstacles arising from the disparity and the limited territorial application of national company law'*.[10] It should permit businesses active across borders within the European Union to incorporate using a legal entity subject to the

---

[4] *Ibid.*, L 199 of 31 July 1985. See also nos 9 and 10 of this report for a brief description of the main characteristics of an EEIG.

[5] *Official Journal*, L 207 of 18 August 2003. Employee involvement is dealt with in Council Directive No. 2003/72 of 22 July 2003 (published in the same *Official Journal*).

[6] In reality, as a result of necessary compromises the Regulation only contains a minimum set of rules, which is identical in each Member State. The Member States will have to supplement the SE statute with national rules, which will differ from one country to another.

[7] Council Directive supplementing the Statute for a European company with regard to the involvement of employees, *Official Journal*, L 294/22 of 10 November 2001.

[8] Article 249 of the EC Treaty provides that a directive is binding as to the result to be achieved on each Member State to which it is addressed but leaves the choice of form and methods to the national authorities.

[9] As a result of the EEA decision of 25 June 2002 (*OJ*, L 266 of 3 October 2002), amending Annex XXII to the EEA Agreement of 2 May 1992.

[10] Seventh Recital of the Regulation.

same rules in each Member State, thus permitting European enterprises to more effectively compete with their US and Japanese counterparts.[11] More particularly, it solves the legal difficulties posed by restructuring and transactions involving companies from different Member States due to the lack of a legal entity governed by the same rules throughout the European Union.[12] The SE will permit cross-border mergers and the cross-border transfer of a company's registered office without the need for liquidation and the formation of a new company. The Regulation does not deal with tax consequences, however.[13]

The Regulation did not entirely succeed in its goals. Indeed, several issues regarding the organisation and structure of an SE are governed by the national law of the country where its registered office is located. The success of the SE will depend on whether European companies and businesses see in it advantages which national corporate forms do not offer. One advantage of the SE is that it is a legal entity governed primarily by the same rules which can move freely from one country to another without the legal restrictions imposed on national entities.

II Application

4. The Regulation entered into force on 8 October 2004 (Art. 70 Reg.). By that date, each Member State should have adapted its national legislation to permit the incorporation of an SE on its territory. In any event, those Member States which have not done so will have to recognise SEs established in other Member States, as the Regulation has direct effect throughout the European Union.[14] No transition period has been provided for the new Member States which acceded to the European Union on 1 May 2004; they must also adapt their legislation accordingly.

The Directive does not have direct effect. In general, it is addressed only to the Member States, which should have adapted their national legislation by the transposition deadline of 8 October 2004 (Art. 14(1) Reg.).

III Definition and characteristics

1 Definition

5. An SE is a public limited-liability company with legal personality and share capital which is based in the European Union (Art. 1 Reg.). As it is governed

---

[11] See the Memorandum from the Commission to Parliament, the Council and the two sides of industry of 15 July 1988 (COM(88) 320 final), p. 11.
[12] Third Recital of the Regulation.   [13] See Chapter 4 of this book.
[14] Art. 249 EC Treaty.

by a Community regulation, an SE should have a substantial link with the European Union or with one of the other countries of the European Economic Area, which can be shown by establishment of its registered office and place of central administration in a Member State (see no. 14 of this report).

In each Member State, an SE will be treated as *'if it were a public limited-liability company formed in accordance with the law of the Member State in which it has its registered office'* (Art. 10 Reg.). A list of qualifying public limited-liability companies in the former fifteen Member States is annexed to the Regulation.[15] This list has been extended by EC Regulation No. 885/2004 of 26 April 2004 to include public limited-liability companies in the new Member States, i.e., Cyprus, Lithuania, the Czech Republic, Malta, Estonia, Poland, Hungary, Slovakia, Latvia and Slovenia.[16]

6. An SE can be formed in several ways. First, an SE can be set up through a merger of two or more public limited-liability companies in the European Union, provided at least two of these companies are located in different Member States. Second, an SE can be formed as a holding company for European limited-liability companies. Third, it can be set up as a subsidiary. Finally, a national company can be converted into an SE. The conditions for formation of an SE differ depending on the method chosen and will be discussed in detail in this report.

2 Legal personality

7. An SE is a legal entity and enjoys legal personality (Art. 1(3) Reg.). This implies that it can acquire rights and liabilities by law, is entitled to sue to enforce its rights, and can be sued in order to ensure compliance with its obligations. An SE is a legal person, separate from its founder(s) and shareholders. An SE can only acquire rights and take on liabilities through its corporate bodies, in accordance with the applicable national rules for representation of the SE towards third parties. The actions of shareholders cannot be imputed to the SE and vice versa.

Legal personality also implies a separate set of assets and liabilities. Only the SE (through its corporate bodies) is entitled to dispose of its assets and liabilities. Shareholders cannot assert claims to the assets of an SE and are not liable for its debts. Shareholder liability is limited to the amount they have subscribed (Art. 1(2) Reg.), which means that creditors of an SE are not entitled

---

[15] See Annex Ia of this book. The public limited-liability company forms of Norway, Iceland and Liechtenstein were added by the Decision of the EEA Joint Committee No. 93/2002 of 25 June 2002 amending Annex XXII (Company Law) to the EEA Agreement (*Official Journal*, L 266/69 of 3 October 2002).

[16] *Official Journal*, L 168/1 of 1 May 2004.

to seek satisfaction of their claims from its shareholders, beyond the capital represented by their shares. If such shares are fully paid up, creditors cannot seek additional payment from shareholders in excess of their paid-in capital. The legal consequences of limited liability are determined in accordance with the rules applicable to public limited companies of the Member State where the SE has its registered office (Art. 10 Reg.).

3 Public company

8. An SE is a public company (Art. 1(1) Reg.), which means that its capital is open to the public, i.e., it can have an unlimited number of shareholders. Thus, an SE should be entitled to seek public financing, which can take the form of a public offering of securities,[17] even upon formation.

In order to determine the implications of the public character of an SE, reference must be made to the rules governing public companies of the Member State where the SE has its registered office (Art. 10 Reg.).

4 Comparison with the European economic interest grouping

9. As of 1 July 1989, European companies have been able to co-operate through a new legal vehicle under Community law, the European economic interest grouping ('EEIG'), introduced by Council Regulation No. 2137/85.[18] The EEIG is a legal entity incorporated *'to facilitate or develop the economic activities of its members and to improve or increase the results of those activities; its purpose is not to make profits for itself. Its activity shall be related to the economic activities of its members and must not be more than ancillary to those activities'*.[19] The purpose of the EEIG must be related to and based on the economic activities of its members to whom all its profits (or losses) revert.[20]

These special characteristics of an EEIG distinguish it from a regular company, whose purpose is to turn a profit for itself (and indirectly for its shareholders).[21] Since an EEIG is not a company, it is not subject to corporate law for issues that are not dealt with in the Regulation or its implementing national legislation.

10. In addition to a specific purpose, an EEIG boasts other special features.

---

[17] Twelfth Recital of the Regulation.
[18] *Official Journal*, L 199 of 31 July 1985; for a detailed discussion of this first vehicle of Community law and its implementation in the various Member States, see D. Van Gerven, C.A.V. Aalders et al., *European Economic Interest Groupings*, Kluwer, Deventer/Boston, 1990.
[19] Art. 3(1) Reg. No. 2137/85.   [20] *Ibid.*, Art. 21(1).   [21] *Ibid.*, Fifth Recital.

Members of an EEIG are jointly and severally liable without limitation for the debts and other liabilities of the EEIG.[22] This liability cannot be limited except in an agreement concluded with a particular creditor. If a member has paid beyond its share as specified in the EEIG contract, it can recover the excess from the other members in proportion to their shares. If the contract does not specify the share of each member, they must contribute an equal amount.[23] Due to this unlimited liability, the EEIG has no capital which must be contributed by its members.

As explained above, the shareholders of an SE are only liable for the amount of their capital contributions, which explains why the SE has a minimum capital requirement of €120,000 unless the law provides for a higher amount (see no. 23 of this report).

Owing to the specific purpose of an EEIG, all profits and losses are presumed to adhere to its members and are allocated amongst them in the proportion specified in the EEIG contract or, in the absence of such a provision, in equal shares.[24] This does not imply that the EEIG cannot retain income to finance its activities; rather it means that the profits from its activities are presumed to adhere to its members.[25] Actual distribution will depend on the EEIG contract. An SE realises profits to finance its own activities and seeks profits on its own behalf. Distribution of net profits requires a decision by the shareholders or, alternatively, by the board of directors, where permitted by national law.

An EEIG is transparent for tax purposes. The profits generated by an EEIG are taxed only in the hands of its members,[26] which also implies that any losses are considered to accrue to the members and can therefore be deducted by them. An SE is taxed on its profits as a separate taxable entity of the Member State where it has its registered and head office or where it has opened a branch, and is not a flow-through entity for tax purposes. As the Regulation does not discuss tax issues, national law will apply.[27]

Organisation of the management of an SE and of an EEIG differs. The management of an EEIG is entrusted to one or more managers who have full managerial authority.[28] The EEIG contract can provide for a board of managers. Any division of authority is not enforceable against third parties; however, the EEIG contract may include a joint signature clause indicating that the signatures of two or more managers are needed in order to bind the EEIG vis-à-vis third

---

[22] *Ibid.*, Art. 24(1).   [23] *Ibid.*, Art. 21(2).   [24] *Ibid.*, Art. 21(1).
[25] D. Van Gerven, 'The European Economic Interest Grouping (EEIG). The first European legal vehicle for co-operation between enterprises', in *European Economic Interest Groupings*, Van Gerven and Aalders (eds.), pp. 33–34.
[26] Art. 40 Regulation No. 2137/85.
[27] Twentieth Recital of the Regulation; see also Chapter 4 of this book.
[28] Art. 19(1) Reg. No. 2137/85; see also, D. Van Gerven, *op.cit.*, *European Economic Interest Groupings*, p. 30 et seq.

parties.[29] The management of an SE can be entrusted to either an administrative organ (one-tier system) or to a management organ overseen by a supervisory board (two-tier system). The administrative or management organ represents the SE in its relations with third parties (see no. 60 *et seq.* of this report).

Similar nationality requirements apply to both an EEIG and an SE. The participation of at least two companies or enterprises situated in at least two different Member States is required for an EEIG.[30] A similar requirement applies to an SE formed by merger (Art. 2(1) Reg.). When an SE is formed as a holding company or a subsidiary it suffices that the founding companies have a subsidiary or branch in another Member State (Art. 2(2) Reg.).

IV Identity

1 Name and corporate form

11. An SE must select a name. Third parties should be able to identify a legal entity so as to avoid confusion when dealing with it. Typically, corporate identity consists of the legal entity's name, registered office, registration number (depending on the country of registration) and corporate form.

The name of an SE must be preceded or followed by the abbreviation SE (Art. 11(1) Reg.). It may also refer in full to *Societas Europaea*, but, in any case, the abbreviation should also be added.

The obligation to mention the abbreviation 'SE' applies to all corporate documents of the SE and to those in which the name of the SE is mentioned. It also applies to other means of communication, such as a website, email account and other means of audio-visual communications.

12. Legal entities that are not incorporated as an SE in accordance with the Regulation are not entitled to use the abbreviation 'SE' in their names. Only an SE may do so (Art. 11(2) Reg.).

Failure to abide by this prohibition may result in a damages award if the confusion caused harm to third parties. For example, a company that holds itself out as an SE may be treated as having capital of at least €120,000, as required by the Regulation. If upon bankruptcy it becomes clear that the company had another corporate form, which it did not reveal and which requires less capital, its management could be held liable for intentionally creating a misleading financial impression.

However, legal entities that have registered in a Member State before 8 October 2004 with names that contain the abbreviation 'SE' will not be required to change their names (Art. 11(3) Reg.). In order to benefit from this exemption,

---

[29] Art. 20 Reg. No. 2137/85.   [30] *Ibid.*, Art. 4.

the legal entity need have included the abbreviation in its corporate name prior to 8 October 2004.

13. An SE is entitled to take action against another legal entity that uses a name identical or confusingly similar to its own. However, such action is not treated by the Regulation and therefore depends on national law.

2 Registered office

14. An SE must be registered in a Member State of the European Union (Art. 7 Reg.) or in one of the other Member States of the European Economic Area.[31] The registration formalities are determined by the law of the Member State where the SE is formed (see below).

Furthermore, an SE's registered office must be located in the same Member State as its head office (Art. 7 Reg.).[32] The head office is defined as the place where the company is effectively managed and controlled; it is the place where the central management and administration are located.[33]

It follows from the above that the registered and head offices of an SE must be situated in the European Union[34] at all times. An SE with its registered office in a Member State cannot have its head office outside the European Union.[35] This is also the case if the SE is registered in a Member State that uses the location of its registered office to determine applicable law.

A Member State may require that an SE registered within its borders register at the place where its head office is located (Art. 7 Reg.).

15. If an SE no longer has its registered office and head office in the same Member State, the Member State where its registered office is located must take the appropriate steps to require the SE to regularise its situation within a specified period of time. Regularisation can take the form of either (a) re-establishment by the SE of its head office in the Member State where its registered office is located or (b) transfer by the SE of its registered office, in accordance with the procedure set forth in Article 8 of the Regulation, to the Member State where its head office is located (see no. 16 *et seq.* of this report) (Art. 64(1)

---

[31] See no 1 *in fine* of this report.
[32] Within five years from the entry into force of the Regulation (i.e., before the end of 2009), the European Commission will analyse the appropriateness of allowing an SE to have its head office and registered office in different Member States (Art. 69(a) Reg.).
[33] Definition used by the European Court of Justice, 27 September 1988, *E.C.R.*, 1988, 5483. In Regulation No. 2137/85 of 25 July 1985 on the European economic interest grouping, the head office is defined as the place of 'central administration' (Art. 4). In the French version of the Regulation, head office is translated as '*administration centrale*'.
[34] See no. 1 *in fine* of this report.
[35] See no. 15 of this report for the sanctions that can be imposed for the establishment by an SE of its head office outside the European Union.

Reg.). The authorities of the Member State to which an SE transfers its head office (or keeps its head office after moving its registered office), in violation of the above requirement, must immediately inform the authorities of the Member State where the SE's registered office is located (Art. 64(4) Reg.) so as to enable them to take the appropriate measures, as described above.

If the SE fails to regularise its situation within the specified period of time, it may be involuntarily liquidated. National law must be adapted to permit liquidation for this reason (Art. 64(2) Reg.). The liquidation and publication thereof shall be organised in accordance with applicable national law (see no. 88 of this report).

Each Member State must provide in its national law for a judicial remedy allowing SEs to challenge the above decisions and procedures. This remedy shall suspend regularisation and liquidation (Art. 64(3) Reg.).

The above also holds true when an SE has its head office outside the European Union. In such a case, the third country is of course under no obligation to inform the authorities of the Member State where the SE's registered office is located. Sanctions may be imposed nevertheless, and the SE can be liquidated if it fails to regularise its situation.

V   Capital

16. An SE has share capital, which must be expressed in euros (Art. 4(1) Reg.).

In those Member States which have yet to introduce the euro as their sole currency, an SE must express its capital in the national currency applicable to public limited-liability companies registered in that state. However, notwithstanding any relevant national legislation, an SE registered in such a Member State can also express its capital in euros (Art. 67(1) Reg.). In such a case, the articles must indicate the capital in both the national currency and in euros. The conversion rate will be that of the last day of the month preceding the month in which the SE was formed (Art. 67(1) Reg.). This rule will also apply to subsequent capital increases. For Member States that do not belong to the euro zone, the conversion rate shall be fixed by the European Commission on the basis of the reference exchange rate published by the European Central Bank.[36]

The capital is represented by shares (Art. 1(2) Reg.).

---

[36] See also the Agreement of 1 September 1998 between the European Central Bank and the national central banks of the Member States outside the euro area laying down the operating procedures for an exchange rate mechanism in stage three of Economic and Monetary Union (*Official Journal*, C 345/6, of 13 November 1998).

The subscription and payment of shares, changes to share capital (including capital increases and decreases), the status of capital in general, the nature of shares and the rights and obligations attached thereto, and the transfer of shares are governed by the law applicable to public limited-liability companies of the Member State where the SE's registered office is located (Art. 5 Reg.). These rules also apply to the issuance of bonds and other securities by an SE, as well as to the rights and obligations attached to such securities and the transfer thereof (Art. 5 Reg.).

17. An SE must have a minimum share capital of at least €120,000 (Art. 4(2) Reg.). This relatively significant amount is intended to ensure that only companies of a reasonable size register as SEs and to discourage small and medium-sized undertakings from opting for SE status.[37]

If the laws of a Member State require greater subscribed capital for public limited companies, this higher amount will apply to SEs registered in that state (Art. 4(3) Reg.).

VI   Formation

1   General remarks

18. An SE can only be incorporated in a Member State of the European Union.[38] As an entity governed by Community law, an SE is restricted to the territory of the European Union and cannot establish its head office outside the European Union (see no. 14 of this report). An SE can be formed in any Member State of the European Union, including the new Member States which acceded on 1 May 2004.

The Regulation stipulates four different methods of formation: (i) by merger; (ii) by incorporation as a holding company; (iii) by formation as a subsidiary; and (iv) by conversion. The Regulation provides specific rules for formation by merger in the event of the absorption by a parent company holding at least 90% of the shares of a subsidiary. These rules will discussed in further detail below.

An SE can only be registered in a Member State if an agreement on employee involvement has been concluded, if required (Art. 12(2) Reg.; see no. 50 of this report). Registration is required for the SE to exist (see no. 49 of this report). Of course, if there are no employees, this requirement does not apply.

19. In general, an SE can only be created by companies incorporated under the laws of a Member State of the European Union and which have both their

---

[37] Thirteenth Recital of the Regulation.   [38] See no 1 *in fine* of this report.

head office and registered office in the European Union (Art. 2 Reg.).[39] It is furthermore required that at least two of the companies involved be subject to the laws of different Member States (Art. 2 Reg.). This requirement excludes the formation of an SE between companies from the same Member State. As a Community legal entity (rather than a national company), an SE requires the involvement of companies from different Member States.

The requirement that the companies involved must have both their head office and registered office in the European Union reflects differences in national law regarding choice of law. Several countries adhere to the incorporation theory, which provides that a legal entity is governed by the law of its place of incorporation (i.e., the location of its registered office). Other countries apply the head office (*siège réel*) theory, according to which the law of the place where the head office is located applies. The head office is defined as the place of effective management.[40]

The above implies that a non-EU company cannot be used to form an SE. However, it could do so by first incorporating a subsidiary in a Member State of the European Union or acting through an affiliate incorporated in a Member State.

A Member State can provide that a company incorporated under the laws of a Member State which does not have its head office in the European Union can participate in the formation of an SE provided (i) it has its registered office in the latter state and (ii) it has a real and continuous link with the economy of a Member State (Art. 2(5) Reg.). Both conditions must be satisfied upon formation. A continuous economic link excludes brass plate companies with no real activity within the European Union. A sufficient continuous economic link shall be found to exist if the company has an establishment in a Member State from which it conducts operations.[41] A formal establishment with no current activity does not qualify. A link cannot be established based solely on the nationality of the company's shareholders, management or members of its supervisory board.[42]

20. For matters not dealt with in the Regulation, the formation of an SE is governed by the law applicable to public limited-liability companies of the

---

[39] See no. 1 *in fine* of this report.

[40] This is the definition used by the European Court of Justice, 27 September 1988, *E.C.R.*, 1988, 5483. In the Twenty-seventieth Recital of the Regulation, the Council explains that the *siège reel* arrangement adopted by the Regulation with respect to SEs is without prejudice to national law and, furthermore, does not pre-empt any choices to be made for other Community texts on company law.

[41] Twenty-third Recital of the Regulation.

[42] See the 1962 General Programme for the abolition of restrictions on freedom of establishment (*OJ*, L 36/62 of 15 January 1962), to which the Twenty-third Recital of the Regulation refers in this respect.

Member State in which its registered office is located (Art. 15(1) Reg.). A list of qualifying public limited-liability companies in the respective Member States is attached to the Regulation as Annex I.[43]

The registration of a new SE shall be made public in accordance with the laws of the Member State where its registered office is located (Art. 15(2) Reg.). The publication formalities are organised by national law in accordance with the First Company Law Directive of 9 March 1968.[44] The creation of an SE need also be mentioned in the *Official Journal of the European Communities*.[45]

21. The rules governing an SE, as drafted by its founders or shareholders, are set forth in its articles (referred to as 'statutes' in the Regulation). The articles include both the instrument of incorporation and permanent rules governing the organisation and management of the company as well as shareholder relations. Reference to the 'statutes' (i.e., the articles) should be construed to include both documents (Art. 6 Reg.; see also no. 57 of this report).

2 Different means of formation

A Formation by merger

22. Public limited-liability companies established in at least two different Member States can form an SE by merger. In order to take part in the merger, each company must have its registered office and head office in the European Union (Art. 2(1) Reg.). A Member State can, however, allow a company formed under the laws of a Member State with its registered office in such latter state but its head office outside the European Union to participate in the merger if it has a real and continuous link with the economy of that or another Member State (Art. 2(5) Reg.; see also no. 26 *in fine* of this report).

Only public limited-liability companies can form an SE by merger. Annex I to the Regulation lists those national companies that qualify.[46]

23. The merger can be organised in one of two ways set forth in the Third Company Law Directive on mergers of public limited-liability companies (the 'Third Company Law Directive'):[47] by acquisition or by the formation of a new company (Art. 17(2) Reg.). The procedure set forth in the Third Company Law Directive and its implementing national legislation must be observed.

A merger by acquisition is defined as *'the operation whereby one or more companies are wound up without going into liquidation*[48] *and transfer to another*

---

[43] See Annex Ib of this book.   [44] See no. 49 *et seq.* of this report.
[45] See no. 52 of this report.   [46] See Annex Ib of this book.
[47] *Official Journal*, L 295 of 20 October 1978.
[48] National law may provide that this type of merger can also be organised by companies which are already in liquidation provided they have not yet begun to distribute their assets to shareholders (Art. 3(2) Third Company Law Directive).

all their assets and liabilities in exchange for the issue to the shareholders of the company or companies being acquired of shares in the acquiring company and a cash payment, if any, not exceeding 10% of the nominal value of the shares so issued or, where they have no nominal value, of their accounting par value.[49] The acquiring company will become an SE by operation of law (Art. 17(2) Reg.). Upon conclusion of the merger, the acquiring company will adopt the corporate form of an SE, which implies that its articles should be amended accordingly.

A merger by formation of a new company is defined as '*the operation whereby several companies are wound up without going into liquidation*[50] *and transfer to the company that they set up all their assets and liabilities in exchange for the issue to their shareholders of shares in the new company and a cash payment, if any, not exceeding 10% of the nominal value of the shares so issued or, where they have no nominal value, of their accounting par value*'.[51] The new company will be an SE (Art. 17(2) Reg.).

An SE is a continuation of the merged companies and therefore will own all the assets and liabilities of these companies, without interruption. All the assets and liabilities of the merged companies are transferred by operation of law to the acquiring company (Art. 29 Reg.).

National law may provide that the competent authorities of a Member State can oppose the formation of an SE by merger if the merger involves a company incorporated in that state. However, this opposition will only be valid if it is expressed prior to the issuance of a certificate by the court, notary or other authority responsible for investigating the legality of the merger in accordance with Article 25(2) of the Regulation (see no. 30 of this report).

Opposition can only be based on grounds of public interest (Art. 19 Reg.). National law can define and limit what constitutes the public interest.

This possibility allows the Member States to oppose participation by certain types of entities, such as banks and insurance companies, in a merger that could undermine their financial stability and consequently the interests of their stakeholders.

This opposition should be subject to judicial review (Art. 19 Reg.).

24. The merger shall be organised in accordance with the rules laid down in the Regulation and in the Third Company Law Directive of 9 October 1978 on

---

[49] Art. 3(1) of the Third Company Law Directive concerning mergers of public limited-liability companies.
[50] National law may provide that this type of merger can also be organised by companies which are already in liquidation provided they have not yet begun to distribute their assets to shareholders (Art. 4(2) Third Company Law Directive).
[51] *Ibid.*, Art. 4(1).

mergers involving public limited-liability companies. For matters not covered by the Regulation, the procedure for each company involved will be governed separately by the laws of the Member State where its registered office is located (Art. 3(1) Reg.). The rules applicable to mergers involving public limited companies in that Member State shall apply (Art. 18 Reg.). In this respect, the Member States should all have transposed the Third Company Law Directive. The validity of the merger will thus be determined in accordance with national law (Art. 25 Reg.), including provisions transposing the Third Company Law Directive and any other national provisions to the extent they do not conflict with the Third Company Law Directive.

National legislation on the protection of creditors, bondholders and the holders of other securities in a merger involving public limited-liability companies[52] shall apply (Art. 24(1) Reg.). The Member States may adopt provisions designed to ensure appropriate protection of minority shareholders who oppose the merger (Art. 24(2) Reg.).[53]

Management must have completed negotiations to reach an arrangement on employee involvement in accordance with the Directive (see no. 50 of this report for more details). This issue is also discussed further in Chapter 3.

25. In any event, the formation of an SE by merger requires the approval of the general meeting of shareholders (see no. 29 of this report). This holds true even if national law allows a merger of public limited-liability companies to be approved solely by the boards of directors.[54]

In preparation for the merger, the management bodies of the companies must prepare draft terms of merger[55] in writing.[56] This is a single document prepared jointly by all companies involved in the merger and must include at least the following information (Art. 20(1) Reg.):

(i) the name and address of the registered office of each company involved and the proposed name and registered office of the SE; national law may also require that the address of the head office be mentioned (Art. 20(2) Reg.);
(ii) the share-exchange ratio and the amount of cash payment to shareholders, if any;
(iii) the terms for the allotment of shares in the SE amongst shareholders;
(iv) the date from which shareholders of the SE will be entitled to share in its profits and any special conditions affecting that entitlement;

---

[52] For a list of qualifying public limited-liability companies, see Annex Ib of this book.
[53] See also Arts. 13, 14 and 15 Third Company Law Directive.
[54] Art. 8 of the Third Company Law Directive, which allows the possibility to specify under national law that the approval of the shareholders of the acquiring company is required (in the event of a merger by acquisition), is inapplicable to a merger to create an SE, as Art. 23(1) of the Regulation requires the approval of the general meeting of each merging company.
[55] The Regulation refers to the *'management or administrative organs of merging companies'* (Art. 20(1)). The competent corporate body will depend on national law.
[56] Art. 5(1) Third Company Law Directive.

(v) the date from which the transactions of the merging companies will be treated for accounting purposes as being those of the SE; as the merger does not imply the liquidation of the merging companies, ongoing transactions will inure to the benefit or cost of the SE, but for accounting purposes a transfer date is required;
(vi) the rights conferred by the SE on the holders of shares to which special rights are attached and of other securities or the measures proposed concerning them;
(vii) any special advantages granted to the experts who examined the draft terms of merger or to members of the administrative, management, supervisory or controlling organs of the merging companies;
(viii) the articles of the SE; in the event of a merger by acquisition, these can take the form of the amended articles of the acquiring company, although the articles should preferably be restated after the merger; the articles with the proposed amendments should be made available for review by shareholders; and
(ix) information on the procedures by which arrangements for employee involvement are determined pursuant to the Directive.[57]

National law may require additional information (Art. 20(2) Reg.). At least two sets of laws will apply as companies from at least two different Member States will participate in the merger. If one or more laws require that additional information be included in the draft terms of merger, such information must be added. This information will be compiled in a single document which is identical for all companies involved.[58] Of course, if national law requires that this document be prepared in a particular language, a translation into that language will be necessary, although the translation should be identical to the original.

The draft terms of merger must be published in accordance with applicable national law at least one month before the general meeting scheduled to vote on the merger.[59] National law may require a longer notice period, however, in which case it suffices that each company involved ensure publication in accordance with its applicable law.

26. The management of each company participating in the merger must prepare a detailed report explaining the draft terms of merger. This report should set out the legal and economic grounds for the merger, in particular the share-exchange ratio,[60] and describe any special valuation difficulties that may have arisen in connection with preparation of the terms of merger.[61]

Furthermore, if the latest annual accounts of one of the merging companies relate to a financial year that ended more than six months before the date of the draft terms of merger, that company must prepare an accounting statement to

---

[57] See no. 50 of this report and Chapter 3 of this book.
[58] Art. 20 of the Regulation refers to '*draft*' terms of merger and states clearly that information on '*each of the merging companies*' should be included in this document (see Art. 20(a), (e) and (g)).
[59] Art. 6 Third Company Law Directive.   [60] *Ibid.*, Art. 9.   [61] *Ibid.*

reflect its financial situation as it existed no earlier than the first day of the third month preceding the date of the draft terms of merger.[62]

The accounting statement must use the same methods and format as the company's last annual balance sheet. National law may provide that (i) it is not necessary to take a fresh physical inventory and (ii) the valuation shown on the last balance sheet may only be altered to reflect new entries in the books. With respect to the latter, the statement must take into account interim depreciation and reserves as well as material changes in actual value not shown on the books.[63]

27. One or more experts must be appointed to examine the draft terms of merger and explain their findings in a report to shareholders.[64] The expert(s) shall be appointed by a judicial or administrative authority in the Member State of the company concerned or by the company itself from a list approved by the aforementioned judicial or administrative authority. Alternatively, the merging companies may jointly request the appointment of an expert by the competent judicial or administrative authority in a Member State where one of them is registered or the proposed SE will be registered, to draft a report for all companies involved (Art. 22 Reg.). In such a case, the report should be drafted in the language of each country in which a merging company is established, depending on the requirements of national law.

The report should (i) state whether the share-exchange ratio is fair and reasonable and (ii) describe any special valuation difficulties. The section regarding the share-exchange ratio must at least (i) indicate the method(s) used to reach the proposed ratio, (ii) state whether such method(s) are adequate, (iii) indicate the values reached using each method, and (iv) give an opinion as to the relative importance attached to each method in arriving at these values.[65]

The experts are entitled to request from each merging company any information they consider necessary to enable them to complete their function.[66]

28. The following information must be published in the official gazettes of the Member States in question (Art. 21 Reg.):

(i) the corporate form, name and registered office of each company involved in the merger;
(ii) the national registry in which information on each company is made available to the public;[67]

---

[62] *Ibid.*, Art. 11(1)(c).   [63] *Ibid.*, Art. 11(2).   [64] *Ibid.*, Art. 10(1).   [65] *Ibid.*, Art. 10(2).
[66] Art. 22 Reg.; Art. 10(3) Third Company Law Directive.
[67] This is the national registry designated in accordance with Art. 3(2) of the First Company Law Directive of 9 March 1968 on the co-ordination of safeguards required by the Member States of companies, within the meaning of Art. 58 of the Treaty, to protect the interests of members and others, with a view to making such safeguards equivalent throughout the Community (*Official Journal*, L 65 of 14 March 1968).

(iii) an indication of the arrangements under national laws on the protection of creditors (Art. 24 Reg.) for the exercise of creditors' rights and the address at which complete information on these arrangements may be obtained free of charge;

(iv) an indication of the arrangements under national laws on the protection of minority shareholders (Art. 24 Reg.) for the exercise of their rights and the address where minority shareholders can obtain complete information on these arrangements free of charge;

(v) the proposed name and address of the registered office of the SE.

National law may require the publication of additional information (Art. 21 Reg.).

As indicated above, the draft terms of merger must also be made public at least one month prior to approval. National law may provide for a longer notice period, however. In general, national law requires that the draft terms of merger be filed with the local registry where information on each participating company is kept.

The shareholders of the merging companies should be able to consult the following documents at least one month before the general meeting scheduled to vote on the terms of merger: (i) the draft terms of merger; (ii) the annual accounts and annual management reports for the last three years of the merging companies; (iii) if the latest accounts relate to a financial year which ended more than six months before the date of the draft terms of merger, accounting statements drawn up as at a date which must not be earlier than the first day of the third month preceding the date of the draft terms of merger (see no. 26 of this report); (iv) the management report explaining the draft terms of merger (see no. 26 of this report); and (v) the expert's report (see no. 27 of this report).[68] Shareholders are entitled to receive copies of these documents[69] free of charge upon request.

29. The terms of merger and any amendments to the articles of association or by-laws of the acquiring company must be approved by a qualified majority of the shareholders of each merging company (Art. 23(1) Reg.). National law will determine the majority required, in accordance with Article 7 of the Third Company Law Directive. This majority should not be less than either (i) two-thirds of the votes attached to the shares and other securities of the company represented at the meeting or (ii) a simple majority of votes cast if those shareholders representing at least 50% of the subscribed capital are present or validly represented. If there is more than one class of shares entitled to vote, the decision will require a separate vote by each class of shareholders whose rights are affected by the decision.[70]

---

[68] Art. 11(1) Third Company Law Directive.   [69] *Ibid.*, Art. 11(3).   [70] *Ibid.*, Art. 7.

If national law does not provide for judicial or administrative oversight of the merger or if such supervision does not extend to all legal acts required for the merger, the minutes of the general meeting must be signed in due form, i.e., usually before a notary or other official authorised to legalise documents.[71] The notary or other official will verify and certify the existence and validity of the legal acts and formalities required for the merger and the draft terms of merger.[72]

Employee involvement in the approval process is regulated by national law in accordance with the Directive (Art. 23(2) Reg.). The general meeting of each merging company may reserve the right to make registration of the SE contingent upon its express ratification of the arrangements on employee involvement. In this case, registration of the SE will only be possible once this ratification has been obtained (Art. 23(2) Reg.).

30. Each Member State shall provide that a court, notary or other competent authority will issue a certificate attesting to the completion of the pre-merger acts and formalities (Art. 25(2) Reg.). This certificate must be issued in those Member States where the merging companies' registered offices are located and in the Member State where the SE will be registered. The attestation is limited to verification of that portion of the procedure initiated by the company subject to the laws of that Member State (Art. 25(1) Reg.). With respect to the acquiring company, i.e., the company that will eventually become the SE (a merger by acquisition) or the new company (the SE that results from a merger by formation), the attestation should also contain a discussion of the legality of the procedure for completion of the merger and formation of the SE (Art. 26(1) Reg.), including verification that the proposed articles do not conflict with the proposed arrangement for employee involvement (Art. 12(4) Reg.; see also no. 59 of this report).

If national law provides for judicial or administrative oversight of the merger, the certificate shall be issued by the supervisory authority. If approval of the merger must take the form of a legalised document, the notary or other official entrusted with drafting the document shall issue the certificate. However, with respect to the acquiring company or the newly formed entity, the certificate can only be issued once the authority has received corresponding certificates from the authorities of the Member States of the other merging companies and has completed its verification procedure.

National law may provide for a procedure to scrutinise and amend the share-exchange ratio or to compensate minority shareholders. Such a procedure will only apply if the other merging companies situated in Member States which do not provide for such a procedure explicitly accept that the shareholders of

---

[71] *Ibid.*, Art. 16(1).   [72] *Ibid.*, Art. 16(2); see also no 30 of this report.

the company situated in the former Member State can have recourse to it. This decision must be taken by the general meeting voting on the terms of merger (Art. 25(3) Reg.). Except if otherwise provided by national law, the shareholders of the other merging companies shall not have recourse to this procedure.

If such a procedure applies, it cannot be invoked to hold up the merger process, and a certificate can be issued before the end of the procedure. Registration of the merger is possible notwithstanding any ongoing procedure to compensate minority shareholders (Art. 25(3) Reg.). The certificate must state that a procedure is pending, however. The decision(s) in such a procedure will be binding on the acquiring company and its shareholders (Art. 25(3) Reg.).

The merging companies shall then submit the certificate and a copy of the terms of merger to the court, notary or other competent authority of the state where the registered office of the SE, i.e., the acquiring or newly formed company, is located within six months from issuance of the certificate (Art. 26(2) Reg.). This authority will verify in particular that (i) the terms of merger have been approved by the general meeting of each merging company on the same terms; (ii) arrangements for employee involvement have been determined pursuant to the Directive;[73] and (iii) the SE has been formed in accordance with the requirements of the Member State where its registered office is located (Art. 26(3) and (4) Reg.). The authority of the Member State where the SE is registered will only issue its certificate once all verification formalities have been satisfactorily completed.

National law may provide that the absence of proper oversight of the legality of the merger pursuant to the above rules is a ground for winding up the SE (Art. 30 Reg.).

31. The merger shall take effect on the date on which the SE is registered with the national registry of the Member State where its registered office is located. This will also be the date on which the SE assumes corporate existence with its amended articles (Art. 27(1) Reg.). Registration is only possible if the formalities set forth under no. 30 above have been completed (Art. 27(2) Reg.) and if an arrangement for employee involvement has been concluded when required (see no. 50 of this report). The national registry will require proof of the issuance of certificates.

After registration, a notice of completion of the merger is published in the official national gazettes of the Member States in which the merging companies are situated and in which the SE has its registered office (Art. 28 Reg.) as well as in the *Official Journal of the European Communities* (Art. 14(1) Reg.). The content of the publication in the national gazettes is determined by national law (see no. 52 of this report). For the legal implications of publication, see no. 53 of this report.

---

[73] See no. 50 of this report.

Completion of these publication formalities can be organised solely by the acquiring or newly formed company,[74] since the other companies will have ceased to exist. If approval of the merger takes the form of a legalised document, the notary or other official who drafted the document may handle the publication formalities, in accordance with national law.

32. Once the merger is complete, the SE will be the sole owner of all assets and liabilities of the merged companies. The other companies that took part in the merger shall cease to exist by operation of law ('*ipso jure*') (Arts. 29(1)(c) and 2(c) Reg.). The acquiring company, in the event of a merger by acquisition, shall assume the corporate form of an SE by operation of law (Art. 29(1)(d) Reg.).

All assets and liabilities of each company that ceases to exist will be transferred by operation of law to the acquiring or newly formed company (Art. 29(1)(a) and (2)(a) Reg.). If national law requires the completion of any special formalities before the transfer of certain assets, rights and obligations can take effect against third parties, these formalities must be carried out by the merging companies or by the SE following registration (Art. 29(3) Reg.). These additional requirements do not affect the merger and cannot be used by the national authorities to postpone registration of the merger or of the SE.

All rights and obligations of the participating companies on terms and conditions of employment arising from national law, practice and individual employment contracts or employment relationships existing on the date of registration shall be transferred to the SE upon registration (Art. 29(4) Reg.).

The shareholders of the merging companies shall become shareholders in the SE by operation of law (Art. 29(1)(b) and (2)(b) Reg.).

The SE will be governed by the rules applicable to public limited-liability companies of the state where its registered office is located (Art. 10 Reg.).

33. A merger cannot be declared void after registration of an SE (Art. 30 Reg.). As a result, national rules on the avoidance of mergers no longer apply once the merger and the SE have been recorded in the national registry.[75]

B Formation by merger through acquisition by a parent company holding at least 90% of the share capital of a subsidiary

34. When at least 90% of the shares and voting securities of a public limited-liability company are held by another public limited-liability company, it is not necessary to commission a report from management[76] or from an independent

---

[74] Art. 18(2) of the Third Company Law Directive.
[75] The Third Company Law Directive allows the Member States to specify in their national laws grounds for the invalidity of a merger under certain conditions (Art. 22).
[76] See no. 46 of this report.

expert[77] on the draft terms of merger of the two companies. Moreover, no further documents necessary for scrutiny are required (Art. 31(2) Reg.). National law may provide otherwise, however.

C   Formation by merger through the acquisition of a wholly owned subsidiary

35. Special rules apply to a merger whereby a parent company absorbs a wholly owned subsidiary. In order to qualify, the parent company must hold all the shares and other voting securities issued by the subsidiary (Art. 31(1) Reg.). Both companies should be public limited-liability companies as defined in the Regulation (see Annex Ib of this book for a complete list). In countries where the shares of public limited-liability companies must be held by at least two shareholders (belonging to the same group), the shares must be transferred to one shareholder in order to take advantage of this simplified merger procedure.

In such a case, the draft terms of merger need not indicate the share-exchange ratio, the amount of the cash payment (if any), the terms for allocating shares in the SE, the date on which shareholders in the SE will be entitled to share in the profits, and any special conditions affecting this entitlement.

Furthermore, no report by an independent expert on the merger is required.[78] Only a management report on the draft terms of merger need be prepared, if so required by national law (Art. 31(2) Reg.). Nor need the documents necessary for scrutiny be issued, unless national law provides otherwise (Art. 31(2) Reg.).

The other rules apply without exception.

D   Formation by incorporation as a holding company

36. Two or more companies established in the European Union[79] can ask their shareholders to contribute their shares to an SE, which will become the parent company, in exchange for shares in the holding SE.

A holding SE can only be formed by two or more public and/or private limited-liability companies, each with its registered office and head office in the European Union[80] (Art. 2(2) Reg.). A list of qualifying companies in each Member State is appended to the Regulation as Annex II (see page 533 of this book).

If a company formed under the laws of a Member State has its head office outside the European Union, it cannot participate in the formation of a holding SE, unless the Member State so allows and such company has its registered office in the Member State in which it is formed and has a real and continuous

---

[77] See no. 27 of this report.
[78] Art. 10 of the Third Company Law Directive does not apply in such a case (Art. 24 of the Third Company Law Directive).
[79] See no. 1 *in fine* of this report.   [80] *Ibid.*

link with the economy of a Member State (Art. 2(5) Reg.; see also no. 19 of this report).

In order to be able to establish a holding SE, at least two of the companies promoting the operation must be governed by the laws of different Member States or at least two of these companies must have owned a subsidiary governed by the laws of another Member State or operated a branch situated in another Member State for at least two years (Art. 2(2) Reg.).

The companies promoting the holding SE shall continue to exist (Art. 32(1) Reg.). The SE is a separate legal entity with its own assets and liabilities.

The Member States can adopt provisions designed to ensure the protection of creditors, employees and minority shareholders who oppose the formation of a holding SE (Art. 34 Reg.).

In general, for matters not dealt with by the Regulation, the national law applicable to public limited companies of the Member State where the SE has its registered office will apply (Art. 3(1) Reg.).

37. The companies promoting the operation must prepare draft terms for the formation of the holding SE and approve the same. This is a single document which is identical for all companies involved.[81] Of course, if national law requires that this document be prepared in a particular language, a translation into that language will be necessary, although the translation should be identical to the original.

These draft terms shall:

(i) include a report explaining and justifying the legal and economic aspects of the formation and indicating the implications of the formation for shareholders and employees;
(ii) mention
   (a) the name and address of the registered office of each of the companies promoting the operation, as well as the proposed name and address of the registered office of the SE;
   (b) the share-exchange ratio and the amount of any cash payment to shareholders;
   (c) the terms for allotment of shares in the SE;
   (d) the rights conferred by the SE on the holders of shares to which special rights are attached and on the holders of securities other than shares or the measures proposed concerning them;
   (e) any special advantages granted to the experts who examined the draft terms of formation (see below) or to members of the administrative, management, supervisory or controlling bodies of the companies promoting the operation;
   (f) the articles of the SE; and

---

[81] Art. 32(2) of the Regulation refers to '*draft*' terms of merger and states clearly that information on '*each of the merging companies*' should be included in this document.

(g) information on the procedures by which arrangements for employee involvement are determined pursuant to the Directive;[82] and

(iii) fix the minimum proportion of shares in each company promoting the operation which its shareholders must contribute to the SE; this should be more than those shares conferring 50% of the permanent voting rights (Art. 32(2) Reg.).

If the minimum number of shares indicated in (iii) is not contributed, the operation will not go through.

Furthermore, an arrangement for employee involvement in accordance with the Directive must be concluded or, failing such agreement or a decision by the employee special negotiating body to rely on the rules of information and consultation of employees in force in the Member States where the SE has employees, a resolution must be passed by the general meeting of all companies involved to apply the reference provisions of the Directive (see no. 50 of this report and Chapter 3 of this book).

38. A report by an independent expert must be commissioned, in which the expert gives an opinion on the draft terms of formation to shareholders. Several experts can be entrusted with this task. Each company promoting the operation can designate its own expert. It is also possible for the companies to agree jointly on the appointment of a single expert or team of experts to act on their behalf. The expert's name should appear on a list approved by the Member State of the company in question; alternatively, the expert can be appointed by a judicial or administrative authority of that Member State, if no such list exists. If one expert or a team of experts is appointed, they should hail from a Member State in which at least one of the companies promoting the operation is established or in which the proposed SE will be registered (Art. 32(4) Reg.).

The report should (i) indicate any particular valuation difficulties, (ii) state whether the proposed share-exchange ratio is fair and reasonable, and (iii) indicate the methods used to arrive at this ratio and whether such methods are adequate in the case at hand (Art. 32(5) Reg.).

The purpose of the expert's report is to inform shareholders, and it must therefore be made available to shareholders before the general meeting scheduled to vote on the formation of the holding SE. As this is not addressed by the Regulation, national law will determine the manner in which the report is made available.

39. The draft terms must be published in each Member State concerned at least one month before the date of the general meeting scheduled to vote on the formation of the holding SE (Art. 32(3) Reg.). These publication formalities are determined by national law in accordance with Article 3 of the First Company Law Directive of 9 March 1968. A filing with the national registry where information on the founding companies is made public is required, as is publication

---

[82] See no. 50 of this report.

in the official gazettes of the Member States in question of the terms in full, an extract thereof or a mention that the terms are available at the national registry.

40. The terms of formation for the holding SE must be presented to the shareholders of each company promoting the operation for approval (Art. 32(6) Reg.). The required majority depends on the law applicable to the company in question.

Employee involvement in the decision-making process is determined by national law in accordance with the Directive. The general meeting of each company promoting the operation can reserve the right to make registration of the holding SE contingent on its express ratification of the arrangements for employee involvement (Art. 32(6) Reg.).

The Member States may adopt special provisions designed to protect employees, creditors and shareholders who oppose the formation of a holding SE (Art. 34 Reg.).

41. Once the terms of formation of the holding SE have been approved, the shareholders of each company promoting the operation will decide whether they wish to contribute their shares to the holding SE in exchange for shares in the latter. They will have three months in which to make a decision, starting the date on which the terms of formation are approved (Art. 33(1) Reg.). If approval is made subject to ratification of the arrangements for employee involvement, this three-month period will start running upon ratification.

A holding SE can only be formed if during this three-month period a sufficient number of shares has been contributed from each company in accordance with the draft terms of formation.[83] If the terms of formation mention other conditions, these must also be fulfilled within this time period (Art. 33(2) Reg.). If this is not the case, the holding SE cannot be formed.

42. If these conditions are met, each company promoting the operation will file the required information in the appropriate form with its national registry and publish a notice to this effect in its official national gazette (Art. 33(3) Reg.). Such filing does not indicate completion of the formation of a holding SE. Indeed, shareholders who have not indicated whether they intend to contribute their shares to the SE shall have an additional month in which to decide (Art. 33(3) Reg.).

Shareholders who contribute their shares will receive shares in the holding SE in return in accordance with the terms of formation (Art. 33(4) Reg.). Only once the aforementioned additional one-month period has expired and all shareholders

---

[83] See no. 37 of this report.

who decided to contribute their shares have received shares in the holding SE can the holding SE be registered with the national registry of the Member State where its registered office is located.

43. The companies promoting the operation must register formation of the holding SE with the national registry of the Member State where the SE's registered office is located (see no. 49 of this report). The national registry can only register the SE if it has been demonstrated that the formalities and conditions for formation are complete (Art. 33(5) Reg.) and if an agreement for employee involvement has been concluded or, failing such agreement or a decision by the employee special negotiating body to rely on the rules of information and consultation of employees in force in the Member States where the SE has employees, a resolution has been passed by the general meeting of all companies involved to apply the standard provisions of the Directive.[84] The manner in which this verification is made will depend on national law.

A notice of incorporation must be published in the national official gazette and in the *Official Journal of the European Communities* (Art. 14(1) Reg.). The content of the publication in the national gazette will be determined by national law.[85] For the legal implications of this publication, see no. 53 of this report.

The SE acquires legal personality on the date on which it is registered (Art. 16(1) Reg.). It is governed by the rules applicable to public limited-liability companies of the Member State where its registered office is located (Art. 10 Reg.).

E Formation by incorporation as a subsidiary

44. Companies or other legal entities situated in the European Union[86] can incorporate an SE. This possibility is open to *'companies and firms within the meaning of the second paragraph of Article [58]*[87] *of the Treaty and other legal bodies governed by public or private law'* (Art. 2(3) Reg.). The only requirements are that these companies and legal entities must be formed under the laws of a Member State and have their registered and head offices in the European Union. If a company formed under the laws of a Member State has its head office outside the European Union, it cannot participate in the formation of a subsidiary SE, unless the Member State in question so allows and that company has its registered office in the Member State in which it is formed and has a real and continuous link with the economy of a Member State (Art. 2(5) Reg.; see no. 19 of this report).

---

[84] See no. 50 of this report.   [85] See no. 52 of this report.
[86] See no. 1 *in fine* of this report.
[87] The Regulation refers to Art. 48 of the EC Treaty. In the new numbering of the Treaty, as amended by the Treaty of Amsterdam, Art. 48 became Art. 58.

The formation of a subsidiary SE is open to all legal entities within the meaning of Article 58 of the EC Treaty. These include '*[c]ompanies or firms formed in accordance with the law of a Member State and having their registered office, central administration or principal place of business within the Community*'. Companies or firms are defined as '*companies or firms constituted under civil or commercial law, including co-operative societies, and other legal persons governed by public or private law, save for those which are non-profit making*'.[88] Since the Regulation adds other legal entities, non-profit organisations with legal personality can also incorporate a subsidiary SE, if the law so permits.

In order to incorporate an SE, at least two of the founding entities must be subject to the laws of different Member States or two of these entities must have owned a subsidiary governed by the laws of another Member State or operated a branch situated in another Member State for at least two years (Art. 2(3) Reg.).

An SE can also incorporate a subsidiary SE. The Regulation states that provisions of national law which require that a public limited-liability company have at least two shareholders shall not apply to a subsidiary SE with its registered in that Member State (Art. 3(2) Reg.). All shares of the subsidiary SE can therefore be validly held by one shareholder, i.e. the incorporating SE. In such case, the provisions of national law implementing the Twelfth Company Law Directive of 21 December 1989 on single-member private limited-liability companies shall apply *mutatis mutandis*.[89]

The capital of a subsidiary SE will be held by the founding entities or founding SE. In the event there are two founders, each will hold a number of shares in proportion to its capital contribution to the SE.

45. The formation of a subsidiary SE is governed by the provisions of national law applicable to public limited-liability companies (Arts. 2(3) and 36 Reg.). The Regulation refers to national law for the conditions and formalities for incorporation of a subsidiary SE.

A subsidiary SE must be registered with the national registry of the Member State where its registered office (and thus its head office) is located (see no. 49 of this report). Registration is only possible if an arrangement for employee involvement has been concluded or, failing such agreement or a decision taken by the employee special negotiating body to rely on the rules of information and consultation of employees in force in the Member States where the SE has employees, a resolution has been passed by the general meeting of all companies involved to apply the reference provisions of the Directive (see no. 56 of this

---

[88] Art. 58 EC Treaty.
[89] Art. 3(2) *in fine* Reg. The Twelfth Company Law Directive was published in the *Official Journal* L 395 of 30 December 1989.

report). The registration must also be published in the national official gazette and in the *Official Journal of the European Communities* (see no. 52 of this report). The legal implications of publication are discussed in no. 53 of this report.

A subsidiary SE will be governed by the rules applicable to public limited-liability companies of the Member State where its registered office is located (Art. 10 Reg.).

F   Formation by conversion

46. A public limited-liability company established in a Member State and which has its registered office and head office in the European Union[90] can be converted into an SE, provided it has held for at least two years a subsidiary subject to the laws of another Member State (Art. 2(4) Reg.). Conversion requires the approval of the general meeting of shareholders (see no. 48 of this report). The Regulation does not define what constitutes a 'subsidiary'. The concept of subsidiary is defined in Article 1 of the Seventh Company Law Directive of 13 June 1983 on consolidated accounts.[91] Most Member States have transposed this definition into national law.

The Regulation wishes to reserve the corporate form of an SE to multinational entities. Therefore, in order for a public limited-liability company to become an SE, it must have a subsidiary in a different Member State. Those public limited-liability companies which can be converted into an SE are listed in Annex I to the Regulation. This list can be found in Annex Ib of this book.

If a public limited-liability company formed under the laws of a Member State with its registered office in a Member State has its head office outside the European Union, it cannot be converted into an SE, unless the Member State where its registered office is located so provides, in which case it must have a real and continuous link with the economy of a Member State (Art. 2(5) Reg.; see also no. 19 of this report).

Conversion is a continuation of the same company in another form. It does not result in the dissolution of the company and the incorporation of a new entity (Art. 37(2) Reg.). The registered office may not be transferred to another Member State during the conversion process (Art. 37(3) Reg.). If transfer of the registered office or the head office[92] is envisaged, it should take place afterwards. The registered office can only be transferred to another Member State in accordance with the procedure set forth in Article 8 of the Regulation (see no. 81 *et seq.* of this report).

---

[90] See no. 1 *in fine* of this report.   [91] *Official Journal*, L 193 of 18 June 1983.
[92] An SE's head office should be located in the same Member State as its registered office (see nos. 14 and 15 of this report). Therefore, the transfer of its head office implies the transfer of its registered office and vice versa.

All rights and obligations of the company to be converted shall be assumed by[93] the newly formed SE, including all rights and obligations regarding terms and conditions of employment arising from national law, practice and individual employment contracts or employment relationships existing on the date of registration of the SE (Art. 37(9) Reg.).

47. The management or administrative organ of the company will prepare draft terms of conversion (Art. 37(4) Reg.). The Regulation does not specify what should be included in these draft terms. As the conversion will require new articles in accordance with the rules applicable to an SE, the terms should at least contain the proposed articles.

The draft terms of conversion must be filed with the national registry, where information on the company is made available to the public (Art. 37(5) Reg.). They must also be published in full, by extract or by mention that they are available from the national registry in the official gazette of the Member State where the company to be converted is located. Publication must occur at least one month before the date of the general meeting called to vote on the conversion (Art. 37(5) Reg.).

Furthermore, the company's management should prepare a report on the draft terms of conversion, explaining and justifying the legal and economic aspects of the conversion and indicating the implications of the conversion for shareholders and employees (Art. 37(4) Reg.).

The company must appoint one or more independent experts, authorised or approved by the judicial or administrative authority of the Member State in which the company is registered, to prepare a report on the conversion. This report should certify that the company has net assets at least equivalent to its capital and reserves which cannot be distributed by law or pursuant to the company's articles (Art. 37(6) Reg.). The expert will prepare a report in accordance with the principles applicable to the report required for capital contributions upon incorporation, as set forth in Article 10 of the Second Company Law Directive of 13 December 1976.[94]

48. The conversion itself, the draft terms of conversion, and the new articles must be approved by the general meeting of shareholders (Art. 37(7) Reg.) by a majority defined by national law, i.e., the law of the Member State where the

---

[93] Art. 37(9) of the Regulation states incorrectly that the rights and obligations are *'transferred'*. As no new legal entity is created in the case of a conversion, it is preferable to use the term *'assumed'*.

[94] Second Council Directive on the co-ordination of safeguards required by the Member States of companies, within the meaning of the second paragraph of Art. 58 of the Treaty, to protect the interests of members and others in respect of the formation of public limited-liability companies and the maintenance and alteration of their capital, with a view to harmonising such safeguards throughout the Community (*OJ*, L 26 of 31 January 1977).

company to be converted is located.[95] This majority cannot be less than either (i) two-thirds of the votes attached to the voting shares and other securities of the company represented at the meeting or (ii) a simple majority of votes cast if those shareholders representing at least 50% of the subscribed capital are present or validly represented. If there is more than one class of shares entitled to vote, the decision will require a separate vote by each class of shareholders whose rights are affected by the decision.[96]

National law may make conversion into an SE subject to a qualified majority or unanimity in the corporate body responsible for organising employee involvement (Art. 37(8) Reg.).

Upon completion, the conversion must be recorded with the national registry of the Member State in which the SE's registered office is located. Registration is only possible if an agreement for employee involvement has been concluded or, failing such agreement or a decision by the employee special negotiating body to rely on the rules of information and consultation of employees in force in the Member States where the SE has employees, a resolution has been passed by the general meeting of all companies involved to apply the standard provisions of the Directive (see no. 50 of this report). A notice of conversion must also be published in the national official gazette and in the *Official Journal of the European Communities* (see no. 52 of this report). The legal consequences of publication are discussed in no. 53 of this report.

3 Registration and publication

A Registration

49. An SE must be registered in the Member State where its registered office is located (Art. 12(1) Reg.). Registration is required for a newly formed SE to enjoy legal personality (Art. 16 Reg.) and in order to complete a merger or conversion into an SE. An SE only exists once it has been registered. The date of registration is the date of formation of the SE.

Registration is effected through a filing with the national registry, where information on companies is made available to the public. These national registries are organised in the Member States in accordance with the First Company Law Directive of 9 March 1968.[97]

50. Registration of an SE is only possible if (i) an arrangement for employee involvement pursuant to Article 4 of the Directive has been concluded or (ii) a decision pursuant to Article 3(6) of the Directive has been taken or

---

[95] Art. 37(7) of the Regulation refers to Art. 7 of the Third Company Law Directive.
[96] Art. 7 Third Company Law Directive.
[97] *Official Journal*, L 65 of 14 March 1968.

(iii) the period for negotiations under Article 5 of the Directive has expired without an agreement having been reached and it has been decided to apply the standard rules contained in this the Directive (Art. 12(2) Reg. and Art. 7(1)(b) Dir.). In general it implies that either an agreement on employee involvement has been reached or a decision taken by the employee special negotiating body to rely on the rules of consultation and information in force in the Member States where the SE has employees, or, in the absence of such an agreement or decision within the period specified in Article 5 of the Directive, that a resolution has been passed by the general meetings of all companies involved to apply the reference provisions of the Directive. For further discussion of these issues, see Chapter 3.

If a Member State exercises its right not to apply to an SE formed by merger within its borders the provisions contained in Part 3 of the Annex to the Directive, registration of the SE is only possible in that state if (i) an arrangement on employee involvement (including participation) pursuant to Article 4 of the Directive has been concluded or (ii) none of the companies participating in the merger was subject to employee participation rules prior to the registration of the SE (Art. 12(3) Reg.).

In the event of the formation of an SE by merger of a holding SE, the general meetings of each merging company may reserve the right to make registration of the SE conditional upon its express ratification of the arrangements on employee involvement (Arts. 23(2) and 32(6) Reg.).

51. Changes to the information on file with the national registry, including deletion of a registration when an SE is wound up or converted into another corporate entity, must also be filed in accordance with national law.

Other information may also need to be filed, such as the identity of the SE's directors and certified auditor(s) as well as of those persons entrusted with daily management, as determined by national law in accordance with the First Company Law Directive of 9 March 1968.

B   Publication

52. The information filed with the national registry must be published in full, by extract or by mention that this information is available at the national registry in the official gazette of the Member State where the SE has its registered office (Art. 13 Reg.), as determined by national law in accordance with Article 3 of the First Company Law Directive.

Notice of the registration of an SE or deletion of a registration must also be published in the *Official Journal of the European Communities*, after publication in the official gazette of the Member State where the SE is or was registered.

This notice must contain the (i) SE's name, (ii) its registration number and the date and place of registration, (iii) the date and place of publication in the national gazette and the title of said publication, (iv) the address of the SE's registered office and (v) its sector of activity (Art. 14(1) Reg.).

The same will apply in the event of a transfer of the registered office of an SE to another Member State in accordance with Article 8 of the Regulation (Art. 14(2) Reg.).

Publication is organised through the Office for Official Publications. The national authorities or the SE, depending on national law, must forward the required information to the Office within one month following publication in the national gazette (Art. 14(3) Reg.).

Publication in the *Official Journal of the European Communities* is for informational purposes only (Art. 14(1) Reg.) and is not a prerequisite for obtaining legal personality or to enforce such information against third parties.

C   Effects of publication

53. Documents and information pertaining to an SE which must be published are only enforceable against third parties after publication.[98] For documents that need only be recorded with the national registry, the filing date serves as the date of publication.

The only derogation from the above rule is where the SE can show that the third party had knowledge of the document or information in question.[99]

Following publication, there is a transition period of 15 days, during which time third parties may attempt to prove that they could not have known of the document. If they can demonstrate this fact, the document cannot be enforced against them.[100]

Third parties may always rely on documents of an SE, even if they have yet to be published, unless publication is required for such documents or for the acts reflected therein to take effect.[101]

54. In the event of a discrepancy between a text as published in the official gazette and the information on file with the national registry, third parties should rely on the latter. Nevertheless, they may still rely on information published in the official gazette, unless the SE can prove that they had knowledge of the information on file.[102] This matter will be further clarified in national law.

---

[98] Art. 3(5) First Company Law Directive.
[99] *Ibid.*   [100] *Ibid.*   [101] *Ibid.*, Art. 3(7).   [102] *Ibid.*, Art. 3(6).

4 Acts committed on behalf of an SE in formation

55. As long as the incorporation of an SE has not been recorded with the national registry, the SE does not enjoy legal personality and cannot enter into contracts or incur obligations. To this effect Article 16(2) of the Regulation provides for a system allowing any party to act on behalf of an SE prior to registration.[103]

When such a party performs acts on behalf of an SE, these acts will be considered those of the SE if, after registration, the SE assumes the obligations arising out of such acts. The SE can only assume acts which have been entered into in its name, i.e., the name of the SE in formation. If the SE in formation does not yet have a name, another form of identification may suffice provided there can be no doubt as to the identity of the SE upon assumption of the rights and obligations resulting from such acts.

Article 16(2) only refers to the assumption of 'obligations' arising out of such acts, which should be understood to include any rights attached thereto, as well. Indeed, if a contract has been entered into on behalf of an SE in formation, it would make no sense to allow the SE to assume only the obligations arising out of such a contract and not the ensuing rights.

If the SE refuses to assume these obligations, the person acting on behalf of the SE in formation will be held solely liable for them. If this person did not act alone, each party will be held jointly and severally liable. The parties can always agree otherwise, and, for example, provide that the agreement entered into on behalf of the SE in formation will be dissolved if the SE is not registered within a specified period of time.

The foregoing rules also apply to an SE formed by merger or by conversion. However, in such cases, it is rather unlikely that the SE will assume obligations incurred by third parties, other than its corporate bodies or special proxies. The latter can indeed act on behalf of the company to be merged or converted into an SE prior to registration of the merger or conversion.

5 Subsidiaries

56. Like any other company with legal personality, an SE can set up subsidiaries. These subsidiaries can take the form of an SE (Art. 3(2) Reg.). The rules applicable to the incorporation of a subsidiary SE shall apply (see no. 45 of this report).

---

[103] This provision is similar to Art. 7 of the First Company Law Directive.

If the subsidiary is an SE, provisions of national law that require shares in a public limited-liability company to be held by more than one shareholder will not apply. In this case, the provisions of national law transposing the Twelfth Company Law Directive of 21 December 1989 on single-member private limited-liability companies[104] will apply *mutatis mutandis* (Art. 3(2) Reg.). Reference is made to the law of the Member State where the subsidiary SE has its registered office.

VII Articles of an SE

57. The articles of an SE, referred to in the Regulation as its 'statutes', are *'the instrument of incorporation and, where they are the subject of a separate document, the statutes of the SE'* (Art. 6 Reg.).

The term 'statutes' has a two-fold meaning.

First, it refers to the rules established by the founders or shareholders upon creation of the SE which determine its structure, the rights and obligations of shareholders and the holders of other securities issued by the SE, and its corporate organisation. The content of these articles is defined by the law applicable to public limited-liability companies of the Member State where the SE's registered office is located.

The term also refers to the memorandum or instrument of incorporation. The instrument of incorporation typically contains, in addition to the articles, other provisions, such as the names of the founders and their capital contributions, the amount of paid-in capital upon incorporation, and the names of the company's first directors and certified auditor.

58. In general, amendments to the articles (in the first sense of the term) can only be made by the general meeting of shareholders. For the quorum and majority required to amend the articles, refer to no. 66 of this report.

In some cases, however, national law may allow the board of directors to amend the articles. For example, the articles may allow the board to increase the company's authorised capital up to a given amount without the approval of the general meeting.

Amendments to the articles must be filed with the national registry and published in the official national gazette (see no. 52 of this report).

59. The articles of an SE may not conflict with the arrangements for employee involvement determined in accordance with the rules set forth in the Directive (Art. 12(4) Reg.; see also no. 50 of this report).

---

[104] *Official Journal*, L 395 of 30 December 1989.

If newly adopted arrangements conflict with the articles, the latter will have to be amended to bring them into line with these arrangements. In this case, national law may provide that a management or administrative body of the SE is entitled to amend the articles without the consent of the general meeting of shareholders (Art. 12(4) Reg.).

VIII Organisation and management

1 General remarks

60. The founders of an SE can opt for a one-tier or a two-tier management structure. In the one-tier system, an SE must have at least two corporate bodies: a general meeting of shareholders and an administrative organ. If the founders opt for a two-tier system, the administrative organ will be replaced by a management organ and a supervisory board (Art. 38 Reg.).

An SE is managed by its administrative or management organ. The general meeting of shareholders has limited powers that pertain to the company's structure, its annual accounts and the composition of its corporate bodies.

2 General meeting of shareholders

A Powers

61. The general meeting of shareholders has limited powers defined by law and the SE's articles. The powers defined by law include those conferred by the Regulation, the Directive and national legislation applicable to public limited-liability companies of the Member State where the SE's registered office is located (Art. 52 Reg.). In general, these powers are exclusive and cannot be delegated to another organ of the SE, except where otherwise provided by law.

The Regulation reserves the following powers to the general meeting: transfer of the registered (and head) office of an SE to another Member State (see no. 82 of this report); amendments to the articles of an SE (see nos. 58 and 66 of this report); the appointment and removal of members of the supervisory board in the two-tier system and of the administrative body in the one-tier system (see nos. 74 and 77 of this report); and conversion of an SE into a public limited-liability company (see no. 48 of this report). National law may also provide that members of the management organ in the two-tier system can be appointed or removed by the general meeting rather than by the supervisory board (see no. 73 of this report).

The articles can extend the powers of the general meeting, unless these powers are reserved by law to another corporate body, such as the administrative or management organ or the supervisory board. In general, management of the SE may not be transferred to the general meeting, as this would render the administrative or management organ redundant.

B   Organisation

62. The general meeting must meet at least once each calendar year within six months from the close of the company's financial year (Art. 54(1) Reg.). This meeting is required to approve the annual accounts of the SE for the preceding financial year. National law (of the Member State where an SE's registered office is located) may require more frequent meetings or may provide that the first general meeting after incorporation may be held at a later date, i.e., at any time during the first 18 months following incorporation (Art. 54(1) *in fine* Reg.).

National law or the SE's articles shall determine which corporate body has authority to call a general meeting. In any event, the management or administrative organ and the supervisory board are always entitled to do so (Art. 54(2) Reg.). In addition, one or more shareholders holding at least 10% of the subscribed capital are entitled to request that a general meeting be convened with an agenda they propose, although national law may provide for a smaller percentage (Art. 55(1) Reg.). This request should state the items on the agenda (Art. 55(2) Reg.). If the relevant corporate body does not convene a general meeting in due time, and, in any event, within two months following the submission of such a request, the competent judicial or administrative authority of the Member State where the SE's registered office is located may, at the request of the shareholders or their representatives, order that a general meeting be held within a given period of time. Such an order shall be without prejudice to any national provisions that allow the shareholders themselves to convene a general meeting (Art. 55(3) Reg.).

If a general meeting has been convened, one or more shareholders holding at least 10% of the subscribed capital may request that other items be placed on the agenda. National law shall define the procedure and time limits applicable to such a request; if not, these matters shall be determined by the SE's articles. The articles can stipulate a lower threshold if the national law applicable to public limited-liability companies of the state where the SE's registered office is located so provides. Moreover, national law can impose a lower threshold (Art. 56 Reg.), although a higher threshold is not permissible.

63. The organisation and conduct of the general meeting, including voting procedures, shall be governed by the law applicable to public limited-liability companies of the Member State where the SE's registered office is located (Art. 53 Reg.).

C   Quorum and voting

64. In general, decisions of the general meeting are validly taken by a majority of votes cast (Art. 57 Reg.). This implies that only votes cast at the meeting are taken into consideration in determining the majority. Votes attached to securities that are not present or validly represented shall not be taken into account. In addition, abstentions and blank or mutilated ballots shall not be counted (Art. 58 Reg.).

The Regulation or national law may provide for a larger majority. This also holds true for amendments to the articles of an SE (see no. 66 of this report). In general, unless provided otherwise by applicable law, the articles may also stipulate a larger majority with respect to certain or all decisions.

If a decision of the general meeting affects specific rights attached to a particular class of shares, the decision must be approved by a separate vote of each class of shares whose rights are affected (Art. 60(1) Reg.).

65. No minimum attendance threshold is required unless provided otherwise. National law may require a quorum with respect to certain decisions, however. Finally, to the extent not prohibited by national law, the SE's articles may also impose a quorum or increase the quorum provided by law.

D   Amendments to the articles of an SE

66. In general, the general meeting has exclusive authority to amend the articles of an SE.[105] Amendments to the articles require a majority of at least two-thirds of the votes cast.[106] National law, i.e., the law applicable to public limited-liability companies of the Member State where the SE has its registered office, may provide a larger majority and/or may permit the articles to stipulate a larger majority (Art. 59(1) Reg.). National law can also stipulate a minimum attendance threshold. If the law of the state where the SE's registered office is located requires a quorum for public limited-liability companies, this quorum shall apply (Art. 53 Reg.).

National law can provide that the articles can be amended by a simple majority of votes cast if a quorum of at least 50% of the subscribed capital is present (Art. 59(2) Reg.). In general, national law may stipulate different majorities depending on the type of amendment; if the law applicable to public limited-liability companies of the state where the SE has its registered office provides for different majorities, these will also apply to the SE, provided these majorities are not lower than those provided in the Regulation (Art. 59(1) Reg.).

---

[105] See nos. 63 and 64 of this report for what is meant by the 'articles' of an SE, referred to as 'statutes' in the Regulation. See also no. 58 of this report for a derogation from the exclusive power of the general meeting to amend the articles.
[106] See no. 64 of this report for information on how to calculate this majority.

If an amendment to the articles affects specific rights attached to a class of shares, a separate vote by each class of shares whose rights are affected is required. The required majority must be obtained in each class in order for the amendment to be validly adopted (Art. 60(2) Reg.).

Amendments to the articles must be filed with the national register and published in the official national gazette (see no. 52 of this report).

3 Management (two-tier system/one-tier system)

A Powers and functioning

67. An SE is managed by a board or by a single manager or several managers, known as the administrative organ (in the one-tier system) or the management organ (in the two-tier system). In the two-tier system, management of an SE is overseen by a supervisory board.

Management of an SE and those powers specifically reserved to the aforementioned corporate bodies cannot be delegated to other corporate organs. A provision in the articles to this effect shall be deemed void.

The Regulation does not deal with the representation of an SE vis-à-vis third parties. The power to represent an SE is held by management. Management and the administrative organ are therefore authorised to represent an SE. In the event of a delegation of daily managerial authority, this manager is entitled to represent the SE with respect to its daily management. The rules applicable to representation shall be defined by national law or, in the absence of specific provisions to this effect, by the law applicable to public limited-liability companies.[107]

68. The decision-making process of the three organs is similar.

In general, at least half the members should be present or represented in order for the organ validly to deliberate and take decisions. A decision must be approved by a majority of those members present or represented. The articles can provide otherwise, however (Art. 50(1) Reg.).

The chair casts the deciding vote in the event of a tie. The articles can provide otherwise, however, unless half the members of the supervisory board are employee representatives (Art. 50(2) Reg.). In the latter case, a tie vote can have serious consequences as it will most probably occur when the shareholder representatives oppose the employee representatives. The above prohibition regarding the deciding vote is limited to the two-tier system and does not apply to the one-tier system even if half the members of the administrative organ are appointed by the employees. With respect to the two-tier system,

---

[107] Art. 9(1)(c) Reg.; see also no. 94 of this report.

it is unclear whether this restriction also applies to the management organ when the supervisory board consists of 50% employee representatives. The wording of the Regulation is unclear in this respect. As the Regulation does not apply this restriction to the administrative organ in the one-tier system, there is no reason it should apply to the management organ in the two-tier system.

If employee participation is provided for in accordance with the Directive, the national law applicable to the SE may provide that the quorum and decision-making authority of the supervisory board shall be governed by the rules applicable to public limited-liability companies subject to the laws of that Member State (Art. 50(3) Reg.).

The Regulation does not contain any rules on conflicts of interest. Therefore, such matters will be governed by national law or, in the absence of specific provisions to this effect, by the rules applicable to public limited-liability companies of that Member State.[108]

B   Appointment, removal and liability

69. The members of the administrative, management and supervisory organs are appointed for a period stated in the SE's articles, which may not exceed six years (Art. 46(1) Reg.). They can be reappointed one or more times, unless the articles provide otherwise (Art. 46(2) Reg.).

A company or other legal entity may serve as a member of an administrative, management or supervisory organ. In order to do so, the articles should expressly authorise the appointment of a legal entity. The national law applicable to public limited-liability companies of the Member State where the SE's registered office is located may prohibit the appointment of a legal entity, however (Art. 47(1) Reg.).

If a company or other legal entity is so appointed, it must designate a natural person to exercise its functions and represent it on the board (Art. 47(1) Reg.).

Persons who are disqualified by law from serving on the board of a public limited-liability company of the state where the SE has its registered office or who are subject to a judicial or administrative order rendered by a court or competent authority in the European Union that effectively prevents them from sitting on a corporate body of a public limited-liability company cannot be appointed members of an SE's administrative or management organ or supervisory board or be designated to represent any legal entity so appointed (Art. 47(2) Reg.).

---

[108] Arts. 39(5), 43(4) and 9(1)(c) Reg.; see also no. 94 of this report.

The articles of an SE may stipulate special eligibility conditions for members of its administrative or management organ or supervisory board in order to ensure that certain shareholders or groups of shareholders are represented. National law will set the limits for such provisions (Art. 47(3) Reg.).

The above rules as contained in the Regulation do not affect national laws allowing minority shareholders or other persons or authorities to appoint directly certain members of an SE's corporate bodies (Art. 47(4) Reg.).

70. Members of the administrative and management organs and of the supervisory board are bound by a duty of confidentiality which continues after the end of their term of office. In general, they may not disclose any information concerning the SE (or its business) if such disclosure could harm the interests of the SE. This rule does not apply if the disclosure is required or permitted by national law applicable to public limited-liability companies or if it is in the public interest (Art. 49 Reg.).

This duty of confidentiality is not limited in time and continues for as long as disclosure could harm the SE or its activities.

71. The liability of members of the administrative or management organ or supervisory board is determined in accordance with the law applicable to public limited-liability companies of the state where the SE's registered office is located (Art. 51 Reg.).

National law will also determine whether such liability is civil or criminal in nature and joint or several, as well as the conditions for avoiding or obtaining a release from liability and who is entitled to file a claim for damages against members of these corporate bodies.[109]

C Two-tier system

72. In the two-tier system, the management organ is overseen by a supervisory board. The latter does not itself manage the company; rather its role is limited to supervision (Art. 40(1) Reg.). The management organ remains solely responsible for managing the SE (Art. 39(1) Reg.).

The articles of an SE should list those categories of transactions which the management organ can only undertake with the approval of the supervisory board. National law (of the state where the SE's registered office is located) may provide that the supervisory board can determine on its own initiative those transactions that require its authorisation (Art. 48(1) Reg.). Moreover, national law may also define categories of transactions that require the prior approval of the supervisory board, and which must be listed in the articles (Art. 48(2) Reg.).

---

[109] G. Keutgen, 'La société européenne. Les règles de fonctionnement', *Act. dr.* 2003, 118.

The management organ may delegate daily management[110] to one or more managing directors in the same manner and under the same conditions applicable to public limited-liability companies of the state where the registered office of the SE is located (Art. 39(1) Reg.).

73. The management organ shall be composed of one or more members who shall elect a chair from amongst their number unless the articles have reserved this power to another organ of the SE. The chair casts the deciding vote in the event of a tie; the articles may provide that the chair does not have a deciding vote, however (Art. 50(2) Reg.).[111]

The articles of an SE shall fix the number of members of its management organ or set rules to determine this number. National law may fix a minimum and/or maximum number (Art. 39(4) Reg.). In the absence of such provisions, it is up to the body responsible for appointments to determine the number of members.

The members of the management organ are appointed and removed by the supervisory board (Art. 39(2) Reg.). However, national law may allow the articles to provide that the member(s) of the management organ shall be appointed and removed by the general meeting under the same conditions applicable to public limited-liability companies with their registered offices in that state (Art. 39(2)(2) Reg.). Consequently, the Regulation does not disallow reservation of the power to appoint or remove members to the general meeting if this is allowed under national law.

Members of the supervisory board may not serve on the management organ. However, the supervisory board can nominate one of its members to serve temporarily on the management organ in the event of a vacancy. During this time, the functions of that person on the supervisory board shall be suspended. National law may impose a time limit on the period that a member of the supervisory board can serve on the management organ (Art. 39(3) Reg.). Even if national law does not do so, however, it goes without saying that this period should be considered temporary and in any event should not exceed the time needed to fill the vacancy.

---

[110] Article 39 refers to 'current' management in relation to the two-tier system, while Article 43 uses the term 'day-to-day' management in relation to the one-tier system. There is no explanation for this difference in wording. In the French version of the Regulation, the words '*gestion courante*' are used to describe both systems. It is therefore probable that both concepts have the same meaning of daily management. This is further confirmed by the Regulation of 22 July 2003 (*OJ*, L 207 of 18 August 2003) on the Statute for a European co-operative society, which also provides for a choice between a one-tier and a two-tier system. In this regulation, the term 'current' management is used to describe both systems (as a translation for '*gestion courante*' in the French version; see Arts. 37(1) and 42(1) of that regulation).

[111] See no. 68 of this report.

74. Members of the supervisory board are appointed by the general meeting. The first members may be appointed by the founders in the articles upon incorporation. National law may permit the direct appointment by minority shareholders, other persons or national authorities. Special provisions may also apply in the framework of employee participation arrangements concluded pursuant to the Directive (Art. 40(2) Reg.). These rules may result in the appointment of employee representatives.

The number of members of the supervisory board or the rules for determining such number shall be defined in the articles of the SE. National law may set a minimum or a maximum number (Art. 40(3) Reg.).

The removal of members of the supervisory board is not discussed in the Regulation. Therefore, the power to remove members will be held by the general meeting. However, national law may provide different rules (in particular in the framework of employee participation), and, in the absence thereof, reference should be made to the rules applicable to public limited-liability companies of the state in question.[112] In states where these rules do not envisage a supervisory board, new rules with respect to the SE may be introduced (Art. 39(5) Reg.). The same applies to conflicts of interest and the functioning of the supervisory board in general.

The supervisory board shall elect a chair from amongst its members. If half the members are appointed by employees, the chair shall be appointed from amongst those members appointed by the general meeting (Art. 42 Reg.). The chair casts the deciding vote in the event of a tie, unless the articles provide otherwise. However, if half the members are appointed by the employees, the chair's right to cast the deciding vote cannot be excluded by the articles (Art. 50(2) Reg.; see also no. 68 of this report).

75. The management organ must report to the supervisory board at least once every three months on its progress and the projected development of the company's business (Art. 41(1) Reg.). It shall promptly[113] inform the supervisory board of events likely to have an appreciable effect on the SE (Art. 41(2) Reg.). Each member of the supervisory board must have full access to this information and be given the time and means to examine it (Art. 41(5) Reg.).

The supervisory board is entitled at all times to request additional information from the management organ, including information of any type which it needs in order to properly supervise the work of the latter. National law may provide that each individual member of the supervisory board is also entitled to request such information (Art. 41(3) Reg.). Requests for information must be addressed to the management body (through the chair unless provided or instructed otherwise by the supervisory board) and not to one or more of its individual members.

---

[112] Art. 9(1)(c) Reg.; see also no. 94 of this report.
[113] In the French version of the Regulation, 'promptly' is translated by '*en temps utile*'.

The supervisory board can also on its own initiative conduct or arrange for investigations necessary for the performance of its duties (Art. 41(4) Reg.).

D One-tier system

76. In the one-tier system, the SE is managed by an administrative organ (Art. 43(1) Reg.). No supervisory board is set up; the general meeting supervises the administrative organ and has limited powers to review the annual accounts and appoint and remove members of this organ.

National law may provide that daily management can be entrusted to one or more managing directors under the same conditions applicable to public limited-liability companies with their registered offices in the state where the SE's registered office is located (Art. 43(1) Reg.).

The articles of an SE should list those categories of transactions that require the express approval of the administrative organ (Art. 48(1) Reg.). National law (of the state where the SE's registered office is located) may define categories of transactions that require the express consent of the administrative organ and which must be listed in the articles (Art. 48(2) Reg.).

77. The administrative organ is composed of one or more members, depending on the articles. The number of members or rules to determine such number shall be fixed in the articles. National law may impose a minimum and/or (*'where necessary'*) a maximum number (Art. 43(2) Reg.). The administrative organ shall, however, consist of at least three members where employee participation is regulated in accordance with the Directive (Art. 43(2) Reg.).

The members of the administrative organ shall be appointed by the general meeting. The first members may be appointed by the founders in the articles upon incorporation. National law may permit the direct appointment by minority shareholders, other persons or national authorities. Special provisions may also apply in the framework of employee participation arrangements concluded pursuant to the Directive (Art. 43(3) Reg.).

The Regulation does not discuss the removal of members of the administrative organ. Other matters such as functioning, representation and conflicts of interest are not dealt with either. National law will have to fill in these gaps, and, in the absence of such provisions, reference should be made to the rules applicable to public limited-liability companies of the Member State in question.[114] In states where such rules do not envisage a one-tier system, new rules may be introduced with respect to the SE (Art. 43(4) Reg.).

The administrative organ shall elect a chair from amongst its members. If half the members are appointed by employees, the chair must be selected from

---

[114] Art. 9(1)(c) Reg.; see also no. 94 of this report.

amongst those members appointed by the general meeting (Art. 45 Reg.). The chair casts the deciding vote in the event of a tie, unless the articles provide otherwise (Art. 50(2) Reg.).

78. The administrative organ shall meet at least once every three months at intervals set forth in the articles to discuss the progress and foreseeable development of the business of the SE (Art. 44(1) Reg.). Each member of the administrative organ should have full access to all information submitted to it and should be able to examine such information (Art. 44(2) Reg.).

IX Annual accounts and consolidated accounts

79. With respect to the preparation and approval of the annual and consolidated accounts of an SE, the rules governing public limited-liability companies having their registered offices in the same state as the SE's will apply (Art. 61 Reg.). These rules also provide for an annual management report and for a report by a certified auditor.

In Member States which have yet to introduce the euro as their sole currency, annual accounts and, where appropriate, consolidated accounts may be stated in euros. However, the national law of such states may require that an SE's annual and consolidated accounts be stated in the national currency as well, under the same conditions as those applicable to public limited-liability companies. In such a case, an SE may opt to state its accounts in both the national currency and in euros (Art. 67(2) Reg.).

80. The annual and consolidated accounts of credit and financial institutions and insurance companies are governed by special rules issued pursuant to Directive No. 2000/12 of 20 March 2000 on the taking up and pursuit of the business of credit institutions[115] and Council Directive No. 91/674 of 19 December 1991 on the annual accounts and consolidated accounts of insurance undertakings.[116] A credit or financial institution or an insurance company that is established as an SE shall prepare its accounts in accordance with this legislation (Art. 62 Reg.).

X Transfer of registered office

81. An SE is entitled to transfer its registered office to another Member State while maintaining legal personality. The cross-border transfer will not result in the liquidation and winding-up of the SE or in the creation of a new legal entity (Art. 8(1) Reg.). The transfer does not affect the SE's legal personality, which continues in effect, except that the law of another Member State, i.e., the state where the new registered office is located, will now apply.

---

[115] *Official Journal*, L 126 of 26 May 2000.   [116] *Ibid.* L 374 of 31 December 1991.

The transfer of an SE's registered office is subject to a complicated procedure, as it entails a change in national law governing issues not addressed by the Regulation (Art. 9 Reg.; see also no. 94 of this report). This procedure does not apply to the transfer of a registered office within the same Member State, unless provided otherwise by the law of that state. The rules applicable to such a transfer, i.e., the formalities and the corporate body responsible for voting on the transfer, are determined by national law (see no. 94 of this report).

The transfer of an SE's registered office to another Member State requires that its head office be relocated to that state as well,[117] and, if the Member State in question so requires, that the head office be located at the same place as the registered office.[118] This implies that an SE's registered office cannot be transferred if its head office remains behind.

82. Transfer of an SE's registered office to another Member State can only be effected with the approval of the general meeting of shareholders. A decision by the majority needed to amend the SE's memorandum and articles of association is required.[119] [120]

Transfer of an SE's registered office is no longer permitted if the SE is in the process of winding up or in liquidation or if an action for winding up, liquidation, insolvency or suspension of payments or similar proceedings has been commenced (Art. 8(15) Reg.). This provision is intended to prevent forum shopping, i.e., choosing a Member State whose law is more favourable as regards winding-up or insolvency.

Furthermore, a Member State may provide that its authorities can oppose the transfer of an SE's registered office in the public interest (Art. 8(14) Reg.). Other grounds for doing so are not permitted. The conditions for such opposition are discussed below (no. 85 of this report).

83. The procedure for transferring the registered office of an SE to another Member State is as follows.

First, the management or administrative organ[121] of the SE must prepare a transfer proposal and a report explaining and justifying the transfer.

The transfer proposal must contain at least the following information (Art. 8(2) Reg.):

---

[117] This is necessary in order to satisfy the criterion that the head office be in the same state as the registered office (Art. 7 Reg.; see also no. 14 of this report).
[118] See no. 14 of this report.
[119] For the rules regarding an SE's memorandum and articles of incorporation, see no. 57 of this report.
[120] Art. 14(6) Reg. which refers to Art. 59 Reg.; for the specific majority and formalities required to amend the articles, see no. 66 of this report.
[121] See no. 67 of this report.

(1) the identity of the SE: name, registered office and registration (or company) number;
(2) the new address of the proposed registered office;
(3) the proposed articles including the new name of the SE and when its name will be changed;
(4) the consequences of the transfer for employee involvement;
(5) the proposed timetable for the transfer;
(6) any rights provided by national law or the SE's articles regarding the protection of shareholders and/or creditors.

The transfer proposal must be published in accordance with Directive 68/151/EEC of 9 March 1968 (the 'First Company Law Directive') in the state where the SE has its registered office.[122] This implies a filing with the national registry, where information on the company is made available to the public, and publication in the relevant national gazette.[123] The Member States may require additional means of publication (Art. 8(2) Reg.).

The transfer report should explain and justify the legal and economic aspects of the transfer and explain the implications of the transfer for shareholders, creditors and employees (Art. 8(3) Reg.). It should, for example, explain any changes to shareholder rights, as the SE will be governed by the laws of the Member State where its new registered office will be located. Moreover, differences between the two legal systems as regards creditors and employees should be explained. With respect to the latter, the report should explain the rules regarding employee involvement in the new country. The report need not be published in the relevant national gazette or filed with the national registry, unless required by law.

The transfer proposal and the report must be made available at the SE's registered office at least one month prior to the general meeting scheduled to vote on the transfer. Shareholders and creditors of the SE are entitled to consult both documents at its registered office and may obtain copies free of charge (Art. 8(4) Reg.). A fee may be charged to third parties, however. Shareholders and creditors should also be able to request by mail or by other means copies of these documents.

The transfer of an SE's registered office to another Member State requires the approval of a qualified majority of the general meeting of shareholders, since this decision is in effect an amendment to the SE's articles.[124] The same applies to any other amendments to the articles that may be required as a result of the change in applicable law. The general meeting can only vote on the proposed

---

[122] EC Directive on co-ordination of the safeguards required by the Member States of companies, within the meaning of the second paragraph of Art. 58 of the EC Treaty, to protect the interests of members and others with a view to harmonising such safeguards throughout the Community (*Official Journal*, L 65 of 14 March 1968).
[123] See no. 49 *et seq.*   [124] See no. 66 of this report.

transfer two months after the date of publication of the transfer proposal (Art. 8(6) Reg.).

As soon as the above formalities are complete, a court, notary or other designated authority in the Member State where the SE had its registered office will issue a certificate attesting that all requisite formalities and acts have been completed (Art. 8(8) Reg.). This will include verification that the new articles meet the requirements for employee involvement.[125] Each Member State will designate the court, notary or authority responsible for issuing such a certificate. Prior to issuing the certificate, the court, notary or other authority must verify that the interests of creditors and the holders of other rights vis-à-vis the SE relating to any liabilities of the SE that arose prior to publication of the transfer proposal have been adequately protected in accordance with the law of the Member State where the SE's registered office was located. National law may extend this verification to all liabilities arising prior to the transfer, i.e., prior to the registration date of the transfer[126] (Art. 8(7) Reg.). The SE must furnish sufficient proof that this is indeed the case. The holders of other rights include shareholders and the holders of other securities issued by the SE, as well as third parties, such as public bodies with claims against the SE, including the tax authorities and the social security administration. The above is without prejudice to the applicability of national legislation on the satisfaction or securing of payments to public bodies (Art. 8(7) Reg.).

A Member State may adopt appropriate legislation in order to protect the rights of minority shareholders in the above procedure (Art. 8(5) Reg.).

84. Transfer of the registered office must be recorded in the company registry of the new Member State (Art. 8(10) Reg.; see no. 49 of this report).

This recordation may only be effected if the competent authority of the Member State where the registered office was formerly located has issued a certificate to the effect that all required formalities and acts have been fulfilled. If the Member State in question has extended its verification procedure to cover all liabilities arising prior to the transfer (see above), the competent authority of that Member State may first wish to know when the transfer will be recorded,[127] which may require some co-ordination.

Furthermore, upon this new registration, the SE will have to produce, in addition to the above-mentioned certificate, proof of compliance with the registration formalities in the state where its new office is located (Art. 8(9) Reg.). The company registry of the new Member State will notify that of the Member State where the registered office was previously located. Upon receipt of such notice, the latter will delete the old registration (Art. 8(11) Reg.).

---

[125] Art. 12(4) Reg.; see also no. 59 of this report.   [126] Art. 8(10) Reg.
[127] See no. 83 of this report.

Both the new registration and the deletion of the old are published in the official gazettes of both Member States (Art. 8(12) Reg.).

Furthermore, the transfer must be mentioned in the *Official Journal of the European Communities* (Art. 14(2 Reg.); see no. 52 of this report).

85. A Member State may provide that a specified authority can oppose the transfer of the registered office of an SE situated in that state on grounds of public interest if the transfer would result in a change in applicable law.[128] The objection must be filed within two months following publication of the transfer proposal (Art. 8(14) Reg.). The authority in question must be designated by national law. The public interest is limited to certain grounds defined by law, and no other grounds may be raised to object to a transfer. If the SE is subject to supervision by a national financial authority, in accordance with applicable Community directives, such an authority will also be entitled to object to the transfer of the SE's registered office to another Member State on grounds of public interest (Art. 8(14) Reg.), provided the laws of that Member State so allow. Judicial review of the objection should be possible (Art. 8(14) Reg.).

86. The transfer only takes effect upon registration in the new Member State (Art. 8(10) Reg.). The same applies to any amendments to the SE's articles resulting from the transfer.

The new registered office may be relied on by third parties as from the date of its publication in the national official gazette. However, if the deletion of the old registration is published after the new registration, third parties may continue to rely on the old registration until the deletion has been published, unless the SE can establish that such third parties were aware of the new registered office (Art. 8(13) Reg.). Proof of actual knowledge is required.[129] If deletion of the old registered office is published before the new registration, the location of the new office is not enforceable against third parties, as publication is required.

As regards any cause of action arising prior to the transfer, the SE will be considered to have its registered office in the Member State where it was registered prior to the transfer (Art. 8(16) Reg.). This shall be the case even if the SE is

---

[128] This will probably always be the case as the transfer of an SE's registered office to another Member State entails a change in the law applicable to the SE (Art. 9 Reg.; see also no. 94 of this report).

[129] The wording 'that such third parties were aware' does not include third parties who should have been aware under the circumstances. Similar wording is used in Art. 3(5) of the First Company Law Directive. In addition, with regard to acts that exceed the corporate purpose, Art. 9(1) of the First Company Law Directive provides that third parties who were aware of a violation of a company's corporate purpose should be treated the same as those could not have been *unaware* of such a violation under the circumstances.

sued after the transfer takes effect. This provision is intended to prevent an SE from transferring its registered office in order to avoid unfavourable judicial decisions based on the law in effect at the time a cause of action arose.

XI Dissolution

87. Winding up, liquidation, insolvency, cessation of payments and similar procedures are governed by the law of the Member State where an SE's registered office is located. The rules applicable to public limited-liability companies[130] formed in accordance with the laws of that state shall apply (Art. 63 Reg.).

The above rules shall also apply to a decision by the general meeting of shareholders to wind up an SE (Art. 63 Reg.).

88. The Regulation contains two grounds for the winding up of an SE in addition to those that may exist under applicable national law.

First, national law may provide that when the legality of a merger is not scrutinised in accordance with the provisions of Articles 25 and 26 of the Regulation as required, an SE can be wound up (Art. 30 Reg.; see also no. 30 of this report).

Second, an SE which no longer has its registered office in the same Member State as its head office may be wound up in accordance with the procedure outlined in no. 14 of this report (Art. 64 Reg.).

89. The initiation and termination of winding-up, liquidation, insolvency or cessation of payment procedures for an SE must be published in the same manner as documents pertaining to an SE are published, in accordance with national law (Art. 65 Reg.; see also no. 52 of this report). The same applies to any decision to continue operating an SE in the case of and notwithstanding its winding-up, liquidation, insolvency or cessation of payments.

National law may impose additional publication formalities.

XII Conversion into a national company

90. An SE may be converted into a public limited-liability company governed by the laws of the Member State where its registered office is located at any time (Art. 66(1) Reg.). Conversion into any other type of company is not permissible under the Regulation. However, an SE that has been converted into a public limited-liability company can be further converted into another corporate entity.

---

[130] For a list of qualifying public limited-liability companies in the various Member States, see Annex Ib of this book.

Conversion is only possible two years after the SE's registration and[131] after approval of two sets of annual accounts (Art. 66(1) Reg.).

Conversion shall not result in the winding up of on SE or in the creation of a new legal person (Art. 66(2) Reg.). Conversion is merely a change in corporate form and does not affect legal personality, which continues without interruption.

91. The management or administrative body of the SE must prepare draft terms of conversion (Art. 66(3) Reg.). The Regulation does not define these terms, but they should include any changes to the articles, including new proposed articles or amendments required to comply with the rules applicable to public limited-liability companies.

The draft terms of conversion must be published in accordance with national law at least one month before the date of the general meeting scheduled to vote on the conversion (Art. 66(4) Reg.; see also no. 52 of this report).

The SE's management must also prepare a report explaining and justifying the legal and economic aspects of the conversion and indicating the implications of the conversion for shareholders and employees (Art. 66(3) Reg.).

One or more experts must be appointed to prepare a report certifying that the company has assets at least equivalent to its capital. The expert(s) are appointed by, or from a list of experts approved by, the judicial or administrative authority of the Member State where the SE has its registered office (Art. 66(5) Reg.).

92. The conversion must be approved by the general meeting of shareholders. At such time, the shareholders must also approve the new articles of the public limited-liability company (Art. 66(6) Reg.).

The majority required to approve the conversion is determined by the national law governing public limited-liability companies of the Member State where the SE's registered office is located. However, this majority should not be less than either (i) two-thirds of the votes attached to the shares and other securities of the company or (ii) a simple majority of votes cast if at least 50% of the subscribed capital is present or validly represented. If there is more than one class of shares entitled to vote, a separate vote of each class of shareholders whose rights are affected by the decision is required.[132]

93. The conversion must be publicised in accordance with the legal provisions applicable to public limited-liability companies in the Member State of incorporation.

---

[131] The conditions are cumulative, as is clearly stated in the French version of the Regulation.

[132] Art. 7 Third Company Law Directive, to which Art. 66(6) Reg. refers.

XIII Applicable law

94. Article 9 of the Regulation defines the law applicable to an SE. The following provisions apply.

First, the provisions of the Regulation apply (Art. 9(1)(a) Reg.), as do the articles of the SE, where expressly authorised by the Regulation (Art. 9(1)(b) Reg.).

For matters not addressed by the Regulation or addressed only in part, national law will apply as follows:

- First, provisions adopted by the Member States to transpose Community measures related specifically to the SE, provided these provisions are in accordance with the directives applicable to public limited-liability companies referred to in Annex I of the Regulation;[133]
- Second, provisions of national law applicable to public limited-liability companies incorporated under the laws of the Member State in which the SE has its registered office; and
- Third, provisions of the articles of the SE, in the same manner as for public limited-liability companies formed under the laws of the Member State in which the SE has its registered office (Art. 9(1)(c) Reg.).

An SE is considered a public limited-liability company in the Member State where its registered office is located and thus subject to the statutory provisions applicable to such corporate entities in that state (Art. 10 Reg.). The sanctions applicable to public limited-liability companies in such state will apply to SEs that violate the provisions of the Regulation.[134]

If the business of an SE is regulated by specific provisions of national law, these provisions will apply in full and the SE must comply with them (Art. 9(5) Reg.). This is, for example, the case for banking[135] and insurance activities.

95. When adapting their national laws, the Member States must ensure that the provisions applicable to SEs do not result in discrimination between SEs and public limited-liability companies or in disproportionate restrictions on the formation of an SE or on the transfer of its registered office.[136]

XIV Conclusion

96. The introduction of the SE was greeted with enthusiasm by those who had been eagerly awaiting an initiative at the Community level to permit the

---

[133] Art. 9(2) Reg.; see Annex Ib of this book for the list.
[134] Eighteenth Recital of the Regulation.   [135] *Ibid.*, Twenty-sixth Recital.
[136] *Ibid.*, Fifth Recital.

cross-border transfer of a company's head or registered office resulting in a change in applicable law or a cross-border merger without liquidation. This is indeed the immediate result of the Regulation.

However, the main purpose of the Regulation, namely to introduce a legal entity governed by a single set of rules throughout the European Union, has in many respects failed. The Regulation undoubtedly did not achieve its main goal due to lengthy discussions between representatives from the various Member States, which resulted in numerous compromises in order to respect different legal cultures. The outcome is indeed a regulation that defers too often to national law, i.e., the law of the state where the SE's registered office is located.

However, in the author's opinion, this is not the main issue. Ultimately, the courts, legal scholars and practitioners will develop a common set of rules taking into account various national limitations, which in turn will dwindle due to increased Community legislation to harmonise the rules applicable to companies throughout the Member States, particularly public limited-liability companies.

A more important obstacle for general use of the SE is the nationality requirement for its shareholders. In the end, this will prevent the SE from becoming a viable alternative to the corporate forms offered by national law for international mergers involving a company outside the European Economic Area. Community lawmakers should be encouraged to drop this requirement when introducing new legal entities under Community law in future.

Other obstacles worth mentioning are the complexity and uncertainty of the procedure for agreeing on rules on employee involvement and the absence of tax harmonisation. The subjection of the SE to corporate income tax in the Member States where it has its registered office and head office, as well in each Member State where it has a permanent establishment, without consolidation at the top, will no doubt be considered a major failure of the new model.

3

Employee involvement: rights and obligations

PHILIPPE FRANÇOIS AND JULIEN HICK
NautaDutilh

I   Introduction   78
II Scope and entry into force of the Directive   79
III Negotiation procedure   80
   1 Composition of the SNB   80
      A Holding and subsidiary SEs and SEs formed by conversion   80
      B SEs formed by merger   81
   2 Appointment or election of members of the SNB   82
   3 Role and functioning of the SNB   83
      A Role   83
          (i) Conclusion of an agreement   83
          (ii) Absence or termination of negotiations   83
      B Functioning of the SNB   84
          (i) Duty to co-operate   84
          (ii) Assistance of experts   84
          (iii) Duration of negotiations   84
          (iv) Funding   84
IV Creation of a system for employee involvement   85
   1 Conclusion of an agreement for employee involvement   85
      A Content and form of the agreement   85
      B Voting rules   86
   2 Absence of an agreement within the negotiations period   86
   3 Decision not to open or to terminate negotiations   87
V   Standard rules   87
   1 Creation of a representative body   87
      A Composition of the representative body and appointment of its members   88
      B Role   88
          (i) General principle   88
          (ii) Renegotiation of an agreement or continued application of the standard rules   89
      C Operation   89
          (i) Duty to co-operate   89
          (ii) Meetings   89

            (iii) Information provided to employee representatives   90
            (iv) Internal measures   91
            (v) Funding of the representative body   91
      2   Employee participation   91
         A   General remarks   91
         B   Scope   92
         C   Content   93
            (i) SEs formed by merger, holding and subsidiary SEs   93
            (ii) SEs formed by conversion   94
VI   European works council   94
VII   National rules on employee involvement   95
VIII   Reservation and confidentiality   95
VIII   Misuse of procedure and compliance with the Directive   96
IX   Protection of employee representatives   96
X   Transposition of the directive   97
XI   Conclusion   97

I   Introduction

1. After years of discussion and countless delays, the European Council finally reached a compromise on 20 December 2000 regarding the creation of a new Community legal entity, the *Societas Europaea* ('SE'). Until that time, the issue of employee involvement had divided the Member States between those who supported a system of employee participation and those who favoured a system based on mere information and consultation.[1]

To resolve this impasse, a group of experts, led by Etienne Davignon, was appointed to examine the various possibilities for employee involvement in the new European company.[2] Many of the solutions proposed by the experts were incorporated in the compromise reached by the Member States.

The issue of employee involvement was eventually solved by recourse to a 'before and after' principle, pursuant to which an SE formed from existing companies will strive to preserve, insofar as possible, their systems and rules for employee involvement. Supplementing Regulation No. 2157/2001 (the

---

[1] For the complete history of the SE, *see* V. Bertrand, 'L'implication des travailleurs dans la société européenne', *Actualités de droit*, 2003, 144–56; M. Bouloukos, 'Le régime juridique de la société européenne (SE): vers une société européenne' à la carte'?', *Revue de droit des affaires internationales*, 2004, 489–92; P. Nicaise, 'La société européenne: une société de type européen!', *Journal des Tribunaux*, 2002, 480–1; F. Blanquet, 'La société européenne n'est plus un mythe', *Revue de droit commercial belge*, 2001, 139–50; P. Paulus de Chatelet, 'La société européenne', *Revue de droit commercial belge*, 2002, 167–70.

[2] Final report of the group of experts on 'European Systems of Worker Involvement' (hereinafter, the 'Davignon report').

'Regulation'),[3] Directive 2001/86/EC (the 'Directive') was published on 10 November 2001, thereby officially condoning and codifying the solution reached by the Member States on employee involvement.[4]

The object of the Directive is to ensure that the establishment of an SE does not entail the disappearance or reduction of practices of employee involvement existing within the companies participating in the establishment of an SE. This object should be pursued through the creation of an employee representation body or rules for information and consultation.

The purpose of the present report is to examine the system for employee involvement created by the Directive. To this end, we first discuss the scope and entry into force of the Directive. We then examine the preliminary information procedure, the creation of a special negotiating body, and the negotiation procedure itself. We next turn our attention to the various systems for employee involvement and the standard rules set forth in the Directive. We subsequently examine the links between the SE and the European works council and a few issues related to compliance with the Directive and the misuse of procedures. Finally, we briefly discuss the deadline for transposition of the Directive into national law.

II Scope and entry into force of the Directive

2. The Directive entered into force on 10 November 2001[5] (Art. 16 Dir.), while the Regulation entered into force on 8 October 2004 (Art. 70 Reg.).

However, the entry into force of the Regulation and the Directive does not allow for the immediate formation of an SE since an SE may not be registered as long as the modalities for employee involvement have yet to be determined (Art. 12(2) and (3) Reg.). As a result, it is theoretically impossible to set up an SE in a country that has not transposed the Directive.

3. Regarding the geographic scope of the Directive, it should be noted that Community legislation with regard to the SE applies to the 25 Member States of the European Union as well as to the member countries of the European Economic Area (EEA).[6]

---

[3] Regulation of October 2001 on the Statute for a European company (SE), *Official Journal*, L 294 of 10 November 2001 (hereinafter the 'Regulation').
[4] Directive of 8 October 2001 supplementing the Statute for a European company with regard to the involvement of employees, *Official Journal*, L 294 of 10 November 2001 (hereinafter, the 'Directive').
[5] I.e., the day of its publication in the *Official Journal of the European Communities*.
[6] EEA decision of 25 June 2002 (*OJ*, L 266 of 3 October 2002), amending Annex XXII to EEA Agreement of 2 May 1992.

| III | Negotiation procedure |

4. Where the management or administrative organs of the participating companies[7] draw up a plan for the formation of an SE, they shall take the necessary steps as soon as possible after publishing the draft terms of merger, creating a holding company or agreeing on a plan to form a subsidiary SE or to convert an existing company into an SE, including the provision of information about the identity of the participating companies, concerned subsidiaries or establishments[8] and the number of their employees, to start negotiations with the companies' employee representatives on arrangements for employee involvement in the SE (Art. 3(1) Dir.).

5. For this purpose and as soon as the aforementioned information is provided, a special negotiating body ('SNB') shall be established, representing the employees of the participating companies and concerned subsidiaries or establishments. This negotiation procedure shall be governed by the legislation of the Member State in which the registered office of the SE is to be situated (Art. 6 Dir.).

| 1 | Composition of the SNB |

6. The Directive sets out rules for the composition of the SNB. A distinction is made between SEs formed by merger and those formed by other means.

| A | Holding and subsidiary SEs and SEs formed by conversion |

7. In transposing the Directive, the Member States must ensure that members of the SNB are elected or appointed in proportion to the number of employees employed in each Member State by the participating companies and concerned subsidiaries or establishments, by allocating in respect of a Member State one seat per portion of employees employed in that Member State which equals 10%, or a fraction thereof, of the number of employees employed by the participating companies and concerned subsidiaries or establishments in all the Member States taken together (Art. 3(2)(a)(i) Dir.).

For example, in the case of an SE formed from a French company with 750 employees, a Belgian company with 250 employees, an Irish company with 700 employees and a German company with 200 employees, the composition of the SNB would be as shown in Table 3.1 below.

As the French company employs 39.47% of the total number of employees in the new SE, France is allocated four seats on the SNB (three seats representing 30% of the employees and one seat for the remaining 9.47%). Only two seats are

---

[7] I.e., the companies directly participating in the establishment of an SE (Art. 2(b) Dir.).
[8] I.e., a subsidiary or establishment of a participating company which is proposed to become a subsidiary or establishment of the SE upon formation (Art. 2(d) Dir.).

Employee involvement: rights and obligations

Table 3.1

Member State	Number of employees	Percentage of the total number of employees	Number of seats on the SNB
France	750	39.47 %	4
Belgium	250	13.16 %	2
Ireland	700	36.84 %	4
Germany	200	10.53%	2

allocated to Belgium (one seat representing 10% of the employees and one seat for the remaining 3.16%). As the Irish company employs 36.84% of the total number of employees in the new SE, Ireland is allocated four seats on the SNB (three seats representing 30% of the employees and one seat for the remaining 6.84%). Only two seats are allocated to Germany (one seat representing 10% of the employees and one seat for the remaining 0.53%).

B   SEs formed by merger

8. In addition to the general rules set out above, particular rules must be taken into account when an SE is formed by merger, since the participating companies will cease to exist after registration of the SE.

In the case of a merger, the SNB must include at least one member from each participating company, which is registered and has employees in that Member State and which shall cease to exist as a separate legal entity following registration of the SE, insofar as:

- the number of such additional members does not exceed 20% of the number of members designated by virtue of the general rules discussed above, and
- the composition of the SNB does not entail double representation of the employees concerned (Art. 3(2)(a)(ii) Dir.).

If the number of such companies is higher than the number of additional seats available, pursuant to the above rules, the additional seats shall be allocated to companies in different Member States by decreasing order of the number of employees they employ (Art. 3(2)(a)(ii) Dir.).

Take, for example, the case of an SE formed by a merger of the following participating companies:

- Company A, registered in Spain and employing 1000 people
- Company B, registered in Poland and employing 60 people
- Company C, registered in Poland and employing 50 people

The seats on the SNB are allocated as shown in Table 3.2 below.

81

Table 3.2

Member State	Company	Number of employees	Percentage of the total number of employees		Number of seats on the SNB
Spain	A	1000	90.09%		10
Poland	B	60	5.41%	9.91%	1
	C	50	4.50%		
Total		1110	100%		11

Table 3.3

Member State	Company	Number of employees	Percentage of the total number of employees		Number of seats on the SNB
Spain	A	1000	90.09%		10
Poland	B	60	5.41%	9.91%	1
	C	50	4.50%		+1
Total		1110	100%		11+1

As the Spanish company employs 90.09% of the total number of employees in the new SE, Spain is allocated ten seats on the SNB (nine seats representing 90% of the employees and one seat for the remaining 0.09%). Only one seat is allocated to Poland.

The Spanish members are all employees of Company A, while the Polish member is an employee of company B.

In principle, each company could claim an additional seat, since they will all cease to exist after the merger. Nevertheless, Companies A and B are not entitled to an additional seat, since such an allocation would lead to double representation (as Spanish and Polish members on the SNB are respectively employees of Company A and Company B). Consequently, only Company C (which is not yet represented on the SNB) could be granted an additional seat.

After allocation of these additional seats, the composition of the SNB is as shown in Table 3.3 above.

2 Appointment or election of members of the SNB

9. The Member States must determine the method to be used for the election or appointment of the members of the SNB who are elected or appointed on their territory. Therefore, they must take the necessary steps to ensure that such members include, insofar as possible, at least one representative from each participating company with employees in that Member State, although such measures may not increase the overall number of members (Art. 3(2)(b) Dir.).

Without prejudice to national laws and/or practice describing thresholds for the establishment of a representative body, the Member States shall provide that employees of undertakings or establishments in which there are no employee representatives through no fault of their own have the right to elect or appoint members of the SNB (Art. 3(2)(b) Dir.).

The Member States may provide that such members can include trade union representatives, regardless of whether they are employed by a participating company or a concerned subsidiary or establishment (Art. 3(2)(b) Dir.).

10. In the exercise of their functions, the members of the SNB shall enjoy the same protection and guarantees provided for employee representatives by national law and/or practice in their respective countries of employment (Art. 10 Dir.).

3 Role and functioning of the SNB

A Role

(i) Conclusion of an agreement

11. The SNB and the competent organs of the participating companies shall determine by written arrangements for employee involvement in the SE. To this end, the competent organs of the participating companies must inform the SNB of the plan and actual process for establishing the SE, up to its registration (Art. 3(3) Dir.).

(ii) Absence or termination of negotiations

12. The SNB can decide not to open negotiations or to terminate negotiations already underway and to rely on the rules for the information and consultation of employees in force in the Member States where the SE has employees. Such a decision shall put an end to the procedure to conclude an agreement on employee involvement (Art. 3(6) Dir.). When such decision has been taken, none of the standard rules shall apply. Such a decision must be approved by two-thirds of the members of the SNB.

In the case of an SE established by conversion, this right does not exist if the company to be converted allows employee participation (Art. 3(6) Dir.). The purpose of this exception is to avoid the diminution or suppression of pre-existing employee participation rights in a company due to a change in its corporate form[9].

Even if a decision not to open or to terminate negotiations is taken, it is not definitive[10]. The SNB may be reconvened at the written request of at least

---

[9] See P. Nicaise, *op. cit.*, 489.   [10] V. Bertrand, *op. cit.*, 161.

10% of the employees of the SE, its subsidiaries and establishments, or their representatives, at the earliest two years after the decision, unless the parties agree to reopen negotiations sooner (Art. 3(6) Dir.).

B   Functioning of the SNB

13. The Directive sets forth a few rules regarding negotiations and the internal functioning of the SNB.

(i)   **Duty to co-operate**

14. The SNB and the competent organs of the participating companies must negotiate in a spirit of co-operation with a view to reaching an agreement on arrangements for employee involvement in the SE (Art. 4(1) Dir.).

The purpose of this rule is obviously to promote a consensual solution. In order to meet this goal, the parties must be willing to work together.[11]

(ii)   **Assistance of experts**

15. The SNB may call upon experts of its choice, such as representatives from appropriate Community-level trade union organisations, to assist it with its work. Such experts may be present at negotiations in an advisory capacity at the request of the SNB to promote coherence and consistency at the Community level, where appropriate (Art. 3(5) Dir.).

The SNB may also choose to inform the representatives of appropriate external organisations, including trade unions, of the start of negotiations (Art. 3(5) Dir.).

It is up to the negotiating parties (i.e. the SNB and the competent organs of the participating companies) to determine the modalities governing the assistance of experts and their remuneration. If no solution can be reached, funding by the participating companies shall be limited to one expert (Art. 3(7) Dir.). However, the Member States may decide to limit the funding to cover one expert only.

(iii)   **Duration of negotiations**

16. Negotiations should commence as soon as the SNB is established and can continue for up to six months thereafter (Art. 5(1) Dir.). Nevertheless, the parties may decide by mutual consent to extend negotiations for up to one year following establishment of the SNB (Art. 5(2) Dir.).

(iv)   **Funding**

17. In principle, any expenses related to the functioning of the SNB, particularly to negotiations, shall be borne by the participating companies in order to enable the SNB to carry out its tasks in an appropriate manner. In accordance with this principle, the Member States may prescribe budgetary rules for the functioning

---

[11] P. Nicaise, *op. cit.*, 489.

of the SNB and, in particular, limit the funding to cover the assistance of one exert only (Art. 3(7) Dir.).

IV Creation of a system for employee involvement

18. Below we examine the creation of a system for employee involvement in an SE: (1) upon the conclusion of an agreement to this end; (2) in the absence of an agreement within the negotiations period; and (3) in the event of a decision not to open negotiations or to terminate negotiations already underway.

1 Conclusion of an agreement for employee involvement

19. The agreement is subject to certain conditions with respect to its form and content. The Directive also sets out voting rules for conclusion of the agreement.

A Content and form of the agreement

20. The following issues must be treated in the agreement on employee involvement entered into by the SNB and the competent organs of the participating companies (Art. 4(2) Dir.):

(a) the scope of the agreement;
(b) the composition, number of members and allocation of seats on the representative body that will serve as the discussion partner of the competent organ of the SE in connection with arrangements for the information and consultation of the employees of the SE and of its subsidiaries and establishments;
(c) the functioning and procedure for the information and consultation of the representative body;
(d) the frequency of meetings of the representative body;
(e) the financial and material resources to be allocated to the representative body;
(f) if the parties decide during negotiations to establish one or more information and consultation procedures rather than a representative body, the arrangements for implementing such procedures;
(g) if the parties decide during negotiations to establish arrangements for employee participation, the substance of such arrangements including (if applicable) the number of members of the SE's administrative or supervisory organ that the employees shall be entitled to elect, appoint, recommend or oppose, the procedures by which the employees can elect, appoint, recommend or oppose these members, and their rights;
(h) the date of entry into force of the agreement and its duration, as well as cases where the agreement should be renegotiated and the procedure for renegotiation.

The agreement concluded by the SNB and the competent organs of the participating companies shall not be subject to the standard rules contained in the Annex to the Directive unless stipulated otherwise[12] (Art. 7(1) Dir.).

21. An additional requirement is imposed in the case of an SE formed by conversion. In this case, the agreement must provide for at least the same level of all elements of employee involvement as those existing within the company to be converted into an SE (Art. 4(4) Dir.). This requirement is in line with the 'before and after' principle expressed in the Third Recital to the Directive, *'[s]pecial provisions have to be set, notably in the field of employee involvement, aimed at ensuring that the establishment of an SE does not entail the disappearance or reduction of practices of employee involvement existing within the companies participating in the establishment of an SE'*.

B Voting rules

22. The majorities required to conclude the agreement are expressly stated in the Directive.

The general rule calls for a double majority, i.e., the SNB takes decisions by an absolute majority of votes cast by its members, provided such a majority also represents an absolute majority of the employees. Each member has one vote (Art. 3(4) Dir.). This formula appears quite dangerous, since a double majority inevitably leads to giving more weight to votes cast by SNB members from countries in which the participating companies employ the most employees.

23. However, this general rule is tempered by particular rules when negotiations would result in a reduction of employee participation rights in the SE as compared to the participating companies (Art. 3(4) Dir.).[13] In such an event, the majority required for a decision to approve such an agreement shall be the votes of two-thirds of the members of the SNB, representing at least two thirds of the employees, including the votes of members representing employees employed in at least the two Member States (Art. 3(4) Dir.).

The rationale for these particular rules is to preserve, insofar as possible, employee participation rights in the participating companies, in accordance with the 'before and after' principle which rendered a compromise solution between the Member States possible at the time of adoption of the Directive.[14]

2 Absence of an agreement within the negotiations period

24. If no agreement on arrangements for employee involvement can be reached within the negotiations period, there are two possible options.

---

[12] See no. 26 *et seq.* of this report.   [13] See nos. 45 and 46 of this report.
[14] *Ibid.*, 315; F. Blanquet, *op.cit.*, 148–9; V. Bertrand, *op.cit.*, 155–6; I. De Meuleneere, 'Verordeningen over de Europese vennootschap', *Bank- en Financieel Recht*, 2002, 114.

Either the competent organs of the participating companies can decide not to pursue formation of the SE or they can decide to go ahead with their plans, in which case they must accept application of the standard rules (Art. 7(1)(b) Dir.).[15]

3 Decision not to open or to terminate negotiations

25. If the SNB decides not to open or to terminate negotiations, the standard rules shall not apply. In this case, the rules on the information and consultation of employees in force in the Member States where the SE has employees shall apply (Art. 3(6) Dir.).

A decision not to open or to terminate negotiations must be approved by two thirds of the members of the SNB representing at least two-thirds of the employees, including those representing employees employed in at least two Member States. This rule does not apply to an SE formed by conversion if the company to be converted allows for employee participation (Art. 3(6) Dir.).

V Standard rules

26. The Annex to the Directive contains standard rules which are applicable, as mentioned above, if the competent organs of the participating companies and the SNB so decide or if no agreement on employee involvement can be reached within the negotiations period (Art. 7(1) Dir.), provided the SNB has not decided not to open negotiations or to terminate negotiations already under way. In these events, the standard rules of the Member State in which the SE has its registered office shall be applicable (Art. 7(1) Dir.).

One objective was to provide the negotiating parties with an alternative solution in order to avoid an impasse in the formation of an SE.[16] Moreover, the Community legislature certainly did not wish to see the SNB and the competent organs of the participating companies deprived of the coherence inherent in a standard system.

Below we examine these standard rules, which deal with the creation of a representative body and a system for employee participation.

1 Creation of a representative body

27. When the standard rules are applicable, a representative body must be established (Part 1 Annex Dir.).

---

[15] See no. 26 *et seq.* of this report.
[16] Eighth Recital of the Directive; see also J-F. Bellis, *op.cit.*, 318–19.

A   Composition of the representative body and appointment of its members

28. The representative body is composed of employees of the SE and its subsidiaries and establishments elected or appointed by the employees' representatives or, in the absence thereof, by the entire body of employees as a whole (Part 1(a) Annex Dir.).

The election or appointment of members of the representative body shall be carried out in accordance with national legislation and/or practice. The competent organs of the SE must be informed of the composition of the representative body (Part 1 (b) and (f) Annex Dir.).

The number of seats on the representative body is determined in the same way as for the SNB (Part 1(c) Annex Dir.). However, contrary to the rules governing the composition of the SNB, no additional seats are allocated for an SE formed by merger.

In order to ensure that the number of members of, and allocation of seats on, the representative body are adapted to changes within the SE and its subsidiaries and establishments, the Members shall lay down appropriate rules (Part 1(b) Annex Dir.).

Where its size so warrants, the representative body shall elect a select committee from amongst its members, comprising at most three members (Part 1(c) Annex Dir.).

29. The Members of the representative body, like members of the SNB, enjoy the same protection and guarantees in the exercise of their function as do employee representatives under national laws and/or practice in their country of employment (Art. 10 Dir.).

B   Role

30. The representative body must be informed or consulted on several issues, as determined by the Directive. Moreover, it can decide to renegotiate the agreement for employee involvement in the SE.

(i) **General principle**

31. The role of the representative body is limited to matters that concern the SE itself and any of its subsidiaries or establishments situated in another Member State and to issues that exceed the powers of the SE's decision-making organs in a single Member State (Part 2(a) Annex Dir.).

Information is defined as '*the informing of the body representative of the employees and/or employees' representatives by the competent organ of the SE on questions which concern the SE itself and any of its subsidiaries or establishments situated in another Member State or which exceed the powers of the decision-making organs in a single Member State at a time, in a manner and with a content which allows the employees' representatives to undertake an in-depth assessment of the possible impact and, where appropriate, prepare consultations with the competent organ of the SE*' (Art. 2(i) Dir.).

Consultation consists in '*the establishment of dialogue and exchange of views between the body representative of the employees and/or the employees' representatives and the competent organ of the SE, at a time, in a manner and with a content which allows the employees' representatives, on the basis of information provided, to express an opinion on measures envisaged by the competent organ which may be taken into account in the decision-making process within the SE*' (Art. 2(j) Dir.).

Thus, the representative body has no actual authority to take decisions.

(ii) **Renegotiation of an agreement or continued application of the standard rules**
32. Four years after the representative body has been established, it shall decide whether to open negotiations for the conclusion of an agreement on employee involvement (in accordance with the same procedure applicable to negotiations with the SNB) or to continue to apply the standard rules (Part 1(g) Annex Dir.). When renegotiating an agreement, the representative body exercises the authority of the SNB.

If no agreement on arrangements for employee involvement can be reached within six months (which period can be extended up to one year), the arrangements initially adopted in accordance with the standard rules shall continue to apply (Part 1(g) Annex Dir.).

C   Operation

33. The Directive sets forth a few rules regarding the operation of the representative body.

(i) **Duty to co-operate**
34. The representative body and the competent organs of the SE shall work together in a spirit of co-operation with due regard for their reciprocal rights and obligations (Art. 9 Dir.).

(ii) **Meetings**
35. Annual meetings must be held. An extraordinary meeting must also be called in the event of exceptional circumstances that affect employees' interests.

Prior to any meeting (annual or extraordinary) with the competent organ of the SE, the representative body or the select committee is entitled to meet without representatives from the competent organ being present (Part 2(d) Annex Dir.).

36. At least once a year, the competent organ of the SE must meet with the representative body in order to inform and consult the latter on the basis of regular reports it has drawn up regarding the progress of the SE's business and its prospects (Part 2(b) para. 1 Annex Dir.).

To this end, the competent organ of the SE shall provide the representative body with the agenda for meetings of the administrative organ or, where appropriate, the management and supervisory organs, along with copies of all documents submitted to the general meeting of shareholders (Part 2(b) para. 2 Annex Dir.).

In concrete terms, the following issues must be discussed at the meeting: the structure of the company, its economic and financial situation, the probable development of the company's business, production and sales, the current situation and probable trends with regard to employment and investments, substantial organisational changes, the introduction of new working methods or production processes, transfers of production, mergers, cut-backs or closures of undertakings, establishments or important parts thereof, and collective dismissals (Part 2(b) para. 3 Annex Dir.).

37. In addition to the annual meeting, the representative body must to be informed if there are exceptional circumstances that affect the interests of employees to a considerable extent, particularly in the event of a relocation, transfer, closure of an establishment or undertaking or a collective dismissal (Part 2(c) para. 1 Annex Dir.).

In this case, the representative body or, if it so decides for reasons of urgency, the select committee, shall have the right to meet at its request with the competent organ of the SE or any more appropriate level of management within the SE having its own decision-making powers so as to be informed and consulted regarding measures that significantly affect the interests of employees (Part 2(c) para. 1 Annex Dir.).

If a meeting is organised with the select committee, members of the representative body who represent the employees directly concerned by the measures in question have the right to attend (Part 2(c) para. 3 Annex Dir.).

If the competent organ of the SE decides not to act in accordance with the opinion of the representative body, the latter shall have the right to an additional meeting with the competent organ with a view to reaching an agreement (Part 2(c) para. 2 Annex Dir.). Nevertheless, if that meeting does not lead to a solution, the competent organ remains free to take the decision that best suits it.

(iii) **Information provided to employee representatives**

38. The members of the representative body shall inform the employee representatives of the SE and of its subsidiaries and establishments of the content and outcome of the information and consultation procedures (Part 2(e) Annex Dir.).

This obligation is nevertheless tempered by the fact that 'Member States shall provide that members of the special negotiating body or the representative body, and experts who assist them, are not authorised to reveal any information which has been given to them in confidence' (Art. 8(1) Dir.).

(iv) **Internal measures**

39. The Directive contains several rules regarding the internal functioning of the representative body.

The Directive provides that *'the representative body shall adopt its rules of procedure'* (Part 1(d) Annex Dir.). Surprisingly, the Directive does not state which questions should be resolved by these procedural rules, which could give rise to problems in the drafting stage.

The representative body, like the SNB, may be assisted by experts, provided the costs of at least one expert are borne by the SE (Part 2(f) and (h) para. 3 Annex Dir.).

Insofar as necessary to fulfil their tasks, members of the representative body are entitled to paid time off for training (Part 2(g) Annex Dir.).

(v) **Funding of the representative body**

40. The costs of the representative body shall be borne by the SE, which shall provide the body's members with the requisite financial and material resources to enable them to perform their duties in an appropriate manner (Part 2(h) para. 1 Annex Dir.). In particular, the SE shall, unless agreed otherwise, bear the cost of organising meetings and providing interpretation facilities as well as travel and accommodation expenses incurred by members of the representative body and of the select committee (Part 2(h) para. 2 Annex Dir.).

The Member States may stipulate budgetary rules regarding the operation of the representative body and, in particular, limit funding to cover the costs of a single expert (Part 2(h) para. 3 Annex Dir.).

2 Employee participation

A General remarks

41. The Directive envisages the participation of employees, i.e. *'the influence of the body representative of the employees and/or the employees' representatives in the affairs of a company by way of:*

– *the right to elect or appoint some of the members of the company's supervisory or administrative organ*, or
– *the right to recommend and/or oppose the appointment of some or all of the members of the company's supervisory or administrative organ'* (Art. 2(k) Dir.).

B   Scope

42. The standard rules on employee participation shall apply depending on how the SE is formed.

43. In the case of an SE formed by conversion, the standard rules on employee participation shall apply only if the company to be converted into an SE was subject to national rules on employee participation in its administrative or supervisory body prior to the conversion (Art. 7(2)(a) Dir.).

44. In the case of an SE formed by merger, the standard rules on employee participation shall apply only if:

- prior to registration of the SE, one or more forms of employee participation were applicable to one or more of the participating companies and covered at least 25% of the total number of employees in all participating companies; or
- prior to registration of the SE one or more forms of employee participation were applicable to one or more of the participating companies but covered less than 25% of the total number of employees in all participating companies and the SNB so decides (Art. 7(2)(b) Dir.).

Nevertheless, the Member States can provide that the standard rules on employee participation shall not apply in the case of an SE formed by merger (Art. 7(3) Dir.).

If there was more than one form of employee participation in the various participating companies, the SNB shall decide which of those forms must be retained in the SE. The Member States can fix rules applicable to SEs registered on their territory in the absence of any decision by the SNB on employee participation (Art. 7(2) Dir.).

If the planned decision does not imply a reduction of participation rights, it can be validly taken by an absolute majority of the members of the SNB, provided such a majority also represents an absolute majority of the employees (Art. 3(4) Dir.).

On the other hand, should negotiations result in a reduction of participation rights, provided employee participation extends to at least 25% of the total number of employees of the participating companies, the majority required to approve the agreement shall be two thirds of the members of the SNB representing at least two thirds of the employees, including the votes of those members representing employees employed in at least two Member States (Art. 3(4) Dir.).

The SNB must inform the competent organs of the participating companies of any decisions taken with regard to employee participation (Art. 7(2) Dir.).

45. In the case of a holding or a subsidiary SE, the standard rules on employee participation shall apply only if:

- prior to registration of the SE, one or more forms of employee participation were applicable to one or more of the participating companies and covered at least 50% of the total number of employees in all participating companies; or
- the SNB so decides and prior to registration of the SE, one or more forms of employee participation applied to one or more of the participating companies but covered less than 50% of the total number of employees in all participating companies (Art. 7(2)(c) Dir.).

If there was more than one form of employee participation in the various participating companies, the SNB shall decide which of those forms must be retained in the SE. The Member States can fix rules applicable to SEs established on their territory in the absence of any decision by the SNB on employee participation (Art. 7(2) Dir.).

If the planned decision does not imply a reduction of participation rights, it shall be validly taken by an absolute majority of the members of the SNB, provided such a majority also represents an absolute majority of the employees (Art. 3(4) Dir.).

However, should negotiations result in a reduction of participation rights, provided employee participation extends to at least 50% of the total number of employees of the participating companies, the majority required to approve the agreement shall be two thirds of the members of the SNB representing at least two thirds of the employees, including the votes of those members representing employees employed in at least two Member States (Art. 3(4) Dir.).

The SNB shall inform the competent organs of the participating companies of the decisions taken with regard to employee participation (Art. 7(2) Dir.).

C   Content

46. Once again, it is necessary to distinguish between SEs formed by conversion and those formed by other means.

(i) **SEs formed by merger, holding and subsidiary SEs**

47. The employees of the SE, its subsidiaries and establishments and/or their representative body shall have the right to elect, appoint, recommend or oppose the appointment of the number of members of the administrative or supervisory organ of the SE equal to the highest proportion in effect in the participating companies prior to registration of the SE (Part 3(b) Annex Dir.). If none of the participating companies was subject to employee participation rules prior to

registration of the SE, the SE shall not be required to establish provisions for employee participation (Part 3(b) Annex Dir.).

The representative body shall decide on the allocation of seats on the administrative or supervisory organ from amongst its members representing employees from the various Member States or on how the SE's employees can recommend or oppose the appointment of members of these bodies according to the proportion of employees in each Member State. If the employees from one or more Member States are not covered by this criterion, the representative body shall appoint a member from one of those Member States, in particular the Member State where the SE's registered office is located. Each Member State can determine the allocation of its seats on the administrative or supervisory body (Part 3(b) Annex Dir.).

48. Every member of the administrative body or, where appropriate, the supervisory body of the SE who is elected, appointed or recommended by the representative body or, depending on the circumstances, by the employees shall be regarded a member in full with the same rights and obligations as members representing shareholders, including the right to vote (Part 3(b) Annex Dir.). This solution, recommended in the Davignon report, provides employees with a real say in the SE's decision-making process.[17]

(ii) **SEs formed by conversion**

49. In the case of an SE formed by conversion, if the rules of a Member State on employee participation in the administrative or supervisory organ applied prior to registration, all aspects of employee participation shall continue to apply to the SE (Part 3(a) Annex Dir.).

Rules regarding the composition of the administrative or supervisory organ and the rights and protection of the members of these organs shall also continue to apply in the same manner (Part 3(a) Annex Dir.).

VI **European works council**

50. Where an SE is a Community-scale undertaking or a controlling undertaking of a Community-scale group of undertakings within the meaning of Directive 94/45/EC[18] or Directive 97/94 EC extending the aforementioned directive to the UK,[19] the provisions of these directives and their implementing

---

[17] No. 81 of the Davignon report.
[18] Directive of 22 September 1994 on the establishment of a European Works Council or a procedure in Community-scale undertakings and Community-scale groups of undertakings for the purposes of informing and consulting employees, *Official Journal*, L 254 of 30 September 1994.
[19] Directive of 15 December 1997 extending, to the United Kingdom of Great Britain and Northern Ireland, Directive 94/45/EC on the establishment of a European Works Council or a procedure in Community-scale undertakings and Community-scale groups of undertakings for the purposes of informing and consulting employees, *Official Journal*, L 010 of 16 January 1998.

national legislation shall not apply to the SE or to its subsidiaries (Art. 13(1) Dir.) as the representative body of the SE fulfils *de facto* the role of the European works council.

However, where the SNB decides not to open negotiations or to terminate negotiations, Directive 94/45/EC or Directive 97/74/EC and the provisions transposing them into national law shall apply (Art. 13 (1) Dir.).

VII National rules on employee involvement

51. The Directive also provides that national rules with regard to participation (other than those implemented by the Directive) do not apply to SEs (Art. 13(2) Dir.).

However, the Directive shall not prejudice provisions on employee participation in the bodies laid down by national law and/or practice applicable to the subsidiaries of an SE (Art. 13(3)(b) Dir.). Moreover, the Directive does not affect existing employee involvement rights provided under national legislation and/or practice in the Member States as enjoyed by employees of the SE and its subsidiaries and establishments, other than participation in the bodies of the SE (Art. 13(3)(a) Dir.).

The Member States may, in order to preserve these rights, take the necessary measures to guarantee that the structures of employee representation in participating companies which will cease to exist as separate legal entities are maintained after registration of the SE (Art. 13(4) Dir.).

VIII Reservation and confidentiality

52. The Member States must also provide that members of the SNB and the representative body, as well as any experts who assist them, are not authorised to reveal any information which has been given to them in confidence, wherever these persons may be, even after expiry of their terms of office (Art. 8(1) Dir.). This also applies to employee representatives in the context of information and consultation procedures (Art. 8(1) Dir.).

National law shall also provide that, under the conditions and limits it determines, the supervisory or administrative organ of an SE or a participating company established in its territory, is not obliged to transmit any information of a nature that, in objective terms, could seriously harm or be prejudicial to the functioning of the SE, its subsidiaries or establishments or a participating company (Art. 8(2) Dir.).

Such dispensation may be subject to administrative or judicial authorisation (Art. 8(2)(2) Dir.).

53 The Member States may also lay down particular rules for SEs established in their territory which pursue directly and essentially the aim of ideological guidance with respect to information and expression of opinions on the condition that such provisions already existed in the Member States concerned on the date of adoption of the Directive (Art. 8(3) Dir.).

54. In any case, the Member States must make provisions for administrative or judicial appeal procedures which may be initiated by the employee representatives in the event the supervisory or administrative organ of the SE demands confidentiality or does not provide information (Art. 8(4) Dir.).

VIII Misuse of procedure and compliance with the Directive

55. The Member States must take appropriate measures in conformity with Community law with a view to preventing the misuse of an SE for the purposes of depriving employees of their rights to involvement or of withholding such rights (Art. 11 Dir.).

The Member States must also ensure that the management of establishments of an SE and the supervisory or administrative organs of subsidiaries and participating companies situated on their territory and the employee representatives or, as the case may be, the employees themselves, abide by the obligations set forth in the Directive, regardless of whether the SE has its registered office in that Member State (Art. 12(1) Dir.).

The Member States must also provide for appropriate measures in the event of failure to comply with the Directive and ensure enforcement of obligations deriving from the Directive by way of administrative or legal procedures (Art. 12(2) Dir.).

IX Protection of employee representatives

56. Employee representatives on the supervisory or administrative organ of an SE who are also employees of the SE or of its subsidiaries or establishments or of a participating company shall enjoy, in the exercise of their functions, the same protection and guarantees provided for employee representatives by national law and/or practice in their country of employment (Art. 10(1) Dir.).

This shall apply in particular to attendance at meetings of the SNB or representative body, any other meetings under the arrangements for employee involvement in the SE or any meeting of the administrative or supervisory organ and to the payment of wages for members employed by a participating company, the SE, its subsidiaries or establishments during a period of absence necessary for the performance of their duties (Art. 10(2) Dir.).

X Transposition of the directive

57. The deadline for transposition of the Directive into national law was 8 October 2004. By that date, the Member States should have ensured that management and labour had introduced the required provisions by way of agreement. Furthermore, the Member States are obliged to take all necessary steps to enable these parties to guarantee at all times the results stemming from the Directive (Art. 14(1) Dir.).

XI Conclusion

58. The issue of employee involvement, and the divergent views held by the Member States on this question, made it difficult to achieve a compromise on the European company statute.

The solution that eventually was found guarantees that employees or their representatives are informed and consulted on the questions affecting them and may lead to a participatory system, which gives employees weight in the decision-making process. The specific modalities of employee involvement in an SE must be determined by the employee representatives and the organs of the participating companies, in accordance with a procedure described in the Directive.

The least one can say is that following this procedure will cost time and money, and reaching agreement will be complicated because negotiating parties will have to overcome differences in their respective laws and social conceptions. This problem will be particularly acute for small companies that do not themselves have employee involvement systems in place.

Clearly, the success of the European company will depend on the capacity of parties to reach an agreement through the channels defined by the Directive. One can wonder if the compromise reached by the Member States on the difficult issue of employee involvement and the modalities required for its execution will not discourage potential candidates from forming SEs.

4

International tax aspects of the Societas Europaea

RODERIK BOUWMAN AND JAN WERBROUCK
NautaDutilh

I   Introduction   98
II Tax treatment of an SE   100
III Tax residence of an SE   102
IV The SE and tax treaties   106
V   The SE and Community directives in the field of taxation   107
    1 General remarks   107
    2 The Parent-Subsidiary Directive   109
    3 The Merger Directive   110
    4 The Interest and Royalties Directive   113

I Introduction

1. In contrast to the proposals of 1970[1] and 1975[2] and to a certain extent those of 1989[3] and 1991,[4] the Regulation does not contain special tax provisions for the SE. Recital 20 of the Regulation expressly states that it 'does not cover other areas of law such as taxation'. Therefore, the provisions of national law and Community law shall apply to areas not covered by the Regulation.

The Regulation differs from Council Regulation No. 2137/85 on the European economic interest grouping (EEIG)[5]. in that it does not contain tax provisions. The EEIG was the first legal entity introduced under Community law, and the EEIG Regulation provides for transparency for tax purposes for profits generated by an EEIG.[6]

The absence of specific tax provisions in the Regulation has been criticised by both legal commentators[7] and the European Commission. In a communication to the Council, the European Parliament and the Economic and Social Committee of October 2001 (the October 2001 Commission

---

[1] *Official Journal* C 124,10 October 1970.   [2] *Bulletin EC Supplement* 4/1075.
[3] *Official Journal* C 263,16 October 1989.   [4] *Ibid.*, C 176, 8 July 1991.
[5] *Council Regulation* (EEC) No. 2137/85 of 25 July 1985 on the European economic interest grouping (EEIG).
[6] Arts. 2(1)(1) and 40 Council Regulation (EEC) No. 2137/85.
[7] K. Lanoo and M. Levin, 'An EU Company Without an EU Tax? A Corporate Tax Action Plan for Advancing the Lisbon Process', *CEPS Research Report*, April 2002.

Communication),[8] the Commission stated as follows in relation to the introduction of the SE:

> By that date, the current and future body of EU company law, such as the Parent-Subsidiary Directive and the Merger Directive, must be amended to allow companies to choose this new legal form. However, this might not be sufficient to make the Statute an attractive company law vehicle. The full benefits of establishing a European company (SE) will only be achieved if existing companies can form such an entity without incurring additional tax costs and can avoid some of the existing tax obstacles of operating in more than one Member State. As things stand, neither of these goals are provided for and the success of the Statute could be jeopardised. The concept of the European company is closely linked to that of a consolidated corporate tax system.

The absence of specific tax provisions in the Regulation has also been greeted with scepticism by some legal scholars,[9] who describe the SE as an alternative corporate form with some Community characteristics which is liable to remain a 'luxury item' for the most part rather than an essential staple for the creation of a single internal market.

2. Following the adoption of the Regulation, the Commission concluded that it had done its utmost to ensure that the SE receives, at the very least, the same tax treatment as any other public limited-liability company formed under the laws of a Member State, despite its failed attempts to include specific tax provisions in the Regulation. The Commission further noted that the SE could be better off in at least one respect in that the transfer of an SE's registered office from one Member State to another for tax purposes (subject to certain conditions) will be better facilitated through an amendment to the Merger Directive[10] (approved by the Council on 17 February 2005). Although only time will tell, this possibility could very well lead in practice to the establishment of SEs in or the transfer of their registered offices to Member States that provide the most flexible legal and attractive (i.e. neutral) tax rules.

In addition, the Commission has proposed testing the consolidated EU tax base with a European company pilot programme.[11] This programme should not be seen solely in relation to the SE but rather in a much wider context

---

[8] Communication from the Commission to the Council, the European Parliament and the Economic and Social Committee, 'Towards an Internal Market Without Tax Obstacles. A Strategy for Providing Companies with a Consolidated Corporate Tax Base for their EU-wide Activities', COM (2001) 582 final.

[9] See Malcolm Gammie QC, 'EU Taxation and the Societas Europaea – Harmless Creature or Trojan Horse', para. 1.3, *European Taxation*, January 2004, vol. 44, 2004, no. 1.

[10] Council Directive of 23 July 1990 on the common system of taxation applicable to mergers, divisions, transfers of assets and exchange of shares concerning companies of different Member States (90/434/EEC).

[11] MEMO/04/235, 8 October 2004.

of providing multinationals with a consolidated corporate tax base for their EU-wide activities.

II Tax treatment of an SE

3. Even though it does not contain specific tax provisions, the Regulation is still relevant in determining the tax treatment of an SE. Articles 9 and 10 of the Regulation arguably apply to the tax treatment of an SE by the Member States.

4. Article 9(1)(c) of the Regulation states that an SE shall be governed,

> ... in the case of matters not regulated by this Regulation or, where matters are partly regulated by it, of those aspects not covered by it, by (i) the provisions of laws adopted by Member States in implementation of Community measures relating specifically to SEs; (ii) the provisions of Member States' law which would apply to a public limited-liability company formed in accordance with the law of the member State in which the SE has its registered office; (iii) the provisions of its statutes in the same way as for a public limited-liability company formed in accordance with the law of the Member State in which the SE has its registered office.

The scope of the first sentence and of subsection (ii) of Article 9(1)(c) is important for tax purposes. The wording is not conclusive as to whether 'matters' and the 'provisions of Member States' law' intend to refer only to corporate law or should be construed more broadly. A broad interpretation would imply that an SE is also subject to the tax laws applicable to public limited-liability companies of the Member State in which its registered office is located.

The Commission favours a broad interpretation in its proposal for adoption of the Interest and Royalties Directive,[12] in which it states:

> Furthermore, the Statute of the European Company (...) will enter into force on 8 October 2004 (...). While there are no provisions in the Statue of the European Company directed specifically at taxation, nevertheless, the instrument does require the SE to be subject to the provisions of Member States' law which would apply to a public limited-liability company formed in accordance with the law of the Member State in which the SE has its registered office.[13]

In the footnote to the above sentence, reference is made to Article 9(1)(c)(ii) of the Regulation.

In the literature, such a broad interpretation has not been accepted without debate. It has been argued that this interpretation would lead to a contradictory result whereby Recital 20 states that the Regulation does not cover tax matters

---

[12] See footnote 59.   [13] COM (2003) 613 final, Introduction, point 20.

while Article 9 subsequently provides that the SE shall be subject to provisions of national tax law.[14]

5. Article 10 of the Regulation provides that *'an SE shall be treated in every Member State as if it were a public limited-liability company formed in accordance of the law of the Member State in which it has its registered office.'*

This article appears to be a general non-discrimination provision through which the Regulation seeks to affirm that the Member States do not have the liberty to introduce specific national rules for the SE which are more or less advantageous, from the SE's perspective, than those applicable to national public limited-liability companies. Recital 5 of the Regulation states that:

> Member States shall be obliged to ensure that the provisions applicable to European companies under this Regulation do not result either in discrimination arising out of unjustified different treatment of European companies compared with the public limited-liability companies or in disproportionate restrictions on the formation of a European company or on the transfer of its registered office.

Moreover, in light of comments made in earlier versions of the Regulation with respect to the fear that the SE would be treated differently (i.e. more favourably) than national public limited-liability companies, Article 10 provides for the equal treatment of SEs and national public limited-liability companies for tax purposes, as well. The sentiment has been expressed in the literature that Article 10 provides a better basis for equal tax treatment of an SE and national public limited-liability companies[15] than Article 9. By stating that the SE shall be treated in *'every Member State'* as a public limited-liability company of the Member State in which its registered office is located, Article 10 would seem to be specifically addressed to those Member States in which the SE is not registered. However, there would appear to be no compelling reason to limit the scope of Article 10 in this way. Essentially, Article 10 can be considered a legal basis for equal tax treatment of the SE and public limited-liability companies formed in accordance with the laws of a Member State.

6. The fact that an SE will in principle be afforded the same tax treatment by each Member State as a public limited-liability company established under the laws of that state is very important and has two significant implications. First, an SE established in a Member State must be treated the same for tax purposes as a national public limited-liability company of that state. Second, an SE registered in a Member State must be treated in other Member States in the same manner as a public limited-liability company of its Member State of

---

[14] *De Europese vennootschap (SE), preadvies van de vereniging 'handelsrecht'*, 2004, part 4, para. 2.2.
[15] *Ibid.*, para. 2.3.

registration. Furthermore, it follows that this principle of equal treatment also applies to shareholders of an SE, who must be treated the same for tax purposes as shareholders of a public limited-liability company formed under the laws of the SE's Member State of registration.

Questions may arise in the Member States, about to the tax treatment of an SE and its shareholders in areas where it is treated differently than national public limited-liability companies, with regards to the transfer of its registered office pursuant to Article 8 of the Regulation.

7. The absence of special tax provisions in the Regulation, coupled with the principle of equal treatment, means an SE is subject to the tax laws of the Member State of which it is considered a resident for tax purposes and, when operating internationally, applicable international regulations, treaties and the laws of the (Member) States in which it operates. Consequently, as a tax resident of the EU, an SE is potentially subject to the tax laws of 28 countries (25 EU Member States and three EEA countries). An SE is also subject to intra-Community and several intra-EEA tax treaties and to provisions transposing into national law the three Community directives in the field of direct taxation. Furthermore, the fundamental freedoms enshrined in the EC Treaty and the EEA Agreement, including interpretations thereof by the European Court of Justice (ECJ), also apply to SEs.[16]

8. The fiscal sovereignty of the Member States in which an SE operates is preserved due to the principle of equal (tax) treatment. Some writers argue that this result is justified since an SE should be viewed as a European form of business organisation rather than as a tax-planning vehicle, a tax incentive or a political instrument to enhance tax competition and/or co-ordination. Therefore, any distortion of the internal market or discrimination against an SE (or favouritism, for that matter) should be prevented from both a Community and national perspective.[17]

III   Tax residence of an SE

9. In the absence of specific tax provisions or tax rules governing the SE, it cannot have European tax residence. Therefore, pursuant to Articles 9 and 10 of the Regulation, the tax residency criteria set forth in the national tax laws of the Member States and in applicable tax treaties shall apply to an SE in the same way as to any other national public limited-liability company.

---

[16] See M. Wenz, 'The European Company (Societas Europaea) – Legal Concept and Tax Issues', *European Taxation*, January 2004.
[17] *Ibid.*, note 16.

10. According to the Regulation, for company law purposes, an SE's registered office (a formal criterion) and its head office (a factual criterion) should be in the same Member State. A similar approach usually applies under the national tax laws of the Member States, which combine formal criteria (often related to company law, such as the place of incorporation or of a company's registered office) with factual criteria. The place of effective management is the most commonly used factual criterion throughout the EU.

Under tax treaties, various criteria can be used to determine tax residence. These criteria, listed in Article 4(1) of the OECD model convention (2003 version), relate to domicile, residence, place of management or any other factors of a similar nature. Pursuant to Article 4(3) of the convention, the place of effective management is often used as a tiebreak rule. In a small number of tax treaties between the Member States, however, the place of effective management is not the deciding factor, and in other cases no tiebreak rule is provided to resolve dual tax residency. Other decisive factors in some treaties include the location of a company's headquarters or management and control and its place of incorporation or of establishment.[18]

11. It follows from the above that the factors used to determine the residency of an SE for company law purposes and its country of residence for tax purposes are similar, for the most part, but not identical. For instance, it is unclear whether the concept of head office as mentioned in the Regulation is identical or similar to the place of effective management referred to in the tax treaties. The commentary to Article 4(3) of the OECD model convention states that:

> [t]he place of effective management is the place where key management and commercial decisions that are necessary for the conduct of the entity's business are in substance made. The place of effective management will ordinarily be the place where the most senior person or group of persons (for example a board of directors) makes its decisions, the place where the actions to be taken by the entity as a whole are determined. However, no definite rule can be given and all relevant facts and circumstances must be examined to determine the place of effective management.[19]

It would appear from this commentary that the place of effective management is the same as an SE's head office, but no definite conclusions can be drawn in this respect. Consequently, at least in theory, a mismatch could occur between the head office of an SE for company law purposes and its place of effective management for tax purposes, which could result in the SE being resident in one Member State for company law purposes and in a different Member State for tax purposes. Likewise, an SE could be an EU resident for company law purposes but not for tax purposes.

---

[18] See also M. Teresa Soler Roh, 'Tax Residence of the SE', *European Taxation*, January 2004.
[19] Commentary to Art. 4.3 of the OECD model convention, para. 24.

12. Article 8(1) of the Regulation provides that an SE's registered office may be transferred from one Member State to another without the need to wind up and create a new legal entity. This provision results in complete freedom of movement within the EU, although an SE's registered office and head office must be in the same Member State. The transfer of an SE's registered office should therefore be accompanied in practice by a simultaneous transfer of its head office in order to meet this condition.

13. The transfer of an SE's registered office to another Member State will, in principle, also result in a change in tax residency (although the possibility of a mismatch exists; see no. 11 above). In most Member States, a change in tax residency results in the imposition of exit tax on hidden reserves and goodwill. A number of Member States, however, do not levy exit tax if and to the extent that a permanent establishment remains behind.[20] Exit tax may be imposed at both the company level and the shareholder level.

14. One relevant question in this respect is whether an exit tax imposed by a Member State on a company, particularly an SE, under the circumstances described above is permitted under Community law. The ECJ has rendered several judgments in such cases but has yet to formulate a clear rule.

The ECJ's case law indicates that the taxpayer must first be able to rely on the EC treaty as such. With regard to the transfer of a company's place of effective management, the ECJ ruled in *Daily Mail*[21] that freedom of establishment confers no right on a company incorporated under the laws of a Member State and having its registered office in the state to transfer its place of central management and control to another Member State.[22] As a result, an exit tax imposed by that Member State cannot be challenged under a provision of Community law. It is unclear whether this holding should apply both to Member States that use the head office theory[23] and to those that apply the incorporation principle.[24] For an SE, reliance on the EC treaty should not be a problem as the right of an SE to transfer its registered office abroad is expressly conferred by Community law. It

---

[20] Soler Roh, *op cit.*, para. 3.2 and footnote 28. [21] ECJ, 27 September 1988, Case 81/87.
[22] With respect to recognition of the legal capacity of a company by the Member State to which the company has transferred its actual centre of administration, see *Überseening*: ECJ, 5 November 2002, Case 208/00.
[23] Under the head office theory, a company shall be treated as a resident for company law purposes of a country if it is effectively run from that country. The company loses legal personality if it transfers its place of effective management abroad.
[24] Pursuant to the incorporation principle, a company shall be treated for company law purposes as a resident of the country in which it is incorporated for the duration of its existence, regardless of where it is effectively managed. The company maintains legal personality in its country of incorporation throughout its life.

should therefore be possible to test the exercise of this right against Community law.[25]

Once a right to rely on the EC treaty has been proved, it must be determined whether the exit tax is a restriction on Community law. Relevant cases in this respect include *X and Y* [26] and in particular *Hughes de Lasteyrie du Saillant*.[27] Although the latter case involved an individual taxpayer, it is widely considered relevant for companies, as well. In that case, the ECJ ruled that an exit tax is a restriction on freedom of establishment by virtue of its dissuasive effect on taxpayers who wish to establish themselves in other Member States. The fact that a taxpayer could obtain a five-year deferral and that at the end of this period the tax due on any shares still held by the taxpayer was waived, did not sufficiently mitigate this dissuasive effect due to the rigorous conditions the taxpayer had to comply with in order to obtain the deferral. However, an automatic deferral, as applied, for instance, by the Dutch tax authorities since *de Lasteyrie*, could be deemed sufficient to mitigate the dissuasive effect of an exit tax so that it no longer constitutes an unlawful restriction on Community law.

Finally, once it has been established that an exit tax restricts freedom of establishment, it must be determined whether the Member State in question is justified in imposing such a restriction. In *de Lasteyrie*, the ECJ rejected the following justifications:

- The exit tax was imposed as an anti-abuse measure. An anti-abuse measure must be proportional and specific. Measures that tax non-abusive situations as well are only permissible if no more specific measure is possible.
- The measure was imposed to protect the national tax base (of France). Protection of the national tax base can never justify a restriction on Community law.
- The measure is necessary for the coherence of the tax system of Member State. It was argued that if gains are taxed only upon realisation, an exit tax is necessary to ensure that all taxpayers are treated fairly. The Court did not expressly address this justification, as coherence of the tax system was not the goal of the French exit tax. In other situations this argument could possibly prevail.

---

[25] See also D. Weber, 'Exit Taxes on the Transfer of Seat and the Applicability of Freedom of Establishment after *Überseering*', *European Taxation*, October 2003, 350–54.
[26] ECJ, 21 November 2002, Case 436/00.
[27] ECJ, 11 March 2004, Case 9/02. For the relevance of *de Lasteyrie* to Dutch exit tax, *see* F.G.F. Peters, *H v J EG 11 maart 2004 (Hughes de Lasteyrie du Saillant): exit voor de Nederlandse emigratieheffing? (1)* and (2), WFR 2004/1274 and WFR 2004/1307.

If an exit tax upon the transfer of an SE's registered office to another Member State is deemed an unjustified restriction on freedom of establishment, Community law shall prevail, and the Member State will not be allowed to impose the tax. Absent confirmation of this point by the ECJ, however, the Member States can continue to levy exit tax. Hence, in order for the SE to become a more attractive vehicle, it is important that exit tax obstacles within the EU be removed. The amended Merger Directive[28] appears to establish in this respect a compromise between freedom of establishment and the financial interests of the Member States by providing an intermediate solution which ultimately may not be compatible with freedom of establishment.[29]

IV   The SE and tax treaties

15. According to the OECD model convention, tax treaties apply to persons who are resident of one or both contracting states.[30] The term 'person' also refers to companies.[31] The term 'company' is defined as 'any body corporate or any entity that is treated as a body corporate for tax purposes'.[32] According to Article 1(1) of the Regulation, the SE is a company with share capital and legal personality. Article 3(1) of the Regulation states that '... an SE shall be regarded as a public limited-liability company governed by the laws of the Member State where it has its registered office'.

According to Article 4(1) of the OECD model convention, a company is a resident of the country where it is subject to tax under the laws of that state by reason of its domicile, residence, place of management or any other criterion of a similar nature. In principle, an SE will be considered a resident subject to corporate tax on an unlimited basis of the state where its head office is located. Consequently, an SE will be a resident for tax treaty purposes of the Member State where its head office (or place of effective management) is situated[33] and will thus be able to benefit from tax treaties concluded by that state.[34]

16. In addition to tax treaties concluded by the Member State of which it is a tax resident, an SE may also be able to benefit from treaties concluded by the Member States in which it maintains permanent establishments. Pursuant to the ECJ's decision in *Saint–Gobain*,[35] permanent establishment of an SE situated

---

[28] See note 52.   [29] *See also* Soler Roh, *op cit.*, para. 3.2.
[30] Art. 1 OECD model convention (2003).   [31] *See also* Soler Roh, *op cit.*, para. 3.2.
[32] *Ibid.*, Art. 3(1)(b).
[33] See no. 11 of this report for more information on the possibility of a mismatch between the location of an SE's head office and its country of residence for tax purposes.
[34] See also M. Helminen, 'The Tax Treatment of the Running of an SE', para. 2.3, *European Taxation*, January 2004, Vol. 44, 2004, No. 1.
[35] ECJ, 21 September 1999, Case C-307/97.

in a Member State should be eligible for the same tax-treaty benefits available to tax residents of that state.

17. Another relevant aspect of treaty application is the most-favoured-nation principle, pursuant to which a taxpayer can apply not only the provisions of the tax treaty concluded between its country of residence and the country from which it derives foreign-source income but also the relevant provisions of all other tax treaties concluded by either of these countries if these provisions are more favourable. Some tax treaties explicitly provide for most-favoured-nation treatment, in one case brought before the ECJ, the advocate general delivered an opinion, in which he advocated application of this doctrine in principle, although not under all circumstances[36]. The Court, however, ruled that the free movement of capital does not necessarily preclude a rule laid down by a bilateral convention for the avoidance of double taxation from not being extended to nationals of a Member State which is not a party to that convention.[37]

V The SE and Community directives in the field of taxation

1 General remarks

18. There are presently three Community directives in force in the field of direct taxation, namely the Parent-Subsidiary Directive,[38] the Merger Directive[39] and the Interest and Royalties Directive.[40] As explained in more detail below, all Member States must respect the provisions of these directives in their tax treatment of the SE.

The SE must meet the requirements of these directives in order to qualify for their benefits. For example, the SE will not be able to benefit from the directives on the basis of a tax treaty with a non-EU Member State if it is not a tax resident of the EU.

One unresolved issue is the tax treatment of the SE in the three EEA member countries with regard to the directives. As these directives do not form part of the EEA Agreement and companies of these countries are not mentioned in the annexes to the directives, they do not apply in the EEA. Nor does the Regulation.

---

[36] 'D' Case, ECJ, Case 376/03.   [37] ECJ, 5 July 2005 Case 376/03.
[38] Council Directive of 23 July 1990 on the common system of taxation applicable in the case of parent companies and subsidiaries of different Member States (90/435/EEC).
[39] Council Directive of 23 July 1990 on the common system of taxation applicable to mergers, divisions, transfers of assets and exchange of shares concerning companies of different Member States (90/434/EEC).
[40] Council Directive of 30 December 2003 on the common system of taxation applicable to interest and royalty payments made between associated companies of different Member States (2003/49/EC).

Hence, the SE will be treated the same way as national public limited-liability companies in these countries and cannot rely on the provisions of the directives.

In addition to the three directives in the field of direct taxation, the Capital Directive[41] may be of relevance to SEs. Pursuant to this directive, the Member States can impose a duty on contributions to a capital company. The term 'capital company' is defined in Article 3 of the Directive. Article 3(1)(a) contains a list of the most commonly used types of national public limited-liability companies in the former 15 Member States. The Capital Directive has yet to be updated to include the SE or the companies of the newly acceded Member States for that matter.[42] It can be argued, however, that the SE, which by its very nature is a capital company, already falls within the scope of this directive. Article 3(1)(b) and/or (c) brings certain general categories of capital companies within its scope. The SE could qualify under one or both of these provisions. Moreover, Articles 9 and 10 of the Regulation would appear to dictate that the Member States must apply the Capital Directive to the SE in the same way as to the national public limited-liability companies listed in Article 3(1)(a) of the Capital Directive.

Consequently, an SE is in principle (i.e. absent the application of an exemption under the Capital Directive)[43] subject to capital duty in the Member State where its centre of effective management is situated at the time of the transaction, unless this centre is outside the EU, in which case the transaction is subject to capital duty in the Member State where the SE's registered office is located.

The impact of the Capital Directive is limited to those Member States that have yet to abolish a tax on capital contributions.

19. Furthermore, the Savings Directive[44] is applicable to SEs in the same way as to national public limited-liability companies incorporated under the laws of a Member State. The Savings Directive only applies to the interest income of beneficial owners who are natural persons. Therefore, this directive applies to the SE only insofar as it acts as a paying agent, as defined in Article 4 of the directive. If an SE pays interest to an individual taxpayer or receives or secures

---

[41] Council Directive of 17 July 1969 concerning indirect taxes on the raising of capital (69/335/EEC).

[42] The European Commission recently launched a proposal to abolish all capital duties in the EU. No final decision has yet been taken. In the meantime, the Council is preparing an updated version of the Capital Directive that incorporates all amendments and relevant ECJ case law. This updated version should contain, *inter alia*, a new list of qualifying capital companies.

[43] The original Capital Directive contained the possibility of such exemptions in Art. 7(1)(b)). Current Art. 7 (as amended by Directive 85/303/EEC) requires the Member States to continue to exempt transactions that were formerly exempt or taxed at a rate of 0.50% or less.

[44] Council Directive of 3 June 2003 on taxation of savings income in the form of interest payments (2003/48/EC).

interest payments for such taxpayers, it must provide information to the tax authorities in compliance with Article 8 of the Savings Directive.

20. Finally, the VAT directives[45] also apply to SEs in the same way as to national public limited-liability companies. VAT liability is based on the type of activities performed by an entrepreneur and the place from which they are performed and is independent of the entrepreneur's corporate form. Therefore, the transfer of an SE's registered office to another Member State does not necessarily imply that taxable activities (and consequently VAT liability) are also transferred.

2 The Parent-Subsidiary Directive

21. The Parent-Subsidiary Directive provides for the elimination of double taxation on profits distributed in the form of dividends by a subsidiary in one Member State to its parent company in another Member State by either the abolition of any withholding tax in the subsidiary's Member State of residence combined with an exemption in the parent company's Member State of residence or imputation of tax already paid in the subsidiary's Member State against tax due in the Member State of the parent company. According to Article 2(a) of the directive, it applies only to companies listed in the Annex thereto.

22. The Parent-Subsidiary Directive was amended by Council Directive 2003/123/EC of 22 December 2003, pursuant to a proposal from the European Commission[46] presented in the October 2001 Commission Communication.[47] Directive 2002/123/EC contains three elements to improve the Parent-Subsidiary Directive, including an updated list of companies to which the directive applies, including new legal entities such as the SE in a category of its own (category (z) in the proposal and category (p) in the final version). This category was originally named (z) as categories (p) to (y) of the Annex were reserved for companies of the acceding Member States.

The Explanatory Memorandum to the proposal to the Parent-Subsidiary Directive stated that the addition of the SE was necessary to formally bring it within the scope of the directive. This necessity was justified as follows:

---

[45] There are 20 Council directives on the harmonisation of the laws of the Member States relating to turnover taxes, of which the most important is the Council directive of 17 May 1977 on the common system of value-added tax: uniform basis of assessment (Sixth VAT Directive, 77/388/EEC).
[46] Proposal for a Council Directive, amending Directive 90/435/EEC of 23 July 1990, COM (2003) 841 final.
[47] Communication from the Commission to the Council, the European Parliament and the Economic and Social Committee, *op. cit.*, footnote 8, 260 final.

As already mentioned, the Statute of the SE has been recently adopted. The Directive's scope should include the companies which will in future operate under this new legal form. Thus the SE is among the new entries proposed for inclusion in the list of entities covered by the Directive.[48]

The necessity of adding the SE to the Annex was also mentioned in Directive 2003/23/EC,[49] in which it is stated:

> Since the SE is a public limited-liability company and (...), (...) similar in nature to other forms of company already covered by Directive 90/435/EEC, the SE (...) should be added to the list set out in the Annex to Directive 90/435/EEC. Pursuant to Article 2 of the proposal to amend the Parent-Subsidiary Directive, the Member States had to bring into force the laws, regulations and administrative provisions necessary to comply with the directive no later than 1 January 2005.

3   The Merger Directive

23. The Merger Directive provides for deferred taxation of capital gains arising from cross-border company restructuring carried out in the form of mergers, divisions, transfers of assets and exchanges of shares. Taxation is, in principle, deferred until eventual disposal of the assets or shares. Transposition of the Merger Directive has not yet been possible throughout the Member States due to failure to reach agreement on the tenth proposal for a Council directive on cross-border mergers of public limited companies.[49] As a result, only cross-border transfers of assets and exchanges of shares are now eligible for tax-neutral treatment in the Member States. As the Regulation provides an autonomous legal base for cross-border mergers, the SE is not dependent on transposition of the proposed directive. Thus, the SE creates a possibility for cross-border mergers of public companies throughout the EU for the first time.

24. Within the framework of its short-term goals as outlined in its Communication of October 2001, the Commission submitted a proposal[51] in October 2003 to broaden the scope of the Merger Directive. The proposal includes a large number of amendments, including (i) an update of the list of companies in the Annex to which the Merger Directive applies and (ii) introduction of tax-neutral treatment for the transfer of an SE's registered office between Member States. The proposal was, subject to certain minor changes, adopted on 7 December 2004 by the Council of Ministers and on 17 February 2005 by the Council.[52] Article 2 of the proposal originally stated that the Member States must transpose

---

[48] Explanatory Memorandum, point 14, COM (2003) 462 final.
[49] Recital 5 of Council Directive 2003/123/EC.   [50] COM (84) 727 final, 8 January 1985.
[51] Proposal for a Council Directive amending Directive 90/434/EEC, COM (2003) 613 final, 17 October 2003, 2003/0239 (CNS).
[52] Council Directive 2005/19/EC of 17 February 2005 amending Directive 90/434/EEC.

the Merger Directive by 1 January 2005. In the final version, however, the schedule for transposition has been split into two. The Member States must now introduce the provisions necessary to allow the tax-neutral transfer of an SE's registered office no later than 1 January 2006. All other provisions of the proposal must be implemented by 1 January 2007.

25. In the amended Merger Directive, the new list of companies to which the directive applies extends to the same legal entities as the amended Parent-Subsidiary Directive. The SE is included in this list (category (z)). The necessity of adding the SE to the list is justified by the same arguments[53] used to include it in the Annex to the Parent-Subsidiary Directive (see no. 19 of this report).

26. Article 2 of the Regulation states four ways in which an SE may be formed, namely by: (i) merger, provided at least two of the merging companies are governed by the laws of different Member States; (ii) as a holding SE; (iii) as a subsidiary SE; or (iv) by conversion of a national public limited-liability company.

With the inclusion of the SE in the Annex to the Merger Directive, the formation of an SE may be accomplished on a tax-deferred basis with respect to the first three means of formation.[54] The fourth method (conversion) is not regulated by the Merger Directive. However, pursuant to the results of a survey on the Societas Europaea[55] conducted in the former 15 Member States, all are expected to grant roll-over relief as conversion only entails a change in corporate form and not a transfer of assets and liabilities. The survey indicates that roll-over relief shall also be granted by the Member States in which a permanent establishment of the company undergoing conversion is situated.

27. The amended Merger Directive introduces tax deferral rules for the transfer of an SE's registered office from one Member State to another. The introduction of tax-neutral treatment for such a transfer is justified as follows:

> This is an expression of the fundamental freedom of establishment. It should not be hampered by discriminatory tax rules or by restrictions or distortions arising from the tax provisions of the Member States which would be in violation of the EC treaty provision. Nevertheless, in order to ensure clarity on this point, it is appropriate to provide in the Directive for provisions that explicitly refer to this case.[56]

---

[53] Explanatory Memorandum, para. 20, respectively Recital (9), COM (2003) 613 final.

[54] For an extensive discussion of this point, see Paolo Conci, 'The Tax Treatment of the Creation of an SE', *European Taxation*, January 2004, Vol. 44, 2004, No. 1.

[55] Survey on the Societas Europaea conducted by the International Bureau of Fiscal Documentation, April 2003, available at hhttp://www.europa.eu.int/comm./taxation_customs/taxation/company_tax/developments.htm.

[56] Explanatory Memorandum, para. 8, COM (2003) 613 final.

This justification matches an earlier statement made by former Commissioner Bolkestein on the subject:[57]

> The first thing to do now is to make sure that the creation of the European company by businesses as from 8 October 2004 will not be hampered by tax problems. For this purpose it is essential that the SE will in future fall under the scope of the Merger Directive. My Services are currently preparing a proposal for the amendment of this Directive. The European company should of course be included in its scope so that businesses will be able to set up a European company in a tax neutral way, without inappropriate taxation on capital gains. Similarly, the scope of the other tax directives and notably the Parent-Subsidiary Directive will have to be extended so as to include the SE.

28. The amendments to the Merger Directive add Articles 10(b), (c) and (d) under new Title IV(b). The applicable tax provisions will be neutral from a competition standpoint while safeguarding the financial interests of the Member State where the SE was resident prior to the transfer. These provisions apply only to SE and the benefit thereof, as well as the benefit of other provisions, may be withdrawn or refused in the event of tax evasion or avoidance or non-fulfilment of the conditions for employee negotiation (Article 14; *see* chapter 1 of this book). The transfer of the registered office of other entities to which the Merger Directive applies (with the exception of the yet-to-be-introduced European cooperative company or 'SCE') is not regulated.

29. Article 10(b) deals with tax deferral when an SE transfers its registered office. Subparagraph (1) guarantees that the transfer of an SE's registered office to another Member State, which may result in a change in tax residency, shall not result in tax liability on income, profits or capital gains provided the assets and liabilities remain effectively connected with a permanent establishment in the former state of residence. Thus, tax deferral is contingent on the assets and liabilities remaining effectively connected with a permanent establishment in the former Member State. It is possible that this condition violates freedom of establishment, and it is uncertain whether the Community legislature is permitted to limit a fundamental freedom in this way. It has been argued that it cannot[58] and that the directives must be interpreted in line with the fundamental freedoms. Thus, if the permanent establishment condition fails when tested against Community law, the Member States will not be allowed to transpose it into national law.

Subparagraphs (2) and (3) provide rules to calculate depreciation and gains or losses in respect of assets that remain effectively connected with a permanent

---

[57] Lecture by former Commissioner Bolkestein on 29 November 2002 in Leiden, taken from the Survey on the Societas Europaea, IFBD, September 2003, 5.

[58] Clemens Ph. Schindler, *EU Report on the Tax Treatment of International Acquisitions of Business*, IFA Convention 2005.

establishment. Subparagraph (2) obliges the Member States continue to tax assets as if the transfer of the registered office had never occurred. As a result, with respect to these assets, the SE remains bound by the depreciation methods applied in its original Member State. Subparagraph (3) applies to cases where the national law of a Member State contains special rules for the computation of depreciation, gains or losses in respect of assets and liabilities connected with a permanent establishment. An SE can opt to apply these rules, in which case the provisions of subparagraph (1) shall not apply.

30. Article 10(c)(1) extends the provisions of Article 5 of the Merger Directive to the transfer of an SE's registered office, guaranteeing that the permanent establishment of the SE continues to enjoy a tax exemption for reserves accumulated prior to the transfer. Subparagraph (2) allows the carry forward of unused losses to the permanent establishment. The proposal contained a subparagraph (3), which dealt with the taxation of existing permanent establishments of an SE in Member States not directly involved in the transfer of its registered office. This subparagraph is not included in the final version of the amended Merger Directive. Taxation by a Member State in which an SE has a permanent establishment at the time its registered office is transferred is therefore not regulated by this directive.

31. Article 10(d)(1) prohibits the Member States from taxing shareholders of an SE by virtue of the transfer of the company's registered office. Subparagraph (2), however, allows the Member States to tax shareholders on the future disposition of their shares in the SE.

4 The Interest and Royalties Directive

32. The Interest and Royalties Directive aims to eliminate withholding taxes on payments of interest and royalties between associated companies within the various Member States and to prevent double taxation of parent companies on their subsidiaries' profits. Article 3(a) of the directive states that it applies only to those companies listed in the Annex thereto.

33. On 31 December 2003, the Commission adopted a proposal for a Council directive to amend the Interest and Royalties Directive.[59] With reference to the two Commission proposals to amend the list of companies annexed to the Parent-Subsidiary Directive and the Merger Directive, the Commission considered it appropriate to follow the same approach in relation to the Interest and Royalties Directive, i.e. by proposing inter alia that the list of companies annexed to this directive be brought into line with the (amended)

---

[59] Proposal for a Council Directive amending Directive 2003/49/EEC on a common system of taxation applicable to interest and royalty payments made between associated companies of different Member States, dated 31 December 2003, COM (2003) 841 final.

Parent-Subsidiary Directive. The addition of the SE to the list is justified as follows:[60]

> While there are no provisions in the Statute of the European Company directed specifically at taxation, nevertheless, the instrument does require the SE to be subject to the 'provisions of Member States' laws which would apply to a public-limited company formed in accordance with the law of the Member State in which the SE has its registered office (footnote 11, Article 9(1)(c)(ii) of Council Regulation No 2157/2001 of 8 October 2001). Such public limited companies in the 15 Member States, which are listed in the Annex to the SE Statute, are also included in the list of companies annexed to the Interest and Royalties Directive. So, in practice the SE already enjoys the benefits of the Interest and Royalties Directive because the Member State where it has its registered office is obliged to grant the same benefits that apply to the respective national public limited company. However, both for the purposes of clarification and to underpin the importance that the Commission attaches to it, the Commission proposes that the SE be specifically mentioned in the list of companies annexed to the Interest and Royalties Directive.

Although the same approach is taken in the proposals to amend the Parent-Subsidiary Directive and the Merger Directive, where the SE is explicitly included in the list of companies covered by the directives, the Commission's justification has changed over time with the statement that the SE already falls within the scope of the three direct tax directives, without it being necessary to amend the Annexes thereto, as a result of the principle of equal tax treatment with public limited-liability companies and as provided by the Regulation.

34. The proposal to amend the Interest and Royalties Directive has yet to be adopted by the Council.

---

[60] Explanatory Memorandum, point 5, COM (2003) 841 final.

PART II
Application in each Member State

National reports for EU Member States

5

Austria

ANDREAS HABLE AND HORST LUKANEC[1]
Binder Grösswang Rechtsanwälte

I   Introduction   120
II Reasons to opt for an SE   121
III Formation   121
   1   General remarks   121
      A   Founding parties   121
      B   Name   121
      C   Registered office   122
      D   Corporate purpose   124
      E   Capital   124
   2   Different means of formation   124
      A   Formation by merger   124
      B   Formation of a holding SE   126
      C   Formation of a subsidiary SE   126
      D   Conversion into an SE   127
   3   Acts committed on behalf of an SE in formation   128
   4   Registration and publication   128
   5   Acquisition of legal personality   128
IV Organisation and management   129
   1   General remarks   129
   2   General meeting   129
      A   General remarks   129
      B   Decision-making process   129
      C   Rights and obligations of shareholders   131
   3   Management and supervision   131
      A   General remarks   131
      B   One-tier system   131
      C   Two-tier system   132
      D   Appointment and removal   133
      E   Liability   134
V   Employee involvement   134
   1   General remarks   134
   2   Special negotiating body   134
      A   Provision of information for the creation of an SNB   134

---

[1] With the assistance of Doris Buxbaum, Viktoria Ebner and Thomas Egerth.

        B   Composition and appointments   135
        C   Members   136
        D   Meetings and decisions   136
        E   Reconvention/reorganisation in the event of substantial changes   137
   3   Standard rules   137
        F   Works council   137
        G   Information and consultation   138
        H   Employee participation   138
   4   Protection of employee representatives and abuse of procedure   139
   5   Reservation and confidentiality   140
   6   Transitional provisions   140
   7   Fines for noncompliance   141
VI   Annual accounts and consolidated accounts   141
   1   Accounting principles   141
   2   Auditors   141
VII   Supervision by the national authorities   141
VIII   Dissolution   142
   1   Winding up, liquidation, insolvency, cessation of payments   142
IX   Applicable law   142
X   Tax treatment   142
   1   Income tax   142
   2   Value added tax and other taxes   144
XI   Conclusion   145

I   Introduction

1. To implement Council Regulation (EC) No. 2157/2001 on the Statute for a European company (the 'Regulation') and transpose Council Directive 2001/86/EC supplementing the Statute for a European company with regard to the involvement of employees (the 'Directive'), both of 8 October 2001, the Austrian legislature passed the *Gesellschaftsrechtsänderungsgesetz 2004–GesRÄG 2004*, which includes the Act on the statute for a European company (*Societas Europaea* or 'SE') (the *SE Gesetz* or 'SEG'). The SEG entered into force on 8 October 2004[2] and amends various other federal laws such as the Commercial Registry Act (*Firmenbuchgesetz* or 'FBG') and the Public Limited-Liability Companies Act (*Aktiengesetz* or 'AktG') in order to accommodate this new legal entity. In transposing the Directive, the legislature also added a sixth chapter to the Labour

---

[2] Gesellschaftsrechtsänderungsgesetz 2004 – GesRÄG 2004, BGBl I 67/2004.

Constitution Act (*Arbeitsverfassungsgesetz* or 'ArbVG') (see nos. 54–81 of this report).

II Reasons to opt for an SE

1. The SE has certain advantages over national corporate forms in Austria. International joint-venture vehicles and multinationals in particular may appreciate the possibility to form an SE with companies from different Member States and the relative ease with which an SE's registered office may be transferred from one Member State to another. Moreover, the introduction of a one-tier management system could also help to promote the establishment of new corporate organisational schemes in Austria. Furthermore, since the abbreviation 'SE' may only be used by companies that take the form of a *Societas Europaea*, the SE could be used as a marketing tool by companies with pan-European operations. Considering the reduction of the corporate tax rate from 34% to 25%, effective 1 January 2005, and the introduction of an advantageous group taxation model, Austria is prepared to enter the competitive fray as the business location of choice for SEs.

2. Despite these advantages, the various legal provisions applicable to the SE and the complex rules with regard to employee involvement could prove to be stumbling blocks and impede the day-to-day functioning of this new legal entity, thereby rendering it less attractive to potential investors.

III Formation

1 General remarks

A Founding parties

3. The founding parties of an SE will depend on the means of formation selected (i.e. by merger, conversion of a national company into an SE or formation of a holding or subsidiary SE). The Regulation sets forth the types of companies in each Member State that may participate in the formation of an SE. There is no room for alternative national rules in this regard. The Austrian legislature has not enacted the option contained in Article 2(5) of the Regulation, according to which a Member State may allow a company whose head office is not in the EU to participate in the formation of an SE.

B Name

4. In accordance with Article 9(1)(c)(ii) of the Regulation, the provisions of Austrian law applicable to national public limited-liability companies apply to

an SE with its registered office in Austria. Pursuant to these rules, the name of an SE must indicate the purpose of the company (Sec. 4(1) AktG)[3] and must be followed by the abbreviation 'SE' (Art. 11(1) Reg.).

C   Registered office

5. The registered office of an SE must be located at the same place as its principal place of business, place of effective management or main centre of administration (Sec. 5(1) SEG). In this respect, the Austrian legislature has enacted a less stringent version of the option contained in Article 7 of the Regulation. If the head office of an SE is transferred to another country, the competent court shall order the SE to relocate its head office to Austria within an appropriate period of time or to transfer its registered office in accordance with Article 8 of the Regulation. If the SE does not comply with this request within the allotted time, the court shall force the SE into liquidation. Any legal remedy against a court order to relocate an SE's head office or to liquidate an SE has suspensive effect (Sec. 5(2) SEG).

6. The SEG contains supplementary rules regulating the transfer of an SE's registered office (Secs. 6–16).[4] When an SE's registered office is transferred from Austria to another Member State, the transfer proposal must contain the information set forth in Article 8(2) of the Regulation. Also, in accordance with Article 8(5) of the Regulation, any shareholder that objects to the transfer has a special right to exit the company by transferring its shares to the company or to a third party in return for cash. The conditions for shareholders to obtain cash from the company or a third party in this case must also be stated in the transfer proposal (Sec. 6 SEG). A certified auditor must examine the share exchange ratio on behalf of the dissenting shareholders to determine whether it is fair and adequate and submit a report to the board of directors and to the supervisory board (Secs. 7(1) and (3) SEG).

7. The supervisory board shall scrutinise the transfer proposal and the board of directors' report explaining and justifying the transfer (Art. 8(3) Reg.) and then draft a report on its findings. This rule applies only to SEs with a two-tier management structure (Sec. 8 SEG). The board of directors or the administrative organ must file the transfer proposal with the competent court at least two months prior to the date of the general meeting scheduled to vote on the transfer. The filing of the transfer proposal must be mentioned in the SE bulletin, which publication also serves to notify

---

[3] O. Röpke, 'Europäische (Aktien-)Gesellschaft (SE) und Arbeitnehmerbeteiligung', *Das Recht der Arbeit*, 2002, 178; C. Greda in *Europäische Aktiengesellschaft SE-Kommentar*, Linde Verlag, Vienna, 2004, §2, no. 6.

[4] Secs. 6 through 15 govern the transfer of an SE's registered office from Austria to another Member State while Sec. 16 deals with the transfer of an SE's registered office from another Member State to Austria.

shareholders and creditors of their rights in relation to an anticipated transfer (Sec. 9 SEG).[5]

At least one month prior to the general meeting scheduled to vote on the transfer, the transfer proposal, the board of directors' report, the auditor's report, the supervisory board's report and the annual accounts must be made available to shareholders and creditors at the company's registered office (Sec. 9(2) SEG).

8. If shareholders' special rights (such as the right to convene a general meeting) are restricted due to a transfer, the shareholders concerned must approve the general meeting's resolution on the transfer (Sec. 10 SEG).[6]

9. If a company has only one shareholder or if all shareholders waive their right to have their shares redeemed, the conditions for the share exchange ratio need not be mentioned in the transfer proposal. Nor is an auditor's report required, so the transfer procedure will be simplified (Sec. 11 SEG).

10. Creditors who give notice in writing of outstanding claims against the company within one month of the general meeting's approval of the transfer must be granted adequate security if the transfer would make recovery of their claims more difficult (Sec. 14 SEG). Creditors may request security for claims that arose up to one month following the general meeting's decision on the transfer (Art. 8(7) Reg.).

11. The application to register the proposed transfer of an SE's registered office must be made by all members of the board of directors. The court will assess whether all requirements for the transfer have been fulfilled and whether the interests of creditors and cash compensation for dissenting shareholders have been adequately secured. If all of these requirements are met, the court will register the transfer and issue a certificate attesting to the completion of the requisite pre-transfer acts and formalities (Art. 8(8) Reg.).

The Austrian legislature has enacted the option contained in Article 8(14) of the Regulation by authorising the capital markets authority *(Finanzmarktaufsicht)* to oppose the transfer of the registered office of an SE engaged in insurance business within two months following publication of the transfer proposal if the interests of policy holders are not sufficiently secured.

Once the transfer has been recorded in the new commercial registry, the board of directors shall file an application to delete the old registration along with a notice of the new registration. If this notice is not in German, a certified German translation must be appended thereto (Sec. 15(5) SEG).

---

[5] C. P. Schindler, 'Das Ausführungsgesetz zur Europäischen Aktiengesellschaft', *Wirtschaftsrechtliche Blätter*, 2004, 257.
[6] C. P. Schindler, *op. cit.*, 258.

	12. Likewise, an application to transfer an SE's registered office from another Member State to Austria must be filed by all members of the company's board of directors or administrative organ (Sec. 16 SEG).[7]
D	Corporate purpose
	13. Pursuant to Articles 9(1)(c)(ii) and 10 of the Regulation, according to which an SE shall be treated as if it were a public limited-liability company under national law, an SE is free to choose its corporate purpose under Austrian law.
E	Capital
	14. The SEG does not contain any further provisions concerning the subscribed capital of an SE. According to Article 4(2) of the Regulation, an SE's subscribed capital shall not be less than €120,000. Consequently, the minimum subscribed capital of an SE is higher than that of an Austrian public limited-liability company, which is €70,000 (Sec. 7 AktG). As Austria is part of the euro zone, the provisions of Article 67 of the Regulation do not apply.
2	Different means of formation
A	Formation by merger
	15. The formation of an SE by merger, as regulated by Articles 17 through 31 of the Regulation, is supplemented by Sections 17 through 24 of the SEG. An SE may be formed by the merger of at least two public limited-liability companies governed by the laws of different Member States. For a formation by merger either a merger agreement *(Verschmelzungsvertrag)* or draft terms of merger *(Verschmelzungsplan)* must be established. The merger agreement as well as the draft terms of merger must contain the conditions for compensating dissenting shareholders who oppose the transfer of the company's assets to an SE in another Member State (Sec. 17 SEG).[8]
	In accordance with the Austrian rules on the merger of public limited-liability companies, the draft terms of merger and the merger agreement must be authenticated by a notary public (Sec. 222 AktG).[9] The board of directors or the administrative organ must draft a report *(Verschmelzungsbericht)* explaining

---

[7] S. Kalss in *Europäische Aktiengesellschaft SE-Kommentar*, Linde Verlag, Vienna, 2004, §16, no. 5.
[8] H. Hügel, in *Europäische Aktiengesellschaft SE-Kommentar*, Linde Verlag, Vienna, 2004, §17 no. 1 et seq.
[9] S. Kalss and C. Greda, 'Die Europäische Gesellschaft (SE) österreichischer Prägung nach dem Ministerialentwurf', *Der Gesellschafter – Zeitschrift für Gesellschafts- und Unternehmensrecht*, 2004, 97.

the legal and economic consequences of the merger.[10] The merger agreement or draft thereof and the draft terms of merger must be examined by an auditor who shall prepare a report to shareholders *(Prüfungsbericht)*. In the two-tier system, the supervisory board must examine the merger based on the board of directors' report. The merger agreement, the draft thereof or the draft terms of merger must also be filed with the court at least one month prior to the general meeting scheduled to vote on the merger. The information mentioned in Article 21 of the Regulation must be included in the publication notice of the filing of the merger documents (Sec. 19 SEG). The general meeting must approve the merger by a qualified majority of three-quarters of the share capital present or represented (Sec. 221(2) AktG).

The Austrian legislature did not enact the option contained in Article 19 of the Regulation, according to which a company may not take part in the formation of an SE by merger if a competent authority of a Member State opposes its participation.

16. Under Austrian law, shareholders who oppose a merger that will result in the transfer of a company's assets to an SE in another Member State have the right to receive cash compensation and to examine the share-exchange ratio (Secs. 21 and 22 SEG, Art. 24(2) Reg.).[11]

17. All members of the board of directors or administrative organ of an Austrian company transferring its assets via a merger to an SE with its registered office in another Member State must file an application to register the proposed merger (Sec. 24 SEG).[12] The court will examine whether all formalities with regard to the merger have been lawfully fulfilled and whether the interests of creditors and dissenting shareholders have been adequately secured (Sec. 24(3) SEG). If all of these conditions have been met, the court will register the merger and issue the certificate mentioned in Article 25(2) of the Regulation.

Once the proposed merger has been recorded in the commercial registry of the other Member State, the board of directors must file a notice of the new registration along with an application to delete the registration of the company in Austria (Sec. 24(5) SEG).

The merger may not be declared null and void once the SE has been registered. The Austrian legislature did not enact the option contained in Article 30 of the Regulation, according to which absence of scrutiny of the legality of a merger may constitute a ground for winding up the resulting SE.

Nor did the legislature adopt the option contained in Article 31(2) of the Regulation regarding a simplified merger procedure.

---

[10] H. Hügel, *op. cit.*, §18, no. 14.
[11] S. Kalss and C. Greda, *op. cit.*, 98.   [12] H. Hügel, *op. cit.*, §24, no. 5.

B   Formation of a holding SE

18. The formation of a holding SE is regulated by Articles 32 through 34 of the Regulation, as supplemented by Sections 25 through 28 of the SEG. Section 26 of the SEG states that the existing Austrian rules on mergers by absorption of public limited-liability companies shall apply to the formation of a holding SE (Secs. 220a-c, 221a, 222 and 225b-m AktG).

The shareholder resolution to form a holding SE must be approved by a qualified majority of three-quarters of the share capital present or represented (Sec. 221(2) AktG; Sec. 98 Private Limited-Liability Companies Act).

19. With respect to the formation of a holding SE, Austria has introduced a two-step system. The commercial registry must be informed of the completion of the requisite acts and formalities for the formation of a holding SE by the companies promoting the operation. Once it has determined that the statutory requirements for forming a holding company have been fulfilled, the registry shall issue a certificate attesting to the completion of the requisite pre-formation acts and formalities (Sec. 27(1) through (3) SEG).[13] After formation of the proposed SE, the companies promoting the operation must apply to incorporate the final holding SE by providing an extract of the SE's registration with the commercial registry (Sec. 27(5) SEG).

The Austrian legislature did not enact the option contained in Article 34 of the Regulation to adopt provisions designed to ensure appropriate protection of creditors, employees and minority shareholders who oppose the formation of a holding SE.

C   Formation of a subsidiary SE

20. The formation of a subsidiary SE is governed by Articles 35 and 36 of the Regulation. Pursuant to Article 36, national laws on the participation of public limited-liability companies in the formation of a subsidiary shall also apply to the formation of a subsidiary SE. Since existing national laws are applied *mutatis mutandis*, there was no need for any additional legislation in this respect.[14]

21. With regard to Article 3(2) of the Regulation, according to which an SE may set up one or more subsidiaries in the form of an SE, the Austrian legislature took the opportunity to amend the Public Limited-Liability Companies Act to introduce the possibility to form a single-member public limited-liability company. The single-member private limited-liability company was first introduced in Austrian law in 1996, further to the transposition of the Twelfth Company Law Directive (89/667/EEC).[15]

[13] C. P. Schindler, *op. cit.*, 264.   [14] S. Kalss, *op. cit.*, Vor §17, no. 27.   [15] *Ibid.*, no. 36.

D   Conversion into an SE

22. The conversion of an existing public limited-liability company into an SE is regulated by Articles 2(4) and 37 of the Regulation, as supplemented by Sections 29 through 33 of the SEG. Since an SE is treated as if it were a public limited-liability company under national law (Art. 10 Reg.), the Austrian legislature did not consider the consequences of the formation of an SE by conversion to be as far-reaching, for example, as those ensuing from the conversion of a private limited-limited liability company into a public limited-liability company and vice-versa.[16] Accordingly, no special rules have been enacted to grant special protection to minority shareholders or creditors when an SE is formed by conversion.[17]

23. When an Austrian public limited-liability company ('AG') is converted into an SE, the obligations of the management or administrative organ as stated in Article 37(4) of the Regulation must be carried out by the board of directors (*Vorstand*). As the Regulation does not contain any provisions regarding the content of the draft terms of conversion, the SEG stipulates that the following information must at least be provided: the previous name of the company; its registered office and registration number; the SE's proposed articles; any possible effects of the conversion on employee involvement; the intended timetable for the conversion; and any intended protection of shareholders and/or creditors (Sec. 29 SEG).

24. Pursuant to Section 30 of the SEG, the regulations contained in the Public Limited-Liability Companies Act regarding review of a contribution in kind shall supplement the provisions of Article 37(6) of the Regulation, which provides that one or more independent experts must certify that the company has net assets at least equivalent to its capital and those reserves which must not be distributed by law (Secs. 25(3)–(5), 26, 27, 42 and 44 AktG).

25. With respect to Article 37(4) of the Regulation, the board of directors must file the draft terms of conversion with the commercial registry at least one month prior to the general meeting scheduled to vote on the conversion. A notice that the draft terms of conversion have been filed must be published in the company bulletin. Moreover, the SEG specifically states which documents must be made available to shareholders one month prior to the general meeting (Sec. 31 SEG).

26. The general meeting must approve the conversion by a qualified majority of three-quarters of the share capital present or represented. Prior to the vote, the board of directors must explain the draft terms of conversion and inform shareholders of any essential changes to the financial situation of the company occurring after the date of the draft terms (Sec. 31(4) SEG).

---

[16] G. Schummer, 'Die Umwandlungsbestimmungen in der SE-VO und im SE-G', *Österreichische Steuerzeitung*, 2004, 391.

[17] Explanatory notes to Bill GesRÄG 2004 466 BlgNR XXII GP, 19.

27. Once the conversion has been approved by the general meeting, the board of directors must apply to the commercial registry to register the SE. Section 32 of the SEG lists the documents that must be filed to register an SE formed by conversion.

3 Acts committed on behalf of an SE in formation

28. An SE is 'in formation' from the time of its act of formation (e.g., if an SE is formed by merger, the 'act of formation' is the approval of the draft terms of merger by the general meetings of the merging companies) until it is recorded with the commercial registry (Art. 16(1) Reg.).[18] According to Article 16(2) of the Regulation, natural persons, companies, firms and other legal entities shall be jointly and severally liable for any acts performed on behalf of an SE prior to registration. As a legal entity may not be a member of an SE's management or administrative organ, such liability only concerns natural persons (Sec. 45(3) SEG).

4 Registration and publication

29. SEs and all other companies registered in Austria must be recorded in the commercial registry or *Firmenbuch*, of which there is only one. The registry is kept electronically. In Vienna, the *Firmenbuch* is administered by the commercial court (*'Handelsgericht'*). Elsewhere, it is administered by the provincial courts of first instance (*'Landesgericht'*).

Documents and information concerning an SE that require publication must be filed with the *Firmenbuch*. Where publication must be made in the national gazette of a Member State, the *Amtsblatt zur Wiener Zeitung* is the official newspaper of record for this purpose in Austria.

5 Acquisition of legal personality

30. An SE having its registered office in Austria shall acquire legal personality on the date on which it is registered with the *Firmenbuch* (Art. 16(1) Reg.). The SEG does not provide any further details on this matter. The Regulation reflects the relevant provisions of the AktG, which contains the same rule for the acquisition of legal personality by a public limited-liability company (Sec. 34(1) AktG).[19]

Regarding the registration of an SE, it should be noted that Austrian law does not allow the management or administrative organ of an SE to amend the company's

---

[18] C. P. Schindler, *Die Europäische Aktiengesellschaft – SE*, LexisNexis, Vienna, 2002, 18.
[19] C. Greda in *Europäische Aktiengesellschaft SE-Kommentar*, Linde Verlag, Vienna, 2004, §2, no. 9.

articles without the approval of the general meeting if the articles conflict with the arrangements for employee involvement (Art. 12(4) Reg.).

IV Organisation and management

1 General remarks

31. In Austria, public limited-liability companies must have a two-tier management structure. Article 38(b) of the Regulation provides that an SE may have either a one-tier or a two-tier system of management; however, it remains to be seen whether the one-tier system will be popular or cause difficulty in practice.

2 General meeting

A General remarks

32. In addition to the powers conferred directly on it by the Regulation (see Chap. 2, no. 61 of this book), the general meeting of an SE can also take decisions on matters for which responsibility is given to the general meeting of a public limited-liability company governed by the laws of the Member State in which the SE's registered office is located, either by law or by its articles in accordance with such national law (Art. 52 Reg.). In Austria, the general meeting of a public limited-liability company (and thus the general meeting of an SE with its registered office in Austria) is thus authorised to take decisions on the following matters: filing of claims against the management and supervisory organs (Sec. 122 AktG); distribution of annual profits (Sec. 126 AktG); release from liability of members of the management and supervisory organs (Sec. 104 AktG) for a given fiscal year; and approval of the annual accounts, if the management or supervisory organ refers this matter to the general meeting or if the supervisory organ has not approved the annual accounts submitted by the management organ (Sec. 125 AktG) or administrative organ (Sec. 41(5) SEG). While general managerial duties may not be delegated to the general meeting, both the management organ and the supervisory organ (only as regards matters requiring its approval) may refer matters to the general meeting for decision (Sec. 103(2) AktG).

B Decision-making process

33. In accordance with Article 54(1) of the Regulation, the general meeting of an SE must meet at least once a year. Austria did not enact the option to allow the first general meeting of an SE to be held at any time during the first 18 months following its incorporation.

34. Normally, the management organ (in the two-tier system) or the administrative organ (in the one-tier system) calls the general meeting (Sec. 105 AktG;

Art. 53 Reg.). In addition, one or more shareholders holding at least 5% of an SE's subscribed capital may request the SE to convene a general meeting (Art. 55 Reg.). The company's articles may provide for a lower percentage, however (Sec. 62 SEG; Sec. 106(2)–(5) AktG).

Notices of general meetings must be published[20] at least 14 days in advance and state the company's name and the time and place of the meeting (Sec. 62 SEG; Sec. 106(2)–(6) AktG).

Those shareholders holding 5% of an SE's subscribed capital may request that additional items be placed on the agenda of a general meeting (Sec. 62 SEG; Art. 56 Reg.). Since Austrian law requires that the agenda be made public seven days before the general meeting (Sec. 108(2) AktG), an additional item can only be placed on the agenda if the request is made in time.

35. The exercise of voting rights may be made subject to the deposit of shares with a notary public or a bank during the general meeting, if the articles so provide.

36. Since the Regulation does not contain specific rules regarding the allocation of voting rights, the national law of the Member State where an SE's registered office is located shall apply.[21] According to Sec. 114 AktG, each share carries one vote which may be exercised in proportion to the face value of other qualified shareholdings or, in the case of shares with no par value, in accordance with the number of shares held. Voting caps are permissible if the company's articles so provide (Sec. 114(1) AktG) but multiple voting rights (golden shares) are not.

Shareholders may be represented by proxy holders who shall vote in their stead on the basis of a written proxy (Sec. 114(3) AktG).

37. Interested shareholders and their proxy holders cannot vote on decisions liable to personally affect them.[22]

38. Notwithstanding Article 59 of the Regulation (see Chap. 2, no. 66 of this book), under Austrian law amendments to an SE's articles must be approved by three-quarters of the votes cast. A higher majority may apply if the company's articles so provide (Sec. 146 AktG). Austria did not enact the option to reduce this majority in cases where at least half the company's subscribed capital is present or represented (Art. 59(2) Reg.).

---

[20] For registered shares only and subject to a provision in the company's articles, the general meeting may also be convened via registered mail.
[21] C. P. Schindler, *Die Europäische Aktiengesellschaft - SE, op. cit.*, 78.
[22] Such as releasing a member of the management organ who is also shareholder or agent of a shareholder from liability.

C Rights and obligations of shareholders

39. Shareholders of public limited-liability companies have (in addition to the right to receive dividends and a share of liquidation proceeds) the right to inspect the company's annual accounts, to sell, pledge and bequeath their shares, and to vote at general meetings.

40. Shareholders' obligations are limited in principle to the payment of capital contributions. Only in exceptional circumstances where the corporate veil is pierced[23] can shareholders be held liable for the bankruptcy or insolvency of the company.

3 Management and supervision

A General remarks

41. The administrative organ (in the one-tier system) or the management organ (in the two-tier system) is responsible for managing the company. Delegation of day-to-day managerial authority to one or more managing directors is only possible in the one-tier system.

In the one-tier system, an SE is represented by its administrative organ and managing director(s) both in legal proceedings and in all other matters (Sec. 43(1) SEG). In the two-tier system, a company is generally represented by its management organ (Sec. 71 AktG). The representative power in both cases generally involves entering into contractual relationships on behalf of the company. Unless the company's articles provide otherwise, members of the management or administrative organ may only represent the company jointly. The articles may grant one or more organ members the power to represent the company individually or jointly with another member or *Prokurist*.[24]

B One-tier system

42. Article 38 of the Regulation states that an SE may have either a one-tier or a two-tier management structure. As Austria followed Germany in this regard and disallowed a one-tier system for public limited-liability companies in 1937, a completely new set of rules for the SE had to be enacted pursuant to Article 43(4) of the Regulation.

---

[23] For a general discussion of this issue, see P. Jabornegg in Aktiengesetz,[3] K. Schiemer, P. Jabornegg and R. Strasser (eds.), Manz, Vienna, 1993, §1, margin no. 52, 70 ss; U. Saurer in *Aktiengesetz*, P. Doralt, C. Nowotny and S. Kalss (eds.), Linde, Vienna, 2003, §48, margin no. 7ss; see also decision of the Austrian Supreme Court (OGH) of 12 April 2001, *Recht der Wirtschaft,* 2001/505, 469 (470).

[24] A *Prokurist* is someone who has been granted special representative authority (limited by statute) without being a board member.

The new one-tier system (Sec. 38-60 SEG) provides that the administrative organ must meet at least once every two months (Sec. 53(3) SEG). This differs from the rules applicable to the supervisory board in the two-tier system (which must meet four times a year) and goes further than Article 44(1) of the Regulation, which states that the administrative organ must meet at least once every three months. As the Regulation does not contain an option for the Member States to provide for more frequent meetings of the administrative organ, the Austrian rule would appear to violate Article 44.

In accordance with Article 43 of the Regulation, Austrian law requires managing directors to be appointed in a one-tier SE (Sec. 59 SEG). The managing directors are responsible for the day-to-day management of the company (Sec. 56 SEG; Art. 43(1) Reg.). If an SE is listed on a stock exchange, the managing directors may not also be members of the company's management board (Sec. 59(2) SEG).

C   Two-tier system

43. In the two-tier system the rules governing national public limited-liability companies (Sec. 70-99 AktG) also apply in principle to SEs. According to these rules, the managing directors as a group are jointly responsible for the day-to-day management of the company (Art. 39(1) Reg.).

44. Managing directors may not be appointed in the two-tier system.

45. In the two-tier system, the supervisory organ oversees the management organ and is responsible for the appointment and remuneration of its members. The SEG refers to the provisions of national law applicable to public limited-liability companies (Sec. 86(1) AktG) and thus allows an SE's supervisory organ to have no less than three and no more than twenty members (Sec. 35 SEG; Art. 40(3) Reg.).

A member of the supervisory organ may only sit on the management organ in the event of a vacancy on the latter body and for a period of time determined in advance (Sec. 90(2) AktG), although there is no maximum time limit under Austrian law (Art. 39(3) Reg.).

In connection with their supervisory functions, individual members of the supervisory organ may request reports from management (Art. 41(3) Reg.), which must be made available to the supervisory organ as such (and not merely an individual member). If the management organ refuses to comply with such a request, the support of a second member of the supervisory organ may be sought. Only the chair of the supervisory organ can request reports from the management organ without the backing of a second member (Sec. 36 SEG).

Austrian law provides that certain categories of transactions (Sec. 95(5) AktG) mentioned in the articles of an SE require the prior consent of the supervisory organ (Secs. 37 and 40 SEG; Art. 48(2) Reg.). The supervisory organ may add activities to this list (Secs. 37 and 40 SEG; Art. 48(1) Reg.).

D   Appointment and removal

46. In the two-tier system, members of the management organ are generally appointed by the supervisory organ (Sec. 75 AktG). The power to appoint and remove members of the management organ may not be delegated to the general meeting (Art. 39(2) Reg.) in Austria.

47. Legal entities are not permitted to sit on the administrative organ (Sec. 45(3) SEG) or management organ (Sec. 75(2) AktG) of an SE. Moreover, natural persons who already sit on more than ten administrative or supervisory organs (being a member of an administrative organ counts as two seats on a supervisory organ) may not be appointed to an SE's administrative organ.[25]

48. Members of the administrative organ shall be appointed for a term set forth in the company's articles, not to exceed five years (Sec. 46(1) SEG). While this provision conforms to the maximum term for members of the management organs of national public limited-liability companies (Sec. 75(1) AktG), it violates Article 46 of the Regulation, which allows a maximum term of six years. It must thus be assumed that the Regulation has direct effect and that members of an SE's administrative organ may serve a six-year term.

49. Managing directors are appointed by the administrative organ for a maximum term of five years (Sec. 59(1) SEG).

50. While members of the management organ may only be removed from office by the supervisory organ for just cause (Sec. 75(4) AktG), members of the administrative organ (Sec. 48 SEG) as well as the managing directors (Sec. 59(5) SEG) may be removed at any time without cause. Members of the administrative organ are removed by the general meeting while managing directors are removed by the administrative organ (even in cases where the managing director is also a member of the latter organ).

51. In accordance with Article 43(2) of the Regulation, Austria has provided that the administrative organ must have at least three and no more than ten members (Sec. 45(1) SEG). A similar provision pursuant to Article 39(4) of the Regulation has not been adopted for the management organ in the two-tier system.

---

[25] Virtually the same reason for exclusion in the two-tier system exists for members of the supervisory organ (Sec. 86(2) AktG), although not of the management organ.

E Liability

52. The applicable standard of care for decisions and actions taken by organ members in the ordinary course of business is that of a reasonably prudent and diligent person (Sec. 84(1) AktG). This duty of care is an objective standard,[26] so managers will not be released from liability if they adhere to a subjective standard. However, managers cannot be held liable for failing to act or to exercise judgment on matters that require special qualifications or training.

Management must always act in the best interest of the company and in accordance with any applicable laws as well as with the company's articles and by-laws.[27] In general, management as a whole shall be held jointly and severally liable for acts or omissions of any individual members. If a delegation of duties to specific members of management is based on the company's articles or a decision of the supervisory board and not merely on a decision of the management organ, in principle only the primary manager shall be held liable.[28] Since the other managers in such a case have a residual duty to supervise and control their colleagues, they may be held liable if they have not duly complied with these obligations, however.

It remains to be seen whether managing directors, even though not necessarily organ members, will be covered by directors' and officers' liability.

53. Management can primarily be held liable vis-à-vis the company. In cases of intentional misconduct or gross negligence, however, management may be liable to creditors if the company's assets are insufficient to satisfy their claims.

V Employee involvement

1 General remarks

54. The provisions of the Directive have been transposed for the most part by an amendment to the Labour Constitution Act *(Arbeitsverfassungsgesetz* or *'ArbVG'*),[29] adding a new chapter on the participation of workers in an SE. This chapter primarily incorporates the definitions and provisions of the Directive.

2 Special negotiating body

A Provision of information for the creation of an SNB

55. To ensure that all information necessary to create a special negotiating body (SNB) is passed on to employees and their representatives, the Labour Constitution Act requires that details about the following subjects be provided:

---

[26] R. Strasser in *Aktiengesetz*,[4] P. Jabornegg and R. Strasser (eds.), Manz, Vienna, 2001, §§77–84, no. 95.

[27] *Ibid.* [28] *Ibid.*, no. 104. [29] BGBl 82/2004.

the intended incorporation of an SE and the procedure up to registration; the identity and form of each participating company (including any subsidiaries and establishments), concerned subsidiaries and establishments; the number of employees working for each participating company, concerned subsidiary or establishment; the identity of the employee representative bodies in these companies and establishments as well as the number of employees they represent; the identity of each participating company with internal arrangements for employee involvement, including the number of employees covered and, if less than all employees of a company are covered, the ratio of employees covered by the participation arrangements compared to the total number of employees; and the date of the first meeting of the special representative body (Sec. 215 ArbVG).

B   Composition and appointments

56. Article 3(2)(a) of the Directive regarding the composition of the SNB was transposed into Austrian law by Section 216 of the Labour Constitution Act.

The composition of the SNB must be adjusted or the SNB must be reconstituted if substantial changes occur to the structure or number of employees of (i) the participating companies, (ii) concerned subsidiaries or (iii) concerned establishments which are liable to effect the previous composition.

Information about substantial changes must be passed on immediately by the management or administrative organ of the participating companies to the SNB and to employees or their representatives in participating companies and concerned subsidiaries and establishments not currently represented on the SNB.

57. Austrian SNB members are appointed by the employees' representative body (e.g., an employee board, works council, central employee board, etc.) in accordance with relatively detailed and complex provisions that distinguish between, for example, sole establishments, undertakings and groups of undertakings (Secs. 217 and 218 ArbVG).

Thus, the election and appointment of SNB members is only possible via (existing) employee representatives. Article 3(2) of the Directive, which obliges the Member States to provide that employees in undertakings or establishments in which there are no employee representatives *through no fault of their own* have the right to elect or appoint members of the SNB, has thus not been transposed into Austrian law.[30]

---

[30] In practice, this incomplete transposition of the Directive will have little effect, as employee representation in Austria is already possible in any given establishment that employs at least five people (Sec. 41(1) ArbVG). Thus, a situation where there are no employee representatives in a given company *through no fault of their own* would in practice be limited to a virtually negligible number of cases.

58. Section 223 of the Labour Constitution Act governs the duration of SNB membership. While membership generally commences with the announcement of an appointment, it can be terminated in various ways, such as when the SNB concludes its work or a member resigns or is removed by the organ responsible for appointments (e.g., because the member is no longer affiliated with a particular works council or trade union). If membership ends for any reason other than conclusion by the SNB of its work, a new member shall be appointed to fill the vacancy.

C   Members

59. Generally, members of the SNB are elected from members of the works council. In accordance with Article (3)(2)(b) of the Directive, members may also be selected from amongst officials or employees of the responsible union.

If more than one Austrian member is to be appointed to an SNB, the appointment shall also mention how many employees are to be represented by each member. Depending on the number of Austrian members appointed, each participating company should be represented by at least one SNB member.

60. Decisions regarding the appointment of SNB members require a quorum of at least half the members of the employees' representative body and are taken by a simple majority of votes cast, which collectively must represent more than half the employees of a group, undertaking or establishment (Sec. 217 ArbVG).

61. After notification of the appointment of SNB members, the management or administrative organ shall invite them to a meeting to elect a chair and adopt rules of procedure (Sec. 219 ArbVG).

D   Meetings and decisions

62. Prior to any meeting, the SNB has the right to hold preparatory meetings with the management and administrative organs. The SNB may call upon the assistance of experts of its choosing (Sec. 220 ArbVG).

Any costs incurred in connection with the work of the SNB that are indispensable for the fulfilment of its obligations, in particular costs related to the preparation of meetings, translations, experts' fees and travel expenses, shall be borne by the participating companies (Sec. 224(3) ArbVG). Furthermore, the participating companies must also provide all necessary equipment to the SNB. Apart from these rather general guidelines the Austrian legislature did not enact the option contained in Article 3(7) of the Directive to lay down budgetary rules regarding the operation of an SNB.

63. With regard to the duration of negotiations, voting procedures, the termination of negotiations and the content of the arrangements on employee involvement concluded with the management or administrative organ, the Austrian legislation more or less reflects the provisions of the Directive.

E   Reconvention/reorganisation in the event of substantial changes

64. Despite Article 3(6) of the Directive, which provides that an SNB shall not be reconvened for a period of two years after a decision has been taken pursuant to Article 3, an SNB can be reconvened earlier if substantial changes to the SE's structure occur that affect the participation rights of employees, provided the request to reconvene is made by: (i) the competent organs of the SE; (ii) at least 10% of the employees or their representatives in the SE, its subsidiaries and establishments; or (iii) the SE's works council (Sec. 228(1) ArbVG).

Examples of substantial changes in this context include the transfer of the company's registered office, changes to the company's administration, the closure, limitation or transfer of undertakings or establishments, etc.

The reconvened SNB or the SE's works council (if already established) shall negotiate an agreement on employee involvement pursuant to Article 4 of the Directive which must reflect the structural changes or changes to the number of employees of the SE, its subsidiaries and establishments.

3   Standard rules

65. Article 7 of the Directive gives little leeway with respect to the applicability of the standard rules set forth in the Annex. The Member States merely have the option to decide not to apply the standard rules on employee participation when an SE is formed by merger (Art. 7(3) Dir.). Austria has not adopted this option.

F   Works council

66. The representative body that must be formed in Austria in accordance with the standard rules set forth in Part 1 of the Annex to the Directive if the SNB cannot reach an agreement is called the *'SE-Betriebsrat'* (SE works council).

67. In principle, the rules on the nomination and election of SNB members (see no. 57 of this report) apply to an SE's works council *mutatis mutandis*. The term 'employee' as used in Part 1(a) of the Annex is interpreted broadly to include employees in the classic sense as well as union representatives if they are already members of a representative organ of a participating company (Sec. 234 ArbVG).

68. Members of an SE works council are normally appointed for a four-year term (Sec. 237 ArbVG). After four years, the works council shall pass a resolution on whether an agreement can be reached regarding the creation of specific information and consultation procedures or whether the standard rules should continue to apply. If the works council decides to enter into an agreement with the competent organ of the SE, the council, rather than the SNB, shall commence negotiations with the company. If an agreement cannot be reached, the standard rules shall continue to apply (Sec. 243 ArbVG).

69. The rules regarding the reimbursement of costs and the establishment of reserves to cover facilities necessary for the work of the SNB shall apply *mutatis mutandis* to the works council and must be borne by the SE.

G   Information and consultation

70. The works council has the right to be informed and consulted with regard to matters concerning the economic, social, health and cultural interests of the employees of the SE or any of its subsidiaries or establishments in another Member State or matters that concern more than one Member State (Sec. 239 ArbVG). Moreover, the works council shall receive at least annual reports on the SE's economic development and prospects (Sec. 240(1) ArbVG). The works council shall inform the (national) employee representatives of the SE, its subsidiaries and establishments of the content and results of any consultation or information procedures (Sec. 242 ArbVG).

71. Four years after its establishment, the SE works council shall pass a resolution on whether an agreement can be reached to create certain information and consultation procedures or whether the standard rules should continue to apply. If the works council decides to enter into an agreement with the competent organ of the SE, it, rather than the SNB, shall commence negotiations with the company. If an agreement cannot be reached, the standard rules shall continue to apply (Sec. 243 ArbVG).

H   Employee participation

72. Pursuant to Part 3 of the Annex to the Directive, 'every member of the administrative body or, where appropriate, the supervisory body of the SE [...] shall be a *full* member with the same rights and obligations as the members representing the shareholders, including the right to vote' (emphasis added). While in conformity with Article 50(3) of the Regulation, this principle of equality, i.e., both shareholder and employee representatives should be treated equally and enjoy equal rights, has not been fully implemented in Austrian law since, as in national public limited-liability companies (Sec. 110 ArbVG), employee

representatives in an SE do not have voting rights in certain specified cases.[31] First, certain decisions not only require a simple majority of votes cast, but also a majority of votes cast by shareholder representatives, such as the appointment or removal of members of the management organ and the election of a chair and deputy chair of the supervisory or administrative organ. Second, employee representatives may be excluded from committees on matters that regard the relationship between members of management and the company, in particular the terms and conditions of employment of members of the management organ and the managing directors.

73. Austria has not made use of the possibility to opt out of the standard employee participation rules where an SE is formed by merger (see also no. 65 of this report).

74. According to Article 7(2) of the Directive, the Member States may set down rules that shall apply in the absence of a decision by the SNB on the form employee participation should taken within an SE where more than one form of such participation exists within the various participating companies. In this regard, Austrian law provides that the form applicable to most employees of the participating companies shall apply (Sec. 244(5) ArbVG). Standard rules on employee participation in national public limited-liability companies are contained in Section 110 of the Labour Constitution Act, which provides for the works council's right to nominate one-third of the members of the supervisory organ.

4 Protection of employee representatives and abuse of procedure

75. According to the Labour Constitution Act, employee representatives are afforded special protection. In particular, they may not be discriminated against with regard to pay or the opportunity for promotion. Furthermore, they enjoy special protection against termination in that they may only be dismissed for a limited number of reasons[32] and dismissal requires prior court approval (Sec. 121 ArbVG).

---

[31] See also U. Runggaldier, 'Die Arbeitnehmermitbestimmung in der SE', *Der Gesellschafter – Zeitschrift für Gesellschafts- und Unternehmensrecht*, 2004, 52.

[32] The reasons for which an employee representative may be dismissed are: (1) closure of the undertaking in which the representative works and the representative is unwilling to continue to work in another undertaking, even though the employer has made an offer to this effect; (2) inability of the representative to continue to work, if ability to work in the near future seems unlikely or assumption of a different post would be unreasonable; and (3) the representative persistently violates his or her obligations at work and continued employment is unreasonable due to lack of discipline.

76. Although employee representatives must generally fulfil their regular duties like any other employees, their pay may not be cut if their representative functions must be performed during regular working hours.

77. In transposing Article 11 of the Directive, the Labour Constitution Act contains a general prohibition on misuse of an SE for the purpose of depriving employees of their right to involvement in the company (Sec. 229 ArbVG). Misuse shall be deemed to exist where structural changes to an SE take place which are capable of depriving employees of their right to be involved in the company or of withholding such a right. An abuse of procedure shall be deemed to exist if such changes occur within the first year following registration of an SE, unless proof to the contrary is provided.

5 Reservation and confidentiality

78. The Directive's rules on confidentiality have been transposed into national law by Section 250 of the Labour Constitution Act, which however does not apply to information requirements vis-à-vis regional employee representatives (who themselves are subject to a duty of confidentiality). Austria did not enact the option to make derogations from the duty to transmit information if such information could seriously harm the functioning of the SE subject to prior administrative or judicial authorisation (Art. 8(2) Dir.).

79. Particular rules for SEs that pursue the aim of ideological guidance with respect to information and the expression of opinions (Art. 8 (3) Dir.) have been transposed into national law (Sec. 249 ArbVG). An SE need not comply with certain information and participation rights of the works council in matters liable to influence corporate policy. In the event of fundamental changes to the company's organisation, work or modes of production or collective dismissals, however, such information and participation rights must be respected.

6 Transitional provisions

80. Transitional provisions have been implemented under national law (Sec. 252 ArbVG), which, *inter alia*, provide that structures for employee representation in participating companies that cease to exist after, for example, the formation of an SE by merger must be maintained after registration of the SE (Art. 13(4) Dir.). In this regard, the administrative or management organ must take the appropriate steps to ensure the continued existence of such structures (Sec. 252(4) ArbVG).

7 Fines for noncompliance

81. If an SE does not comply with the applicable rules on employees representation, it can be fined up to €2,180.

VI Annual accounts and consolidated accounts

1 Accounting principles

82. The accounting principles set forth in the Austrian Commercial Code (*Handelsgesetzbuch* or 'HGB') are applicable to the preparation of an SE's annual accounts. If the company must prepare consolidated accounts, it may use internationally accepted accounting standards (IFRS or US GAAP). Within five months after the closing date of the annual balance sheet, the board of directors (in the two-tier system) or the managing directors (in the one-tier system) must prepare annual accounts and appendices as well as an annual report and submit these documents, along with a proposal on the distribution of profits, to the supervisory board (in the two-tier system) or the administrative organ (in the one-tier system) (Sec. 41(1) SEG). The supervisory board or the administrative organ, as the case may be, must approve or reject the annual accounts within two months. The general meeting must vote on the distribution of profits within eight months after the closing of the balance sheet (Sec. 42 SEG). The adopted annual accounts and annual report must be filed with the *Firmenbuch* within nine months after the closing date of the balance sheet (Sec. 277 HGB).

2 Auditors

83. The annual accounts and annual report of an SE must be examined by a certified auditor. 'Certified auditors' are e.g. certified public accountants, tax accountants or auditing firms and tax advisors. However, there are certain restrictions on which types of certified auditors may audit an annual report. For example, the auditor may not hold more than 20% of the company's subscribed capital or be a member of its management organ or supervisory board (for further restrictions see Sec. 271 HGB).

VII Supervision by the national authorities

84. The registration of an SE, as well as all matters which, according to the Regulation, require the approval of a court, notary or any other competent authority, shall be referred to the court of first instance of the place where an SE's registered office is located (Sec. 4 SEG) (see also no. 29 of this report).

VIII   Dissolution

1   Winding up, liquidation, insolvency, cessation of payments[33]

85. The winding up, liquidation, insolvency and cessation of payments of an SE registered in Austria are governed by the laws applicable to Austrian public limited-liability companies (Art. 63 Reg.).

86. Section 203 *et seq.* of the Public Limited-Liability Companies Act apply to the winding up of an SE. Accordingly, the general meeting of an SE must approve the decision to wind up by a qualified majority of at least three-quarters of the share capital present or represented. The board of directors or the administrative organ must register the decision to wind up with the *Firmenbuch* and publish a notice to this effect in the *Amtsblatt zur Wiener Zeitung*. However, an SE's articles or the general meeting may also allow winding up to be carried out by a third party. Accordingly, in the one-tier system, the managing directors may be responsible for winding up an SE. However, a provision to this effect must be included in the SE's articles or a specific decision taken by the general meeting.

87. All national insolvency rules also apply to SEs registered in Austria, in particular the Bankruptcy Act *(Konkursordnung)*, the Composition Act *(Ausgleichsordnung)* and Council Regulation (EC) No. 1346/2000 on insolvency proceedings.

IX   Applicable law

88. Apart from the Regulation and the Directive, SEs registered in Austria are governed by their articles (Art. 9(1)b Reg.). In matters not dealt with by the Regulation, the Directive or the company's articles, the SEG and the relevant sections of the Labour Constitution Act shall apply. In addition, an SE established in Austria shall also be governed by the rules of law applicable to national public limited-liability companies, in particular the Public Limited-Liability Companies Act, the Commercial Registry Act and the Commercial Code.

X   Tax treatment

1   Income tax

89. Taxation of corporate income is regulated by the Corporate Income Tax Act (CITA), which refers in part to the Income Tax Act (ITA). Taxation of an SE is subject to the same rules applicable to Austrian public limited-liability

---

[33] For a general discussion, see S. Kalss, *op. cit.*, Nach §63, nos. 3–5.

companies. As of 1 January 2005, the Austrian corporate tax rate is generally 25% (Sec. 22(1) CITA).

Dividends received by an Austrian SE from another domestic corporation are not subject to tax (pursuant to the national participation exemption). Dividends and capital gains received by an Austrian SE from foreign subsidiaries are also generally tax exempt if a minimum shareholding of at least 10% has been maintained for at least one year (the international participation exemption).

Dividends distributed by an Austrian company to a foreign parent company are generally subject to withholding tax at a rate of 25%. Within the EU, withholding tax is generally not levied if the receiving company has maintained a direct shareholding in the distributing company of at least 10% for at least one year.[34] In addition to this exemption, the rate of withholding tax may be reduced by an applicable double tax treaty.

Effective 1 January 2005, a new group taxation model was introduced in Austria. Under this model, group profits and losses are pooled by adding those of the subsidiaries to the parent company's until all profit and loss has been attributed to the head of the group. Within certain limits, foreign companies can also be included in an Austrian group. Foreign losses will reduce the group's tax base but are subject to recapture when the foreign subsidiary sets off its losses against future earnings.

90. The formation of an SE by merger with a transfer of assets and liabilities from a domestic to a foreign company (an 'export merger') or a transfer of assets and liabilities from a foreign to a domestic company (an 'import merger') is in principle subject to the provisions of Article I of the Reorganization Tax Act (RTA).

An export merger is tax neutral as long as hidden reserves in the transferred assets remain subject to tax in Austria (Secs. 1(1) and 3 RTA). For income tax purposes, assets are transferred at their book value to the receiving company (i.e., the SE).

Hidden reserves, however, are subject to exit tax insofar as the right to tax unrealised capital gains is restricted in Austria due to the merger (Sec. 1(2) RTA; Secs. 19 and 20 CITA). If the company's assets and liabilities are transferred to an EU or EEA[35] resident company, exit tax will not be levied until effective realisation of the inherent capital gains (Sec. 1(2) RTA), which shall be deemed to have retroactive effect. Accordingly, capital gains realised after expiry of the statute of limitations (ten years) shall not be subject to tax.

---

[34] Those companies listed in the Annex to Directive 90/435/EEC of 23 July 1990 are eligible for the exemption.

[35] Provisions related to tax exemption or deferral in the RTA referred to in this report shall apply to EEA Member States only if the country in question grants extensive assistance with respect to tax administration and enforcement.

An exchange of shares in the course of a merger is generally tax neutral insofar as hidden reserves in the transferred assets remain subject to tax in Austria (Sec. 5 RTA; Sec. 1 RTA). However, if Austria's right to tax transferred assets is restricted, non-EU/EEA shareholders will be subject to corporate tax in Austria if the applicable tax treaty so allows. If the assets are transferred to an EU- or EEA-resident company, an exchange of shares in the course of a merger shall be tax neutral for domestic and EU- or EEA-resident shareholders.

In an import merger, insofar as Austria acquires the right to tax the transferred assets, the assets shall be recorded on the balance sheet of the receiving company (i.e. the SE) at their fair market value (Sec. 3(1) RTA). Repatriated assets that have been subject to deferred exit tax are recorded at their book value.

91. The formation of a holding SE can be made subject to Article III of the Reorganisation Tax Act, which contains regulations for certain contributions made to a company in exchange for shares. Pursuant to this article, a contribution of shares by a shareholder residing in Austria or in another EU/EEA Member State is not subject to (income) tax.

However, if the contribution is made by a non-EU/EEA resident shareholder, liquidation tax shall be levied in accordance with Austrian administrative practice (Sec. 16(2)(2) RTA). Taxation under such circumstances does not comply with Article 8(1) of the Directive of 23 July 1990 if both the receiving company (the SE) and the acquired company (the company whose shares are contributed) are residents of the EU or the EEA.[36] In most cases, however, direct application of Community law is not necessary since under most double tax treaties the right to tax capital gains is granted to the shareholder's country of residence so Austria will have no right to tax.

92. The formation of an SE by conversion constitutes a continuation of the same company in another corporate form and therefore has no tax consequences.

93. The transfer of the registered office of an SE from Austria to another Member State or from another Member State to Austria will generally be treated under the same rules as an export or import merger.

2 Value added tax and other taxes

94. An SE is subject to Austrian VAT at the same conditions applicable to other Austrian companies. Generally, the rate of VAT is 20%. Pursuant to the RTA, the formation of an SE is not subject to VAT (Secs. 6(3), 11(3), 22(3), 26(1)(2), 31(1)(2) and 38(3)).

95. The acquisition of shares by a shareholder and contributions from shareholders to an SE with its registered office or place of effective management in

---

[36] C. P. Schindler, *op. cit.*, Steuerrecht nos. 120–127.

Austria are generally subject to a 1% capital duty (Sec. 2 Capital Duty Act).[37] Pursuant to the RTA, however, an exemption from this tax is granted in most cases.

XI Conclusion

96. The first Austrian SE was registered on 12 October 2004, only four days after the SE legislation entered into force. A second SE was registered in December 2004.

It remains to be seen whether the advantages of the SE will attract significant numbers of international companies and joint ventures. The rather complicated rules governing the SE may prevent it from becoming a real and viable alternative to national corporate forms. Despite these difficulties, however, the SE is an important first step towards European harmonisation and unification.

---

[37] The Austrian legislature has not amended Sec. 4 of the Capital Duty Act (which lists those legal entities subject to tax) to include the SE. Nevertheless, the tax authorities are not expected to treat an SE differently from any other public limited-liability company.

6
Belgium

DIRK VAN GERVEN AND ELKE JANSSENS
NautaDutilh

I   Introduction   147
II   Reasons to opt for an SE   147
III Formation   149
    1 General remarks   149
        A Founding parties   149
        B Name   149
        C Registered office and transfer   149
            (i) Registered office   149
            (ii) Transfer of registered office   150
        D Corporate purpose   152
        E Capital   152
    2 Different means of formation   152
        A Formation by merger   152
            (i)   Procedure and publication requirements   152
            (ii) Right to object to a company participating in a merger   155
            (iii) Minority shareholders   156
            (iv) Rights of creditors   156
            (v)   Acquisition by a company holding 90% or more of the shares in another company   156
            (vi) Avoidance of a merger   156
        B Formation of a holding SE   157
            (i) Procedure and publication requirements   157
            (ii) Minority shareholders   157
        C Formation of a subsidiary SE   158
        D Conversion into an SE   158
    3 Acts committed on behalf of an SE in formation   159
    4 Registration and publication   159
    5 Acquisition of legal personality   160
IV   Organisation and management   160
    1 General remarks   160
    2 General meeting   160
        A Decision-making process   162
        B Rights and obligations of shareholders   162
    3 Management and supervision   162
        A Two-tier system/one-tier system   162

		(i) General remarks	162
		(ii) One-tier system	162
		(iii) Two-tier system	162
	B	Appointment and removal	164
	C	Representation	165
	D	Liability	165
V	Employee involvement		165
	1	Special negotiating body	166
	2	Employee participation	166
	3	Protection of employee representatives	166
VI	Annual accounts and consolidated accounts		167
	1	Accounting principles	167
	2	Auditors	168
VII	Supervision by the national authorities		169
VIII	Dissolution		169
	1	Winding up	169
	2	Liquidation	169
	3	Insolvency	169
	4	Cessation of payments	170
IX	Applicable law		171
X	Tax treatment		171
	1	Income tax	171
	2	Value added tax	173
	3	Other taxes	173
XI	Conclusion		173

I Introduction

1. The Regulation was implemented under Belgian law by a royal decree of 1 September 2004 (the 'Royal Decree') pursuant to powers vested in the King by the Act of 22 December 2003.[1]

As provided by the Directive, Belgium granted the power to transpose the Directive to representatives of employers and employees. The result is Collective Bargaining Agreement (CBA) No. 84 of the National Labour Council ('CBA No. 84'), which transposed the Directive only in part. Those provisions which have yet to be transposed into national law shall form the subject of a statutory initiative shortly. The Royal Decree and CBA No. 84 entered into force on 8 October 2004.

II Reasons to opt for an SE

2. The SE has certain advantages over national corporate forms in Belgium. Its main advantage is its European character. No other limited-liability legal entity

---

[1] The Royal Decree was ratified by Parliament by Article 300 of the Act of 27 December 2004.

presents the same European dimension. European corporate groups can express their European identity by choosing to take the form of an SE. The SE may thus turn out to be a useful marketing tool, particularly for listed companies.

Moreover, the registered office of an SE can be transferred to another Member State without a loss of legal personality and, as of 1 January 2006, without adverse tax consequences.[2] If a company that is not an SE decides, for any reason whatsoever, to transfer its headquarters from one Member State to another, in most cases it will have to face the burdensome procedure of dissolution and reincorporation.

Moreover, the relative ease with which an SE can transfer its registered office means it can be used as a special purpose vehicle (SPV). In structured financing transactions, SPVs are often incorporated to carry out business related to a specific transaction (e.g. project and real estate finance, acquisition finance, etc.). Currently, SPVs are usually incorporated as limited-liability companies (*société anonyme/naamloze venootschap*) under Belgian law. The SE is a valid alternative to an SA in such transactions. In addition, if it becomes difficult for the SPV to conduct its business in Belgium or if the financing costs increase due to a significant change in the tax rules applicable to SPVs, it may wish to relocate abroad. The relocation process will be facilitated if the company takes the form of an SE. Finally, the lenders could decide to transfer the SPV's registered office to a more transaction-friendly Member State if a significant change in tax or company law is expected. It should be stressed, however, that the transfer of an SE's registered office will only be tax neutral if the SE's assets and liabilities remain effectively connected with a permanent establishment in the Member State from which the registered office is transferred.

Finally, an SE can be formed through a cross-border merger, for which the Regulation provides an autonomous legal basis. The tenth proposal for a Council directive on cross-border mergers of public limited companies also provides a legal basis for such mergers, but no agreement has yet been reached on this proposal.[3] The SE allows companies to clear this hurdle. Furthermore, a cross-border merger should be tax neutral pursuant to the Merger Directive, which, however, has yet to be transposed into Belgian law in this respect.[4]

---

[2] Council Directive 2005/19/EC of 17 February 2005, amending Directive 90/434/EEC 1990 on the common system of taxation applicable to mergers, divisions, transfers of assets and exchanges of shares concerning companies of different Member States, *O.J.*, 4.3.2005, L58/19.

[3] COM (84) 727 final, 8 January 1985.

[4] Council Directive 2005/19/EC of 17 February 2005, amending Directive 90/434/EEC 1990 on the common system of taxation applicable to mergers, divisions, transfers of assets and exchanges of shares concerning companies of different Member States

III Formation

1 General remarks

A Founding parties

3. Belgian law refers to the provisions of the Regulation as far as the requirements the founders must comply with are concerned (see Chap. 2, no. 18 *et seq.* of this book).

4. If a merging party does not have its head office within the European Union, it can still take part in the formation of an SE provided: (i) it has been incorporated in accordance with the laws of a Member State; (ii) its registered office is established in that Member State; and (iii) it has a real and continuous link with the economy of a Member State (Art. 894 Company Code).

B Name

5. An SE shall be referred to as a *Europese vennootschap* in Dutch or a *Société européenne* in French (Art. 1(2) Company Code). The name of an SE shall be preceded or followed by the abbreviation 'SE'. Only SEs may include this abbreviation in their name (Art. 11 Reg.).[5] Furthermore, the company's name should differ sufficiently from that of other legal entities to avoid confusion (Art. 65 Company Code).

C Registered office and transfer

(i) **Registered office**

6. Belgium applies the head office (*siége réel*) theory to determine whether a legal entity, such as a company, is governed by Belgian law (Art. 110 Private International Law (PIL) Code). Belgian law does not prohibit the transfer of a company's head office from or to Belgium and such a transfer does not necessitate the winding up of the company under Belgian law if the same rule is accepted in the country from where or to which the head office is transferred (Art. 112 PIL Code). Under the Regulation, the registered office of an SE should be located in the same Member State as its head office (Art. 7 Reg.).

Under Belgian law, the registered office of an SE should be located at the same place as its head office or central administration, and the SE should be registered at the place where its head office is located (Art. 67 Company Code; Art. 4(3) PIL Code).

If the head office of an SE with its registered office in Belgium is situated outside Belgium, the competent commercial court can declare the SE

---

[5] With the exception of legal entities which included the abbreviation in their names prior to the entry into force of the Regulation (see Chap. 2, no. 12 of this book).

dissolved at the request of any interested party or the public prosecutor's office. Such a decision is not enforceable unless no ordinary legal remedy, such as appeal, is possible (Art. 941 Company Code). The commercial court can grant the SE an extension within which to regularise its situation (Art. 64(1) Reg.).

When the head office but not the registered office of an SE is located in Belgium, the public prosecutor's office will inform the competent authorities of the Member State where the SE's registered office is situated (Art. 876 Company Code).

(ii) **Transfer of registered office**
7. The rules relating to the transfer of an SE's registered office to another Member State are set forth in Article 8 of the Regulation. The Company Code provides specific rules regarding the transfer of the registered office of an SE within Belgium as well as to another Member State. Some of the rules applicable to the transfer of an SE's registered office to another Member State would also seem to apply to a domestic transfer. The explanatory memorandum to the Royal Decree seems to indicate that it was not the intention of the legislature to apply such stringent rules to purely domestic transfers, however. However, since there is no explicit exclusion of such transfers from the rules applicable to cross-border transfers, the latter will be deemed applicable to the transfer of an SE's registered office within Belgium.

8. A transfer proposal, drawn up in accordance with Article 8(2) of the Regulation, should be filed with the clerk's office of the commercial court of the place where the SE's registered office is situated. A mention of the filing (i.e., a notice of the transfer) must be published in the Annexes to the *Belgian State Gazette* (Art. 75 Company Code). The board of directors or the management board must prepare a report in which it explains and justifies the legal and economic aspects of the transfer as well as its implications for shareholders, creditors and employees. This report must be made available to the shareholders pursuant to Article 8(4) of the Regulation (see Chap. 2, no. 83 of this book).

9. The general meeting must vote on the transfer. Prior to the meeting, shareholders shall receive a copy of the transfer proposal and the report of the board of directors or management board.

The general meeting must approve the transfer by at least 75% of the votes cast. The articles of association may state that a simple majority is acceptable if at least half the share capital is present or represented at the general meeting (Art. 929 Company Code). Finally, for a domestic transfer (i.e. a transfer within Belgium), the articles may provide that the board of directors or the management board is empowered to vote on the transfer without the prior authorisation of the general meeting.

10. A Belgian notary shall provide a certificate attesting to the completion of all requisite pre-transfer acts and formalities (Art. 934 Company Code).

In the event of a transfer to another Member State, the old entry on file with the commercial court must be deleted and a notice thereof published in the Annexes to the *Belgian State Gazette* (Art. 936 Company Code).

Any transfer of an SE's registered office to Belgium must be formalised in a notarised document (Art. 937 Company Code). Such a document can only be prepared if a certificate from the competent foreign authority is produced confirming that all necessary acts and formalities have been completed. The notarised document and the amended articles of association must be filed with the clerk of the commercial court where the SE's registered office will be situated in Belgium. In addition, an extract of the document and of the articles must be published in the Annexes to the *Belgian State Gazette*.

11. The Regulation allows the Member States to adopt provisions designed to protect minority shareholders who oppose the transfer of an SE's registered office. Belgium has not adopted any specific rules in this respect.

12. Within two months following publication of the transfer proposal in the Annexes to the *Belgian State Gazette* (*see* no. 7 of this report), creditors and other right holders can request security or other guarantees from the SE. They must have an outstanding claim against the SE which is not yet due. The SE can avoid the need to grant security by settling the claims at face value less a discount for early payment. If the creditor and the SE cannot reach an agreement in this respect, the competent commercial court shall determine whether security should be granted and, if so, how much and within which timeframe. If security or priority has already been granted to a claimant or if the SE is solvent, the court may decide not to require the provision of (additional) security. These are summary proceedings that do not delay the transfer process (Art. 933 Company Code).

13. The Regulation provides that the Member States can object to the transfer of an SE's registered office on grounds of public interest. In Belgium, the Ministry of Economic Affairs has the right to object to a transfer of such grounds during a period of two months following publication in the Annexes to the *Belgian State Gazette* of the transfer proposal (Art. 935 Company Code). Any objection should be made by means of an official notice filed with the clerk of the competent commercial court. A mention of the filing must also be published in the Annexes to the *Belgian State Gazette*. The procedure to appeal such opposition will be set forth in a royal decree (which has yet to be published).

As long as the opposition has not been withdrawn or a negative decision taken within the scope of the aforementioned proceedings, the notary cannot furnish the certificate (see no. 10 of this report) necessary to transfer an SE's registered office to another Member State.

14. Article 210(4) of the Income Tax Code states that the cross-border transfer of the registered or head office of a Belgian company will be treated as the liquidation of the company, implying that all unrealised capital gains on the company's assets will become taxable and that withholding tax at a rate of 10% shall be levied on any (deemed) liquidation proceeds (subject to certain exemptions). This provision must be amended to reflect the tax neutrality provided for by Council Directive 2005/19/EC of 17 February 2005.

D Corporate purpose

15. The Belgian rules on corporate purpose shall apply equally to SEs, which means that an SE's corporate purpose must be clearly defined and that it may only engage in acts that fall within or are incidental to its corporate purpose, as set forth in its articles. There are no SE-specific rules. Any acts outside an SE's corporate purpose will bind the company unless it can establish that the third party was aware or should have been aware of the *ultra vires* nature of the act. Publication of the SE's corporate purpose in the Annexes to the *Belgian State Gazette* does not constitute sufficient proof of such knowledge (Art. 536 Company Code).

E Capital

16. The share capital of an SE must be at least €120,000, of which €61,500 must be paid up (Art. 875 Company Code). Furthermore, at least one quarter of each share should be paid up at the time of incorporation. Shares which represent contributions in kind should be fully paid up within five years from subscription (Arts. 448 and 586 Company Code). Shares can be issued in bearer or registered form.

2 Different means of formation

A Formation by merger

(i) Procedure and publication requirements

17. Among Belgian corporate forms, only a *société anonyme* or 'SA' can participate in the formation of an SE by merger. The *société commandité par actions*, although considered a public limited-liability company, is not listed in Annex I to the Regulation. Therefore, it cannot form an SE by merger and must first be converted into an SA.

Each participating company must help to prepare the draft terms of merger.[6] Only the board of directors (*conseil d'administration*) or management organ (*conseil de direction*), if any, is authorised to prepare the draft terms (Art. 879

---

[6] The draft terms of merger is a document containing relevant information for all participating companies (see Chap. 2, no. 25 of this book).

Company Code). There is no obligation to have the draft terms prepared in the presence of a notary. In addition to the particulars mentioned in no. 25 of Chapter 2 of this book, the draft terms should include the following information with respect to Belgian participating companies: (i) the corporate purpose of each participating company; and (ii) the address of its head office, which should correspond to its registered office (Arts. 693 and 706 Company Code). Under Belgian law, the draft terms should be drafted in an official language of Belgium, i.e. Dutch, German or French, depending on where the head office of the participating company is situated.

The board of directors or management organ must prepare a report explaining the draft terms of merger. In addition to the information mentioned in no. 26 of Chapter 2 of this book, the draft terms should define the financial situation of the company and the merger conditions, the manner in which the merger will take place, the consequences of the merger, the methods used to determine the share-exchange ratio and the relative importance attached to each method and the values resulting from each method (Arts. 694 and 707 Company Code).

The draft terms of merger must be examined by the company's auditor or, if the company does not have an auditor, by a certified auditor or chartered accountant appointed by the board of directors or management organ of each Belgian participating company. The participating companies may jointly petition the competent commercial court for permission to appoint a single expert. The auditor or accountant's report should include at least the information mentioned in no. 27 of Chapter 2 of this book. To this end, the auditor or accountant is entitled to access corporate documents and books at the company's offices (Arts. 695 and 708 Company Code).

The draft terms of merger must be filed with the clerk of the competent commercial court at least six weeks prior to the general meeting scheduled to vote on the merger (Arts. 693 and 706 Company Code). The information mentioned in Article 21 of the Regulation must be published in the Annexes to the *Belgian State Gazette* (Art. 880 Company Code; see also Chap. 2, no. 28 of this book).

18. The draft terms of merger, the abovementioned reports, and the annual accounts and reports for the last three years of each participating company should be made available to shareholders at the company's head office one month before the general meeting scheduled to vote on the merger (see Chap. 2, no. 28 of this book). If the latest annual accounts relate to a financial year that ended more than six months prior to the date of the draft terms of merger, a financial statement valid as at a date no earlier than the first day of the third month preceding the date of the draft terms should be made available. In order to prepare such a financial statement it is not necessary to take a new inventory. Furthermore, the valuations shown on the last balance sheet must only be altered to the extent necessary to reflect interim entries in the books. In any event, interim depreciation and reserves and material changes in value not shown on the

books must be taken into consideration (Arts. 697(2)(5) and 710(2)(5) Company Code).

Notices of the general meeting scheduled to vote on the merger must indicate that the draft terms, the management report and the auditor's reports are available at the company's offices. These documents must be sent to the holders of registered shares no later than one month prior to the date of the meeting and to all persons who meet the attendance requirements (Arts. 697(1) and 710(1) Company Code). Any shareholder is entitled to obtain a copy upon request free of charge of any document that must be made available at the company's offices in accordance with the above rules, with the exception of documents previously sent to them (Arts. 697(3) and 710(3) Company Code).

The board of directors or the management organ must inform the general meeting and the management organ of the other participating companies of any material changes to the company's assets and liabilities occurring subsequent to the date of the draft terms of merger but before the general meeting scheduled to vote on the merger (Arts. 696 and 709 Company Code).

19. Under Belgian law, the merger must be approved by three-quarters of the votes cast at a general meeting of each participating company at which at least half the subscribed capital is present or represented (unless the articles provide for a greater majority or quorum). If the latter requirement is not met, a second general meeting shall be called at which no quorum is required (Arts. 699 and 712 Company Code). Immediately after the decision to approve the merger, the shareholders must approve the new articles of association by the same majority, failing which the merger shall have no effect (Arts. 701 and 714 Company Code). If the merger results in changes to rights attached to a particular class of shares, the above quorum and majority requirements should be satisfied for each class. Non-voting bonus shares are entitled to vote in their class. The board of directors shall draft a report explaining the reasons for the changes, which should be made available along with the draft terms and mentioned in the notice of the general meeting (Art. 560 Company Code).

The minutes of the general meeting must be in notarised form. The conclusion of the auditor's or accountant's report should be mentioned in the notarial instrument, in which the notary must also confirm the internal and external legality of the merger and the completion of all requisite formalities (Arts. 700 and 713 Company Code). The notary will also issue a certificate attesting to completion of the pre-merger acts and formalities and, if this notary also prepares the instrument for the acquiring company, a certificate attesting to completion of the merger and formation of the SE in accordance with the applicable rules (Art. 882 Company Code; see also Chap. 2, no. 30 of this book). The notary preparing the merger instrument of an SE, i.e. the acquiring company or the newly formed company resulting from the merger, shall confirm completion of the merger at the request of the participating companies, which must provide the notary with all relevant documents confirming that the merger resolution of each participating company has been published in accordance with the laws of the relevant Member State, including certificates attesting to completion of the requisite pre-merger acts and formalities. This confirmation should take the form of a notarial instrument filed with the clerk of the commercial court of the judicial district where the SE's registered office is located (Art. 884 Company Code).

The participating companies' management shall oversee the allocation of shares amongst shareholders in an SE with its registered office in Belgium. Any costs incurred shall be charged to the SE. No shares are allocated to a participating company for shares, including own shares, held in another participating company (Arts. 703(2) and 717(2) Company Code).

20. The merger is made public by filing the minutes of the general meeting with the clerk of the commercial court of the judicial district where the head office of the participating company is located and by publication of an extract in the Annexes to the *Belgian State Gazette* (Arts. 702 and 716 Company Code).

The articles of the SE resulting from the merger are filed with the clerk of the competent commercial court, together with notarial confirmation of completion of the merger. Filing is only possible if the rules on employment involvement have been complied with (Art. 895 Company Code; Art. 12(2) Reg.). An extract of the relevant provisions of the articles of the SE must be published in the Annexes to the *Belgian State Gazette* (Art. 884 Company Code).

(ii) **Right to object to a company participating in a merger**

21. The minister of economic affairs has the right to object to participation by a given company in the formation of an SE by merger (Art. 878 Company Code). If such objection is filed, the company in question cannot take part in the merger. The objection should be made by means of an official notice filed with the clerk of the commercial court of the judicial district where the company's head office is located. A mention of the filing must also be published in the Annexes to the *Belgian State Gazette*. The company must be informed of the ministry's objection within one month following publication of the information set forth in Article 21 of the Regulation in the Annexes to the *Belgian State Gazette*. The procedure to appeal such an objection shall be set forth in a royal decree.

As long as the opposition has not been withdrawn or a negative decision taken within the scope of the aforementioned proceedings, the notary cannot furnish the certificate necessary to proceed with the merger.

(iii) **Minority shareholders**

22. The Member States are free to adopt appropriate provisions to protect minority shareholders who oppose the formation of an SE by merger. Belgium has not adopted any specific rules in this respect.

(iv) **Rights of creditors**

23. Creditors of Belgian participating companies with claims that arose prior to publication of the merger enjoy special protection and are entitled to claim security (Art. 684 Company Code). Alternatively, the SE (or participating company) can settle the claim less a discount for early payment. If the parties cannot reach agreement, the dispute can be submitted to the president of the competent commercial court who will decide if security need by granted or if the creditor has sufficient guarantees or that the company is sufficiently solvent to refuse to secure the claim. If the court orders the company to grant security and the company refuses to do so, the claim will become immediately payable. Such special protection does not apply to financial institutions subject to oversight by the Banking, Finance and Insurance Commission (CBFA).

(v) **Acquisition by a company holding 90% or more of the shares in another company**

24. Belgian law does not contain an exception to the reporting requirements for a merger by acquisition of a company that already holds at least 90% of the shares in another company. However, a specific procedure exists for the merger by acquisition of a wholly-owned subsidiary, in which case the merger proposal may be drawn up in a simplified form and no merger report is required (Art. 676 Company Code).

(vi) **Avoidance of a merger**

25. Under Belgian law, a merger can be declared void by the court in the event that (i) the decisions have not been enacted in a notarial deed or (ii) the required management and audit reports have not been prepared. The court can grant the participating companies an extension by which to regularise their situation (Art. 689 Company Code).

In addition, the commercial court can declare a merger void if additional cash compensation exceeding one-tenth of the par value of the shares is distributed to shareholders or if the shares have no nominal value (Art. 688 Company Code).

A decision to avoid a merger must be published (Art. 691 Company Code). Once an SE resulting from a merger has been registered, however, it may no longer be declared void by the courts (Art. 30 Reg.).

B Formation of a holding SE

(i) Procedure and publication requirements

26. In Belgium only a *société anonyme* and a *société privée à responsabilité limitée* are entitled to participate in the creation of a holding SE.[7] The *société commandite par actions* and the *société coopérative* cannot do so. The board of directors, the management organ or the managers[8] of each participating company prepare draft terms of formation (Art. 885 Company Code).[9] By law, the draft terms must be prepared in an official language of Belgium, i.e. Dutch, German or French, depending on where the head office of the participating company is situated. The draft terms are filed with the clerk of the competent commercial court and published in the Annexes to the *Belgian State Gazette* (Art. 886 Company Code).

Under Belgian law, the draft terms must be examined by the company's auditor or, if no auditor has been appointed, by a certified auditor or chartered accountant appointed by the board of directors, the management organ or the managers of the relevant participating company (Art. 887 Company Code). The auditor's or accountant's report should contain the information mentioned in Chapter 2, no. 38 of this book (Art. 32(5) Reg.).

27. Each participating company, upon completion of the necessary steps to form a holding SE, must file a document with the clerk of the commercial court of the judicial district where its head office is located stating that it has fulfilled the conditions for formation (Art. 888 Company Code). A notice to this effect must be published in the Annexes to the *Belgian State Gazette*.

If an SE has its registered office in Belgium, its articles of association must be filed with the competent commercial court. Filing is only possible if the rules on employment involvement have been complied with (Art. 895 of the Company Code; Art. 12(2) Reg.). The articles of the holding SE must state that shareholders have contributed the required number of shares within a three-month period, as set forth in the draft terms, and that all other requirements have been fulfilled. The aforementioned statement should also be mentioned in the extract of the articles published in the Annexes to the *Belgian State Gazette* (Art. 889 Company Code).

(ii) Minority shareholders

28. Belgium has no specific provisions to protect minority shareholders, creditors or employees who oppose the formation of a holding SE.

---

[7] Annex II of the Regulation.
[8] A *société privée à responsabilité limitée* is managed by one or more managers. The articles of association may provide that when several managers are appointed, they must take decisions by a majority.
[9] See Chap. 2, no. 37 of this book.

C Formation of a subsidiary SE

29. The rules on the formation of a Belgian *société anonyme* apply to the formation of a subsidiary SE with its registered office in Belgium, with one exception. An SE can itself form one or more subsidiaries that take the form of an SE. In this case, all shares of the SE shall be held by a sole shareholder. The rules of the Company Code applicable to single-member private limited-liability companies (BVBA/SPRL) shall apply *mutatis mutandis* to the formation and organisation of such a company. The Belgian legislature has not provided for any special rules in this respect.

D Conversion into an SE

30. In Belgium, only a *société anonyme* can be converted into an SE (Art. 2(4) Reg.). To this effect, the board of directors[10] must prepare draft terms of conversion (Art. 890 Company Code). By law, the draft terms must be prepared in one of the official languages of Belgium, i.e. Dutch, German or French, depending in where the company's head office is situated. The draft terms must be filed with the clerk of the competent commercial court and a notice to this effect published in the Annexes to the *Belgian State Gazette* (Art. 891 Company Code).

The board of directors shall prepare a report on the draft terms of conversion explaining and justifying the legal and economic consequences of the conversion and the implications for shareholders and employees (Art. 37(2) Reg.). Moreover, one or more independent experts shall be appointed to draw up a report on the conversion. Under Belgian law, this expert shall be the company's auditor or, if no auditor has been appointed, a certified auditor or chartered accountant appointed by the board of directors (Art. 892 Company Code). The auditor or accountant must certify that the company has net assets at least equivalent to its capital plus those reserves which cannot be distributed by law or pursuant to the company's articles of association (Art. 37(6) Reg.).

The Regulation states that the Member States can condition conversion on approval by the organ within which employee participation is organised. Since the Belgian works council does not qualify as such, this provision does not apply.

31. The draft terms of conversion and the new articles must be approved by three-quarters of the votes present or represented at a general meeting at which at least half the subscribed capital is present or represented (unless the articles provide for a greater important majority or a higher quorum). If the latter requirement is not met, a second meeting shall be called at which no quorum is required

---

[10] This is also the case if the *société anonyme* has appointed a management committee (*comité de direction*).

(Arts. 699 and 893 Company Code). If changes to special rights attached to a class of shares are proposed, the above quorum and majority requirements should be satisfied with respect to each class. Non-voting bonus shares are entitled to a vote in their class. The board of directors should explain the reasons for the changes in a report made available simultaneously with the draft terms of merger and mentioned in the notice of the general meeting (Art. 560 Company Code).

The draft terms of conversion and the articles of association are filed with the clerk of the competent commercial court and an extract thereof is published in the Annexes to the *Belgian State Gazette*. Filing is only possible if the rules on employment involvement have been complied with (Art. 895 Company Code; Art. 12(2) Reg.).

3 Acts committed on behalf of an SE in formation

32. If acts are performed in an SE's name prior to registration, the natural persons or legal entities that committed the acts shall be held jointly and severally liable (together with the SE) if the SE does not assume the obligations arising out of these acts. Upon ratification, the acts will be considered by operation of law to have been entered into by the SE.

Article 60 of the Company Code does not apply to SEs. This article provides that acts performed in a company's name prior to registration shall be deemed to have been entered into by the company only if it is registered within two years' time and expressly assumes the acts within two months of registration.

4 Registration and publication

33. An SE shall be registered in the Member State in which its registered office is situated. In Belgium, the articles of an SE must be filed with the clerk of the commercial court in the judicial district where its registered office is located. Filing is only possible if the rules on employee involvement have been observed (Art. 895 Company Code; Art. 12(2) Reg.). The clerk's office will publish an extract of the articles in the Annexes to the *Belgian State Gazette*. A notice of the registration of an SE (or of a change to the location of its registered office) must be published in the *Official Journal of the European Communities* (Art. 14(1) Reg.).

An SE is also recorded in the registry of legal entities (the 'Registry'). All legal entities must be registered with the Registry or with the Crossroads Enterprise Bank (*Kruispuntbank van Ondernemingen/Banque-Carrefour des Entreprises*).

5 Acquisition of legal personality

34. Belgian companies acquire legal personality upon the filing of their articles with the clerk of the competent commercial court. This is not the case for an SE. An SE acquires legal personality on its date of recordation with the Registry (Art. 2(4) Company Code). In general, this will be the filing date of its articles of association with the clerk of court.

IV Organisation and management

1 General remarks

35. The organisation of an SE largely complies with existing Belgian rules applicable to the *société anonyme*. In Belgium, the decision-making power in a *société anonyme* (a public limited-liability company) is divided between the general meeting of shareholders and the board of directors; the latter has residual powers. Belgium has traditionally only recognised a one-tier management system. Until 1 September 2002, the only model a *société anonyme* could adopt was thus a one-tier board model. In this model, the board of directors has the most extensive powers to manage the company. However, since the entry into force of the Corporate Governance Act of 2 August 2002, a *société anonyme* can opt for either the classic one-tier system or a two-tier system with a management organ (*comité de direction*).

2 General meeting

A Decision-making process

36. The convening and conduct of shareholder meetings of an SE with its registered office in Belgium are in general governed by the provisions applicable to the *société anonyme*, subject to specific rules set forth in the Regulation.

At least one general meeting must be held each year in order to adopt the annual accounts (Art. 92 Company Code). The first general meeting can be held at any time during the first 18 months following incorporation of an SE (Art. 925 Company Code).[11]

37. The general meeting can be convened by the board of directors (in the one-tier system), the management or supervisory board (in the two-tier system) or the company's auditors (Art. 922 Company Code). One or more shareholders holding at least 10% of the subscribed capital can request that a general meeting be held. Belgium did not enact the option contained in Article 55(1) to allow a lower threshold. If the shareholders request a general meeting, one must be

---

[11] Belgium has enacted the option to this effect contained in Article 54 of the Regulation.

held within two months. If the SE fails to do so, the president of the commercial court in summary proceedings may order the company to convene the general meeting within a specified period of time or authorise the shareholders or their proxy holders to do so (Art. 922 Company Code). Once a meeting has been convened, one or more shareholders holding at least 10% of the subscribed capital can request that additional items be placed on the agenda. Once again, Belgium has not enacted the option contained in Article 56 of the Regulation to allow a lower percentage. Such a request must be communicated to the board of directors or the management board within 48 hours of convening, unless the articles provide otherwise. The proposal must be published in the same newspaper as the notice of the meeting no later than eight days in advance or, where applicable, sent by registered mail to the holders of registered securities (Art. 923 Company Code).

The annual general meeting examines and approves the annual accounts and releases directors and members of the supervisory board and the management organ from liability (Art. 926 Company Code). The board of directors or the management organ is entitled to adjourn the annual meeting for three weeks. Such an adjournment will void any decisions related to the annual accounts; all other decisions shall remain valid unless the general meeting decides otherwise. Shareholders may request that the annual accounts be approved when the meeting reconvenes; no further adjournment is possible (Art. 927 Company Code). Shareholder(s) holding at least 1% of an SE's share capital or a shareholding with a value of €1,250,000 and who did not vote to release the directors from liability are entitled to file, on behalf of the company, a claim against any director or member of the management organ or supervisory board for negligence (Art. 930 Company Code).

38. Resolutions of the general meeting are passed by a majority of votes validly cast (Art. 57 Reg.). Amendments to the articles must be approved by a two-thirds majority of votes cast at a meeting where at least half the subscribed capital is present or represented. If the meeting is adjourned and subsequently reconvened, resolutions can be passed regardless of the number of shares present provided they are approved by a two-thirds majority, although the company's articles may provide for a greater majority (Art. 558 Company Code).

The articles of association may furthermore provide that amendments to an SE's articles shall be approved by a simple majority of votes cast if at least half the subscribed capital is present or represented (Art. 929 Company Code; Art. 59(2) Reg.). The foregoing implies that the articles of a Belgian SE can be amended by a simple majority if the articles expressly provide for this possibility. If the aforementioned quorum is not met, a second meeting must be called at which shareholders can take decisions by a two-thirds majority if less than half the subscribed capital is present or represented or, if more than half the subscribed capital is present or represented, by a simple majority of votes cast. Finally, if the articles conflict with the arrangements for employee involvement, the board of directors or the management organ is entitled to amend the articles without the approval of the general meting (Art. 877 Company Code; see Chap. 2, no. 59 of this book).

B   Rights and obligations of shareholders

39. The rights and obligations of shareholders are set forth in an SE's articles of association and the Company Code. In particular, shareholders have the right to submit questions to members of the board of directors (in the one-tier system) or the management organ and supervisory board (in the two-tier system) regarding their duties and any items on the agenda. Directors and members of the management organ and the supervisory board have the right to refuse to divulge any information concerning the SE if such disclosure could seriously harm the interests of the company, its shareholders or personnel (Art. 924 Company Code).

3   Management and supervision

A   Two-tier system/one-tier system

(i)   **General remarks**
40. The founders of an SE may opt for either a one-tier or a two-tier management structure. In the one-tier system, management is entrusted to a board of directors (*conseil d'administration* or *raad van bestuur*). In the two-tier system, management is entrusted to a management organ (*conseil de direction* or *directieraad*) overseen by a supervisory board (*conseil de surveillance* or *raad van toezicht*). An SE is bound by the acts of its organs that fall within their scope of authority, even if these acts are outside the SE's corporate purpose, unless it can establish that the third party was or, given the circumstances, should have been aware of the *ultra vires* nature of the act (Art. 897 Company Code).

Directors and members of the management organ or supervisory board may be legal entities, in which case they must appoint a representative who shall be liable in the same way as the legal entity they represent (Art. 896 Company Code).

(ii) **One-tier system**
41. In the one-tier system, the board of directors is entrusted with overall management of the company. The rules applicable to a *société anonyme* shall apply. It is not possible to delegate management to a management committee (*comité de direction*). However, daily management may be delegated to a managing director, who is also a member of the board of directors, or to a general manager or several persons, who may be members of the board of directors, acting

as a corporate body (Art. 898 Company Code; Art. 43(1) Reg.). Daily management has been defined by Belgium's highest court (*Cour de cassation*) as the power to manage the daily needs of the company or to take decisions which are of minor importance or that require immediate action.[12]

The board of directors should be composed of at least three directors, unless the SE has only two shareholders (Art. 518 Company Code). The articles of an SE can always set a higher number or impose a maximum number (Art. 43(2) Reg.).

(iii) **Two-tier system**

42. The management organ of an SE must comprise at least one member (Art. 899 Company Code; Art. 39(4) Reg.). The supervisory board must have at least three members (Art. 900(2) Company Code; Art. 40(3) Reg.). The articles of an SE can set a higher number or cap the number of directors (Arts. 39(4) and 40(3) Reg.). The management organ may delegate daily management, as is the case in a *société anonyme* (Art. 900(1) Company Code; Art. 39 (1) Reg.).

The remuneration of members of the management organ can be fixed or variable and is determined by the supervisory board within the limits set forth in the articles of association. The supervisory board cannot alter the remuneration of a member of the management organ without the consent of the latter. The remuneration of members of the supervisory board is set by the general meeting (Art. 914 Company Code).

43. The management organ is entrusted with the same powers as the board of directors of a *société anonyme* (Art. 901 Company Code; Art. 41(3) Reg.), which implies that the supervisory board can only oversee the work of the management board but cannot engage in actual management of the SE. The management organ has extensive powers to manage the SE and perform all acts necessary or useful to further the company's corporate purpose (Art. 903(1) Company Code). Pursuant to the Regulation, the articles of an SE may define certain categories of transactions that require the approval of the supervisory board. However, Belgium did not enact this option (Art. 48(2) Reg.). The supervisory board may also define categories of decisions that require its prior approval (Art. 48(1) Reg.). However, the absence of authorisation by the supervisory board cannot be invoked against third parties (Art. 903(2) Company Code).

No person can sit simultaneously on both the management organ and the supervisory board (Art. 904 Company Code). In the event of a vacancy on the management organ, the supervisory board may appoint one of its members to

---

[12] Cass., 21 February 2000, *Tijdschrift voor rechtspersoon en vennootschap*, 2000, 283; Cass., 17 September 1968, *Revue pratique des sociétés*, 1970, 197.

temporarily fill the position. During this period of time, which may not exceed one year, the functions of that person on the supervisory board shall be suspended (Art. 39(3) Reg.). Members of the management organ can attend meetings of the supervisory board if asked to do so, in which case they are not entitled to vote (Art. 913 Company Code).

44. If the management organ is composed of more than one member, these members form a corporate body which takes decision by a majority of votes cast. The articles may provide that the management organ can take decisions in writing in the event of an emergency and if the corporate interest so requires. In this case, the decision must be approved by a unanimous vote of the management organ. This procedure cannot be applied to approve the annual accounts, an increase of capital within authorised limits or any other decision specifically excluded by a provision in the articles of association (Art. 907 Company Code).

The supervisory board should meet at least once each quarter. It takes decisions by a simple majority of votes cast or by the majority stipulated in the articles (Art. 912 Company Code). Members of the administrative organ are entitled to attend meetings of the supervisory board if asked to do so, although they are not entitled to vote (Art. 913 Company Code). The supervisory board is not permitted to take decisions in writing.

The rules on conflicts of interest applicable to the members of a *société anonyme*'s board of directors apply to members of the supervisory board and the management organ. If a board member has a conflict of interest, the minutes of the meeting must include a justification of the decision taken (Art. 523 Company Code). If the SE is a listed company, special mandatory rules apply including a prohibition on the interested member from taking part in deliberations and voting (Arts. 915 and 916 Company Code). Moreover, if a member of the management organ has a conflict of interest, the management organ cannot deliberate and vote on the matter, which shall be referred to the supervisory board.

B   Appointment and removal

45. Members of the board of directors or the supervisory board are appointed by the general meeting of shareholders. Members of the management organ are appointed and removed by the supervisory board (Art. 905 Company Code). The articles of association shall determine the conditions for appointment and removal. As provided in Article 39(2) of the Regulation, the articles can allow the general meeting to appoint members of the management organ. If no provision is made, the supervisory board shall have the power to do so.

Members of the board of directors or supervisory board, respectively, can be removed from office at any time by the general meeting (Art. 910 Company Code). Any restriction on such power is null and void. In the event of a vacancy, the board of directors or supervisory board may recruit a new member to sit out the remaining term. The articles may provide otherwise (Arts. 519 and 911 Company Code).

C Representation

46. In the one-tier system, the board of directors represents the SE (Art. 522 Company Code). In the two-tier system, the management organ represents the SE. The articles may provide that an SE is represented by a one or more members of its management organ. Any other restrictions or provisions with respect to representation are not enforceable against third parties (Arts. 908 and 909 Company Code). The supervisory board is entrusted with supervision of the management organ and does not act towards third parties. However, in the event of a conflict between the SE and a member of its management organ, the supervisory board can act on behalf of the SE (Art. 914 Company Code).

D Liability

47. The liability of members of the board of directors, the management organ and the supervisory board is subject to the rules applicable to the directors of a *société anonyme*. Special rules apply to members of the management organ and the supervisory board in the two-tier system, who shall be jointly liable for any violations of the Company Code and the company's articles of association. A member of the supervisory board who did not participate in the violation can avoid liability by disclosing the violation at the next general meeting; a member of the management organ who was not a party to the violation must disclose the violation at the next meeting of the supervisory board (Art. 919 Company Code).

V Employee involvement

48. The Directive has been transposed into Belgian law by Collective Bargaining Agreement (CBA) No. 84 of 6 October 2004 of the National Labour Council, which is very detailed and adopts most of the provisions of the Directive.

Structures for employee representation in Belgian participating companies which will cease to exist as separate legal entities following the formation of an SE must be maintained in the newly formed SE, provided the criteria for such structures are still valid (Art. 13 (4) Dir.).

1 Special negotiating body

49. The composition of the special negotiating body ('SNB') is governed by special rules. If the Belgian company has a works council, the latter shall appoint a representative from amongst its members. If there is a committee for prevention and protection at work but no works council, the committee shall appoint a representative to the SNB. If there is no works council or committee for prevention and protection at work, the relevant joint committee can authorise the company's trade union representatives to appoint members to the SNB. Finally, the employees of the company can themselves appoint representatives (Art. 3(2)(b) Dir.). Members of the special negotiating body need not necessarily be employees of the company (Art. 9 CBA No. 84; Art. 3(2)(b) Dir.).

All expenses related to the SNB shall be borne by the participating companies. The SNB may enlist the assistance of experts of its choosing. In accordance with Article 3(7) of the Directive, Belgium has limited the number of experts whose expenses shall be borne by the participating companies to one.

2 Employee participation

50. Belgian law does not currently recognise participation rights or the right of workers to sit on management bodies. Thus, if formal negotiations fail, the standard rules regarding employee participation as set forth in the Directive and CBA No. 84 shall apply to the extent such participation exists in the other companies forming the SE (Art. 7(2) Dir.). Belgium did not enact the option contained in Article 7(3) of the Directive.

3 Protection of employee representatives

51. Pursuant to Article 10 of the Directive, members of the SNB are protected in the same way as works council members under Belgian law. They are entitled to reasonable paid time off to perform their duties and are protected against abusive dismissal or harassment (mobbing) by the employer when acting as employee representatives under the law, standing for election to such a position, seeking to exercise rights conferred by the law, and in certain other circumstances. A claim for wrongful termination or a complaint of harassment may be brought before the labour courts.

Changes must still be made to national law to reinforce these provisions (i.e. regarding Art. 8(2) and (3) Dir.).

VI Annual accounts and consolidated accounts
1 Accounting principles

52. The section on the SE in the Company Code contains only three provisions regarding its annual accounts, consolidated accounts and auditors. Moreover, these provisions only apply to two-tier SEs, which implies that SEs in general are subject to the same rules as a *société anonyme*.

In a two-tier SE, the supervisory board shall prepare a report on the annual accounts and management report (Art. 938 Company Code). This report must be made available to shareholders before the general meeting scheduled to approve the annual accounts and must be filed with the National Bank of Belgium along with the annual accounts. The annual accounts are prepared by the management organ.

53. Accounting and auditing are regulated by the law of 17 July 1975 on accounting. This law is supplemented by a number of royal decrees which regulate various aspects of accounting practices and financial reporting. The royal decree of 12 September 1983 mainly regulates the simplified system of accounting applicable to small businesses and partnerships and sets forth the requirements regarding preparation and maintenance of books of account. The royal decree of 30 January 2001 defines the content and presentation of minimum tables of annual accounts and consolidated annual accounts, including the reporting and disclosure requirements for commercial companies. Furthermore, interpretative guidelines for accounting and auditing rules are set forth in several opinions and recommendations of the Commission for Accounting Standards. These guidelines are not legally binding but are highly authoritative nonetheless. Banks, credit institutions and insurance companies, as well as listed companies, are subject to specific accounting, reporting and auditing rules which fall outside the scope of this report.

Each company must use the accounting system best suited to its character and size and one that takes into account all of the company's operations, assets, rights, liabilities, obligations and commitments. In general, the SE's accounting system must include a system of books and accounts which must be kept in accordance with the principle of double-entry bookkeeping. All transactions must be recorded chronologically, in an accurate and complete manner. Entries must be consolidated in a central register at least once a month. Each entry must be justified by a dated supporting document. All supporting documents must be kept for at least ten years, save when they have no evidentiary value (in which case they need be kept for only three years).

Accounts must be prepared in accordance with minimum tables of accounts set forth in the royal decree of 30 January 2001.

Annual accounts consist of a balance sheet, income statement and any notes thereto.

An SE's annual accounts are prepared by its board of directors or management organ and must be approved by the general meeting within six months following the close of its financial year. Annual accounts must be filed with the National Bank within thirty days of approval.

54. Subject to certain exceptions, a parent company is required to prepare consolidated accounts for its group and other companies it controls. The concept of 'control' is defined in the Company Code. Control can be exercised jointly or independently. A distinction should be made between cases in which control shall be deemed to exist automatically and cases where the existence of control shall be presumed under the circumstances. A minimum table of consolidated accounts is set forth in the royal decree of 30 January 2001. Consolidated accounts comprise a consolidated balance sheet, income statement and notes and must provide a true and fair view of the group's financial situation at the end of the financial year. They need not be approved by the general meeting. The royal decree of 30 January 2001 also contains specific rules governing the audit and publication of consolidated accounts.

2 Auditors

55. An SE must appoint one or more auditors if it employs annually more than 100 full-time equivalents or if more than one of the following conditions are met: (i) the SE employs on average at least 50 full-time equivalents annually; (ii) the SE has turnover of at least €6,250,000 (excluding VAT); and (iii) the SE's balance sheet total is at least €3,125,000. The auditor must be a member of the Institute of Certified Auditors.

The auditor shall monitor the company's financial position, annual accounts and the conformity of operations reflected in its annual accounts. The auditor is appointed by the general meeting for a renewable three-year term and cannot be removed from office except for just cause. The general meeting shall also determine the auditor's remuneration. The auditor should be independent, and various rules exist to guarantee such independence. For example, auditors are not allowed to serve as a director, manager, consultant or employee of the company during a period of two years following the end of their term of office.

The auditor must draft a report for shareholders each year, stating whether, in the auditor's opinion, (consolidated) annual accounts have been prepared in accordance with the requirements of Belgian law. If the auditor feels that any of these requirements have not been fulfilled, a statement to this effect must be made in the report.

VII   Supervision by the national authorities

56. The national authority competent to supervise application of the Regulation depends on the provision in question. Pursuant to Article 68(2) of the Regulation, the competent national authorities in Belgium are: (i) Belgian notaries (for purposes of Articles 8(8), 25(2) and 26(1) of the Regulation); (ii) an SE's auditor(s) (Art. 54 Reg.); (iii) the president of the competent commercial court (Art. 55(3) Reg.); and (iv) the public prosecutor (Art. 64(4) Reg.).

VIII   Dissolution

1   Winding up

57. The dissolution of a company may be voluntary or involuntary. Dissolution requires sufficient assets to cover all debts. If the company cannot pay its debts, it will most likely be declared bankrupt. Voluntary dissolution is initiated by the company itself, in most cases by the board of directors or the management board. The general meeting must vote on and approve dissolution by the same majority required to amend the company's articles. In the event of a loss of capital, special rules apply and the SE can be forced into liquidation by a minority of shareholders.

The court can order a company to dissolve, in which case it shall appoint a liquidator and determine the conditions for liquidation. Any interested party can petition the court to order the dissolution of an SE if the value of the company's net assets has fallen below €61,500 or the SE has not filed its annual accounts for the past three financial years.

2   Liquidation

58. The rules regarding the liquidation of a *société anonyme* shall also apply to SEs (Art. 63 Reg.). In addition, any interested party or the public prospector can petition the commercial court to order the involuntary liquidation of an SE whose registered office is in Belgium but whose head office is located abroad. The court can grant the SE an extension by which to regularise its situation (Art. 941 Company Code).

Any decision or judgment regarding winding up, liquidation, insolvency or cessation of payments of an SE must be filed with the clerk of the relevant commercial court. An extract of the decision must be published in the Annexes to the *Belgian State Gazette* (Art. 942 Company Code).

3   Insolvency

59. A company can be declared bankrupt if it qualifies as a merchant (as defined in the Commercial Code) and is in a situation of permanent cessation of

payments that undermines its creditworthiness. Only the commercial court can declare a company bankrupt. An adjudication in bankruptcy can be sought by the company itself, one or more of its creditors, the public prosecutor or a temporary receiver. Once declared bankrupt, the court shall appoint one or more trustees in bankruptcy and a supervising judge. A list of the company's assets shall be prepared. In addition, the court shall set a deadline by which creditors must inform the court of any claims and a date on which the list of outstanding claims will be closed. The court can also rule that a date for cessation of payments, used to determine which transactions performed prior to the adjudication in bankruptcy are valid, be fixed prior to commencement of proceedings. After the adjudication in bankruptcy, the company shall be administered by a trustee in bankruptcy. The board of directors, the supervisory board and the management board are divested of all authority. As a result of the bankruptcy, all existing claims against the company become immediately due. Interest on unsecured or secured claims ceases to accrue once an adjudication in bankruptcy has been rendered.

The trustee in bankruptcy shall liquidate all assets and pay off all debts. The trustee shall then convene a creditors' meeting and file a report detailing his or her fees, the company's debts, the liquidation of assets and the distribution of the proceeds to various creditors. If it has been established prior to the creditors' meeting that the assets of the company are insufficient to cover its debts and expenses, the trustee shall apply another procedure, in which case the commercial court shall hear the trustee, the supervising judge and the company and close the proceedings. A decision to close bankruptcy proceedings effectively puts an end to the company.

4 Cessation of payments

60. The purpose of a composition with creditors is to create a framework in which to allow companies facing temporary financial difficulties to recover. The law on judicial composition of 1998 takes into account the interests of creditors and of the company as well as the general interest. Such proceedings involve a transition period during which the company is protected against creditors' claims. During this time, the company can draft a recovery plan. Only merchants facing financial difficulties likely to result in a definitive cessation of payments or that threaten the continuity of their business can obtain the benefit of judicial composition, provided they are not acting in bad faith. After this initial period, during which time payment of a company's debts is temporarily suspended, the payment of existing claims is definitively suspended by a recovery plan, which must be approved by the company's creditors and the court.

Creditors vote on the recovery plan during a meeting. The plan will be approved if half the creditors present (whose claims have been acknowledged and accepted) vote in favour. In addition, the total value of claims represented by the favourable votes must represent at least half the company's outstanding debts. In some cases, the approval of individual secured creditors may be required. If the required majority is obtained, the court has two weeks within which to approve or reject the final suspension of payments. Such a suspension can last no longer than 24 months as from the date of the judgment and can be extended once for an additional 12 months. A recovery plan so approved is binding on all creditors, including those who voted against it or failed to state their claims. If the recovery plan is executed in full, the company is definitively discharged from all declared and undeclared claims. New claims are not covered by the composition. Execution of the plan is overseen by a court-appointed commissioner, who reports directly to the court.

IX Applicable law

61. In general, SEs registered in Belgium shall be governed by Belgian law. In certain cases, however, the laws of another Member State will apply, such as, for example, when an SNB is established (i.e. employee representatives from the various participating companies are appointed in accordance with the laws of the Member States concerned). Moreover, Article 12 of the Regulation requires that the Member States ensure that the management of SEs and the management organs of SE subsidiaries and concerned establishments situated within their territory, as well as employee representatives and employees themselves, abide by the obligations set forth in the Directive. This rule applies regardless of whether the registered office of an SE is located within the territory of a particular Member State.

X Tax treatment[13]

1 Income tax

62. A Belgian SE is, in principle, subject to corporate tax at a rate of 33.99% on its worldwide income, unless an exemption is provided in an applicable tax treaty. The Belgian permanent establishment of a nonresident SE will be subject to nonresident corporate tax at a rate of 33.99% on profits attributable to the permanent establishment.

Belgium has not enacted any specific direct or indirect tax measures with respect to SEs. From a tax perspective, a Belgian SE or the Belgian branch of a foreign SE will be treated like any other Belgian entity or branch having separate legal personality. There is no specific risk of discrimination against the SE compared to national or foreign public limited-liability companies formed under Belgian or foreign law.

---

[13] Written by Jan Werbrouck, a tax partner with NautaDutilh Brussels.

Belgium is particularly interesting as a location for SEs since Belgian companies with foreign branches may deduct the losses of these branches from their worldwide taxable income in Belgium, even if the income is exempt from tax in Belgium pursuant to a tax treaty (subject to possible recapture rules). Furthermore, there are no complex allocation rules, apart from the general arm's-length principle.

Formerly, Belgian-source losses had to be set off against foreign-source income exempted under a tax treaty, which meant that only the balance of any unused losses could be carried forward to the next tax year. In this way, the benefit of a treaty exemption for foreign-source income was obviously lost. However, this provision was declared invalid by the ECJ on 14 December 1999 in *Amid* on the ground that it violates Community law (Case C-141/99). Pursuant to this decision, Belgian companies with permanent establishments in other Member States are no longer required to set off Belgian losses against the tax-exempt income of their foreign branches.

Belgian law also provides that a company's foreign-source losses must first be set off against foreign-source income exempt from tax under a treaty for the avoidance of double taxation and only afterwards against Belgian-source profits. However, it is doubtful that this provision complies with Community law.

63. As far as the creation of an SE by means of a cross-border merger is concerned, the Belgian tax authorities have long taken the view that, absent an agreement on the tenth proposal for a Council directive on cross-border mergers of public limited companies, such a merger is not possible under Belgian law. Consequently, they have refused to introduce tax-neutral treatment for such mergers. As a result, Article 2(a) of the Merger Directive has yet to be transposed into national law. A bill was recently drafted on this subject but has not yet been approved by Parliament. The Regulation, however, provides an autonomous legal basis for cross-border mergers. Consequently, the Belgian legislature is expected to take the necessary measures to ensure that such mergers have no adverse tax consequences.

The creation of a holding SE by an exchange of shares should not trigger any adverse tax consequences since Belgian law generally provides for a full exemption of capital gains on shares.

The creation of a subsidiary SE will be tax neutral provided the assets and liabilities contributed constitute a branch of activity or a universality of goods. In the event of a contribution to a foreign SE, the assets and liabilities contributed should be maintained in Belgium in the form of a Belgian permanent establishment in order to benefit from the tax exemption.

64. Under Belgian tax law, the transfer of an SE's registered office is treated as the liquidation of the company, resulting in taxation of all hidden reserves and

the imposition of withholding tax at a rate of 10% on the liquidation proceeds (in excess of the company's capital). Belgian law will have to be amended to provide for tax-neutral treatment of such a transfer in accordance with Directive 2005/19 of 4 March 2005, amending the Merger Directive.

2 Value added tax

65. An SE will be subject to Belgian VAT on the same terms as other Belgian companies, in accordance with the Sixth VAT Directive.

3 Other taxes

66. Contributions to the capital of a Belgian SE are subject to a 0.5% capital duty. A contribution of more than 75% of the shares held in a company established in the EU may benefit from an exemption (*'fusion à l'anglaise'*).

XI Conclusion

67. The SE has been greeted in Belgium with moderate enthusiasm. The complexity and uncertainty with regard to the procedure for concluding arrangements on employee involvement and the absence of tax harmonisation are the main causes for concern of Belgian companies examining the possibility of forming an SE. The fact that the SE and its subsidiaries or branches are subject to corporate tax in each Member State of establishment, without the possibility of consolidation at the parent level, is considered a major drawback. If attractive tax rules for the SE can be created, Belgium will be able to retain the headquarters of some international groups.

Although the rules governing the SE may appear complicated and the formalities with respect to employee involvement burdensome, these should not prove an obstacle to setting up an SE, if handled correctly. The formation process will usually take six to twelve months, but may be accomplished sooner, particularly if the founding parties do not have any employees, as will be is the case, for example, when an SE is used as an SPV in financing transactions.

The first SEs have already been incorporated in Belgium. Other groups are examining the possibility of forming an SE in the near future. Since, as a rule of thumb, companies in different Member States are involved, it is necessary to wait for the implementation of specific regulations with respect to the SE in each Member State concerned.

7
Denmark

VAGN THORUP, NIKOLAJ HANSEN, CLAUS JUEL HANSEN
(EMPLOYMENT MATTERS) AND ARNE OTTOSEN (TAX LAW)
Kromann Reumert

I   Introduction   175
II   Reasons to opt for an SE   175
III   Formation   176
     1   General remarks   176
        A   Founding parties   176
        B   Name   177
        C   Registered Office   178
        D   Corporate purpose   180
        E   Capital   180
     2   Different means of formation   183
        A   Formation by merger   183
        B   Formation of a holding SE   185
        C   Formation of a subsidiary SE   185
        D   Conversion into an SE   186
     3   Acts committed on behalf of an SE in formation   187
     4   Registration and publication   187
     5   Acquisition of legal personality   187
IV   Organisation and management   188
     1   General remarks   188
     2   General meeting   189
        A   Decision-making process   189
        B   Rights and obligations of shareholders   190
     3   Management and supervision   191
        A   Two-tier/one-tier system   191
        B   Appointment and removal   192
        C   Representation   193
        D   Liability   194
V   Employee involvement   194
     1   Special negotiating body   194
     2   Employee participation   196
     3   Protection of employee representatives   196
VI   Annual accounts and consolidated accounts   196
     1   Accounting principles   196
     2   Auditors   197
VII   Supervision by the national authorities   198
VIII   Dissolution   198

       1   Winding up   198
       2   Liquidation   199
       3   Insolvency   199
       4   Cessation of payments   200
IX   Applicable law   201
X   Tax treatment   201
       1   Income tax   201
       2   Value added tax   202
       3   Other taxes   202
XI   Conclusion   202

I Introduction

1. Denmark implemented the Regulation by the Act on the European Company (the 'SE Act')[1] and the Act amending the Danish Companies Act.[2] The Directive was transposed into national law by the Act on Employee Involvement in the SE[3] (the 'Employee Involvement Act'). The Danish legislation entered into force on 8 October 2004.

In implementing the Regulation and transposing the Directive, Denmark sought to make the rules governing SEs as similar as possible to those applicable to Danish public limited-liability companies ('A/S').[4] In most cases where the Regulation gives Member States an option to apply existing national law to SEs registered on their territory, this option has been adopted.

This report is a practical guide to the possibilities and obstacles inherent in establishing an SE in Denmark and in using Danish legal entities to form an SE. Furthermore, it reflects where Danish law contains preconditions for the formation or operation of an SE. Finally, pursuant to Article 9(1) of the Regulation, some essential provisions of the Danish Companies Act[5] and other pieces of legislation applicable to SEs are outlined.

II Reasons to opt for an SE

2. The European character of an SE distinguishes it from other corporate forms in Denmark. Unfortunately, the initial lack of uniform rules throughout the EU will undoubtedly discourage, to a certain extent, use of the SE. Its main selling point, namely a reduction in costs due to an ability to operate in all Member States in accordance with a uniform set of rules, is not yet a reality.

---

[1] Act No. 363 of 19 May 2004 ('*lov om det europæiske selskab*').
[2] Act No. 364 of 19 May 2004 ('*lov om ændring af aktieselskabsloven mv.*').
[3] Act No. 281 of 26 April 2004 ('*lov om medarbejderindflydelse i SE-selskaber*').
[4] '*Aktieselskab*' in Danish, abbreviated 'A/S'.
[5] Consolidated Act No. 1001 of 8 October 2004, as amended ('*aktieselskabsloven*').

Uncertainty as to the handling of cross-border tax issues will most likely cause many of those considering the use of an SE to reconsider their position or at least to postpone taking a decision until tax harmonisation is a reality.

The ability to manage risk through several legal entities which are not jointly liable is lost in an SE structure. As many Danish businesses are small and medium-sized enterprises, the costs related to formation of an SE will probably constitute a barrier to extensive use of this corporate form.

On the other hand, savings on administrative costs with respect to the preparation of annual accounts, auditing, etc. may be particularly advantageous for an SE. For financial undertakings, the possibility of being subject to supervision primarily by the authorities of only one Member State and the ability to go cherry picking in this regard bode in favour of the SE.

As cross-border mergers and takeovers are common and on the rise in Denmark, we believe the SE will at least be worth considering when contemplating a cross-border transaction or reorganisation. Takeover rules for listed companies do not apply to control obtained in connection with a merger, so that it may be possible to avoid an otherwise mandatory takeover bid if the transaction is structured as the formation of an SE by merger. In cross-border transactions, the potential positive psychological effects of two companies merging as opposed to one being taken over by the other should not be disregarded.

The possibilities related to cross-border mergers and transfer of an SE's registered office are interesting new features. Furthermore, the ability of a Danish SE to distribute dividends tax free to its shareholders makes Denmark a country worth considering when deciding where to register an SE.

III Formation

1 General remarks

A Founding parties

3. In general, participation in the formation of an A/S is not subject to any restrictions. A company with its head office outside the European Union[6] can participate in the formation of an SE in Denmark, provided certain conditions are met (Art. 4 SE Act; Art. 2 Reg.), such as that the company must have a real and continuous link with the economy of a Member State (Art. 2(5) Reg.;

---

[6] References to the 'Community' and 'Member States' should be construed as synonymous with the European Union (EU), which is deemed to include the EEA countries.

see also Chap. 2, no. 19 of this book).[7] The restrictions on the participation of legal entities in the various SE formation procedures also apply in Denmark (see Chap. 2, no. 22 *et seq.* of this book).

Any legal entity or person who has filed for bankruptcy or has ceased payments may not act as the founder of an SE (Art. 3(2) Companies Act). The same holds true for persons convicted of certain criminal offences (Art. 79(2) Criminal Code).[8]

4. An SE is a legal entity separate from its founders, who, as a general rule, are only liable for their initial capital contributions. Absent an agreement to the contrary, creditors with claims against shareholders cannot reach the assets of an SE, and shareholders are not liable for an SE's debts (see Chap. 2, no. 7 of this book). A founder can be held liable for negligence, however.

B Name

5. An SE is obligated and solely entitled[9] to use the abbreviation 'SE' in its name.[10] An SE's name must clearly distinguish it from other companies. An SE is not allowed to include in its name any family or business name or any references to real property, trademarks, etc. that do not belong to it. The name also must not be misleading (Art. 153(2) and (3) Companies Act).[11]

The Danish Commerce and Companies Agency (the 'Agency')[12] shall decide whether a name can be registered. At the request of an interested party, the Agency can decide to delete a registration if the company's name is confusingly similar to that of another legal entity.

In certain circumstances, an SE must add a description to its name, such as '*under flytning*' (transfer pending) after publication of a transfer proposal (Art. 7(4) SE Act) and '*under stiftelse*' (in formation) during formation (Art. 12(4) Companies Act). Likewise, during liquidation and in bankruptcy a reference to this effect must be added (see nos. 51 and 55 of this report).

---

[7] Twenty-third Recital of the Regulation and Bill No 142, *Danish Parliamentary Gazette* 2003/2004, Addendum A, 4995 *et seq.*

[8] Consolidated Act No. 960 of 21 September 2004, as amended ('*straffeloven*').

[9] However, other Danish companies with the abbreviation 'SE' in their names can maintain this abbreviation if the name was registered prior to 8 October 2004.

[10] If those acting on behalf of an SE do not use the abbreviation 'SE' or otherwise indicate to third parties that they are dealing with a limited liability company, they may be held personally liable. However, under Danish law is it uncertain whether a company holding itself out as an SE will be treated as having minimum share capital of €120,000; rather, the company's management risks incurring personal liability.

[11] A change of name is required if the business to which a name is linked undergoes a material change.

[12] '*Erhvervs- og Selskabsstyrelsen*' in Danish.

Secondary names are allowed but must be followed by the primary name in parentheses.[13] An SE is not obliged to use a secondary name. An SE's full primary or secondary name, address and registration number must be indicated on certain corporate and business documents[14] (Art. 153(6) Companies Act; Art. 7 e-Commerce Act;[15] see also Chap. 2, no. 11 of this book).

C Registered Office

6. The registered office and head office of a Danish SE must be in the same place (Art. 7 Reg.).[16] If both are not located in Denmark, the Agency can request the competent probate court to liquidate the SE (Art. 15 SE Act; Art. 64(2) Reg.), although the SE will be granted a deadline by which to regularise its situation. In similar circumstances, an A/S will normally be given four weeks; however, in view of the extensive formalities an SE must accomplish,[17] a longer deadline will probably be granted. Administrative review of the Agency's decision is not possible. However, in accordance with the Regulation's requirement that such a decision be subject to judicial review (Art. 64(3) Reg.), an appeal can be lodged with the competent court (Art. 20(2) SE Act).

The requirement that an SE have its registered office and head office in the same Member State has been called into question in the Danish literature,[18] with specific references to the *Überseering*,[19] *Inspire Art*[20] and *Centros Ltd.*[21] cases. The argument is that this requirement violates freedom of establishment (Arts. 43 and 48 EC Treaty) and thus cannot be maintained or enforced.

If an SE does not have its registered office and head office within the same municipality, the Agency can fine the SE and the members of its organs until the situation has been regularised but, in these circumstances, it cannot force the SE into liquidation.

---

[13] For example if the primary name of an SE is 'Kromann Reumert SE' and its secondary name is 'KR SE', the secondary name must be used in the following manner: 'KR SE (Kromann Reumert SE)'.

[14] Examples include letters, e-mails, faxes, business cards, web pages, etc.

[15] Act No. 227 of 22 April 2002 on e-commerce (*'e-handelsloven'*).

[16] In Denmark, this implies that the registered office and head office must be in the same municipality (*'kommune'*).

[17] These formalities relate to the transfer of a head office or of a registered office to the country where the head office is located (Art. 8 Reg.).

[18] S. Friis Hansen, 'Free movement of companies – the head office theory is dead; long live the registration theory', *Nordisk Tidsskrift for Selskabsret*, no. 4, 2003, 444, and E. Werlauff, 'Cross-boarder transfer of an SE – a registered office requirement in violation of the Treaty', *Ugeskrift for Retsvæsen 2004*, chap. B, 242.

[19] European Court of Justice, 5 November 2002, *European Court Reports*, I-9919.

[20] European Court of Justice, 30 September 2003, *European Court Reports*, I-10155.

[21] European Court of Justice, 9 March 1999, *European Court Reports*, I-1459.

7. The proposed transfer of the registered office of an SE outside Denmark must be published in the national official gazette at least two months in advance. The notice must call upon creditors and other rights holders to file their claims. Claims that arose prior to publication of the transfer proposal and within two weeks thereafter are admissible (Art. 7 SE Act). A transfer may not take place until all claims have been settled or adequate security provided, if so requested. The competent probate court decides whether security must be granted and whether the security offered is adequate. Disputes must be filed with the competent probate court within two weeks from the filing of a claim (Art. 7(2) SE Act).

Shareholders who oppose[22] the transfer at a general meeting may claim redemption of their shares within four weeks thereafter (Art. 6(1) SE Act). If the shareholders were asked before the general meeting whether they intended to redeem their shares, they must have issued a statement to this effect in order for the redemption to go through (Art. 6(1) *in fine* SE Act; cf. Art. 5(2) SE Act).

The shares will be redeemed at their fair market value. In the absence of an agreement, assessors approved or appointed by the competent probate court will determine the value. The suggested share exchange ratio can be challenged before the probate court within three months following its announcement.

If requested, security for the value of shares must be provided. If the adequacy of the security is called into question, the assessors[23] shall decide the matter. The Agency can only issue the required certificate (Art. 8(8) Reg.) once such a decision has been taken. A challenge to a decision before the probate courts does not generally affect the Agency's power to issue the certificate.

The Agency will register and make public the transfer of an SE to Denmark upon receipt of a certificate from the foreign competent authority evidencing that all requisite acts and formalities have been duly completed.

8. The content of a transfer proposal, its availability to shareholders and creditors, etc. are fully dealt with in the Regulation (Art. 8 Reg.), and no provisions on these matters have been included in the SE Act (see Chap. 2, no. 81 *et seq.* of this book).

A transfer proposal must be approved by shareholders at a general meeting by the same majority required to amend the company's articles,[24] i.e. a double

---

[22] The shareholders need not vote against a proposal to oppose it. For evidentiary purposes, however, it is important to have the opposition recorded in the minutes.
[23] The assessors are appointed by the probate court of the place where the SE's registered office is located.
[24] The articles form part of the founding document ('*stiftelsesdokument*') or instrument of incorporation. However, the founding document, as referred to in this report, is not part of the articles.

179

two-thirds majority[25] (Art. 78 Companies Act; see also no. 31 of this report). A decision to transfer the registered office must be filed with the Agency within two weeks following its adoption.

The option to grant the authorities of a Member State the right to oppose a transfer on the grounds of public interest has not been adopted in Denmark. Accordingly, a veto applies only with respect to financial institutions (Art. 19 SE Act; cf. Art. 8(14) Reg. and Chap. 2, no. 82 *in fine*).

D   Corporate purpose

9. The corporate purpose of an SE must be stated in its articles and must cover the entire business of the SE, including that of its subsidiaries and branches. A corporate purpose which is too broad[26] cannot be registered.

E   Capital

10. Denmark has not introduced the euro as its national currency. The share capital of an SE may be denominated in both euros and Danish kroner[27] (Art. 2 SE Act). The minimum share capital is €120,000 or the equivalent in DKK.[28,29] The share capital must be fully paid in (Art. 11(2) Companies Act). If an SE is established in a Member State which does not impose such a requirement, the SE must ensure that its share capital is fully paid in before it can transfer its registered office to Denmark.

11. If an SE has more than one class of shares, its articles must define the rights of the various classes,[30] their size and any rights of first refusal accorded the shareholders of each class (Art. 17 Companies Act). The difference between the voting rights of two classes of shares may not exceed a ratio of 1:10 (Art. 67 Companies Act).

12. A shareholder who holds more than 5% of the share capital of an SE (with a nominal value of at least €24,000 or the equivalent in DKK)[31] must notify the SE of this fact within four weeks of acquiring such a shareholding and must inform the company if the shareholding falls below or increases above 5% or rises above or falls below one-third or two-thirds in aggregate. The SE must

---

[25] Two-thirds of both (i) the votes cast and (ii) the share capital entitled to vote which is present or represented at the general meeting. Contrary to the normal practice under Danish law, blank ballots are not taken into account (Art. 58 Reg.).
[26] According to the Agency's practice, examples of a corporate purpose that is too broad include 'earn dividends for shareholders' and 'trade, industry and related business'.
[27] Abbreviated '*DKK*'.
[28] For the calculation procedure, see Chap. 2, no. 16 of this book.
[29] Certain entities, e.g. financial institutions and insurance companies, must have and maintain a higher share capital.
[30] Such as a preferred right to dividends, differences in voting rights, etc.
[31] For the calculation procedure, see footnote 28.

keep a publicly available record of such notices (Art. 28a and 28b Companies Act) and a shareholders' register (Art. 25 Companies Act).

If a shareholder holds 90% or more of the share capital and voting rights of an SE, that shareholder, along with the administrative or supervisory organ, as the case may be, can force the minority shareholders to transfer their shares. Minority shareholders are given four weeks' notice. The notice must set out the conditions for the transfer, including the purchase price[32] (Arts. 19(2) and 20b Companies Act). Minority shareholders who do not voluntarily transfer their shares shall be given an additional three or six months' notice via the official gazette. Upon expiry of this period, their shares shall be deemed transferred automatically (Art. 20c Companies Act). Minority shareholders can also force a shareholder who holds 90% or more of an SE's share capital to acquire their shares. A similar share-exchange ratio procedure applies. Takeover bids are under certain conditions regulated by statute with respect to holding or acquiring shares in a listed SE.[33]

Absent exceptional circumstances, an SE may not hold more than 10% of its own shares. In any event, the total share capital less the face value of its own shares must exceed the minimum capital requirement (Art. 48 Companies Act). Exceptional circumstances will be found to exist if an SE is forced to acquire more than 10% of its own shares in a stock redemption following a transfer or a merger (Art. 48b(3) Companies Act; see nos. 7 and 19 of this report). If an SE in this manner ends up holding more than 10% of its own shares, it must dispose of the surplus as soon as possible and in any event within three years following acquisition. This implies that the shares must be sold to the first acceptable buyer. If no buyer can be found, the share capital must be decreased accordingly (Art. 48f Companies Act).

13. If an SE has lost 50% or more of its share capital, the management or administrative organ must call a general meeting to explain the financial situation of the SE. If necessary, measures to remedy the situation must be adopted (Art. 69a Companies Act).[34]

14. It is prohibited to extend loans to or secure the obligations of shareholders, members of management and persons or entities closely related to an SE or its parent company (Art. 115(1) Companies Act).[35] This prohibition does not

---

[32] Absent agreement on the share exchange ratio, assessors appointed by the competent probate court shall establish the fair market value. If they arrive at a higher ratio than that offered by the majority shareholders, this ratio shall apply to all minority shareholders, not only those who objected to the proposed ratio (Art. 20b(3) Companies Act).

[33] Such as the acquisition of voting rights, decisive influence and holding of more than one-third of the share capital, the right to appoint or remove the majority of members of the administrative or supervisory organ, etc. (Art. 31 Securities Act).

[34] Such as a decision to wind up the company, if necessary.

[35] In this respect, the term 'parent company' includes parent companies, 'grandparent' companies, etc.

apply to EU-based parent companies[36] and shareholders, members of management, and persons or entities closely related thereto in parent companies located outside the European Union (Art. 115a(1) Companies Act). Transactions in the ordinary course of business[37] fall outside the scope of the prohibition, as well.[38] Consequently, under certain conditions, an SE can participate in cash pooling arrangements.

An SE is barred from financing the acquisition of its own shares or of shares in a parent company located within the European Union (Art. 115(2), cf. Art. 115a(2) Companies Act).[39]

15. Normally, the annual general meeting decides whether to distribute dividends when it approves the annual accounts. Only the aggregate net profits[40] less amounts deducted from equity or otherwise provided for may be distributed and only as suggested by the management or administrative organ (Arts. 109 and 110 Companies Act). However, the general meeting may, by way of an inclusion in the articles, authorise the management or administrative organ to distribute interim dividends in the period preceding the next ordinary general meeting. Such distribution must be based on an interim balance sheet, examined and endorsed by the company's auditor, showing sufficient funds (Art. 109a Companies Act), and no distribution may take place until the amendment to the articles has been recorded and published by the Agency. When deciding to distribute interim dividends, the management or administrative organ must issue a statement confirming that the distribution does not exceed justifiable limits, taking into account the financial situation of the SE and its subsidiaries.

16. Decisions regarding capital increases and decreases and convertible bonds and securities are taken in accordance with and must follow the rules set forth in the Companies Act.[41]

If a capital increase is effected through a contribution in kind, a valuation report stating that the value of the contributed assets is at least equal to the amount of the increase and any premium, dated no more than four weeks prior to the general meeting scheduled to vote on the increase, must be prepared by certified valuators (Arts. 6–6b and 33 Companies Act). If a capital increase in cash is

---

[36] In this context, however, the ultimate parent company based in the European Union or the EEA is only included if it resembles a Danish A/S or ApS.
[37] Such as would have been performed by another entity in the same line of business.
[38] Bill No. L 119, *Danish Parliamentary Gazette* 1981/82, Addendum A, 2884.
[39] The Agency considers the position on shareholder loans/security and self-financing unfortunate and is currently considering how to revise the Danish rules in this respect.
[40] Including net profits not distributed in previous years.
[41] Capital increases (Chapter 5), convertible bonds, etc. (Chapter 6) and capital decreases (Chapter 7).

made to facilitate an acquisition of specific assets,[42] a similar report on the value of the assets to be acquired is required. The latter requirement may pose a problem in transactions where an 'unvalued' premium for goodwill constitutes a significant portion of the purchase price.

A capital decrease for the purpose of distributing dividends to shareholders must be proposed or approved by the management or administrative organ. Before distribution can occur, a notice must be published in the official gazette informing creditors that they have at least three months to file claims. Distribution must await settlement of any claims submitted or the provision of adequate security.

17. Decisions regarding a capital increase or decrease must be filed with the Agency within four weeks of adoption (Art. 156 and Chapter 19 Companies Act). Failure to meet this deadline shall not cause a decision to be invalid, but the SE and/or the members of its organs may be fined accordingly. Most decisions regarding capital increases or decreases become null and void if not registered within one year following adoption, however.

2 Different means of formation

A Formation by merger

18. The Regulation extensively governs the formation of an SE by merger and the related procedures (see Chap. 2, nos. 22–33 of this book), and most of the merger provisions in the Danish Companies Act also apply. Consequently, only a few additional provisions on formation by merger have been included in the SE Act.

If an A/S participates in the formation of an SE by merger, its board of directors is responsible for preparing draft terms of merger and a management report (*see* Chap. 2, no. 25 *et seq.* of this book).

The option to grant the national authorities a veto has been introduced only with respect to financial institutions (Art. 19 SE Act). Certain conditions apply (see Chap. 2, no. 23 of this book), and in Denmark the only possible reason for exercising the veto is to ensure the safety and proper functioning of the financial sector.[43]

As the Danish rules facilitating a merger between a parent company and a subsidiary apply only to wholly owned subsidiaries, the option set forth in the Regulation (Art. 31(2) Reg.) has not been adopted in Denmark. The abridged

---

[42] Such as the acquisition of the shares or assets of a business.
[43] Such as the security of the payments system or the functioning of capital markets (Bill No. 142, *Danish Parliamentary Gazette* 2003/2004, Addendum A, 4995 *et seq.*).

procedure applies only to mergers with wholly owned subsidiaries, with the modification that the board of directors can approve the merger (Art. 31(1) Reg.).

19. Shareholders who oppose a merger may ask to have their shares in the merging companies redeemed. The same requirements with regard to the nature and scope of the opposition, the valuation procedure, and the issuance of a certificate by the Agency, etc. apply (see, e.g. no. 7 of this report).

Under Danish law, the independent experts who examine the draft terms of merger (Art. 22 Reg.) may be, and often are, the auditor(s) of any of the merging companies.[44]

20. A number of provisions of the Companies Act apply to the formation of an SE by merger (Art. 134–134i Companies Act), the most significant being: (1) the draft terms of merger must include any secondary names of the continuing company; (2) the share exchange ratio must be explained and justified in the report on the draft terms of merger and an accounting report with a balance sheet that predates the signing of the draft terms of merger by no more than six months must be attached thereto; (3) the experts must issue a statement on the protection of creditors; (4) a certified copy of the signed draft terms of merger must be received by the Agency within four weeks after signing; (5) the draft terms of merger, the last three years' annual accounts of all participating companies, the report of the board of directors and all expert statements must be made available to shareholders at the offices of all participating Danish companies at least four weeks prior to the general meeting scheduled to vote on the merger; and (6) the general meeting voting on the merger may not be held within the first four weeks following publication by the Agency of the draft terms of merger and the expert statements.

All merger documents shall be published through the Agency's electronic system (Arts. 158 and 158a Companies Act and Art. 32 Filing Order).

The general meeting must approve the merger by a double two-thirds majority (see no. 31 of this report), and the Agency must be notified of this fact within two weeks' time (Art. 134i(1) Companies Act). If organ members and auditors have not been appointed in a new SE formed by merger, a general meeting to fill these positions must be held no later than two weeks after adoption of the merger proposal (Art. 134h(5) Companies Act).

A merger to form an SE cannot be declared void after registration (Art. 30 Reg.), contrary to what is normally the case in Denmark (Art. 81 Companies Act).

A merger implies the assumption of all rights and obligations of the merging companies, so registration of any 'change' in ownership of certain types of

---

[44] E. Werlauff, 'SE-selskabet – det europæiske aktieselskab', *Jurist- og Økonomforbundets Forlag*, 2002, 47.

assets, e.g., real property, cars, aircraft, listed shares, etc., is not required. The registration formalities that do apply do not constitute acts of security and are for informational purposes only. To be able to grant security in such assets, however, the 'new' entity must be registered as the owner.

B Formation of a holding SE

21. The Regulation sets forth many provisions applicable to the formation of a holding SE, e.g. draft terms of formation, decision procedures, etc. (see Chap. 2, no. 36 *et seq.*).

Shareholders that oppose the formation of a holding SE can decide not to contribute their shares and thus will remain shareholders in the holding SE's subsidiary. No further protection of such shareholders has been introduced.

As the contribution to the holding SE will be shares in other companies, the transaction is a contribution in kind, which requires a valuation report (Arts. 6–6b Companies Act; see also no. 16 of this report). If a new holding SE acquires assets from its founders or shareholders in the period between signature of the draft terms of formation and the first 24 months following registration without this acquisition being directly linked to its formation, the general meeting must approve the acquisition if the consideration equals at least 10% of the SE's share capital. In addition, a valuation report must be prepared for any assets so acquired (see no. 16 of this report).

22. The articles of an SE must contain the following information: (1) the company's name and secondary names; (2) the address of its registered office; (3) its corporate purpose; (4) its share capital; (5) the voting rights attached to its shares; (6) whether the shares are registered or bearer; (7) whether the shares are non-transferable; (8) the minimum and maximum number of auditors and organ members and the length of their term of office as well as any limitations on their signatory powers; (9) the procedure for calling general meetings; and (10) the company's financial year (Art. 4 Companies Act).

An application to register a holding SE must be filed within six months of signature of the draft terms of formation (Art. 11 Companies Act). Pending registration, the SE must add '*under stiftelse*' (in formation) to its name (see no. 5 of this report).

C Formation of a subsidiary SE

23. The rules on formation of an A/S apply to the formation of a subsidiary SE. Only one founder is required. Both SEs and other legal entities[45] can form

---

[45] Such as an A/S, a private limited company (*ApS*), a limited partnership (*P/S*) or a cooperative limited liability company (*andelsselskab*).

a subsidiary SE without any cross-border restrictions, but the founder must be a legal entity within the meaning of Article 58 of the EC Treaty (see Chap. 2, no. 44 of this book).

Application of the Regulation implies that sole shareholders must be listed in a publicly available register (Art. 3(2) *in fine* Reg.). If an SE has only one shareholder, decisions taken by that shareholder as well as agreements between the SE and its shareholder must be in writing.

The draft terms of formation must contain the following information: (1) the name, title and address of the founder; (2) the subscription price and deadline for subscription; (3) the deadline for the first general meeting; (4) whether the company must pay formation costs; (5) who can subscribe the shares; (6) contributions in kind, if any; and (7) special rights or agreements entailing material financial obligations entered into with the founder(s) or others. The articles of a subsidiary SE must meet certain requirements (Art. 4 Companies Act; see also no. 22 of this report). If the main content of a document referred to in the draft terms of formation is not set forth therein, the document must be attached (Art. 6 Companies Act).

Contributions in kind must be valued (see no. 16 of this report) and cannot consist of a claim against or an obligation of founders or shareholders to perform services (Art. 5 Companies Act).

The terms of formation and the SE's articles must be adopted at the first general meeting. The subscription of shares can occur immediately thereafter (Art. 9(2) Companies Act) or by a certain date.

The submission deadline is four weeks. Pending registration, the SE must add '*under stiftelse*' (in formation) to its name (see no. 5 of this report).

D　　Conversion into an SE

24. The Regulation contains a number of provisions governing the conversion of an A/S into an SE (see Chap. 2, no. 46 *et seq.* of this book). Only a few provisions of Danish law are applicable to this procedure.

The articles of an SE must meet certain requirements (Art. 4 Companies Act; see also Chap. 2, no. 22 of this book).

The option contained in the Regulation to make conversion contingent on approval by a qualified majority or unanimity in the organ of the company to be converted within which employee participation is organised (Art. 37(8) Reg.) has not been adopted in Denmark. The general meeting holds exclusive power in this respect and must approve the conversion by a double two-thirds majority (see no. 31 of this report).[46]

---

[46] If the company's articles require a higher majority to approve a merger, this threshold will probably also apply to conversion of an A/S into an SE, see E. Werlauff, *op. cit.*, 69.

An SE cannot be converted back into an A/S within the first two years following its registration and even then only if it has submitted at least two annual accounts (Art. 66 Reg., see also Chap. 2, no. 90 of this book). Furthermore, an SE most likely cannot be converted into an ApS or a P/S until the conditions for conversion into an A/S have been satisfied, even though this would imply that an SE has fewer rights than an A/S. Even though the Companies Act applies to a P/S and to co-operative limited liability companies, these entities cannot be converted into an SE.[47]

Under certain conditions, the general meeting must approve acquisitions from shareholders on the basis of a valuation report (see nos. 16 and 21 of this report).

3 Acts committed on behalf of an SE in formation

25. Prior to registration, an SE cannot incur rights or obligations or be a party to legal proceedings, other than in relation to the subscription of its shares (Art. 12(1) Companies Act). Those who incur obligations on behalf of an SE in formation, either themselves or in co-operation with others, shall be held jointly, severally and personally liable. Upon registration, the SE shall assume the obligations referred to in the draft terms of formation and any obligations towards third parties who knew they were dealing with an SE in formation (Art. 12(2) Companies Act; Art. 16(2) Reg.). Upon the SE's assumption of liability, personal liability for those who incurred the obligations shall cease to exist. Pending formation, the SE must add '*under stiftelse*' (in formation) to its name (see no. 5 of this report).

4 Registration and publication

26. The Agency is responsible for filings, submissions, notifications, registrations, etc. in relation to SEs. Publication is done by electronic means, and certain information (e.g., the company number, name, and address) is available to the public on the Agency's website (www.publi-com.dk). In some cases, publication in the official gazette is also required.[48] The Agency must receive filings and the like by established deadlines (Art. 154–159b Companies Act; see also the Filing Order).

5 Acquisition of legal personality

27. An SE acquires legal personality upon registration (Art. 16 Reg., cf. Art. 12 Reg.). Legal personality implies the ability to acquire rights, incur obligations

---

[47] To become an SE, these types of entities must first be converted into an A/S in accordance with the procedure set out in the Companies Act.
[48] Such as the transfer of an SE's registered office from Denmark, a capital decrease for the purpose of distributing dividends to shareholders, etc.

and carry out transactions in this respect. Only a registered SE can be a party and act in relation to legal proceedings (see Chap. 2, no. 7 of this book).[49]

IV Organisation and management

1 General remarks

28. Any matter regarding an SE can be presented to the general meeting for decision. In addition to the general meeting, an A/S has a board of directors and manager(s). Danish law allows the articles to provide that minority shareholders or others are entitled to appoint board members. This also holds true for the higher organs of an SE.

29. The managers of an A/S are entrusted with the day-to-day running of the company,[50] including ensuring that accounting methods comply with applicable regulations and that assets are managed properly (Art. 54(3) Companies Act).

The board of directors of an A/S has authority in all other matters, including the supervision of and issuance of general and specific instructions to management. Other responsibilities of the board include: (1) ensuring proper organisation of the company's business and issuing general guidelines for the conduct thereof; (2) taking decisions on matters that fall outside the scope of day-to-day operations; (3) determining whether the company's financial position is sound; and (4) ensuring proper oversight of accounting methods and asset management (Art. 54(1)–(3) Companies Act).

The board of directors plays an active role in an A/S and must be composed of at least three members, the majority of whom cannot be managers. Furthermore, a manager cannot serve as chairman of the board. However, members of the board may serve as managers and vice versa.

For the purposes of the Regulation and to ensure a practical rather than a formal approach, the management structure of an A/S is deemed a one-tier system, regardless of its two constituent 'bodies'. This choice requires the fewest changes to existing law and offers the greatest degree of flexibility and security to Danish SEs.[51]

---

[49] A summons served by an unregistered SE as plaintiff will be dismissed and a deed naming an unregistered SE the owner of real property will not be recorded.

[50] Such operations do not include transactions that are unusual or of great significance in light of the company's financial situation, such as the purchase or sale of real property and businesses, etc. (Art. 54(1) Companies Act).

[51] Erhvers- OG Selskabsstyrelsen, 'Det europæiske selskab (SE) – Debatoplæg vedrørende selskabsretlig indarbejdelse af Rådets forordning (EF) nr. 2157/2001 om statut for det europæiske selskab (SE)', *Økonomi- og Erhvervsministeriet*, 42.

30. The articles of an A/S may provide that the general meeting can also elect a committee of at least five shareholders, who cannot be board members or managers (Art. 59 Companies Act). This committee supervises the other corporate organs of the A/S, somewhat like the supervisory organ in a two-tier SE. If the articles so provide, the shareholder committee can appoint members of the board of directors and establish their remuneration, but it cannot exercise other powers. Regardless of the obvious similarities between a shareholder committee and the supervisory organ of an SE, it will probably be possible to establish such a committee in a two-tier SE.[52]

2 General meeting

A Decision-making process

31. Unless otherwise provided, the general meeting adopts resolutions by a simple majority of votes cast.[53] Under certain circumstances, such as an amendment to the articles of association, a double two-thirds majority is required (e.g., Art. 78 Companies Act; see also Chap. 2, no. 8 of this book). The general meeting must approve amendments to the articles resulting from the arrangements on employee involvement, contrary to the option set forth in the Regulation (Art. 12(4) Reg.). It is not possible for the general meeting to adopt decisions that normally require a qualified majority by a simple majority of votes cast if 50% or more of the share capital is present or represented.

National law may require a greater majority to amend the SE's articles, etc. than does the Regulation (Art. 59(1) Reg.). It has been debated in Denmark[54] whether the double two-thirds majority qualifies as such. This majority affords extended protection to minority shareholders (Art. 59(1) Reg.) and should thus arguably be maintained. However, blank ballots may not be taken into account (Art. 58 Reg.; see also Chap. 2, no. 64 of this book).

Certain decisions, such as the placement of restrictions on the rights of shareholders and the transferability of shares, must be approved by 90% of the votes cast, and the same majority of (voting) shares must be present or represented at the general meeting. All shareholders must adhere to decisions to increase their obligations to an SE (Art. 79 Companies Act). To further protect minority shareholders, the general meeting is not allowed to adopt (or refrain from

---

[52] *Ibid.*, 94; however, E. Werlauff, *op. cit.*, 71 rules out the possibility of electing a shareholder committee.

[53] This implies that a simple majority has been obtained if three proposals receive four, three and two votes, respectively, out of a total of nine votes.

[54] Support for this point can be found in Erhvers- OG Selskabsstyrelsen, *op. cit.*, 52 and 118. For an opposite view, see E. Werlauff, *op. cit.*, 117.

adopting) a decision if to do so would grant certain shareholders or others an unfair advantage (Art. 80 Companies Act).[55]

32. Under the Companies Act, the general meeting of an SE has exclusive authority for certain matters, the most significant being: (1) approval of certain acquisitions from founders or shareholders (Art. 6c(1)); (2) approval of the annual accounts and the distribution of profits or the appropriation of losses[56] (Art. 69(2)); (3) the discharge of directors from liability (Art. 69(5)); (4) the appointment of auditors (Art. 82(1)); (5) the resumption of business during liquidation (Art. 126(1)); (6) conversion of the company into another corporate form (Arts. 134l and 134m); (7) demerger (Art. 136); and (8) the commencement of legal proceedings against members of the corporate organs (Art. 144).

The SE's highest organ usually convenes the general meeting (Art. 72 Companies Act), but under certain circumstances shareholders (see no. 33 of this report), auditors, organs or their members, and the Agency are entitled to do so (Arts. 69a and 70 Companies Act).

B Rights and obligations of shareholders

33. As required by the Regulation, Danish law provides that minority shareholders can call a general meeting (Art. 70 Companies Act). Any shareholder is entitled to have an item placed on the agenda of a general meeting if the request is made in time (Art. 71 Companies Act).

Otherwise, shareholders primarily have a right to speak and vote at the general meeting. A shareholder may attend a general meeting in person, together with an adviser, or be represented by a person in possession of a dated and signed proxy (Art. 66 Companies Act). If the articles so provide, the right to vote on acquired shares may be limited to cases where the transfer has been recorded in the shareholders' register or where the shareholder has notified the SE of the transfer and produced evidence to this effect (Art. 67(2) Companies Act). Shareholders have the right to receive dividends if a decision to distribute dividends is adopted by the general meeting (see no. 15 of this report).

Unless otherwise set forth in the articles, the management or administrative organ may decide that shareholders can participate in the general meaning by electronic means (Art. 65a Companies Act), and meetings can be held in the same manner if the articles so allow. Communication between the SE and its shareholders may occur electronically if the articles or an individual shareholder so permit (Art. 65b Companies Act). A decision to amend the articles to reflect the above provisions requires, in addition to the aforementioned double

---

[55] To a lesser extent, the purpose of this restriction is also to protect a majority shareholder against an 'angry' minority.
[56] This must occur at least once each year.

two-thirds majority, that shareholders holding 25% or more of the voting shares do not vote against it.

Shareholders are not obliged to make further capital contributions to an SE or to assume or guarantee the company's liabilities. If a shareholder commingles its funds with those of an SE or acts negligently, that shareholder may be held liable for the obligations of the SE or to third parties under general rules of Danish law (see nos. 4 and 41 of this report).[57]

3 Management and supervision

A Two-tier/one-tier system

34. The management system of an A/S is deemed a one-tier system (see no. 29 of this report). However, as the existing structure of an A/S is in reality a cross between a one-tier and a two-tier system, it was to a certain extent necessary to set forth the responsibilities of the supervisory, management and administration organs in the SE Act.

35. The supervisory and management organs in the two-tier system have certain rights and responsibilities (see Chap. 2, no. 67 *et seq.* of this book). In a Danish two-tier SE, it is not possible to appoint general managers. Rather, the management organ holds the rights and responsibilities of both the board of directors and the managers.

However, certain rights and responsibilities have been granted specifically to members of both the supervisory and management organs, such as: (1) the obligation to notify the SE of ownership interests in the SE and its group; (2) a prohibition against engaging in speculative transactions; (3) the obligation to submit information to the SE's auditor(s) and the general meeting; (4) the right to resign at any time; (5) the obligation to keep minutes and adopt rules of procedure; (6) the obligation to submit annual accounts; (6) the right to file for bankruptcy; and (7) a duty of confidentiality (Art. 8(4) SE Act).

In the two-tier system, the supervisory organ must have at least three members and the management organ one member. There is no maximum number. Each member of the supervisory organ has the right to request information from the management organ, and such information must be distributed to all members of the supervisory organ. The supervisory organ can decide that certain actions require its approval (Art. 10 SE Act).

There is no limit on the period of time during which a member of the supervisory organ can fill a vacancy on the management organ, but during this time that member cannot continue to sit on the supervisory organ. Members of the

---

[57] For more information regarding the concept of negligence under Danish law, see no. 41 of this report.

management organ are entitled to attend the meetings of the supervisory organ (Art. 56 Companies Act).

36. The administrative organ in a one-tier SE has certain rights and responsibilities (see Chap. 2, no. 67 *et seq.* of this book). In a one-tier SE, the administrative organ must appoint one or more general managers to handle the day-to-day running of the company. The administrative organ must have at least three members, the majority of whom may not also be general managers. There is no maximum number. The duties of the board of directors and the managers in an A/S are allocated to the administrative organ and the general managers of an SE, respectively (see no. 29 of this report).

37. If certain decisions are to be reserved to the supervisory or administrative organ, a mention to this effect must be made in the articles (Art. 48(1) Reg.), but no requirements with regard to such decisions have been established.

The supervisory and administrative organs must (and the management organ may) elect a chair. In an A/S, the chair casts the deciding vote if the articles so provide. In an SE, however, the chair has the deciding vote unless the articles provide otherwise (Art. 50(2) Reg.). The chair is responsible for ensuring that the organs meet when required (see Chap. 2, nos. 75 and 78 of this book) and that all members are duly summoned (Art. 56(2) Companies Act).

The supervisory, management and administrative organs are obliged to establish internal rules of procedure, but requirements to the content thereof apply only to listed SEs (Art. 56(7) Companies Act).

38. Under Danish law, only a shipping A/S can have a legal entity (a sole proprietorship or a general partnership) serve as a general manager. Thus, the option contained in the Regulation to have legal entities serve on the management organs of an SE (Art. 47 Reg.) is open only to a shipping SE (see Chap. 2, no. 69 of this book).

A group relation with an SE exists if a shareholder can appoint or remove more than half the members of its supervisory or administrative organ (Art. 2(2)(2) Companies Act).

B   Appointment and removal

39. Members of the supervisory and administrative organs are appointed by the general meeting, which can also remove them at any time and establishes their remuneration. The supervisory or administrative organ appoints and removes members of the management organ and the general managers and approves their remuneration. The general meeting has no such powers.

Danish law governs the appointment of general managers in a one-tier SE (Art. 43(1) Reg.). As is customary in Denmark, general managers may be appointed 'until further notice' even if members of SE organs are generally appointed for a limited term not to exceed six years (Art. 46(1) Reg.).

Members of management organs and general managers must be legally competent and not under any form of guardianship (Art. 52(1) Companies Act). Prior to appointment to an SE organ, nominees must inform the SE of any affiliation with the management bodies of other Danish companies (Art. 49(6) Companies Act). No residence requirements apply to members of SE organs.

C Representation

40. More than half the members must be present to form a quorum (Art. 57 Companies Act).

The articles must set forth who has the power to bind the SE.[58] The general rule is that any member of an SE organ has the power to sign alone (Art. 60(2) Companies Act). Members of the higher organ always hold a joint-signature right. The signatory power of individual members of an SE's organs may be limited only with respect to numbers, names and/or positions (Art. 60(3) Companies Act).[59] It is not possible to limit the signatory power of an organ member with reference to certain matters.[60]

A transaction entered into by one or more organ members on behalf of an SE is binding on the SE unless the member(s) acted either in violation of limitations on their authority as provided in the Companies Act or outside the corporate purpose of the SE and the third party in question knew or ought to have known of this fact (Art. 61(1) Companies Act).

In addition to the signatory rules, general rules on acting in accordance with a written, oral or implied power-of-attorney apply. To this end, any member of the organ responsible for the day-to-day running of an SE can usually bind the company with respect to the signing of purchase orders and other agreements in the ordinary course of business, the hiring of non-key personnel, etc. An employee who is usually allowed to act in relation to certain matters[61] can bind an SE by virtue of this implied authority.

Organ members may not participate in adopting decisions in which they or a person or entity closely related to them has a material interest liable to be contrary to that of the SE (Art. 58 Companies Act).

---

[58] When signing on behalf of an SE, it is important to clearly state that obligations are assumed on behalf of the SE, e.g. by signing 'for' or 'on behalf of'.
[59] Examples of such limitations include: 'joint signature by at least two organ members', 'joint signature by the chair and one organ member', 'the signatures of an organ member appointed by X and an organ member appointed by Y' or 'joint signature by Mr X and Ms Y'.
[60] Such as the purchase of real estate, transactions beyond a certain value, the removal of general managers, etc.
[61] Such as a purchaser, seller, HR manager, etc.

D Liability

41. All members of an SE's organs are liable for damage caused to the SE and its shareholders, creditors and other parties due to misconduct or negligence on their part. Liability towards the three latter groups is incurred under Danish law (Art. 140 Companies Act), whereas liability towards the SE is governed directly by the Regulation (Art. 51 Reg.). The concept of negligence, however, is the same, as in both cases it will be interpreted in accordance with general rules of Danish law.

An act shall be deemed negligent if a reasonably prudent person would have acted differently under the circumstances.[62] Moreover, in order to incur liability, it must have been possible to reasonably foresee the damage caused, taking into account the nature of the act or omission. The party claiming damages bears the burden of proof. Anyone who makes or maintains a transaction in violation of the prohibition against extending shareholder loans and engaging in self-financing (see no. 14 of this report) shall be held responsible for repaying the funds received plus interest at a fixed rate.

A decision to initiate legal proceedings against organ members must be adopted by the general meeting (Art. 144 Companies Act).

42. Non-compliance by organ members with certain obligations shall be punishable by a fine. Examples of punishable non-compliance include failure to meet deadlines and breach of the duty of confidentiality (Art. 160(1) Companies Act; Arts. 21–23 SE Act). Violation of Articles 11, 39–45 and 49 of the Regulation may result in the imposition of a fine (Art. 21(1) SE Act). In this respect, it should be noted that the duty of confidentiality expressed in the Companies Act is probably narrower in scope than that provided in the Regulation (Art. 49 Reg.).

V Employee involvement

1 Special negotiating body

43. Once the competent bodies of the companies participating in the formation of an SE have drawn up a plan for employee involvement, they must take the necessary steps as soon as possible to initiate negotiations with the employee representatives (Art. 3 Dir.; Art. 3 Employee Involvement Act).

The composition of the special negotiating body ('SNB') is rather complex. As a rule, an SNB is comprised of employee representatives from each applicable Member State, so that for each 10% (or part thereof) the employees from a

---

[62] Often the relevant question is whether organ members continued operations beyond the point of no return (by a reasonableness standard), took decisions without having an adequate basis for doing so or neglected their supervisory role.

Member State account for the aggregate number of employees involved, they are awarded one seat.[63] In the formation of an SE by merger, the total number of employee seats on the SNB is increased to ensure that employees from each discontinuing company are awarded at least one seat (Art. 7 Employee Involvement Act).

In order to register an SE, arrangements for employee involvement must have been concluded (Art. 12 Reg.). If the SNB of a Danish SE decides not to open negotiations or to terminate negotiations already underway, the employees of the participating companies must rely on Danish rules of information, consultation and employee participation (see nos. 44 and 46 of this report.).

44. The rules on information and consultation are currently contained in collective bargaining agreements and basically either entitle employees to elect trade union representatives and/or facilitate the establishment of works councils in larger companies. Generally, collective bargaining agreements provide that union representatives are entitled to participate in negotiations regarding conditions at work, wages, working hours, etc. The employees or their representatives must also be informed of intended collective dismissals[64] and the transfer of an SE's business.[65]

Recently, employees in companies not subject to a collective bargaining agreement have been granted rights similar to those described above, which are typically included in a collective bargaining agreement.[66]

45. Danish works councils differ from those in other Member States in that they consist of an equal number of employee and management representatives. An SE with a works council is obliged to inform its works council of the financial situation of the SE, the current state and probable trend of employment, and substantial organisational changes, including new production or administration methods. In extraordinary circumstances, an SE can impose a duty of confidentiality on members of its works council.

The Works Council Act[67] governs the conditions of undertakings or groups of undertakings considered to be Community-scale based on thresholds for

---

[63] For example, 24% implies three seats.
[64] Act No. 414 of 6 January 1994, as amended, with regard to notification in relation to large-scale redundancies ('*lov om varsling i forbindelse med afskedigelser af større omfang*').
[65] Consolidated Act No. 710 of 20 August 2002 on employee rights in relation to transfers of undertakings ('*virksomhedsoverdragelses-loven*').
[66] Act No. 303 of 2 May 2005 on information and consultation of employees, transposing Direction 2002/14/EC of the European Parliament and of the Council of 11 March 2002 establishing a general framework for the information and consultation of employees in the European Community.
[67] Act No. 371 of 22 May 1996, as amended ('*lov om europæiske samarbejdsudvalg*'), transposing Council Directive 94/45/EC of 22 September 1994 on the establishment of a European Works Council or a procedure in Community-scale undertakings and Community-scale groups of undertakings for the purposes of informing and consulting employees.

workforce size, unless a collective bargaining agreement contains obligations and rights at least equal to those set forth in the act. At present, only a few collective bargaining agreements contain rules on European works councils. Consequently, an SE is likely to be subject to the Works Councils Act.

2 Employee participation

46. Employees of an SE, its subsidiaries and establishments and/or their representative body are under certain circumstances entitled to elect, appoint, recommend or oppose the appointment of a certain number of members of the administrative or supervisory organ of an SE equal to the highest proportion applicable in the companies participating in the establishment of the SE (Art. 7 Dir.; Part 3b Annex and Art. 33(2) Employee Involvement Act).

The employees of an A/S are entitled to elect representatives to the board of directors if the A/S has employed at least 35 people on average over the last three years (Art. 49(2) Companies Act). The number of employee representatives so elected may equal up to half the number of members of the board of directors (elected by the general meeting) and, at the employees' request, may not be less than two.

Employee participation on the board of directors is based on the principle of equality, meaning that employee representatives have the same rights and obligations as other board members. Accordingly, employee representatives must safeguard the SE's interests, even to the detriment of its employees.

Furthermore, employees of a subsidiary SE registered in Denmark are entitled to elect a number of employee representatives to the board of directors of its (Danish) parent company (Art. 49(3) Companies Act).

3 Protection of employee representatives

47. Employee representatives are entitled to adequate paid time off to perform their duties. As employee representatives enjoy the same job protection as do union representatives and security committee members, they cannot be dismissed before consultation with their union or, in the absence of such an affiliation, before negotiation and mediation with the employee in question.

VI Annual accounts and consolidated accounts

1 Accounting principles

48. A financial year is usually 12 months. However, the first financial year of an A/S may last up to 18 months (Art. 15(2) Accounting Act).[68]

---

[68] Consolidated Act No. 196 of 23 March 2004, as amended ('*årsregnskabsloven*').

The financial year can be changed. An extension may only exceed 12 months under certain circumstances,[69] however, and can never exceed 18 months.

The first general meeting of an SE must be held within 18 months of its formation (Art. 13 SE Act). The annual accounts must be submitted to the Agency immediately after they have been approved by the general meeting, which may be held no later than five months after the close of the financial year (Art. 138 Accounting Act). Consequently, for practical purposes, an SE's first financial year probably cannot exceed $17^1/_2$ months.[70] An A/S may wait up to 23 months[71] after formation to submit its first annual accounts.

As envisaged above, a Danish SE must submit its annual accounts no later than five months (four months for a listed SE) following the end of the financial year. This rule results in a shortening of the six-month deadline for holding the ordinary general meeting (Art. 54(1) Reg.) and possibly violates freedom of establishment (Art. 54(1) Reg. and Arts. 43 and 48 EC Treaty). If so, this requirement cannot be maintained.

All Danish companies must draw up and submit annual accounts, and a parent SE must draw up consolidated annual accounts for its group. An SE is allowed to denominate its annual accounts in euros. Annual accounts must include at least: (1) an income statement; (2) a balance sheet; (3) notes; (4) a management statement; and (5) an auditor's endorsement. Further requirements may apply depending on the turnover and workforce of the SE. Pre-determined accounting principles must be applied. Bookkeeping requirements also apply to an SE, including the obligation to keep a double-entry system with supporting documents, to be able to track transactions, and to keep accounting documents for at least five years.

2 Auditors

49. The general meeting of an SE must appoint one or more auditors to audit the company's annual accounts. The auditor(s) may be either natural persons or an auditing firm. In a listed SE the auditors must be publicly certified, whereas either publicly certified or registered accountants can audit an unlisted SE (Art. 135 Accounting Act).

The auditor is a 'public watchdog' and must ascertain that the company's annual accounts present a true and fair view of its assets, liabilities, financial position and results (Art. 11(1) Accounting Act) as well as that quality control

---

[69] Such as the establishment of a new group relationship or a merger (Art. 15(3) Accounting Act).
[70] This leaves two weeks to prepare, adopt and submit the audited annual accounts.
[71] A financial year of 18 months plus a general meeting no later than five months from the close of the financial year.

requirements (Art. 12 Accounting Act) and basic preconditions (Arts. 13–16 Accounting Act) are met. If the annual accounts present a true and fair view, the auditor will give an unqualified endorsement. Otherwise, reservations must be made or additional information may be required. The audit is further documented by audit minutes, setting forth in detail the work carried out as well as any findings or remarks of the auditors in this respect.

VII Supervision by the national authorities

50. The Agency is the competent authority with which SEs must register.[72] The Agency is also responsible for handling the various supervisory obligations incumbent on the Member States (Art. 68(2) Reg.). The Agency has issued an executive order containing general and SE-specific content requirements, deadlines, etc. with respect to filings and submissions (the 'Filing Order').[73]

VIII Dissolution

1 Winding up

51. Winding up of an SE takes the form of liquidation (Chapter 14 Companies Act). The general meeting must approve the liquidation by a double two-thirds majority (see no. 31 of this report) and appoint one or more liquidators (Art. 120 Companies Act).[74] The liquidator assumes the responsibilities and obligations of the organ members (Art. 121(1) Companies Act). Pending liquidation, an SE must add 'i likvidation' (in liquidation) to its name.

The liquidator prepares an audited income statement for the period since the close of the last financial year. This statement is then made available to shareholders and the Agency (Art. 122 Companies Act). The liquidator must also publish a notice to creditors in the official gazette stating that they have three months to file their claims. The liquidator will notify creditors whether their claims have been accepted. Creditors whose claims are rejected have an additional three-month period within which to file a complaint with the bankruptcy court (Art. 123 Companies Act). Distribution to shareholders of liquidation proceeds can only take place once all accepted claims have been settled. Claims filed after the deadline stipulated in the official gazette will be settled with undistributed proceeds, if any (Art. 124 Companies Act).

---

[72] The draft terms of merger for merging insurance companies must be submitted to the Danish FSA, however.
[73] Executive Order No. 200 of 21 March 2005.
[74] Shareholders holding at least 25% of the nominal share capital may appoint their own liquidator, who will act in conjunction with the liquidator appointed by the general meeting.

If the circumstances that gave rise to liquidation are no longer present, the general meeting may decide that the SE shall resume business. In this situation, new organ members and auditor(s) must be appointed. If the share capital is below the minimum threshold, it must be re-established in full[75] (Art. 126 Companies Act).

52. The Agency can decide that an SE which fails to submit its annual accounts or to appoint members to applicable organs or auditors should be involuntarily liquidated and must decide so if the SE does not have its registered office and head office in the same Member State (see no. 6 of this report). The Agency can appoint an expert to draw up the required accounts and review the SE's accounting methods, books, etc. (Art. 118a Companies Act).

Otherwise, similar procedures as described above apply. However, if the general meeting wishes to halt the process of involuntary liquidation, the circumstance(s) that gave rise to the Agency's decision must be addressed. A decision by the general meeting to resume business must be taken and notified to the Agency no later than three months after the date on which the Agency asked the bankruptcy court to initiate liquidation proceedings. If within the preceding five years the SE has been subject to similar proceedings, the general meeting cannot decide to resume business (Art. 126(3) Companies Act).

53. Decisions on liquidation matters must be notified to the Agency within two weeks following adoption. Companies in liquidation cannot participate in mergers (Art. 134e(1) Companies Act). If the company's liabilities cannot be paid in full, the liquidator is legally obliged to file for bankruptcy (see no. 55 of this report).

2 Liquidation

54. Please refer to no. 52 *et seq.* of this report.

3 Insolvency

55. An SE can be declared bankrupt by the bankruptcy court if it is incapable of paying its debts as they fall due, unless this incapacity is only temporary (Art. 17(2) Bankruptcy Act).[76] During bankruptcy, the SE must add 'under konkurs' (in bankruptcy) to its name.

---

[75] However, if an SE has share capital in excess of the minimum required by law (i.e., €120,000), its share capital may be reduced to this amount in order to cover deficits, meaning that only the minimum share capital need be re-established.

[76] Consolidated Act No. 118 of 4 February 1997 as amended (*'konkursloven'*).

Generally, the date of notice[77] is the date when the bankruptcy court receives a petition for either bankruptcy, composition with creditors or cessation of payments (for the latter two scenarios, when they lead to bankruptcy).

A petition for bankruptcy must be filed with the bankruptcy court in the jurisdiction where the SE's registered office is located, either by the responsible organ of the SE, a liquidator or a creditor. Requirements as to the content of the petition apply (Arts. 22 and 23 Bankruptcy Act). If a debtor seeks a composition with creditors, the bankruptcy decision may be delayed one or more times for up to three months but cannot be postponed for more than twelve months in total (Arts. 24 and 25, cf. Art. 16e(2), Bankruptcy Act).

A declaration of bankruptcy implies that the company and its organs are deprived of their rights to act, including the right to dispose of assets. This responsibility is assumed by a trustee in bankruptcy appointed by the bankruptcy court. The trustee handles the estate, including the payment of debts, drawing up of accounts, etc. All debts become due and are settled in accordance with their priority. Creditors cannot seek satisfaction of their claims against the debtor's assets (save for secured debts). Transactions that took place prior to the notice date, e.g. certain grants of security and settlements of debts, may be invalidated depending on the timing and other circumstances.

4 Cessation of payments

56. An SE can file a petition for cessation of payments with the bankruptcy court of the place where its registered office is located (Chapter 2 Bankruptcy Act). Such a petition suspends the payment of debts,[78] and creditors cannot seek satisfaction of their claims against the SE's assets, save for those over which an unavoidable security has been established (Art. 16 Bankruptcy Act). The bankruptcy court will appoint a trustee[79] to send out accounting and asset information to all known creditors, together with an explanation of the reasons for the cessation of payments. Absent the trustee's consent, the SE may not carry out any material transactions (Art. 15(1) Bankruptcy Act). The bankruptcy court can halt the cessation of payments, e.g. if it lacks a reasonable purpose or if the entity in cessation of payments has acted unfairly. A cessation of payments cannot last more than 12 months.

Cessation of payments may occur without court involvement, in which case it has no legal consequences in respect of enforcement by creditors, etc.

---

[77] The notice date is used to compute certain periods of invalidity and to determine when a debtor will be deprived of the ability to act and of its rights, etc.

[78] Debts may still be settled in accordance with the rules of priority in order to avoid losses (Art. 15(1) Bankruptcy Act).

[79] The trustee may be someone proposed by a debtor filing for cessation of payments.

IX Applicable law

57. Except where otherwise provided (Art. 9(1) Reg.), an SE will be governed by applicable provisions of Danish law (see Chap. 2, nos. 94 and 95 of this book).

X Tax treatment

1 Income tax

58. Neither the Regulation nor the SE Act deals with the tax treatment of an SE. A Danish SE will generally be treated as an A/S for tax purposes. If an SE is registered in Denmark or if its place of effective (daily) management is in Denmark, it will as a rule be considered a resident of Denmark for tax purposes and thus subject to Danish tax rules, unless an applicable tax treaty provides otherwise. The foregoing applies both to the taxation of an SE following incorporation and to the taxation of a Danish company participating in the formation of an SE. The Danish company tax rate is 30%. Capital gains by Danish companies on the sale of shares in companies in which they have had an ownership interest of 20% or more for at least three years are not subject to tax.

59. An A/S can be converted into an SE without triggering any tax consequences. Participation by a Danish company in the formation of an SE can be a taxable or a tax-exempt event. The Danish Act on Taxation of Mergers[80] provides for tax-exempt 'mergers' and 'contributions of assets' and the Act on Taxation of Capital Gains on Shares[81] provides for tax-exempt 'exchanges of shares'. The provisions of these acts are based on the EU Merger Directive.[82] Generally speaking, in order for a transaction to be tax-exempt, the assets and liabilities in question must remain subject to tax in Denmark. Consequently, following a merger or other transaction, assets and liabilities must be attributable to a Danish permanent establishment and may not leave Denmark without taxation.

60. The Parent-Subsidiary Directive[83] (as amended)[84] has been transposed into Danish law and entered into effect on 1 January 2005.[85] An SE is covered by

---

[80] Consolidated Act No. 821 of 30 September 2003, as amended, on mergers, demergers and contributions of assets, etc. (*'fusionsskatteloven'*).
[81] Consolidated Act No. 974 of 21 September 2004 (*'aktieavancebeskatningsloven'*).
[82] Directive 90/434/EEC of 23 July 1990 on the common system of taxation applicable to mergers, divisions, transfers of assets and exchanges of shares concerning companies of different Member States.
[83] Directive 90/435/EEC of 23 July 1990 on the common system of taxation applicable in the case of parent companies and subsidiaries of different Member States.
[84] Directive 2003/123/EC of 22 December 2003 amending Directive 90/435/EEC on the common system of taxation applicable in the case of parent companies and subsidiaries of different Member States.
[85] Bill No. 27 of 7 October 2004 (under review in the Danish Parliament, currently before the Fiscal Committee).

Danish tax rules allowing for tax-free distributions between Danish and foreign group companies, provided the parent company has held at least 20% of the shares in the subsidiary for at least 12 months and certain other criteria are met.[86]

2 Value added tax

61. An SE will be subject to Danish VAT rules. According to these rules, an exchange of services between different branches, etc. of the same legal entity is not considered a taxable supply. This also holds true for the exchange of services between an SE and its permanent establishment(s).

3 Other taxes

63. Other Danish taxes, levies, duties and fees will apply to an SE as to other Danish legal entities.

XI Conclusion

63. In Denmark, use of an SE will depend on the ability of practitioners to explain the inherent cross-border advantages of this legal entity. Lack of European-wide harmonisation and uncertainty with respect to tax treatment have caused the welcoming to be far from warm, however. Whereas the general argument in favour of an SE is that it saves administrative costs, merging financial institutions will probably also see an advantage in being subject to supervision by authorities in (primarily) one Member State.

In Denmark, cross-border moves cannot occur without a concomitant effect on legal personality. In cases where this feature is important, use of an SE should be considered. If a takeover of a listed company can be structured as the formation of an SE by merger, this could mean that an otherwise mandatory takeover bid would be avoided. Moreover, the ability of a Danish SE to distribute dividends tax free to shareholders makes Denmark a place worth considering when deciding where to register a proposed SE. No SEs have been established in Denmark thus far.

---

[86] Legislative history of Bill No. 27 of 7 October 2004.

8
Finland

BERNDT HEIKEL AND JOHAN NYBERGH
Hannes Snellman

I Introduction 204
II Reasons to opt for an SE 205
III Formation 205
   1 General remarks 205
      A Founding parties 205
      B Name 206
      C Registered office 207
         (i) Transfer of an SE's registered office from Finland 207
         (ii) Transfer of an SE's registered office to Finland 209
      D Corporate purpose 209
      E Capital 210
   2 Different means of formation 211
      E Formation by merger 211
         (i) SEs registered in Finland 211
            (a) Preparation and registration of the draft terms of merger 211
            (b) Approval of the draft terms of merger 213
            (c) Authorisation to execute the merger 213
            (d) Execution of the merger 214
         (ii) SEs to be registered outside Finland 214
         (iii) Special rights in connection with the formation of an SE by merger 215
         (iv) Acquisition by a company holding 90% or more of the shares in another company 216
      B Formation of a holding SE 216
      C Formation of a subsidiary SE 217
      D Conversion into an SE 217
   3 Acts committed on behalf of an SE in formation 218
   4 Registration and publication 218
   5 Acquisition of legal personality 219
IV Organisation and management 219
   1 General remarks 219
   2 General meeting 219
      A Decision-making process 219
      B Rights and obligations of shareholders 221
   3 Management and supervision 222

        A Two-tier system/one-tier system   222
        B Appointment and removal   223
        C Representation   225
        D Liability   225
V   Employee involvement   226
    1 Creation of a special negotiating body   226
    2 Standard rules on employee participation   227
    3 Miscellaneous provisions   228
VI   Annual accounts and consolidated accounts   229
    1 Accounting principles   230
    2 Auditors   230
VII Supervision by the national authorities   231
VIII Dissolution   231
    1 Winding up   231
    2 Liquidation   232
        A Voluntary liquidation   232
        B Involuntary liquidation   232
        C Liquidation procedure   232
    3 Insolvency   233
        A Debt restructuring   233
        B Liquidation in bankruptcy   234
    4 Cessation of payments   234
IX   Applicable law   234
X   Tax treatment   235
    1 Income tax   235
        A General remarks   235
        B Formation of an SE   235
    2 Value added tax   236
    3 Other taxes   236
XI   Conclusion   236

I   Introduction

1. This report discusses the provisions applicable to an SE that has or will have its registered office in Finland and to Finnish entities participating in the formation of an SE.

In Finland, Council Regulation (EC) No. 2157/2001 on the Statute for a European company or *Societas Europaea* ('SE') (the 'Regulation') was implemented[1] by the European Company Act (13.8.2004/742) (the 'SE Act'). Council Directive 2001/86/EC of 8 October 2001 supplementing the Statute for a European company, with regard to the involvement of employees (the 'Directive') was transposed into national law by the act on employee involvement

---

[1] Article 9 of the Regulation provides the basis for implementation of the Regulation and transposition of the Directive into national law.

in the European company (13.8.2004/758) (the 'Employee Involvement Act' or 'EIA'). Both acts entered into force on 8 October 2004.

II Reasons to opt for an SE

2. The SE differs from national corporate forms in that it is a genuinely European entity.

An SE can transfer its registered office and head office from one Member State to another with relative ease, without the need to liquidate and/or form a new company. Such a transfer is tax neutral pursuant to recent amendments to the Merger Directive.[2] A Finnish limited-liability company may not transfer its registered office to another Member State.

The Regulation also provides a legal framework for tax-neutral mergers of companies registered in different Member States (cross-border mergers).

III Formation

1 General remarks

3. The Regulation contains provisions governing the formation of an SE, including but not limited to the founding parties, share capital, registered office, company name and means of formation.

A Founding parties

4. Article 2(1) through (4) of the Regulation lists the entities that can participate in the formation of an SE. In Finland, the following types of entities qualify:[3]

Formation by merger

Public limited-liability companies (*julkinen osakeyhtiö*)[4] as regulated by the Finnish Companies Act (29.9.1978/734, as amended) and SEs.

Formation of a holding SE or a subsidiary SE

Limited-liability companies (*osakeyhtiö*[5] or *julkinen osakeyhtiö*) as regulated by the Finnish Companies Act (29.9.1978/734, as amended), including both public and private limited-liability companies. Article 3 of the Regulation

---

[2] Council Directive 2005/19/EC amending Council Directive 90/434/EEC 1990 on the common system of taxation applicable to mergers, divisions, transfers of assets and exchanges of shares concerning companies of different Member States.
[3] See Chap. 2, no. 19 of this book for additional requirements regarding ties to different Member States.
[4] Abbreviated 'Oyj' in the company name or 'Abp' (*publikt aktiebolag*) in Swedish.
[5] Abbreviated 'Oy' or 'Ab' (*aktiebolag*) in Swedish.

provides that an SE shall be considered a public limited-liability company for this purpose.

In addition, partnerships, limited partnerships, cooperative companies, associations, municipalities and other public or private law bodies or legal entities formed under the laws of and having their registered and head offices in Finland may participate in the formation of a subsidiary SE.[6]

Conversion of an existing public limited-liability company into an SE

Only a public limited-liability company (*julkinen osakeyhtiö*), as regulated by the Finnish Companies Act (29.9.1978/734, as amended), can be converted into an SE.

5. Article 2(5) of the Regulation gives the Member States the option to allow a company whose head office is not in the EU to participate in the formation of an SE provided that company is formed under the laws of a Member State and has a real and continuous link with the economy of a Member State.

Finland has opted to allow Finnish limited-liability companies or their foreign equivalents to participate in the formation of an SE provided that the company meets the requirements of Article 2(5)[7] of the Regulation. The same holds true for other companies as defined in Article 48 of the treaty where a subsidiary SE is formed in accordance with Article 2(3) of the Regulation.

B   Name

6. An SE with its registered office in Finland must be registered with the National Board of Patents and Registration (the 'Trade Register'). The name to be registered must *inter alia*:

(a) be clearly distinguishable from other registered names;
(b) not interfere with protected trade names, secondary trademarks or trademarks;
(c) not be contrary to good practice or public policy or be misleading;[8] and
(d) include the abbreviation 'SE'.[9]

Once registered, a company name is inalienable and cannot be transferred to another entity or person except in connection with the transfer of the business associated with that name.[10,11]

---

[6] Due to the sheer number of entities that qualify to participate in the formation of a subsidiary SE, the list is not thought to be exhaustive, merely illustrative.
[7] Sec. 3 SE Act; see also Art. 2(5) Reg.
[8] A company's name may not include any word or abbreviation liable to mislead the public. In addition, words that may be regarded as offensive (in Finnish or Swedish) may not be registered.
[9] Sec. 7(7a) of the Corporate Names Act (2.2.1979/128, as amended).   [10] *Ibid.*, Sec. 13.
[11] The purpose of this prohibition is to protect the public interest; see Martti Castrén, *Toiminimi*, Suomen lakimiesliiton kustannus, Helsinki, 1984, 156–63.

C Registered office

7. Finland applies the registered office theory in determining whether Finnish company law shall apply to an entity. Therefore, Finnish law does not as a rule restrict a company's right to transfer its head office outside Finland, and such a transfer shall not in general affect the legal status of the company or lead to its winding up.

The general principles regarding the transfer of an SE's registered office are discussed in Chapter 2 of this book.

8. If the registered office of an SE is in Finland, the company's head office must also be within the Finnish territory.[12] Finnish law does not require that the registered office and head office be at the same place.[13] An SE's registered office must be registered with the Trade Register.

The transfer of an SE's registered office within Finland does not affect the company's status as there is no requirement that a Finnish SE have its registered office and head office at the same place, since Finland has not enacted the option contained in Article 7 of the Regulation.

All documents to be filed with the Trade Register in connection with the transfer of a company's registered office must be translated into Finnish or Swedish.[14]

(i) **Transfer of an SE's registered office from Finland**

9. Shareholders of an SE registered in Finland may vote against the transfer from Finland of the company's registered office and demand that the company redeem their shares at fair market value. Holders of options, convertible bonds or other rights comparable to the rights of shareholders have the same right to demand redemption.[15]

The transfer of an SE's registered office from Finland entails the following formalities:

(a) The SE must submit a transfer proposal[16] to the Trade Register within one month following signing of the same. If the proposal is not submitted within this time period or if registration is refused, the transfer cannot go through.[17]
(b) The general meeting must approve the transfer proposal within two months of its registration by two-thirds of the votes cast.[18]

---

[12] Art. 7 Reg.
[13] Article 7 of the Regulation provides that the Member States may require SEs registered within their territory to locate their head office and registered office in the same place.
[14] Sec. 20a(4) Trade Register Decree 208/1979, as amended.
[15] Art 8(5) Reg. and Sec. 10 SE Act and Chap. 14, Secs. 12 and 13 Companies Act.
[16] Art. 8(2) Reg. [17] Sec. 9(1) SE Act.
[18] Unless the articles of the SE require a larger majority.

(c) Execution of the transfer proposal is subject to authorisation from the Trade Register. The SE shall apply for authorisation to execute the transfer within one month[19] following approval of the transfer proposal by the general meeting. If an application is not submitted within this time period or if permission is refused, the transfer resolution shall expire.[20]

(d) When requesting authorisation, the report referred to in Article 8(3) of the Regulation and the general meeting's resolution approving the transfer proposal must be attached to the application. Approval of the transfer proposal by class of shares must be mentioned in the minutes of the general meeting. Mention should also be made of the number of shares per class to be redeemed.[21]

(e) The Trade Register shall issue a public notice to all of the company's creditors. If a creditor objects to the transfer, it must notify the Trade Register at least one month prior to the date fixed for the transfer, which shall be at least four months after registration of the notice.

(f) Before the Trade Register can issue the certificate attesting to the completion of the requisite pre-transfer acts and formalities pursuant to Article 8(8) of the Regulation, any floating charges registered on the property of any participating Finnish company must either be transferred to the property of a branch to be established in Finland or cancelled.[22]

(g) The investigation conducted by the Trade Register prior to issuance of the aforementioned certificate comprises all liabilities that arose before the transfer, not only prior to publication of the transfer proposal.[23]

(h) Once the deadline has passed, the Trade Register shall issue the certificate attesting to the completion of the requisite pre-transfer acts and formalities. This certificate must be submitted to the competent authority of the Member State where the new registered office will be located within six months or it shall expire.[24]

(i) The company must register the transfer within four months from the authorisation date.

---

[19] In this regard, the SE Act refers to the merger procedure, according to which the company must apply for permission within four months following approval of the draft terms of merger or the merger resolution shall expire. However, a one-month time limit is expressly stated in the SE Act for the transfer of an SE's registered office and should therefore be applicable, regardless of this inconsistency.

[20] Sec. 9(2) SE Act.

[21] This corresponds to the protection of minority shareholders allowed under Article 24(2) of the Regulation.

[22] *Ibid.*, Sec. 9(4).

[23] Finland has enacted the option contained in Article 8(7) of the Regulation to extend the scope of the verification procedure (Sec. B(4) of the working paper of the European company work group of the Department of Justice of 17 October 2003).

[24] Sec. 9(5) SE Act.

(j) Once the registered office of an SE has been transferred from Finland, final accounts for the period after approval of the company's last annual accounts up to the transfer must be prepared regardless of whether the SE will continue its accounting period in the Member State to which its registered office has been transferred.[25] These accounts must be approved by the general meeting and registered in Finland.

The transfer of an SE's registered office from Finland may result in the need to register a branch in Finland.

(ii) **Transfer of an SE's registered office to Finland**

10. A decision to transfer an SE's registered office to Finland must be filed with the Trade Register within one month following issuance of the certificate attesting to the completion of the requisite pre-transfer acts and formalities by the authority in the Member State where the SE's registered office is located (prior to the transfer).

In addition to the information required by the Regulation,[26] the registration application must include the same documents presented in connection with the formation of a national limited-liability company. The articles of an SE transferring its registered office to Finland must also comply with the requirements for the articles of a Finnish limited-liability company carrying on the same type of business.[27]

Before the Trade Register can record the transfer of an SE's registered office to Finland, the SE must deregister any branch offices it may have in Finland, as a Finnish company may not maintain a branch in Finland.[28] In addition, a certificate regarding the registered share capital in the other Member State must be submitted to the Trade Register.[29]

11. Article 8(14) of the Regulation provides that the Member States may provide that a competent authority can object to the transfer of an SE's registered office on the grounds of public interest. Finland has not adopted any rules in this respect.

D Corporate purpose

12. The articles of an SE with its registered office in Finland must mention the company's areas of activity. There is no limit on the number of areas in which a

---

[25] *Ibid.*, Sec. 11 and Bill 55/2004, 31–32.
[26] The transfer proposal (Art. 8(2)), explanation (Art. 8(3)) and certificate (Art. 8(8)).
[27] This requirement also leads *inter alia* to the conclusion that the issued share capital must be fully paid up before the transfer can go through (Chap. 2, Sec. 9(3) and Chap. 4, Sec. 9 Companies Act).
[28] Bill 55/2004, 37.   [29] Sec. 20a(3) Trade Register Decree 876/1979, as amended.

company can conduct business. However, all fields actually covered by an SE's activities must be mentioned in its articles.[30]

Unlike its areas of activity, a company's corporate purpose is usually not mentioned in its articles. However, if the company's purpose is not to turn a profit, a mention to this effect must be made in the articles.[31]

An SE shall be bound by any *ultra vires* acts it commits unless the other party was or should have been aware that the act in question exceeded the company's corporate purpose. It has been argued that registration and publication of a company's articles (including its corporate purpose) do not constitute sufficient proof of such knowledge.[32]

E   Capital

13. According to Article 4(2) of the Regulation, the subscribed capital of an SE may not be less than €120,000 and must, according to the Companies Act, be paid up in full before the SE can be registered.

Pursuant to the Companies Act, a company's share capital may not be freely decreased or otherwise distributed. A strict procedure must be followed.

As an SE is subject to the legislation applicable to national limited-liability companies in the Member State where its registered office is located, the requirements of the Companies Act regarding the ratio between shareholders' equity and the share capital of public limited-liability companies shall apply equally to SEs registered in Finland, meaning that an SE's shareholders' equity cannot be less than half its subscribed capital. If this requirement is not met, the administrative or management organ shall ensure that the situation is remedied within the time limit set forth in the Companies Act. If no solution is found, the company shall be forced into liquidation.[33]

14. No certificates representing shares in an SE need be issued unless a shareholder so requests.

---

[30] As a general rule, the management or administrative organ's right to represent the company is limited by the areas of activity mentioned in the company's articles. For a more detailed analysis, see J. Kyläkallio, O. Iirola and K. Kyläkallio, *Osakeyhtiö*, Helsinki: Edita Publishing Oy, 142–3.

[31] Companies whose corporate purpose is not to generate profits for shareholders include joint stock companies and other companies whose purpose is to render services to shareholders at a reasonable price.

[32] J. Kyläkallio, O. Iirola and K. Kyläkallio, *op cit.*, 139.

[33] When calculating the ratio between shareholders' equity and subscribed capital, certain adjustments must be made, such as the addition of outstanding subordinated loans to the company's equity. For a more detailed analysis of these adjustments, see J. Kyläkallio, O. Iirola and K. Kyläkallio, *op cit.*, 927–35. It is also possible to allocate payments against shares to a premium fund rather than to share capital, in which case the share capital against which shareholders' equity is compared will be lower; see J. Kyläkallio, O. Iirola and K. Kyläkallio, *op cit.*, 496–8.

2 Different means of formation

E Formation by merger

15. The only type of Finnish company that can participate in the formation of an SE by merger is a public limited-liability company (julkinen osakeyhtiö),[34] as regulated by the Companies Act (29.9.1978/734, as amended).

16. The SE Act does not allow the competent authorities to oppose the formation of an SE by merger.[35] Nor has Finland enacted a simplified procedure pursuant to Article 31(2) of the Regulation for a merger by absorption by a company holding at least 90%, but less than all, of the shares and voting securities of the absorbed company.

(i) SEs registered in Finland

17. If the acquiring company is not registered in Finland but the SE to be formed by merger will be, a certificate regarding the share capital registered in the other Member State must be filed with the Trade Register.[36]

(a) Preparation and registration of the draft terms of merger

18. The management or administrative organ of each merging company must prepare draft terms of merger. If a Finnish public limited-liability company is participating in the formation of an SE by merger and the SE's registered office will be located in Finland, the Finnish company must submit the draft terms[37] to the Trade Register within one month following signing of the same or the merger cannot go through.[38]

The Trade Register shall scrutinise the draft terms of merger.

The draft terms of merger must, in addition to the information mentioned in Article 20 of the Regulation, include the following information for Finnish companies:

(a) the registration number of each participating company;
(b) information on any (subordinated loan) creditors liable to oppose the merger;

---

[34] Abbreviated 'Oyj' or 'Abp' (*publikt aktiebolag*) in Swedish.
[35] Article 19 of the Regulation stipulates that a Member State may provide that a company governed by the law of that state may not take part in the formation of an SE by merger if a competent authority of that state opposes participation by the company in the merger on grounds of public interest.
[36] Sec. 20a(3) Trade Register Decree 876/1979, as amended.
[37] Registration of documents appended to the draft terms of merger is not mandatory at this stage, but any documents not registered at this time must be registered in connection with the application for authorisation to execute the merger.
[38] If the draft terms of merger lapse, they must be signed again, which will lead to a situation whereby the initial draft terms cannot be used and the new terms (even if identical to the original) are treated as completely different.

(c) information on shares in the acquiring company and its parent company held by the acquired company and its subsidiaries; and

(d) information on the reason for the merger and the grounds on which the decision shall be taken.

In addition, certain documents must be attached to the draft terms, including those listed under Articles 10 and 11 of Council Directive 78/855/EEC (the 'Merger Directive') and Article 22 of the Regulation:

(a) A report by one or more independent experts[39] on the draft terms of merger of each participating company, including an assessment of whether the draft terms give correct and sufficient information on facts liable to have a substantial influence on the evaluation of the merger, such as the value of the transferred assets and the amount and modalities for distribution of consideration. The report on the acquiring company must state separately whether the merger is likely to endanger repayment of the company's debts.[40]

(b) Copies of documents related to the last three sets of annual accounts or, if the annual accounts are to be approved at the general meeting scheduled to vote on the merger, copies of documents related to the current annual accounts and the two preceding financial periods.

(c) Copies of documents regarding the intermediate closing of accounts for a period ending within the past three months and prepared and audited in compliance with the provisions on and requirements for annual accounts, where appropriate. These documents are required only if the financial period to which the last annual accounts relate ended more than six months before the general meeting scheduled to vote on the merger and approval of the annual accounts is not on the agenda for the meeting.

(d) A copy of an interim report prepared after the closing of the last financial period, if such a report is not included in the accounting statement.

(e) A report by the management or administrative organ on events that have taken place after submission of the last annual accounts, accounting statement or interim report and which are liable to have a material effect on the company's financial position.

(f) An opinion of the company's auditors and supervisory board[41] on the accounting statement, interim report and the report of the management or administrative organ.

---

[39] Pursuant to Article 22 of the Regulation, a joint report can be drafted on behalf of all participating companies by an independent expert.

[40] Exceptions to the required content of the experts' report may be made in certain cases; see J. Kyläkallio, O. Iirola and K. Kyläkallio, *op cit.*, 1003–9 and 1023–4.

[41] The opinion of the supervisory board is, of course, only required if the company has such a board (G. af Schultén, *Osakeyhtiölain kommentaari II*, Helsinki: Talentum, 2004, 508).

(g) All documents related to companies other than Finnish companies must be submitted to the Trade Register in their original language along with a translation into Finnish or Swedish.

(b) **Approval of the draft terms of merger**

19. After registration, the draft terms of merger must be approved by the general meeting of both the acquiring and acquired companies.[42] The draft terms of merger and all documents appended thereto must be made available to shareholders for inspection at least one month prior to the general meeting scheduled to vote on the merger. The merger must be approved by two-thirds of the votes cast and shares represented at the general meeting.[43] Finland has not enacted the option to allow approval of draft terms by a simple majority of votes cast in the cases set out in the Regulation.[44]

(c) **Authorisation to execute the merger**

20. The Finnish participating companies must apply to the Trade Register for authorisation to execute the merger within four months following approval of the draft terms by the general meeting of each merging company or the merger resolution shall expire. The application must be accompanied by any documents appended to the draft terms of merger not previously registered as well as the certificate referred to in Article 25(2) of the Regulation, the resolution approving the draft terms and translations of these into Swedish or Finnish.[45]

21. Upon receipt of an application to execute a merger, the Trade Register shall issue a public notice informing all creditors of the merging companies of their right to object to the merger within a period of three months.

Pursuant to Section 4(1) of the SE Act, participating companies from other Member States must approve the right of shareholders in the Finnish company to demand redemption of their shares.[46]

---

[42] These criteria are more restrictive than those contained in the Companies Act, as a resolution approving the draft terms in a purely domestic merger can be passed in certain cases by the merging companies' boards of directors. For a more detailed study, see J. Kyläkallio, O. Iirola and K. Kyläkallio, *op cit.*, 1015–22.

[43] Chap. 9, Sec. 14 Companies Act. The Companies Act allows for different classes of shares. If the company has more than one class of shares, the resolution must be approved by at least two-thirds of each class represented at the general meeting.

[44] This would, however, be possible according to Article 59(2) of the Regulation and Article 7(1) of Council Directive 78/855/EEC; see also C. Da Costa and A. Bilreiro, *The European Company Statute,* The Hague: Kluwer Law International, 2003, 30–1.

[45] Pursuant to Section 17 of the Finnish Constitution (11.6.1999/731), both Finnish and Swedish are official languages of Finland so any documents may be filed in either language.

[46] See no. 9 of this report.

The Trade Register shall approve the merger if no creditors of the participating Finnish companies object to the merger within the specified time period or if those creditors who do oppose the merger receive payment or satisfactory security for their claims in accordance with a final court order.

(d) **Execution of the merger**

22. The merging companies as well as the acquiring company must notify the Trade Register of execution of the merger within six months from the date on which (i) the authorisation to execute the merger is issued in Finland and (ii) the certificate referred to in Article 25(2) of the Regulation on completion of the requisite pre-merger acts and formalities is issued to another participating company, or the merger resolution shall expire.[47]

23. Prior to recording the merger, the Trade Register shall ascertain that the SE in formation complies with the rules of any regulated business the company may conduct, such as banking or insurance activities.

As regards compliance with the law by the other merging companies, the Trade Register must rely on the certificates issued by the competent authorities in the other Member States.[48]

As a rule, the Trade Register will not question the legality of the agreement on employee involvement and shall rely instead on information provided about the agreement or, alternatively, on a notice that no agreement has been reached after six months of negotiations and no consensus to extend negotiations has been reached.[49]

24. If any participating foreign company has a branch in Finland, the Trade Register shall de-register the branch in connection with execution of the merger based on an application to this end.

(ii) **SEs to be registered outside Finland**

25. If a Finnish company participates in the formation of an SE by merger and the acquiring company is registered in another Member State or in Finland but its registered office will be transferred to another Member State in connection with the formation of the SE, specific conditions apply.[50] These additional conditions are discussed below.

26. Before the Trade Register can issue the certificate regarding completion of the requisite pre-merger acts and formalities pursuant to Article 25(2) of the Regulation, any floating charges on the property of any participating Finnish

---

[47] Sec. 4(1) SE Act.   [48] Arts. 25(2), 26(1) and 26(2) Reg.
[49] According to Article 5(2) of the Directive, negotiations may be extended for up to one year by joint agreement of the parties.
[50] See the consultation paper of the European company work group of 2 December 2003, 45–7.

company must be rearranged.[51] The company in whose name a floating charge is registered shall provide the Trade Register with either an agreement regarding transfer of the floating charge to the property of a branch to be registered in Finland[52] or an application to cancel the floating charge.[53]

27. If the acquiring company is a Finnish company and the SE's registered office will be located in another Member State, the Finnish company shall prepare final accounts in the manner required for acquired companies in national mergers.[54] These accounts must be prepared regardless of whether the SE will continue its accounting period in the Member State to which its registered office shall be transferred.

28. If a participating company has its registered office in Finland and the SE will be registered in another Member State, the competent authority in Finland, i.e. the Trade Register, shall issue a certificate conclusively attesting to the completion of the requisite pre-merger acts and formalities in Finland.[55] This certificate can be issued in either Finnish or Swedish.[56]

(iii) **Special rights in connection with the formation of an SE by merger**

29. According to national law, shareholders in a company being acquired in a merger have the right to demand that the company redeem their shares at fair market value.[57]

This right also adheres to the shareholders of a Finnish *acquiring* company if the registered office of the SE will not be located in Finland.[58]

---

[51] Sec. 4(2) SE Act.
[52] In most cases, a branch created in connection with the formation of an SE by merger must be registered in the Member State of each merging company (other than the state in which the SE will be registered). Transfer of a floating charge to a branch to be registered in Finland requires that an application to establish a branch be filed prior to issuance of the authorisation to execute the merger. According to the consultation paper of the European company working group of 2 December 2003, a floating charge can also be transferred to an existing Finnish branch of a participating company (46).
[53] In addition, all promissory notes secured by a floating charge must be filed with the Trade Register.
[54] Consultation paper of the European company work group of 2 December 2003, 47.
[55] Art. 25(2) Reg.
[56] The applicant, i.e. the SE, is responsible for providing a translation of the certificate into the language of the Member State where it will be registered.
[57] Chap. 14, Sec. 12(1) Companies Act.
[58] Shareholders of the *acquired* company in a domestic merger have the same right to demand redemption of their shares. Shareholders of the *acquiring* company, on the other hand, do not generally enjoy this right in domestic mergers. However, as the rights and obligations of shareholders in the acquiring company are liable to change as a result of the merger if that company is registered as an SE in another Member State, shareholders of the acquiring company are exceptionally allowed to request redemption of their shares in this instance; see Bill 55/2004, 25–26 and Sec. 5 SE Act.

The right of creditors to object to the merger and demand payment or satisfactory security for their claims is discussed above (see no. 9 of this report).

(iv) **Acquisition by a company holding 90% or more of the shares in another company**

30. Finnish law does not contain a simplified merger procedure for an acquisition by a company that holds 90% or more of the shares in another company. However, a simplified procedure exists for the merger of a wholly owned subsidiary,[59] and certain sections of the draft terms are not required.

B   Formation of a holding SE

31. In Finland only public or private limited-liability companies (*osakeyhtiö* or *julkinen osakeyhtiö*)[60] as defined in the Companies Act can participate in the formation of a holding SE. Article 3 of the Regulation provides that an SE shall be considered a public limited-liability company for this purpose.

32. The administrative or management organ of each participating company must prepare draft terms of formation to be recorded with the Trade Register without delay.[61] The registration notice shall also state the number of shares and voting rights contributed by each participating company to the holding SE.[62] To the extent documents to be filed have not been drafted in Finnish or Swedish, an official translation must be attached to the application.[63]

33. After the shares in the holding company have been subscribed, a constitutive meeting shall be held at which a decision to form a holding SE is taken. The decision to form a holding SE must be filed with the Trade Register within six months from the date of the draft terms of formation or it shall expire.

In connection with the registration, all members of the management or administrative organ, the managing director and the auditors shall ascertain that the subscribed capital of the company to be formed has been paid up in full. As shares in a holding SE are obtained by way of exchange, a statement by an independent expert on the contribution of share capital is also required.[64]

34. Finland has no specific provisions to protect creditors, employees or minority shareholders who oppose the formation of a holding SE.[65]

---

[59] Art. 31(2) Reg. and Chap. 14, Sec. 4 Companies Act.
[60] '*Aktiebolag*' or '*publikt aktiebolag*' in Swedish.
[61] Sec. 6 SE Act.   [62] Sec. 20a(2) Trade Register Decree.
[63] *Ibid*., Sec. 20a(4).   [64] See also Art. 32(4) Reg.
[65] Sec. B(3) of the working paper of the European company work group of the Department of Justice of 17 October 2003.

C   Formation of a subsidiary SE

35. The formation of a subsidiary SE is nothing new insofar as the same procedure applies to national companies. The main issue is to integrate the newly formed SE into the existing legal structure.[66]

The formation of a subsidiary SE is governed by the laws of the Member States applicable to national public limited-liability companies. Therefore, the provisions of the Companies Act on the formation of a Finnish limited-liability company shall apply.[67] The procedure to form a subsidiary SE corresponds to that set out above for the formation of a holding SE, except that a statement by an independent expert on the valuation of the consideration is not required if the share capital is paid in cash.

The Companies Act does not require that a public limited-liability company have more than one shareholder. Thus, Article 3(2) of the Regulation did not necessitate any amendments to the Companies Act.

D   Conversion into an SE

36. In Finland, only a public limited-liability company (*julkinen osakeyhtiö*)[68] may be converted into an SE.[69] Contrary to the methods of formation described above, the conversion of an existing public limited-liability company into an SE involves only one company.[70]

37. The administrative or management organ of the company undergoing conversion shall prepare draft terms of conversion, which must be submitted to the Trade Register without delay.[71] The management or administrative organ shall also prepare a report explaining and justifying the legal and economic aspects of the conversion and indicating the implications for shareholders and employees. In addition, an independent expert must certify that the company has net assets at least equivalent to its capital plus those reserves which may not be distributed pursuant to the SE's articles.[72]

---

[66] Allowing the formation of a subsidiary SE did not entail any material changes to national law.
[67] In short, the formation of a limited-liability company in Finland entails the following steps. First, the founder(s), which can be either natural persons or legal entities, prepare a memorandum of association. Once the shares have been subscribed, the shareholders hold a meeting at which they officially decide to form a company. If the founders subscribe all of the company's shares, no separate meeting to form the company is required, and the new company can be formed immediately. A company can be registered only after its subscribed capital has been paid up in full. The company acquires legal personality upon completion of registration with the Trade Register.
[68] '*Publikt aktiebolag*' in Swedish   [69] Art. 2(4) Reg.
[70] Pursuant to Article 37(3) of the Regulation, the registered office of a company may not be transferred from one Member State to another while it is being converted into an SE.
[71] Sec. 6 SE Act.   [72] Art. 37(6) Reg.

To the extent the documents that must be filed are not drafted in Finnish or Swedish, an official translation must be appended to the registration application.[73]

38. A decision to convert a company into an SE must be approved by the general meeting by the same majority required to amend the company's articles, i.e. two-thirds of the votes cast and shares represented at the meeting.[74] Finland does not require a greater majority in the organ within which employee participation is organised.[75]

3 Acts committed on behalf of an SE in formation

39. An SE that has not yet been recorded in the Trade Register does not enjoy legal personality. However, as a need to enter into contracts or incur obligations may arise prior to registration of an SE, the Regulation provides for a procedure for an SE to assume such rights and obligations.

40. According to Article 16 of the Regulation, an SE has the option, but is not obliged, to assume obligations arising out of acts performed in its name prior to registration. If the SE does not assume such rights and obligations, the persons or entities that performed these acts shall be jointly and severally liable for the consequences thereof.[76]

4 Registration and publication

41. An SE with its registered office in Finland is registered in the same register as Finnish limited-liability companies, i.e. the Trade Register maintained by the National Board of Patents and Registration.

42. In the formation by merger of an SE with its registered office in Finland, the merger and simultaneous formation of the SE are effective on the date the SE is recorded in the Trade Register.

43. Upon registration of an SE all assets and liabilities of the acquired companies are transferred to the acquiring company by operation of law, the shareholders of the acquired company become shareholders of the acquiring company,

---

[73] Sec. 20a(4) Trade Register Decree.
[74] In certain cases, however, a decision may require the consent of specific shareholders. A decision to convert a company into an SE, however, usually does not require additional consent.
[75] Art. 37(8) Reg. and Sec. B(8) of the working paper of the European company work group of the Department of Justice of 17 October 2003.
[76] This differs somewhat from the rule applicable to Finnish limited-liability companies. Rights and obligations incurred in the name of such a company between the signing date of its memorandum of association and registration are assumed automatically by the company upon registration. (Chap. 2, Sec. 14 Companies Act).

the acquired company ceases to exist, and the acquiring company becomes an SE.[77]

44. As the competent authority in the Member State where an SE is registered is not obliged to inform the authorities in the Member State of each acquired company of the registration, it is quite possible for the registration of an acquired company not to be deleted from the register of a Member State until the competent authority in that state learns of the registration of the SE via the *Official Journal of the European Communities*.[78]

5 Acquisition of legal personality

45. An SE, like a Finnish limited-liability company,[79] acquires legal personality upon registration.[80] Prior to that time, an SE cannot acquire rights or obligations, enter into agreements or be represented in court or before the public authorities.

IV Organisation and management

1 General remarks

46. An SE may select the best model for its organisation and management within the limits provided by the Regulation. The Regulation did not necessitate the introduction of any new organisational models under Finnish law, as both a one-tier and a two-tier management structure have existed (and been used by) Finnish limited-liability companies for quite some time. In addition, the separation of powers described in the Regulation between the general meeting and the administrative, management and supervisory organs is in general in line with the provisions of the Companies Act.

2 General meeting

A Decision-making process

47. The general meeting of shareholders of an SE must meet at least once each calendar year within six months following the close of the company's financial year. Finland does not require that the first general meeting of an SE be held within 18 months of the company's formation. However, as an SE's financial year may be shortened or extended to up to 18 months, the first general meeting

---

[77] Art. 29 Reg.   [78] Bill 55/2004, 24.
[79] Certain other Finnish legal entities, such as partnerships, acquire legal personality upon the signing of their memorandum of association, i.e. prior to recordation in the Trade Register.
[80] Art. 16(1) Reg.

of an SE with its registered office in Finland may thus be held at any time within 24 months of formation.[81]

48. In order to be valid, decisions of the general meeting must be based on the agenda as set out in the notice to convene the meeting. Notices of a general meeting shall be sent no earlier than two months and no later than one week in advance, unless the company's articles provide otherwise. If the company's shares are book-listed, notices of a general meeting must be sent at least 17 days in advance. Certain resolutions also require that a notice be sent no later than one month prior to the meeting.

49. The general meeting can be convened only by the management or administrative organ based on a resolution passed by the management, administrative or supervisory organ or on a request from the auditors or those shareholders holding at least 10% of the company's shares. Should the management or administrative organ, as the case may be, not convene a general meeting in due time, the county administrative board may allow a moving party to convene a meeting at the company's expense.[82]

50. Resolutions of an SE's general meeting must, in most cases, be passed by an absolute majority of votes cast. Certain resolutions, however, require a qualified majority or the explicit consent of certain shareholders.[83] In case of a tie, the chair shall cast the deciding vote, except in elections, where the main rule is that the person receiving the most votes shall be deemed the winner.

All amendments to the articles of an SE must be approved by the general meeting by at least two-thirds of both the votes cast and shares represented.[84] Under Finnish law, the management or administrative organ cannot amend the articles without the approval of the general meeting if they conflict with the arrangements for employee involvement.[85]

Resolutions that consist of various parts subject to different procedural requirements shall be approved by applying the requirements that would otherwise apply had the resolution been passed in separate parts.[86]

---

[81] *Ibid.*, Art. 54(1) and Sec. B(17) of the working paper of the European company work group of the Department of Justice of 17 October 2003.

[82] Chap. 9, Sec. 8(2) Companies Act.

[83] It is also possible to include in an SE's articles a requirement that certain resolutions be approved at two or more consecutive general meetings in order to be valid.

[84] Article 59(2) of the Regulation allows the Member States to provide that a simple majority shall suffice if at least half the subscribed capital is present or represented. Finland has not enacted this option, however. Article 12(4) of the Regulation gives the Member States the option to provide that the management or administrative organ can amend the company's articles if the latter conflict with the arrangements on employee involvement.

[85] Art. 12(4) Reg. and Sec. B(6) of the working paper of the European company work group of the Department of Justice of 17 October 2003.

[86] J. Kyläkallio, O. Iirola and K. Kyläkallio, *op cit.*, 747.

51. There is no quorum required for a general meeting. Thus, as long as at least one shareholder is present or represented, the meeting can validly take decisions. The articles of an SE may require that certain decisions be approved by a greater majority or an absolute number of shares, however.[87]

B Rights and obligations of shareholders

52. Shareholders holding at least 10% of the subscribed capital of an SE have the right request the company to convene a general meeting and draw up an agenda. The same rule applies to shareholders of Finnish limited-liability companies.[88]

53. Every shareholder is entitled to take part in the general meeting of an SE, either personally or by proxy. Shareholders have the right to: (i) attend meetings; (ii) speak and ask questions at meetings; (iii) receive information about the company at meetings; (iv) request that items be placed on the agenda of a general meeting; (v) vote (or abstain from voting) at meetings; (vi) challenge decisions taken by the general meeting in court; and (vii) read and receive a copy of the minutes of a meeting. An SE may not vote at a general meeting shares held by the company itself, a subsidiary or a trust controlled by the company or any of its subsidiaries.[89]

In order to attend the general meeting of an SE, shareholders must register their shareholdings in the register maintained by the company or provide proof of title to their shares.

If an SE's shares are book-listed, shareholders must be recorded in the system ten days before the meeting in order to be eligible to attend.[90] Holders of nominee-registered[91] shares must be temporarily entered in the system under their actual names prior to the date of the meeting in order to be able to attend.

Shareholders have no obligations with regard to the general meeting. They may decide, for example, not to participate in or vote at a meeting and may leave at any time.[92]

54. Shareholders shall be liable for damage caused to the company, another shareholder or third parties due to wilful misconduct or gross negligence on

---

[87] *Ibid.*, 748.
[88] Art. 55(1) Reg. and Sec. B(18) of the working paper of the European company work group of the Department of Justice of 17 October 2003.
[89] Chap. 9, Sec. 1(3) Companies Act.
[90] There are exceptions to this rule, however, as shareholders recorded in the shareholders' register on the last day to register for a general meeting may attend by presenting valid proof of title to their shares.
[91] Shares in a Finnish company held by foreign shareholders may be recorded in a book-entry system without indicating the name of the ultimate owner but rather a nominee acting on behalf of the owner. Such a registration, however, may in certain cases limit the possibility for the ultimate owner to exercise its rights.
[92] During general meetings, shareholders must abide by the rules of order fixed by the chair.

their part in violation of the Companies Act or the SE's articles. The liability of each shareholder shall be assessed on a case-by-case basis.

55. According to Article 56 of the Regulation, shareholders holding at least 10% of the subscribed capital may request that additional items be placed on the agenda of a general meeting. As this threshold may be lowered by national law, any shareholder of an SE with its registered office in Finland, regardless of its shareholding, may request that additional items be placed on the agenda of a general meeting provided the request is made in time to be included in the notice of the meeting.[93]

3 Management and supervision

A Two-tier system/one-tier system

56. Finnish public limited-liability companies can choose either a one-tier or a two-tier system of management. In the one-tier system, the statutory organs according to the Companies Act are the general meeting and the board of directors. In the two-tier system, the statutory organs are the general meeting, the supervisory board and the board of directors.[94] The administrative organ (in the one-tier system) and the management organ (in the two-tier system) are governed by the provisions of the Companies Act applicable to the board of directors of a public limited-liability company, while the supervisory organ is governed by the provisions applicable to the supervisory board.

In Finland, the two-tier system has been adopted mainly by larger corporations, but only some of them. A clear trend over the past ten years has been to switch from a two-tier to a one-tier management structure. One of the reasons behind this shift is the general feeling that the juxtaposition of a supervisory board between shareholders and the board of directors results in unnecessary bureaucracy, unclear management liability and less effective and distinct decision-making.

The administrative or management organ must have at least three members and the supervisory organ five.[95]

57. The administrative or management organ is responsible for the management and proper running of the company. This organ is also responsible for supervising accounting practices and overseeing the company's financial affairs.

The supervisory organ oversees the management or administrative organ and the managing director. The supervisory organ has very limited powers to engage in

---

[93] Sec. 8(1) SE Act and Chap. 9, Sec. 7 Companies Act.

[94] Chap. 8, Secs 1 and 11 Companies Act; for a detailed analysis of the powers of these organs, see J. Kyläkallio, O. Iirola and K. Kyläkallio, *op cit.*, 576 ff and 657 ff.

[95] Arts. 39(4), 40(3) and 43(23) Reg.

actual management. The supervisory organ of an SE with its registered office in Finland may not make certain categories of transactions subject to its approval.[96]

The same person may not serve as both managing director and chair of the administrative or management organ, nor may the managing director or a member of the management or administrative organ be a member of the supervisory organ.[97]

In an SE with a two-tier system of management, the supervisory organ and each individual member of this organ are entitled to request any information from the management organ or the managing director they deem necessary in order to properly supervise the latter.[98]

B Appointment and removal

58. The Regulation allows legal entities to serve as members of an SE's organs provided the law applicable to public limited-liability companies in the Member State in which the SE's registered office is located so allows.

According to the Companies Act, members of the board of directors and the managing directors of public limited-liability companies must be natural persons.[99] Individuals who lack capacity or have been declared bankrupt may not sit on the administrative, management or supervisory organs or serve as the managing director of an SE with its registered office in Finland. These requirements apply to all SE organs.[100]

59. An SE with its registered office in Finland must have a managing director responsible for the day-to-day[101] management of the company in accordance with the instructions and orders of the administrative or management organ and for ensuring that the company's accounts comply with applicable laws and regulations and that its financial affairs are handled in a reliable manner.[102] The managing director is appointed by the administrative organ (in the one-tier system) or by the management organ or, if the company's articles so provide,

---

[96] Art. 48(2) Reg. and Sec. B(15) of the working paper of the European company work group of the Department of Justice of 17 October 2003. Finland has not enacted specific provisions based on Art. 50(3) Reg.

[97] Art. 39(3) Reg. Finland has not imposed a time limit on the period during which the supervisory organ can nominate one of its members to sit on the management organ in the event of a vacancy on the latter body.

[98] Chap. 8, Sec. 11a(1) Companies Act and Art. 41(3) Reg.

[99] Bill 743/2004.   [100] Sec. 7(1) SE Act and Chap. 8, Sec. 4(2) Companies Act.

[101] Article 39(1) of the Regulation refers to 'current management' while Article 43(1) mentions 'day-to-day management'. Apparently, however, there is no clear distinction between these terms.

[102] Sec. 7(2) SE Act. The obligation for an SE to have a managing director responsible for the day-to-day management of the company reflects the same requirement for Finnish public limited-liability companies.

by the supervisory organ (in the two-tier system). A managing director can only be removed from office by the same body that appointed him of her.

At least one member of the administrative or management organ, as well as the managing director,[103] must be a resident of the European Economic Area.

60. In the one-tier system, members of the administrative organ are appointed by the general meeting.[104]

In the two-tier system, the members of the supervisory organ are appointed by the general meeting.[105] The general rule is that the supervisory organ then appoints the members of the management organ unless national law allows the general meeting do so.[106]

In Finland, the general meeting in the two-tier system can appoint members of the management organ if the SE's articles so provide.[107]

61. In both the one-tier and two-tier systems, members of the supervisory, management and administrative organs may only be removed from office by the body that appointed them.[108]

62. As the Companies Act does not contain any restrictions on the term of office for members of an SE's organs, their term may not exceed six years, the maximum period allowed by the Regulation.[109] A company's articles may include restrictions on the re-election of members of its organs and limit their term of office to less than six years, however.

Organ members may resign at any time prior to expiry of their term of office. The body that appointed the member in question shall be notified of the resignation.

63. The remuneration of the managing director and of members of the management, administrative and supervisory organs shall be determined by the body responsible for electing or appointing such members.

---

[103] Chap. 8, Sec. 4(1) Companies Act.
[104] Art. 39(3) Reg. This procedure differs to a certain extent from that applicable to Finnish public limited-liability companies, as the Companies Act allows up to half the members of the administrative organ to be appointed by other means as defined in the company's articles. For a detailed analysis of this point, see J. Kyläkallio, O. Iirola and K. Kyläkallio, *op cit.*, 596–7.
[105] *Ibid.*, Art. 40(2). This procedure differs to a certain extent from that applicable to Finnish public limited-liability companies, as the Companies Act allows up to half the members of the supervisory organ to be appointed by other means, as defined in the company's articles. For a detailed analysis of this point, see J. Kyläkallio, O. Iirola and K. Kyläkallio, *op cit.*, 677–8.
[106] This rule corresponds to that contained in the Companies Act regarding the procedure that the supervisory organ must follow to appoint members of the management organ unless the articles provide otherwise (Chap. 8, Sect. 11a Companies Act).
[107] Art 39(2) Reg., Sec. 7 SE Act and Bill 55/2004, 27.
[108] Chap. 8, Secs. 2(1) and 11(3) Companies Act. [109] Art. 46(1) Reg.

C   Representation

64. A public limited-liability company registered under Finnish law is represented by its board of directors.[110] As the Regulation does not include any further rules on representation of an SE, an SE with its registered office in Finland shall be represented by its management or administrative organ.

In addition to representing an SE, the management or administrative organ may appoint others to sign on the company's behalf. The only restriction that can be recorded, and thus rendered official, in this regard is a joint signature clause.[111] Acts committed in the name of the company are binding on it provided they fall within the representative's registered authority; acts that fall outside the company's purpose but within the representative's registered authority are also binding on it if the third party in question was unaware that the representative was acting with restricted authority. It has been argued that the recordation and publication of a company's corporate purpose in its articles does not constitute sufficient proof of such knowledge.[112]

D   Liability

65. Pursuant to Section 15 of the SE Act, members of the administrative, management and supervisory organs are liable for acts and omissions they commit in the same way as members of the board of directors or supervisory board of a Finnish limited-liability company. Thus, organ members must make good all damage to *the company* caused while in office, either intentionally or via negligence. In order to impose liability, the company must have suffered a loss; an organ member must have caused the loss while in office; there must be a causal link between the measures taken by the organ member and the damage sustained by the company; and the organ member must have acted intentionally or with negligence.

A member of the administrative, management or supervisory organ can be held directly liable to *a shareholder* or *a third party* for damage caused by an act that violates the Companies Act or the company's articles. In this regard, the liability of organ members is more limited since a violation of the Companies Act or the articles is required *in addition to* the requirements for a finding of liability vis-à-vis the company.[113]

---

[110] Chap. 8, Sec. 12 Companies Act.
[111] Third parties are generally deemed to be aware of recorded restrictions.
[112] J. Kyläkallio, O. Iirola and K. Kyläkallio, *op cit.*, 139.
[113] Although organ members are normally released from liability at the annual general meeting, such a discharge covers only acts and omissions of the organ members known to the general meeting at the time.

As far as liability is concerned, the Regulation and the SE Act are treated like the Companies Act in that a violation of either piece of legislation is treated as a violation of the Companies Act.[114]

The managing director shall be held liable under the same conditions as organ members.

In addition to civil liability, criminal liability can also be incurred. If a crime is committed in the course of business or in connection with the activities of a Finnish company, the general rule is that the party or parties responsible for the criminal acts or negligence shall be held liable. In each case, criminal liability must be based on an assessment of whether the party in question acted in a manner corresponding to the relevant provisions of the Criminal Code or other applicable provisions. Liability for violation of stock exchange rules or the legislation applicable to publicly traded shares can also arise.

V Employee involvement[115]

66. The Directive has been transposed into Finnish law through the SE Employee Involvement Act (13.8.2004/758, hereinafter the 'Employee Involvement Act' or 'EIA'). The Employee Involvement Act covers mainly SEs registered in Finland. However, some parts of the act (e.g. the sections dealing with the special negotiating body, the election of the representative body, and employee representatives on the board of directors or supervisory board) are applicable irrespective of the Member State in which an SE is registered.

The Employee Involvement Act reflects, for the most part, the provisions of the Directive. However, there are some differences, such as the method used to elect Finnish members of the special negotiating body (SNB).

1 Creation of a special negotiating body

67. Pursuant to the Employee Involvement Act, an SNB is created in accordance with the provisions of the Directive. In accordance with Article 3(2)(b) of the Directive, the act provides rules for the allocation of seats among Finnish companies[116] as follows.

If the number of Finnish participating companies exceeds the number of seats on the SNB allocated to such companies or if the number of allocated seats equals the number of Finnish participating companies, the seats shall be allocated one at a time amongst the Finnish companies in descending order and in proportion

---

[114] Sec. 15(2) SE Act.
[115] This section was written by Irmeli Timonen, an employment law specialist with Hannes Snellman.
[116] Sec. 7 EIA.

to the number of employees they employ. If the number of the seats allocated to Finnish participating companies is higher than the number of participating companies, each Finnish company shall be allocated one seat, and the remaining seats shall thereafter be allocated amongst the companies in proportion to the number of employees they employ.

The employees may, however, agree to deviate from the above procedure. If possible, representation shall be secured by way of agreement for all Finnish participating companies and employee groups.

Furthermore, there is a special section concerning the election of SNB members in Finland.[117] Employees of an SE who work in Finland are entitled to appoint representatives to the SNB by way of agreement or through elections. Unless the employees are able to agree on the procedure, the labour protection delegates representing the largest number of employees and officials shall jointly arrange the elections (or other procedure) so as to ensure that all employees have the right to participate.

2 Standard rules on employee participation

68. The standard rules[118] on employee participation set forth in the Employee Involvement Act are nearly identical to those contained in the Directive, with some additions or specifications.

Regarding the selection of the form of employee participation, the Employee Involvement Act states that if the SNB does not take a decision, the participating companies shall decide.[119]

The composition of the employee representative body is similar to that of the SNB and is determined in accordance with the rules set forth in Part 1 of the Annex to the Directive. The rules governing the allocation of seats among Finnish companies are similar to those applicable to the creation of an SNB.

The Employee Involvement Act states that if no agreement is reached, the representative body shall verify once a year whether there have been changes to the SE, its subsidiaries or establishments that require the composition of the representative body to change.[120]

The standard rules in the Employee Involvement Act on information and consultation are similar to those set forth in Part 2 of the Annex to the Directive. There is one additional rule,[121] specifying that the costs mentioned in the Directive,[122] which are borne by the SE, shall include the fees of any expert the employees may be entitled to consult in the information and consultation process.[123]

---

[117] *Ibid.*, Sec. 8.   [118] Annex Dir.   [119] Sec. 19 EIA and Art. 7(2) Dir.
[120] *Ibid.*, Sec. 21.   [121] *Ibid.*, Sec. 27.   [122] Part 2, Sec. (h) Annex Dir.
[123] Finland has not enacted the option contained in Article 3(7) of the Directive. However, the costs borne by the SE must, according to Bill 107/2004, be reasonable.

The standard rules on employee participation, described in Part 3 of the Annex to the Directive, are incorporated in the Employee Involvement Act, with two exceptions.

First, in addition to the standard rules on the allocation of seats to employee representatives,[124] the Employee Involvement Act stipulates that the employees of an SE who work in Finland are entitled to appoint a representative to the board of directors or the supervisory board through consensus or by election. If the employees are unable to agree on the procedure, the labour protection delegates representing the greatest number of workers shall organise the elections or other procedure in such a manner that all employees are entitled to participate.[125]

Second, pursuant to Part 3, Section 4 of the Annex to the Directive, employee representatives on the administrative organ of an SE have the same rights and obligations as shareholder representatives. One exception, however, is that employee representatives may not vote on or participate in discussions on matters related to collective labour agreements or industrial actions or any other issue where their interests are liable to conflict with those of the SE.[126]

3   Miscellaneous provisions

69. The duty of confidentiality expressed in the EIA corresponds to Article 8(1) of the Directive. However, there is an exception[127] in that the supervisory board or board of directors is allowed to withhold information if disclosure of such information would cause material harm to the SE, a participating company or any of its subsidiaries or establishments. This information must be disclosed immediately after the grounds for non-disclosure cease to exist and reasons for the non-disclosure must be provided. Finland has not enacted any specific provisions based on Article 8(3) of the Directive.

Employee representatives enjoy protection against dismissal. The employer can terminate the employment contract of an employee representative on subjective grounds (i.e. related to the representative's person) only if a majority of the employees represented so agree. Furthermore, the employer shall be entitled to terminate the employment contract of an employee representative on financial and economic grounds or due to a reorganisation or bankruptcy only if the representative's post is eliminated and the employer is unable to find another arrangement that corresponds to the representative's skills or is otherwise suitable or to train the representative for another function.[128]

To prevent misuse of an SE, the EIA provides that if a material change occurs within a year following registration of the company liable to result in a need for wider employee representation, new negotiations must be held on arrangements

[124] Part 3, Sec. 3 Annex Dir.   [125] Sec. 29(2) EIA.
[126] Ibid., Sec. 30(2).   [127] Ibid., Secs. 32. and 8(2) EIA.   [128] Ibid., Sec. 33.

for employee involvement in the order that should have been followed had the change occurred prior to registration of the SE.

New negotiations need not be held, however, if the SE can prove that there is an acceptable ground for the material change and that it was not possible to implement the change prior to registration of the SE.[129]

Article 13(4) of the Directive did not necessitate any amendments to Finnish law.

VI Annual accounts and consolidated accounts

70. An SE with its registered office in Finland must abide by the provisions of Finnish law on annual accounts and consolidated accounts. The national currency of Finland is the euro (Art. 67(1) Reg.).

The annual accounts are prepared by the management or administrative organ and must be completed within four months following the close of the financial year and submitted to the company's auditors. The annual general meeting approves the income statement and balance sheet and, for a parent company, the consolidated income statement and balance sheet, within six months following the close of the company's financial year. Annual accounts (including consolidated accounts) must be filed with the Trade Register within two months of adoption.

A parent company is a company that holds more than half the shares or voting rights of another company based on ownership, membership, its articles or another agreement or has the right to appoint the majority of members of that company's management or administrative organ.[130]

Consolidated accounts must be prepared for a limited-liability parent company unless no more than one of the following thresholds has been exceeded during the last two financial years:

(a) a balance sheet total of €12,500,000;
(b) turnover of €25,000,000;
(c) employment on average of more than 250 people (during the last financial year).

Moreover, if (i) the parent company is based in the EEA and holds at least 90% of the subsidiary, (ii) the shareholders of the parent company so agree, and (iii) the consolidated accounts of the parent company are registered in Finland, a

---

[129] *Ibid.*, Sec. 36.
[130] Chap. 1, Sec. 5 Accounting Act. As the Companies Act refers to both the administrative organ and the management organ as the 'board of directors', provisions regarding the latter body shall apply to both organs.

Finnish subsidiary that is itself a parent company need not prepare consolidated accounts for its group.[131]

1 Accounting principles

71. A company whose shares are quoted on a stock exchange in any Member State must prepare annual accounts in accordance with IAS/IFRS as of financial years commencing 1 January 2005, at the latest.[132]

Other companies that have an auditor certified by the Finnish Central Chamber of Commerce have the option of applying IAS/IFRS but are not obliged to do so. A company that has opted to use IAS/IFRS must not as a rule switch back to national standards.[133]

2 Auditors

72. All limited-liability companies registered in Finland must appoint an auditor.[134] If a certified public accounting firm ('CPA firm') is not named auditor, at least one deputy auditor must be appointed.

The auditor must:

(a) be a natural person or CPA firm;
(b) have sufficient knowledge of accounting, economics and law as well as requisite skill and experience in auditing based on the business of the company; and
(c) not be legally incompetent or declared bankrupt or subject to any prohibitions on doing business.

In addition, at least one auditor must reside in the EEA.[135]

Thus, there is no general requirement that only a person certified by a public authority can serve as an SE's auditor. However, companies exceeding certain thresholds are obliged to appoint auditors certified by a local chamber of commerce or the Central Chamber of Commerce.[136]

Only a public accountant certified by the Central Chamber of Commerce can serve as auditor if two of the following three thresholds are met:

---

[131] Chap., 6 Sec. 1 Audit Act.
[132] Regulation (EC) No. 1606/2002 of the European Parliament and of the Council of 19 July 2002 on the application of international accounting standards.
[133] Sec. 3.2 Bill 126/2004, amending the Accounting Act and related acts.
[134] Chap. 1, Sec. 1 Audit Act and Chap. 1, Sec. 1 Accounting Act.
[135] *Ibid.*, Chap. 3, Sec. 10(2).
[136] There are several requirements for certified auditors, although only the requirement that they be certified by the Central Chamber of Commerce is discussed in this report. For further details on the above thresholds, see Secs. 11 and 12 Audit Act.

(a) the company's balance sheet total for the last financial year exceeds €25,000,000;
(b) the turnover for the last financial year exceeded €50,000,000;
(c) the company employed on average more than 300 people (during the preceding financial year).[137]

In corporate groups, at least one auditor from the parent company must be appointed to audit each subsidiary.[138]

VII Supervision by the national authorities

73. An SE with its registered office in Finland is overseen by the public authorities responsible for supervising national limited-liability companies.

All SEs registered in Finland are supervised by the Trade Register, which maintains current information on the members of a company's management, administrative and supervisory organs, auditors, its articles, annual accounts and administration.

Depending on the business of an SE, it may be subject to supervision by other national authorities, such as the Financial Supervisory Authority (FSA) or the Insurance Supervisory Authority.

The FSA supervises all companies whose shares are quoted on the Helsinki Stock Exchange, regardless of their field of activity.

The national authorities competent to supervise application of the Regulation in accordance with Article 68(2) of the Regulation are: (i) the Trade Register (for all registration-related matters); (ii) the county administrative boards (for convening the general meeting); and (iii) the district courts (for liquidation-related procedures).[139]

The Ministry of Labour is the competent authority for matters concerning employee involvement in an SE

VIII Dissolution

1 Winding up

74. The procedure to dissolve a Finnish limited-liability company (other than through bankruptcy) is liquidation, which can be either voluntary or involuntary.

---

[137] Sec. 12 Audit Act. For companies that do not exceed these thresholds, there are different requirements for auditors depending on the parameters mentioned in connection with the obligation to appoint only public accountants certified by the Central Chamber of Commerce.
[138] Ibid., Chap. 3, Sec. 13(2).
[139] Secs. A(1) and A(3) of the working paper of the European company work group of the Department of Justice of 17 October 2003 and Secs. 2, 8 and 14 SE Act.

2 Liquidation

75. An SE with its registered office in Finland is liquidated as a national limited-liability company under the Companies Act, i.e. voluntarily or involuntarily.[140]

A Voluntary liquidation

76. An SE's general meeting may decide to place the company in voluntary liquidation. The decision must be approved by a qualified two-thirds majority of the shares represented and votes cast at the general meeting. If the company has different classes of shares, the decision must be approved by at least two-thirds of each class of shares represented at the meeting.

B Involuntary liquidation

77. If the management or administrative organ notices when preparing an SE's annual accounts or otherwise has reason to assume that the company's equity is less than half its share capital,[141] it must prepare a balance sheet to ascertain the financial situation of the company as soon as possible. If the company's equity according to the balance sheet is indeed less than half its share capital, the balance sheet must be submitted to the auditors, and a general meeting must be held within two months to decide whether to place the company in liquidation.

The company shall be placed in liquidation unless a general meeting held no later than 12 months following the meeting referred to above adopts an audited balance sheet indicating the company's financial position when the notice of the meeting was sent, according to which the company's equity is at least half its share capital.

A company may also be placed in involuntary liquidation on grounds set out in its articles.

The decision to place a company in involuntary liquidation must be approved by half the votes cast at a general meeting.

C Liquidation procedure

78. The organ (or authority, as the case may be) deciding to place a company in liquidation shall appoint one or more liquidators to replace the administrative

---

[140] Sec. 13 of the Companies Act outlines liquidation procedures for Finnish limited-liability companies. Only the most common methods of liquidation are mentioned in this report. Certain procedures pertaining to e.g. abuse of shareholder authority are not discussed.

[141] When calculating the ratio between shareholders' equity and subscribed capital, certain adjustments must be made, such as adding any loans to shareholders' equity must be made. For a more detailed analysis of these adjustments, see J. Kyläkallio, O. Iirola and K. Kyläkallio, *op cit.*, 927–35.

organ or management and supervisory organs and the managing director. A financial statement shall be prepared for the period after the latest adopted accounts.[142] The liquidator(s) shall realise the company's assets and pay its debts. The company may continue to do business during the liquidation process only to the extent necessary for liquidation.

Should the assets of the company not suffice to pay its debts, the company shall be placed in bankruptcy. After all corporate debts have been paid, the liquidator(s) shall distribute the remaining proceeds to shareholders. The general meeting may decide to terminate the liquidation process and to continue to run the company.

3 Insolvency

79. Finnish law allows for both liquidation in bankruptcy, aimed at dissolving a company, and liquidation for the purposes of restructuring.

The latter procedure takes precedence over liquidation in bankruptcy, and an application to initiate the procedure may be filed even after a petition in bankruptcy. If applications for both procedures be pending, the application to restructure shall be given priority.

A Debt restructuring

80. An SE with its registered office in Finland may be subject to voluntary or involuntary insolvency proceedings.[143]

Insolvency proceedings may be initiated by the company, a creditor or a presumed creditor on the following grounds:

(a) voluntarily by the company itself or by one or more creditors representing at least one-fifth of the company's known claims;
(b) the company is under threat of insolvency; or
(c) the company is insolvent.[144]

The purpose of insolvency proceedings is to adjust the company's debt to correspond to its ability to pay in order to avoid bankruptcy.

After proceedings have been initiated, the company may not, subject to certain limited exceptions, pay down its debts or grant security. The company does not lose the right to govern its assets; however, legal restrictions protecting the rights of creditors shall apply. The court shall confirm the debt restructuring

---

[142] In the event of voluntary liquidation, the general meeting can decide that such a financial statement need not be prepared (Chap. 13, Sec. 8(3) Companies Act).
[143] Corporate Restructuring Act (47/1993, as amended).
[144] This report does not discuss insolvency proceedings in depth or the special regulations concerning the grounds for insolvency and other detailed provisions.

plan. Once confirmed, the plan shall govern the terms and conditions of the company's debts and other liabilities.

B Liquidation in bankruptcy

81. Liquidation in bankruptcy aims to pay all debts of the company and to liquidate the company in connection therewith.

Once proceedings have been commenced, the company automatically loses the right to govern its assets, which now belong to the bankruptcy estate. The assets are governed by a trustee in bankruptcy appointed by the relevant district court.

Bankruptcy proceedings may be initiated if the company is unable to meet its obligations on time and such inability is not merely temporary.

A petition to commence bankruptcy proceedings can be made by a creditor with a claim:

(a) based on a final judgment or other enforceable claim;
(b) based on a written agreement that the debtor does not contest; or
(c) the validity of which cannot reasonably be disputed.

4 Cessation of payments

82. Finnish law does not provide for procedures applicable in the event of insolvency or a cessation of payments other than those mentioned under nos. 80 and 81 of this report.

IX Applicable law

83. An SE with its registered office in Finland is governed by the following legislation and/or provisions:

(a) the Regulation;
(b) its articles, where expressly authorised by the Regulation;
(c) the SE Act;
(d) the Companies Act;
(e) its articles (by default).

If the SE's business is regulated by specific provisions of national law, these provisions shall apply in full and the SE must comply with them. This is the case, for example, with banking and insurance activities.[145]

---

[145] Recital 26 Reg.

X Tax treatment[146]

1 Income tax

A General remarks

84. An SE will be treated as a company (defined in Section 3 of the Income Tax Act) for tax purposes in Finland. An SE with its registered office and place of effective management in Finland is generally subject to tax in Finland. Therefore, it must pay corporate tax (presently at a rate of 26%) in Finland on its worldwide income. Applicable conventions for the avoidance of double taxation between Finland and other countries where an SE may have permanent establishments can prevent taxation in Finland of income attributable to a foreign permanent establishment. Depending on the tax treaty, double taxation is avoided either by exempting the income from Finnish tax or by granting the SE a tax credit for taxes paid in the county where the permanent establishment is located. If an SE conducts business in Finland, it is taxed in accordance with the Business Income Tax Act. An SE is subject to the same income tax laws applicable to national public limited-liability companies.

B Formation of an SE

85. The establishment of an SE by conversion does not entail any income tax consequences for the company or its shareholders. This has been confirmed by the Central Taxation Board (CTB 35/2004).

If an SE is formed by merger of a Finnish public limited-liability company with a company from an EU (or EEA) Member State in accordance with Article 2(1) of the Regulation, the merger should not result in any adverse tax consequences for the company or its shareholders, provided the following requirements are met:

(1) The other participating company (or companies) appears on the list referred in Article 3(a) of the Merger Directive.
(2) The consideration, if any, given to shareholders of the merging companies consists of cash and new shares issued by the SE, and the cash consideration does not exceed 10% of the nominal or book value of the shares.

The Finnish tax treatment of the formation of an SE by merger has yet to be confirmed by the tax authorities in a tax or advance ruling, so there is some uncertainty in this regard.

---

[146] This part was written by Antti Lehtimaja, a tax specialist with Hannes Snellman.

2   Value added tax

86. An SE is liable for value added tax (VAT) on the sale of goods and the provision of services in Finland and must register to pay VAT in Finland like any other company registered in a Member State. The current rate of VAT is 22%.

3   Other taxes

87. The liability of an SE for transfer taxes, real estate taxes and excise duties is similar to that of any other company registered in a Member State.

XI   Conclusion

88. The introduction of the SE was welcomed in Finland in public statements issued by several companies. However, by 12 April 2005, only two listed companies had publicly expressed interest in becoming an SE. The main reasons for this dampened enthusiasm are the complexity of the formation process, uncertainty about the procedure for concluding arrangements on employee involvement, and tax aspects. In addition, certain companies may be deterred by the fact that the Regulation and the Directive have not been implemented in all Member States.

At the beginning of April 2005, no SEs had been registered in Finland. However, on 15 April 2005, the first draft terms for the formation of an SE by merger were recorded with the Trade Register. Experience thus far indicates that implementation of the Regulation in the Member States involved has left certain issues of national company law unresolved. When such issues arise, the participating companies must resort to improvisation and strive to get the national authorities to co-operate.

9
Germany

WILHELM HAARMANN AND CLEMENS PHILIPP SCHINDLER
Haarmann Hemmelrath

I   Introduction   238
II Reasons to opt for an SE   239
III Formation   240
    1   General remarks   240
       A   Founding parties   240
       B   Name   241
       C   Registered office   241
          (i)   Location   241
          (ii) Transfer   242
          (iii) Protection of minority shareholders   242
          (iv) Protection of creditors   242
       D   Corporate purpose   243
       E   Capital   243
    2. Different means of formation   243
       A   Formation by merger   243
          (i) Protection of minority shareholders   244
              (a) Review of the share-exchange ratio   244
              (b) Right of appraisal   245
          (ii) Protection of creditors   246
       B   Formation of a holding SE   247
       C   Formation of a subsidiary SE   248
       D   Conversion   248
    3   Acts committed on behalf of an SE in formation   248
    4   Registration and publication   248
    5   Acquisition of legal personally   249
IV Organisation and management   249
    1   General remarks   249
    2   General meeting   249
       A   Decision-making process   250
       B   Rights and obligations of shareholders   250
    3   Organisation and management   250
       A   Two-tier system/one-tier system   250
          (i) Two-tier system   250
          (ii) One-tier-system   251
       B   Appointment and removal   253

         C   Representation   253
         D   Liability   253
V   Employee involvement   253
VI   Annual accounts and consolidated accounts   255
         1   Accounting principles   255
         2   Auditors   255
VII Supervision by the national authorities   255
VIII Dissolution   255
         1   Winding up   255
         2   Liquidation   256
         3   Insolvency   256
         4   Cessation of payments   256
IX   Applicable law   256
X   Tax treatment   256
         1   Inbound mergers   257
             (i) Prior to transposition of the Merger Directive and the directive of 17 February 2005   257
             (ii) Following transposition of the Merger Directive and the directive of 17 February 2005 into national law (i.e., as of January 2006)   258
         2   Outbound mergers   258
             (i) Prior to transposition of the Merger Directive and the directive of 17 February 2005   258
             (ii) Following transposition of the Merger Directive and the directive of 17 February 2005   259
         3   Transfer of registered office and place of effective management   260
         4   Holding SE   261
         5   Subsidiary SE   261
         6   Conversion of a German public limited company into an SE   262
XI   Conclusion   262

I Introduction

1. The rules governing the formation and structure of an SE are set forth in Regulation No. 2157/2001 of 8 October 2001 on the Statute for a European company (SE) (the 'Regulation') and Directive 2001/86/EC of 8 October 2001 supplementing the Statute for a European company with regard to the involvement of employees (the 'Directive'). Whereas the Regulation automatically entered into force on 8 October 2004 in all Member States, the Directive had to be transposed into national law. Although a regulation generally does not necessitate implementation, in this case the Regulation required action on the part of the national legislatures. In some cases, the Regulation expressly allows the Member States to enact national rules applicable only to SEs. In other instances, it requires the Member States to do so. In some areas, the Regulation is incomplete and

additional provisions will be necessary in order to ensure effective application (particularly since many national rules do not cover cross-border transactions), in which case Article 68(1) of the Regulation provides a legal basis for enacting such legislation The issues raised by implementation of the Regulation were addressed by the German legislature in a discussion draft published in March 2003.[1] A revised version of this draft was subsequently enacted as the SE Implementation Act (*'Gesetz zur Ausführung der Verordnung (EG) 2157/2001 des Rates vom 8 Oktober 2001 über das Statut der Europäischen Gesellschaft (SE) – SE-Ausführungsgesetz'* or 'SEAG'), which forms the first part of the SE Introductory Act (*'Gesetz zur Einführung der Europäischen Gesellschaft'* or 'SEEG'). The Directive was transposed into national law by means of the SE Employee Involvement Act (*'Gesetz über die Beteiligung der Arbeitnehmer in einer Europäischen Gesellschaft – SE-Beteiligungsgesetz'* or 'SEBG'), which forms the second part of the SEEG. A draft of the SEEG was published on 26 May 2004. The Regulation and the SEEG both entered into force on 8 October 2004.

The German legislature limited the scope of the SEEG to matters required to transpose the SE statute and abstained from extending the reforms to the German Stock Corporations Act. Therefore, an SE with its registered office in Germany will have very similar characteristics to a German public limited-liability company or stock corporation (*'Aktiengesellschaft'* or 'AG'), as an SE is subject to national law in the absence of specific provisions in the Regulation or the SEEG. Regarding taxation of an SE, no draft rules dealing with this issue have been published thus far.

II Reasons to opt for an SE

2. Even prior to implementation of the Regulation, German public and private limited-liability companies could engage in cross-border mergers under domestic company law. However, since no special rules exist governing the assumption of all of a company's assets and liabilities in cross-border transactions, complex, cost-intensive structures have to be set up to achieve financially comparable results. The frequently voiced criticism that an unmanageable set of rules renders the SE unattractive does not hold true in large transactions. The 'alternative solutions' traditionally used to implement cross-border mergers have entailed not only comparably higher outlay, in terms of time and organisation (depending on the structures adopted), but also a great deal of legal

---

[1] For a detailed analysis of the discussion draft, see U. Brandt, 'Der Diskussionsentwurf zu einem SEAusführungsgesetz', *Deutsches Steuerrecht*, 2003, 1208; H.-Ch. Ihrig and J. Wagner, 'Diskussionsentwurf für ein SE-Ausführungsgesetz', *Betriebs-Berater*, 2003, 969; H.-W. Neye and Ch. Teichmann, 'Der Entwurf für das Ausführungsgesetz zur Europäischen Aktiengesellschaft', *Die Aktiengesellschaft*, 2003, 169; C. Ph. Schindler, 'Vor einem Ausführungsgesetz zur Europäischen Aktiengesellschaft', *ecolex*, 2003, no. 6, script 26, 1.

uncertainty. Until the eventual adoption of the Tenth Company Law Directive on cross-border mergers, the SE represents a significantly more flexible vehicle for cross-border transactions than national corporate forms in Germany.

Another important advantage is the possibility for an SE to transfer its registered office from one Member State to another without the need to first dissolve or liquidate. Germany continues to deny this right to purely national public and private limited companies, despite the case law of the European Court of Justice (ECJ) in favour of freedom of establishment. Although it is not possible to prevent a company from transferring its registered office to another Member State, the country of incorporation has exclusive authority to decide whether to allow a transfer in the absence of dissolution or liquidation. In Germany, a national company that wishes to transfer its registered office must first liquidate and then reincorporate. However, although the SE would seem to have an advantage in this regard, the requirement that the registered office and head office of an SE be in the same Member State tends to undermine this advantage, as the company must transfer its center of administration along with its registered office.

The right to select either a two-tier or a one-tier system of management enables companies to retain or standardise their corporate form throughout Europe. This option may also work to the advantage of German companies. As it has only one executive organ, the one-tier system represents a more streamlined management structure.

The two issues that are likely to most severely limit the success of the SE in Germany are the lack of appropriate tax rules and the unattractive provisions on employee involvement. The latter, of course, may also be viewed as a reason to opt for an SE, if structures can be found that render the level of employee involvement acceptable. Changes are also likely to occur in the field of taxation as a result of recent ECJ case law and new legislation in various areas of direct taxation.

III   Formation

1   General remarks

A   Founding parties

3. In general, only companies incorporated under the laws of a Member State and whose registered and head offices are located in the European Union can form an SE. However, the Member States can provide that a company whose head office is not located in the European Union is entitled to participate in the formation of an SE, provided that company is incorporated under the laws of a Member State, has its registered office in that Member State and has a real and continuous link with the economy of a Member State (Art. 2(5) Reg.). As

such a provision could be viewed as prejudicial to German companies, which are not permitted to have their registered office and centre of administration in different countries, the German legislature did not adopt this option.[2]

B   Name

4. No special rules apply.

C   Registered office
(i)   **Location**

5. Article 7 of the Regulation provides that the registered office and head office of an SE must be located in the same Member State. This provision has been roundly criticised by many authorities. The prevailing opinion is that Article 7 does not run contrary to the case law of the ECJ.[3] Therefore, German lawmakers have enacted appropriate national rules (especially to implement the provisions of Article 64 of the Regulation).

Germany has also exercised the option set forth in Article 7 of the Regulation that an SE's registered office and head office must be in the same place. The corresponding provision in the Stock Corporations Act (*Aktiengesetz* or 'AktG')

---

[2] Ch. Teichmann, 'Germany', in *The European Company – All Over Europe*, Oplustil and Teichmann (eds.), de Gruyter, Berlin, 2004, 111.

[3] H. Eidenmüller, 'Mobilität und Restrukturierung von Unternehmen im Binnenmarkt: Entwicklungsperspektiven des europäischen Gesellschaftsrechts im Schnittfeld von Gemeinschaftsgesetzgeber und EuGH', *Juristenzeitung*, 2004, 24; M. Lind, *Die Europäische Aktiengesellschaft*, Neuer Wissenschaftlicher, Verlag, Vienna, 2004, 72; C. Ph. Schindler, 'Überseering und Societas Europaea: Vereinbar oder nicht vereinbar, das ist hier die Frage', *Recht der Wirtschaft*, 2003, 124 *et seq.*; C. Ph. Schindler, 'Das Ausführungsgesetz zur Europäischen Aktiengesellschaft', *Wirtschaftsrechtliche Blätter*, 2004, 254 *et seq.*; Ch. Teichmann, 'The European Company – A Challenge to Academics, Legislatures and Practitioners', 4 *German Law Journal*, 2003, 315; CH. Teichmann, 'Minderheitenschutz bei Gründung und Sitzverlegung der SE', *Zeitschrift für Unternehmens- und Gesellschaftsrecht*, 2003, 399 *et seq.*; O. Thömmes, 'EC Law Aspects of the Transfer of Seat of an SE', *European Taxation*, 2004, 27. With reference to C. Ph. Schindler, 'Überseering und Societas Europaea: Vereinbar oder nicht vereinbar, das ist hier die Frage', *Recht der Wirtschaft*, 2003, 124 *et seq.*; S. Lombardo and P. Pasotti. 'The "Societas Europaea": A Network Economics Approach', ECGI Law Working Paper No. 19/2004, 12, available at http://ssrn.com/abstract=493422; M. Wenz, 'The European Company (Societas Europaea) Legal Concept and Tax Issues', *European Taxation*, 2004, 9; see also (concurring) S. Kalss and C. Greda, 'Die Europäische Gesellschaft (SE) österreichischer Prägung nach dem Ministerialentwurf', *Der Gesellschafter*, 2004, 94; S. Leible, 'Niederlassungsfreiheit und Sitzverlegungsrichtlinie', *Zeitschrift für Unternehmens- und Gesellschaftsrecht*, 2004, 548; (dissenting) K. Hempel, in H. Mayer, EUV EGV, Manz, Vienna, 2003, no. 46; T. Ratka, 'Der dritte Streich: EuGH entscheidet Inspire Art', *GeS aktuell*, 2003, 434; E. Wymeersch, 'The Transfer of the Company's Seat in European Company Law', ECGI – Law Working Paper No. 08/2003, 25 *et seq.*, available at http://ssrn.com/abstract=384802; E. Wymeersch, 'Cross-border Transfer of the Seat of a Company – EU Case Law and SE Regulation', in Rickford (ed.), *The European Company*, Intersentia, Antwerp, 2003, 91; H. Ziemons, 'Freie Bahn für den Umzug von Gesellschaften nach Inspire Art?!', *Zeitschrift für Wirtschaftsrecht*, 2003, 1918.

is less onerous, however, since it only requires that the registered office be in the same place as the company's plant, place of effective management or centre of administration. While the discussion draft initially extended this rule to SEs, the SEAG takes the option contained in the Regulation at face value.

(ii) **Transfer**

6. The cross-border transfer of the registered office of a German company is not regulated by national law. German conflict-of-laws rules basically follow the head office theory (*Sitztheorie*) and prohibit the cross-border transfer of the registered office of a German company in the absence of dissolution and liquidation. Therefore, the flexibility afforded by Article 8 of the Regulation is an exclusive privilege of the SE and a powerful incentive to select this corporate form in Germany.

(iii) **Protection of minority shareholders**

7. The Regulation affords protection to minority shareholders by requiring the provision of information in advance and giving them a say in the decision-making process. In addition, the Member States have the option to extend these rights. The German legislature deemed it necessary to do so since an SE becomes subject to another country's laws when its registered office is transferred to another Member State. According to the list of applicable legislation set forth in Article 9 of the Regulation, the transfer will also affect shareholder rights, as the rules on this subject have yet to be harmonised and so can differ significantly from one Member State to another. In addition, certain disadvantages, such as language barriers or a greater distance from the company's headquarters, may arise. Therefore, the German legislature opted to provide for an appraisal remedy to allow dissenting shareholders to exit the company in return for reasonable cash compensation. The legislature did not distinguish between listed and unlisted companies in this respect. At a shareholder's request, the adequacy of the amount paid for the shares is subject to judicial review. On the other hand, it is not possible to challenge resolutions passed by the general meeting on the ground that the cash payment is inadequate (Sec. 11(2) in conjunction with Sec. 7(5) SEAG). The procedure set forth in Section 12 of the SEAG is based on the same principles as those applicable to mergers (see below).

(iv) **Protection of creditors**

8. Article 8(7) of the Regulation requires adequate protection of creditors before the court or other competent authority can issue a certificate confirming that all acts and formalities necessary to transfer an SE's registered office have been completed. Section 13 of the SEAG offers preliminary protection and requires the provision of security before registration of a transfer can go through. Only creditors who can establish that satisfaction of their claims would be jeopardised by the transfer are entitled to request security. It should also be kept in mind that Article 8(16) of the Regulation affords additional protection to creditors

by providing that with respect to any cause of action that arose prior to the transfer, an SE shall be deemed to have its registered office in the Member State where the claim arose. In addition, Article 8(7) gives the Member States the option to extend their rules on the protection of creditors and the holders of other rights with respect to an SE to all liabilities that arose prior to the transfer. Section 13(2) of the SEAG adopts this option in a modified form and restricts creditor protection to claims that arose up to 14 days following publication of the transfer proposal. This period is based on Section 15(2) of the German Commercial Code ('HGB'), which sets forth the fundamental principle that facts shall be deemed known 14 days after publication.[4]

D   Corporate purpose

No specific rules apply.

E   Capital

9. The SEAG does not deal with the raising and maintenance of capital since Article 5 of the Regulation refers directly to the harmonised national rules applicable to public limited-liability companies. In Germany, the respective provisions of the Stock Corporations Act shall apply.

2   Different means of formation

A   Formation by merger

10. The formation of an SE by merger requires the involvement of at least two public limited-liability companies governed by the laws of different Member States which have both their registered office and head office in the European Union. A merger can be carried out through the acquisition by one company of another or through the formation of a new company. In the latter case, the new company, i.e. the SE, can establish its registered office and head office in a third Member State.

Each merging company is governed by the rules applicable to mergers involving public limited companies of the Member State in which it has its registered office. For German public limited companies participating in a merger, these rules are set forth in the Transformation Act (*Umwandlungsgesetz* or 'UmwG'), which transposed into national law Directive 78/855/EEC.

Accordingly, when forming an SE by merger, the German merging company must prepare the following documents: (i) draft terms of merger, (ii) a management ('*Vorstand*') report; and (iii) a report on the merger by an independent court-appointed expert. In addition, certain information about the merger must

---

[4] Ch. Teichmann, *op cit.* (footnote 2), 128.

be published at least one month in advance (Sec. 61 Transformation Act in conjunction with Sec. 123 Stock Corporations Act). Since one of the main purposes of this procedure is to protect creditors' rights, this one-month period must be observed even if all shares in the merging companies are held by a sole shareholder.

The merger plan and terms of merger must be approved by the general meeting of each merging company. Following approval, the terms of merger must be filed with the relevant local register. According to Section 4 of the SEAG, this is the trade register (*'Handelsregister'*) of the competent court of registry (*'Registergericht'*)). After scrutinising the legality of the merger as regards the merging company, the court of registry shall issue a certificate conclusively attesting to completion of the requisite pre-merger acts and formalities (Art. 25(2) Reg.).

Once such a certificate has been issued for each merging company, the competent court of registry shall scrutinise the legality of the merger as regards that part of the procedure concerning the completion of the merger and formation of the SE (Art. 26(1) Reg.). In particular, the court must ensure that arrangements for employee involvement have been concluded pursuant to the Directive. The merger and simultaneous formation of the SE shall take effect on the date the SE is recorded in the trade register (Art. 27(1) Reg.).

(i) **Protection of minority shareholders**

11. In addition to the provisions of the Regulation, as supplemented by national rules on mergers, the Member States can adopt rules to protect minority shareholders who oppose a merger (Art. 24(2) Reg.).

(a) Review of the share-exchange ratio

12. Section 15 of the Transformation Act grants shareholders the right to have the share-exchange ratio reviewed by a court. If the court finds that the ratio is unfair, the shareholders are entitled to receive cash compensation.[5] However, shareholders cannot contest resolutions passed by the general meeting on the grounds that the share-exchange ratio is inadequate or that the company failed to comply with the information obligations contained in the preparatory documents. Review of the share-exchange ratio forms the subject of a special procedure, referred to as the 'decision body procedure' (*'Spruchstellenverfahren'*), and cannot prevent or delay registration of a merger.

Section 6 of the SEAG extends this procedure to the formation of an SE by merger. However, Section 6 only protects shareholders of the *transferring* companies and not those of the acquiring or receiving company. While the discussion draft intended to extend protection to all shareholders, the German legislature

---

[5] *Ibid.*, 112.

decided otherwise in order to avoid departing from the national rules applicable to public limited-liability companies in this regard.

According to Article 25(3) of the Regulation, a procedure to amend the share-exchange ratio or compensate minority shareholders shall only be given effect if the other merging companies situated in Member States which do not provide for such a procedure explicitly accept it when approving the draft terms. Thus, explicit acceptance will be necessary whenever a company whose registered office is not in Germany or Austria (the only Member States that provide for such a procedure) is involved in a merger.

As previously stated, Article 24(2) of the Regulation provides that the Member States can adopt provisions to protect minority shareholders who oppose a merger. However, it is doubtful that the procedure set forth in Section 6 of the SEAG was the sort of protection envisaged by the Regulation, which only refers to provisions designed to ensure appropriate protection for minority shareholders who *oppose* a merger. This is clearly not the case with Section 6, which has been sharply criticised by many authorities.[6] The German legislature obviously believes Section 6 conforms to the Regulation; this issue will ultimately need to be referred to the ECJ.

Nevertheless, further details regarding this procedure are warranted. Section 6(4) of the SEAG, in conjunction with Section 4 of the Decision Body Procedure Act ('*Spruchverfahrensgesetz*' or '*SpruchG*'), requires an application for review to be filed within three months following registration of a merger. If the share-exchange ratio is found to be inadequate, the additional compensation due shareholders shall be increased by interest accrued from the date of registration of the merger (or publication of the registration notice, depending on applicable law) (Sec. 6(3) SEAG).

(b) Right of appraisal

13. Minority shareholders who oppose a merger can exit the company in return for cash compensation (Sec. 7 SEAG). This procedure is derived from Section 29 *et seq.* of the Transformation Act. As in the case of review of the share-exchange ratio, only shareholders of the transferring company have such a right. In addition, it is restricted to shareholders of a company whose assets

---

[6] U. Brandt, *op cit.*(footnote 1), 1210; Deutscher Anwaltsverein, 'Stellungnahme zum Diskussionsentwurf eines Gesetzes zur Ausführung der Verordnung (EG) Nr.2157/2001 des Rates vom 8 Oktober 2001 über das Statut der Europäischen Gesellschaft', available at http://www.anwaltverein.de/03/05/2003/65-03.pdf; H.-Ch. Ihrig and J. Wagner, *op cit.*, 972; C. Ph. Schindler, *op cit.* (footnote 3), 5 *et seq.* Dissenting: CH. Teichmann, *op cit.* (footnote 1), 384 *et seq.*; S. Kalss, 'Der Minderheitenschutz bei Gründung und Sitzverlegung der SE nach dem Diskussionsentwurf', *Zeitschrift für Unternehmens – und Gesellschaftsrecht*, 2003, 603; cf. Ch. Teichmann, 'Die Einführung der Europäischen Aktiengesellschaft Grundlage der Ergänzung des europäischen Statuts durch den deutschen Gesetzgeber', *Zeitschrift für Unternehmens- und Gesellschaftsrecht*, 2002, footnote 181, 426.

are transferred to an SE with its registered office outside Germany. The initial discussion draft extended this right to all shareholders, i.e. it did not distinguish between shareholders of the transferring company and those of the acquiring company and did not limit the right of appraisal to cases where an SE is formed with its registered office outside Germany. Regarding this amendment, doubts have been raised as to whether the adopted provision is discriminatory and hence violates the fundamental freedoms enshrined in the EC treaty.[7]

The shareholders have two months following registration of the merger in which to accept the cash offer. As the merging companies cease to exist upon registration of the SE, the latter is responsible for making the cash payment. In principle, payment by a company in return for its own shares constitutes a stock redemption. Therefore, the SEAG refers to Section 71 of the Stock Corporations Act, which permits a company to acquire its own shares for this purpose. As with the share-exchange ratio, shareholders have the right to have the adequacy of the offer reviewed by a court. Section 7(7) of the SEAG, read in conjunction with Section 4 of the Decision Body Procedure Act, requires an application for judicial review to be filed within three months following registration of the SE. In this case, recourse to judicial review (but not the cash offer) is subject to explicit acceptance by the general meeting of all companies situated in Member States that do not provide for such a procedure (i.e. all Member States other than Germany and Austria). If the other companies accept, shareholders cannot challenge the merger based on the alleged inadequacy of the cash payment or the share-exchange ratio. The court's decision is binding on the SE and its shareholders (Art. 25(3) Reg.).

(ii) **Protection of creditors**

14. In this regard, Section 8 of the SEAG refers to the procedure set forth in Section 7 (see above) if the registered office of the acquiring company is or shall be located outside Germany. (Like Section 7, Section 8 could be deemed discriminatory and this to violate the fundamental freedoms of the EC treaty.) If, on the other hand, the SE's registered office shall be in Germany, the procedure described in Section 22 of the Transformation Act applies. As the latter provision only grants creditors deferred protection, the legislature believed additional safeguards were necessary in order to provide adequate protection against the risks inherent in cross-border transactions. Even if one adheres to this view, however, the problem with Section 8 is its lack of a legal basis,[8] as Article 24(1) of the Regulation refers to the law of the Member State governing each merging company with regard to the protection of creditors.[9] The German legislature

---

[7] See H. Hügel, in Sekonmentare, Kalss and Hügel (eds).

[8] Deutscher Anwaltsverein, *op cit.* (footnote 6), 78; H.-Ch. Ihrig and J. Wagner, *op cit.* (footnote 1), 973; C. Ph. Schindler, *op cit.* (footnote 1), 7.

[9] C. Ph. Schindler, *Die Europäische Aktiengesellschaft*, LexisNexis, Vienna, 2002, 28; O. Vossius in *Umwandlungsrecht*, Widmann and Mayer (ed.), Stollfuß, Bonn, 2002, §20 UmwG no. 446.

contends that a legal basis for this provision can be derived from the phrase 'taking into account the cross-border nature of the merger', which follows the reference to national law in Article 24(1). This phrase could be construed to extend national rules and may justify preliminary protection in certain cases, but it clearly does not form the basis for an SE-specific set of creditor-protection rules.[10]

B Formation of a holding SE

15. Pursuant to Article 34 of the Regulation, the Member States can adopt provisions designed to ensure adequate protection of minority shareholders who oppose the formation of a holding SE. The German legislation offers dissenting shareholders an appraisal right (Sec. 9 SEAG, which refers to Sec. 7 SEAG) and all shareholders the possibility of judicial review of the share-exchange ratio (Sec. 11 SEAG, which refers to Sec. 6 SEAG).

The appraisal right[11] is available in two instances. First, shareholders have the right to dispose of their shares in the founding companies if the registered office of the proposed SE will be located outside Germany. An appraisal right also exists if the SE becomes a 'dependent company', as defined in Section 17 of the Stock Corporations Act.

The protection afforded minority shareholders in connection with the formation of a holding SE may appear excessive, since the formation of a holding SE is much less risky than a cross-border merger.[12] In the formation of a holding SE, shareholders cannot be forced to exchange their shares, and the founding companies do not cease to exist as a result. Therefore, each shareholder can freely decide whether to exchange its shares for shares in the newly formed SE. Thus, the procedure for judicial review of the share-exchange ratio (Sec. 11 SEAG) would seem to lack any real justification since the exchange of shares is voluntary and based on a disclosed, predetermined ratio.[13]

In addition to the protection of minority shareholders, the SEAG treats two other issues with respect to the formation of a holding SE (Sec. 10 SEAG).

According to Article 32(6) of the Regulation, the general meeting of each company promoting the formation of a holding SE must approve the underlying

---

[10] Cf. C. Ph. Schindler, *op cit.* (footnote 3), 261.
[11] Regarding the possible conflict with the capital markets law, see Ch. Teichmann, 'Austrittsrecht und Pflichtangebot bei Gründung einer Europäischen Aktiengesellschaft', *Die Aktiengesellschaft*, 2004, 73.
[12] Stressing the similarities with a merger Ch. Teichmann, *op cit.* (footnote. 3), 16 *et seq.*
[13] Deutscher Anwaltsverein, *op cit.* (footnote 6), p. 78; F. Kübler, 'Leitungsstrukturen der Aktiengesellschaft und die Umsetzung des SE-Statuts', *Zeitung für das gesamte Handelsrecht und Wirtschaftsrecht*, 2003, 631; K. Oplustil, 'Selected Problems Concerning Formation of a Holding SE (Societas Europaea)', *German Law Journal*, 2003, 122 *et seq*, *available at* http://www.germanlawjournal.com; C. Ph. Schindler, *op cit.* (footnote 1), 8.

draft terms. However, no mention is made of the majority required to pass such a shareholder resolution. There are two possible explanations for this. One is to regard the lack of reference to Article 7 of Directive 78/855/EEC, as is contained in Article 31(3) of the 1991 draft of the Regulation, as an inadvertent omission on the part of the Community legislature and to fill in the gap with reference to the majority required to approve the formation of an SE by merger.[14] Another solution would be to argue that the omission was intentional and that a simple majority of votes cast is thus sufficient to pass a shareholder resolution in this respect.[15,16] The German legislature opted for the first solution and, therefore, a qualified majority of no less than three quarters of the votes cast is required (Sec. 10(1) SEAG).

The second issue is procedural in scope. With respect to the formation of a holding SE, the Regulation does not require the issuance of a certificate confirming the completion of certain pre-formation acts and formalities. However, a holding SE may not be registered until it has been shown that the formalities referred to in Article 32 of the Regulation have been completed (Art. 33(5) Reg.).[17] Thus, Section 10(2) of the SEAG requires that an SE's management board file a statement along with the application for registration to the effect that no lawsuits challenging the shareholder resolution have been filed or that any such proceedings have been abandoned or dismissed. This requirement is based on Section 16(2) of the Transformation Act.

C   Formation of a subsidiary SE

16. No special rules apply.

D   Conversion

17. No special rules apply.

3   Acts committed on behalf of an SE in formation

18. No special rules apply.

4   Registration and publication

19. Article 12 of the Regulation provides that an SE shall be registered in the Member State in which it has its registered office. In this regard, Section 3

---

[14] C. Ph. Schindler, *op cit.* (footnote 8), 35 *et seq.*; A. Schulz and B. Geismar, 'Die Europäische Aktiengesellschaft Eine kritische Be standsaufnahme', *Deutsches Steuerrecht*, 2001, 1081; Ch. Teichmann, *op cit.* (footnote 6), 435; Ch. Teichmann, *op cit.* (footnote 3), 391 *et seq.*

[15] M. Casper, 'Der Lückenschluß im Statut der Europäischen Aktiengesellschaft', in *Festschrift für Peter Ulmer*, Habersack *et al.* (ed.), de Gruyter, Berlin, 2003, 60; J. Neun, 'Gründung', in *Die Europäische Aktiengesellschaft*, Theisen/Wenz (ed.), Schäffer Pöschl, Stuttgart, 2002, 141.

[16] For further references, see K. Oplustil, *op cit.* (footnote 12), 116 *et seq.*

[17] Ch. Teichmann, *op cit.* (footnote 2), 116.

of the SEAG refers to the trade register, in accordance with the relevant provisions governing German public limited-liability companies. According to Section 4 of the SEAG, the trade register is also the competent authority for all other procedures mentioned in Articles 8, 25, 26, 54, 55 and 64 of the Regulation (Art. 68(2) Reg.). For example, the trade register must issue a certificate attesting to completion of the acts and formalities required to transfer the registered office of an SE (Art. 8(8) Reg.) or to form an SE by merger (Art. 25(2) Reg.).

The SEAG did not adopt the proposal made in the literature[18] that a special body should be established to hear proceedings involving SEs. While it is certainly true that questions may arise in connection with an SE that would not with respect to national companies, these questions will normally concern the interpretation of Community law, on which the ECJ is the ultimate arbiter.[19] To resolve such questions, use should be made of the preliminary ruling procedure described in Article 234 of the EC Treaty.[20]

5 Acquisition of legal personality

20. No special rules apply.

IV Organisation and management

1 General remarks

21. The internal organisation of an SE is comparable to that of a German stock corporation. The main difference is that the shareholders of an SE may select either a one-tier or a two-tier system of management. Depending on their choice, the SE will have either two or three corporate bodies: the general meeting of shareholders, a management board and a supervisory board (in the two-tier system) or the general meeting and an administrative organ (in the one-tier system).

2 General meeting

22. The Regulation does not give much leeway to the national legislatures with regard to the general meeting of shareholders,. According to Article 53 of the Regulation, the organisation and conduct of general meetings as well as voting procedures shall be governed by the law applicable to public limited-liability companies of the Member State in which an SE's registered office is located.

---

[18] U. Brandt, 'Überlegungen zu einem SE-Ausführungsgesetz', *Neue Zeitschrift für Gesellschaftsrecht*, 2002, 995.
[19] Cf. C. Ph. Schindler, *op cit.* (footnote 1), 3, footnote 23.
[20] Ch. Teichmann, *op cit.* (footnote 21), 118.

Articles 55 and 56 of the Regulation provide that one or more shareholders who collectively hold at least 10% of an SE's subscribed capital may require the company to convene a general meeting and draw up an agenda or request that additional items be placed on the agenda of an upcoming general meeting. According to the Regulation, national law may provide for a smaller percentage under the same conditions applicable to public limited-liability companies. The German legislature has adopted this option and reduced the threshold to 5% (or a corresponding value of €500,000), in keeping with Section 122 of the Stock Corporations Act.

A Decision-making process

23. According to Article 59 of the Regulation, amendments to the articles of an SE must be approved by at least two-thirds of the votes cast at a general meeting, unless the law applicable to public limited-liability companies of the Member State in which the SE's registered office is located requires or permits a larger majority. In Germany, Section 179(2) of the Stock Corporations Act requires a qualified majority of no less than three-quarters of the votes cast. The articles may provide that a simple majority of votes cast is sufficient if at least half the share capital is present or represented at the general meeting (Sec. 51 SEAG). This reduced quorum is not applicable to changes to an SE's corporate purpose, a resolution to transfer its registered office pursuant to Article 8(6) of the Regulation or where a higher majority is required by law.

B Rights and obligations of shareholders

24. The SEAG does not provide detailed rules regarding the rights and obligations of shareholders. The relevant provisions of the SEAG concern the right to require the company to convene a general meeting (see above) and the rights of shareholders during formation of an SE.

3 Organisation and management

The Regulation provides that an SE may have either a two-tier (a supervisory board and a management board) or a one-tier (an administrative organ) system of management. This choice will not affect the scope of employee involvement rights.

A Two-tier system/one-tier system

(i) **Two-tier system**

25. Article 39(5) of the Regulation states that where national law does not provide for a two-tier system of management in relation to public limited-liability companies established within the territory of that Member State, the national legislature may adopt appropriate measures in relation to SEs. The

two-tier system set forth in the Regulation corresponds to the German *Vorstand-*and-*Aufsichtsrat* model. Article 39(5) only applies to Member States where no provision is made in national company law for a two-tier system. If such a system already exists, as is the case in Germany, national law applies in addition to Articles 39 to 42 of the Regulation, and SE-specific rules are permitted.[21]

However, the Regulation offers certain possibilities to Member States where provision is made for a two-tier-system. Thus, the SEAG refers to certain provisions of the Stock Corporations Act. For example, Section 15 of the SEAG adopts the wording of Section 105(2) of the Stock Corporations Act (on the assumption by members of the supervisory board of managerial functions) and Sections 16 and 17 of the SEAG mirror Sections 76(2) and 95(1) of the Stock Corporations Act (on the number of members of the management and supervisory boards, which also depends on employee participation rights). Section 18 of the SEAG states that the supervisory board can request reports from the management board in accordance with Section 90 of the Stock Corporations Act, while Section 19 is based on Section 111(4) of the Stock Corporations Act, which provides that the supervisory organ may stipulate certain categories of transactions that require its authorisation.[22]

(ii) **One-tier-system**

26. In general, the administrative organ (*Verwaltungsrat*) must have at least three members. If the capital of an SE is €3 million or less and its articles do not provide otherwise, the number of members of the administrative organ can be reduced to one. On the other hand, Section 23 of the SEAG stipulates the maximum number of members of the administrative organ, which is based on the SE's share capital. In any event, the number of members cannot exceed twenty-one for an SE with share capital in excess of €10 million. The members of the administrative organ are appointed by the general meeting (Art. 43(3) Reg.). Removal is addressed by Section 29 of the SEAG, which corresponds to Section 103 of the Stock Corporations Act (on the removal of supervisory board members). Consequently, board members who have been appointed by non-binding means may be removed prior to expiry of their term of office by a qualified majority of at least three-quarters of the votes cast.

The administrative organ manages the company, issues guidelines governing its activities, and supervises implementation of the same (Sec. 22(1) SEAG). While the administrative organ is responsible for determining the company's long-term business strategy and policy, the managing directors are in charge of day-to-day management. Section 40 of the SEAG requires the appointment of at least one managing director. The managing directors may be chosen from amongst the members of the administrative organ or from outside candidates. However, a majority of members of the administrative organ cannot also be

---

[21] *Ibid.*, 119. [22] *Ibid.*

managing directors. Members of the administrative organ shall be held jointly liable notwithstanding any delegation of managerial authority to the managing directors or amongst themselves. Ultimate responsibility for management of the company therefore rests with the administrative organ. This constitutes a significant difference with the two-tier system, in which managerial authority is divided amongst two organs.[23] The provisions of the SEAG on the administrative organ largely reflect the provisions applicable to the supervisory board of a German public limited company, with changes where necessary. For example, the appointment (Sec. 28 SEAG), removal (Sec. 29 SEAG) and qualifications (Sec. 27 SEAG) of members of the administrative organ, as well as its composition (Sec. 24 SEAG), internal procedures (Sec. 34 SEAG), and rules for calling meetings (Sec. 37 SEAG) and passing resolutions, are based on corresponding provisions of the Stock Corporation Act.

Section 22(6) of the SEAG allocates to the administrative organ the responsibilities of the supervisory board as well as those of the management organ, some of which are expressly listed, including the preparation and implementation of resolutions for the general meeting and the convening of the general meeting if the company's subscribed capital falls by more than fifty percent. However, the administrative organ need not engage in daily management tasks itself. Certain tasks, such as preparing trade register applications and providing information to shareholders prior to a general meeting, are entrusted to the managing directors (Sec. 40 SEAG). The managing directors are also responsible for preparing the annual accounts and submitting information to the trade register (Sec. 47 SEAG).

The German legislature did not base the provisions of managing directors on Article 47(1) of the Regulation, which provides that if a company or other legal entity sits on the management organ of an SE, it must appoint a natural person to perform its duties in its stead, as this article only applies if no provision is made under the law governing public limited-liability companies of the Member State in which the SE has its registered office. As this is not the case in Germany, Article 47(1) is not applicable. Rather, the German legislature relied on Article 43(4) of the Regulation, which states that where no provision is made for a one-tier system in relation to public limited-liability companies with their registered offices within its territory, a Member State may adopt the appropriate measures with respect to SEs.

The managing directors are subject to oversight by the administrative organ, which appoints them and can remove them at any time without cause (Sec. 40(1) and (5) SEAG). The managing directors have unlimited authority to represent the company vis-à-vis third parties (Sec. 44(1) SEAG), but as far as internal matters are concerned, they must comply with the instructions of and restrictions

---

[23] *Ibid.*, 121.

imposed by the administrative organ. Thus, their position is comparable to the managing directors of a private limited-liability company (*Gesellschaft mit beschränkter Haftung* or 'GmbH').

B Appointment and removal

27. Members of the management board are appointed in accordance with national law by the company's supervisory board for a maximum term of five years. The right to remove members from office prior to expiry of their term is severely restricted (Sec. 84(3) AktG).

Members of the administrative organ are appointed by the general meeting (Art. 43(3) Reg.) and can be removed from office at any time with the approval of at least three-quarters of the votes cast (Sec. 29(1) SEAG). If the administrative organ does not have enough members to take a decision, vacancies can be filled by court appointment, in accordance with similar rules to those applicable to the supervisory board of a German stock corporation. The managing directors in the one-tier system are appointed by the administrative organ (Sec. 40(1) SEAG) and can be removed without cause by the administrative organ (Sec. 40(5) SEAG).

C Representation

28. A two-tier SE is represented by its management board (Sec. 78 AktG), while a one-tier SE is represented by its managing director(s) (Sec. 41 SEAG).

D Liability

29. No special rules apply.

V Employee involvement

30. Individual employment relationships remain unaffected by the formation of an SE, regardless of the means of formation selected. However, special rules apply to the involvement of employees as a whole. In this context, a distinction must be made between involvement through a works council and involvement via the supervisory or administration organ.

The Works Constitution Act (*Betriebsverfassungsgesetz*) and the various Codetermination Acts (*Mitbestimmungsgesetz, Drittelbeteiligungsgesetz, Montan-Mitbestimmungsgesetz*) contain mandatory rules on employee involvement in national companies and on the formation, rights and duties of various corporate bodies. The SEBG, on the other hand, offers a more flexible approach with regard to employee involvement in an SE by providing for negotiations between management and labour. If the parties cannot reach an agreement on employee involvement, the SEBG provides for the application of alternative rules.

When forming an SE, a special negotiating body ('SNB') must be established. The SNB's sole task is to negotiate an agreement on employee involvement within the competent organ of each participating company.

According to Section 4 of the SEBG, immediately after publication of the draft terms of merger (or other relevant document, depending on the means of formation), the management or administrative organ of each participating company shall inform its employee representatives of the identity of the other participating companies, concerned subsidiaries and establishments and the number of employees they employ. Thereafter, the employee representatives shall form a representative body (Sec. 8 SEBG) to elect members to the SNB (Sec. 11 SEBG). Elections shall be held within ten weeks following the provision of the information specified above (Sec. 11(1) SEBG). If no works council exists, SNB members shall be elected by the employees directly (Sec. 8(7) SEBG).

Negotiations start as soon as the SNB is established and may continue for up to six months (Sec. 20(1) SEBG). The parties may jointly decide to extend negotiations for up to one year following establishment of the SNB (Sec. 20(2) SEBG).

The agreement on employee involvement shall contain provisions regarding its scope, the composition, number of members and allocation of seats on the works council, the functions and procedure for informing and consulting the representative body, etc. (Sec. 21(1) SEBG). The agreement shall specify the number of employee representatives on the supervisory or administrative organ, the election procedure and the rights of these representatives (Sec. 21(3) SEBG).

If no agreement can be reached, the rules set forth in the SEBG shall apply (Secs. 22 and 34 SEBG), in which case the formation of a works council is mandatory. The authority of an SE works council is not comparable to that of the works council in a regular German company, which has codetermination rights. An SE works council need only be informed and consulted about current business and future developments.

With regard to employee participation in the administrative or supervisory organ, the rules contained in the SEBG shall apply:

(i) to an SE formed by conversion if rules on codetermination in the supervisory or administrative organ applied prior to conversion;
(ii) to an SE formed by merger if, prior to registration of the SE, codetermination rights existed in one or more participating companies involving at least 25% of the total number of employees of all participating companies; if this threshold is not met, the SNB shall decide whether the SEBG rules should apply;
(iii) to a holding or subsidiary SE if, prior to registration of the SE, codetermination rights existed in one or more participating companies involving

at least 50% of the total number of employees of all participating companies; if this threshold is not met, the SNB shall decide whether the rules set forth in the SEBG should apply.

For an SE formed by conversion, the rules applicable before the conversion shall continue to apply thereafter (Sec. 35(1) SEBG). For an SE formed by merger or a holding or subsidiary SE, the number of employee representatives is based on the highest number of representatives in any participating company (Sec. 35(2) SEBG). Therefore, if a German company participates in the formation of an SE, the German rules will most likely apply.

In this context, it should be mentioned that, according to the SEBG, the employees of participating companies and their subsidiaries are taken into account in determining whether the above thresholds are met. It remains unclear, however, whether this provision conforms to Article 7 of the Directive, which only refers to 'participating companies', defined in Article 2(b) of the Directive as 'companies directly participating in the establishing of an SE'.

VI Annual accounts and consolidated accounts

31. After the managing directors submit the annual accounts, the administrative organ must call a general meeting (Sec. 47 SEAG). The managing directors must also submit a proposal on the use to which the company's profits should be put. These rules apply *mutatis mutandis* to consolidated annual accounts. The annual accounts shall be deemed final once approved by the administrative organ, which may, however, delegate this duty to the general meeting (Sec. 47(4) SEAG).

1 Accounting principles

32. No special rules apply.

2 Auditors

33. No special rules apply.

VII Supervision by the national authorities

34. No special rules apply.

VIII Dissolution

1 Winding up

35. No special rules apply.

2 Liquidation

36. According to Article 7 of the Regulation, the registered office of an SE must be located in the same Member State as its head office. The German legislature has implemented the provisions of Article 64 of the Regulation, which provides that the Member State in which an SE's registered office is located shall take appropriate measure to force the company to regularise its position if it no longer complies with the requirement set forth in Article 7. According to Section 52 of the SEAG, a violation of Article 7 shall be treated as a defect in an SE's articles as provided in Section 262(1) and (5) of the Stock Corporations Act. The liquidation procedure set forth in Section 144a of the *Gesetz über die Angelegenheiten der Freiwilligen Gerichtsbarkeit* shall apply accordingly. If the SE does not regularise its situation within a reasonable period of time, the competent court shall declare it in violation of Article 7. This decision may be appealed, although the company shall be deemed liquidated once it enters into effect.[24]

3 Insolvency

37. No special rules apply.

4 Cessation of payments

38. No special rules apply.

IX Applicable law

39. No special rules apply.

X Tax treatment

40. Neither the SEEG nor the Regulation contains provisions regarding the taxation of an SE. Therefore, national rules shall apply, and an SE shall be treated like any other national company (*Kapitalgesellschaft*) for tax purposes.

This report does not address the Merger Directive[25] or the directive of 17 February 2005 amending the Merger Directive.[26] Please refer to the general report on taxation in this book for more information in this regard.

---

[24] Cf. *ibid.*, 118.

[25] Council Directive 90/434/EEC of 23 July 1990 on the common system of taxation applicable to mergers, divisions, transfers of assets and exchanges of shares concerning companies of different Member States, *Official Journal* L 225/1 of 20 August 1990.

[26] Council Directive 2005/19/EC of 17 February 2005 amending Directive 90/434/EEC 1990 on the common system of taxation applicable to mergers, divisions, transfers of assets and exchanges

1 Inbound mergers

(i) **Prior to transposition of the Merger Directive and the directive of 17 February 2005**

41. It could be argued that the Merger Directive should have been transposed into national law by now and thus has direct effect. However, the SE was not mentioned in the original text of the Merger Directive (prior to amendment), so this argument is moot.

In an inbound merger, public limited companies merge to form an SE that is a resident of Germany for tax purposes. The merger of two or more German public limited companies to form an SE can be achieved on a book-value basis without the realisation of hidden reserves in the companies' assets. In addition, there are convincing arguments that assets attributable to the German permanent establishment of a foreign public limited company can be transferred to a newly formed SE with no adverse tax consequences. However, there is neither precedent nor clear wording in the tax code to support this contention.

At the shareholder level, formation of an SE by merger is not a taxable event. However, if shareholders of a merging public limited-liability company are residents of Germany for tax purposes, an exchange of shares (i.e., shares in a foreign company are contributed to a newly formed SE in exchange for shares in the latter) shall result in realisation of capital gains. Ninety-five percent of the gain is tax exempt for corporate shareholders (Sec. 8b(2) KStG), while individual shareholders are only subject to tax in the following three cases: (i) the shareholder holds 1% or more of the company's share capital and has not increased its shareholding in the last five years; (ii) the shareholder has held the shares for less than one year at the time of disposal; or (iii) the shares are held as business assets. In these cases, individual shareholders are subject to tax on 50% of their capital gain. In the third case, trade tax will also apply unless the shareholder held 10% or more of the company's share capital at the beginning of the tax year and the company is engaged in active business.

Losses from a foreign company that merges with a German public limited company cannot be carried forward. However, this rule could be viewed as discriminatory under Community law.

A German SE is subject to tax in Germany on its worldwide income, including income from foreign permanent establishments. However, such income

---

of shares concerning companies of different Member States, *Official Journal* L 58/19 of 4 March 2005. For a detailed analysis of the Merger Directive and its recent amendments, see C. Ph. Schindler, 'EU Report on Subject II: International Business Acquisitions', IFA Congress 2005, Buenos Aires, in *Cahiers de droit fiscal international Volume LXXXIXb*, International Fiscal Association, Kluwer, The Hague/London/Boston, 2005 1, 49 *et seq.*

will be exempt from tax if a double tax treaty applies, as is usually the case.

If a company owns real property in Germany, real estate transfer tax may apply.

(ii) **Following transposition of the Merger Directive and the directive of 17 February 2005 into national law (i.e., as of January 2006)**

42. Once the Merger Directive is transposed into national law, a cross-border merger will be tax neutral in Germany. An exchange of shares by German shareholders will not be subject to capital gains tax. Shares in the merging companies will be exchanged for shares in the receiving company. Furthermore, it will be possible to transfer losses carried forward from a German permanent establishment of a foreign company if the establishment or part thereof that recorded the loss will continue to exist for at least five years following the merger in a comparable size considering the totality of economic circumstances.

With regard to taxation of an SE and real estate transfer tax, see above.

2 Outbound mergers

43. In an outbound merger, a public limited-liability company that is a resident of Germany for tax purposes merges to form an SE which is not a tax resident of Germany.

Germany has yet to transpose into national law the Merger Directive with respect to cross-border mergers. Therefore, the Reorganisation Tax Act ('*Umwandlungssteuergesetz*' or 'UmwStG') does not apply to cross-border mergers. If the necessary amendments to German tax law are not made by 1 January 2006, most legal scholars are of the opinion that the Merger Directive will be directly applicable to cross-border transactions.[27]

(i) **Prior to transposition of the Merger Directive and the directive of 17 February 2005**

44. The current tax treatment of cross-border mergers in Germany can be summarised as follows.

---

[27] C. Ph. Schindler, 'Part III (Steuerrecht)' in *SE-Kommentar*, Kalss/Hügel (ed.), Linde, Vienna, 2004, 926; see also C. Ph. Schindler, *op cit.* (footnote 8), 88 *et seq.*; W. Schön, 'Die Europäische Aktiengesellschaft im Steuerrecht' in *Die Europa AG – eine Perspektive für deutsche Unternehmen?*, Deutsches Aktieninstitut (ed.), DAI Eigenverlag, Frankfurt, 2002, 87 *et seq.*; W. Schön, 'Tax Issues and Constraints on Reorganizations and Reincorporations in the European Union', *Tax Notes International*, 12.4.2004, 197 *et seq.*; O. Thömmes, 'Besteuerung', in *Die Europäische Aktiengesellschaft*, Theisen/Wenz (ed.), Schäffer Pöschl, Stuttgart, 2002, 465.

For German companies, such a merger will not result in liquidation tax according to Section 11 of the Corporate Tax Act (*Körperschaftsteuergesetz* or 'KStG'), as the German company is not liquidated. Nor will the merger result in exit tax pursuant to Section 12 of the KStG, as the German company does not transfer its registered office and place of effective management abroad.

However, an outbound merger could possibly be treated as a taxable realisation of hidden reserves in the assets of the German company, which are deemed distributed in kind to shareholders in accordance with general principles of German tax law.

The transfer shall be subject to real estate transfer tax if the German company owns real property in Germany.

At the shareholder level, an exchange of shares in connection with a merger (i.e., shareholders in a German public limited-liability company contribute their shares to a newly formed SE in exchange for shares in the latter) is a taxable event for individual shareholders in the following four cases: (i) the shareholder holds 1% or more of the company's share capital and has not increased its shareholding in the preceding five years; (ii) the shareholder has held the shares for less than one year at the time of disposal; or (iii) the shares are held as business assets; or (iv) the shares were obtained in return for the contribution of a permanent establishment or any part thereof or a partnership interest or substantial shareholding in a company below its fair market value. In these cases, individual shareholders are subject to tax on 50% of their capital gain. For corporate shareholders, 95% of the capital gain is tax exempt (Sec. 8(b)(2) KStG). In the third scenario, trade tax will also apply unless the shareholder held 10% or more of the company's share capital at the beginning of the tax year.

(ii) **Following transposition of the Merger Directive and the directive of 17 February 2005**

45. Once the Merger Directive is transposed into national law, a merger will not be subject to tax to the extent hidden reserves are attributable to a German permanent establishment. The wording of the directive presupposes that assets with hidden reserves that are not attributable to a German permanent establishment will give rise to taxation. The ECJ's case law (*XY* and *Hughes de Lasteyrie du Saillant*) seems to imply, however, that such hidden reserves should not be taxed at the time of the merger.

Real estate transfer tax will also apply if the merging German company owns real property in Germany.

Losses carried forward by a merging company can be transferred to the German permanent establishment of a 'foreign' SE if the establishment or part thereof that recorded the loss will continue in existence for five years following the merger in a comparable size taking into account the totality of economic circumstances.

German shareholders will no longer be taxed on capital gains resulting from an exchange of shares in connection with a merger.

3 Transfer of registered office and place of effective management

46. In general, all hidden reserves in an SE that is a resident of Germany for tax purposes shall be deemed realised if the company transfers its registered office and/or place of effective management abroad and thus is no longer a tax resident of Germany (Secs. 11 and 12 KStG, the so-called '*Liquidationsbesteuerung*'). However, as early as the beginning of the 1990s, it was argued in the literature – although this view is obviously not shared by the tax authorities – that no liquidation tax should apply to hidden reserves in assets with respect to which Germany retains the right to tax (because such assets are attributable to a permanent establishment in Germany) or with respect to which Germany never had the right to tax.[28]

This issue was clarified by an amendment to the Merger Directive, which must be transposed into German law by 1 January 2006. The deferral of tax under the Merger Directive is based on the existence of a permanent establishment, meaning that only assets effectively connected with a permanent establishment in the exit country are eligible for deferred taxation. After the ECJ's decisions in *Hughes de Lasteyrie du Saillant*[29] and *XY*[30], it is doubtful whether this concept is in keeping with the fundamental freedoms of the EC treaty.[31] European Commission officials argue that the wording of the Merger Directive does not imply that hidden reserves in assets that do not belong to a permanent establishment must or may be taxed.

If an SE that is not a resident of Germany for tax purposes transfers its registered office or place of effective management to Germany, it is uncertain whether it can step up the book values of its assets to reflect their fair market value in order to avoid taxation of hidden reserves that accrued outside Germany. Such a transfer is not a taxable event for German shareholders of the SE.

---

[28] B. Knobbe-Keuk, 'Restrictions on the Fundamental Freedoms Enshrined in the EC Treaty by Discriminatory Tax Provisions – Ban and Justification', *EC Tax Review*, 1994, 83 *et seq.*

[29] ECJ, 11 March 2004, Case C-9/02. For a detailed analysis of this decision, see C. Ph. Schindler, 'Hughes de Lasteyrie du Saillant als Ende der (deutschen) Wegzugsbesteuerung?', *Internationales Steuerrecht*, 2004, 300 *et seq.* (*x4/ Rykskattwerke*).

[30] ECS, Case E200/98, 18 November 1999.

[31] See W. Schön and C. Ph. Schindler, 'Zur Besteuerung der grenzüberschreitenden Sitzverlegung einer Europäischen Aktiengesellschaft', *Internationales Steuerrecht*, 2004, 571 *et seq.*, (argument for non-conformity).

For shareholders that are not residents of Germany for tax purposes, capital gains on future disposals of shares are taxable in Germany, unless an applicable treaty for the prevention of economic double taxation provides otherwise. (Individual shareholders are subject to tax only if they hold at least 1% of the SE's share capital.) It is unclear whether the fair market value of the shares at the time of the transfer should be used to compute the capital gain.

4 Holding SE

47. In the formation of a holding SE, shares in national public or private limited-liability companies are contributed to an SE in exchange for shares in the latter. Such an exchange of shares generally results in a realisation of capital gains, which can be avoided pursuant to Section 20(l) or Section 23(4) of the UmwStG. Section 20(I) applies when shares are contributed to a German holding company under certain conditions. Section 23(4) applies to contributions of shares from other European companies. However, Section 23(4) contains strict requirements for such an exchange of shares to qualify for tax-neutral treatment.

One requirement for the non-taxation of hidden reserves is that the receiving company maintain the book value of the contributing company's assets as the acquisition cost on its books. A further requirement is that Germany retains the right to tax with respect to the shares in the SE. If the requirements of Section 23(4) are not met, the exchange of shares shall lead to the realisation of a capital gains. For corporate shareholders, 95% of the capital gain is exempt pursuant to Section 8(b)(2) of the KStG. For individual shareholders, if one of the four abovementioned conditions is met (i.e., the shareholder holds 1% or more of the company's share capital, the shareholder has held the shares for less than one year at the time of disposal, the shares are held as business assets or the shares stem from certain reorganisations), only 50% of the gain is taxable.

5 Subsidiary SE

48. If an SE is formed as a subsidiary, business assets and shares in public or private limited companies can be contributed to the SE in exchange for shares in the latter. If the subsidiary SE is not a resident of Germany for tax purposes, the contribution of business assets shall result in the realisation of hidden reserves. If the business assets remain in a German permanent establishment, the realisation of hidden reserves can be avoided under certain circumstances (Sec. 23 UmwStG). If the subsidiary SE is a tax resident of Germany, a contribution in

exchange for shares can be tax neutral if certain requirements are met (Sec. 20 UmwStG).

6 Conversion of a German public limited company into an SE

49. The conversion of a German public limited-liability company into an SE is not a taxable event.

XI Conclusion

50. The pros and cons of forming an SE in Germany have been extensively described in this report. In short, the SE need not fear competition from national corporate forms. As far as tax treatment is concerned, the SE is on equal footing with national companies, whilst in terms of company law, the SE has a clear advantage. Despite the criticism levelled against the SE, one thing is certain: the flexibility and potential for cross-border reorganisations inherent in this new supranational corporate form will render it increasingly popular. Inclusion of the abbreviation 'SE' in a company's name will have a positive effect on the image of groups operating throughout Europe and may even help to overcome psychological barriers to doing business.

10

The Netherlands

MARIANNE DE WAARD, FRITS OLDENBURG AND PAUL STORM
NautaDutilh

I   Introduction   265
II Reasons to opt for an SE   266
III Formation   266
   1   General remarks   266
      A   Founding parties   266
      B   Name   266
      C   Registered office   266
         (i)   General remarks   266
         (ii) Transfer of an SE's registered office abroad   267
         (iii) Transfer of an SE's registered office to
             the Netherlands   269
      D   Corporate purpose   270
      E   Capital   270
   2   Different means of formation   270
      A   Formation by merger   270
         (i)   Procedure and publication requirements   270
         (ii)   Opposition on grounds of public interest   272
         (iii) Protection of creditors   273
         (iv)   Protection of minority shareholders   273
         (v)   Intra-group mergers   273
         (vi)   Holders of depositary receipts   273
      B   Formation of a holding SE   274
         (i)   Procedure and publication requirements   274
         (ii) Protection of minority shareholders, creditors and
             employees   275
         (iii) Prospectus and offer document   275
      C   Formation of a subsidiary SE   275
      D   Conversion into an SE   276
   3   Acts committed on behalf of an SE in formation   276
   4   Registration and publication   277
   5   Acquisition of legal personality   277
IV Organisation and management   277
   1   General remarks   277
      A   Structure regime   277
      B   Reasonableness and fairness   278
   2   General meeting   279

263

   A Decision-making process 279
   B Rights and obligations of shareholders 280
  3 Management and supervision 281
   A Two-tier system/one-tier system 281
    (i) General remarks 281
    (ii) Two-tier system 281
    (iii) One-tier system 282
   B Appointment and removal 282
    (i) Two-tier system 282
    (ii) One-tier system 283
   C Representation 283
   D Liability 283
V. Employee involvement 284
  1 General remarks 284
  2 The Works Councils Act 284
  3 The European Works Councils Act 285
  4 The Employee Involvement Act 285
   A Special negotiating body 285
   B Employee participation 286
   C Protection of employee representatives 287
VI Annual accounts and consolidated accounts 288
  1 Accounting principles 288
  2 Auditors 288
VII Supervision by the national authorities 288
VIII Dissolution 289
  1 Winding up 289
  2 Liquidation 289
  3 Insolvency 290
  4 Cessation of payments 290
IX Applicable law 291
X Tax treatment 291
  1 Income tax 291
   A Corporate tax 291
    (i) Tax residency 291
    (ii) Tax group (taxation as a single entity) 292
    (iii) Special rules for investment institutions 292
    (iv) Double taxation 292
    (v) Community directives 292
    (vi) Conversion of an NV into an SE (and vice versa) 293
    (vii) Transfer of an SE's registered office and/or business 293
     (a) Transfer abroad (outbound transfer) 293
     (b) Transfer to the Netherlands (inbound transfer) 294
   B Personal income tax 295
    (i) General remarks 295
    (ii) Transfer of registered office 295
     (a) Outbound transfer 295

            (b) Inbound transfer   296
    2   Value added tax   296
        A   General remarks   296
        B   Tax group (taxation as a single entity)   296
        C   Transfer of registered office   296
    3   Other taxes   297
        A   Tax on capital contributions   297
            (i)   General remarks   297
            (ii) Conversion of an NV into an SE (and vice versa)   297
            (iii) Transfer of registered office   297
        B   Dividend withholding tax   297
            (i)   General remarks   297
            (ii) Parent-Subsidiary Directive   297
            (iii) Transfer of registered office   298
                (a)   Outbound transfer   298
                (b)   Inbound transfer   298
XI Conclusion   298

I Introduction

1. The Regulation and the Directive were implemented in the Netherlands on 1 April 2005 by means of the European Company (SE) Regulation Implementation Act (the Regulation Implementation Act or 'RIA')[1] and the SE Employee Involvement Act ('EIA'), respectively.[2] The provisions of these acts are supplemented by national rules applicable to public limited-liability companies incorporated under Dutch law (*'naamloze vennootschappen'* or 'NVs'), as set out in the Civil Code (*'Burgerlijk Wetboek'*).

In drawing up the RIA, the legislature adopted a somewhat minimalist approach. For example, it did not take the opportunity to enact provisions on the one-tier system of management, which exists in practice in the Netherlands but for which no specific provision is made in the Civil Code. (However, the Dutch government has announced that legislation with respect to the one-tier system may be expected in the near future.)

Consequently, many pre-existing rules of Dutch law apply unchanged to SEs, such as the requirement that a certificate of no objection be obtained from the Ministry of Justice prior to the incorporation of a new company or the amendment of a company's articles of association[3] and that the relevant notarial instrument be drafted in Dutch.

---

[1] *Uitvoeringswet verordening Europese vennootschap, Staatsblad (Legal Bulletin)* 2005, 150.
[2] *Ibid., Wet rol werknemers bij de Europese vennootschap*, 166.
[3] Please note that the term 'articles' is used to refer to both the articles of association of domestic companies and the SE's 'statutes'. Furthermore, there are plans to change the system of issuing certificates of no objection; see Part VII of this report.

II   Reasons to opt for an SE

2. Unlike the two national corporate forms with share capital under Dutch law, the NV and the BV,[4] the SE is essentially a 'European' entity in that it is governed by rules which, for the most part, apply across the European Union ('EU') and the European Economic Area ('EEA'). Thus, the SE is an attractive option for businesses with cross-border activities for both practical (legal, financial and commercial) and psychological reasons.

More specifically, the SE offers companies (i) the possibility to transfer their registered office to another Member State without having to wind up the existing company and (ii) the ability to participate in cross-border mergers. These options are not available to an NV or a BV. Furthermore, under certain circumstances, large companies in the Netherlands are subject to what is known as the 'structure regime', meaning they are required, among other things, to have a supervisory board (i.e. a two-tier management structure is obligatory). Under the RIA, however, the structure regime in principle does not apply to an SE with its registered office in the Netherlands. Thus, the SE can also be seen as a means to avoid application of these constrictive rules.

III   Formation

1   General remarks

A   Founding parties

3. In order to facilitate cross-border activities, the Dutch legislature has chosen to enact the option contained in Article 2(5) of the Regulation. Accordingly, a company whose head office is located outside the EU may participate in the formation of an SE in the Netherlands provided (i) it is formed under the laws of a Member State, (ii) has its registered office in that Member State and (iii) has a real and continuous link with the economy of a Member State (Art. 2 RIA).

B   Name

4. An SE with its registered office in the Netherlands is a '*Europese naamloze vennootschap*'. Its name must be preceded or followed by the abbreviation 'SE'.

C   Registered office

(i)   **General remarks**

5. The Member States may require SEs registered within their territory to have their registered office and head office at the same place (Art. 7 Reg.). The

---

[4] A Dutch private limited-liability company ('*besloten vennootschap met beperkte aansprakelijkheid*').

Netherlands has not enacted this option on the grounds that to do so would needlessly restrict the freedom of an SE to choose and/or change the location of its head office. It should be noted that under Dutch law, NVs and BVs must have their registered office[5] in the Netherlands, although their head office may be located elsewhere.

The Civil Code does not contain any provisions regarding the transfer of a company's registered office.[6] Thus, the rules governing the transfer of an SE's registered office to or from the Netherlands are set forth in the RIA (Arts. 3–6).

(ii) **Transfer of an SE's registered office abroad**
6. An SE that wishes to transfer its registered office abroad must file a transfer proposal with the relevant trade registry[7] and make a copy available at its registered office (Art. 3 RIA). Furthermore, the company must publish a notice of the filing in a national daily newspaper, indicating the address of the relevant trade registry and of its registered office. No additional forms of publication are required.

The interests of creditors are protected in the following manner (Art. 4 RIA):

1. An SE must provide (on demand) security for or guarantee the satisfaction of any claims that arise or are liable to arise prior to the transfer, failing which a creditor can successfully oppose the transfer (see below). The foregoing does not apply if the claim is sufficiently secured or if the SE's financial position provides adequate guarantees.
2. Up until two months following publication of the filing notice, any creditor may oppose the transfer by petitioning the competent district court.
3. Prior to making a decision, the court may allow the SE to grant security specified by the court within the period set by it.
4. If a creditor has objected to the transfer in a timely manner, the certificate attesting to the completion of the requisite pre-transfer acts and formalities (pursuant to Art. 8(8) Reg.) may not be issued until the opposition has either been withdrawn or a court order dismissing the creditor's claim become enforceable. This certificate must be issued by a civil law notary in the Netherlands (Art. 20 RIA).

---

[5] The Dutch legislation refers to the corporate 'seat' ('*zetel*') of a company whereas the Community legislation refers to a company's registered office. For the sake of convenience, the term 'registered office' is used throughout this report.
[6] Specific rules on the transfer of the registered office of an NV or BV to the Netherlands Antilles or Aruba or – in the event of war, revolution or immediate threat of war – to another foreign country are contained in the Voluntary Transfer of Registered Office of Legal Entities Act (*Rijkswet vrijwillige zetelverplaatsing van rechtspersonen*) and the Voluntary Transfer of Registered Offices (to Third Countries) Act (*Wet vrijwillige zetelverplaatsing derde landen*), respectively, rather than the Civil Code.
[7] Art. 2 Trade Register Act 1996 (*Handelsregisterwet 1996*).

5. In dismissing a petition, the court can declare its decision immediately enforceable. In such a case, the certificate can be issued and the transfer proposal executed. However, it is also possible to appeal the court's decision. If the appeal is successful, the transfer will already have become irrevocable by virtue of execution of the transfer proposal. Article 4(5) of the RIA foresaw this situation and gives the appellate courts the power to order that security be granted and to impose a fine for non-compliance. In this respect, Article 8(16) of the Regulation provides that an SE which has transferred its registered office to another Member State shall be considered as having its registered office in the Member State where it was registered prior to the transfer with respect to any cause of action that arose prior thereto, even if sued after the transfer.

The transfer of an SE's registered office to another Member State will not have effect if the Dutch minister of justice objects to the transfer on grounds of public interest within two months following publication of the notice of filing of the transfer proposal (Art. 5 RIA). If such opposition is filed, the SE can petition the Business Section of the Amsterdam Court of Appeal to review it.

A certificate attesting to the completion of the requisite pre-transfer acts and formalities will only be issued once the opposition has been withdrawn or a court order dismissing it become irrevocable. This rule prevents a transfer from being effected and creating an irrevocable situation on the basis of a judicial decision that is later overturned on appeal.

The Netherlands has chosen not to adopt additional provisions to protect minority shareholders who oppose a transfer (Art. 8(5) Reg.). According to the legislative history of the RIA,[8] the justification for this choice is that the transfer of an SE's registered office abroad does not affect the company's equity (*vermogen*). However, this does not mean that the position of minority shareholders will always remain the same after a transfer, as the law of the Member State to which the registered office is transferred may grant minority shareholders rights different than those enjoyed under the law of the original Member State.

7. The issuance of depositary receipts in return for shares, a means of separating the voting rights attached to shares from the rights inherent in economic ownership, is a common practice in the Netherlands. Under this system, legal ownership of the shares is vested in a trust office (*administratiekantoor*) which exercises the voting rights and in turn issues depositary receipts entitling the holders to share in the company's profits.

If depositary receipts are issued for shares in an SE having its registered office in the Netherlands, the trust office will remain a shareholder even if the company's registered office is transferred to another Member State.

---

[8] Explanatory memorandum to the RIA bill, Parliamentary document (Tweede Kamer der Staten Generaal, vergaderjaar 2003–2004, doc. 29 309, no. 3).

Under Dutch law, the holders of depositary receipts issued with the company's consent have certain rights vis-à-vis the company (e.g., the right to participate in shareholder meetings, receive certain information and request inquiries). The relevant question is whether these rights can be guaranteed if the company's registered office is transferred abroad. The answer to this question will depend on the law of the Member State to which the office is transferred, specifically whether that country's law recognises the rights granted to receipt holders under Dutch law. If it does not, receipt holders will have fewer or no rights. This would be the case, for example, if that country's law contains mandatory provisions restricting participation in shareholder meetings to shareholders.

8. The transfer of an SE's registered office from one Member State to another requires an amendment to the company's articles. If the registered office is being transferred from the Netherlands, a certificate of no objection must first be obtained from the Ministry of Justice (Art. 2:125 Civil Code). The amendment can then be effected through a notarised instrument, drafted in Dutch and executed before a Dutch civil law notary.

(iii) **Transfer of an SE's registered office to the Netherlands**
9. In order to transfer an SE's registered office to the Netherlands, a notarised document containing the SE's articles (in Dutch) executed before a Dutch civil law notary (Art. 6(2) RIA) must be filed with the trade registry. The transfer, as well as the requisite amendment to the SE's articles, takes effect on the date of recordation (Art. 8(10) Reg.). A certificate of no objection from the Ministry of Justice is not required.

Article 6(2) of the RIA states that Articles 2:65 and 2:69 of the Civil Code, pertaining to the incorporation of NVs, shall apply *mutatis mutandis* to the transfer of an SE's registered office to the Netherlands. Article 2:65 provides, among other things, that a power-of-attorney with respect to the execution of a notarised instrument must be in writing. Article 2:69 provides that managing directors (or members of the management organ)[9] are responsible for handling registration formalities with the trade registry, including the filing of a statement indicating the total established and estimated expenses incurred in connection with the company's formation to be borne by the company.

Pursuant to Article 2:69(2) of the Civil Code, managing directors are jointly and severally liable for all legal acts binding on the company performed during their term of office until: (a) the filing of the initial registration with the

---

[9] The relevant body for NVs and BVs is usually referred to as the management board, but for the sake of convenience the term 'management organ' will be used herein. It should also be noted that the term 'managing director' as used herein refers to *any member of the management organ* and *not* a particular director (or directors) charged with running the company's day-to-day affairs in situations where there are both inside and outside directors. As explained further on, there is, strictly speaking, no such distinction under Dutch law.

trade registry, along with all other required documents; (b) the paid-up capital reaches the minimum amount prescribed upon incorporation; and (c) at least one quarter of the nominal value of the capital issued upon incorporation is paid up.

In our opinion, the Dutch legislature cannot have intended the consequences of these provisions to extend to SEs incorporated in other Member States.

D Corporate purpose

10. Since the Regulation and the RIA are silent on this matter, SEs shall be subject to the provisions applicable to NVs. In this respect, Article 2:66 of the Civil Code provides that an NV's articles of association should state its purpose. A company may declare void a transaction concluded in its name if the transaction was beyond the scope of its corporate purpose and the other party knew or should have known of the *ultra vires* nature of the act (Art. 2:7 Civil Code).

E Capital

11. The subscribed capital of an SE must be at least €120,000 (Art. 4(2) Reg.). SEs are subject to the same rules with regard to the paying up of their capital as NVs (Art. 2:80(1) Civil Code). Article 2:80(1) of the Civil Code allows less than all of a company's subscribed capital to be paid up upon formation, provided at least 25% is paid in. In addition, the amount paid up for NVs (and therefore SEs) must not be less than €45,000[10] (Art. 2:67 Civil Code). The remaining portion must be paid up at the company's request.

2 Different means of formation

A Formation by merger

12. With regard to the formation of an SE by merger, Article 18 of the Regulation provides that where the Regulation is silent on a particular matter, a merging company shall be subject to the provisions of domestic law applicable to national limited-liability companies, in accordance with the Third Company Law Directive. These provisions are contained in Article 7 of the RIA and Articles 2:309 to 2:334 of the Civil Code.

(i)   Procedure and publication requirements
The following documents must be filed with the trade registry (Art. 2:314(1) Civil Code):

---

[10] This amount is the minimum authorised capital for an NV and is valid as of April 2005, although it may be increased pursuant to Article 2:67(2) of the Civil Code.

(a) draft terms of merger containing the information required pursuant to Article 20 of the Regulation;
(b) the last three sets of adopted annual accounts, together with the auditors' reports, and the last three annual reports of companies that are party to the merger (exemptions may apply in certain circumstances);
(c) an interim statement of assets and liabilities if a company's last financial year closed more than six months prior to the date of filing (although annual accounts that have not yet been adopted may be submitted instead); the interim statement or annual accounts must be dated no earlier than the first day of the third month preceding the month of filing;
(d) an auditor's report (see below).

The management organ of each merging company must draw up an explanatory memorandum setting out the reasons for the merger, the expected consequences for the company's activities and an explanation of the legal, economic and employment implications of the merger (Art. 2:313(1) Civil Code; Art. 18 Reg.). The memorandum must also contain information on the method(s) used to determine the share exchange ratio, the appropriateness of each method, the resulting valuation, and the acceptability of the relative weight assigned to each method.

Each merging company must make the documents[11] filed with the trade registry and the explanatory memorandum prepared by its management organ available at its offices or, in the absence thereof, at the address of a managing director. If the company has a works council and the latter has submitted advice or recommendations in writing with regard to the merger, these must also be made available. These documents must remain available for inspection by shareholders and others with special rights vis-à-vis the company, such as subscription rights or rights to share in profits, until the date of the merger and for six months thereafter.

The merging companies must publish a notice of the filing of the draft terms and supporting documents (indicating where they are available for consultation) in a national daily newspaper in the Netherlands (Art. 2:314(3) NCC). The information set out in Article 21 of the Regulation must be published in the *Staatscourant*, the official gazette of the Netherlands.

Each company must retain an auditor to examine its draft terms of merger and explanatory memorandum (Art. 2:328 Civil Code; Arts. 18 and 22 Reg.) and determine whether the proposed share exchange ratio is reasonable. Furthermore, the auditor must certify that the value of the company's net assets is at least equal to the total nominal value of the SE's shares plus any cash consideration to be issued to shareholders (Art. 2:328(1) Civil Code).

---

[11] Where an exemption applies with regard to the filing of annual accounts and/or annual reports with the trade registry, these must still be made available at the company's office.

Finally, the auditor must render an opinion on the statements made in the explanatory memorandum with respect to the valuation method(s). In principle, each merging company should have its own auditor. However, the merging companies may jointly petition the president of the Business Section of the Amsterdam Court of Appeal for permission to appoint a single auditor (Art. 2:328(3) Civil Code; Art. 22 Reg.) to act on behalf of all companies involved.

Where the merger is to result in the incorporation of a new SE with its registered office in the Netherlands, a certificate of no objection from the Ministry of Justice is required (Art. 2:64(2) Civil Code). A certificate of no objection is also required if the surviving company in the merger is an NV that will be converted into an SE having its registered office in the Netherlands (Arts. 2:124 and 2:332 Civil Code).

An SE's instrument of incorporation and all amendments to its articles of association must be executed in Dutch.

Pursuant to Article 20 of the RIA, the scrutinisation of the legality of the creation of an SE by merger referred to in Articles 25 and 26 of the Regulation must be undertaken by a Dutch civil law notary. Where the acquiring company is to be an SE with its registered office in the Netherlands, the notary will execute a notarial merger instrument. The Dutch legislature has not indicated whether such an instrument must be executed before a Dutch civil law notary if the acquiring company will be an SE with its registered office abroad and the Dutch company/ies shall cease to exist following the merger. Such a document should not be required if a notarial merger instrument is executed in the country where the acquiring SE's registered office will be located.

The SE can then be recorded in the trade register. The date of registration is the date on which the merger and formation of the SE legally take effect (Art. 6(1) RIA; Art. 27(1) Reg.). A notice of the registration must be published in the *Staatscourant* (Art. 28 Reg.). Within one month following registration, the SE must notify all relevant public registries of the merger (Art. 2:318(4) Civil Code; Art. 29(3) Reg.).

(ii) **Opposition on grounds of public interest**

13. Pursuant to Article 7 of the RIA, a company with its registered office in the Netherlands may not participate in the formation of an SE by merger if the Dutch minister of justice opposes that company's participation in the merger on grounds of public interest.

The company in question may have the opposition reviewed by the president of the Business Section of the Amsterdam Court of Appeal. Its participation in the merger will only have legal effect after the opposition has been withdrawn or once a court order dismissing the opposition has become irrevocable.

(iii) Protection of creditors

14. In the Netherlands, any creditor of a merging company may oppose the merger and petition the competent court for security. If a creditor opposes the merger, the merger instrument may only be executed once the opposition has been withdrawn or a court order dismissing it become irrevocable (Art. 2:316(4) Civil Code). There are no special protective measures for bondholders other than the foregoing right of opposition (Art. 24(1)(b) Reg.). Holders of securities other than shares which carry special rights in a company that will cease to exist as a result of a merger are entitled to compensation if they are not granted an equivalent right vis-à-vis the acquiring company (Art. 2:320 Civil Code; Art. 24(1)(c) Reg.).

(iv) Protection of minority shareholders

15. In keeping with general principles of Dutch company law, the RIA does not contain any specific measures designed to protect minority shareholders.

(v) Intra-group mergers

16. Mergers between a parent company and a wholly-owned subsidiary are exempt from certain statutory requirements (Art. 2:333 Civil Code; Art. 31(1) Reg.). Dutch law does not contain any special provisions with respect to mergers between a parent company and a subsidiary in which it holds 90% or more, but not all, of the shares. Consequently, such mergers are not exempt from certain requirements, unlike mergers involving wholly-owned subsidiaries.

Article 2:334 of the Civil Code provides for a special type of merger – the triangular merger – in which shareholders of the company that will disappear in the merger acquire shares in a company (usually the parent company) other than the one acquiring the assets of the disappearing company. This type of merger is not based on the Third Company Law Directive and is not provided for by the Regulation. Indeed, Article 29(1)(b) of the Regulation explicitly states that one of the consequences of a merger pursuant to Article 17(2)(a) is that shareholders in the acquired company become shareholders in the acquiring company. As a triangular merger does not meet the requirements of the Regulation, this type of merger cannot be used to form an SE.

Dutch law also provides for a simplified procedure for mergers between two affiliates (wholly-owned subsidiaries) without the issuance of new shares. Again, this type of merger is not based on the Third Company Law Directive and is not provided for by the Regulation. Therefore, it cannot be used to create an SE.

(vi) Holders of depositary receipts

17. If a Dutch NV in which depositary receipts have been issued in return for shares will disappear in a cross-border merger, the trust office (*administratiekantoor*) will become a shareholder in the acquiring foreign SE. This

raises the same question regarding the position of receipt holders as in the transfer of a company's registered office (see Part III.1.C.(ii) of this report). Their rights under Dutch law (e.g. participation in shareholder meetings, the right to request an inquiry, etc.) will be lost, unless such rights are recognised under the relevant foreign law. The most obvious way of guaranteeing the rights of receipt holders is to convert the receipts into shares prior to or after the merger.

B   Formation of a holding SE

(i)   Procedure and publication requirements

18. Pursuant to Article 32(4) and (5) of the Regulation, a report on the draft terms of formation must be prepared for the shareholders of each company promoting the operation by an independent auditor, as referred to in Article 2:393 of the Civil Code. A single auditor may draw up a report for all companies involved if a joint request to this effect has been approved by the Business Section of the Amsterdam Court of Appeal (Art. 2:328(3) Civil Code).

Companies having their registered offices in the Netherlands and promoting the formation of a holding SE must file draft terms of formation and an auditor's report with the trade registry (Art. 8 RIA). In addition, each company must make these documents available at its registered office or, in the absence thereof, at the address of a managing director. These documents must remain available for inspection by shareholders until the date of incorporation of the holding SE, during which time shareholders may obtain a copy upon request free of charge.

The companies are also required to publish, in a national daily newspaper in the Netherlands, a notice of the filing and availability of the above documents, indicating the registry or address at which each is available for inspection.

Once the conditions for formation of a holding SE set out in Article 33(2) of the Regulation have been fulfilled, each company promoting the operation must file a declaration to that effect with the trade registry and publish a notice of the filing in a national daily newspaper.

19. The formation of a holding SE entails the contribution of shares in the promoting companies in return for the issuance of shares in the newly formed SE. Such an exchange constitutes a contribution in kind under Dutch law. Accordingly, if the holding SE will have its registered office in the Netherlands, the following documents must be appended to the instrument of incorporation and filed with the trade registry (Art. 2:94a Civil Code):

    (a) a description of the contribution, prepared and signed by the founders (the promoting companies), stating the value of the contribution and the valuation method(s) used, which must be in line with generally accepted standards; the description must pertain to the condition of the contribution as at a date no earlier than five months prior to incorporation of the SE;

(b) a auditor's report on the above description stating that the value of the contribution, applying generally accepted valuation methods, is at least equal to the amount to be paid up for the shares issued upon formation.

A description of the contribution and an auditor's report are not required if certain conditions are met (Art. 2:94a Civil Code).

20. If the holding SE will have its registered office in the Netherlands, a certificate of no objection from the Ministry of Justice is required (Art. 2:64(2) Civil Code). The instrument of incorporation must be executed in Dutch before a Dutch civil law notary.

(ii) **Protection of minority shareholders, creditors and employees**

21. The RIA does not set out any specific measures for the protection of minority shareholders since, unlike in a merger, the companies promoting the formation of a holding SE continue to exist after incorporation of the SE. The Dutch legislature was therefore of the opinion that in the absence of specific protection for minority shareholders in general Dutch company law, there was no reason to introduce such protection in this case. The same holds true for creditors and employees of the companies in question.

(iii) **Prospectus and offer document**

22. Under Dutch law, it is prohibited to offer securities or to make announcements with respect to such an offering unless a prospectus has been published or an exemption applies (Art. 3 Securities Transactions Supervision Act 1995[12] or 'STSA'). It could be argued that the notice of the filing and availability of the terms of formation referred to above constitutes an offering of securities or an announcement of an offering which requires the publication of a prospectus pursuant to the STSA.

Furthermore, Article 6a of the STSA states that a public bid may not be made for securities that are listed on a Dutch stock exchange or that are regularly traded in the Netherlands, unless an offering memorandum has been published and a number of rules observed. The offer to shareholders of the companies promoting the holding SE could be considered a public bid for shares, if these shares are listed or traded regularly in the Netherlands.

C Formation of a subsidiary SE

23. If a subsidiary SE will have its registered office in the Netherlands and the shares in the company are paid up in cash prior to or upon incorporation,

[12] *Wet Toezicht Effectenverkeer 1995.*

a statement (or where applicable, multiple statements) from a bank subject to oversight within the EU must be submitted to a civil law notary indicating that:

(a) the amounts to be paid under the instrument of incorporation for the issued shares will be placed immediately at the disposal of the SE upon incorporation; or
(b) the amounts to be paid under the instrument of incorporation for the issued shares will be held, for a specified date, no later than five months prior to incorporation of the SE, in a separate account placed at the sole disposal of the SE after incorporation, subject to acceptance of such payment by the SE in its instrument of incorporation.

If payment is made in a foreign currency, the statement must indicate the exchange rate against the euro on the date of payment or, if payment is made more than one month prior to incorporation, on the date of incorporation.

Where a contribution in kind is made in return for shares upon incorporation of a subsidiary SE, a description of the contribution and an auditor's report are required, subject to the same conditions as described above (Part III.2.B(i) of this report) with regard to the formation of a holding SE.

Where a subsidiary SE will have its registered office in the Netherlands, incorporation requires a certificate of no objection from the Ministry of Justice (Art. 2:64(2) Civil Code). The instrument of incorporation must be executed in Dutch before a Dutch civil law notary.

D   Conversion into an SE

24. Pursuant to Article 10 of the RIA, the draft terms of conversion of an NV into an SE must be filed with the trade registry and a notice of the filing published in a national daily newspaper in the Netherlands.

A report regarding the NV's assets and capital (Art. 37(6) Reg.) must be issued by an auditor, as referred to in Article 2:393 of the Civil Code.

Amendments to an NV's articles of association require a certificate of no objection from the Ministry of Justice (Art. 2:64(2) Civil Code). The instrument amending the articles and converting the company into an SE must be executed in Dutch before a Dutch civil law notary.

3   Acts committed on behalf of an SE in formation

25. Article 16(2) of the Regulation reflects pre-existing Dutch law on the performance of legal acts on behalf of a company prior to incorporation. In addition, Article 93(3) of the Civil Code provides that if the company ratifies the acts in question but does not perform the obligations arising therefrom, those persons

who acted in the name of the company in formation will be held jointly and severally liable for any resulting losses to third parties who knew, or should have known, that the company would not be able to perform its obligations. The foregoing is without prejudice to any liability on the part of the company's managing directors towards third parties in the same regard. If the company is declared bankrupt within one year following incorporation, there is a statutory presumption of such knowledge on the part of those persons who acted on behalf of the company in formation.

4 Registration and publication

26. The registration of an SE in the Netherlands is carried out by the trade registry (Art. 6(1) RIA) and must be published in the *Staatscourant* (Art. 17 Trade Registry Act; Arts. 15(2) and 13 Reg.).

5 Acquisition of legal personality

27. Under Dutch law, legal personality is usually acquired by means of the execution of a notarised instrument of incorporation. However, pursuant to Article 16(1) of the Regulation, an SE acquires legal personality on the date of its recording in the trade registry.

IV Organisation and management

1 General remarks

28. Before discussing the main corporate bodies/organs of an SE, we briefly address two aspects of Dutch company law that are, or could be, of significance to SEs in the Netherlands, namely (i) the structure regime and (ii) principles of reasonableness and fairness.

A Structure regime

29. As stated above, certain large companies in the Netherlands are subject to what is termed the 'structure regime', application of which is mandatory for companies that have (i) issued capital of at least €16 million, (ii) a works council, and (iii) at least 100 employees in the Netherlands for at least three consecutive years,

Companies subject to the structure regime must establish a supervisory organ,[13] whose members (known as supervisory directors) are appointed by the general

---

[13] In NVs and BVs, this body is usually known as the 'supervisory board', but it is referred to herein as the supervisory organ for the sake of convenience. Members of the supervisory organ are referred to as supervisory directors.

meeting on the basis of nominations submitted by the supervisory organ. The works council and the general meeting can also recommend candidates to the supervisory organ; the works council has an enhanced right to recommend one-third of organ members. The supervisory organ is authorised to appoint and remove members of the management organ, and the management organ must obtain the supervisory organ's approval prior to adopting particular management resolutions.

Under certain circumstances, a company may be eligible for a full or partial exemption from the structure regime, e.g. if it belongs to an international group. In the case of a partial exemption, members of the management organ are appointed and removed by the general meeting rather than by the supervisory organ.

In implementing the Regulation and the Directive, an important question for the Dutch legislature was whether the structure regime would automatically apply to SEs meeting the criteria outlined above. It was ultimately decided that it should not (Art. 1(6) EIA).

As for the participation rights of the works council in companies subject to the structure regime, Article 1(6) of the EIA provides that such rights are not of mandatory application in an SE with its registered office in the Netherlands. Pursuant to Article 40(2) of the Regulation, such rights only apply insofar as they stem from the Directive. Under the Directive, however, where the employees of one or more companies involved in the formation of an SE have participation rights, there is a presumption that at least the same level of participation shall be granted to the SE's employees. Derogations from this rule must, in some cases, be approved by a special majority within the special negotiating body. In the formation of an SE by conversion, no deviation from this rule is possible. In concrete terms, this means that there are situations in which the works council's enhanced right of recommendation will in fact apply to an SE. For further details, please refer to Part V of this report.

B   Reasonableness and fairness

30. Pursuant to Article 2:8 of the Civil Code a company and its shareholders as well as members of its management and supervisory organs (if any) must act in accordance with the principles of reasonableness and fairness (*redelijkheid en billijkheid*) in their dealings with one another. A rule that binds the parties by virtue of law, usage, the company's articles of association or by-laws or a shareholder resolution is inapplicable to the extent compliance would be incompatible with these principles under the circumstances. Article 2:8 of the Civil Code, which is applicable to all Dutch companies, also applies to SEs by virtue of Article 9 of the Regulation.

These principles may therefore result in the application of additional rights and obligations which are not expressly provided for by law or in an SE's articles and may also limit the applicability of otherwise binding rules if to apply such rules would be unacceptable according to these principles. In both situations, these principles have internal effect only and are not effective against third parties.

2 General meeting

A Decision-making process

31. In keeping with Article 54(1) of the Regulation, Article 15 of the RIA provides that the first general meeting of an SE may be held at any time during the first 18 months following incorporation. The articles may require that general meetings be held more frequently. If it appears that the capital of an SE has fallen below less than half its paid-in and called-up capital, a general meeting must be held within three months to discuss the measures to be taken (Art. 2:108a Civil Code; Art. 9 Reg.).

The general meeting may be convened by either the management organ or the supervisory organ (if any), or, as the case may be, the administrative organ. In addition, the articles may also vest this power in another organ or competent authority (Art. 54(2) Reg.). The same rule applies to NVs under the Civil Code (Art. 2:109).

As Article 54(2) of the Regulation allows the general meeting to be convened by any organ or competent authority if the SE's articles so provide, a request by shareholders of a two-tier SE to convene a general meeting must be directed to the management organ alone, and not the supervisory organ. This is contrary to the relevant provision in the Civil Code (Art. 2:110(1)), which provides that such a request must be submitted to both the management and supervisory organs. If a general meeting is not held within two months following receipt of such a request, the competent judicial authority (the district courts, in the Netherlands) may (i) order that a meeting be convened within a given period of time or (ii) authorise those shareholders who submitted the petition or their representatives to convene a general meeting (Art. 55(3) Reg.). Article 2:111(1) of the Civil Code provides that the court must verify that the applicants have a reasonable interest in holding a meeting.

Pursuant to Article 16 of the RIA and Article 2:114a of the Civil Code, shareholders of an SE who, alone or with others, hold at least 1% of the company's share capital or – in the case of listed shares – shares with a value of at least €50 million, may request that one or more additional items be placed on the agenda of a general meeting, provided (i) the SE receives the request no later than 60 days prior to the date scheduled for the meeting and (ii) inclusion of the additional items would not conflict with a substantial interest of the SE. The articles may provide for a lower percentage or value and/or a period shorter than 60 days.

32. Save where the Regulation or the Civil Code requires a greater majority, the general meeting can take decisions only by a majority of votes validly cast (Art. 57 Reg.).

The Civil Code requires a greater majority in the following cases: (a) changes to a legal entity's corporate form must be approved by at least nine-tenths of the votes cast (Art. 2:18(2) Civil Code); and (b) if less than 50% of the issued capital is present or represented at a general meeting, a two-thirds majority is required to pass resolutions on the following subjects:

 (i) the placement of restrictions on or elimination of shareholders' pre-emptive right in the event of a new issue of shares or to designate an organ other than the general meeting to restrict or eliminate such rights (Art. 2:96a(7) Civil Code);
 (ii) reductions to a company's issued share capital (Art. 2:99(6) Civil Code);
 (iii) execution of a statutory merger (Art. 2:330(1) Civil Code); and
 (iv) execution of a statutory division or split-up (*splitsing*) (Art. 2:334ee(1) Civil Code).

An SE's articles may require a larger majority or even unanimity (within certain limits, in the case of resolutions to suspend or remove a managing director)[14] (Art. 2:134(2) Civil Code).

Article 17 of the RIA provides that unless the articles require a larger majority, resolutions to amend an SE's articles must be approved by a majority of votes cast at a general meeting at which at least half the subscribed capital is present or represented. Although not expressly stated in the RIA, we assume the articles may provide for a larger quorum.

33. Article 2:128 of the Civil Code allows resolutions to be passed without a meeting provided (i) the articles so provide, (ii) the resolution is approved unanimously by all shareholders entitled to vote, (iii) the votes are cast in writing, and (iv) the company has not issued bearer shares or depositary receipts.

B   Rights and obligations of shareholders

34. The principles of reasonableness and fairness (see Part IV.1.B of this report) apply to ensure the rights and compliance with the obligations of an SE's shareholders.

---

[14] If the articles provide that such a resolution may be passed only by a greater majority at a meeting where a quorum is required, this majority may not exceed two-thirds of the votes cast representing more than 50% of the issued share capital.

3 Management and supervision

A Two-tier system/one-tier system

(i) General remarks

35. Under Dutch law, all companies must have a management organ[15] charged with the daily management of the company. Managing the company is the joint responsibility of the management organ as such and of its members.[16] Although Article 2:9 of the Civil Code allows the division of duties to a certain extent, the management organ and its individual members remain, in principle, collectively responsible for the performance of all managerial duties.

If a company wishes to provide for directors with supervisory rather than management responsibilities it must establish a supervisory organ.[17] Establishment of such an organ is optional, except in companies subject to the structure regime (see above). The general duties of the supervisory organ include overseeing management's policy and the general affairs of the company (and of its associated enterprises).

Dutch company law does not specifically provide for a one-tier system, in the sense of a single management organ comprised of both inside and outside directors. Nevertheless, some Dutch multinationals do have structures providing for outside managing directors who, in principle, are jointly responsible (and liable) for the daily management of the company.

(ii) Two-tier system

36. Article 39(1) of the Regulation allows a Member State to provide that one or more managing director(s)[18] of an SE will be responsible for the daily management of the company under the same conditions as for public limited-liability companies. In keeping with the principle of joint liability described above, the Dutch legislature chose not to enact this option.

Nor has the Netherlands enacted the option contained in Article 41(3) of the Regulation (regarding the provision of information to individual members of the supervisory organ) as it was felt that Article 2:141 of the Civil Code, which requires the management organ to provide the supervisory organ in a timely manner with all information it needs to perform its duties, was sufficient.

---

[15] This body is usually referred to as the management board in an NV or BV; see footnote 9.
[16] As stated above, the term 'managing director' is used as a synonym for 'a member of the management organ'; see footnote 9.
[17] This body is usually referred to as the supervisory board in an NV or BV; see footnote 13.
[18] Note that the term 'managing director' as used in Article 39(1) of the Regulation carries a different meaning in this report; see footnote 9.

(iii) One-tier system

37. Once again, in keeping with the principle of joint liability and responsibility, the Dutch legislature chose not to enact the option contained in Article 43(1) of the Regulation. Accordingly, no distinction is made between the responsibilities of inside and outside members of the administrative organ of an SE based in the Netherlands.

B Appointment and removal

(i) Two-tier system

38. There is no minimum or maximum with regard to the number of members of the management and supervisory organs of an SE with its registered office in the Netherlands. The articles of a Dutch SE may permit a company or other legal entity to serve as a managing director, although legal entities may not sit on the supervisory organ of an SE as members of this organ in an NV must be natural persons (Art. 2:140(1) Civil Code).

The managing directors of an SE are appointed and removed by the supervisory organ. With regard to the option contained in Article 39(2) of the Regulation, the Netherlands has chosen to permit an SE's articles to provide that managing directors are to be appointed and removed by the general meeting (Art. 11 RIA). If the articles make such provision, the general meeting can also suspend and remove managing directors pursuant to Article 2:134 of the Civil Code, which applies *mutatis mutandis* to SEs further to Article 11 of the RIA.

If an SE's articles provide that a decision to suspend or remove a managing director may only be passed by a heightened majority at a general meeting where a quorum is required, this majority may not exceed two-thirds of the votes cast representing more than half the subscribed capital (Art. 2:134 Civil Code).

The articles may provide that the general meeting shall appoint managing directors from a list of candidates drawn up by a designated organ or third party and containing the names of at least two persons for each vacancy to be filled. The general meeting can override such a list by a resolution approved by at least two-thirds of the votes cast representing more than half the subscribed capital (Art. 11 RIA).

The articles must stipulate the manner in which the SE will be temporarily managed if one or more managing directors are absent or unable to fulfil their duties (Art. 2:134(4) Civil Code).

Members of the supervisory organ are appointed by the general meeting (Art. 40(2) Reg.), as in an NV. The company's articles may provide that one or more members of the supervisory organ, not to exceed one-third in total, however, can be appointed by other means (Art. 2:143 Civil Code; Art. 47(4) Reg.). Members of the supervisory organ can only be suspended and removed from office by the body that appointed them (Art. 2:144 Civil Code).

(ii) **One-tier system**

39. The administrative organ of a Dutch SE must have at least three members (Art. 13 RIA). In contrast, the board of a one-tier NV or BV may consist of a single member.

Members of the administrative organ not charged with executive functions in an SE must be natural persons (Art. 14 RIA). Members of the administrative organ are appointed by the general meeting, which also has the power to suspend or remove them (Art. 2:134(1) Civil Code).

C   Representation

40. In a two-tier SE, the management organ, as well as each individual member, has the power to represent the SE, i.e. to bind it in transactions with third parties (Art. 2:130 Civil Code). The only possible restriction on this power is a joint signature clause in the articles (i.e. a clause stipulating that an SE can be bound only by the signatures of two (or more) managing directors or one director acting with another person, such as an employee armed with a power-of-attorney).

Unless the articles provide otherwise, an SE will be represented by its supervisory organ if there is a conflict of interest between the company and one or more managing directors (Art. 2:146 Civil Code). The general meeting is always authorised to appoint one or more other persons to represent the SE in the event of a conflict of interest.

In a one-tier SE, both the administrative organ and each individual member thereof (including any outside members) have the power to represent the SE. Limitations on this power, e.g. in the form of a joint signature clause, may be stipulated in the articles.

D   Liability

41. Members of an SE's management, supervisory and administrative organs are liable to the company for any breach of their statutory duties, the company's articles or any other obligations inherent in their role in accordance with the provisions applicable to NVs.

In the two-tier system, individual members of the management and supervisory organ can be held liable to the company for the proper performance of their duties (Arts. 2:9 and 2:259 Civil Code). However, the courts have held that such organ members can only be held liable for gross negligence (seriously culpable conduct) in the performance of their duties. Such an assessment must be based on principles of reasonableness and fairness.

If a matter falls within the scope of the duties allocated to two or more members of the management or supervisory organ, the organ members in question shall be held jointly and severally liable unless it can be proved that the failure was not attributable to a particular member and that that member was not negligent in preventing its consequences. Some division of duties is permissible, but, in principle, members of the management and supervisory organs are collectively responsible for ensuring proper performance of the duties of the organ as a whole. In practical terms, it is more difficult for members of the supervisory organ to argue that a failure did not fall within the scope of their allocated duties owing to the different character and functions of these two organs.

Under Dutch law, members of the management and supervisory organs can be held liable to third parties for certain offences, such as misrepresentation of the company's annual accounts, torts and the provision of misleading information regarding goods and services.

In a one-tier SE, the liability of members of the administrative organ (both inside and outside directors) is governed by the same rules applicable to the managing directors of an NV. It is expected, however, that outside members will be better able to avoid joint and several liability as they will find it easier to prove that a violation was not attributable to them and that they were not negligent in acting to prevent the consequences thereof.

V Employee involvement

1 General remarks

42. In the Netherlands, the Directive has been transposed into national law by the SE Employee Involvement Act (the 'EIA'), which closely follows the structure of the Directive. Pre-existing national rules on employee involvement are contained, for the most part, in the Works Councils Act and the European Works Councils Act. These rules are discussed briefly below. As stated above, the structure regime provides for employee participation in NVs and BVs.

2 The Works Councils Act

43. The Netherlands has a long tradition of employee involvement in the running of enterprises. Under the Works Councils Act[19] ('WCA'), which dates back to 1950, certain employers must establish a works council (i.e. a representative body elected by the company's employees from amongst their number) and consult it regularly. Furthermore, certain important business decisions may not be taken before seeking the council's advice. As a general rule, a company must

---

[19] *Wet op de ondernemingsraden.*

establish a works council if it has at least 50 employees (including part-time workers). The WCA also contains rules on employee involvement in companies employing fewer than 50 people.

Pursuant to Article 1(6)(3) of the EIA, existing employee involvement rights under Dutch law shall apply to an SE having its registered office in the Netherlands. As a result, a situation may arise whereby both an SE works council, established pursuant to the EIA, and one or more works councils established pursuant to the WCA are invited to render advice or to consult on a proposed transaction. The legislative history of the EIA[20] indicates that this should not be considered redundant as the advisory rights of a Dutch works council under the WCA are substantially broader than the consultation rights of an SE works council under the Directive's reference provisions. An SE works council represents all employees of the SE (and its subsidiaries, if any) whereas a Dutch works council represents only Dutch employees.

3 The European Works Councils Act

44. The European Works Councils Act[21] ('EWCA'), which transposed Directive 94/45/EC[22] into Dutch law on 23 January 1997, provides for the establishment of a European works council or certain information and consultation procedures in Community-scale undertakings and groups of undertakings. Pursuant to Article 1(6)(1) of the EIA, SEs that would otherwise qualify as Community-scale undertakings within the meaning of the EWCA are in principle not subject to the provisions of this Act. However, the EWCA will apply to an SE that normally falls within its scope if the SE's special negotiating body ('SNB') decides not to open negotiations or to terminate negotiations already under way.

4 The Employee Involvement Act

A Special negotiating body

45. The EIA describes the procedure to create an SNB following a decision to form an SE with its registered office in the Netherlands. Dutch members of the SNB are appointed by the works councils of the Dutch participating companies and, if applicable, their subsidiaries and establishments which will become subsidiaries or establishments of the SE (Art. 2(4)(2) EIA).

---

[20] Explanatory memorandum to the EIA bill, Parliamentary document (*Tweede Kamer der Staten Generaal, vergaderjaar* 2003–2004, doc. 29 298, no. 3).
[21] *Wet op de Europese ondernemingsraden.*
[22] Council Directive 94/45/EC of 22 September 1994 on the establishment of a European Works Council or a procedure in Community-scale undertakings and Community-scale groups of undertakings for the purposes of informing and consulting employees.

If the SNB opens negotiations with the participating companies, arrangements for employee involvement in the form of an SE works council can be put in place via a specific written agreement or the application of standard rules. Article 2(12) of the EIA sets out the items that must be covered if a written agreement is drawn up; the standard rules are laid down in Article 3(1)–(14) of the EIA.

Alternatively, the SNB can decide not to open negotiations or to terminate negotiations and to rely instead on the information and consultation rules in force in the relevant Member State(s). In this case, Article 1(6)(2) of the EIA states that the provisions of the EWCA shall apply if the SE meets the criteria for the establishment of a European works council.

If the deadline for negotiations has expired without the conclusion of an agreement on employee involvement and the SNB has not decided to terminate negotiations (see above), the participating companies can decide to apply the standard rules, in which case the consent of all companies involved is required.

B Employee participation

46. As explained in Part IV.1.A above, the structure regime provides for employee participation in Dutch companies in the form of the works council's right to issue binding recommendations with respect to the appointment of one-third of the supervisory organ's members. In principle, Article 1(6)(2) of the EIA, which transposes into national law Article 13(2) of the Directive, excludes application of the structure regime to SEs. However, owing to the rule that participation rights cannot be reduced where an SE is formed by conversion, the works council of an SE formed by conversion of an NV subject to the structure regime must maintain at least the same right with respect to the appointment of members of the SE's supervisory organ or, as the case may be, outside members of its administrative organ.

In accordance with Article 7(2)(c) of the Directive, the EIA's standard rules provide that if there is more than one form of employee participation in the participating companies, the SNB may decide which form(s) shall be carried over to the SE, subject to the proviso that special majority requirements shall apply where a reduction in participation rights affecting a certain percentage of the total number of employees is proposed (Art. 2(8)(3) EIA; Art. 3(4) Dir.).

If the SNB does not reach a decision in this regard, the EIA provides that if one (or more) of the participating companies are subject to the structure regime, the works council is entitled to issue binding recommendations with respect to the appointment of one-third of the supervisory organ's members or outside members of the administrative organ (Art. 3(2) EIA). If none of the participating companies is subject to the structure regime, the form of employee participation that gives employees the most election, appointment or recommendation rights with respect to the relevant corporate organ shall apply. This is a purely quantitative test. No distinction is made as to whether recommendations made pursuant to such rights are binding or as to the powers enjoyed by the relevant corporate organ.

Under Dutch law, the supervisory organ of a company that is subject to the structure regime has certain additional powers. With regard to SEs, however, the EIA is silent as to the powers of the supervisory organ or, as the case may be, the outside members of the administrative organ. Therefore, reference must be made to the SE's articles. Accordingly, it is possible that even where an SE works council has the right to make bindings recommendations with respect to the appointment of one-third of the members of the supervisory or administrative organ, it will still have less influence than the works council of an NV.

Article 7(3) of the Directive gives the Member States the option to exclude application of the reference provisions where an SE is formed by merger. The Dutch legislature has not chosen to enact this option. Accordingly, Article 3(12)–(14) of the EIA also applies when an SE is formed by merger.

C Protection of employee representatives

47. Members of the SNB, the employee representative body (i.e. the SE works council), any employee representatives involved in the information and consultation procedure, and any employee representatives sitting on an SE's supervisory or administrative organ who are also employees of the SE, its subsidiaries or establishments or of a participating company are entitled to the same level of protection as employee representatives under national law in their country of employment (Art. 10 Dir.).

Article 10 has been transposed into national law by Articles 1(4) and 4(2) of the EIA. Article 1(4) provides that the above categories of personnel are entitled to receive their regular salary for the period during which they are unable to perform their usual functions due to organ duties. In addition, they must be given the opportunity to consult with others during normal working hours on matters involving the exercise of their functions and to receive additional training. Article 1(4) also sets out rules regarding their duty of confidentiality. Lastly, Article 4(2) of the EIA amends Article 7:670 of the Civil Code, which provides protection against dismissal to certain groups of employees, by extending this protection to the same categories of employees in an SE.

VI Annual accounts and consolidated accounts

1 Accounting principles

48. Pursuant to Article 61 of the Regulation, an SE having its registered office in the Netherlands is subject to the national rules applicable to NVs (set out in Part 9, Book 2 of the Civil Code) as regards the preparation of annual and consolidated accounts (including the annual report) and the auditing and publication of the same.

In keeping with Community law, all listed companies (including SEs) in the Netherlands must apply International Financial Reporting Standards (IFRS) when drawing up consolidated annual accounts. Under a bill currently (April 2005) being debated in Parliament, a company will in all other cases have the option to apply either IFRS or Dutch accounting standards when preparing its annual accounts.

2 Auditors

49. As a general rule, a company's annual accounts must be reviewed by an auditor who meets the requirements set out in Article 2:393 of the Civil Code. In principle, the auditor is appointed by the general meeting of shareholders (Art. 2:393(2) Civil Code).

A company is not required to have its annual accounts audited if at least two of the following three criteria are met, among other factors: (i) the company has net turnover of less than €7.3 million; (ii) employs fewer than 50 people on average; and (iii) the value of its assets does not exceed €3.65 million (Art. 2:396(9) Civil Code).

VII Supervision by the national authorities

50. Companies in the Netherlands are supervised by the Ministry of Justice. At present, the minister of justice may prevent the formation of a company or the amendment of its articles by refusing to grant a certificate of no objection. In the first case, a certificate may be refused only if there is a risk that the company will be used for an unlawful purpose or that its activities may be detrimental to creditors, taking into account the background and intentions of the parties responsible for shaping the company's policy.

With regard to proposed amendments to a company's articles, the minister may refuse to issue a certificate only if, as a result of the amendment, (i) the company would be of a prohibited nature or (ii) there is a real risk that the company will be used for an unlawful purpose.

In March 2005, the Dutch government announced that this system of preventive supervision will be replaced by repressive supervision. In addition, the Ministry of Justice must be notified of the incorporation of a company and of certain changes with respect to companies.

VIII Dissolution

1 Winding up

51. Two stages can be distinguished in the voluntary dissolution (or winding up) of a company: (i) a decision to dissolve; and (ii) liquidation of the company's assets and liabilities. As a general rule, a decision to dissolve takes the form of a resolution by the general meeting, which should also designate the person or entity responsible for overseeing the company's books and accounts, which must be kept for a period of seven years. If the company has no assets or liabilities at the time the resolution is passed, it shall immediately cease to exist. The management organ (or the administrative organ, as the case may be) must file a notice with the trade registry that the company has ceased to exist, stating the identity of the person or entity in charge of keeping the company's books and accounts.

Under certain circumstances, an SE can be dissolved at the initiative of the public authorities (the public prosecutor's office or the chamber of commerce), the courts or an interested party. At the request of the public prosecutor's office, the competent district court will dissolve an SE that has its registered office in the Netherlands but its head office elsewhere (Art. 18 RIA; Art. 64(2) Reg.). Before issuing an order to this effect, the court may grant the SE the opportunity to transfer its head office to the Netherlands within a specified period of time or to transfer its registered office abroad in accordance with Article 8 of the Regulation. In addition, an SE can be dissolved for violations of certain rules (e.g. if it has an illegal purpose or fails to comply with filing and registration requirements) under the same conditions as an NV. These situations are for the most part set forth in the Civil Code.

2 Liquidation

52. If an SE has assets and/or liabilities at the time a decision is taken to dissolve, the company shall remain in existence long enough to liquidate its assets. One or more liquidators must be appointed for this purpose, as a rule by the general meeting. The following steps must then be taken.

The liquidator will draw up liquidation accounts and, if there are more than two parties entitled to receive liquidation proceeds, a distribution plan. These documents must be filed with the relevant trade registry and made available at the company's offices. A notice of the filing and of the fact that these document(s) have been made available at the company's offices must be published in a national daily newspaper in the Netherlands.

No final distributions can be made within the first two months following publication of the abovementioned notice. During this time, any creditor or party entitled to receive liquidation proceeds may file a petition objecting to the distribution plan with the court. In such a case, no distributions can be made until all such petitions have been finally adjudicated.

Under the distribution plan, the company's assets are realised and the proceeds are used to settle any outstanding claims. The excess (if any) is distributed to shareholders in proportion to their shareholdings. Once the liquidation proceeds have been distributed, the company shall cease to exist. At this time, the company should have no remaining assets, to the best of the liquidator's knowledge. The liquidator must then file a notice with the trade registry that the company has ceased to exist, identifying the entity charged with keeping the company's books and accounts for the statutory period of seven years.

3 Insolvency

53. The Bankruptcy Act[23] provides for three separate sets of insolvency rules: (i) bankruptcy; (ii) cessation of payments (*surséance van betaling*); and (iii) debt rescheduling for natural persons. Only the first two will be addressed here, as the third does not apply to SEs.

The purpose of bankruptcy is to liquidate the debtor's assets through a court-appointed trustee in bankruptcy. A petition in bankruptcy can be submitted by the debtor itself, one or more creditors or the public prosecutor's office. If an NV wishes to file for bankruptcy, its management organ must obtain the consent of the general meeting of shareholders, unless the company's articles provide otherwise (Art. 2:136 Civil Code). This holds true for SEs as well. As a general rule, a debtor will be declared bankrupt if the court finds that it has ceased to pay its creditors, as will be the case if the debtor has at least two unpaid debts, one of which is due and payable. Bankruptcy operates as a general attachment in that previously rendered pre-judgment attachment orders lapse and execution is suspended. Except where a composition with creditors has been reached, the debtor shall cease to exist upon the termination of bankruptcy proceedings.

4 Cessation of payments

54. The purpose of a cessation of payments is to enable a debtor to avoid bankruptcy by giving it temporary relief from any pressing claims and the

---

[23] *Faillissementswet.*

opportunity to reorganise its business, restructure its debts and, ultimately, satisfy its creditors. A cessation of payments only affects unsecured debts and may be granted for a maximum period of 18 months. Only the debtor can apply for a cessation of payments and must satisfy the court that it cannot continue to pay its debts as they fall due, but that it will eventually be able to pay them or that a composition can be reached with its creditors. If the petition is granted, the court will appoint one or more receivers to administer the debtor's affairs. During a cessation of payments, the debtor can no longer exercise exclusive control over its assets and must co-operate with the receiver. Cessation of payments ends (i) by court order (with the debtor either continuing its activities or being declared bankrupt), (ii) with the acceptance and court approval of a composition with creditors, or (iii) by lapse of time.

IX Applicable law

55. Pursuant to Article 9 of the Regulation, an SE having its registered office in the Netherlands will be governed by (i) the Regulation, (ii) its articles (where expressly authorised by the Regulation), (iii) the RIA, (iv) national rules of law applicable to NVs (in most cases the Civil Code), and (v) its articles (under the same conditions applicable to NVs). It should be noted that certain areas of activity, e.g. insurance, pensions and financial services, are subject to additional legislation in the Netherlands (Art. 9(3) Reg.).

X Tax treatment

1 Income tax

A Corporate tax

(i) Tax residency

56. Two criteria are used to determine the country of residence of a company for Dutch corporate tax purposes: the incorporation principle and the 'facts and circumstances' test.

The incorporation principle is laid down in Article 2(4) of the Corporate Tax Act 1969[24] ('CTA'). The general rule is that a company incorporated under Dutch law will be deemed a resident of the Netherlands for corporate tax purposes. An SE incorporated and with its registered office in the Netherlands will be deemed incorporated under Dutch law. Consequently, even if its registered office is transferred abroad, the SE will remain a Dutch resident for corporate tax purposes. The second criterion is the facts and circumstances test. In accordance with the principle of equal treatment, this test, which is set forth in Article 4

---

[24] *Wet op de Vennootschapsbelasting 1969.*

of the State Taxes Act 1959[25] ('STA'), applies to both NVs and SEs alike. The decisive factor is the place of effective management.

(ii) **Tax group (taxation as a single entity)**
57. An SE may be included in a group that is taxed as a single consolidated entity (*fiscale eenheid*), either as a parent company or as a subsidiary. In order to be included in such a consolidated tax group, the SE must have its place of effective management in the Netherlands. For this reason, an SE that satisfies only the incorporation criterion cannot be included in a tax group.

(iii) **Special rules for investment institutions**
58. Article 28 of the CTA lays down special rules for investment institutions. Only certain types of legal entities, including NVs, are eligible. Accordingly, an SE may also qualify for such special treatment.

(iv) **Double taxation**
59. Like an NV resident in the Netherlands for tax purposes, a Netherlands-resident SE can claim a tax exemption or tax credit under a treaty for the avoidance of double taxation concluded between the Netherlands and another country. In the absence of such a treaty, the SE may apply the Avoidance of Double Taxation Decree 2001,[26] which provides unilateral relief from double taxation in cases where no treaty applies.

(v) **Community directives**
60. An SE having its registered office in the Netherlands is subject to Dutch legislation transposing Community directives in the field of taxation, even if the SE is not yet listed in the annex to the relevant directive.

The amended Parent-Subsidiary Directive[27] (as of April 2005) has not yet been transposed into Dutch law. In December 2004, the Dutch secretary of state for finance issued a temporary decree[28] announcing certain consequences for Dutch taxpayers resulting from the amendments, pending the passage of the transposing legislation, and explicitly confirmed that the current Dutch rules transposing the 'old' Parent-Subsidiary Directive apply to SEs. In March 2005, a bill to transpose the amended Parent-Subsidiary Directive into Dutch law was introduced in Parliament.[29]

---

[25] *Algemene Wet inzake Rijkbelastingen 1959.*
[26] *Besluit voorkoming dubbele belasting 2001.*
[27] Council Directive 2003/123/EC of 22 December 2003 amending Council Directive 90/435/EEC of 23 July 1990.
[28] Decree No. CPP2004/2730M of 18 December 2004.
[29] Bill to amend certain tax laws in connection with the transposition of Council Directive 2003/123/EC, Parliamentary document (*Tweede Kamer der Staten Generaal, vergaderjaar* 2004–2005, doc. 30 031, no. 2).

Thus far, no steps have been taken to transpose the amended Merger Directive[30] into Dutch law. Although the scope of the transposition measures is, therefore, still uncertain, the transfer of an SE's registered office is already largely provided for under Dutch tax law, as described below.

As the proposed amendments to the Interest and Royalties Directive[31] are still under consideration by the Council of Ministers, no new national measures of transposition have been proposed.

(vi) **Conversion of an NV into an SE (and vice versa)**
61. The conversion of an NV into an SE or of an SE into an NV can take place on a tax-neutral basis as, pursuant to the Regulation (Arts. 37 and 66), such a conversion does not result in the winding up of the existing entity or in the creation of a new one.

(vii) **Transfer of an SE's registered office and/or business**
(a) **Transfer abroad (outbound transfer)**
62. Articles 15c and 15d of the CTA contain the Dutch exit tax provisions, which also apply to SEs incorporated under Dutch law. In this regard, the following three situations can arise:

(a) an SE transfers part of its business to another country (an EU Member State or non-EU country);
(b) an SE transfers its registered office and head office and part of its business to another Member State while maintaining a presence in the Netherlands;
(c) an SE transfers its registered office and head office and all of its business to another Member State.

In situation (a), the SE will, in principle, have or create a permanent establishment in the other country or Member State. As its registered office and head office remain in the Netherlands, Articles 15c and 15d of the CTA are not applicable. However, any hidden reserves and/or goodwill inherent in the transferred assets will be subject to Dutch corporate tax through a reduction of double taxation relief over time.

In situation (b), the SE will cease to be a resident of the Netherlands for tax purposes due to the transfer of its registered office and head office to another Member State. The tiebreak rule incorporated in tax treaties between the Netherlands and other Member States gives priority to the place of effective management over the place of incorporation. Pursuant to Article 15c of the CTA, the assets and liabilities of the transferred branch of activity (the income and gain from which will, as a result of the transfer, cease to be included in the company's tax

---

[30] Council Directive 2005/19/EC of 17 February 2005, amending Council Directive 90/434/EEC of 23 July 1990.
[31] Council Directive 2003/49/EC of 3 June 2003.

base for Dutch corporate tax purposes) will be deemed to have been sold at their fair market value on the date directly preceding transfer of the SE's registered office. Consequently, hidden reserves and/or goodwill attributable to the transferred assets will be subject to exit tax in the Netherlands. Assets remaining in the Netherlands will not be subject to exit tax provided they constitute a permanent establishment.

In the event of a full outbound transfer (situation (c)), exit tax will be due on all hidden reserves and goodwill. In this regard, Article 15d functions as a safety net in that exit tax will be levied only to the extent it has not already been imposed pursuant to Article 15c.

In these circumstances, exit tax may constitute an unjustified restriction on the fundamental freedoms set forth in the EC treaty, in particular freedom of establishment (Art. 43 EC). The views expressed in the literature vary widely.[32] Some scholars state that it is unclear whether the ECJ should find Articles 15c and 15d of the CTA to be compatible with freedom of establishment, while others are of the opinion that this question simply cannot be answered yet.[33] In theory, however, the imposition of exit tax is only justified if the other country or Member State allows the receiving company to step-up the value of the transferred assets to reflect their fair market value for tax purposes.

As stated above, an SE incorporated under Dutch law will be deemed a resident of the Netherlands for Dutch corporate tax purposes. Therefore, after such an SE's registered office and place of effective management have been transferred to another Member State, the company will remain subject to corporate tax in the Netherlands, even if it no longer has any connection with this country. In practice, this is only of importance in cross-border situations where there is no tax treaty for the avoidance of double taxation or where the tax residency provision in the relevant treaty differs from that contained in the OECD model convention, as amended.

(b) **Transfer to the Netherlands (inbound transfer)**

63. Although the CTA does not address the consequences of an inbound transfer, it follows from the legislative history and the case law[34] that in an inbound transfer an SE should be allowed to step-up the basis of its assets and liabilities to their fair market value for corporate tax purposes. This step-up should include not only hidden reserves but also goodwill (self-generated or otherwise). Although the legislation and case law provide exceptions to the above rule for self-generated goodwill, such an exception should not apply in the case

---

[32] A. C. van Ede, 'De eindafrekening is nog steeds niet EU-proof', *Weekblad voor Fiscaal Recht*, 2002, 735.

[33] J.A.M. van Eijndthoven, 'De Europese Vennootschap, een keizer met of zonder kleren', Weekblad voor Fiscaal Recht, 2004, 785.

[34] *Inter alia* Dutch Supreme Court, 21 November 1990, BNB 1991 90.

of an SE transferring its registered office to the Netherlands if it paid exit tax in the other Member State.

Likewise, if a non-resident SE already has a permanent establishment (which term includes a permanent representative) in the Netherlands, the transfer of its registered office to the Netherlands will entail the conversion of the permanent establishment into a Netherlands-resident SE. Such a conversion should also allow a step-up of the company's assets (albeit only those transferred into the country) to their fair market value for Dutch tax purposes.

B Personal income tax

(i) **General remarks**

64. For the purpose of determining income from individual shareholdings, the Personal Income Tax Act 2001[35] ('PITA') applies the same two criteria used to establish tax residency in the CTA. Article 4.35 of PITA explicitly extends the incorporation principle to SEs.

(ii) **Transfer of registered office**

(a) Outbound transfer

65. If an SE transfers its registered office from the Netherlands to another Member State, there will be no effect on the tax position of shareholders resident in the Netherlands for tax purposes (resident shareholders).

For nonresident shareholders, a distinction should be made between substantial shareholdings as defined in PITA (box 2 shareholdings) and other shareholdings (box 3 shareholdings).[36] A substantial shareholding exists if a resident or non-resident individual, either alone or together with his or her partner (as defined by statute) or certain other related persons, directly or indirectly (i) holds a stake of 5% or more in a company's total issued capital or 5% or more of any class of shares, (ii) has the right to acquire, directly or indirectly, such a shareholding, or (iii) holds certain profit-sharing rights in a company (Art. 4.6 PITA).

For non-resident taxpayers with substantial shareholdings, an outbound transfer of an SE will be considered a deemed disposition of their shares. Income tax will be imposed on the basis of a suspended tax assessment. Payment in whole or in part is only required if all or part of the shares are disposed of within ten years. After expiry of this period, the assessment will lapse. At the same time, the value of the shareholding for tax purposes will be stepped up to its deemed

---

[35] *Wet op de Inkomstenbelasting 2001*.

[36] Under PITA, the taxable income of individuals is divided into three categories – box 1, 2 and 3 – each of which is subject to a particular tax rate(s). Box 1 is taxable income from employment and home ownership (different rates apply depending on the amount). Box 2 is taxable income from substantial shareholdings (taxed at a fixed rate of 25%) and box 3 is taxable income from savings and investments (taxed at a fixed rate of 30%). These rates are valid as of April 2005.

disposition value. If the shareholder is a resident of a country with which the Netherlands has concluded a tax treaty, the Dutch tax authorities may have the right to impose a suspended tax assessment.

For non-residents whose shares do not constitute a substantial shareholding, the outbound transfer of an SE will not have any consequences for Dutch income tax purposes.

(b) Inbound transfer

66. Like resident shareholders, nonresident shareholders will become subject to personal income tax in the Netherlands if their stake in an SE constitutes a substantial shareholding at the time of the transfer. In the absence of relief under a tax treaty, nonresident holders of substantial shareholdings will fall within box 2 and will thus be liable for income tax at a rate of 25% in respect of any income or gain deriving from their shareholdings. Any dividend withholding tax can be credited against the shareholder's income tax liability. Shareholders who are deemed to be residents of the Netherlands for tax purposes pursuant to a tax treaty are normally exempt from box 2 taxation. This does not apply to former tax residents of the Netherlands who have left the country and settled in a state that has concluded a tax treaty with the Netherlands.

2 Value added tax

A General remarks

67. As stated above, the Regulation does not contain specific tax provisions for SEs. This holds true for VAT, as well. Dutch VAT legislation does not differentiate as to corporate form. The only criterion is whether the taxpayer is an entrepreneur for VAT purposes. Therefore, no amendments to the legislation were necessary to implement the Regulation and transpose the Directive.

B Tax group (taxation as a single entity)

68. An SE conducting business in the Netherlands may be included in a tax group (*fiscale eenheid*)[37] with other Netherlands-resident companies provided they are sufficiently closely connected by financial, organisational and economic ties. If these conditions are met, the relevant companies will be considered to form a single entity for VAT purposes.

C Transfer of registered office

69. The transfer of an SE's registered office may have VAT consequences in cross-border transactions in which consideration is charged. However, as the SE will remain the same legal entity, no consideration will in principle be charged.

---

[37] See Part X.1.A(iii) of this report.

The transfer will only be deemed an intra-Community transaction if goods are physically transferred by an SE from one Member State to another. Dutch VAT will be due if the goods are acquired or deemed to have been acquired by an SE in the Netherlands.

3 Other taxes

A Tax on capital contributions

(i) General remarks

70. Pursuant to the Legal Transactions Tax Act[38] ('LTTA'), tax on capital contributions is levied at a rate of 0.55% on formal and informal contributions, whether in cash or in kind, to the capital of Netherlands-resident companies (including SEs). For the purposes of this tax, a company will be considered a tax resident of the Netherlands if it has its registered office or place of effective management in the country.

The relevance of this tax to SEs is limited, as plans were announced on 24 March 2005 to abolish it as of 1 January 2006.

(ii) Conversion of an NV into an SE (and vice versa)

71. The above changes to corporate form are exempt from the tax on capital contributions (Art. 37(1)(b) LTTA).

(iii) Transfer of registered office

72. The transfer of a corporate entity to the Netherlands will normally lead to the imposition of a capital contributions tax (at a rate of 0.55%), unless the entity was either a tax resident of, or had its registered office in, another Member State (Art. 34(e) LTTA). Consequently, this tax will not be levied on the inbound transfer of an SE's registered office.

B Dividend withholding tax

(i) General remarks

73. In determining whether an SE is required to withhold tax on dividends paid in the Netherlands, the Dividend Withholding Tax Act 1965[39] ('DWTA') applies the same two criteria used to establish tax residency under the CTA.

(ii) Parent-Subsidiary Directive

74. SEs that are residents of the Netherlands for tax purposes are eligible for an exemption from dividend withholding tax pursuant to the Parent-Subsidiary Directive.

---

[38] *Wet op belastingen van rechtsverkeer.*   [39] *Wet op de Dividendbelasting 1965.*

(iii) **Transfer of registered office**
(a) Outbound transfer

75. The DWTA does not contain exit tax provisions, i.e. no dividend withholding tax will be due in respect of corporate profits on the occasion of the transfer of an SE's registered office to another Member State.

An SE with its registered office in the Netherlands will be deemed to remain a Dutch resident for dividend withholding tax purposes. This implies that even if such an SE transfers its registered office to another Member State, it will still be required to withhold tax on its dividend distributions. In practice, this is only important in cross-border situations where the Netherlands has not concluded a treaty for the avoidance of double taxation or where the applicable treaty does not prohibit the extraterritorial taxation of dividends. The tax treaties concluded by the Netherlands normally prohibit this under a provision equivalent to Article 10.5 of the OECD model convention.

(b) Inbound transfer

76. Following the transfer of an SE's registered office to the Netherlands, both resident and non-resident shareholders will become subject to dividend withholding tax upon the distribution of dividends by the SE. The DWTA does not distinguish between corporate profits accrued in the former Member State and those accrued in the Netherlands. Therefore, the inbound transfer will not result in a step-up in the basis of the shares for withholding tax purposes.

XI   Conclusion

77. From a Dutch perspective, the main advantages of the SE are the possibility for it to transfer its registered office from one Member State to another without the need to first dissolve and reincorporate and its ability to participate in cross-border mergers. Neither option is available to an NV or a BV. In addition, an SE, in principle, is not subject to the structure regime, which is of mandatory application for certain large Dutch public and private limited-liability companies.

11
Estonia

SVEN PAPP AND MAARJA OVIIR-NEIVELT
Raidla & Partners

I   Introduction   300
II   Reasons to opt for an SE   302
III   Formation   302
    1   General remarks   302
       A   Founding parties   302
       B   Name   302
       C   Registered office and transfer   303
           (i)   Registered office   303
           (ii)   Transfer   304
       D   Corporate purpose   305
       E   Capital   305
    2   Different means of formation   306
       A   Formation by merger   306
           (i)   Procedure and publication requirements   306
           (ii)   Publication   307
           (iii)   Right to object to participation in a merger   307
           (iv)   Minority shareholders   308
           (v)   Rights of creditors   309
           (vi)   Acquisition by a company holding 90% or more of the shares in another company   309
           (vii)   Avoidance of a merger   310
       B   Formation of a holding SE   310
           (i)   Procedure and publication requirements   310
           (ii)   Minority shareholders   311
       C   Formation of a subsidiary SE   311
       D   Conversion into an SE   311
    3   Acts committed on behalf of an SE in formation   312
    4   Registration and publication   313
    5   Acquisition of legal personality   314
IV   Organisation and management   315
    1   General remarks   315
    2   General meeting   315
       A   Decision-making process   315
       B   Rights and obligations of shareholders   317
    3   Management and supervision   317
       A   Management (two-tier system/one-tier system)   317

   (i) General remarks 317
   (ii) One-tier system 317
   (iii) Two-tier system 319
  B Appointment and removal 319
   (i) One-tier system 319
   (ii) Two-tier system 320
  C Representation 320
  D Liability 320
V Employee involvement 322
  1 Special negotiating body 322
  2 Employee participation 322
  3 Protection of employee representatives 322
VI Annual accounts and consolidated accounts 322
  1 Accounting principles 322
  2 Auditors 324
VII Supervision by the national authorities 324
VIII Dissolution 324
  1 Winding up 324
  2 Liquidation 325
  3 Insolvency 325
IX Applicable law 328
X Tax treatment 328
  1 Income tax 328
  2 Value added tax 329
  3 Other taxes 329
XI Conclusion 329

I Introduction

1. Two special laws have been passed by the Estonian parliament (*Riigikogu*) to enable the formation and operation of SEs in Estonia. The Implementation Act[1] (or 'IA') for the Community regulation on a European company or ('SE')[2] was adopted on 10 November 2004.[3] The act on employee involvement in Community-scale undertakings and groups of undertakings and in the European

---

[1] 'Euroopa Liidu Nõukogu määruse (EÜ) no. 2157/2001 'Euroopa äriühingu (SE) põhikirja kohta' rakendamise seadus'.

[2] Council Regulation No. 2157/2001 of 8 October 2001 on the Statute for a European company (SE) (the 'Regulation').

[3] Although the Regulation has direct effect in the Member States and no specific implementing measures are thus required to enforce it, the Member States are given a number of options in the Regulation and certain issues are governed by the national law of the Member State where an SE is registered. The Estonian legislature adopted the Implementation Act to enact many of the options contained in the Regulation and to provide rules for certain areas (explanatory letter to the draft Implementation Act dated 17 June 2004 of the Ministry of Justice).

company[4] (the Employee Involvement Act or 'EIA') was passed on 12 January 2005 and entered into force on 11 February 2005. The Employee Involvement Act was adopted to transpose the Directive[5] into national law and is designed to ensure the involvement of employees in issues and decisions affecting an SE.[6]

2. The Regulation does not govern all matters related to the establishment and operation of an SE. Aspects not covered by the Regulation are determined by the national laws of the Member States.[7]

The main Estonian legislation regulating commercial entities (including public limited-liability companies and SEs) is the Commercial Code (*Äriseadustik*),[8] the General Principles of the Civil Code Act ('GPCCA') (*Tsiviilseadustiku üldosa seadus*) and the Obligations Act ('OA') (*Võlaõigusseadus*). In addition, certain commercial entities, such as banks, investment funds and insurance companies, are subject to various industry-specific laws and regulations.

Companies listed on the Tallinn Stock Exchange (TSE), Estonia's only active stock exchange and the country's principal centre for the public trading of securities, are also subject to special rules which provide for higher standards of corporate governance than the Commercial Code.

Estonia acceded to the European Union on 1 May 2004. As a condition of EU membership, Estonian law must reflect the *acquis communautaire*. Officials from the Ministry of Justice have confirmed that Estonia has transposed all principal company law directives into national law, and Estonian business law (including the Commercial Code) complies with the applicable Community legislation in all essential respects.

3. An SE is the third type of company with share capital that may be incorporated under Estonian law, the other two being a private limited-liability company (*osaühing* or 'OÜ') and a public limited-liability company (*aktsiaselts* or 'AS').

---

[4] '*Üleühenduselise ettevõtja, üleühenduselise ettevõtjate grupi ja Euroopa äriühingu tegevusse töötajate kaasamise seadus*'.
[5] Council Directive 2001/86/EC of 8 October 2001 supplementing the Statute for a European company with regard to the involvement of employees.
[6] Twenty-first Recital of the Regulation. [7] See Art. 9(1) Reg. for the hierarchy of laws.
[8] Please note that a draft law amending the Commercial Code (the 'LACC') has been prepared and submitted to the Riigikogu. The proposed amendments aim to reduce the formalities related to the commercial register and to company management. Furthermore, the provisions on the liability of members of management and supervisory bodies have been changed and issues regarding the protection of minority shareholders clarified. According to the Ministry of Justice, these amendments will be adopted in September 2005 and will enter into force on 1 January 2006 at the earliest.

II Reasons to opt for an SE

4. An Estonian company may consider taking the form of an SE to conduct Community-scale business for a number of reasons. Below we discuss only the most relevant ones when considering SE status.

First, an SE can operate as one company under a single set of (management and reporting) rules throughout the EU rather than as a burdensome and costly network of subsidiaries subject to different national laws. Consequently, the SE could help companies reduce operating costs and become more efficient.

Second, the Regulation envisages a comprehensive system of corporate mobility. A company may decide to transfer its registered office to another Member State due to unwelcome changes to tax law or in the legal climate. In the case of an Estonian public limited-liability company, the transfer of its registered office to another Member State will trigger an obligation to liquidate and reincorporate abroad. The SE will allow companies active across borders to transfer their headquarters from one Member State to another without having to undergo costly and complex liquidation and reincorporation procedures.

Third, the Regulation provides a mechanism to establish an SE by way of a cross-border merger. At present, cross-border mergers are not regulated at the Community level.

Last but not least, a company may wish to express its European identity by choosing to incorporate as an SE. Thus, the SE could be used as a powerful marketing tool to attract investors and raise capital on the international markets.

III Formation

1 General remarks

A Founding parties

5. Only a company whose registered office and head office are located in the same Member State can participate in the formation of an SE (Art. 2 Reg.; see also Chap. 2, no. 19 of this book). Estonian law does not contain any exceptions to this rule (Art. 2(5) Reg.).

B Name

6. An SE will be referred to as a *Euroopa äriühing* in Estonian (Art. 1 IA). The name of an SE must be preceded or followed by the abbreviation 'SE'. Only SEs may include the abbreviation 'SE' in their names (Art. 11 Reg.).

7. If an SE is formed in Estonia, it must take into account the rules of Estonian law on the choice of a corporate name.

Under Estonian law, a company's name must distinguish it from other legal entities (Art. 9 Commercial Code). The Commercial Code sets forth a number of requirements regarding corporate names, such as: (i) a company's name must be clearly distinguishable from those of other businesses entered in the Estonian commercial register; (ii) a name may not be misleading with regard to a company's legal form or area or scope of activity; (iii) a name may not be contrary to public policy or morality; (iv) a sign or combination of signs consisting of letters, words or numbers and protected as a trademark in Estonia may not be used in a corporate name without the notarised consent of the trademark holder; (v) a name must be written in the Estonian (Latin) alphabet, etc. A complete list of requirements with regard to corporate names is contained in Articles 12 and 13 of the Commercial Code and in Article 30 of the GPCCA.

An SE may take action against another legal entity that uses a name identical or confusingly similar to its own in accordance with the Code of Civil Procedure (*Tsiviilkohtumenetluse seadustik*).

C Registered office and transfer

(i) Registered office
8. Pursuant to Estonian law, a legal entity shall be governed by the law of the country where it was founded. If a legal entity is managed in Estonia or if its main activities are carried out in Estonia, it shall be governed by Estonian law (Art. 15 Private International Law Act).

If the registered office of an SE in formation will be located in Estonia, the company must register with the Estonian commercial register in order to enjoy legal personality. The registration formalities are discussed in Part III, Section 4 of this report.

If an SE has been incorporated under Estonian law, both its registered office and head office must be located in Estonia at all times (Art. 7 Reg.). The registrar of the commercial register[9] shall oversee compliance with this requirement. If an SE's registered office and head office are no longer both in Estonia, the registrar shall give the company a time limit (at least two months) within which to regularise its situation by either (i) transferring its head office to Estonia or (ii) transferring its registered office to the Member State in which its head office is located, in accordance with the procedure set forth in Article 8 of the Regulation. If the SE fails to meet this deadline, the registrar can force the company into liquidation (Art. 29 IA). Unless special rules apply, involuntary liquidation will be carried out in accordance with the provisions of the Commercial Code.

---

[9] See footnote 29 for more information about the commercial register.

(ii)   Transfer

9. An SE may transfer its registered office to another Member State while maintaining legal personality. For a detailed description of the transfer procedure, please refer to Chap. 2, no. 10 of this book. The Implementation Act provides that an SE's management board must submit a transfer proposal to the registration division of the court of first instance (i.e., the registrar) with territorial jurisdiction over the company's registered office, and a notice of the transfer must be published in the Estonian official gazette, the *Ametlikud Teadaanded*. The notice must mention that the transfer proposal is available for inspection at both the commercial register and a location designated by the SE's management board (Art. 5 IA).

10. As soon as all formalities regarding the transfer have been fulfilled, the registrar will issue a certificate to this effect (Art. 4(1) IA; Art. 8(8) Reg.; see also Chap. 2, no. 83 of this book). The registrar may issue such a certificate only after receiving the approval of the Tax and Customs Board. In order to receive board approval, the registrar must submit a request in writing. The board may not withhold its consent unless it has claims against the SE or considers it likely that violations of tax law will be found during administrative proceedings initiated before the date of the request.[10] If authorisation is not received within 20 days from the date of the request, the board shall be deemed to have approved the transfer (Art. 8 IA; Art. 8(14) Reg.). A refusal by the board may be challenged pursuant to the Administrative Procedure Code.

11. Prior to issuing the certificate referred to above, the registrar must verify that the interests of creditors and the holders of other rights vis-à-vis the SE have been adequately protected (Art. 8(7) Reg.). Creditors of an SE that plans to transfer its registered office must notify the company of their claims and request security within two months following publication of the transfer proposal. The SE must provide security for claims notified within this period, provided the creditor is not entitled to satisfaction of its claim and proves that the transfer is liable to jeopardise recovery (Art. 7 IA).

12. The Member States may adopt appropriate legislation in order to protect the rights of minority shareholders that oppose the transfer of an SE's registered office (Art. 8(5) Reg.) To this end, the Implementation Act provides that any shareholder who opposes the transfer of an SE's registered office from Estonia to another Member State may require the company to buy back its shares within two months following recordation of the SE in the new register. Such compensation must be at least equal to the amount the shareholder would have received

---

[10] Pursuant to Article 8(14) of the Regulation, opposition may only be based on grounds of public interest. With respect to the Tax and Customs Board, the public interest within the meaning of this provision is deemed to be the board's obligation to prevent tax evasion (explanatory letter to the draft Implementation Act of the Ministry of Justice, dated 17 June 2004); see also Chap. 2, no 85.

from distribution of the liquidation proceeds had the SE been liquidated at the time the transfer resolution was passed. A list of shareholders who oppose the transfer and wish to exercise their right to compensation must be appended to the transfer resolution. Each shareholder must confirm its opposition by signing. An SE must pay interest on any unpaid amounts due at the statutory rate in force at the time of its recordation in the new register. If a shareholder who opposes the transfer does not request compensation, it may still transfer its shares to the company within two months regardless of any transfer restrictions provided by law or the SE's articles of association (*põhikiri*)[11] (Art. 6 IA).

D Corporate purpose

13. The Regulation and the Implementation Act do not provide any special rules with regard to corporate purpose. Hence, the provisions of Estonian law applicable to public limited-liability companies shall apply (Art. 9(1) Reg.). Pursuant to Estonian law, a company may operate in all fields not prohibited to it by law (Art. 4(1) Commercial Code). Therefore, the activities of a public limited-liability company need not be confined to the areas stipulated in its articles of association, and the notion of *ultra vires* acts is not applicable to private law legal entities (including public limited-liability companies).

However, the law may set forth areas of activity for which a licence is required or in which only a particular type of company may operate. The areas of activity listed in a company's articles of association or the commercial register may not be misleading with regard to their type or scope (Art. 4 Commercial Code).

E Capital

14. The third phase of economic and monetary union (EMU) is not yet applicable in Estonia.[12] Therefore, the capital of an SE formed in Estonia must be expressed in Estonian kroons[13] (Art. 67(1) Reg.; see also Chap. 2, no. 16).

Contributions to the share capital of an SE may be made in cash or in kind. A public limited-liability company's share capital must be fully paid up in order to record the company with the commercial register, unless the certificate of incorporation stipulates otherwise (Art. 246 Commercial Code).

The shares of a public limited-liability company must be registered with the Estonian Central Register of Securities (ECRS). The ECRS holds and records securities transactions, maintains ownership registration and pledge records,

---

[11] Under Estonian law, an instrument of incorporation and articles of association are separate documents.
[12] Estonia is expected to join EMU and adopt the euro as its national currency in 2007.
[13] Estonia's official currency is the kroon (EEK), a freely convertible currency whose exchange rate is fixed against the euro at EEK 15.65 per one euro.

2 Different means of formation

A Formation by merger

(i) Procedure and publication requirements

15. Among Estonian companies, only an *aktsiaselts* ('AS') or public limited-liability company can participate in the formation of an SE by merger.[14]

Each merging company must prepare draft terms of merger (see Chap. 2, no. 25). The management board (*juhatus*) of a participating company registered in Estonia shall prepare the draft terms, which must be signed in the presence of a notary (Arts. 392(1) and 392(4) Commercial Code).[15]

The management board must also prepare a report explaining the legal and economic consequences of the merger as well as the methods used to determine the share-exchange ratio and the amount of compensation and describe any special valuation difficulties that may have arisen in connection with preparation of the draft terms (Art. 393(1) Commercial Code).

The draft terms of merger must be examined by an auditor. The auditor will prepare a report on the merger (Arts. 395 and 396 Commercial Code). Article 22 of the Regulation provides that a judicial or administrative authority in the Member State of a merging company or of the proposed SE may appoint one or more independent experts to draw up a single report on behalf of all shareholders of the merging companies. Pursuant to Article 4(2) of the Implementation Act, the Tallinn City Court is the competent authority for this purpose.

16. The draft terms of merger must be filed with the commercial register at least one month prior to the general meeting scheduled to vote on the merger. Furthermore, by that date[16] the draft terms of merger, the management board's report, the auditor's report, and the annual accounts and management reports for the last three years of each Estonian participating company must be made available to shareholders at the company's head office. If the latest annual report of a participating company relates to a financial year that ended more than six months prior to the date of the draft terms of merger, a financial statement (i.e. an interim balance sheet) as of the last quarter must be prepared and presented to shareholders for examination. Shareholders are entitled to obtain copies of these documents upon request at the company's offices (Art. 419 Commercial Code).

---

[14] Annex II of the Regulation.

[15] Under Estonian law, the draft terms of merger are referred to as the merger agreement (*ühinemisleping*).

[16] That is, at least one month prior to the general meeting scheduled to vote on the merger.

17. Pursuant to Estonian law, the merger resolution and any amendments to the company's articles of association must be approved by no less than two-thirds of the share capital present or represented at a general meeting at which at least half the share capital is present or represented (provided the articles do not require a higher majority or quorum) (Arts. 297 and 421 Commercial Code).[17] If the required quorum is not met, another general meeting shall be called at which no quorum is required (Art. 297(2) Commercial Code).

There is no requirement under Estonian law that the minutes of a general meeting be notarised.

18. The power to scrutinise the legality of a merger within the meaning of Articles 25 and 26 of the Regulation has been vested with the registrar of the commercial register who shall, among other things, issue a certificate conclusively attesting to the completion of the requisite pre-merger acts and formalities (Art. 4 IA).

19. The management board of an Estonian participating company may submit a petition to record the merger in the relevant commercial register no earlier than three months following publication of the last merger notice.[18] The documents set forth in the Commercial Code (e.g. a notarised copy of the draft terms of merger, the merger resolution, the authorisation of the Competition Board, if required, etc.) must be appended to the petition.

Provided all legal formalities have been fulfilled, the requisite entries will be made in the commercial register. The registration formalities, effects of registration, and publication requirements are discussed in Part III, section 4 of this report.

(ii) **Publication**

20. After adoption of the merger proposal by the general meeting, the management board of an Estonian participating company must publish two merger notices in at least 15 day intervals in the Estonian official gazette. In compliance with Article 21 of the Regulation, the Implementation Act provides that the merger notice must, in addition to the information set forth in Article 21, inform creditors that they have two months from its date of publication to submit their claims (Art. 10 IA; see also Chap. 2, no. 28 of this book).

(iii) **Right to object to participation in a merger**

21. Pursuant to Article 19 of the Regulation, the legislature adopted Article 9 of the Implementation Act, which provides that the competent authority in Estonia

---

[17] However, if a public limited-liability company has several classes of shares, the merger resolution must be approved by at least two-thirds of the holders of each class (unless the company's articles provide for a greater majority) (Art. 421 Commercial Code).

[18] See no. 20 of this report.

can oppose the participation by an Estonian company in the formation of an SE. Article 9 states that if a merger involves a company listed in the Estonian commercial register which shall cease to exist as a result of the formation of an SE in another country, the registrar may issue the certificate referred to in Article 25(2) of the Regulation only with the prior authorisation of the Tax and Customs Board. In order to obtain this authorisation, the registrar must submit a written request to the board, which may not withhold its consent unless it has claims against the SE in formation or considers it likely that administrative proceedings initiated prior to the date of the request will reveal violations of tax law.[19] If authorisation is not received within 20 days following submission of a request, the board shall be deemed to agree to the formation of the SE.

According to Article 19 of the Regulation, the aforementioned right of the Tax and Customs Board to oppose the formation of an SE by merger must be subject to judicial review. Indeed, the board's refusal to grant authorisation may be challenged pursuant to the Administrative Procedure Code.

(iv) **Minority shareholders**

22. Pursuant to Article 24(2) of the Regulation, the Member States may adopt provisions designed to ensure appropriate protection of minority shareholders who oppose a merger. In keeping with this article, the Implementation Act provides that if a dissenting shareholder feels the share-exchange ratio is too low, it may request additional compensation from the acquiring company. Such compensation may exceed a standard limit of one-tenth of the aggregate nominal value of the exchanged shares.[20] Moreover, dissenting shareholders may force the acquiring company to purchase their shares within two months following recordation of the merger. Such compensation must equal the amount the dissenting shareholders would have been entitled to receive had the company been forced to liquidate at the time the merger resolution was passed. In any event, dissenting shareholders who do not request compensation are still entitled to transfer their shares to the company within two months, regardless of any transfer restrictions provided by law or the company's articles of association (Art. 11 IA).[21]

---

[19] The Tax and Customs Board's obligation to prevent tax evasion is deemed to be in the public interest within the meaning of Article 19 of the Regulation (explanatory letter to the draft Implementation Act of the Ministry of Justice, dated 17 June 2004).

[20] In a 'standard' merger where a regular public limited-liability company acts as the acquiring company, the compensation may *not* exceed one-tenth of the sum of the nominal value of the exchanged shares (Art. 398(3) Commercial Code).

[21] Pursuant to Article 25(3) of the Regulation, if a company that proposes to form an SE by merger is subject to national procedures giving minority shareholders a right to compensation (without preventing registration of the merger) these procedures shall apply only if the other merging

However, dissenting shareholders cannot seek to have the merger resolution of the target company declared void on the ground that the share-exchange ratio is too low (Art. 11 IA).

(v) **Rights of creditors**

23. Article 24(1) of the Regulation provides that the law of the Member State governing each merging company shall apply as in the case of a merger involving public limited-liability companies (taking into account the cross-border nature of the merger) with regard to the protection of creditors, bondholders and the holders of securities other than shares in the merging companies.

Pursuant to the Commercial Code, the management board of a merging company must send a written notice of the merger to all known creditors whose claims predate the passage of the merger resolution within 15 days following its adoption. Furthermore, the management board must publish two notices of the merger in at least 15-day intervals in the Estonian official gazette, informing creditors that they have two months to submit their claims.[22] The merging company must provide security to creditors whose claims are submitted within this period. If the deadline has passed or insufficient security has been granted, creditors may still seek satisfaction of their claims if they can prove that the merger will jeopardise recovery, unless the claim is past due (Art. 399 Commercial Code).[23]

(vi) **Acquisition by a company holding 90% or more of the shares in another company**

The Commercial Code sets forth a simplified procedure for the merger by acquisition of a wholly-owned subsidiary. Simplified draft terms of merger must be prepared, but no merger report is required. If the acquiring company already holds 90% of the shares in the other company, there is no need for the former to approve the draft terms of merger, provided its management board has published a notice concerning execution of the draft terms and has made them available to shareholders along with the merger report and the company's annual reports and management reports for the last three years (Art. 421(4) Commercial Code; Art. 31(2) Reg.).

---

companies (resident in Member States without such procedures) accept that shareholders of the first company shall have recourse to them.

[22] See no. 20 of this report.

[23] The current rules are subject to amendment by the LACC, pursuant to which the notification procedure has been simplified (one notice is sufficient). In addition, the acquiring company must guarantee claims submitted within six months (rather than two months) following publication of the merger notice.

(vii) Avoidance of a merger

24. Under the Regulation and Estonian law, a merger cannot be declared null and void once an SE has been recorded in the commercial register (Art. 403(5) Commercial Code; Art. 30 Reg.).

B Formation of a holding SE

(i) Procedure and publication requirements

25. In Estonia, only an *aktsiaselts* ('AS') and an *osaühing* ('OÜ') may participate in the formation of a holding SE.[24] The management boards of the companies promoting the operation must prepare draft terms of formation.[25] Under Estonian law, the draft terms and the articles of association must be notarised and signed by all founders (Art. 243 Commercial Code).

The draft terms must be examined by an auditor, who will then prepare a report containing the information mentioned in Chap. 2, no. 38 of this book (Art. 32(4) Reg.).

26. At least one month prior to the general meeting scheduled to vote on formation of the holding SE, the management board of each Estonian participating company must submit to the registrar of the commercial register draft terms of formation and publish a notice to this effect in the Estonian official gazette. This notice must contain information on the availability of the draft terms at the commercial register and at the company's registered office (Art. 14 IA; Art. 32(3) Reg.).

27. The draft terms of formation must be approved by the general meeting of each company promoting the operation by more than 50% of the votes validly cast (Art. 57 Reg.). Estonian law does not require a different majority in this instance.

28. If the conditions for formation of a holding SE have been fulfilled in accordance with Article 33(2) of the Regulation, a notice to this effect must be published in the Estonian official gazette.

Upon completion of the necessary preconditions stipulated in the Regulation, the holding SE may be recorded in the commercial register. The draft terms of formation (the formation agreement) may not be declared void after registration of a holding SE (Art. 27(2) GPCLA).

Registration takes place in accordance with the provisions of the Commercial Code regulating the formation of public limited-liability companies (see also Part III, Section 4 of this report for more information on registration).

---

[24] Annex II of the Regulation.
[25] Under Estonian law, the draft terms of formation are referred to as the formation agreement (*asutamisleping*); see also Chap. 2, no. 37 of this book for more information on the draft terms of formation.

(ii) **Minority shareholders**

29. In accordance with Article 34 of the Regulation, the Implementation Act contains provisions to protect minority shareholders who oppose the formation of a holding SE.[26] In this case, the protection granted is essentially the same as for formation of an SE by merger: minority shareholders may (i) request additional compensation from the holding SE if they feel the share-exchange ratio is too low (Art. 12 IA) and, (ii) within two months following recordation of the holding SE in the commercial register, force the company to purchase their shares for an amount equal to what they would have received had the company been compelled to liquidate at the time of formation of the holding SE. Where a private or public limited-liability company acquires its own shares, the standard restriction that the nominal value of the acquired shares may not exceed one-tenth of the company's share-capital does not apply. A list of those shareholders who oppose the formation of a holding SE and wish to exercise their rights pursuant to Articles 12 and 13 of the Implementation Act must be appended to the formation resolution and each shareholder must confirm its opposition by signing. Upon recordation of the holding SE in the commercial register, the company must pay interest as damages at the statutory rate on any outstanding amounts due. If dissenting shareholders do not request compensation, they may still transfer their share(s) within two months regardless of any transfer restrictions provided by law or the SE's articles of association (Art. 13 IA).

C Formation of a subsidiary SE

30. If the registered office of a subsidiary SE will be located in Estonia, the provisions of the Commercial Code on the incorporation of public limited-liability companies shall apply (Arts. 2(3) and 36 Reg.). The Estonian legislature has not passed any special rules in this respect. For more information regarding the incorporation and registration procedure, please refer to Part III, Section 4 of this report.

D Conversion into an SE

31. In Estonia, only an *aktsiaselts* ('AS') with its registered office and head office in a Member State may be converted into an SE.[27]

32. In order to convert a public limited-liability company into an SE, the management board of the company to be converted must prepare draft terms of

---

[26] According to the Explanatory Letter to the draft Implementation Act of 17 June 2004, such protective clauses are necessary since the formation of a holding SE could have a greater effect on the interests of minority shareholders than the regular conversion of a company under national law.

[27] Annex II of the Regulation.

conversion (*ümberkujundamiskava*) and submit the same to the relevant commercial register. The board must also publish a notice to this effect in the Estonian official gazette containing information on the availability of the draft terms at the commercial register and at the company's registered office (Art. 15 IA; Art. 37(5) Reg.).

In addition, the management board must prepare a report explaining and justifying the legal and economic aspects of the conversion and its implications for shareholders and employees (Art. 37(2) Reg.). Furthermore, an auditor must examine the draft terms of conversion and draft a report for shareholders of the company to be converted. Among other things, the auditor must confirm that the company has net assets at least equivalent to its capital plus those reserves that may not be distributed by law or pursuant to the company's articles (Art. 37(6) Reg.).

The conversion itself, the draft terms of conversion and the new articles of association must be approved by the general meeting by a majority defined by the law of the Member State where the company to be converted is located (Art. 37(7) Reg.). Since Estonian law does not provide for a greater majority in this respect, a simple majority is sufficient to approve the conversion and the draft terms. Any amendments to the company's articles of association, however, must be approved by two-thirds of the votes cast at a meeting where more than half the share capital is present or represented (unless the articles stipulate a higher majority or quorum) (Arts. 297 and 300(1) Commercial Code).[28] If the quorum is not met, another general meeting shall be called at which no quorum is required (Art. 297(2) Commercial Code). The Estonian legislature has not enacted the option contained in Article 37(8) of the Regulation to make conversion subject to approval by a qualified majority or unanimity in the organ of the company to be converted within which employee participation is organised.

33. Upon completion, the conversion must be recorded with the commercial register. Thereafter, a notice of conversion must be published in the Estonian official gazette. The registration and publication formalities are discussed in Part III, Section 4 of this report.

3 Acts committed on behalf of an SE in formation

34. As long as an SE has not been recorded in the commercial register, it shall not enjoy legal personality and cannot enter into contracts or incur obligations (see no. 36 and Chap. 2, no. 55 of this book). The Regulation does not state how an SE may assume rights and obligations arising out of acts performed

---

[28] However, if a public limited-liability company has several classes of shares, the merger resolution must be approved by at least two-thirds of the holders of each class (unless the company's articles stipulate a greater majority) (Art. 421 Commercial Code).

on its behalf prior to registration. Therefore, reference is made to the respective provisions of national law (Art. 18 Reg.). Pursuant to the Commercial Code, obligations arising out of transactions performed in the name of an SE in formation will be assumed by the SE if its general meeting approves the transactions (Art. 253(3)). If the SE refuses to assume these obligations, the persons acting on behalf of the SE in formation will be held jointly and severally liable, in the absence of an agreement to the contrary (Art. 16(2) Reg.; Chap. 2, no. 55 of this book). The Commercial Code provides that the statute of limitations for such claims is five years from recordation of an SE in the commercial register (Art. 253(4)).

4 Registration and publication

35. An SE must be registered in the Member State where its registered office is located (Art. 12(1) Reg.). If an SE is incorporated in Estonia, it must be recorded in the Estonian commercial register.[29] Recordation is also required if the registered office of a holding or subsidiary SE is established in Estonia and where an SE is formed by merger or conversion. An SE acquires legal personality as of its date of recordation in the commercial register and loses legal personality when its registration is deleted (Arts 26(2) and 45(2) GPCCA; Art. 16(1) Reg.). Recordation in the commercial register is only possible if the rules on employee involvement have been complied with (Art. 12(2) Reg.).

In order to register an SE or to effect a merger or conversion, a notarised application along with the documents[30] prescribed by law must be submitted to the registrar. Regardless of the means of formation selected, the law provides a detailed list of documents that must be submitted. After reviewing the application, the court of first instance will rule on the registration, i.e. it will approve

---

[29] The commercial register is maintained by the registration departments of the various courts of first instance. Information in the commercial register is public. Anyone can examine the register and the commercial files and obtain copies of registry cards and documents on file. The B-card of a commercial file contains *inter alia* the following information on a company: (i) its name and registration code; (ii) the address of its registered office; (iii) its areas of activity; (iv) its share capital; (v) the identity of its management board members; (vi) the authority of members of the management board to represent the company; (vii) any amendments to its articles of association and the date on which they were approved; and (viii) the opening and closing dates of its financial year.

[30] The commercial register is maintained in the Estonian language. Hence, documents must be submitted to the registrar in Estonian or a notarised translation must be appended. If the transaction documents must be notarised (e.g. a formation agreement, draft terms of merger, etc.), the powers of the parties' representatives must be certified to the notary. For foreign companies, documents must be apostilled (if the party is a resident of a country that is a signatory of the Hague Convention) or legalised.

the application in whole or in part or reject it.[31] On the basis of this judgment, an entry will be made in the commercial register. As a rule, recordation usually occurs within 20 days from submission of an application.

36. Information on the transfer of an SE's registered office (Art. 8(2) Reg.), a merger (Art. 21 Reg.), formation of a holding SE (Art. 33(3) Reg.), and conversion of an existing public limited-liability company into an SE (Art. 37(5) Reg.) shall be published in the Estonian official gazette, *Ametlikud Teadaanded*.[32] Since 1 July 2003, *Ametlikud Teadaanded* has appeared only in electronic form (i.e. on line). Publication in *Ametlikud Teadaanded* is for informational purposes only and is not a prerequisite for obtaining legal personality or to enforce information against third parties.[33] Notices shall be published 'as is'. Anyone who submits a notice for publication is responsible for its accuracy (Art. 24^1(2) Riigi Teataja Act).

After publication in *Ametlikud Teadaanded*, the information on the SE is published in the *Official Journal of the European Communities*. The national authorities or the SE must forward the required information to the Office for Official Publications of the European Communities within one month following publication in the Estonian official gazette.[34]

5 Acquisition of legal personality

37. An SE acquires legal personality on the date on which it is recorded in the commercial register (Art. 26(2) GPCCA; Art. 16(1) Reg.). An SE with legal personality may acquire rights and liabilities, is entitled to sue to enforce its rights and can be sued to ensure the performance of its obligations. The legal consequences of limited liability are set forth in the Commercial Code, which states that a shareholder cannot be held personally liable for the obligations of a public limited-liability company (Art. 221(2) Commercial Code).[35] For further information please refer to no. 34 above and Chap. 2, no. 7.

---

[31] The court may approve the application only if an agreement on employee involvement within the SE has been concluded (unless none of the participating companies is subject to employee participation rules prior to registration of the SE) (Art. 12(3) Reg.).

[32] Pursuant to Article 24(2) of the Riigi Teataja Act, notices and announcements that must be published by law or pursuant to a ministerial or governmental decree but for which publication in the *Riigi Teataja* or another publication is not required shall be published in *Ametlikud Teadaanded*, the official gazette.

[33] Information is effective against third parties as from the date of its recordation in the commercial register. An entry shall be deemed ineffective with regard to legal acts performed within 15 days after recordation if a third party can prove that it was unaware and could not have been aware of the content of the entry (Art. 34 Commercial Code).

[34] At present, Estonian law does not provide for a detailed procedure regulating the submission of information to the Office for Official Publications of the European Communities.

[35] Different rules apply, however, where a shareholder has caused damage to a third party, another shareholder or the company. Those injured by a shareholder's actions may file a claim against the shareholder pursuant to the Commercial Code.

IV Organisation and management

1 General remarks

38. According to the Regulation, an SE may have either a one-tier or a two-tier system of management (a management board or a management board and a supervisory board, respectively). The companies forming the SE are free to choose the structure they prefer.

All 'standard' public limited-liability companies (*aktsiaselts*) incorporated in Estonia must have a two-tier system of management. According to the Regulation, where no provision is made under national law for a one-tier or a two-tier system of management in relation to public limited-liability companies with their registered offices within its territory, a Member State may adopt the appropriate measures in relation to SEs (Arts. 39(5) and 43(4) Reg.). In the one-tier structure, the management board fulfils the duties of both the administrative board and the supervisory board. As it was not possible to directly apply the existing provisions on the management of public limited-liability companies to SEs, the Estonian legislature had to enact (through the Implementation Act) detailed rules on the functioning and authority of an SE's management (or administrative) board (*haldusnõukogu*).[36]

2 General meeting

A Decision-making process

39. The organisation and conduct of the general meeting of an SE with its registered office in Estonia are governed by the provisions of the Commercial Code applicable to national public limited-liability companies (Art. 53 Reg.).

According to the Commercial Code, the general meeting must meet at least once a year within six months from the close of the SE's financial year in order to approve the company's annual report (Art. 291 Commercial Code; Art. 54(1) Reg.).[37]

The general meeting can be convened by the management board (in both the one-tier and two-tier systems),[38] the supervisory board (in the two-tier system), shareholders holding at least 10% of an SE's share capital, or the company's auditor(s) (Arts. 291 and 292 Commercial Code; Arts. 54(2) and 55(1) Reg.). If the management board does not convene a general meeting within one month following receipt of a request to do so, the shareholders, the

---

[36] Explanatory letter to the draft Implementation Act dated 17 June 2004.
[37] The first general meeting of an SE, however, may be held at any time during the first eighteen months following its incorporation (Art. 13(2) Accounting Law; Art. 54(1) Reg.).
[38] The Implementation Act refers to the management board of an SE in the one-tier system as its 'administrative board' (*haldusnõukogu*).

supervisory board or the auditor can convene the meeting (Art. 292(2) Commercial Code).

As a rule, the supervisory board in the two-tier system or the management board in the one-tier system determines the agenda of the general meeting, unless the shareholders or the auditor convene the meeting. The management board (in the two-tier system) or one or more shareholders holding at least 10% of an SE's share capital may request that items be placed on the agenda of a forthcoming general meeting (Art. 293 Commercial Code; Art. 56 Reg.). Currently, Estonian law does not allow an SE's articles of association to provide for a lower threshold for shareholders to place items on the agenda of a general meeting (Art. 56 Reg.). Since Estonian law does not specify the procedure applicable to request the company to convene a general meeting, the SE's articles of association must do so (Art. 56 Reg.).

The management board must send a notice of the general meeting by registered mail to all shareholders listed in the shareholders' register. If an SE has more than 100 shareholders, the notice may be published in a national daily newspaper instead (Art. 294 Commercial Code).[39] Notice of an annual general meeting must be provided at least three weeks in advance and of an extraordinary general meeting at least one week in advance, unless the articles of association provide otherwise. The notice must contain the information set forth in Article 294 of the Commercial Code.

If the requirements of law or the company's articles are violated in convening a general meeting, the meeting shall have no authority to pass resolutions, unless all votes represented by the shares are present or represented (Art. 296 Commercial Code). The Estonian Supreme Court (*Riigikohus*) has ruled that a decision adopted by a general meeting convened in violation of law or the company's articles shall be deemed null and void (unless all votes represented by the shares are present or represented).[40]

40. The general meeting may adopt decisions if more than 50% of the votes represented by the shares are present or represented, unless the SE's articles of association require a higher threshold. If the required quorum is not met, the management board must call another meeting with the same agenda within three weeks' time but not before seven days (Art. 297 Commercial Code).

The general meeting takes decisions by a majority of votes validly cast, provided the Regulation or national law does not require a greater majority (Art. 57 Reg.). In addition to those decisions that require a greater majority pursuant to the Regulation, Estonian law requires that the following decisions be approved by two-thirds of the votes present or represented at a general meeting: (i) an

---

[39] The draft LACC provides that a notice must be published if a public limited-liability company has more than 50 shareholders.
[40] Rules to this effect are also provided in the draft LACC.

increase or decrease in the company's share capital; (ii) the winding up of an SE and the continuation of activities of a dissolved SE; (iii) the merger, division or conversion of an SE; and (iv) the removal of members of the management board (in the one-tier system) or supervisory board (in the two-tier system). Restrictions on shareholders' pre-emptive right to subscribe new shares must be approved by at least three-quarters of the votes present or represented at a general meeting. A decision to alter the rights attached to a class of shares must be approved by a four-fifths majority, provided nine-tenths of the shareholders of the class of shares whose rights are affected vote in favour. An SE's articles of association may stipulate a greater majority, however, for any or all of the foregoing decisions. The Estonian legislature has not enacted the option contained in Article 59(2) of the Regulation to allow amendments to an SE's articles to be approved by a simple majority of votes cast, provided at least half the SE's subscribed capital is present or represented.

B   Rights and obligations of shareholders

41. The rights and obligations of shareholders are set forth in an SE's articles of association and in the Commercial Code. Shareholders can take decisions on all matters that fall within the competence of the general meeting by law or pursuant to the company's articles. Moreover, shareholders holding at least 10% of the share capital may request a special audit on matters regarding the management or financial situation of an SE. If the general meeting does not authorise the audit, shareholders holding at least 25% of the share capital can petition the court to appoint a special auditor (Art. 330 Commercial Code).

3   Management and supervision

A   Management (two-tier system/one-tier system)

(i)   **General remarks**
42. According to the Regulation, an SE may have either a one-tier system of management (comprised of a management board or *haldusnõukogu*) or a two-tier system (comprised of a management board or *juhatus* and a supervisory board or *nõukogu*).

Under Estonian law, members of the management and supervisory boards must be natural persons. Legal entities may not sit on the management or supervisory board.

(ii)   **One-tier system**
43. In the one-tier system, the management board handles day-to-day managerial duties and represents the company in its dealings with third parties. The management board must act in the company's best interest at all times. The

Implementation Act contains detailed rules on the duties of the management board (Art. 43(1) Reg.; see also no. 38 of this report). Pursuant to the Implementation Act, the management board of an SE has the following authority: (i) to organise accounting; (ii) to prepare issues to be discussed at general meetings and ensure implementation of resolutions passed by the general meeting; (iii) to propose measures, particularly with regard to internal organisation and control, on matters liable to jeopardise the functioning of the company; and (iv) if the company is insolvent and the insolvency is not temporary, to immediately file a petition in bankruptcy with the competent court and in any event no later than three weeks following the start of insolvency (Art. 19 IA). The articles of an SE may list categories of transactions that require the approval of the management board (Art. 48(1) Reg.).

44. The management board must have at least three members, unless the SE's articles provide for a greater number. The Implementation Act does not set forth a minimum or maximum number of board members (Art. 43(2) Reg.). At least half the board members must reside in Estonia, another EEA country or Switzerland (Art. 21 IA). In addition to the conditions for eligibility set forth in Article 47 of the Regulation, an SE's articles may stipulate grounds for disqualification. Under Estonian law, legal entities may not be appointed to an SE's management board (Art. 47(3) Reg.).

45. The management board must meet at least once every three months (Art. 44(1) Reg.). The chair (or substitute chair) of the board calls the meetings. A meeting must be called if a request to this effect is made by a member of the management board, the company's auditor or one or more shareholders representing at least 10% of the share capital. In addition, any of the foregoing persons may call a meeting if the management board fails to do so within two weeks following receipt of a request. An item may be added to the agenda of a management board meeting only if all board members are present and at least three-quarters approve the inclusion. Minutes of board meetings must be kept, and dissenting opinions must be entered in the minutes and confirmed by signing (Art. 23 IA).

If a meeting of the management board is called in violation of law or an SE's articles, the meeting is not entitled to adopt decisions unless all board members are present. Decisions passed at a meeting convened in violation of law or the company's articles shall be deemed null and void, unless those board members whose rights have been violated approve the decisions (Art. 23(6)).

46. Issues regarding quorums and decision-making authority are governed by Article 50 of the Regulation. Members of the management board, however, may not abstain from voting or remain undecided. Board members who cannot attend a meeting may vote in writing. Board members may not vote on transactions between third parties and the SE if they have a conflict of interest with the company. Shareholders or management board members can petition the court

to declare null and void board resolutions that conflict with applicable laws or the company's articles. The petition must be filed within three months following adoption of the decision (Art. 24 IA). The management board can take decisions without a meeting, unless the SE's articles provide otherwise, provided all board members are in agreement.[41]

(iii) **Two-tier system**

47. With regard to the duties, appointment and removal of members, and the decision-making process (quorums and voting requirements) of corporate bodies in the two-tier system, reference must be made to the provisions of the Regulation (see also Chap. 2, nos. 67 to 75 of this book). The Estonian legislature has opted to apply Article 48(1) of the Regulation, which provides that the supervisory board can stipulate categories of transactions that require its authorisation (Art. 17 IA), as well as Article 39(3), which states that the supervisory board can nominate one of its members to serve on the management board for a limited period of time, not to exceed one year, in the event of a vacancy on the latter body. Renewal or extension of an appointment is possible, provided the overall term does not exceed one year (Art. 16 IA). Issues not governed by the Regulation or the Implementation Act shall be governed by national rules of law applicable to public limited-liability companies (Art. 9(1) Reg.).

B   Appointment and removal

(i) **One-tier system**

48. In the one-tier system, members of the management board are appointed and removed by the general meeting.[42] The general meeting can remove a member of the management board for any reason. Any rights and obligations arising from a former board member's contract will be terminated pursuant to the terms thereof. A decision to remove a board member must be approved by two-thirds of the shares present or represented at a general meeting (see no. 40 of this report). Those shareholders representing at least 10% of the share capital may petition the court to order the removal for cause of a member of the management board. Pursuant to a petition filed by the management board, a shareholder or any other interested party, the court may appoint a replacement to serve on the board until a new member is appointed by the general meeting (Art. 22 IA).

---

[41] A detailed procedure to pass resolutions without calling a meeting is outlined in Article 25 of the Implementation Act.

[42] Employee participation rules must be applied on the occasions specified in the Directive and in the Employee Involvement Act (i.e. some members of the management board may be elected or appointed by the employees of an SE, its subsidiaries and establishments and/or by their representative body).

(ii) Two-tier system

49. In the two-tier system, members of the management board are appointed and removed by the supervisory board (Art. 39(2) Reg.). Members of the supervisory board are appointed and removed by the general meeting (Art. 298 Commercial Code; Art. 52 Reg.).

C Representation

50. Since the Regulation does not govern the representation of an SE vis-à-vis third parties, the rules applicable to representation of public limited-liability companies under national law shall apply (Art. 9(1) Reg.).

The Implementation Act provides rules with regard to the representation of a one-tier SE. Representation of a two-tier SE is governed by the provisions of the Commercial Code applicable to Estonian public limited-liability companies. The two sets of rules are quite similar. In both systems, any member of the management board may represent an SE in its dealings with third parties, unless the company's articles provide that all or some members may or must represent the company jointly. Joint representation is enforceable against third parties only if recorded in the commercial register. Upon entering into transactions on behalf of an SE, members of the management board must abide by restrictions set forth (i) in the company's articles of association and (ii) by the general meeting or the management board (in the one-tier system) or (iii) by the supervisory board (in the two-tier system).[43] Restrictions on representation are not enforceable against third parties. Moreover, members of the management board may not represent an SE in transactions that legally require the appointment by shareholders of a representative (Art. 22 IA; Art. 307 Commercial Code).[44]

Members of the supervisory board may not represent an SE vis-à-vis third parties.

D Liability

51. If an SE's registered office is located in Estonia, the liability of members of its management and supervisory boards shall be determined in accordance with Estonian law (Art. 51 Reg.).

Liability of members of the management and supervisory boards is governed by the Commercial Code, the GPCCA and the Criminal Code (*Karistusseadustik*).

---

[43] The draft LACC (see footnote 8) provides that the management board must also abide by any restrictions set forth in the company's articles of association, resolutions of the general meeting and supervisory board decisions.

[44] Similar rules have been provided for the two-tier system in the draft law LACC (see footnote 8) as follows: 'A member of the management board may not represent a public limited-liability company in transactions which by law require the appointment of a representative by shareholders or the supervisory board.'

52. Under current law, members of corporate organs are held jointly and severally liable for losses sustained by the company due to breach of their obligations. Thus, any member of a corporate organ can be required to make good a loss in full, in which case that member can assert a claim for indemnification against the other organ members. In addition, management board members may be held personally liable regardless of whether they are at fault.[45] Supervisory board members can only be held personally liable if they actually engaged in wrongdoing, however. Under the Commercial Code, liability shall be incurred for participation in unlawful decisions. Members of a company's management organ will be released from liability if they acted in accordance with a lawful decision taken by the general meeting or other competent body and can avoid liability altogether by dissenting from the resolution out of which the illegal activity arose.[46]

Members of an SE's corporate bodies and the SE itself may also incur criminal liability in certain cases. The Criminal Code sanctions unlawful acts performed by members of corporate organs on behalf of a company, such as engaging in business without a licence and violations of tax or competition law. In addition, failure to convene a general meeting when the net value of an SE's assets falls below the minimum threshold required by law or to file for bankruptcy constitute criminal offences under the code. Members of an SE's corporate organs who commit an offence may be charged along with the company if the facts provide an adequate basis for liability. Specific laws (environmental legislation, etc.) may also contain rules on misdemeanours for which organ members may be held liable.

In addition, the Bankruptcy Act establishes a specific procedure for claiming compensation from members of the management board if a court rules that the insolvency of the company was caused by gross negligence on the part of management board members. Certain acts that contribute to the insolvency of a company (such as destroying, damaging or squandering assets or granting/assigning assets without justification, assuming unjustified obligations, etc.) may also be sanctioned under the Criminal Code.

53. Claims against members of corporate organs must be brought within five years of the time the illegal activity occurred or the obligation in question was breached. During this period, an SE may assert claims against members of its management or administrative organ. Creditors may also assert claims against members of the management or administrative organ if their claims cannot be satisfied out of the SE's assets. Creditors can maintain such claims even if the SE has abandoned or settled its own claims against the member in question.

[45] As a rule, breach of an obligation may be sufficient to give rise to liability.
[46] More detailed rules regarding the liability of members of the corporate organs of public limited-liability companies have been proposed in the draft LACC (see footnote 8). However, the main principles of liability remain the same.

V Employee involvement

54. The Directive has been transposed into Estonian law by the Employee Involvement Act (see no. 1 of this report), which provides detailed rules on employee involvement in an SE.

1 Special negotiating body

Pursuant to the EIA, the general meeting of employees elects members to the special negotiating body ('SNB') of an Estonian participating company in accordance with the procedure approved by the meeting. If there is more than one Estonian participating company, a joint committee composed of three employee representatives from each participating company shall elect the SNB. The number of votes allotted to employee representatives is based on the number of employees they represent (Art. 54 EIA; Art. 3(2)(b) Dir.). The participating companies must reimburse reasonable expenses incurred in relation to the creation and functioning of an SNB. If an expert is involved at the SNB's initiative, the participating companies must reimburse the fees of at least one expert (Art. 61 EIA; Art. 3(7) Dir.).

2 Employee participation

Estonia does not currently recognise the right of employees to sit on corporate organs or other participation rights. The EIA transposes most of the standard provisions of the Directive governing the employee participation when formal negotiations fail. No special rules have been provided when the SNB does not decide which form of employee participation should be established in an Estonian SE (Art. 7(2) Dir.), nor has the Estonian legislature adopted the option contained in Article 7(3) of the Directive.

3 Protection of employee representatives

Estonian SNB members, employee members of corporate organs and other employee representatives in an SE enjoy the same protection as employee representatives under Estonian law (Art. 80 EIA; Art. 10 Dir.). Thus, they are entitled to a paid time off to perform their duties and are protected against unjustified dismissal and harassment by their employer.

VI Annual accounts and consolidated accounts

1 Accounting principles

55. If an SE's registered office is located in Estonia, Estonian law on the preparation and approval of the annual and consolidated accounts of public

limited-liability companies shall apply (Art. 61 Reg.). The principal law governing financial reporting and auditing in Estonia is the Accounting Act (*Raamatupidamise seadus*). Requirements regarding specific auditing aspects are set forth in other laws.

An SE must prepare an annual report at the end of each fiscal year.[47] Until Estonia joins EMU and adopts the euro as its national currency, the annual accounts of an SE must be denominated in Estonian kroons (Art. 67(2) Reg.; see also no. 14 of this report). However, under the Regulation, an SE may denominate its accounts in euros (see Chap. 2, no. 79 of this book). The annual report must be approved by the SE's general meeting and submitted to the commercial register for recordation within six months from the close of its financial year.

As a rule, parent companies and certain other entities[48] must prepare a consolidated annual report for their group.[49] In certain instances, however, an entity may be exempt from this obligation.[50]

56. Accounting and financial reporting must be conducted in accordance with Estonian generally accepted accounting principles as set forth in the Accounting Act. These principles reflect Community accounting directives and international financial reporting standards (i.e. standards and interpretations such as SIC Interpretations) approved by the International Accounting Standards Board.

---

[47] The annual report is comprised of a statement of annual accounts and a management report. A distribution proposal for the coming fiscal year must be appended to the report. Statements of annual accounts are prepared on the basis of the company's business transactions and book entries during the fiscal year. Such statements comprise the company's balance sheet, income statement, cash flow statement and statement of changes in ownership equity, as well as notes to the accounts.

[48] The Accounting Act provides that parent companies and other accounting entities exercising dominant influence over other accounting entities are required to prepare consolidated accounts (Art. 27(1) Accounting Act).

[49] A consolidating entity together with one or more consolidated entities form a consolidated group (Art. 27(3) Accounting Act).

[50] The following entities are eligible for an exemption: (i) a company at least 90% of whose voting stock is held by a consolidating entity registered in Estonia or in another EU Member State and which is subject to an obligation to prepare and disclose the audited annual report of its consolidated group under the laws of that country; (ii) a consolidating entity if, as of the date of its balance sheet for the accounting year, the entity did not exceed two of the following three criteria: sales revenue (net turnover) of EEK 95 million, balance sheet total of EEK 45 million, and 75 employees; (iii) a consolidating entity if the balance sheet total of none of its consolidated entities exceeds one per cent of its balance sheet total and if the balance sheet total of all consolidated entities taken together does not exceed 5% of its balance sheet total. The exemptions provided under (i) and (ii) above do not apply to consolidating entities that are credit institutions, financial holding companies, mixed-activity holding companies or insurance companies or to those whose issued shares or other securities are quoted on a stock exchange in Estonia or in a Member State of the European Union (Art. 29 Accounting Act).

323

2 Auditors

57. Pursuant to the Commercial Code, all public limited-liability companies must have an auditor. The general meeting appoints the auditor. Only auditors with the requisite qualifications whose names appear on the Board of Auditors'[51] (*Audiitorkogu*) list can perform audits. In addition to auditing an SE's annual accounts, auditors may, at the company's request, perform other services such as reviewing financial information and compiling financial reports.

VII Supervision by the national authorities

58. The national authorities in charge of ensuring application of the Regulation differ depending on the applicable provision. In Estonia, the competent authorities are: (i) the registrar of the commercial register with territorial jurisdiction over the registered office of an SE (for the purposes of Arts. 8(8), 25(2) and 26 Reg.); (ii) the Tallinn City Court (for purposes of Art. 22 Reg.); and (iii) the court ruling on the violation (for purposes of Art. 7 Reg.) (Art. 64(4) Reg.).

VIII Dissolution

1 Winding up

59. The rules of Estonian law on the winding up of public limited-liability companies also apply to SEs (Art. 63 Reg.). An SE may be wound up voluntarily or involuntarily. Winding up may occur pursuant to: (i) a decision of the general meeting; (ii) a decision of the creditors' meeting in the case of bankruptcy proceedings; (iii) by court order in the event of involuntary dissolution; and (iv) any other grounds provided by law or the SE's articles of association (Art. 364 Commercial Code; Art. 39 GPCLA). The decision to wind up must be approved by at least two-thirds of the share capital present or represented at a general meeting. If an SE has several classes of shares, the decision must be adopted by two-thirds of the votes represented by each class of shares. An SE's articles, however, may prescribe a greater majority (Art. 365(1) Commercial Code).

An SE may be subject to involuntary dissolution by court order if: (i) the general meeting does not adopt a decision to wind up when required to do so by law or the company's articles; (ii) the value of the company's net assets falls below the minimum level required by law and the general meeting has not passed a resolution in this respect as required by law; (iii) a general meeting has not been held for the last two financial years; (iv) the term of the management board ended more than two years ago and a new board has not been elected; and

---

[51] The Board of Auditors is a self-governing association that organises the professional activities of auditors and protects their rights. All auditors on the list are members of the Board of Auditors.

(v) in all other cases provided by law (Art. 366 Commercial Code). If both the registered office and the head office of an SE are not located in Estonia at all times, the company may be ordered to wind up pursuant to Article 64 of the Regulation (see no. 8 of this report).

2 Liquidation

60. The rules of Estonian law on the liquidation of public limited-liability companies shall also apply to SEs (Art. 63 Reg.).

After the general meeting resolves to wind up an SE or the SE is ordered to wind up by court order, an entry regarding the decision will be made in the commercial register and the liquidation will be carried out. The liquidators must promptly publish a notice on the initiation of liquidation proceedings in the Estonian official gazette and notify all of the company's known creditors that they have four months following publication of the notice to submit their claims.[52] After completion of liquidation, but no earlier than six months following publication of the notice of liquidation and at least three months following presentation of the final balance sheet and asset distribution plan to shareholders, the liquidators must submit a request to delete the SE's registration from the commercial register. In addition, a notice of completion of the liquidation formalities must be published in the Estonian official gazette and the *Official Journal of the European Communities* (see Part III, Section 4 of this report).

If the assets of an SE in voluntary or involuntary liquidation are not sufficient to satisfy its creditors' claims, the liquidators must file for bankruptcy.

3 Insolvency

61. On 1 January 2004, a new Bankruptcy Act (*Pankrotiseadus*) entered into effect in Estonia. This act is the principal legislation on insolvency proceedings and reorganisation in bankruptcy of companies.[53] On 1 May 2004, Estonia acceded to the EU. Therefore, as from that date, the provisions of Council Regulation (EC) No. 1346/2000 of 29 May 2000 on insolvency proceedings are applicable in Estonia with respect to cross-border insolvency proceedings involving legal entities or natural persons whose operations are connected to more than one EU Member State.

---

[52] Pursuant to the draft LACC, failure to submit a claim on time shall not affect the validity of the claim or the creditor's right to petition the court for satisfaction against an SE in liquidation.

[53] Other legislation may supplement or partly replace the rules set forth in the Bankruptcy Act. For instance, certain rules are contained in the Credit Institutions Act and the Insurance Activities Act with regard to insolvency proceedings of credit institutions and insurance companies, respectively. In addition, requirements in the Securities Markets Act, the Unemployment Insurance Act and other specific laws may apply to insolvency proceedings.

The Bankruptcy Act recognises two types of bankruptcy proceedings: (i) those aimed at liquidation of the debtor; and (ii) those aimed at the reorganisation and restructuring of troubled but viable companies. Reorganisation of a debtor's business without filing for bankruptcy is not currently possible under Estonian law. However, Estonian law does not exclude the possibility of out-of-court reorganisation by agreement of the debtor with all relevant creditors. If it is obvious that a debtor is permanently insolvent, however, the members of its management board are legally bound to file for bankruptcy. Failure to do so can expose board members to both civil and criminal sanctions.

Pursuant to Estonian law, bankruptcy cases are handled by the general civil courts. There are no special bankruptcy courts or bankruptcy judges.

A petition in bankruptcy may be filed by an insolvent debtor or a creditor.[54] Pursuant to the Bankruptcy Act, if the debtor files a petition in bankruptcy, it shall be presumed insolvent. A creditor must substantiate the debtor's insolvency in its petition, for instance by showing that at least one of the following conditions has been met: (i) the debtor has not fulfilled an obligation within 30 days after it fell due, the creditor informed the debtor in writing of its intent to commence bankruptcy proceedings, and the debtor thereafter failed to meet its obligation within ten days; (ii) the enforcement of a claim against the debtor has been impossible for three months due to insufficient assets or it has become evident during mandatory execution proceedings that the debtor's assets are insufficient to satisfy its liabilities; (iii) the debtor has destroyed, hidden or squandered its assets, made grave management errors or performed other acts as a result of which it has become insolvent; (iv) the debtor has notified the creditor or the general public that it is unable to pay its debts; or (v) the debtor has left Estonia or is in hiding in order to avoid paying its debts (Art. 10 Bankruptcy Act).

Upon the filing of a petition in bankruptcy, the court will first hold preliminary hearings before rendering an adjudication in bankruptcy (if the petition is filed by a creditor).[55] The court shall declare the debtor bankrupt on the basis of a creditor's petition if it finds that the debtor is insolvent based on the report of a temporary trustee and upon hearing the debtor and the creditor(s) who submitted the petition. At the time of the adjudication in bankruptcy, the court shall appoint a trustee in bankruptcy (who must be approved by the creditors' meeting) and set a date and place for the first creditors' meeting.

---

[54] Under the Bankruptcy Act, insolvency is defined as the inability of a debtor to pay its due and payable debts if such inability is not temporary considering the debtor's financial position. Legal entities shall also be deemed insolvent if their assets are insufficient to cover their liabilities and this situation is not temporary considering the financial position of the entity.

[55] The court must render its decision within ten days from the filing of a petition in bankruptcy.

The court shall immediately publish a notice of bankruptcy in the Estonian official gazette. Furthermore, the trustee shall notify all known creditors about the bankruptcy and the time and place of the first creditors' meeting. If there are more than 100 known creditors, publication of a notice is sufficient. However, the trustee shall in any case inform all known secured creditors and creditors whose place of residence or registered office is in another Member State.

The most important consequences of an adjudication in bankruptcy are: (i) from the time the adjudication is handed down the debtor's assets become the bankruptcy estate (*pankrotivara*) over which the debtor forfeits control; (ii) the right to administer the bankruptcy estate and to execute transactions with assets belonging to the estate is transferred to a court-appointed trustee in bankruptcy; (iii) all obligations of the debtor become due and interest and penalties stop to accruing; (iv) the trustee has the right to decide whether to perform the debtor's obligations or to terminate contractual relationships; (v) all creditors are obliged to notify the trustee of claims against the debtor within two months from publication of the notice of bankruptcy in the Estonian official gazette; (vi) third parties who hold any of the debtor's property or have unperformed obligations vis-à-vis the debtor must transfer these obligations to the trustee; and (vii) the court will not accept claims against the debtor submitted outside of bankruptcy proceedings.

Creditors may exercise certain decision-making powers in bankruptcy proceedings through the general meeting of creditors and the bankruptcy committee.

The Bankruptcy Act lists certain claims which must be paid from the proceeds of the bankruptcy estate before other claims such as: (i) claims of third parties arising from the exclusion of property from the bankruptcy estate and claims based on voidable transactions for the recovery of property; (ii) support to the debtor and its dependants (if the bankruptcy has deprived the debtor of a minimum allowance); (iii) payments made to creditors of the estate (so-called 'mass claims'); and (iv) the costs of the bankruptcy proceedings (Art. 146(1) Bankruptcy Act).

The claims of creditors are satisfied in the following order: (i) accepted claims secured by a pledge (i.e. a security interest) and filed on time; (ii) other accepted but unsecured claims filed on time; and (iii) accepted claims not filed on time.

Proceeds from the sale of assets in the bankruptcy estate are distributed pursuant to a distribution proposal drafted by the trustee and approved by the court. The distribution proposal must set forth, among other items, information on accepted claims, their priority and distribution ratios, proceeds from the sale of all collateral, and an overview of the sale of all assets (or any unsold assets) in the bankruptcy estate. Distribution is only allowed in accordance with a court-approved proposal. In the event of a compromise, distributions to creditors may be made only in accordance with a court-approved compromise proposal.

IX Applicable law

62. SEs registered in Estonia shall be governed by Estonian law, if the Regulation requires or authorises the application of national law.

X Tax treatment

63. The Regulation does not cover the taxation of SEs or their shareholders. An SE and its shareholders are subject to the national tax laws of the Member States and to any applicable Community legislation in this field (Recital 20 and Art. 9(1) Reg.).

1 Income tax

64. Pursuant to the Income Tax Act (*Tulumaksuseadus*), the standard income tax rate in Estonia is currently 24%. The Income Tax Act provides, however, for a gradual reduction of this rate by 1% per annum over the next several years. The rate will fall to 23% in 2006, 22% in 2007, 21% in 2008 and to 20% on 1 January 2009.

Estonia takes a unique approach to corporate income tax, designed to encourage investment and maximise corporate profits. Pursuant to the Income Tax Act, corporate tax by Estonian resident companies[56] is due when the income is distributed rather than earned. Resident companies are therefore not taxed on their profits unless these profits are distributed as dividends or by other means. Estonian companies are currently taxed at a rate of 24% on distributions of profit, so the effective rate is 24/76.[57] An exemption or tax credit for a particular fraction of each dividend distribution may be available in some cases for companies affiliated with the distributing company, such as subsidiaries. For example, no corporate tax is due on dividends distributed by an Estonian resident company or profits distributed by a nonresident company through an Estonian permanent establishment if income tax has been paid in Estonia or abroad on that share of the profit which forms the basis for the dividend or on which income tax has been withheld by a company in which the distributing company holds at least 20% of the shares or votes. If an Estonian

---

[56] Pursuant to the Regulation, an SE is considered a resident of the Member State in which its registered office is located (Art. 10 Reg.).

[57] As noted above, the rate will decrease each year until 2009, at which time a rate of 20% (20/80) will apply.

resident company or a foreign company with an Estonian permanent establishment holds less than 20% of a nonresident distributing company, it is eligible for a tax credit when declaring a dividend of its own or making another allocation of profits in the amount of tax withheld by the distributing company abroad.

Under Estonian tax law, a distribution of profits encompasses more than the mere distribution of dividends and includes various enumerated costs and expenses not directly related to the business activities of a company, as well as fringe benefits, gifts and donations made by a company.

2 Value added tax

65. Most goods and services sold or provided in Estonia are subject to value added tax ('VAT') at a rate of 18%, though specific items, such as books and certain medications listed in regulations issued by the Ministry of Social Affairs, are taxed at a reduced rate of 5%. VAT is imposed upon all imports, regardless of whether the importer is registered for VAT purposes. Exports are technically also subject to VAT, but the applicable rate is 0%. Various transactions are exempt from VAT, including property transfers incidental to mergers or divisions of business entities, real estate transfers, and the provision of insurance services, the importation of certain goods and services, and transfers of securities. Companies whose taxable turnover exceeds EEK 250,000 (approximately €16,000) as measured from the start of the calendar year must register with the VAT administration. Dispatches and acquisitions of EU products are not considered exports or imports and are subject to a specific set of rules, under which VAT is generally imposed in the country of destination.

3 Other taxes

Excise tax

66. Excise tax at varying rates is levied on alcohol, tobacco, packaged goods, fuel, and sales of heavy vehicles used to transport goods.

XI Conclusion

67. The Implementation Act, effective 10 December 2004, and the Employee Involvement Act, effective 11 February 2005, allow the formation and operation of SEs in Estonia.

The SE is the third type of company with share capital that may be incorporated under Estonian law, in addition to the private limited-liability company (*osaühing* or 'OÜ') and the public limited-liability company (*aktsiaselts* or 'AS').

Although the necessary implementing laws were passed in Estonia only recently, Estonian companies with Community-scale operations have already shown great interest in the SE, which could allow them to reduce operating costs and improve efficiencies. At the same time, companies are reluctant to be the first to establish an SE since, at present, this corporate form 'exists only on paper'. To date, no SEs have been formed in Estonia, and it remains to be seen how the Community legislation on SEs and the Estonian implementing legislation will work in practice.

12

Hungary

JACQUES DE SERVIGNY
Gide Loyrette Nouel

I   Introduction   332
II Formation   333
   1   General remarks   333
      A   Founding parties   333
      B   Name   333
      C   Registered office and transfer   333
         (i)   Registered office   333
         (ii) Transfer   334
            (a)   Protection of minority shareholders   334
            (b)   Protection of creditors   335
            (c)   Accounting   335
      D. Corporate purpose   336
      E   Capital   336
   2   Different means of formation   337
      A   Formation by merger   337
      B   Formation of a holding SE   337
      C   Formation of a subsidiary SE   337
      D   Conversion into an SE   337
      E   Acts committed on behalf of an SE in formation   337
      F   Registration and publication   337
      G   Acquisition of legal personality   338
III Organisation and management   338
   1   General remarks   338
   2   General meeting   338
      A   Decision-making process   338
      B   Rights and obligations of shareholders   339
   3   Management and supervision   339
      A   One-tier system/two-tier system   339
         (i)   One-tier system   339
         (ii) Two-tier system   339
      B   Appointment and removal   341
IV Employee involvement   341

         1 Special negotiating body   341
         2 Protection of employee representatives   342
         3 Judicial remedy   342
    V   Annual accounts and consolidated accounts   342
         1 Accounting principles   342
         2 Auditors   342
    VI Supervision by the national authorities   343
    VII Dissolution   343
    VIII Applicable law   343
    IX Tax treatment   343
         1 Income tax (corporate tax and dividend withholding tax)   343
              A Special rules related to adjustment of the corporate tax base   344
              B Carry forward of losses   344
         2 Value added tax   344
         3 Other taxes   345
    X   Conclusion   345

I   Introduction

1. Council Regulation (EC) No. 2157/2001 of 8 October 2001 on the Statute for a European Company (the 'Regulation'), introducing a new legal entity under Community law, the *Societas Europea* or 'SE', and Directive 2001/86/EC of 8 October 2001 supplementing the Statute for a European company with regard to the involvement of employees (the 'Directive') have finally been adopted by the Council of Ministers. The SE is a *sui generis* form of company which can be established in addition to companies formed under the national laws of a Member State. However, the SE differs from other (national) corporate forms in that it is based on and largely governed by a Community regulation rather than domestic law.

Hungary has enacted legislation to allow the incorporation of SEs on its territory. Act XLV of 2004 on the European Company *('európai részvénytársaság')* (the 'SE Act') entered into force on 8 October 2004.

The provisions of the Act apply when the Regulation does not directly regulate the issue at hand and does not refer to the SE's articles or to the provisions of national law applicable to public limited-liability companies. Thus, Section 1(1) of the Act stipulates that the Regulation and the Act govern the formation, organisation, management and dissolution of SEs established in Hungary. The Act also contains provisions applicable to the founders of an SE who are established in Hungary, even if the SE itself is based abroad (Section 1(2)).

II Formation

1 General remarks

A Founding parties

2. The Act refers to the provisions of the Regulation as regards the requirements the founders must comply with (see Chap. 2, no. 19 of this book). No specific rules have been enacted in Hungary.

B Name

3. The Act does not contain any specific rules regarding the name of an SE. The general rules applicable to Hungarian companies therefore apply, as stated in Section 2 of the Act. These rules can be found in Act CXLV of 1997 on the company register, public company information and court registration proceedings (the 'Registration Procedure Act').

4. Under Hungarian law, the name of a company must denote its principal activity and actual form and may not be misleading.

A company's name starts with a lead word, i.e. an expression or abbreviation that facilitates identification of the company and distinguishes it from other companies engaged in identical or similar activities. A company can be named after its owners or members.

Other than a lead word, a company's name may only consist of Hungarian words in accordance with the rules of Hungarian grammar. A company may also have an abridged name, consisting of a lead word followed by its corporate form.

5. A company's name (and abridged name, if any) must be clearly distinguishable from the names of other companies engaged in similar activities within the country. If more than one company applies to register the same name, priority shall be given to the company that first submitted its application. This provision does not affect the right of owners or members to use their name as the lead word in a company's name.

6. Finally, by direct application of Article 11 of the Regulation, the name of an SE registered in Hungary must be preceded or followed by the abbreviation 'SE'.

C Registered office and transfer

(i) **Registered office**

7. Registration of a newly formed SE must take place in accordance with the Registration Procedure Act (Sec. 2 SE Act). The competent authority is the county court, which acts as the court of registry having jurisdiction on the territory where an SE is established in Hungary.

8. According to Article 7 of the Regulation, an SE's registered office must be located in the same Member State as its head office. A Member State may require that an SE registered within its borders be registered at the place where its head office is located. Accordingly, the SE Act provides that the registered office of an SE in Hungary must also serve as its head office (Sec. 4). According to Section 16(1) of the Registration Procedure Act, the registered office of a company is its main centre of business administration. For the sake of consistency with national law, the same rule applies to SEs registered in Hungary pursuant to the option contained in the Regulation.

9. If an SE no longer complies with the provisions of Article 7 of the Regulation (i.e. its registered office is not in the same Member State as its head office), the Member State in which the SE's registered office is situated shall take appropriate steps to oblige the SE to regularise its situation within a specified period of time. In the interest of effective application of Article 7, Hungarian law allows the involuntary liquidation of an SE registered in Hungary if the company fails to regularise its situation within a specified period of time and provides a judicial remedy allowing an SE in such a position to challenge the measures taken by the authorities in this regard (Art. 64(1)–(3) Reg.). These requirements are satisfied under Hungarian law by mandatory application to SEs of the provisions of the Registration Procedure Act (Secs. 2 and 3 SE Act).

(ii) **Transfer**
(a) **Protection of minority shareholders**

10. Article 8(5) of the Regulation entitles the Member States, with respect to SEs registered within their territory, to adopt provisions designed to ensure the protection of minority shareholders who oppose the transfer of an SE's registered office. In this vein, Section 13(1) of the SE Act contains the same provisions as Section 5, which deals with the protection of minority shareholders who oppose a merger.

11. Certain information and documents must be provided to minority shareholders who oppose a transfer. Thus, the company's officers must prepare a draft source and application of funds statement and a draft statement of the company's assets, valid as of a reference date determined by the general meeting, as well as a proposal to minority shareholders. Information must also be provided with respect to the ratio of equity to subscribed capital as per the draft source and application of funds statement and of equity to the balance sheet total (Sec. 5(2) SE Act). The draft source and application of funds statement and the draft asset statement must be prepared in accordance with the requirements of Act C of 2000 on Accounting (the 'Accounting Act'). The balance sheet of the report prepared pursuant to the Accounting Act may also be accepted as the

draft source and application of funds statement for the SE if its reference date is no more than six months prior to the decision to approve the transfer (Sec. 5(3) SE Act).

12. The general meeting must pass a resolution approving the draft source and application of funds statement and the draft statement of assets. Except in the case set forth in Section 5(3) of the SE Act, the draft source and application of funds statement must be approved within three months of its reference date (Sec. 5(4) SE Act).

13. Based on the data contained in the draft source and application of funds statements and on the officers' proposal, the general meeting will establish in detail that share of the company's assets to which dissenting minority shareholders are entitled and modalities for distribution of the same (Sec. 5(5) SE Act). Distribution must be completed within 30 days following registration of the transfer, unless an agreement with the parties concerned provides for a later payment date (Sec. 5(6) SE Act).

(b) **Protection of creditors**

14. Section 6 of the SE Act contains provisions to protect creditors when an SE is formed by merger. Section 13(1), which refers to Section 6, provides similar protection in the event of the transfer of an SE's registered office.

Thus, an SE must grant security to creditors with outstanding claims that arose prior to publication of the transfer proposal (Sec. 6(1) SE Act). No security shall be granted if the creditor has already been afforded protection on the basis of statutory provisions or by contract or if the company's financial situation provides adequate guarantees (Sec. 6(2) SE Act). If the company refuses to grant a creditor's request for security, the creditor has eight days within which to petition the competent court of registry to review the company's decision. The court shall take a decision within 30 days following receipt of the petition (Sec. 6(3) SE Act). Minority shareholders are not entitled to receive their share of the company's assets unless and until the SE has complied with the aforementioned provisions for the protection of creditors (Sec. 6(4) SE Act).

(c) **Accounting**

15. The accounting rules applicable to the transfer of an SE's registered office are set forth in the SE Act since the Accounting Act applies only to going concerns. Following the transfer, an SE is no longer governed by the laws of the Member State where its registered office was located but rather by the laws of the Member State where its new registered office is established. As far as accounting is concerned, this means that an SE must prepare opening and closing balance sheets.

Section 13(2) of the SE Act therefore stipulates that when an SE located in Hungary transfers its registered office to another Member State, it must satisfy within 150 days the auditing, deposit, disclosure and annual reporting requirements of the Accounting Act effective as of the date of registration of the new office.

16. Section 13(3) of the SE Act regulates the transfer of an SE's registered office from another Member State to Hungary. In such a case, an SE must prepare, in accordance with the Accounting Act, an opening balance sheet and statement of assets and liabilities, effective as of the day on which the transfer is recorded by the competent court of registry. The SE's opening accounts must reflect the figures contained in its opening statement of assets and liabilities (historical costs, depreciation, write-offs, adjustments in value, evaluation differences, etc.) (Sec. 13 (4) SE Act).

If the currency used to denominate the accounts and in the annual report changes upon the transfer of an SE's registered office to Hungary, the opening balance sheet and statement of assets and liabilities referred to in Section 13(3) of the SE Act must be completed using the previous currency and subsequently converted on the same date into the new currency in accordance with the provisions of the Accounting Act (Sec. 13(5) SE Act).

D Corporate purpose

17. The Hungarian general rules on corporate purpose shall apply equally to SEs. These rules are set forth in the Registration Procedure Act, which provides that the a company's principal activity and any activities mentioned in its articles of association must be listed in the company register in accordance with the nomenclature of the Hungarian Central Statistics Office (*KSH*) (the so-called TEAOR code).

There are no specific rules applicable to SEs.

E Capital

18. According to Section 203 of Act CXLIV of 1997 on Business Associations (the 'BAA'), the share capital of a Hungarian public limited-liability company may be no less than 20 million Hungarian forints (€80,000). The Regulation contains specific rules for the minimum share capital of an SE which are directly applicable in Hungary. Pursuant to Article 4(2) of the Regulation, an SE must have minimum share capital of at least €120,000.

19. The BAA governs the subscription of and payment for shares, changes to share capital, the status of capital in general, the nature of shares and the rights and obligations attached thereto, and transfers of shares.

2 Different means of formation

A Formation by merger

20. When a public limited company participates in the formation of an SE by merger, certain accounting documents and information must be provided to minority shareholders who do not wish to become shareholders in the new company (Sec. 5 SE Act). For the detailed procedure, see Part II Section (ii) of this report.

Furthermore, the SE Act extends protection to creditors where an SE is formed by merger (Sec. 6). For further information, see Part II Section (ii) of this report.

B Formation of a holding SE

21. The companies promoting the formation of a holding SE must provide certain accounting documents and information to minority shareholders who oppose the transaction. They must also ensure appropriate protection of creditors (Sec. 7 SE Act). For further information, see Part II Section c.2 of this report.

C Formation of a subsidiary SE

22. The SE Act does not contain any special provisions governing the formation of a subsidiary SE. For further information, see Chap. 2, nos 45 and 46 of this book.

D Conversion into an SE

23. The SE Act does not contain any special provisions governing the conversion of a Hungarian public limited-liability company into an SE. For further information, see Chap. 2, no. 46 of this book.

E Acts committed on behalf of an SE in formation

24. The SE Act does not contain any special provisions governing acts committed on behalf of an SE in formation. For further information, see Chap. 2, no. 55 of this book.

F Registration and publication

25. Pursuant to Article 12 of the Regulation, an SE must be registered in the Member State in which its registered office is located.

In Hungary, the registration of a newly formed SE is governed by the Registration Procedure Act (Sec. 2 SE Act). The court of registry of the place where the company's registered office is located must be notified of the formation of the SE within 30 days following the date of conclusion of its articles of association.

The court of registry shall then proceed to publish the notice of incorporation in the Hungarian company gazette (*Cégközlöny*) and to register the company. Pursuant to the Registration Procedure Act, the court must register the company within 68 days following submission of a formal request by the applicant, failing which the company shall be registered automatically on the basis of the information provided.

Notice of an SE's registration must also be published in the *Official Journal of the European Communities* (Art. 14(1) Reg.).

G   Acquisition of legal personality

26. The Act does not contain any specific rules regarding the acquisition of legal personality by an SE. The general rules governing business associations in Hungary, as set forth in the BAA, shall therefore apply.

Pursuant to Section 14 of the BAA, a business association, including an SE, can operate as a 'pre-company' as of the date of either countersignature of its articles of association or of such being drawn up in a public document.

Following submission of an application to register a business association, the pre-company may pursue business-like economic activities. Until registration is completed, the officers of the business association shall be deemed to be acting on its behalf and for its benefit. The rules applicable to business associations apply equally to pre-companies, with a few exceptions.

A company, including an SE, is officially brought into existence when recorded in the company register.

III   Organisation and management

1   General remarks

As set forth in the Regulation and the SE Act, the founders of an SE established in Hungary can opt for either a one-tier or a two-tier system of management (see Chap. 2, no. 60 of this book).

2   General meeting

A   Decision-making process

27. The decision-making process of an SE is very similar to that of a public limited-liability company under Hungarian law. Decision-making authority lies with the general meeting. The Regulation governs the convening of as well as participation in and representation and voting at general meetings. However, the organisation and conduct of general meetings, together with voting procedures, are governed by the laws applicable to public limited-liability companies of the Member State in which the SE's registered office is located (Art. 53 Reg.).

28. The general meeting takes decisions by a simple majority of votes validly cast (Art. 57 Reg.). However, amendments to an SE's articles require at least a two-thirds majority (Art. 59 Reg.), unless the law applicable to public limited-liability companies in the Member State in which the SE's registered office is located requires a larger majority. Pursuant to Section 19(1) of the BAA, the general meeting passes resolutions by a simple majority of votes cast. Nevertheless, Section 237 of the BAA states that resolutions related to the exclusive authority of the general meeting must be approved by at least three-quarters of the votes adopting the draft resolution. As these provisions are stricter than those contained in the Regulation, the foregoing issues are governed by national law.

29. Pursuant to Articles 55 and 56 of the Regulation, one or more shareholders holding jointly at least 10% of an SE's subscribed capital may force the company to convene a general meeting and place certain items on the agenda. Nevertheless, an SE's articles or national law may provide for a smaller percentage under the same conditions as those applicable to public limited-liability companies. The BAA allows these rights to be exercised by shareholders holding at least 5% of the votes attached to the company's shares (Secs. 51(6) and 295(3)). Section 8 of the SE Act requires application of these provisions, with the difference that 5% of the subscribed capital (rather than 5% of the votes) is the relevant threshold. In keeping with the provisions of the Regulation, an SE's articles may stipulate a lower percentage, however.

B   Rights and obligations of shareholders

30. The rights and obligations of shareholders are set forth in an SE's articles of association and in the provisions of the BAA applicable to Hungarian public limited-liability companies.

For more information regarding the protection of minority shareholders, see Part II Section (ii) of this report.

3   Management and supervision

A   One-tier system/two-tier system

(i)   One-tier system

31. Pursuant to Article 43(4) of the Regulation, where no provision is made for a one-tier system of management for public limited-liability companies with registered offices within the territory of a Member State, appropriate measures may be adopted in relation to SEs.

Thus, Sections 9 and 10 of the SE Act establish certain basic rules for companies that opt for a one-tier system of management.

In the one-tier system, the administrative organ (the board of directors or *igazgatótanács*) manages the SE (Sec. 9(1) SE Act). In accordance with the Regulation, the SE Act states that the administrative organ must have at least five and may have no more than eleven members (Sec. 9(2)).

As there is no supervisory organ in the one-tier system to oversee management on behalf of shareholders, members of the administrative organ serve in both a managerial and a supervisory capacity. Consequently, Section 9(3) of the SE Act provides that the majority of members of the administrative organ (the board of directors) should be independent, although an SE's articles may set a higher threshold.

The SE Act lists examples of dependent relationships, including where an organ member is an employee, expert or committee member of the SE, holds, directly or indirectly, at least 30% of the votes attached to the company's shares or is a close relative of such a person, will benefit directly from the profitable functioning of the SE, or is controlled or overseen in another company by a non-independent member of the SE's administrative organ (Sec. 9(4) and (5)).

If an SE's articles allow a managing director *(vezérigazgató)* to be appointed, only an employee of the SE can serve in this capacity (Sec. 9(6) SE Act).

When the nature of an SE's activities or any other reasonable cause so justifies, an SE's articles may allow the creation of committees (e.g. a nominations committee, a remuneration committee, etc.) (Sec. 10(1) SE Act). The creation of an audit committee is mandatory.

(ii) **Two-tier system**
32. Article 39(1) of the Regulation provides that in an SE with a two-tier system, the management organ is responsible for managing the company. The number of members of the management organ must be specified in the SE's articles. Nevertheless, national law may specify a minimum and/or maximum number. Thus, pursuant to Section 11 of the SE Act, the management organ (the executive board or *igazgatóság*) must have at least three and may have no more than 11 members.

Article 40 of the Regulation contains similar provisions regarding members of the supervisory organ, which oversees the management organ. Consequently, Section 12(1) of the SE Act provides that the supervisory body *(felügyelöbizottság)* must have at least three and may have at most 15 members. This rule applies without prejudice to any arrangements for employee involvement.

According to Article 39(3) of the Regulation, no person may sit simultaneously on both the management organ and the supervisory organ of an SE. The supervisory organ may, however, nominate one of its members to temporarily fill a vacancy on the management organ. Pursuant to the Regulation, Section 12(3) of the SE Act provides that this period may not exceed 60 days, although an SE's articles may stipulate a longer period of time.

B   Appointment and removal

33. According to the Regulation, members of the management organ in the two-tier system shall be appointed and removed by the supervisory organ. Nevertheless, a Member State may require or permit an SE's articles to provide that members of its management organ are to be appointed and removed by the general meeting under the same conditions as those applicable to public limited-liability companies having their registered offices in that country (Art. 39(2) Reg.). The BAA provides that the election and removal of members of the management organ fall within the exclusive competence of the general meeting (Art. 233(d)). Consequently, for the sake of consistency with this provision, Section 12(2) of the SE Act states that an SE's articles may provide that members of the management organ can be appointed and removed by the general meeting rather than by the supervisory organ.

IV   Employee involvement

The second part of the SE Act contains provisions similar to those set forth in Council Directive 2001/86/EC supplementing the Statute for a European company with regard to the involvement of employees.

1   Special negotiating body

34. As required by the Directive, the SE Act fixes the method to be used to determine the composition of the special negotiating body (SNB), which must consist of elected or appointed members. Section 21 of the SE Act provides that SNB members must be appointed or elected by either the works council or the central works council(s) (where applicable). Following appointment of these members, the SE Act specifies that alternates must be designated.

35. Section 22 of the SE Act provides that when a participating company has no works council, the employee representatives of the company, subsidiary or establishment must be invited to attend the caucus of the works council or central works council(s). These representatives are elected by the employees of the participating entities. The SE Act contains various rules governing their election (including the creation of an elections committee). Employee representatives must be treated in all respects as other members of the caucus.

36. As set out in the Directive, necessary and justified expenses related to the functioning of the SNB and to negotiations in general (such as rental fees, experts' and interpreters' fees, travel and accommodation expenses, etc.) shall

be borne by the participating companies in proportion to the number of employees they employ (Sec. 28 SE Act). The amounts that can be borne by participating companies in Hungary are determined pursuant to Section 63 of the Hungarian Labour Code.

2 Protection of employee representatives

37. Like other employee representatives, SNB members are protected under Hungarian labour law (Art. 10 Dir.). They must be given sufficient paid time off to discharge their duties and to attend training programmes. The amount of paid leave to which they are entitled shall be calculated in accordance with Section 62 of the Hungarian Labour Code, unless a signed agreement provides otherwise (Sec. 33 SE Act)

3 Judicial remedy

38. Pursuant to Article 12(2) of the Directive, the Act provides a judicial remedy for violations of the Directive's obligations on employee involvement. In the event of a violation, the employee representatives may lodge a complaint with the labour courts, in accordance with the relevant provisions of the Hungarian Labour Code, against an SE's board of directors and the administrative organs of any participating companies (Sec. 34(1) SE Act).

An SE's board of directors and the administrative organs of participating companies may also file claims against the SNB, the employees' representative body and the employee representatives themselves (Sec. 34(2) SE Act).

V Annual accounts and consolidated accounts

1 Accounting principles

39. The only special provisions contained in the SE Act concern the transfer of an SE's registered office (see Part II, Section C of this report).

The Accounting Act applies to all other issues. In particular, the Accounting Act requires Hungarian public limited-liability companies to have their accounts certified at least once a year by an auditor registered in Hungary. This provision also applies to SEs. The company's financial records, prepared in accordance with the applicable legal requirements, must be submitted to the relevant court of registry by 31 May of each year.

2 Auditors

40. The creation of an audit committee is mandatory in an SE with a one-tier system. The audit committee oversees the company's accounting methods and is

composed of at least three members appointed by the administrative organ from amongst its members (Sec. 10(2) SE Act). The audit committee is authorised to issue an opinion on the company's annual report (prepared in accordance with the Accounting Act), to recommend the appointment of an independent auditor and his or her remuneration, to draft the auditor's employment contract and sign it on the basis of authority granted to it by the articles, to evaluate internal audit procedures and make suggestions, and to assist the administrative organ in order to ensure proper oversight of internal audit procedures (Sec. 10(3) SE Act). An SE's articles may stipulate additional responsibilities for the audit committee, however (Sec. 10(4) SE Act).

VI Supervision by the national authorities

41. As prescribed by Article 68(2) of the Regulation, Hungary has designated a competent authority for the purposes of Articles 8, 25, 26, 54, 55 and 64 of the Regulation. According to Section 3 of the SE Act, the competent authority is either the county court or the Budapest court, as the case may be, acting as a court of registry.

VII Dissolution

42. Article 63 of the Regulation provides that as regards winding up, liquidation, insolvency, cessation of payments and similar procedures, an SE shall be governed by the legal provisions applicable to public limited-liability companies formed in accordance with the laws of the Member State in which its registered office is located. The Act provides that Act XLIX of 1991 on Bankruptcy Proceedings, Liquidation Proceedings and Members' Voluntary Dissolution and the Registration Procedure Act shall apply to SEs.

VIII Applicable law

43. The Regulation and the SE Act apply to the formation, organisation, management and winding up of SEs established in Hungary (Sec. 1(1) SE Act).

IX Tax treatment

1 Income tax (corporate tax and dividend withholding tax)

44. In general, an SE is treated like a regular public limited-liability company under Hungarian law for the purposes of Act LXXXI of 1996 on Corporate Tax and Dividend Tax (the 'Corporate and Dividend Tax Act').

Indeed, under Hungarian tax law, the corporate form of an entity is irrelevant. Hungarian companies, regardless of their form, are generally subject to the same tax rules and are taxed on their profits regardless of the nature of their economic activities. Thus, an SE based in Hungary will be subject to Hungarian corporate tax at a rate of 16% on its worldwide profits. However, taxes paid abroad may be deducted, even in the absence of an applicable tax treaty.

Certain SE-specific rules should also be taken into account.

A Special rules related to adjustment of the corporate tax base

45. Pursuant to Section 16(4) of the Corporate and Dividend Tax Act, the tax liability of an SE and any successor non-resident enterprise carrying on its activities following the transfer of its registered office shall be determined as if the transfer had not taken place. Consequently, despite the transfer of its registered office abroad, an SE's tax liability will continue to be determined in the same way as a Hungarian company's.

If the enterprise is no longer subject to the provisions of the Corporate and Dividend Tax Act for any reason except winding up due to a transformation or transfer of its registered office abroad, it shall be considered to have liquidated without a successor in interest for corporate tax purposes. The foregoing shall not apply when an SE transfers its registered office to another country in connection with activities it pursues as a non-resident entrepreneur or to foreign taxpayers whose activities are taken over by an SE (Sec. 17(4) Corporate and Dividend Tax Act).

B Carry forward of losses

46. When the Hungarian permanent establishment of a non-resident enterprise ceases to exist after the establishment of an SE or the transfer of an SE's registered office to Hungary, any losses realised by the permanent establishment in Hungary that have not yet been offset can be carried forward by the SE, without the need to obtain an authorisation from the tax authorities.

When an SE having its registered office in Hungary transfers its registered office abroad and continues its Hungarian activities through a permanent establishment, the permanent establishment is entitled to apply the above loss carry-forward rules to any losses incurred by the SE.

2 Value added tax

47. Act LXXIV of 1992 on value added tax does not contain any specific provisions for SEs. An SE is therefore subject to Hungarian VAT under the same conditions as other Hungarian companies, in accordance with the Sixth VAT Directive.

3 Other taxes

48. An SE having its registered office in Hungary, like other Hungarian companies, is subject to local business tax at a maximum rate of 2%. The actual tax rate depends on the municipality where the company operates. However, in most locations, e.g. Budapest, the rate is 2%. This tax is levied on the company's net turnover, which includes certain financial income (e.g., 50% of interest received). Only the costs of re-invoiced (mediated) services, goods sold and materials used may be deducted from the company's net turnover.

As of 2005, 50% of any local business tax paid is deductible from a company's corporate tax base.

X Conclusion

49. It is still too soon to measure the practical effects of the introduction of the SE in Hungary. However, it appears that the SE will finally create a legal framework in Hungary for cross-border transactions between larger companies.

13

Lithuania

ZILVINAS KVIETKUS AND MINDAUGAS CIVILKA
Norcous & Partners

I   Introduction   347
II Formation   347
   1   General remarks   347
   2   Founding parties   347
   3   Name   348
   4   Registered office and transfer   348
   5   Capital   348
   6   Different means of formation   349
      A   Formation by merger   349
      B   Formation of a holding SE   350
      C   Formation of a subsidiary SE   350
      D   Conversion into an SE   350
   7   Acts committed on behalf of an SE in formation   351
   8   Registration and publication; acquisition of legal personality   351
III Organisation and management   352
   1   General remarks   352
   2   General meeting   352
      A   Decision-making process   353
      B   Rights and obligations of shareholders   353
   3   Management and supervision   354
      A   Two-tier system/one-tier system   354
      B   Appointment and removal   355
      C   Representation   355
      D   Liability   356
IV Employee involvement   356
V   Annual accounts and consolidated accounts   358
   1   Accounting principles   358
   2   Auditors   359
VI Supervision by the national authorities   359
VII Dissolution   360
   1   General remarks   360
   2   Reorganisation   360
   3   Liquidation   361
   4   Cessation of payments   362
VIII Applicable law   362

IX	Tax treatment 363	
	1 General remarks 363	
	2 Corporate tax 363	
	3 Withholding tax 364	
	4 VAT 364	
	5 Property and land tax 365	
	6 Tax framework for the formation of an SE 365	
	8 Consequences of a tax-free merger 366	
	9 Transfer of head office and change in corporate form 366	
	10 Establishment of a subsidiary SE 366	
	11 Transfer of registered office and cross-border merger 367	
X	Conclusion 367	

I Introduction

The European Company (SE) Act (*Europos Bendrovi 1 statymas*) (the 'SE Act') was adopted on 29 April 2004 and entered into force on 8 October 2004. The SE Act implements Council Regulation No. 2157/2001 of 8 October 2001 on the Statute for a European company (the 'Regulation'). Provisions of Lithuanian law governing public limited companies, mainly the Companies Act, are also applicable *mutatis mutandis* to SEs with their registered offices in Lithuania. In addition, the Civil Code, the core of Lithuanian civil law, regulates general issues applicable to SEs registered in Lithuania.

II Formation

1 General remarks

As of February 2005, it has been possible to form an SE in Lithuania pursuant to amendments to the regulations governing the register of legal entities (the 'Register') for the purpose of allowing the registration of SEs. In practice, however, registration of an SE became possible only after complete transposition into national law of Council Directive 2001/86 supplementing the Statute for a European company with regard to the involvement of employees (the 'Directive'). On 12 May 2005, the Lithuanian Parliament passed the SE Employee Involvement Act ('EIA'), which entered into force on 28 May 2005.

2 Founding parties

Any legal entity within the meaning of Article 2(3) of the Regulation formed under Lithuanian law may participate in the formation of a subsidiary SE, unless it is explicitly prohibited from doing so by law or pursuant to its articles. By law, state and municipal enterprises may not hold an interest in legal entities and, therefore, such enterprises may not be founders of an SE.

3 Name

In terms of Lithuanian law, the name of a legal entity is protected as of the date on which an application to register the entity is filed with the Register. The name of a company is its sole property and may not be sold or disposed of by any party other than the legal entity itself. According to Article 2.39 of the Civil Code, a legal entity must have a name that is not contrary to public policy or morality and is not misleading as to the identity of its founders, owners and corporate purpose or deceptively similar to a recognised or well-known trademark in Lithuania. The abbreviation 'SE' does not carry any other meaning in Lithuanian, and the name of an SE must be preceded or followed by this abbreviation.

4 Registered office and transfer

Article 7 of the Regulation has been implemented under national law through Article 4 of the SE Act, which provides that the registered and head office of an SE must be in the same place. According to Article 2 of the Companies Act, the registered office of a Lithuanian limited-liability company must be situated in the Republic of Lithuania at all times.

If an SE no longer has its registered office and head office in Lithuania, it may not remain registered as a Lithuanian company. Article 2 of the SE Act sets forth a detailed procedure to transfer the registered office of an SE from Lithuania to another country. The transfer resolution must be approved by two-thirds of votes cast at the general meeting and followed by a tender offer (submitted by those shareholders who voted in favour of the transfer) to purchase the shares of those shareholders who either voted against the transfer or abstained.

The Ministry of Justice can oppose the transfer of an SE's registered office on grounds of public interest. Thus far, the government has not approved any grounds and/or procedures on which such opposition could be based.

5 Capital

Lithuania is not yet a member of the euro zone (the introduction of the euro as the sole national currency is tentatively scheduled for 1 January 2007), so the capital of an SE must be expressed in litas. Applying the official exchange rate, the minimum share capital of an SE is 414,336 litas. In comparison, the minimum share capital of a national public limited-liability company is only 150,000 litas (approximately €43,443).

The capital of an SE is represented by shares. The shares must be fully paid up within the time period stipulated in the documents of incorporation, which may not exceed 12 months from the signing date of any such document.

6 Different means of formation

Pursuant to the SE Act, an SE may be formed (i) by merger, (ii) as a holding company, (iii) as a subsidiary, and (iv) by conversion. The provisions of the Civil Code and the Companies Act on the formation of national public limited-liability companies shall apply *mutatis mutandis* to the formation of an SE.

A Formation by merger

The Third Company Law Directive has been implemented in the Civil Code (Chapter VIII) and the Companies Act (Chapter Eight). The relevant provisions (e.g. requirements pertaining to corporate decision-making, merger procedures, etc.) should be observed when forming an SE through a merger of two or more public limited-liability companies.

The boards of the Lithuanian public limited companies involved in a merger must draw up draft terms of merger, including at least the information stipulated in Article 20(1) of the Regulation. The merger documents must be drafted in or translated into Lithuanian.

The draft terms of merger must be approved by a qualified majority of no less than two-thirds of the votes present or represented at a general meeting (the company's articles may stipulate a greater majority, however). If the company has different classes of shares, a resolution can be passed only if approved by a separate vote of each class. Voting by secret ballot is not allowed. Each participating company must appoint an independent auditor to examine the draft terms. However, the participating companies can jointly petition the registrar of the Register to appoint a single auditor on behalf of them all.

The draft terms of merger must be published at least three times in at least three-month intervals. Alternatively, a single public announcement can be made if all creditors are notified individually in writing.

The Ministry of Justice may, in the manner prescribed by the government, oppose the participation of a public limited company in the formation of an SE by merger. Thus far, however, the government has yet to approve any grounds and/or procedures on which such opposition could be based.

According to Lithuanian law, the companies participating in a reorganisation must provide additional protection to safeguard the rights of creditors with claims outstanding on the date of publication of the reorganisation plan, if the creditor has valid reasons to believe that the reorganisation will jeopardise recovery of its claim.

B   Formation of a holding SE

A public or private limited company registered in Lithuania may promote the formation of a holding SE. All companies promoting the operation must prepare draft terms for the holding SE and approve them. According to Article 3 of the SE Act, the draft terms of formation should be examined by an independent auditor appointed by each company involved in the formation. Lithuanian law does not include any specific requirements with regard to the draft terms, except that all documents must be drafted in or translated into Lithuanian.

The draft terms of formation must be submitted to the Register no later than their publication date. Statutory requirements with regard to notification of a contemplated reorganisation, the protection of creditors, and corporate decision-making apply *mutatis mutandis* to the formation of a holding SE.

C   Formation of a subsidiary SE

The requirements of the Civil Code and the Companies Act regarding the incorporation of a national public limited company govern formation of a subsidiary SE. Accordingly, formation of a subsidiary SE in Lithuania involves the following steps: (i) execution of an incorporation agreement (memorandum of association) and articles; (ii) opening of an account with a Lithuanian bank and payment of initial capital contributions in return for shares; (iii) convening of a statutory meeting to approve the incorporation report and appoint members of the corporate organs; (iv) approval of the company's offering prospectus by the Lithuanian Securities Commission, except in the cases indicated in the Securities Market Act (transposing Directive 2003/71/EC of 4 November 2003); (v) attestation by a notary that the documents of incorporation conform to Lithuanian law; and (vi) registration of the company with the Register and the tax authorities (if necessary).

D   Conversion into an SE

A public limited company registered and having its head office in Lithuania may be converted into an SE, provided it has held a subsidiary for at least two years in another Member State. This is the simplest way for a public limited company to form an SE.

According to the SE Act, the board of a public limited-liability company must draw up draft terms of conversion including at least such basic corporate information as the company's name, legal personality, the address of its head office and registered office, its authorised capital, legal status and liability, VAT number and liability, the name of the proposed SE, the procedure for allocating shares in the public limited company, and any special rights conferred on the auditor evaluating the SE's authorised capital. The draft terms should be submitted to the Register by their publication date.

The draft terms of conversion must be approved by a qualified majority of two-thirds of the votes cast and shares represented at a general meeting. The Regulation also gives the Member States the option to condition conversion on a favourable vote of a qualified majority or unanimity in the organ within which employee participation is organised. This option has not been enacted in Lithuania, however.

7 Acts committed on behalf of an SE in formation

The SE Act does not specifically regulate the issue of acts committed on behalf of an SE in formation. According to Article 7 of the Companies Act, the persons authorised to sign for a company in formation should be listed in its incorporation documents. Moreover, the company's management organ can approve *post factum* contracts entered into in the company's name by other (non-authorised) individuals prior to incorporation.

8 Registration and publication; acquisition of legal personality

No registration formalities are discussed in the Regulation, as this issue is reserved to national law. According to the Article 11 of the Register's regulations, an SE must be registered prior to commencing any activities. The registration date is the date of formation of an SE. Registration is certified by a certificate.

The documents that must be submitted to the Register include: (i) an application form; (ii) draft terms of merger or formation or articles of association; (iii) a licence (for engaging in certain types of business), if one must be acquired prior to formation of an SE or transfer of an SE's registered office; (iv) a valuation report; (v) a formation report or a report by the management board on the transfer of the company's registered office; (vi) an audit report on the draft terms of merger or formation; (vii) a certificate issued by the competent authority of an EU or EEA Member State attesting to the completion of the requisite pre-merger or pre-transfer acts and formalities; and (viii) a receipt certifying that stamp duty has been paid. In addition to the foregoing, the Register keeps other basic information about registered businesses on file (e.g. the identity of board/management members, information on their annual accounts, etc.). Any changes to the information on file must be submitted to the Register.

A newly formed SE acquires legal personality on its date of recordation with the Register. According to Article 3 of the SE Act, a company promoting the formation of a holding SE acquires legal status as such on the date the Register announces the drawing up of the draft terms of formation.

In general, information filed by national limited-liability companies with the Register is publicly available only through the Register's website and is not published in an official national gazette. However, pursuant to Article 6 of the SE Act, the registrar is obliged to ensure publication of the documents and particulars of an SE (including any branches and affiliates) and forward the relevant information to the Office for Official Publications of the European Communities. The registrar is also responsible for providing information pursuant to Article 64(4) of the Regulation.

III Organisation and management

1 General remarks

The management structure of an SE is not discussed in detail in SE Act. National company law is flexible enough to accommodate an SE with either a one-tier or a two-tier management structure. Article 19 of the Companies Act requires that a public limited-liability company must have at least a general meeting of shareholders and a managing director (CEO). Other corporate bodies – a supervisory board (the supervisory council) and a management organ (or board of directors) – are optional. Accordingly, provisions of the Companies Act on the board of directors shall apply to the management organ (in a two-tier SE) and the administrative organ (in a one-tier SE), and provisions on the supervisory council shall apply to the supervisory board of a two-tier SE.

2 General meeting

The SE Act does not include any specific requirements regarding the general meeting of an SE. Thus, provisions of national company law on the management of domestic public limited-liability companies shall apply.

The general meeting wields supreme decision-making power in a public limited-liability company. An annual shareholders' meeting must be held within four months from the close of the company's financial year to approve the annual accounts, decide on the distribution of profits and release board members from liability. An extraordinary general meeting can be convened whenever the board (in the two-tier system) or the CEO (in the one-tier system) sees fit or at the written request of shareholders representing at least 10% of the company's share capital.

The powers of the general meeting are described in detail in the Companies Act and are rather narrow in scope, the most significant being the power to appoint and remove members of the management or administrative and supervisory organs, to amend the company's articles, to decide to wind up the company, etc. National company law acknowledges the separation of supervisory and managerial functions. Accordingly, the general meeting is not allowed to interfere in the activities of other corporate bodies or to adopt decisions falling within their competence.

A   Decision-making process

The general meeting can validly take decisions if shareholders holding at least 50% of the votes represented by the shares are present or represented, unless the articles require a greater quorum. If this quorum is not met, the general meeting cannot take decisions, and another meeting must be convened (to which no quorum applies), although this meeting shall be authorised to take decisions only on issues that appeared on the agenda of the first meeting.

In general, in order for a resolution to be valid and enforceable, more shareholders must have voted for it than against it (and abstentions do not count). As an exception to this rule, the Companies Act lists a number of issues for which a qualified majority is required, including an increase in the share capital, the distribution of profits and amendment to the articles (all of which require the approval of at least two-thirds of the votes cast and shares represented at a general meeting). A decision to issue new shares, warrants or convertible bonds in derogation from the pre-emptive right of existing shareholders must be approved by three-quarters of the votes cast and shares represented at a general meeting. The articles may provide for a greater majority, however.

B   Rights and obligations of shareholders

Shareholders exercise their principal rights through the general meeting. These rights include the right to attend meetings, to make proposals and to vote and request that the board or CEO provide information on matters being handled at the meeting. In addition, all shareholders have a right to share in profits (in the form of dividends), a pre-emptive right to acquire shares issued by the company, and a right to receive a share of the liquidation proceeds, if any. Shareholders can also challenge in court decisions taken by the general meeting or invoke the liability of board members or the CEO for damage caused to the company.

Pursuant to Lithuanian law, established case law and the literature, there is no explicit definition of the term 'minority shareholder'. Lithuanian law assesses whether a specific right or cause of action should be granted to a shareholder and whether a person or entity qualifies as a minority shareholder on a case-by-case basis. In general, rules for the protection of minority shareholders are defined narrowly in Lithuanian company law and in terms of the percentage of issued share capital held. For instance, the holders of 10% of a company's share capital are usually given certain rights, such as the right to request the inclusion of items on the agenda of a general meeting, the right to convene an extraordinary general meeting, and the right to initiate a judicial inquiry into the company's affairs.

There are no provisions of Lithuanian law permitting the direct appointment of minority shareholders, other persons or national authorities to the management organs of a company, with the exception of certain companies in which the state holds shares.

In general, the shareholders of a public limited-liability company enjoy limited liability, i.e. they have no other proprietary obligations to the company, except their duty to pay for subscribed shares, and cannot be held liable for the company's obligations. Certain exceptions may be found in the Civil Code, which provides that certain shareholders shall be held jointly liable for obligations incurred by the company if the latter is unable to perform its duties due to unfair actions on the part of said shareholders.

3 Management and supervision

A Two-tier system/one-tier system

Lithuanian law provides for both a one-tier and a two-tier management structure, and the founders of an SE can opt for the model they prefer. A one-tier SE must have at least two corporate organs – a general meeting of shareholders and an administrative organ. In the two-tier system, the SE must have a management organ (or board) and a supervisory organ (referred to as the 'supervisory council' under national law). Article 4 of the SE Act provides that the management or administrative organ of an SE must have at least three members, while the supervisory organ must have at least three and no more than 15 members.

The concept of the administrative organ, as described in the Regulation, required certain changes to the current Companies Act, pursuant to which the day-to-day management of a national public limited company is entrusted to a single person, namely the managing director (or CEO). Under the SE Act, on the other hand, daily management of an SE is entrusted to a member of the management or administrative organ (both of which must have at least three members). In the two-tier system, the management or supervisory organ must appoint a managing director from amongst the members of the management organ, whereas in the one-tier system, a member the administrative organ must be appointed to fill this position.

In general, at least two-thirds of the management organ members and more than half the members of the supervisory organ must be present in order to take valid decisions in these corporate bodies. A decision must be approved by a majority of the members present. The chair (elected by the members from amongst themselves) casts the deciding vote in the event of a tie. Neither the

SE Act nor the Companies Act establishes a quorum or voting requirements for the administrative organ. Presumably, the administrative organ can validly take decisions if at least half the members are present or represented; decisions must be approved by a majority of votes validly cast.

Powers specifically reserved to specific corporate organs in an SE's articles cannot be delegated to other corporate organs. The frequency of organ meetings is not stipulated under national law.

B Appointment and removal

Pursuant to the Companies Act, members of the administrative organ in the one-tier system are appointed and removed by the general meeting. In the two-tier system, members of the supervisory organ are appointed (and removed) by the general meeting, while members of the management board are appointed (and removed) by the supervisory organ (or council). The number of members of the administrative, management and supervisory organs should be stipulated in an SE's articles and may not be less than three. (The supervisory organ may have no more than 15 members.) No special nationality or residence requirements apply to organ members under Lithuanian law.

Legal entities may be members of the supervisory organ. However, pursuant to Article 31 of the Companies Act, the CEO and members of the management organ of an SE, its subsidiaries and parent company may not also sit the company's supervisory organ.

Only natural persons can sit on the management organ (or board). Article 33 of the Companies Act expressly provides that members of the supervisory organ cannot serve on the management board. Neither the SE Act nor the Companies Act allows the supervisory organ to nominate one of its members to temporarily fill a vacancy on the management organ.

Members of the management and supervisory organs may resign prior to expiry of their term of office by giving at least 14 days' advance notice in writing. There are no special provisions under Lithuanian law regarding the involvement of employee representatives in the removal process.

C Representation

In general, a single manager, the managing director (or CEO), wields the ultimate power to represent a public limited-liability company vis-à-vis third parties under Lithuanian company law (Art. 37 Companies Act). In addition, the company's articles may set forth rules for joint representation pursuant to which other organ members can represent the company with the managing director or CEO (Art. 37 Companies Act).

The managing director has discretion to decide whether to enter into transactions. Article 37 of the Companies Act sets forth certain categories of transactions that require the express consent of the board, including the transfer, lease or mortgage of fixed assets and the securing or guaranteeing of obligations of other entities accounting for more than one-twentieth of the company's share capital in both cases.

Pursuant to Article 4 of the SE Act, daily management of an SE is entrusted to a member of its management or administrative organ. Thus, depending on the management system selected, the management or supervisory organ (in a two-tier SE) shall appoint a member of the management organ, or the administrative organ (in a one-tier SE) shall appoint one of its members, in the manner set forth in the company's articles, to serve as managing director. The managing director is bound to perform managerial tasks in the same manner and under the same conditions as applicable to Lithuanian public limited-liability companies.

D Liability

According to general principles of the Civil Code, members of a corporate organ are obliged to act in good faith and in a reasonable manner with respect to the company and other organ members (Art. 2.87). In addition, members of the management and supervisory organs are bound by duties of loyalty and confidentiality and must avoid situations in which their interests are liable to conflict with those of the company. Organ members must always avoid such conflicts of interest and are subject to relevant disclosure requirements.

In general, members of the administrative, management and supervisory organs shall be held liable for failure to perform their duties or for improper performance of statutory or corporate obligations. Pursuant to the Civil Code, corporate organ members must make good all damage caused the company, unless otherwise provided by law, the documents of incorporation or a specific agreement (Art. 2.87). Civil liability may not be limited or restricted by virtue of an agreement in cases of gross negligence or intentional torts.

IV Employee involvement

Employment and labour issues in Lithuania are governed by the Labour Code (*Darbo kodeksas*), amended as of 2 June 2002 (effective 1 January 2003). In general, all employers must abide by the provisions of the Labour Code, irrespective of their legal status and line of business. These provisions can to a certain extent be superseded by collective bargaining agreements.

All Lithuanian and foreign nationals employed by domestic companies must enter into an employment contract. This requirement does not apply to members of the management and supervisory organs of public limited-liability companies, unless they perform duties prior to taking office. However, by law, the managing director (or CEO) of a company and the chairman of the board (or supervisory council or an authorised representative of the general meeting) must sign an employment contract with the company. Remuneration shall be determined by the board (or if there is none by the supervisory council or, in the absence thereof, by the general meeting of shareholders).

An employment contract must be in writing and shall be deemed concluded at the time the employer and employee agree on the duties to be performed and the remuneration. If a written contract has not been signed, the employee has the right to request one. However, if at least one party has started to perform the agreed duties, an oral agreement shall have the same force as a written contract. An employment contract may be of either definite or indefinite duration or until further notice. The parties may also agree on a trial period of up to three months.

Employees are generally paid an hourly wage or a monthly salary. The monthly salary cannot be less than the national minimum wage for regular working hours. The maximum working time is eight hours per day, 40 hours per week.

An employment contract of indefinite duration may be terminated by either party by providing notice. In general, however, an employment contract can be terminated by several means, including mutual consent of the parties or at the initiative of one party. If the employer terminates or rescinds the employment contract on insufficient grounds, the employee is generally entitled to compensation corresponding to two to six months' salary.

Codetermination within companies is established by the Trade Union Act (21 November 1991), the European Works Councils Act (19 February 2004), and the Works Councils Act (26 October 2004). These acts establish information and consultation rights only and do not cover the right of employees to nominate representatives to corporate organs or otherwise significantly affect corporate decision-making.

Employee participation in an SE is addressed by the SE Employee Involvement Act (12 May 2005), which transposed the Directive into national law. The provisions of the EIA cover both information and consultation rights and the right to participate in the decision-making process of an SE's management organs.

Within 30 days of submission of a formation plan (by merger, conversion or the formation of a holding or subsidiary SE) to the Register, the administrative or management organ should start negotiations with employee representatives. As a first step, information should be provided about the participating companies and the number of employees they employ. The EIA contains detailed provisions on the special negotiating body ('SNB'), which represents all employees of the participating companies in their negotiations with management. As a general rule, most significant decisions (e.g. to reduce or abolish participation rights, not to negotiate, etc.) must be approved by two-thirds of SNB members. Standard decisions can be passed by a simple majority. The SNB may decide either (i) to enter into an agreement with the competent organs of the participating companies or not to start negotiations or (ii) to terminate negotiations already under way or (iii) to accept the standard rules. An agreement between the parties should focus on the establishment of a works council. Should the parties agree on employee participation, the agreement must deal with the allocation of seats to employee representatives on the supervisory and administration organs. Alternatively, the SNB and management may agree to apply the EIA's standard rules, meaning that a representative body must be set up to handle questions concerning the SE itself and any of its subsidiaries or establishments.

An SE cannot be registered unless the participating companies can prove that the SNB (formed by the employees) has taken one of the aforementioned decisions.

V Annual accounts and consolidated accounts

1 Accounting principles

The main guidelines for accounting and financial reporting are set forth in the Accounting Act (6 November 2001) and the Financial Reporting Act. All entities engaged in economic activities in Lithuania must keep accounts. Legal entities must organise their accounts so as to ensure the provision of appropriate, exhaustive, objective and comparable information concerning their financial position, economic performance and cash flow. Accounts should be kept in a double-entry system.

Accounts should be denominated in the national currency of Lithuania (the lita) and drawn up in Lithuanian. A second language may be used in the accounts, although the foregoing requirement must be observed.

Starting 1 January 2005, companies that list and publicly trade securities on regulated markets must comply with International Accounting Standards (IAS).

All companies must prepare an annual report following the close of each fiscal year. In general, a fiscal year coincides with the calendar year, unless the company's articles provide otherwise. The annual report consists of a statement of accounts and a management report as well as a balance sheet, income statement, statement of cash flow, statement of changes in equity, and explanatory notes. The management report should provide an overview of the company's activities, circumstances material to assess its financial position and business activities, significant events that occurred during the preceding fiscal year, and projected developments for the coming year.

The procedures governing the drafting, adoption and publication of consolidated annual accounts are set forth in the act of 6 November 2001. A company having one or more subsidiaries registered in Lithuania or other countries is obliged to prepare consolidated accounts, including a consolidated (i) balance sheet, (ii) income statement, (iii) statement of cash flow, and (iv) statement of changes in equity as well as explanatory notes.

Annual reports (including annual accounts and consolidated accounts and the management report) must be approved by the annual general meeting, which must be held within four months following the close of the company's fiscal year. Following approval of the annual accounts, they must be submitted to the Register and made public to all interested parties.

2 Auditors

All public limited-liability companies must hire an auditor. At the end of each fiscal year and prior to the annual general meeting, the auditor must audit the company's annual (and consolidated) accounts. The performance of audits and related activities of the auditing profession are governed by the Audit Act (8 April 2004).

Annual accounts are prepared by the company itself. The auditors are responsible for preparing a report on the company's annual accounts. The purpose of the audit is to verify that the annual accounts give, in all material respects, a true and fair view of the company's financial position, business results and cash flow. An audit of annual accounts should cover all areas of a company's operations, including accounting, to check whether they comply with basic regulatory requirements. In addition, the auditors should verify that the information in the management report corresponds to the annual accounts. An audit of annual accounts may be performed according to either national or international standards.

Auditors are appointed and their remuneration is approved by the general meeting. Only auditors with the requisite qualifications whose names appear on a list maintained by the Chamber of Auditors are authorised to perform audits. An audit firm may start auditing activities only after inclusion on the aforementioned list.

VI Supervision by the national authorities

According to the Civil Code, public and municipal institutions may not use administrative methods to regulate the activities of legal entities, unless otherwise specifically provided by law (Art. 2.80). Specific supervision of public limited-liability companies is performed by the Lithuanian Securities Commission. Financial institutions are subject to oversight by sector-specific supervisory institutions.

Article 2 of the SE Act provides that the Ministry of Justice can oppose the transfer of an SE's registered office to another country if the transfer would be contrary to the public interest. Furthermore, the Securities Commission and the National Bank may also oppose such a transfer if the SE is subject to supervision by either of these institutions. The Ministry of Justice may also oppose participation by a public limited-liability company in the formation of an SE by merger (Art. 2(1) Reg.).

VII Dissolution

1 General remarks

As far as SEs are concerned, all dissolution and winding-up procedures in Lithuania are governed by national law, in particular general provisions of the Civil Code and specific provisions of the Companies Act on the dissolution and liquidation of public limited companies.

Lithuanian civil law distinguishes between two types of winding up: reorganisation and liquidation. Liquidation occurs when no entities assume the rights and obligations of the company, except in specific cases prescribed by law where certain obligations must be fulfilled after liquidation (such as when the payment of damages for bodily harm is ensured by way of immediate recovery or an insurance policy). Reorganisation is winding up without entering liquidation. A company shall be deemed wound up on the date its entry is deleted from the Register.

2 Reorganisation

The reorganisation of a company may take the form of a merger or a division. A merger may occur by acquisition or by formation. A merger by acquisition is where one or more companies merge with another company, which assumes all assets and liabilities of the acquired companies. A merger by formation occurs where two or more companies form a new company, which assumes all assets and liabilities of the merging companies. A division may take the form of either a spin-off or a split-up. A spin-off is the transfer of a company's assets and liabilities to other operating entities. A split-up is defined as the formation of two or more new legal entities to assume the assets and liabilities of the split-up company in an agreed proportion.

Lithuanian company law establishes certain pre-requisites for reorganisations: (i) a company may be reorganised or take part in a reorganisation only after its share capital has been fully paid up at the price of the last issue of shares; and (ii) reorganisation is incompatible with liquidation and is prohibited if liquidation is started in any way other than by a shareholder resolution (see below for the permissible grounds for liquidation) or if at least one shareholder has received property of the company in liquidation.

The relevant provisions of the Civil Code and the Companies Act indicate the following stages in the reorganisation of a public limited-liability company (and hence of an SE): (i) the management or administrative organ of the SE that is being reorganised or taking part in the reorganisation prepares terms of reorganisation and a report on the goals and purpose of the reorganisation; (ii) the terms are examined by an audit firm; (iii) the terms are published three times in at least three-month intervals or, alternatively, a public announcement is made and written notice is sent to all creditors; (iv) a resolution on the reorganisation is passed by the shareholders of each participating company; assets and liabilities are assumed; (v) the reorganisation is deemed complete when a new company formed as a result is recorded with the Register or when the amended articles of a company continuing to exist following reorganisation are so recorded.

Creditors of companies participating in a reorganisation are entitled to request termination of an agreement or the performance of obligations prior to maturity as well as damages where so provided in the contract or if there are indications that performance of contractual duties is liable to become more difficult due to the reorganisation, and the company has failed to grant security following the creditor's request. Moreover, a reorganisation may not be carried out if additional security is not granted or before the entry into force of a judicial decision on the provision of such security. The company may lawfully refrain from providing additional security if the creditor's claim is adequately secured by a pledge, mortgage, surety or guarantee.

3 Liquidation

The Civil Code contains a limited list of grounds for liquidation of a public limited-liability company. The following grounds are applicable to the liquidation of an SE: (i) a shareholder resolution to wind up the company has been passed by the majority set out in the company's articles, which may not be less than two-thirds of the votes present or represented at a general meeting; (ii) the competent court or the creditors' meeting has resolved to declare the company bankrupt and liquidate it; (iii) a court of competent jurisdiction has rendered a judgment to liquidate the company following a special inquiry into its activities; (iv) a court of competent jurisdiction has ordered the company to liquidate pursuant to an application submitted by the Register due to lack of activity; (v) the time limit (established in the articles) for a company's activities has expired; or (vi) a court has declared formation of the company unlawful.

The liquidator assumes the functions of the management or administrative board of a public limited-liability company once its identifying data has been recorded with the Register or when a court order to liquidate the company enters into force.

The decision to liquidate must be published three times in at least three-month intervals or a public announcement can be made once and all creditors given written notice.

4 Cessation of payments

The Corporate Bankruptcy Act (20 March 2001) defines insolvency as failure by a company to settle its debts as they fall due within three months of the deadline for payment set by statute or pursuant to an agreement (or within three months following a creditor's request for payment if there is no statutory or contractual deadline) and the company's overdue liabilities exceed the value of its net assets by at least half. A petition in bankruptcy may be filed by either a creditor, a shareholder holding more than 10% of the voting rights, a member of the management or administrative organ (responsible for day-to-day management of the company) or a liquidator (if the company is in liquidation). Extrajudicial bankruptcy proceedings (where the court's role is assumed by the creditors' meeting) are allowed if no legal actions are pending against the company.

On the date the adjudication in bankruptcy enters into force, the following changes occur: (i) all powers of the management organs (i.e. the management (administrative) bodies of the SE) are transferred to a trustee appointed by the court; and (ii) any payments by the company, including interest, penalties and taxes, are prohibited. On the other hand, all the company's debts shall be deemed overdue as of the date of commencement of bankruptcy proceedings.

If the company fails to reach a composition with creditors within three months from the date of entry into force of the court order approving the creditors' claims, the court shall force the company into liquidation.

VIII Applicable law

Pursuant to Article 9 of the Regulation, the following legislation applies to SEs established in Lithuania:

1. Acts adopted to implement SE-specific Community measures, including:
   1.1 the SE Act, to ensure application of the Regulation in Lithuania;
   1.2 the SE Employee Involvement Act, transposing the Directive;
   1.3 relevant provisions of the Register's regulations governing registration of an SE, transfer of its registered office and other procedural issues;
   1.4 relevant provisions of the Insurance Act (18 September 2003).
2. General legislation applicable to public limited-liability companies formed in accordance with Lithuanian law includes:
   2.1 the Civil Code;
   2.2 the Companies Act;
   2.3 the Securities Market Act (16 January 1996) and related Securities Commission decrees;
   2.4 the Corporate Bankruptcy Act.

IX Tax treatment

1 General remarks

In general, an SE is subject to the national tax law of its country of registration. Furthermore, like other companies, an SE is subject to tax in Lithuania if it acts through a branch or other kind of permanent establishment in Lithuania.

When an SE is formed by means of a cross-border merger or transfers its registered office, the formation or transfer shall result in a branch or other type of permanent establishment located in at least one of the countries of registration of the merging companies or in the country where the SE's registered office was located. As far as taxation is concerned, (i) a Lithuanian SE will generally be regarded as any other national public limited-liability company, and (ii) a foreign SE shall be regarded like any other multinational company.

Therefore, in general, Lithuanian tax law shall apply to Lithuanian and foreign SEs in the same way as to Lithuanian and foreign public limited-liability companies.

2 Corporate tax

According to the Corporate Tax Act (20 December 2001), the standard tax rate for companies registered in Lithuania is 15%. The income of a foreign company operating in Lithuania through a permanent establishment is subject to tax at a rate of 15%. Small businesses, in general, benefit from a rate of 13%. An additional 4% tax will be imposed on the profits of all companies registered in Lithuania in 2006; the rate will be reduced to 3% in 2007.

Business activities of a foreign entity in Lithuania shall be qualified as permanent only if such activities last for more than six months and comprise a complete cycle of commercial operations. A permanent establishment shall not be deemed a corporate organ but rather a structure for calculating and paying tax in Lithuania without legal personality. Income of a foreign company operating in Lithuania through a permanent establishment is subject to tax at a rate of 15%.

Dividends received by a Lithuanian company from another Lithuanian and/or a foreign company are taxed at a rate of 15%, unless the beneficiary is registered in a tax haven. However, dividends paid by a company to another company that has held for an uninterrupted period of at least 12 months (at the time of the distribution) more than 10% of the voting rights in the distributing company are not subject to tax and are not included in the tax base of the receiving company.

3 Withholding tax

For foreign companies, the following principal types of income (excluding income received through permanent establishments) originating in Lithuania are subject to withholding tax at a rate of 10%: interest income (with certain exceptions), income from distributed profits, royalties, income received as remuneration for rights or information, know-how granted under a licensing agreement, and income received from the sale, any other transfer of ownership or lease of immovable property in Lithuania.

Dividends are subject to withholding tax at a rate of 15%. However, dividends paid by a Lithuanian company to a foreign company that has held for an uninterrupted period of at least 12 months (at the time of the distribution) more than 10% of the voting rights in the distributing company are not subject to tax, unless the foreign receiving company is registered or otherwise organised in a tax haven.

The rate of withholding tax may be reduced pursuant to a double tax treaty. Lithuania is currently a party to more than 30 such treaties.

4 VAT

The Value Added Tax ('VAT') Act (5 March 2002) has been harmonised with Community law, mainly the Sixth VAT Directive. The standard rate of VAT is 18%. Reduced rates of 5% and 9%, as well as 0%, may be applied in certain cases. A foreign taxable person that exceeds the limit of LTL 125,000 (approximately €36,202) for distance sales must register with the VAT administration in Lithuania if such person sells goods from another Member State to Lithuanian residents who are not taxable persons or VAT payers. Thus, the transfer of a Lithuanian SE's registered office to another Member State could have VAT implications.

5 Property and land tax

Property tax is assessed annually on the value of real estate owned by a company, both in Lithuania and abroad, at a rate of 1% of the value of the real estate for tax purposes. The tax is payable quarterly. Legal entities or natural persons that own land are subject to an annual land tax at a rate of 1.5% of the value of the land.

6 Tax framework for the formation of an SE

In general, Lithuanian tax law allows an SE to be formed by merger, a transfer of assets or an exchange of shares without adverse tax consequences. National tax law does not specifically apply to the transfer of an SE's registered office from Lithuania to another Member State and vice-versa. However, the following basic rules are applicable in respect of purely domestic mergers and transfers of assets.

The Lithuanian corporate tax system is aimed at 'neutralisation' of the tax consequences of business reorganisations so that a reorganisation results in neither advantages nor disadvantages from a tax perspective.

The principle of tax neutrality implies that (i) no tax is levied at the time of the reorganisation and (ii) after the reorganisation, the taxable gain of the receiving company and its shareholders is assessed based on tax elements present in the transferor and its shares prior to the reorganisation.

In general, both type of mergers (by acquisition or through the formation of a new company) qualify for tax-free treatment. Moreover, spin-offs, split-offs, and split-ups can also qualify.

A reorganisation will not be subject to tax in Lithuania if the following basic conditions are met:

(a) the shareholders of the transferring company receive shares in the receiving company in proportion to their share of the transferred company's assets;
(b) for a transfer of assets that forms the basis of an autonomous branch of activity: (i) shareholders of the transferring company are offered shares in the receiving company in proportion to their shareholdings and (ii) the transferring company reduces its share capital and reserves by the value of the transferred assets; shareholders are entitled to receive compensation for up to 10% of the difference in the nominal value of the shares exchanged and those received;

(c) for the transfer of a branch of activity: (i) the transferring company is offered shares in the receiving company and (ii) any difference between the nominal value of the shares exchanged and those received (up to 10%) is paid in cash;

(d) for an exchange of shares: (i) the acquiring company gains 66% of the voting rights in the acquired company and (ii) shareholders of the acquired company are offered shares in the acquirer, with any difference in the nominal value (up to 10%) paid in cash.

8 Consequences of a tax-free merger

In general, capital gains realised in an exchange of shares or a transfer of assets as a result of a merger are not subject to tax. For income earned as a result of a transfer of assets and rights between Lithuanian legal entities, the following rules shall apply: (i) for shareholders of the participating companies, an increase in the value of the transferred assets shall not be regarded as taxable gain; and (ii) for the participating companies, any increase in the value of the transferred assets shall not be regarded as taxable gain.

For gain received as a result of a transfer of assets and rights between Lithuanian legal entities and entities from other Member States (taxpayers, as envisaged by Article 3(c) of Council Directive 90/434/EEC of 23 July 1990 on the common system of taxation applicable to mergers, divisions, transfers of assets and exchanges of shares concerning companies of different Member States), the following rules shall apply: (i) for shareholders of the legal entities participating in the reorganisation, any increase in the value of the assets shall not be regarded as taxable income; (ii) for the participating entities, any increase in the value of the transferred assets shall not be regarded as taxable income; and (iii) the difference in the nominal value of the shares exchanged and those received may be paid in cash, provided this amount does not exceed 10% of the par value of the acquired shares.

9 Transfer of head office and change in corporate form

The transfer of a company's head office should not have significant tax consequences as long as the office remains in Lithuania. A mere change in corporate form is also unlikely to give rise to any tax liability. All assets and liabilities of the business remain within a single legal entity, although a different one, and shareholders maintain their equity interest unchanged. Thus, conversion of an existing local company into an SE will most likely not have any direct tax consequences under Lithuanian law.

10 Establishment of a subsidiary SE

In general, there are no direct tax consequences when an SE establishes a subsidiary SE in Lithuania.

11 Transfer of registered office and cross-border merger

Under Lithuanian tax law, if a Lithuanian SE transfers its registered office to another Member State there should be no direct tax consequences, in theory, provided all of the transferring company's assets and activities situated in Lithuania prior to the transfer remain there, i.e. in the form of a branch or other permanent establishment. However, it is still unclear whether the Lithuanian tax authorities will uphold such a view.

A transfer of assets abroad from a Lithuanian SE could constitute a taxable transfer, although no clear answer has been formulated yet. Transfer of a company's registered office may also affect the taxation of dividends.

X Conclusion

Formation of an SE can give rise to new opportunities:

1. All legal requirements as to corporate governance, shareholder rights, the powers and liability of management organs, auditing and financial reporting standards, etc. are governed by an SE's articles, the Regulation and the law of the Member State where the company's registered office is located. As a result, an SE will have to bear fewer administrative and similar expenses than companies operating a network of subsidiaries in different Member States.
2. An SE is subject to a single management and corporate governance structure and reporting system for operations in different jurisdictions and can therefore avoid the need to set up a financially costly and administratively time-consuming complex network of subsidiaries governed by different national laws and possibly raise economy-of-scale opportunities if it operates in multiple jurisdictions.
3. An SE is subject to a single and uniform employment policy and incentives and reporting mechanism.
4. The SE makes it easier to forum shop around the EU for friendlier company law (e.g. choosing a jurisdiction that provides appropriate safeguards against hostile takeovers or claims by minority shareholders).

As the SE will undoubtedly be viewed by financing institutions as a single legal and business unit, it will be able to attract new sources of financing and fundraising opportunities, particularly given its significant financial resources, share capital and other financial characteristics.

1. In the absence of a choice of law, an SE can only be sued in the Member State where its registered office is located.
2. If both companies participating in the formation of an SE have contractual relationships subject to scrutiny with regard to transfer-pricing rules, such mutual arrangements and any associated risks shall expire after the merger.

3. The registered office of an SE may be transferred from one Member State to another without the need to wind up the company, thus enabling an SE to adjust to changes in the business, legal and tax environment faster and more efficiently.
4. The formation of an SE is currently the only way to carry out a cross-border merger in Lithuania.

On the other hand, the formation of an SE could result in the following disadvantages:

1. Compared to a national company, an SE must ensure a significantly higher level of employee participation in decision-making and management.
2. As far as taxation is concerned, an SE is regarded like any other multi-national company, i.e. it is taxed under the laws of every country where it engages in business; bearing in mind that the tax laws of the Member States are far from harmonised, an SE may need to engage tax specialists in each country where it operates.
3. If during formation of an SE two or more stand-alone companies merge, a problem of separating professional and legal liability shall arise. Financial and business risks pertaining to separate activities in different jurisdictions are no longer separate in that the failure of a unit operating in a Member State other than Lithuania will directly effect the SE as a whole and not only the Lithuanian parent company as in the traditional structure of associated undertakings in multiple jurisdictions. With regard to civil and/or administrative liability arising out of the activities of formerly separate business units in different jurisdictions, the SE, will be liable for any outstanding obligations as the only successor in interest to the former companies.
4. In other Member States, a Lithuanian SE will be regarded as a foreign company and could therefore face certain restrictions in this regard (e.g. on the acquisition or use of land, the acquisition or operation of necessary infrastructures, the use of rights of way, etc.).
5. From a regulatory perspective, obligations imposed on a company participating in the formation of an SE by a national regulatory authority (such as the competition authorities) could bring about uncertainty after formation of the SE, as the manner in which said obligations will be assumed and implemented by the SE may not be clear.

14
Poland

AGNIESZKA SZYDLIK, JACEK BONDAREWSKI, MAGDALENA
MOCZULSKA, MALGORZATA KOZAK, MICHAL BERNAT AND
MORVAN LE BERRE
Wardyński & Partners

I   Introduction   370
II   Reasons to opt for an SE   371
III   Formation   372
     1   General remarks   372
        A   Founding parties   372
        B   Name   372
        C   Registered office   372
        D   Corporate purpose   373
        E   Capital   373
     2   Different means of formation   374
        A   Formation by merger   374
        B   Formation of a holding SE   375
        C   Formation of a subsidiary SE   376
        D   Conversion into an SE   376
     3   Acts committed on behalf of an SE in formation   377
     4   Registration and publication   377
     5   Acquisition of legal personality   377
IV   Organisation and management   378
     1   General remarks   378
     2   General meeting   378
        A   Decision-making process   378
        B   Rights and obligations of shareholders   379
     3   Management and supervision   380
        A   Two-tier system/one-tier system   380
           (i)   General remarks   380
           (ii)   One-tier system   380
           (iii)   Two-tier system   383
        B   Amendment of articles   384
        C   Representation   384
        D   Liability   384
V   Employee involvement   385
     1   Special negotiating body   385
           (i)   Appointment of SNB members   385
           (ii)   Election of SNB members   386
     2   Employee participation   386

     3   Protection of employee representatives   386
VI   Annual accounts and consolidated accounts   387
     1   Accounting principles   387
     2   Auditors   388
VII Supervision by the national authorities   388
VIII Dissolution   389
     1   Winding up   389
     2   Liquidation   389
     3   Insolvency   390
IX   Applicable law   391
X   Tax treatment   391
     1   Income tax   391
     2   Value added tax   395
     3   Other taxes   396
XI   Conclusion   396

I Introduction

1. The original text of the Regulation does not mention the types of companies under Polish law which qualify to form an SE. However, Council Regulation (EC) No. 885/2004 of 26 April 2004[1] subsequently amended the Regulation so that a *spółka akcyjna* (SA) or joint stock company is now mentioned in Annex I. Similarly, the SA and the *spółka z ograniczoną odpowiedzialnością*, (or limited-liability company, *sp. z o.o.*) were added to Annex II of the Regulation.

Appropriate amendments to Polish law designed to accommodate Community rules of company law were introduced by the European Economic Interest Grouping and European Company Act of 4 March 2005 (the 'SE Act'). The president of Poland signed the SE Act into law on 24 March 2005, and it was published in the Polish *Official Journal* on 18 April 2005 and entered into force on 19 May 2005. Since no regulatory powers have been delegated to ministers or to the Council of Ministers, no further implementing decrees regarding the SE Act are expected.

---

[1] Council Regulation (EC) No. 885/2004 of 26 April 2004 adapting Regulation (EC) No. 2003/2003 of the European Parliament and of the Council, Council Regulations (EC) No. 1334/2000, (EC) No. 2157/2001, (EC) No. 152/2002, (EC) No. 1499/2002, (EC) No. 1500/2003 and (EC) No. 1798/2003, Decisions Nos. 1719/1999/EC, 1720/1999/EC, 253/2000/EC, 508/2000/EC, 1031/2000/EC, 163/2001/EC, 2235/2002/EC and 291/2003/EC of the European Parliament and of the Council, and Council Decisions 1999/382/EC, 2000/821/EC, 2003/17/EC and 2003/893/EC in the fields of free movement of goods, company law, agriculture, taxation, education and training, culture and audiovisual policy and external relations, by reason of the accession of the Czech Republic, Estonia, Cyprus, Latvia, Lithuania, Hungary, Malta, Poland, Slovenia and Slovakia (*Official Journal of the European Union*, L 168 of 1 May 2004).

The SE Act implements both the Regulation and the Directive, i.e. it contains not only rules of company law but also a framework for employee involvement. No further collective bargaining agreements are necessary to apply the provisions of the Directive, although general rules on industrial relations may be required, for instance, once an SE has been established.

A number of statutory provisions were also amended to facilitate the operation of SEs in Poland, including legislation on the National Court Register, stock exchange regulations and the European Works Council Act.

Insofar as a matter is not governed directly by the Regulation or the Directive, Polish SEs shall be subject to provisions of national law applicable to joint stock companies, without the need for amendments to these laws.

II   Reasons to opt for an SE

2. Since enlargement of the EU in 2004, many greenfield investors and existing businesses have considered establishing or relocating their activities to another Member State or simply extending their operations across the enlarged EU. The SE is a potentially convenient vehicle for integrating pan-European operations, restructuring corporate groups, and acquiring businesses in or expanding into a new Member State such as Poland.

The SE offers substantial advantages in terms of mobility as it can transfer its registered office to another Member State with relative ease. In this respect, it differs from national corporate forms which are generally not permitted to transfer their registered offices abroad or merge directly with foreign companies, especially when this would result in the transfer of the entity abroad. In this way, the Regulation makes it more convenient for investors to acquire businesses in Poland. Moreover, corporate groups can be restructured using holding SEs in Poland so as to enjoy favorable tax treatment and non-fiscal benefits.

Such non-fiscal advantages include the rule of company law which not only provides that the acquiring company assumes the assets of the acquired company, as required by the Regulation, but also stipulates that the merger implies an *ex lege* transfer of any administrative permits, authorisations and relief to the acquired company, unless provided otherwise by law or an applicable judicial decision. The Regulation stipulates that the companies participating in the formation of an SE by merger shall be governed by national law in certain respects. Hence, the formation of an SE by merger involving Polish acquiring companies active in heavily regulated sectors allows a smooth and cost-effective transition for foreign investors, as they can continue to use existing licences and authorisations which often pose a significant entry barrier in regulated sectors.

The SE Act is generally business friendly and appears to have implemented the Regulation in as liberal and non-restrictive a way possible for business.

In this spirit, the Polish legislature chose to allow the national authorities to oppose the formation of an SE by merger only when the merger involves a financial institution with its registered office in Poland and would lead to the incorporation of an SE with its registered office in another Member State.

In addition, the only third party afforded protection under the SE Act is minority shareholders who, pursuant to the Regulation, have the right to object to a merger. The SE Act, however, does not confer a similar right on employees (outside the scope of the Directive) or creditors.

An SE established in Poland is taxed like a Polish joint stock company. Hence, an SE is subject to corporate tax at a rate of 19%, and profits distributed as dividends by Polish SEs to qualified parent companies located in other Member States are exempt from withholding tax. Moreover, the necessary rules are, in principle, already in place to ensure tax neutrality when an SE is formed by merger, including through an exchange of shares. Certain issues may still arise with respect to the transfer of an SE's registered office from Poland to another Member State, but corresponding tax measures are expected to be enacted by the end of 2005, as required by Community law.

Finally, the establishment of an SE may reduce the administrative costs and burdens usually associated with the operation of a network of subsidiaries.

III Formation

1 General remarks

A Founding parties

3. Pursuant to the amended Regulation, only a joint stock company ('*spółka akcyjna*') shall be considered a public limited-liability company in Poland (Art. 2(1) Reg.). According to the SE Act, it is also possible for a company with its head office outside the Community to participate in the formation of an SE in Poland (Art. 15) provided the conditions listed under Article 2(5) of the Regulation are fulfilled.

B Name

4. The SE Act does not contain any specific rules regarding an SE's name. However, the name of an SE must consist of the company name and the abbreviation 'SE'.

C Registered office

5. The SE Act contains specific provisions designed to protect minority shareholders who oppose transfer of an SE's registered office (Part III, Sec. 3 SE Act; Art. 8(5) Reg.).

According to Article 48 of the SE Act, shareholders who voted against the transfer may demand that the company redeem their shares if no third-party purchaser can be found.

6. Moreover, shareholders who voted against the transfer proposal and whose opposition to the transfer is recorded in the minutes of the meeting may challenge the transfer resolution in accordance with the rules applicable to joint stock companies contained in the Commercial Code of 15 September 2000. According to the procedure set forth in the SE Act, an application for the certificate referred to in Article 8(8) of the Regulation, attesting to the completion of the requisite pre-transfer acts and formalities, cannot be obtained prior to expiry of the deadline for challenging the transfer resolution.

7. The transfer resolution must be published. Creditors whose claims arose before the publication date of the resolution and who submitted their claims at least one month prior to this date and can prove that recovery of their claims would be jeopardised by the transfer may request immediate satisfaction or security.

8. If the SE in question is a financial institution, the competent corporate organ should inform the relevant financial supervisory authority (such as the Insurance and Pension Funds Supervisory Commission or the Banking Supervisory Commission), prior to publication of the transfer proposal, of the company's intent to transfer its registered office to another Member State. The supervisory authority has two months from the date of publication of the transfer proposal to express its opposition to the transfer. Such a decision may be appealed to the competent administrative court.

9. The courts of registry are the authority responsible for issuing the certificate attesting to completion of the requisite pre-transfer acts and formalities. Decisions of the courts of registry can be appealed.

D Corporate purpose

10. The SE Act does not contain any specific rules regarding the corporate purpose of an SE. According to general rules of Polish company law, a company may be formed for any commercial purpose.

E Capital

11. The share capital of an SE must be at least €120,000. The SE Act does not provide any additional indications with respect to an SE's share capital. There are no limitations on the maximum amount of share capital. Shares subscribed by means of contributions in kind must be paid up in full within one year of registration. For shares subscribed in cash, at least one quarter of their face value should be paid up prior to registration.

12. An SE is obliged to create a reserve with at least one-third of its share capital. The company can also create other reserves.

Higher requirements as to share capital apply to certain types of organisations, such as banks and electronic lending institutions.

2 Different means of formation

A Formation by merger

13. Annex I of the Regulation lists only a joint stock company ('*spółka akcyna*' or 'SA') with reference to Poland. Therefore, only this type of company can form an SE by merger in Poland, provided the requirements of Article 2(1) of the Regulation are met.

Under Polish law, the formation of an SE by merger must be approved by a qualified majority of votes cast at the general meeting of the Polish company.

If the registered office of an SE formed by merger will be located abroad, the vote on the merger resolution must be conducted by roll call. In this case, each share carries one vote. Adoption of the resolution should be mentioned in the minutes of the general meeting, drafted by a notary public.

14. Polish law requires publication of the merger proposal in the *Court and Commercial Monitor* ('*Monitor Sądowy i Gospodarczy*'). Publication may be effected at the request of either the acquiring or the newly formed company.

15. Pursuant to Article 24(2) of the Regulation, the SE Act contains detailed procedures designed to protect minority shareholders. In essence, minority shareholders who voted against the merger may request redemption of their shares.

16. Polish company law allows judicial review of a merger resolution. Plaintiffs may seek to have the resolution either set aside or declared invalid, depending on their arguments. In any case, such actions may only be brought within one month from the date of the resolution.

17. A Polish company must petition the competent court of registry, but not within the first month following passage of the merger resolution, for a certificate attesting to completion of the requisite pre-merger acts and formalities, as mentioned in Article 25(2) of the Regulation (the 'merger certificate').

The SE Act requires that the following documents be appended to the application:

- evidence of publication in a national newspaper of the information set forth in Article 21 of the Regulation;
- the merger resolution itself;

- evidence of redemption of the shares of minority shareholders who voted against the merger and have requested that the company redeem their shares;
- a statement from the directors of the Polish participating company regarding any legal proceedings pending against the merger resolution; and
- a resolution by the general meeting of the Polish merging company approving the agreement on employee involvement, insofar as this right has been expressly reserved to the general meeting pursuant to Article 23(2) of the Regulation.

If proceedings are pending against the merger resolution, the court of registry will issue a certificate only if it finds the claim to be unsubstantiated.

However, if the court declares the merger resolution void or repeals it after issuing the merger certificate, shareholders who were harmed by registration of a merger based on a defective resolution may request compensation from the SE, without the need to prove negligence or misconduct on the part of the SE's officers.

The procedure for issuing the merger certificate is governed by Polish rules of civil procedure.

Pursuant to Article 27(2) of the Regulation, a merger certificate from the competent court of registry is required to record an SE in the national (court) register.

18. Under Polish company law, upon completion of a merger, the newly formed company must be recorded in the national court register. Insofar as provided by Polish law, a merger only becomes effective following registration, which also entails deletion of the Polish company from the same register.

Pursuant to Article 12 of the Regulation, an SE must be registered in the Member State in which its registered office is located. According to Article 27 of the Regulation, the merger and subsequent formation of an SE become effective only following registration.

B   Formation of a holding SE

19. Polish joint stock companies and limited-liability companies are entitled to participate in the formation of a holding SE, provided the conditions set forth in Article 2(2) of the Regulation are fulfilled.

In general, the guidelines for the creation of a holding SE are novel as regards the creation of a holding joint stock company, hitherto unknown under national law.

20. For registration purposes, the SE Act requires submission of the following:

- proof that the requirements of Article 2(2) of the Regulation have been fulfilled;
- draft terms of formation for a holding SE and the opinion of an auditor(s), drawn-up in accordance with Article 32 of the Regulation;
- a resolution of the general meeting of each participating company approving the draft terms;
- a statement issued by the competent organ of each participating company that the minimum percentage of shares specified in the draft terms of formation has been contributed within the time limit specified in Article 33(1) of Regulation;
- a statement by the competent organ of each participating company that no proceedings to have the resolution approving the draft terms of formation set aside or declared invalid are pending;
- a resolution of the general meeting of each participating company approving the arrangements on employee involvement, if this right has been reserved to the general meeting in accordance with Article 32(6) of the Regulation.

21. Despite Article 34 of the Regulation, which allows the introduction of measures intended to protect creditors or employees, the SE Act does not envisage any protection in addition to that already afforded under Community or Polish law.

C   Formation of a subsidiary SE

22. Polish law does not contain any particular provisions with respect to the creation of a subsidiary SE. If a founding company contributes an undertaking or an organised part thereof to an SE, the general meeting must approve the contribution by a qualified majority of votes cast. If the registered office of a subsidiary SE shall be located in Poland, Polish rules on the creation of a joint stock company shall apply in accordance with Article 15 of the Regulation.

D   Conversion into an SE

23. In accordance with Article 2(4) of the Regulation, only a joint stock company may be converted into an SE, provided the conditions specified in the Regulation are met. In this regard, the SE Act refers to the applicable provisions of the Commercial Code on changes in corporate form that require the management board to draft a conversion plan and commission a report from an independent auditor. The plan must be published in the *Court and Commercial Monitor*. The

plan, together with the proposed SE's articles, must be approved by the general meeting (see above).

For registration purposes, documents confirming that the requirements set forth in Article 2(3) of the Regulation have been fulfilled must be submitted. If these documents are drafted in a foreign language, an official translation into Polish must be attached.

3 Acts committed on behalf of an SE in formation

24. A joint stock company in formation has no legal personality but may acquire rights and incur liabilities in its own name as well as sue and be sued.

The management board represents the company in formation. Persons acting in the name of a company in formation shall be held jointly and severally liable for any debts incurred during formation unless the company assumes these obligations after registration (Art. 13 Commercial Code; Art. 16(2) Reg.). The personal liability of management board members, except towards third parties, ceases once their pre-registration activities are approved by the general meeting.

The management board must register the company with the competent court of registry within six months following execution of its articles of association or the articles shall be deemed void.

4 Registration and publication

25. Companies must be entered in the commercial register of the national court of registry. The register is computerised and covers certain categories of entrepreneurs and other legal entities operating in Poland. It is maintained by designated departments in the district courts, known as courts of registry. The company's management board must report the formation of the company to the court of registry of the place where its registered office is located. All management board members must sign the petition.

5 Acquisition of legal personality

26. The following steps are required for a joint stock company to gain legal personality: formation of a company (including the signing of its articles by the founders), submission of shareholder contributions to cover initial share capital, establishment of management and supervisory boards, and recordation in the commercial register.

IV Organisation and management

1 General remarks

27. Pursuant to Article 38 of the Regulation, an SE's organs include the general meeting of shareholders and, depending on the type of management structure selected, either supervisory and management boards or an administrative board. The two-tier system of management was already recognised under Polish law, while the one-tier system was introduced for the first time in the SE Act. Therefore, the SE Act contains considerably more provisions regulating the one-tier system.

2 General meeting

A Decision-making process

28. The general meeting has authority to take decisions on matters entrusted to it by (i) the Regulation, (ii) national rules transposing the Directive into Polish law, (iii) provisions of Polish law applicable to public limited-liability companies, and (iv) the company's articles of association.

Shareholder meetings may be either ordinary or extraordinary.

29. An ordinary general meeting should be held within six months following the close of each financial year (Art. 395 Commercial Code). The agenda of the meeting should include the following items:

- review and approval of the management report on the company's activities as well as review of the financial statements for the previous financial year;
- adoption of a resolution on the distribution of profits or coverage of losses;
- acknowledgement of the fulfillment of duties on the part of corporate bodies.

Shareholder resolutions should be mentioned in the minutes, which must be drafted by a notary. The minutes should state that the meeting was validly convened and can pass resolutions and should list the resolutions passed as well as the number of votes cast in favour and against each one. An attendance list signed by the shareholders present or their representatives should be appended to the minutes (Art. 421 Commercial Code).

A general meeting is normally held at the company's registered office. However, the general meeting of a public company may also take place at the stock exchange where its shares are traded. The company's articles may include provisions regarding the location of shareholder meetings (Art. 403 Commercial Code).

30. The general meeting has sole authority to pass resolutions on the following matters:

- the redemption of shares;
- reductions in the company's share capital;
- removal from office or suspension of management and administrative board members, regardless of the body that appointed them;
- approval of actions to be taken by the management board should the supervisory board deny such consent;
- claims for damage caused during formation of the company or of its management and supervisory boards;
- the sale or lease of the company's business or any branch of activity, as well as the establishment of limited property rights;
- the purchase and sale of real property, life estates or shares in real property, unless the articles provide otherwise;
- issuance by the company of convertible bonds with a right of preference and subscription options;
- continuation of the company if the balance sheet prepared by the management board indicates losses exceeding the sum of capital reserves and one-third of the company's share capital;
- amendments to the company's articles, increases in share capital and denial to shareholders of the right to subscribe shares in whole or in part;
- dissolution of the company or transfer of its registered office abroad;
- merger, division or conversion of the company.

B Rights and obligations of shareholders

31. The SE Act does not refer to the rights and obligations of shareholders, as these are set forth in the Commercial Code and generally comply with the Regulation.

Only one entered in the shareholders' register kept by the management board or a holder of bearer shares has the status of shareholder. In accordance with general principles of law, similarly situated shareholders must be treated equally (the principle of equal treatment).

Shareholders may participate in the general meeting and vote either in person or by proxy. A power-of-attorney must be in writing in order to be valid. Management board members and employees may not represent shareholders at a general meeting (Art. 412 Commercial Code).

Shareholders may not, either in person or by proxy or as proxy for a third party, vote on resolutions concerning the following: (i) their liability towards the company on any grounds whatsoever; (ii) acknowledgement of fulfillment of duties or release from liability; and (iii) disputes between themselves and the company (Art. 413 Commercial Code).

The company's articles may grant certain rights to individual shareholders, in particular, the right to appoint or remove management or supervisory board members (Art. 354 Commercial Code). Such rights are inalienable and are extinguished when the shareholder in question exits the company.

Shareholders holding at least one-tenth of the company's share capital may request that the company call a general meeting or place certain items on the agenda of the next general meeting. The company's articles may grant similar rights to shareholders holding less than one-tenth of the share capital, however (Art. 400 Commercial Code).

Shareholders may review the minutes of meetings and request extracts of resolutions authenticated by the management board.

3 Management and supervision

A Two-tier system/one-tier system

(i) General remarks

32. The founders of an SE may select either a one-tier or a two-tier system of management. A mention to this effect must be made in the company's articles. In the two-tier system traditionally recognised under Polish law, management is entrusted to a management board (*zarząd*), which is overseen by a supervisory board ('*rada nadzorcza*'). In the one-tier system, management is entrusted to an administrative board ('*rada administrująca*').

33. Pursuant to Article 18 of the Commercial Code, members of the management and supervisory boards and the audit committee as well as liquidators must be natural persons with full capacity to undertake legal action. Moreover, no person who has been convicted by a valid judgment for certain offences specified in the Criminal Code or listed in the Commercial Code can sit on a company's management or supervisory board or serve as liquidator. According to the SE Act, the provisions of Article 18 of the Commercial Code shall also apply to the administrative board in the one-tier system.

The Commercial Code does not allow legal entities to serve as organ members of an SE with its registered office in Poland.

The SE Act does not list categories of transactions that must be indicated in the articles of an SE registered in Poland.

(ii) One-tier system

34. The one-tier system of management was hitherto unknown under Polish law. The introduction of a one-tier system in Poland may thus prove to be an exceptionally difficult task.

In the one-tier system, the company is managed by an administrative board.

The SE Act stipulates that unless the law provides otherwise, appropriate provisions of the Commercial Code, together with regulations pertaining to management and supervisory boards and their members, shall apply *mutatis mutandis* to the administrative board of an SE and its members. In case of doubt as to whether management or supervisory board regulations should apply, management board regulations are to be preferred.

Notwithstanding the above, the SE Act contains additional rules governing the administrative board and managing directors, as described below.

The administrative board must have at least three members (five in publicly traded companies). Administrative board members are removed by the general meeting, unless the articles provide otherwise.

35. The administrative board has sole authority to pass resolutions concerning:

- the appointment and removal of managing directors;
- the establishment of the remuneration of managing directors;
- the determination of annual and long-term business plans;
- the payment to shareholders of interim dividends against an envisaged dividend at the end of a financial year;
- approval of management reports on an SE's activities and the financial report for a given financial year prior to presentation to the annual general meeting for review and approval;
- designation of the issue price of new shares when so authorised by a shareholder resolution on a capital increase;
- actions surrounding contracts with sub-issuers, subject to shareholder prerogatives;
- actions concerning the allocation of additional shares to the shareholders who subscribed such shares if the remaining shareholders do not claim their shares;
- actions pertaining to a target increase in capital;
- conclusion by a subsidiary SE of credit agreements, loans, guarantees and other similar contracts with a member of the management or administrative board, a managing director, a signing clerk or liquidator of the parent company;
- other matters reserved by the company's articles to the administrative board.

The administrative board can also:

- adopt resolutions concerning capital reductions or redemption of the company's shares where, on the basis of separate regulations, the general meeting is not authorised to do so;
- adopt resolutions to call a general meeting and grant or withdraw proxies, unless the articles provide otherwise.

The administrative board performs its duties as a body, unless the articles provide otherwise.

36. In performing its duties, the administrative board may examine all corporate documents, request reports or explanations from the managing directors and employees, and audit the company's accounts. Each administrative board member may also request the presentation of documents, reports or explanations to the administrative board at its next meeting.

Without prejudice to the exclusive powers listed above and the company's articles, the administrative board may delegate certain duties to committees comprised of at least two of its members. An administrative board member who is also a managing director may not serve on a committee that supervises the company's activities.

Administrative board committees must be specified in the company's articles. This does not apply to committees that include managing directors who are not members of the administrative board. The prerogatives of these committees include solely the preparation and performance of administrative board resolutions.

The organisation and conduct of the administrative board's tasks are governed by its internal rules, which are adopted by the general meeting. The articles may stipulate other means of adoption, however.

37. The administrative board may entrust management of the SE's affairs to one or more managing directors. The number of managing directors and their powers must be set forth in an administrative board resolution, unless the articles provide otherwise. The administrative board may alter or withdraw this delegation of authority at any time.

A managing director may be either a member of the administrative board or an outsider. Nonetheless, at least half the administrative board members should not serve as managing directors. The articles may set stricter requirements in this respect.

The administrative board shall adopt regulations governing the managing directors. If there are two or more managing directors, the regulations may grant one of them (the general manager) specified managerial authority and a deciding vote in the event of a tie. The general manager cannot also serve as chair of the administrative board, unless the articles provide otherwise. This restriction also applies if the SE has only one managing director.

The administrative board (but not the general meeting) can issue mandatory instructions to managing directors concerning the running of an SE's affairs. Managing directors must submit to the administrative board a report on their duties within three months of the close of each financial year.

The remuneration of managing directors is determined by the administrative board in a resolution adopted with the participation of only members who are not also managing directors.

The general meeting may authorise administrative board members who are not managing directors to allow the latter to share in an SE's annual profit earmarked for distribution to shareholders.

An administrative board member who is not a managing director can represent the company in an agreement between the SE and its managing directors as well as in disputes amongst them. In the event of a conflict of interests between the SE and a managing director or the spouse, relative or other close personal relation of a director, the director in question should abstain from participating in decisions on the matter and may request that such abstention be recorded in the minutes.

Managing directors may not, without the SE's consent, and administrative board members may not, without the consent of the general meeting, engage in business that competes with the company's, participate in competitive partnerships or serve as members of the management or supervisory bodies of such partnerships or as managing directors of a company or members of its management or supervisory boards. This also holds true for participation in companies if a managing director or administrative board member holds at least 10% of the shares of that company or the right to appoint at least one member to its management or administrative board.

Unless the articles provide otherwise, consent for the managing directors to assume any of the above positions is granted by an administrative board resolution passed solely by those board members who are not also managing directors.

(iii) **Two-tier system**
38. The section of the SE Act regulating the two-tier system is quite limited. Since the two-tier management structure is extensively regulated by the Commercial Code, the SE Act accommodates only those issues for which the Regulation allows the Member States to adopt separate solutions. The Commercial Code generally complies with the Regulation.

Members of the management board of an SE registered in Poland can be appointed by the general meeting (Art. 24 SE Act; Art. 368(4) Commercial Code). The powers of the general meeting must be expressly stated in the SE's articles.

The supervisory board of an SE registered in Poland must have at least three members (five if the company is publicly traded).

According to the SE Act, a supervisory board member may fill a vacancy on the management board, but for no more than three months (Art. 25 SE Act; Art. 40 Reg.).

B Amendment of articles

39. Amendments to a company's articles require a shareholder resolution and a corresponding entry in the national register. A resolution to amend the articles must be approved, in principle, by three-quarters of the votes cast. However, in certain cases the Commercial Code requires a higher majority, such as resolutions that increase the obligations of shareholders or curb rights granted to specific shareholders, which must be approved by all shareholders so affected.

Resolutions on substantial changes to a company's activities must be approved by two-thirds of the votes cast. In this case, each share carries one vote, and voting by secret ballot is not allowed. The results of the vote must be announced afterwards. Moreover, the effectiveness of the resolution is contingent on redemption of the shares of dissenting shareholders.

C Representation

40. In the one-tier system, representation of a Polish SE that does not have managing directors is regulated by the provisions of the Commercial Code applicable to management board members, as described below.

Managing directors who are not also administrative board members can represent an SE in all legal and extrajudicial matters within the scope of their authority. The articles may impose restrictions in this regard that are effective against third parties. The articles shall also determine the manner of representation. In the absence of any provisions in the articles, two managing directors or one director together with a proxy can issue statements in the name of an SE.

In the two-tier system, management board members have the right to represent the company in all legal and extrajudicial matters. Any limitations on this right are not binding against third parties. If the management board has more than one member, the articles shall determine the manner of representation. If the articles contain no provisions on this matter, two management board members or one member together with a proxy can issue statements in the name of the company.

The above rules do not prevent a company from issuing sole or joint proxies and do not limit the rights of proxies stemming from proxy regulations. All persons entitled to represent an SE must be mentioned in the commercial register along with a brief description of the scope of their representative authority and the manner in which it may be exercised.

D Liability

41. Management and administrative board members are not, in principle, liable for obligations of the company, with the notable exception that board members can be held personally and jointly liable (with the company) for the deliberate or negligent provision of false information regarding the payment for shares in an application to register a company or record a capital increase.

Managing directors, like management, supervisory and administrative board members and liquidators, are liable to the company for damage caused by acts or omissions in violation of law or the company's articles, unless they can prove that they were not at fault.

V Employee involvement

42. The Directive has been transposed into Polish law through Part IV of the SE Act concerning employee participation in an SE.

1 Special negotiating body

43. As far as the creation of a special negotiating body ('SNB') is concerned, Polish law distinguishes between two phases. The first covers the allocation of seats on the SNB while the second includes the election and appointment of SNB members.

Participating companies must determine a start date for the procedure.

Each participating company submits certain information to the employee representatives (or, in the absence thereof, to the employees themselves) in a manner that is accepted within the company. In determining the total number of employees, both full-and part-time workers are taken into account, with the latter converted into full-time equivalents.

In principle, pursuant to the Directive, one seat on the SNB is allocated to each group of employees employed in a given Member State that comprises 10% of the total number of employees in all participating companies, concerned subsidiaries and establishments. The SE Act also contains provisions to cover the situation whereby the number of employees in Poland does not equal or exceed 10% of the total number of employees in all participating companies.

(i) Appointment of SNB members

44. SNB members are generally appointed by representative trade unions or by the employee representative bodies (collectively).

A representative trade union within the meaning of the Labour Code[2] is a trade union that:

(1) is an organisational unit or membership organisation of a sector-wide trade union which is recognised as representative in that at least 7% of a company's employees are members; or
(2) counts at least 10% of a company's employees as members.

---

[2] Polish *Official Journal*, 1998, no. 21, item 94, as amended.

If there is no such organisation, SNB members are elected by the employees directly.

The SE Act specifies that the majority of SNB members should be employees of participating companies or concerned subsidiaries and establishments.

(ii) Election of SNB members

45. If there is no trade union or if the employee representative bodies do not collectively appoint SNB members, elections must be held. The SE Act contains detailed rules regarding the election of SNB members. The elections are organised by the relevant body within each participating company or subsidiary or by management. Elections are direct and voting takes place by secret ballot. Resolutions regarding the election of SNB members are adopted by an absolute majority of votes cast.

Finally, the participating companies must call a meeting of the SNB within fourteen days of its establishment in order to conclude an arrangement on employee involvement.

2 Employee participation

46. The provisions of the SE Act on employee participation reflect those of the Directive. If the SNB resolves not to undertake negotiations or to terminate negotiations already underway before an agreement has been reached, the SE Act provides that national rules on information and consultation of employees shall apply. Polish employees participate in corporate affairs through trade unions. They also have the right to be informed and consulted on issues liable to affect them. The scope of this obligation has yet to be determined under Polish law, although a proposal is currently under discussion.

If an SE is formed by conversion of a public limited-liability company, the level of employee participation in the SE cannot be less than that in the company being converted.

3 Protection of employee representatives

47. SNB members, like other employee representatives, enjoy protection against dismissal for the duration of their term of office and for a period of one year thereafter.

During this time, SNB members may not be dismissed or receive notice of termination. Nor may the employer unilaterally change an employee representative's working conditions or salary to the detriment of the latter without the consent of the employee's trade union or, if the employee is not a union member, the district labour inspector of the place where the employer's registered office is located.

VI Annual accounts and consolidated accounts

1 Accounting principles

48. An SE incorporated under Polish law must meet the standard requirements set forth with respect to joint stock companies in the Accounting Act of 29 September 1994 and its implementing regulations. Additional or alternative accounting rules may apply to specific types of entities, such as banks, pension funds and insurance companies.

An SE is therefore required to maintain accounts in accordance with general rules. It must also draft an annual report, including a balance sheet, profit and loss statement and notes, which must be reviewed by a certified auditor. A management report describing the company's activities over the course of the financial year is also required.

The annual report must be adopted by the general meeting and submitted to the competent registry court. These documents must also be filed with the tax authorities no later than three months following the close of the company's fiscal year.

Polish SEs are subject to general rules governing the opening and closing of their accounts and financial year. An SE will most likely be required to close and open accounts when converted into a Polish joint stock company and vice versa.

The SE Act expressly indicates that accounts must be closed when an SE's registered office is transferred to (or from) Poland.

The issue of where and under which rules the accounts of a Polish SE should be maintained, if there are branches in other Member States, may also be relevant. The law currently provides that Polish companies must keep their books in Poland and comply with substantive and procedural Polish accounting rules, although no specific mention is made of SEs. Therefore, a Polish SE will need to maintain a uniform system of accounts in Poland for both its domestic and cross-border operations.

Specific rules apply, however, to SEs with branches or establishments outside Poland if the latter prepare financial reports in their respective countries. Under the Accounting Act, figures should be retrieved and transferred from the balance sheets and profit and loss statements of the foreign branches (and establishments) and converted into Polish currency, taking into account currency fluctuations.

Provided certain technical and organisational requirements are met, accounts may be maintained in electronic form, which could facilitate the management of foreign branches.

Further to the rules discussed above, a Polish SE with subsidiaries or branches (establishments) in other Member States must prepare a consolidated annual report that includes both its domestic and foreign operations, with accounting data indicated as if all operations formed a single entity.

A foreign SE may also be required to maintain accounts in Poland for activities performed in Poland.

2 Auditors

49. In practice, an SE must appoint a certified auditor to examine its annual report and issue an opinion as to whether the report gives a clear and correct overview of the company's financial situation.

Accounting law requires auditors to be impartial and independent. The Accounting Act specifies that auditors who *inter alia* (i) hold shares in the company being audited, (ii) manage its accounts, (iii) assisted in the preparation of its financial report, or (iv) received 50% or more of their annual revenue during any preceding five-year period from the company are disqualified from auditing its accounts. Any audit performed in violation of the above restrictions shall be deemed invalid.

VII Supervision by the national authorities

50. The SE Act does not specifically indicate or refer to the national authorities competent to supervise the activities of an SE. Therefore, an SE incorporated in Poland shall be subject to control or supervision as provided under Polish law, including stock exchange rules and specific legislation pertaining to financial services, banking, retail trade, electronic communications, the media, labour conditions, the environment, the construction industry, taxes and customs duties, the social security system, public procurement and other regulated areas.

51. Moreover, a Polish SE may be subject to supervision by the national competition authority, the Office for Competition and Consumer Protection (*Urząd Ochrony Konkurencji i Konsumentów*), especially insofar as the company's activities affect the market. An SE will presumably engage in cross-border operations and thus its activities could potentially affect trade between the Member States. Hence, certain aspects of its operations may be supervised by the European Commission and the competition authorities of other Member States.

52. Pursuant to the SE Act, the registry courts are competent to oversee compliance with the Regulation. For the purposes of Articles 8, 55 and 64, the registry court of the place where an SE's registered office is located is competent. For Articles 25 and 26, the court where the registered office of the joint stock company participating in formation of the SE by merger is located shall be competent.

VIII Dissolution

53. Winding up, liquidation, insolvency, cessation of payments and similar procedures for SEs situated in Poland are governed by Polish law.

The Regulation indicates that if the head office of an SE is transferred and is no longer located in the same Member State as its registered office, the Member State in which the SE's registered office is located can order the company to rectify the situation within a specified period of time. If the SE fails to do so, it may be forced into liquidation.

The Polish courts can order an SE, on their own initiative or pursuant to a motion by any interested party, to relocate its head office or registered office within a specified period of time. Should the SE fail to do so, the court can impose a fine. Ultimately, the court can appoint an administrator for a period of three months, which period can be further extended by up to three months.

If the SE does not rectify the situation referred to above, the competent registry court can force the company into liquidation on its own initiative and appoint a liquidator.

1 Winding up

54. Dissolution of an SE may occur for reasons stipulated in its articles or pursuant to a resolution of the general meeting to dissolve the company or transfer its registered office abroad, a declaration of bankruptcy or other conditions under Polish law.

Dissolution follows liquidation. A company is officially dissolved when its entry is deleted from the national register.

2 Liquidation

55. Liquidation commences on the date a judicial decision to dissolve the company becomes enforceable, the general meeting adopts a resolution to dissolve the company, or another lawful condition for liquidation occurs. Liquidation is conducted in the company's name, which henceforth must be followed by the words 'in liquidation'.

The company maintains legal personality during liquidation. While liquidation is under way, no payments from profits can be made to shareholders, nor may company assets be divvied up prior to payment of all debts.

56. Management board members become the company's liquidators, unless the articles or a shareholder resolution provide otherwise, and must file certain information with the commercial register such as the date on which liquidation commences, the names of the liquidators and their mailing addresses, the manner in which the liquidators are entitled to represent the company, and any other relevant information in this regard.

Liquidators must prepare a balance sheet as of the start of liquidation and present it to the general meeting for approval. They must also publish two notices regarding the impending dissolution of the company and the commencement of liquidation during a period of no less than two weeks and not to exceed one month. Creditors shall be asked to submit their claims within six months from the date of the final notice.

The activities of the liquidators should be limited to concluding ongoing affairs, collecting receivables, ensuring the fulfillment of obligations, and realising the company's assets. New business can only be undertaken if necessary to conclude ongoing transactions. Liquidators have the right, within the limits of their authority, to conduct business and represent the company. In internal affairs, liquidators must abide by resolutions of the general meeting. This rule does not apply to court-appointed liquidators.

If the company's capital has not been paid up in full and its assets are insufficient to cover its liabilities, the liquidators shall issue a capital call to shareholders, starting with non-preferred shares, to the extent necessary to cover the company's liabilities.

A bond should be posted with the court to satisfy or secure the claims of known creditors who do not come forward or which are not due or disputed.

The financial statements must be approved by the general meeting the day before any remaining liquidation proceeds are distributed to shareholders. At this point, liquidation is complete. The liquidators then file a liquidation report with the competent registry court along with a motion to delete the company's entry from the commercial register. Books and records of a dissolved company must be consigned to a party indicated in the articles or a shareholder resolution for storage. If no such mention is made, the court shall designate a storage facility.

3 Insolvency

57. In accordance with the Bankruptcy and Recovery Act of 28 February 2003, the management board is required to file a petition in bankruptcy no later than two weeks from the date on which the grounds for bankruptcy arose.

Polish law defines insolvency as a consistent failure to fulfill one's obligations or when the value of a company's liabilities exceeds that of its assets, even if the company can meet current liabilities. If the management board fails to file a timely petition in bankruptcy, it shall be liable for any damage resulting from such delay.

A company is dissolved upon completion of bankruptcy proceedings, and the trustee in bankruptcy files an application to delete the company's entry from the commercial register.

A company shall not be dissolved where bankruptcy proceedings result in a composition with creditors, are abandoned or discontinued for other reasons.

IX Applicable law

58. In principle, SEs registered in Poland are governed by Polish law. However, in certain cases the laws of other Member States may apply. For instance, if no agreement is reached with the SNB, the rules of a given Member State on information and consultation of employees shall apply to the SE.

X Tax treatment

1 Income tax

59. An SE incorporated under Polish law shall be governed by national tax rules, like any other Polish joint stock company, and will be subject to corporate tax at a rate of 19% (in 2005) on its worldwide income, except where the income in question is exempt by virtue of a tax treaty. A Polish SE will furthermore be subject to general rules on the determination of taxable income and corresponding deductible business expenses.

Although Poland has not specifically transposed Council Directive 2003/123/EC, allowing SEs to benefit from the Parent-Subsidiary Directive, an SE based in Poland should not be prevented from relying directly on Community tax law to claim an exemption from dividend withholding tax.

60. SEs registered in Poland should be able to apply for an exemption from withholding tax on dividends distributed to qualifying companies in other Member States, including other SEs, or to their Polish permanent establishments (PE) if they comply with the criteria set forth in the Parent-Subsidiary Directive.

The minimum required shareholding in this respect is currently 20%, but the Polish tax code already provides for a reduction to 15% as of 1 January 2007, and ultimately to 10% as of 1 January 2009.

61. As for interest and royalties, Poland has transition periods during which royalties and interest distributed by Polish companies to qualifying companies in other Member States, while not exempt from withholding tax at source, are taxed at a reduced rate, as authorised by Council Directive 2004/76/EC.[3]

As a result, interest and royalties distributed by a Polish SE to companies in other Member States will by taxed at source at a rate of 10% as of 1 July 2005 until 30 June 2009 (unless a lower rate or an exemption is available under an applicable tax treaty). After 30 June 2009, interest and royalties will be subject to withholding tax at a rate of 5%. As of 1 July 2013, a Polish SE will be able to distribute profits by way of interest payments or royalties to companies in other Member States free of withholding tax.

Once again, Polish law does not directly ensure that an SE based in (an)other Member State will qualify, as a recipient of interest or royalties from a Polish SE or other Polish company, for a reduced rate of or exemption from withholding tax in Poland. Indeed, the Interest and Royalties Directive must still be amended to specifically include the SE in its list of qualifying entities.

However, pending the adoption of amendments to the Interest and Royalties Directive and their transposition into domestic law, SEs from other Member States can still qualify for a reduction of or exemption from withholding tax on interest or royalties, as the case may be, paid by Polish companies (SEs or not) based on the current wording of Polish corporate tax laws which entered into force on 1 July 2005 and require that the recipient of interest or royalties from another Member State be subject to income tax in a Member Sate on its worldwide income.

62. A Polish permanent establishment of a foreign SE will, in principle, also be subject to general corporate tax at a rate of 19%.

No specific rules have been laid down to determine the revenue or income of a PE or regulate its force of attraction. As the tax treaties suggest, a general *arm's length* basis is likely to apply.

Nevertheless, businesses should take into account specific rules introduced as recently as 1 January 2005, which allow Polish PEs of foreign companies, possibly including SEs, to benefit from a tax credit for tax paid abroad by a foreign subsidiary distributing dividends to a Polish PE.

Moreover, as tax laws effective 1 July 2005 seem to indicate, a Polish PE of a foreign SE distributing interest or royalties may claim the benefit of a reduction

---

[3] Council Directive 2004/76/EC of 29 April 2004 amending Directive 2003/49/EC as regards the possibility for certain Member States to apply transition periods for application of a common system of taxation applicable to interest and royalty payments made between associated companies of different Member States.

of or exemption from withholding tax in Poland provided the interest or royalties are deductible in Poland.

63. Under Polish law, an SE incorporated in Poland may carry forward past losses for no more than five fiscal years. Carry back is not allowed, however.

64. Revenue and expenses generated by a Polish SE from foreign activities will, in principle, be aggregated with those from domestic operations, unless an applicable tax treaty exempts foreign-source income from taxation in Poland, as would be the case where the foreign activities are deemed to amount to a permanent establishment in another Member State. In such a case, a Polish SE would not be required to account for either income or expenses taxed abroad and exempted in Poland. This implies in essence that losses of a Polish SE from foreign activities in other Member States may not be deducted in Poland.

65. If a Polish company acquires a company from another Member State by way of a merger *per unionem,* becoming a Polish-based SE, it would not be allowed to utilise any tax losses of the acquired company, as is the case when a Polish company acquires another Polish corporation. Therefore, for the purposes of set off, the optimal scenario would involve a Polish SE with losses acquiring a profitable foreign company. Income from foreign operations, if taxed in Poland, would eventually allow effective utilisation of available tax losses.

Similarly, a Polish-based SE created by way of a merger *per incorporationem* would most likely be prevented from deducting losses of both Polish and foreign parties to the transaction.

66. Intra-group set-off of losses is not usually allowed in Poland, regardless of whether a group includes foreign members. Therefore, when an SE is formed in or transfers its registered office to Poland by way of a merger, as a holding or subsidiary SE or pursuant to Article 8 of the Regulation, it would not be able to claim in Poland any current losses of other group members, whether established in Poland or elsewhere within the EU.

Notwithstanding the above, Polish law allows for the creation by limited-liability and joint stock companies of so-called 'tax capital groups'. Such an option allows consolidation of current taxable profits and losses within a group of companies: losses and profits incurred or generated before a tax capital group was created or after it was discontinued are not available for set-off. It should be mentioned, however, that the strict and numerous conditions for establishing tax capital groups have rendered them unpopular, and only a few are known to exist.

In any event, tax capital groups are open only to companies incorporated in Poland. Therefore, in the case of a Polish SE with subsidiaries in other Member States, no mechanisms to facilitate intra-group set-off of tax losses are available.

This is obviously worrisome as far as compliance with the treaty principles of non-discrimination, freedom of establishment and free movement of capital, as interpreted by the European Court of Justice, are concerned.

67. Polish tax law has not yet been amended to specifically comply with Council Directive 2005/19/EC,[4] which must be transposed by the Member States no later than 1 January 2006. At present, the SE is not mentioned in Polish tax law as a qualifying company for purposes of the Merger Directive.

However, as mentioned above, as soon as the transposition period expires, it may be possible to rely on provisions of the amended Merger Directive, insofar as they can be considered directly applicable in cross-border mergers involving Polish parties.

Under laws in force since 1 January 2004, a Polish SE formed or involved as an acquiring company in a cross-border merger may not be subject to tax on any potential surplus in the value of assets received from an acquired company (or companies) based in another Member State above the nominal value of the shares allocated to shareholders of the latter company. This rule applies regardless of the foreign parties' corporate form as long as their registered office or place of effective management is located in a Member State. Moreover, no tax on the above surplus is due when an SE from another Member State acquires a Polish company.

Polish tax law aims to prevent tax avoidance in mergers and acquisitions by providing that a merger is not tax neutral for the company or shareholders involved when it is not based on valid economic reasons, and its only or major aim is tax abuse or avoidance. These safeguards will likewise apply to SEs in cross-border mergers.

68. The creation of a subsidiary SE in Poland will usually have no adverse tax consequences. Thus, companies making contributions in kind to a newly established SE will not be immediately taxed on any income they may receive in return. Capital gains will only be deemed realised and taxed in Poland when the Polish parent company disposes of its shares in the SE. Capital gains realised by parent companies in other Member States usually remain outside Polish tax jurisdiction pursuant to Article 13 of tax treaties modeled on the OECD model convention.

69. The characterisation for tax purposes of the transfer of the registered office of a Polish SE remains unclear pending the transposition into Polish law of Council Directive 2005/19/EC, which is expected by 1 January 2006. In the

---

[4] Council Directive 2005/19/EC of 17 February 2005 amending Directive 90/434/EEC 1990 on the common system of taxation applicable to mergers, divisions, transfers of assets and exchanges of shares concerning companies of different Member States.

absence of corresponding amendments to national law, the transfer of a Polish SE's registered office abroad may trigger taxation of capital gains if the tax authorities choose to view the transfer as equivalent to liquidation of the Polish company. The Regulation provides that such a transfer does not necessitate liquidation of the SE, but it also specifically excludes its own application in tax matters.

However, even in the above scenario, capital gains of Polish shareholders are usually taxed at a flat rate of 19%, whereas other shareholders are only subject to tax on capital gains, if any, in their country of residence, subject to the application of a tax treaty.

Similarly, no provisions explain the tax exposure, if any, liable to arise upon the transfer of an SE's registered office from another Member State to Poland. It appears, however, that such an operation should not trigger taxation of the SE or its shareholders in Poland. Still, the SE should become a Polish tax resident following the transfer and will thereafter be taxed in Poland on its worldwide income.

On the other hand, when an SE is transferred to Poland from another Member State, the tax treatment in several areas remains unclear (i.e. book depreciation of assets and depreciable intangibles, business losses incurred outside Poland, continuation of past reserves, etc.).

2 Value added tax

70. A Polish SE will generally be recognised as an ordinary VAT taxpayer in Poland and subject to standard VAT rules.

Certain additional information may be useful regarding the VAT status of a Polish SE in Member States where foreign companies acquired through merger carry on activities.

First, in certain business schemes involving supplies to an SE by acquired companies, the supplies will constitute taxable activity in accordance with Polish VAT laws and Community provisions. Although supplies made by independent companies from other Member States have traditionally been subject to tax, the merger and creation of an SE may effect the place of taxation. Supplies following a merger will most likely be taxed in Poland, whereas supplies made by independent entities may be taxed in other Member States, subject to conditions contained in national VAT laws and the Sixth VAT Directive.

Furthermore, the creation of an SE may make it necessary for the company to register itself or its branches for VAT purposes in the Member States where acquired entities carried out taxable activities.

3 Other taxes

71. Under Polish tax law, contributions (in cash or in kind) to the capital of a Polish SE whether upon formation or pursuant to a subsequent capital increase are subject to tax at a rate of 0.5%. The same applies to additional payments made to an SE by its shareholders.

Moreover, a Polish SE that undergoes a merger, division or change in corporate form may also be subject to this tax if the value of the company's assets or share capital is increased. The 0.5% tax would then be imposed on the value of the contributed assets or share capital, as the case may be.

Under Polish tax law, the transfer of an SE's registered office or place of effective management to Poland will only be subject to the capital contributions tax if the creation of the SE in another Member State was exempt from a similar duty, in which case the tax base shall be the amount of the company's share capital.

XI Conclusion

72. While the Regulation and the Directive have been implemented, for the most part, under Polish law, certain issues remain unresolved which will require the scrutiny of practitioners and business leaders when considering whether to form an SE in Poland. Questions raised elsewhere regarding the use and development of an SE are also relevant in Poland.

The novelty of the one-tier management system in Poland may mean that the two-tier model will be the most practical under certain circumstances, in particular with regard to existing undertakings.

Despite the foregoing, there is no doubt that the SE has significant potential in Poland, especially in light of the increased business opportunities across the enlarged internal market and the reduced corporate tax rate.

15
Slovak Republic

KATARÍNA ČECHOVÁ AND MICHAELA JURKOVÁ
Čechová Rakovsky

I   Introduction   398
II   Reasons to opt for an SE   398
III   Formation   399
    1   General remarks   399
        A   Founding parties   399
        B   Name   400
        C   Registered office   400
            (i)   Protection of minority shareholders   401
            (ii)   Protection of creditors   401
            (iii)   Obligatory transfer of an SE's registered office   402
        D   Corporate purpose   402
        E   Capital   402
    2   Different means of formation   403
        A   Formation by merger   403
            (i)   Protection of minority shareholders   404
            (ii)   Protection of creditors   405
        B   Formation of a holding SE   406
        C   Formation of a subsidiary SE   406
        D   Conversion into an SE   407
    3   Acts committed on behalf of an SE in formation   408
    4   Registration and publication   408
    5   Acquisition of legal personality   409
IV   Organisation and management   409
    1   General remarks   409
    2   General meeting   410
        A   Decision-making process   410
        B   Rights and obligations of shareholders   411
    3   Management and supervision   411
        A   Two-tier system   411
        B   One-tier system   412
        C   Appointment and removal   414
        D   Representation   414
        E   Liability   414
V   Employee involvement   415
VI   Annual accounts and consolidated accounts   416

       1 Accounting principles   416
       2 Auditors   417
   VII Supervision by the national authorities   418
   VIII Dissolution   418
       1 Winding up   418
       2 Liquidation   419
       3 Insolvency   420
       4 Cessation of payments   421
   IX Applicable law   422
   X   Tax treatment   422
       1 Income tax   422
       2 Value added tax   422
       3 Other taxes   423
          A Real estate tax   423
          B Excise taxes   423
   XI Conclusion   423

I Introduction

1. The main legislation regulating the establishment and functioning of a European company or *Societas Europaea* ('SE') in the Slovak Republic comprises Council Regulation (EC) No. 2157/2001 on the Statute for a European company (SE) (the 'Regulation'), which is directly applicable in all EU Member States, including Slovakia, and Council Directive 2001/86/EC of 8 October 2001 supplementing the Statute for a European company with regard to the involvement of employees (the 'Directive').

The Directive has been transposed into national law by Act No. 562/2004 Coll. on the European company (the 'SE Act'), which also regulates certain issues left by the Regulation up to national law of the Member States. The SE Act entered into effect on 1 November 2004. On many points, the Regulation refers to general provisions of national law applicable to public limited-liability companies of the Member State in which an SE's registered office is located. The SE Act expressly states that matters regarding the legal status and relations of an SE which are not directly addressed by the Regulation or the SE Act shall be governed by the provisions of Act No. 513/1993 Coll. (the Commercial Code), as amended, applicable to joint stock companies (the equivalent of a public company limited by shares).

II Reasons to opt for an SE

2. The Regulation has been implemented in the Slovak Republic with a view to persuading foreign and domestic companies to create and establish SEs in Slovakia. Therefore, the legislature has not generally adopted the options

contained in the Regulation to impose certain limitations and restrictions on SEs established in Slovakia.

Use of an SE can give a company greater flexibility to respond to market demands and developments due to the fact that an SE can transfer its registered office from one Member State to another without the need to first wind up or create a new legal entity, which would entail additional costs.

The relative ease with which an SE's registered office can be transferred to another Member State may allow further development of the company with regard to investments and acquisitions, as well as the possibility to select the Member State with the best possible conditions for its business, taking tax considerations into account as an SE is subject to tax in the country where its registered office is located.

For Slovak companies, establishment of an SE means the possibility to opt for a different system of management, since an SE, unlike other Slovak companies, may select either a two-tier or a one-tier system of management.

Thanks to more centralised management, internal processes within an SE can be handled with greater efficiency of corporate governance, thus ensuring that the company's business culture allows for better working conditions.

Finally, formation of an SE can also be seen as a strong marketing tool, enhancing a company's European identity and strengthening its global image.

III Formation

1 General remarks

3. Unless otherwise provided in the Regulation, the formation of an SE shall be governed by provisions of national law applicable to public limited companies of the Member State where its registered office is located. Therefore, in the Slovak Republic, the provisions of the Commercial Code regulating the formation of joint stock companies shall apply to the formation of an SE with its registered office in Slovakia.

A Founding parties

4. In general, the Regulation stipulates that only companies whose head office and registered office are located within the European Union may create or participate in the creation of an SE. However, the Slovak legislature has adopted the option expressed in Article 2(5) of the Regulation to allow a company whose head office is located outside the EU to participate in the formation of an SE provided that company is formed under Slovak law, has its registered office in the Slovak Republic and has a real and continuous link with the Slovak economy.

Annexes I and II of the Regulation list those companies that can participate in the formation of an SE in the various Member States. In Slovakia, joint stock companies (*akciová spoločnosť*) can participate in the formation of an SE by merger, and both joint stock companies and private limited-liability companies (*spoločnosť s ručením obmedzeným*) can form a holding SE.

B Name

5. The SE Act does not contain any special provisions regarding the name of an SE registered in Slovakia. Therefore, the name of an SE established in the Slovak Republic need only be preceded or followed by the abbreviation 'SE', as required by the Regulation.

The competent registry court shall verify whether the proposed name of an SE is identical to another name already registered (regardless of the abbreviation indicating the entity's corporate form).

C Registered office

6. The term 'Slovak legal entity' is defined in the Commercial Code as a legal entity whose registered office is located within the territory of the Slovak Republic. The internal relations of a foreign legal entity, i.e. a legal entity whose registered office is outside the Slovak Republic, are governed by the national law of the country where it is established, even after the transfer of its registered office to Slovakia.

The SE Act does not require a Slovak SE to locate its head office and registered office in the same place (Art. 7 Reg.). However, an SE's registered office must be located in the same Member State as its head office, otherwise the court could order the company to dissolve (see also no. 52 *et seq.* of this report.).

If an SE registered in the Slovak Republic intends to transfer its registered office to another Member State, the SE's management or administrative organ must draft a transfer proposal (Art. 8(2) Reg.). In addition to the information listed in Article 8(2) of the Regulation, the transfer proposal must indicate a reasonable price at which the SE is obliged to purchase the shares of minority shareholders (see below) as well as the period for which the offer shall remain open.

The competent authority will not register the new registered office unless and until the SE submits a certificate attesting to the completion of all requisite pretransfer formalities. In the Slovak Republic, notaries public are the competent authority for this purpose and will only issue the certificate once the SE has proven, *inter alia*, that its creditors have been provided appropriate security and that the general meeting's resolution approving the transfer is valid and has not been challenged in court, or, if it has been, that the action has been dismissed or abandoned.

(i) Protection of minority shareholders

7. The aim of the provisions concerning the protection of minority shareholders is to protect shareholders who oppose the transfer of an SE's registered office and give them the option to end their stake in the company and sell their shares (Art. 8(5) Reg.).

Pursuant to the Regulation, the protection of creditors and minority shareholders of an SE that transfers its registered office is governed by the national law of the Member States.

Pursuant to the SE Act, any shareholder who voted against the decision to transfer an SE's registered office at the general meeting approving the transfer and who requested that its opposition be recorded in the minutes (an 'entitled minority shareholder') has the right to request that the SE buy back its shares at an appropriate price. Mention of this right must be made in the notice or announcement of the general meeting scheduled to vote on the transfer.

8. An SE must submit an offer to acquire the shares of entitled minority shareholders within one month following publication of the notice of registration of its new office in the commercial register of the Member State where this office is located. Entitled minority shareholders must be given at least 14 days to decide whether to accept the offer.

If the offer price is considered insufficient, any shareholder may file a claim with the competent court within one year following publication of the notice of registration. If the claim is deemed admissible, the shareholder may be entitled to compensation in the form of an additional payment. Such a decision is applicable to all shareholders who accepted the SE's original offer, and the SE must compensate them on equal terms.

In order to provide legal certainty and protection for re-registered SEs, a judicial decision that the share price is inadequate cannot serve as a ground to invalidate the resolution by the general meeting approving the transfer.

(ii) Protection of creditors

9. The SE Act contains provisions to protect creditors of an SE when the company's registered office is transferred, as a result of which the settlement and/or recovery of their debts could prove more difficult (Art. 8(7) Reg.).

If the possibility of settlement becomes more remote as a result of the transfer of an SE's registered office, creditors with outstanding claims against the company are entitled to request settlement in an appropriate manner within one month following publication of a notice that the general meeting's resolution has been filed with the registrar of deeds. This does not hold true for claims backed by adequate security or for claims that did not exist on the day of publication of the notice.

(iii) **Obligatory transfer of an SE's registered office**

10. Under Slovak law, the head office of an SE need not be in the same place (i.e. at the same address) as its registered office. However, the head office and registered office of an SE must be located in the same Member State. Pursuant to the SE Act, if an SE whose registered office is located in the Slovak Republic transfers its head office to another Member State, the Slovak court will, without a motion, order the SE to either transfer its head office back to Slovakia or transfer its registered office to the other Member State following the procedure stipulated in Article 8 of the Regulation.

If the SE fails to comply with this request within the stipulated time limit, the court will order the company to dissolve in accordance with the applicable provisions of the Slovak Commercial Code (see no. 52 of this report).

11. Article 8(14) of the Regulation has not been transposed into Slovak law, and the Slovak authorities are not entitled to oppose the transfer of the registered office of an SE on the grounds of public interest.

Pursuant to Council Directive 2005/19/EC of 17 February 2005 amending Directive 90/434/EEC on the common system of taxation applicable to mergers, divisions, transfers of assets and exchanges of shares concerning companies of different Member States, the Member States shall adopt and bring into force legislation regarding the tax issues relevant to the transfer of an SE's registered office by 1 January 2006 to allow for tax-neutral treatment of such a transfer. However, the actual effects of such legislation will have to be evaluated after adoption.

D Corporate purpose

12. The main purpose for establishing an SE is to carry on business activities, which are defined in the Commercial Code as systematic activities independently conducted for the purpose of turning a profit by an entrepreneur in its own name and on its own behalf. Slovak private and public limited-liability companies may be established for other purposes, however.

E Capital

13. The SE Act does not contain any special provisions concerning the subscribed capital of Slovak SEs. Therefore, the provisions governing the registered capital of joint stock companies shall apply, except for those pertaining to the amount of capital (Art. 67(1) Reg.). According to the Regulation, the subscribed capital of an SE may not be less than €120,000. This amount is significant compared to the minimum subscribed capital of Slovak joint stock companies, which is only SKK 1,000,000 or €25,000. (Even though Slovakia has yet to join the European Monetary Union, the share capital of Slovak joint stock companies may be denominated in either Slovakia koruna or in euros.)

2 Different means of formation

A Formation by merger

14. Only those companies listed in Annex I to the Regulation may participate in the formation of an SE by merger. For the Slovak Republic, Annex I, as amended,[1] lists the *akciová spoločnosť* or joint stock company, which is equivalent to a public company limited by shares.

Matters concerning the formation of an SE by merger which are not covered by the Regulation shall be governed by provisions of national law applicable to mergers involving public limited companies. In the Slovak Republic, the Commercial Code also applies.

15. Section 69(3) of the Commercial Code defines two types of mergers:

   (i) *Zlúčenie* is a procedure whereby on the basis of winding up without going into liquidation, one or more companies cease to exist and their assets are transferred to another existing company which becomes their legal successor. This description corresponds to a merger by acquisition as defined in Article 3(1) of Third Council Directive 78/855/EEC of 9 October 1978 based on Article 54(3)(g) of the Treaty concerning mergers of public limited-liability companies.
   (ii) *Splynutie* is a procedure whereby on the basis of winding up without going into liquidation, two or more companies cease to exist and their assets are transferred to another, newly created company that becomes the legal successor of these entities. This description corresponds to the definition of a merger by formation of a new company as contained in Article 4(1) of Directive 78/855/EEC.

16. As in the case of the transfer of an SE's registered office and under the same terms, a certificate confirming the completion of all pre-merger acts and formalities in the Slovak Republic must be issued by a notary. Among other prerequisites, the SE must declare that appropriate security has been provided to creditors and that there are no pending suits challenging the validity or legality of the general meeting's resolution approving the merger.

---

[1] By Council Regulation (EC) No. 885/2004 of 26 April 2004 adapting Regulation (EC) No. 2003/2003 of the European Parliament and of the Council, Council Regulations (EC) No. 1334/2000, (EC) No. 2157/2001, (EC) No. 152/2002, (EC) No. 1499/2002, (EC) No. 1500/2003 and (EC) No. 1798/2003, Decisions No. 1719/1999/EC, No. 1720/1999/EC, No. 253/2000/EC, No. 508/2000/EC, No. 1031/2000/EC, No. 163/2001/EC, No. 2235/2002/EC and No. 291/2003/EC of the European Parliament and of the Council, and Council Decisions 1999/382/EC, 2000/821/EC, 2003/17/EC and 2003/893/EC in the fields of the free movement of goods, company law, agriculture, taxation, education and training, culture and audiovisual policy, and external relations, by reason of the accession of the Czech Republic, Estonia, Cyprus, Latvia, Lithuania, Hungary, Malta, Poland, Slovenia and Slovakia (*Official Journal*, L 168 of 1 May 2004).

17. Under Slovak law, a merger agreement must take the form of a special notarised document. The agreement must be approved by two-thirds of shareholders present or represented at the general meeting of each merging company and, if a new company is created, the general meeting of that company as well. Approval of the merger must be recorded in a notarised instrument.

If the last financial statement of any merging company was prepared more than six months prior to the date of the draft merger agreement, a preliminary financial statement dated no earlier than the first day of the third month preceding the date of the draft merger agreement must be prepared and made available to shareholders.

18. An application to register an SE in the commercial register must be submitted to the competent registry court in accordance with Act No. 530/2003 Coll. on commercial registry, as amended (the 'Commercial Registry Act'), and Decree No. 25/2004 Coll. of the Ministry of Justice (the 'Commercial Registry Decree'). A proposal to register an SE must be submitted on a specific form along with the documents stipulated in the legislation. Before an SE formed by merger can be registered, the registry court must examine, in addition to the general terms of registration, whether the merging companies have approved the (same wording of the) draft terms of merger and whether the conditions set forth in Article 12(2) of the Regulation have been fulfilled (existence of an agreement on employee involvement).

The boards of directors of the merging companies must arrange for publication of information about the merger in the *Commercial Newsletter* (Art. 21 Reg.) as well as for submission of the draft merger agreement to the registrar of deeds of the relevant commercial register.

19. Slovak law does not allow the national authorities to oppose the participation of a Slovak company in the formation of an SE by merger (Art. 19 Reg.).

The SE Act provides protection to minority shareholders and creditors where an SE is formed by merger.

(i) **Protection of minority shareholders**

20. Any shareholder of a company participating in the formation of an SE by merger who (i) was a shareholder of any merging company when the general meeting of that company approved the merger, (ii) was present at that general meeting, (iii) voted against the merger, and (iv) requested that its opposition be recorded in the minutes (an 'entitled shareholder') has the right to request the newly formed SE to buy back its shares at an appropriate price (Art. 24(2) Reg.).

The Commercial Code (Sec. 218j, in conjunction with Sec. 218i(4) and (5)) regulates mergers involving Slovak joint stock companies. Accordingly, the provisions of the Commercial Code apply to the formation of an SE by merger for issues not covered by the Regulation or the SE Act. Thus, within one month following recordation of the merger in the commercial register, the SE must send or publish a draft share purchase agreement for the acquisition of its shares from entitled shareholders in the manner described in its articles of association (referred to as 'statutes' in the Regulation and as 'articles' hereafter) to convene the general meeting. Entitled shareholders must be given at least 14 days to consider the offer. The purchase price must correspond to the share exchange ratio of the participating companies and of the newly formed SE, possibly increased by a supplement. If it does not, any shareholder who has accepted the offer may be entitled to compensation in the form of an additional payment.

Shareholders have the right to seek compensation through the courts. However, this right expires if a petition is not filed within one year following recordation of the merger in the commercial register. A judicial decision confirming the right of a shareholder to compensation is binding on the SE and applicable to all entitled shareholders, so that the SE must offer the same compensation to all shareholders who accepted its offer.

If the share-exchange ratio set out in the merger agreement, together with any supplement, is not adequate, any shareholder of a participating company is entitled to seek compensation from the SE in the form of an additional payment. Only those shareholders who (i) were shareholders of any merging company at the time the general meeting of that company approved the merger, (ii) did not transfer any of their shares in the merging company or the SE prior to filing the petition with the court, and (iii) have not waived their right to compensation are eligible.

According to Section 218i(3) of the Commercial Code, which applies to the formation of an SE by merger, a shareholder may waive its right to compensation. Such a waiver must be in writing and delivered to the company or recorded in the minutes of the general meeting if made at that time. The waiver extends to future assignees of the shares in question.

The validity of the general meeting's resolution to approve the merger agreement cannot be challenged on the ground that (i) the purchase price set forth in the draft share purchase agreement was inadequate, (ii) the share exchange ratio, along with any possible supplement, as set forth in the merger agreement, was insufficient, or (iii) the information contained in the auditor's report was incomplete (Sec. 218a(3) Commercial Code).

(ii) **Protection of creditors**

21. The SE Act extends protection to creditors of a Slovak joint stock company participating in the formation of an SE by merger if the SE's registered office will not be located in the Slovak Republic. Creditors with outstanding claims against the company are entitled to satisfaction or security if recovery of their claims would prove more difficult as a result of formation of the SE.

This right is not available to creditors with secured claims or to those whose claims arose after the date of publication of the filing notice of the draft merger agreement with the registrar of deeds.

B Formation of a holding SE

22. Pursuant to Annex II of the Regulation, as amended,[2] two types of Slovak companies may participate in the formation of a holding SE: an *akciová spoločnosť* (or joint-stock company, equivalent to a public limited-liability company) and a *spoločnosť s ručením obmedzeným* (or private limited-liability company).

The SE Act contains provisions to protect minority shareholders where a holding SE is formed and sets forth the responsibility of the companies' statutory representatives (either the board of directors, for a joint stock company, or the executives for a private limited-liability company) to publish a notice confirming the completion of all conditions for formation of the holding SE (Art. 33(2) Reg.).

(i) **Protection of minority shareholders**

23. If the proposed share exchanged ratio set forth in the formation agreement, together with any supplement, is not sufficient, the individual shareholders of all companies involved have the right to receive an additional payment.

Only those shareholders who (i) were shareholders of a company participating in the formation of the holding SE when the general meeting of that company approved the agreement, (ii) announced their intention to contribute their shares to the holding SE, (iii) did not transfer any of their shares in the companies participating in the formation of the holding SE or in the holding SE itself prior to filing the petition, and (iv) have not waived their right to compensation, may claim compensation in court. Shareholders can waive their right to compensation only in writing and vis-à-vis the holding SE.

The provisions regulating the protection of minority shareholders with respect to the formation of a holding SE are similar to those pertaining to the formation of an SE by merger and the transfer of an SE's registered office (Art. 34 Reg.).

Prior to recordation of a holding SE with the commercial register, the competent registry court shall verify whether the conditions set forth in Articles 32 and 33 of the Regulation have been fulfilled.

C Formation of a subsidiary SE

24. Pursuant to Article 36 of the Regulation, the entities participating in the formation of a subsidiary SE shall be subject to the provisions governing the

---

[2] See footnote 1 above.

formation of a subsidiary in the form of a public limited-liability company under national law.

A joint stock company, i.e. a public limited-liability company, is a legal entity whose stock is divided into a certain number of shares with a specified face value. A joint stock company is liable to its creditors to the full extent of its assets, while its shareholders bear no liability.

The registered share capital of a joint stock company may be increased by (i) subscription or (ii) without subscription if the share capital is fully paid up by the founders of the company. The share capital can be paid up by either in cash or by way of contributions in kind. Founders or subscribers must pay in at least 30% of all cash contributed to the share capital of a joint stock company upon incorporation. The remainder must be paid up within one year following recordation of the company in the commercial register.

Upon incorporation, it is obligatory for a joint stock company to establish a reserve equal to at least 10% of its share capital. This reserve must be replenished annually by the amount stipulated in the company's articles, which must be at least 10% of its net profits until the threshold set forth in the articles is reached (i.e. at least 20% of the company's share capital).

A joint stock company is established by signing a founder's deed or a foundation agreement in the form of a notarised instrument prepared by a notary and executed by an authorised representative or attorney of the founders. The company's articles must be attached to this instrument.

D   Conversion into an SE

25. Pursuant to Article 2(4) of the Regulation, a Slovak joint stock company can be converted into an SE provided both its registered office and head office are located within the European Union and it has had a subsidiary governed by the laws of another EU Member State for at least two years.

The SE Act does not contain any special provisions regarding the formation of an SE by conversion. Taking into account the general rule that matters not covered by the Regulation shall be governed by national law, the provisions of the Commercial Code regarding changes to the corporate form of a Slovak joint stock company shall apply.

The board of directors of a joint stock company that wishes to be converted into an SE must prepare draft terms of conversion and make the same available to shareholders at the company's registered office within at least the period stipulated in its articles or by law for sending and publishing notices of a general meeting. In addition, the shareholders must be able to obtain or request a copy of the report upon request free of charge. The supervisory board will examine the report and submit a statement to shareholders concerning the change in corporate form.

The decision regarding the change in corporate form must be approved by two-thirds of those shareholders present and voting at the general meeting and must be recorded in the form of a notarised instrument. The company's articles may stipulate a higher majority, however. The SE Act does not contain any special provisions regarding approval of a change in corporate form by the corporate organ within which employee participation is organised (Art. 37(8)).

3 Acts committed on behalf of an SE in formation

26. The SE Act does not contain any specific provisions regarding acts committed on behalf of an SE in formation. Therefore, the respective provisions of the Regulation will apply, according to which any acts performed in an SE's name prior to registration that give rise to obligations not assumed by the SE after registration shall be binding on the natural persons and legal entities that performed those acts, unless agreed otherwise.

4 Registration and publication

27. An SE with its registered office in the Slovak Republic must be registered with the relevant commercial register in accordance with the Commercial Code. An SE acquires legal personality upon recordation with the commercial register, although this does not hold true for the transfer of an SE's registered office. The commercial registers are maintained by the registry courts (i.e. district courts based in the regional capitals), and the company is registered based on where its registered office is located.

Recordation with the commercial register is regulated by the Commercial Registry Act and its implementing decree. This legislation was recently amended, effective 1 November 2004, to incorporate provisions specifically related to the registration of SEs in the Slovak Republic.

Under Section 6 of the Commercial Registry Act, before registering an SE the registry court will examine any changes to or deletion of data from the register and whether the application was submitted by an authorised party, whether it is complete and all documents required by law have been appended in due form, whether the data mentioned in the application corresponds to the enclosed documents, etc.

If all legal requirements are met, the court will authorise registration within five business days from the filing date of the application. The court will then issue and deliver a confirmation of registration to the applicant, stating the content of the registration and containing an extract from the commercial register.

28. Apart from publication in the *Official Journal of the European Union* as required by the Regulation, the competent registry court must publish the data in the *Commercial Newsletter* (*Obchodný vestník*) as well as a notice that all

required documents have been filed with the registrar of deeds. The *Commercial Newsletter* is regulated by Decree No. 42/2004 Coll. on the *Commercial Newsletter* (effective 1 February 2004) (the 'Commercial Newsletter Decree').

Data recorded in the commercial register is effective vis-à-vis third parties as of its publication date. The content of a document for which publication is required is effective against third parties as of the publication date of the notice that the document has been filed with the registrar of deeds.

If there is a discrepancy between published and recorded data or documents, third parties can rely on the published wording unless it can be proven that they were aware of the registered data or filed documents.

Data which must be published *ex lege* by the courts or the public authorities must appear in the *Commercial Newsletter* within five business days following the delivery of supplementary documents in accordance with the Commercial Newsletter Decree.

Data regarding entrepreneurs (save financial statements, annual reports and securities prospectuses, for which the time limit is 90 days) must be published within five working days following delivery of supplementary documents executed in compliance with the Commercial Newsletter Decree and payment of the publication fee.

The Ministry of Justice is authorised to notify the *Official Journal* of the recordation with or deletion from the commercial register of an SE and of the recordation or deletion of an SE's registered office in the event of a transfer.

5 Acquisition of legal personality

29. Like any other Slovak company, an SE acquires legal personality upon registration with the commercial register. An application for registration must be submitted by the company's founders to the competent registry court (depending on where the SE's registered office is located) within 90 days following formation of the company or receipt by the company of a business permit.

IV Organisation and management

1 General remarks

30. In the Slovak Republic, joint stock companies (public limited-liability companies) must have a two-tier management system, and the Commercial Code contains a great many rules in this respect. The SE Act implements only some of the options afforded the Member States by the Regulation in connection with the two-tier system.

Since a one-tier management structure does not exist in Slovakia for public limited-liability companies, it was necessary to provide extensive rules in the SE Act for SEs that opt for this structure.

2 General meeting

31. The general meeting is the highest authority of a public limited-liability company in Slovakia. A general meeting must be held at least once a year and is convened by the board of directors (or the administrative board in an SE with a one-tier system) in the manner and within the periods specified in the company's articles, unless provided otherwise by law. The option contained in Article 54(1) of the Regulation allowing the first general meeting be held at any time during the first 18 months following incorporation of an SE has not been adopted in Slovakia. The board of directors shall send a notice of the meeting to all shareholders at least 30 days prior to the proposed date. The notice must contain the proposed agenda of the meeting, as well as other required information.

A Decision-making process

32. The general meeting is empowered:

- to amend the company's articles of association;
- to decide whether to increase or decrease the company's registered share capital and issue bonds;
- to appoint and remove members of the board of directors, if the articles so provide;
- to appoint and remove members of the supervisory board, with the exception of members elected as employee representatives, and other corporate bodies if the articles so provide;
- to approve the annual accounts and decide on the distribution of profits and royalties;
- to decide whether to replace share certificates with book-entered shares and vice versa;
- to decide whether to wind up the company or change its corporate form;
- to decide whether to delist the company's shares;
- to determine rules for the remuneration of members of the corporate organs;
- to approve an agreement on the transfer of an undertaking or any part thereof;
- to decide on any other matters entrusted to it by law or the company's articles.

For most of the above-mentioned decisions, approval by a simple majority of shareholders present or represented is sufficient, provided the SE's articles do not stipulate otherwise. However, pursuant to the Commercial Code, the approval of two-thirds of shareholders present or represented is required to amend a company's articles (i.e. the legislature did not adopt the option contained in Article 59(2) of the Regulation to allow amendments to a company's articles to be approved by a simple majority of votes cast), increase or decrease its share capital or authorise the board of directors to increase the share capital, issue preferred or convertible bonds, and wind up the company or change its corporate form. The foregoing decisions must be recorded in a notarised instrument.

B Rights and obligations of shareholders

33. Pursuant to Articles 55(1) and 56 of the Regulation, the SE Act provides that one or more shareholders holding at least 5% of an SE's share capital have the right to request that a general meeting be held and draw up its agenda or to request that additional items be placed on the agenda. The SE's articles may extend this right to a shareholder or shareholders who jointly hold less than 5% of the company's share capital.

3 Management and supervision

A Two-tier system

34. The two-tier management structure for SEs established under Slovak law is governed by the relevant provisions of the Regulation, as supplemented by the rules on the management of public limited-liability companies contained in the Commercial Code (Art. 39(5) Reg.).

The board of directors is responsible for managing a Slovak public limited-liability company. The board of directors is a statutory authority that acts on the company's behalf and is entitled to take decisions on all matters not reserved by law or the company's articles to the general meeting or to the supervisory board.

Under the Slovak Commercial Code, only natural persons may serve as members of a company's board of directors. No minimum or maximum number of board members is stipulated (Art. 39(4) Reg.).

The length of time during which a member of the supervisory board can temporarily fill a vacancy on the board of directors pursuant to Article 39(3) of the Regulation is limited under the SE Act to one year, and such a posting will terminate automatically upon the appointment of a new member to the board of directors by the competent body.

The board of directors is responsible for managing the company's business, ensuring that its accounts are duly kept and submitting reports on its activities to the supervisory board. The board of directors must call an extraordinary general meeting if the company's losses exceed one third of its share capital, or if such losses can be expected, and propose necessary measures in this regard to the general meeting. It must also notify the supervisory board accordingly without delay (Art. 39(1) Reg.).

35. The supervisory board oversees the board of directors and the company's business. Section 21 of the SE Act provides that each individual member of the supervisory board may request any necessary information from the board of directors on behalf of the entire supervisory board (Art. 41(3) Reg.).

The supervisory board is entitled to consult any documents and records related to the company's activities and to monitor the company's accounting and business practices and compliance of the same with law, the company's articles and resolutions of the general meeting. The supervisory board must convene a general meeting whenever the interests of the company so require and propose any necessary measures at that meeting. The SE Act does not contain a list of transactions that require the authorisation of the supervisory board, although the supervisory board can make certain decisions of the board of directors subject to its approval, even if no mention is made to this effect in the company's articles (Art. 48(1) and (2) Reg.).

In compliance with Article 40(3) of the Regulation, the Commercial Code stipulates that the supervisory board must have at least three members. If the company has more than 50 employees, two-thirds of the supervisory board's members shall be appointed and removed by the general meeting and one-third by the employees. However, the foregoing rule applies only if the agreement on employee involvement concluded between the SE's special negotiating body and management does not provide otherwise.

Only natural persons may sit on the supervisory board. Members of the supervisory board are appointed for a term set out in the company's articles which may not exceed six years (Art. 46 Reg.). Decisions of the supervisory board must be approved by a majority of its members, unless the articles provide otherwise.

B   One-tier system

36. Since no provisions existed under Slovak law for a one-tier system of management for joint-stock companies, the SE Act contains a complete set of rules in this regard supplementing the provisions of the Regulation (Art. 43(4) Reg.).

The administrative board (i.e., the administrative body of an SE established in the Slovak Republic) is a statutory body that acts on behalf of an SE, manages its activities and defines the course of its development. Unless otherwise provided in the SE's articles, each individual member of the administrative board is entitled to act on behalf of the company.

The administrative board takes decisions on all matters except those reserved by law or the SE's articles to the managing directors or to the general meeting. The administrative board can make certain decisions of the managing directors subject to its approval, even if this is not stated in the SE's articles.

The administrative board consists of three members, unless the company's articles provide otherwise (Art. 43(2) Reg.). Only natural persons may sit on a company's administrative board in Slovakia.

Each member of the administrative board is entitled to supervise the company's activities, to review all corporate documents and accounts, and to request information and explanations from the managing directors. The administrative board prepares and submits to the general meeting a report summarising its oversight activities and must also inform the general meeting of the SE's plans for development, its business activities, financial situation and assets.

The administrative board calls the general meeting at the times and in the manner set forth in the SE's articles. It must convene an extraordinary general meeting if the company's losses exceed one third of its registered share capital or if such losses can be expected.

The administrative board meets regularly, depending on the needs of the company, but must meet at least once every three months.

37. The administrative board may appoint one or more managing directors to act on behalf of the company. Only natural persons may serve as managing directors. The managing directors manage the company's business. Their decisions must be approved by a majority of all such directors unless the company's articles require a higher threshold.

Managing directors may be removed by the administrative board for no specific reason. One or more members of the administrative board may be appointed managing directors, provided the number of board members who are not serving simultaneously as managing directors constitutes a majority.

Managing directors are responsible for ensuring that the company's accounts are duly kept, preparing its financial statements, and submitting proposals regarding the distribution of profits as well as certain other documents to the administrative board. They are obliged to report to the administrative board on all matters liable to influence the company's business, particularly if the company's losses exceed or are expected to exceed one-third of its share capital.

If the administrative board decides not to appoint managing directors, it shall exercise their authority instead.

C   Appointment and removal

38. In accordance with the Regulation, members of the board of directors of an SE with a two-tier management structure are removed and appointed by the supervisory board. A director's term of office may not exceed six years. Pursuant to the option contained in Article 39(2) of the Regulation, the SE Act allows a company's articles to provide that members of the board of directors can be appointed by the general meeting. The body that appoints members of the board of directors shall also be responsible for designating a chair.

39. In the one-tier system, members of the administrative board are appointed by the general meeting, unless the company's agreement on employee involvement or the law stipulates otherwise. The administrative board is entitled to appoint and remove the managing directors.

Pursuant to general provisions of the Commercial Code, if a member of a company's board of directors, supervisory board or administrative board resigns, the resignation shall be effective as of the date of the first meeting of the body responsible for appointments following tender of the resignation. If no meeting and subsequent appointment or election takes place within three months, the resignation shall be effective upon expiry of this period.

D   Representation

40. In the two-tier system of management, each individual member of the board of directors is entitled to act on behalf of the company, unless the company's articles provide otherwise. The names of board members and the manner in which they represent the company must be recorded with the commercial register. The power of the board of directors to act on behalf of the company may be restricted by the company's articles, resolutions of the general meeting or decisions of the supervisory board, although such restrictions are not effective against third parties.

41. An SE with a one-tier system of management is represented by either its administrative board or its managing directors if the administrative board has appointed one or more managing directors to act on behalf of the company.

E   Liability

42. Members of the board of directors of an SE with a two-tier system must exercise due professional care in carrying out their duties and must act in accordance with the interests of the company and its shareholders. They must acquire any and all information needed to take decisions, keep confidential information and facts the disclosure of which could harm the company, its interests or the interests of its shareholders, and perform their duties without giving preference to their own interests or the interests of certain shareholders or third parties.

Directors who violate these obligations may be held jointly and severally liable to the company for any damage caused. Board members are not liable for damage if they can prove that they acted with due (professional) care and in good faith in the interest of the company. Under Slovak law, agreements between the company and any member(s) of its board of directors to restrict or eliminate liability are impermissible. Nor may the company's articles restrict the liability of board members.

43. In addition, members of the board of directors are not allowed to compete with the company, in particular they may not: (i) carry out in their own name or on their own behalf commercial activities related to the SE's business; (ii) act as an intermediary for third parties with respect to the company's business; (iii) participate in another company as a partner with unlimited liability; or (iv) serve as a member of a statutory body of another legal entity performing similar activities to the company's unless such entity is a subsidiary of the company. The SE's articles may provide further limitations in this respect.

Provisions concerning directors' liability and the prohibition on competing with the company shall apply *mutatis mutandis* to members of the supervisory board in an SE with a two-tier system.

44. In an SE with a one-tier system, the liability of administrative board members for the exercise of their functions and the ban on competing with the company are regulated by the same provisions applicable to members of the board of directors in the two-tier system.

The liability of managing directors for the performance of their duties and the ban on competing with the company are governed by the provisions of the Commercial Code applicable to the executives of private limited-liability companies. These provisions are construed similarly to those applicable to members of the board of directors of companies with a two-tier management structure (Art. 43(1) Reg.).

V Employee involvement

45. General labour relations in an SE are governed by the national law of the Member State in which the SE is formed. In the Slovak Republic, the relevant legislation is Act No. 311/2001 Coll. (the Labour Code), as amended. Employee involvement in the management of an SE as per the Directive is regulated by the SE Act, which may stipulate that provisions of the Labour Code shall apply.

46. The provisions of the SE Act regarding employee involvement in an SE reflect the respective provisions of the Directive.

The employees of an SE may participate or otherwise be involved in the company's decision-making process through an employee committee or employee representatives or pursuant to an agreement on employee involvement concluded between the SE's special negotiating body (SNB) and management.

Employee representatives of Slovak companies participating in the creation of an SE shall appoint members to the SNB at a joint meeting. The SNB of a Slovak SE must have between three and 17 members. Employees from each Member State are represented by one member; an additional one, two or three members are appointed on behalf of employees from the Member State where at least 25%, 50% or 75% respectively of all employees work (Art. 3(2)(b) Dir.).

Employee representatives in the Slovak Republic include trade unions, works councils and employee trustees.

47. If the employees of an SE are entitled to appoint or elect certain members of its organs due to the result of negotiations on employee involvement, such election or appointment shall be governed by the provisions of the Commercial Code pertaining to the election by employees of members of the supervisory board of a joint stock company, unless the application of Slovak law is forbidden under the laws of the home country.

Election of supervisory or administrative board members, as the case may be, is organised by the board of directors in collaboration with the trade unions, or, if no trade union is represented in the company, with those employees who are entitled to vote. Trade unions and any group representing at least 10% of the employees may submit proposals for the appointment or removal of members of the supervisory or administrative board. The appointment or removal of a board member is valid if the decision is approved by at least 50% of all employees entitled to vote or their representatives.

The SE Act provides that the management organ of a company participating in the creation of an SE can refuse to transmit information which, according to objective criteria, would seriously harm the functioning of SE, its subsidiaries and establishments and may classify any transmitted information as confidential. The SNB or the employees' committee can lodge a complaint with the supervisory organ or before the courts if it is of the opinion that the management organ classified certain information as confidential without a valid reason for doing so (Art. 8(2) Dir.).

VI Annual accounts and consolidated accounts

1 Accounting principles

48. As indicated in Article 61 of the Regulation, preparation of annual and/or consolidated accounts and of the annual report for an SE having its registered office in the Slovak Republic is governed by the provisions of Slovak law applicable to public limited-liability companies (Art. 67(2) Reg.).

The general rules are contained in the Commercial Code and specified in more detail in Act No. 431/2002 Coll. on accountancy, as amended.

Either the board of directors (in a two-tier SE) or the managing directors (in a one-tier SE) are responsible for ensuring that the company's accounts are duly kept and for preparing financial statements and an annual report. Oversight and review functions with respect to accountancy are executed by the supervisory board and the administrative board, respectively.

The board of directors or managing directors shall submit the financial statements for approval to the SE's general meeting within six months following the close of the respective accounting period, which may correspond to a calendar year, or, if the company so decides, a financial year.

In addition, every public limited-liability company and SE must publish its final balance sheet and income statement in the *Commercial Newsletter* within 30 days following their approval. The same applies to a company submitting consolidated financial statements, in which case the deadline for publication is one year following the end of the relevant accounting period.

49. Consolidated financial statements and the consolidated annual report are prepared by the parent company which:

   (a) holds a majority of voting rights; or
   (b) has the right to appoint or remove the majority of members of a subsidiary's statutory or supervisory body and is also a shareholder of the latter company; or
   (c) has the right to control the company in which it is a shareholder on the basis of an agreement concluded with that company or as per the memorandum of association or articles of the latter; or
   (d) is a shareholder of that company and has appointed the majority of members to its statutory or supervisory body; or
   (e) is a shareholder in and has executed the majority of voting rights in a subsidiary based on an agreement with shareholders in another company.

2 Auditors

50. Auditing services in the Slovak Republic can be provided only by accredited auditors – either natural persons whose names appear on the Slovak Chamber of Auditors' list or auditing firms, i.e. a general or limited partnership or private limited-liability company registered with the Slovak Chamber of Auditors.

Public limited-liability companies, including SEs, must have their ordinary and extraordinary financial statements audited. The company must provide any and all documents and explanations the auditors request, and any costs incurred shall be borne by the company.

An SE must file its financial statements, after they have been approved by the competent body (i.e. the general meeting) and verified by the auditor, with the registrar of deeds of the relevant commercial register, together with the auditor's report and identification data. Financial statements may be filed as part of the annual report, which is audited to ensure compliance with the company's financial statements.

Financial statements must be audited within one year from the close of the accounting period to which they relate and filed with the registrar of deeds within 30 days following their approval.

Consolidated financial statements must be verified by an auditor.

VII Supervision by the national authorities

51. The Ministry of Justice is authorised and obliged to inform the *Official Journal* of the registration with or deletion of an SE from the commercial register and the registration or deletion of its registered office in the event of a transfer.

Notaries public are the authority competent to issue a certificate confirming that all conditions for the creation of an SE or the transfer of its registered office have been fulfilled.

VIII Dissolution

52. As regards winding up, liquidation, cessation of payments and similar procedures, Slovak SEs shall be governed by the legal provisions applicable to Slovak public limited-liability companies, i.e. the Commercial Code in conjunction with Act No. 328/1991 Coll. on bankruptcy and composition, as amended (the 'Bankruptcy and Composition Act'), which will be replaced by the recently adopted Act No. 7/2005 Coll. on bankruptcy and restructuring, effective 1 January 2006. If the SE performs special activities (such as banks, insurance companies, etc.), the provisions of other laws may apply.

1 Winding up

53. Pursuant to the SE Act, if an SE with its registered office in the Slovak Republic transfers its head office to another Member State, a Slovak court will, without a motion, order the SE to either transfer its head office back to Slovakia or transfer its registered office to the other Member State in accordance with the procedure set forth in the Regulation (Art. 8 Reg.).

If the SE fails to comply with the court order within the stipulated time limit, the court will order the company to dissolve in accordance with the provisions of the Commercial Code regarding the winding up of joint-stock companies.

54. A company ceases to exist when it is deleted from the commercial register. Prior to dissolution, the company must be wound up, either with or without going into liquidation. Liquidation shall occur if all of the company's assets have not been transferred to its legal successor. The general meeting of an SE is authorised to decide whether the company should be wound up and enter liquidation.

55. A company is wound up either: (a) upon expiry of the term for which it was established; (b) by a decision of the general meeting; (c) by court order; (d) by abandonment of bankruptcy proceedings, either after compliance with a resolution on the distribution of proceeds or if the company's assets are not sufficient to cover the costs of the proceedings or if the petition in bankruptcy was rejected due to insufficient assets; or (e) for any other reason stipulated by law.

The Commercial Code lists several situations in which the courts may order the involuntary dissolution of a company, including where:

(a) a general meeting was not held in the respective calendar year or corporate bodies were not established during a period exceeding three months;
(b) the company's business permit was revoked;
(c) the prerequisites stipulated by law for the creation of the company become invalid;
(d) the company violated its obligation to create or supplement reserves;
(e) the company failed to file its financial statements with the registrar of deeds for two accounting periods.

Before rendering a decision, the court will give the company a period of time in which to regularise its situation and remedy the grounds for dissolution. The court will then examine whether the company has sufficient assets to cover the costs of liquidation. If so, it will order the company to enter liquidation. If not, the court will order the company to dissolve and delete its entry from the commercial register.

If the company itself proposes to delete its entry from the commercial register, it must submit an authorisation to do so from the tax authorities.

2   Liquidation

56. A company shall be liquidated if all its assets have not been transferred to its legal successor. The general meeting of an SE has authority to decide whether the company should be wound up and enter liquidation.

Liquidation is handled by a liquidator appointed by the general meeting. If no liquidator is appointed, liquidation shall be handled by the company's statutory body. If no such body exists or if it has no members or if a liquidator is not appointed without delay, one shall be appointed by the court.

The liquidator is entitled to act on behalf of the company in all matters regarding the liquidation. The company's statutory body continues to perform its functions insofar as its duties have not been transferred to the liquidator.

The liquidator must petition the court for an adjudication in bankruptcy if it is ascertained that the company's liabilities exceed its assets.

The liquidator will notify all known creditors of the commencement of liquidation and publish the notice along with a request to creditors to file their claims. The liquidator will also prepare balance sheets as of the start and end dates of the liquidation and submit a final report and proposal for distribution of any remaining proceeds to shareholders. The liquidator is entitled to call a general meeting to approve the financial statements, the final report and the distribution proposal.

57. The competent registry court shall delete the entry of a joint stock company from the commercial register only if the company's share certificates have been declared void or destroyed and registered shares cancelled. A petition to delete a company from the commercial register must be submitted by the liquidator within 90 days following approval of the financial statements, final report and distribution proposal. The above documents must also be filed with the registrar of deeds of the relevant commercial register.

3 Insolvency

58. Insolvency proceedings in the Slovak Republic are currently regulated by the Bankruptcy and Composition Act. A new act on bankruptcy and restructuring, which shall come into effect on 1 January 2006, has been adopted recently with the aim to speed up bankruptcy proceedings and make them more creditor-friendly and flexible. Below is a brief description of bankruptcy proceedings, as currently regulated by the Bankruptcy and Composition Act.

Bankruptcy proceedings are commenced by filing a petition in bankruptcy with the debtor's regional court. Such a petition can be filed by (i) the debtor, (ii) a creditor, (iii) the debtor's liquidator, or (iv) any other person entitled to do so by law. If the petition is submitted by a creditor, it must submit proof of the debtor's bankruptcy and documentation relating to its claim and identify at least one other creditor of the debtor.

A company is deemed bankrupt if (i) it has been unable to meet its financial obligations to a number of creditors for at least 30 days or (ii) it is insolvent (the act does not define this term but it likely means that the debtor's liabilities exceed its assets).

Once the petition has been filed, the debtor must refrain from any acts that could lead to a decrease in the value of its assets, although it is permitted to carry on its day-to-day business. The debtor is required to prepare and file with the court within a given period of time a list of its assets and liabilities, identifying its debtors and creditors and providing an address for each.

When ruling on the petition in bankruptcy, the court will appoint a trustee in bankruptcy. A copy of the court's decision will be sent to the debtor, the petitioner(s), the debtor's tax office and all known creditors. The decision becomes effective upon publication on the official calendar of the court, and from this day forward, the debtor is officially bankrupt and the consequences of bankruptcy effective. The decision is also recorded in the commercial register and in the trade register of the place where the debtor is located, as well as in the relevant land register if the debtor owns real property.

The adjudication in bankruptcy requests the debtor's creditors to file their claims within 60 days. Creditors must identify all claims, the amounts due, the factual and legal basis of each claim, any security held, the class of each claim, and whether they are seeking a separate settlement.

59. Control of the debtor's estate is transferred to the trustee in bankruptcy for the duration of the bankruptcy proceedings. The Bankruptcy and Composition Act lists the consequences of the effectiveness of the adjudication in bankruptcy, including: (i) any unsettled claims and liabilities become immediately due and payable; (ii) all outstanding instructions, powers-of-attorney and proposals for the conclusion of contracts that have yet to be acted upon are deemed null and void; (iii) any obligations owed to or by the debtor which would ordinarily be subject to set off no longer are if the claim, debt or right arose after the adjudication in bankruptcy entered into effect; (iv) execution against the debtor's assets cannot occur; (v) all acts by the debtor relating to its assets and business are of no effect; and (vi) any party that has concluded a contract with the debtor after the adjudication in bankruptcy is entitled to withdraw from the contract.

The trustee in bankruptcy shall draw up a list of the debtor's assets with the latter's assistance for review by the court. Any disposal of assets through sale or otherwise requires the consent of the court. Claims shall be satisfied in compliance with the provisions of the Bankruptcy and Composition Act.

4 Cessation of payments

60. Slovak law does not regulate the cessation of payments as such. However, as of 1 January 2006, new bankruptcy and restructuring legislation will enter into effect. Slovak companies facing financial difficulties, including SEs established under Slovak law, will have the option to restructure, during which time they will be protected against creditors' claims (i.e. no enforcement or bankruptcy

proceedings may be commenced) and can prepare and submit a restructuring plan to the court for approval.

IX Applicable law

61. An SE established under Slovak law with its registered office in Slovakia shall be governed mainly by the Regulation, and, where so permitted, by Slovak law on SE-specific issues and those relating to transposition of the Directive. If no special rules are contained in the aforementioned legislation, general provisions of Slovak company law shall apply.

X Tax treatment

62. Since the Regulation does not provide any common rules regarding the taxation of SEs, an SE established under Slovak law with its registered office in Slovakia shall be subject to domestic tax law.

The Slovak tax system is generally based on the systems of taxation of the other EU Member States and includes corporate and personal income tax, value added tax ('VAT'), taxes on selected assets (such as real estate and vehicles) and excise taxes on specific goods such as alcohol and tobacco products.

1 Income tax

63. Following the tax reform effective 1 January 2004, income tax at a rate of 19% is imposed on both legal entities and natural persons that have their registered office, residence or place of effective management, as the case may be, in the Slovak Republic, including an SE with its registered office in the Slovakia.

The tax liability of a business is assessed on the basis of its profits. The tax base can be reduced *inter alia* by depreciation. For this purpose, assets are divided into four categories with the depreciation period ranging from four to 20 years (e.g. real property can be depreciated over 20 years). Two methods are available for tax depreciation: straight-line and accelerated. The choice of method must be made on an asset-by-asset basis and cannot be changed once made.

It is worth mentioning that dividends are not subject to tax in the Slovak Republic.

2 Value added tax

64. A business entity with turnover of more than SKK 1,500,000 (approximately €37,500) in the 12 preceding calendar months is obliged to register with the

VAT authorities. Since 1 January 2004, VAT at a flat rate of 19% has been levied on all taxable supplies. Supplies exempt from VAT include postal, financial and insurance services.

In the Slovak Republic, VAT is currently levied on taxable supplies, which can be divided into four categories: (a) supplies of goods in return for remuneration performed on the territory of the Slovak Republic by entities liable for VAT; (b) the provision of services in return for remuneration performed on the territory of the Slovak Republic by entities liable for VAT; (c) the acquisition of goods in return for remuneration performed on the territory of Slovakia from other Member States; and (d) the import of goods to Slovakia from outside the EU.

Registered entities may claim a deduction for input VAT paid on goods and services purchased to perform a taxable supply. A VAT deduction may be claimed on the date the taxable supply is made.

3 Other taxes

A Real estate tax

65. Real estate tax is payable by real property owners to the municipal authorities on an annual basis. The current tax rate is 0.25% of the value of the property (as established by an expert opinion or pursuant to the Ministry of Agriculture's decree on farm land). This rate may be changed by the municipal authorities.

B Excise taxes

66. Excise taxes are levied on certain goods such as mineral oils, spirits, liqueurs, beer, wine and tobacco products. The tax is payable in a lump sum. Liability for excise tax depends on the quantity of goods imported or produced.

XI Conclusion

67. Despite the high expectations that accompanied implementation of the Regulation in Slovakia, the position of the SE in this country remains complex and tenuous, particularly due to mixed application of Community and national legislation. Apart from the benefits inherent in the creation of an SE discussed at the beginning of this chapter, certain factors may be viewed as disadvantages or obstacles to the formation of an SE in Slovakia, in particular the following:

– To date, there has been little or no practical experience in setting up SEs in the Slovak Republic. The decision to establish an SE or to convert a public limited-liability company into an SE would encounter difficulties arising from a lack of experience in both legal and economic terms of the steps to be taken and the practical functioning of an SE.

- Establishment of an SE could possibly mean costly and lengthy efforts with uncertain results, coupled with the threat of uncertain and complicated negotiations with employee representatives. Companies based in countries whose laws provide for minor involvement and influence by employees could be faced with a significant rise in the importance of the latter's role if they take part in the formation of an SE, which is subject to stricter regulation in this regard.
- Companies that participate in the formation of an SE with its registered office in another Member State will become subject to different national laws and will need to bring their by-laws and practice into line with the applicable legislation, thereby incurring additional legal and managerial costs.
- The final form of proposed Community legislation, such as the directive on cross-border mergers (the Tenth Company Law Directive) and the directive on cross-border transfers of a company's registered office (the Fourteenth Company Law Directive), could offer companies operating on a pan-European level some of the advantages inherent in an SE without the need to cope with the aforementioned uncertainty in setting one up.
- The SE is subject to a complex mixture of rules and regulations arising from the EC Treaty, general principles of Community law, the Regulation, the Directive, the company's articles of association, and related national legislation, which could result in an extended period of uncertainty and additional legal costs.

Slovak legislation implementing the Regulation and transposing the Directive:

Act No. 562/2004 Coll. on the European company, amending and supplementing certain other acts – *Zákon č. 562/2004 Z.z. o európskej spoločnosti a o zmene a doplnení niektorých zákonov*

Also, in part:

Act No. 530/2003 Coll. on the commercial register, amending and supplementing certain other acts, as amended - *Zákon č. 530/2003 Z.z. o obchodnom registri a o zmene a doplnení niektorých zákonov, v znení neskorších predpisov*

Decree No. 25/2004 Coll. of the Slovak Ministry of Justice, stipulating the forms of petitions for recordation in the commercial register and the documents to be appended thereto – *Vyhláška Ministerstva spravodlivosti Slovenskej republiky č. 25/2004 Z.z., ktorou sa ustanovujú vzory tlačív na podávanie návrhov na zápis do obchodného registra a zoznam listín, ktoré je potrebné k návrhu na zápis priložiť'*

16
Sweden

KLAES EDHALL, ANNE RUTBERG, HELENA REMPLER, ANNIKA ANDERSSON, ANNA-KARIN LILJEHOLM AND KERSTIN KAMP-WIGFORSS
Mannheimer Swartling

I   Introduction   426
II   Reasons to opt for an SE   427
III Formation   427
    1   General remarks   427
        A   Founding parties   427
        B   Name   428
        C   Registered office   428
            (i)   General remarks   428
            (ii)   Transfer of registered office   429
        D   Corporate purpose   432
        E   Capital   432
            (i)   General remarks   432
    2   Different means of formation   432
        A   Formation by merger   432
            (i)   Procedure and publication requirements   432
            (ii)   Right to object to a company participating in a merger   436
            (iii) Minority shareholders   436
            (iv)   Rights of creditors   436
            (v)   Acquisition of a wholly owned subsidiary   436
            (vi)   Avoidance of a merger   437
        B   Formation of a holding SE   437
            (i)   Procedure and publication requirements   437
            (ii)   Minority shareholders   438
        C   Formation of a subsidiary SE   438
        D   Conversion into an SE   438
    3   Acts committed on behalf of an SE in formation   439
    4   Registration and publication   439
    5   Acquisition of legal personality   440
IV   Organisation and management   440
    1   General remarks   440
    2   General meeting   441
        A   Decision-making process   441
        B   Rights and obligations of shareholders   442
    3   Management and supervision   442

           A Two-tier system/one-tier system   442
              (i)   General remarks   442
              (ii) One-tier system   442
              (iii) Two-tier system   443
           B Appointment and removal   444
           C Managing director   444
           D Representation   445
           E Liability   445
   V   Employee involvement   445
       1   Formation of a special negotiating body   446
       2   Standard rules   446
       3   Employee participation on the board of directors or
           supervisory board   447
       4   Protection of employee representatives; jurisdiction;
           confidentiality; damages   447
   VI Annual accounts and consolidated accounts   448
       1   Accounting principles   448
       2   Auditors   449
   VII Supervision by the national authorities   449
   VIII Dissolution   450
       1   Liquidation and winding up   450
       2   Insolvency   450
       3   Cessation of payments   451
   IX Applicable law   451
   X   Tax treatment   451
       1   Income tax   451
       2   Tax issues when forming an SE   452
           A Formation by merger   452
           B Formation of a holding SE   453
           C Formation of a subsidiary SE   453
           D Conversion into an SE   453
           E Transfer of registered office and head office   453
       3   Value added tax   453
       4   Other taxes   453
   XI Conclusion   454

I   Introduction

1. On 8 October 2004, the Act on Employee Involvement in an SE (*Lag (2004:559) om arbetstagarinflytande i europabolag*), transposing into national law Council Directive 2001/86/EC of 8 October 2001 on employee involvement in an SE (the 'Directive'), entered into force along with the SE Act (*Lag 2004:575 om europabolag*) (the 'SE Act'), complementing Council Regulation No. 2157/2001 of 8 October 2001 on the Statute for a European company (SE) (the 'Regulation'), and a national SE regulation (*Förordning (2004:703) om*

europabolag) (the 'Swedish SE Regulation'). The SE Act and the Swedish SE Regulation are applicable to SEs with their registered offices in Sweden (Sec. 1(2) SE Act).[1] On the same date, certain amendments to Swedish tax law entered into effect so as to bring domestic tax law into line with the Regulation. As of 8 October 2004, it has thus been possible to form an SE in Sweden.

II Reasons to opt for an SE

2. In our opinion, the SE could be an interesting alternative for corporate groups with European-wide operations. Above all, we believe that in certain sectors, such as banking, use of an SE could allow existing corporate groups to streamline their operations. The Nordic banking group Nordea has made public its intention to restructure as an SE with its registered office in Sweden as of 2006. Moreover, Alfred Berg, a Nordic investment firm, has announced its intention to become an SE in September 2005, by turning its subsidiaries in Denmark, Finland and Norway into branches of an SE with its registered office in Sweden. The SE could also be an interesting vehicle for businesses in other sectors that wish to simplify their corporate administration and obtain a solid legal framework for their operations.

We believe the SE will prove to be an interesting and viable corporate vehicle in connection with cross-border acquisitions within the European Union, particularly cross-border mergers. While the Council directive on cross-border mergers of public limited-liability companies also provides a legal basis for such transactions, it has yet to be transposed into national law in Sweden. In theory, it should also be possible to carry out tax-neutral cross-border mergers pursuant to the Merger Directive, which has been transposed into Swedish law.

Another advantage of the SE is that it can transfer its registered office from one Member State to another with relative ease. Most national corporate forms must first dissolve or liquidate in order to transfer their registered office abroad.

III Formation

1 General remarks

A Founding parties

3. Swedish law refers to the provisions of the Regulation as far as the requirements the founders must comply with are concerned (see Chap. 2, no. 18 *et seq.* of this book).

---

[1] With respect to insurance companies, the SE Act and the Swedish SE Regulation apply only to the extent permitted by the Insurance Business Act (*Försäkringsrörelselag (1982:713)*) (Sec. 1(3) SE Act).

427

If a limited-liability company (or, with respect to the formation of a subsidiary SE, other companies and firms within the meaning of Article [58][2] of the EC Treaty) has its head office outside the European Union it may still, pursuant to Section 4 of the SE Act, participate in the formation of an SE provided that company: (i) is formed under the laws of a Member State; (ii) has its registered office in that Member State; and (iii) has a real and continuous link with the economy of a Member State. A company has a real and continuous link with the economy of a Member State if it has an establishment in that Member State from which it conducts business.[3]

B Name

4. The name of an SE must contain the abbreviation 'SE' and must differ sufficiently from the names of other entities listed in the Swedish SE register (Sec. 3 SE Act). Furthermore, an SE registered in Sweden may not bear a name that is deceptively similar to the name or trademark of another business entity (Sec. 3 Corporate Names Act (*Firmalag (1974:156)*).

C Registered office

(i) General remarks

5. An SE must be registered in the Member State where its registered office is located (Art. 12(1) Reg.). An SE must have its registered office and head office in the same Member State (Art. 7 Reg.). An SE registered in Sweden may have its registered office and head office[4] at different locations in Sweden.[5]

6. If an SE registered in Sweden has its head office in another Member State, the Companies Registration Office shall determine that there has been a breach of Article 7 of the Regulation (Sec. 29 SE Act). Once this decision has been given force of law, the Companies Registration Office shall order the SE to either transfer its registered office or head office, as the case may be, within a specified period of time. If the SE does not comply with this order, the Companies Registration Office shall force it into liquidation. Decisions of the Companies Registration Office may be appealed to the relevant district court (Sec. 32(2) SE Act). The Companies Registration Office will not render a decision on liquidation, however, if the basis for liquidation ceases to exist while the matter is pending. Furthermore, a decision to force an SE into liquidation may not be executed until it has attained force of law.[6]

---

[2] The Regulation refers to Article 48 of the EC Treaty. In the new numbering of the treaty, as amended by the Treaty of Amsterdam, Article 48 became Article 58.

[3] Preparatory work to the SE Act (*Proposition ('Prop.') 2003/04:112*, 120) and Recital 23 of the Regulation.

[4] For a definition of the term 'head office', see Chap. 2, no. 14 of this book.

[5] Prop. 2003/04:112, 54.

[6] Companies that conduct banking and insurance business and certain other financial services must, in principal, have their registered office and head office in the same Member State. If they

If the Companies Registration Office learns that an SE with its head office in Sweden is registered in another Member State, it shall inform the competent authority in that state (Sec. 10 Swedish SE Regulation).

7. In order for an SE with its registered office in another Member State to conduct business in Sweden, it must establish a branch in Sweden.[7] The business of the branch is subject to the Foreign Branches Act (*Lag (1992:160) om utländska filialer m.m.*). The branch must be registered with the Companies Registration Office (Sec. 15 Foreign Branches Act) and have independent administration. An SE must appoint a managing director to manage the business of its branch. The SE shall authorise the managing director to represent the company and sign on its behalf for all matters concerning its business in Sweden. The managing director must be a resident of the European Economic Area (EEA) (Secs. 8–10 Foreign Branches Act). The branch shall maintain accounting records with respect to its business in Sweden. An SE is required to keep separate books for its branches (Sec. 11 Foreign Branches Act).

(ii) **Transfer of registered office**

8. An SE may transfer its registered office from Sweden to another Member State. Such a transfer shall not result in the winding up of the SE or in the creation of a new legal person (Art. 8(1) Reg.). For SEs registered in Sweden, Sections 9 through 15 of the SE Act contain supplementary provisions with respect to the transfer of an SE's registered office.[8]

The transfer is initiated by the board of directors or (for a company with a two-tier management structure) the management board which prepares a transfer proposal (Art. 8(2) Reg.). For more information regarding the content of this proposal, please refer to Chap. 2, no. 83 of this book. The board of directors or the management board also prepares a report explaining and justifying the legal and economic aspects of the transfer and its implications for shareholders, creditors and employees (Art. 8(3) Reg.).[9] The transfer proposal must be filed with the Companies Registration Office, which shall publish a notice of registration

---

do not, the Swedish Financial Supervisory Authority ('*Finansinspektionen*') (the 'FSA') can impose sanctions, the most important being withdrawal of the company's permit to conduct the business in question. Pursuant to the SE Act, these rules also apply to an SE conducting banking or insurance business or engaged in certain other financial services (Prop. 2003/04:112, 103).

[7] Prop. 2003/04:112, 106–7.

[8] With respect to the transfer of the registered office of an SE engaged in banking or certain other financial services, Chapter 10, Sections 33–35 and Chapter 11, Section 1 of the Banking and Financial Services Act (*Lag (2004:297) om bank och finansieringsrörelse*) apply instead (Sec. 9 SE Act); see also footnote 13.

[9] An SE transferring its registered office from Sweden to another Member State will be required to prepare accounting statements for any period not included in earlier annual accounts. The Swedish legislature will prepare rules in this respect (Prop. 2003/04:112, 110).

without delay in the Swedish official gazette (*Post- och Inrikes Tidningar*) (Sec. 8 SE Act).[10]

The transfer requires a decision by the SE's general meeting and an amendment to the company's articles of association. The SE's shareholders and creditors are entitled to examine the transfer proposal and the management report at the SE's registered office and obtain copies upon request free of charge at least one month prior to the general meeting scheduled to approve the transfer (Art. 8(4) Reg.). No decision on the transfer may be taken for two months following publication of the proposal (Art. 8(6) Reg.). The resolution on the transfer and the amendment to the articles of association must be approved by two-thirds of votes cast and shares represented at the general meeting (Chap. 9, Sec. 30 Companies Act; Art. 59(1) Reg.). The Swedish legislature has not adopted the option contained in Article 8(5) of the Regulation to enact further protection for minority shareholders who oppose a transfer.[11]

If the general meeting has approved the transfer of an SE's registered office to another Member State, the SE shall notify all of its known creditors[12] to this effect in writing (Sec. 10(1) SE Act). The notice must mention the creditors' right pursuant to Article 8(4) of the Regulation to examine the transfer proposal and the report by the board of directors or the management board at the SE's registered office and to obtain copies upon request free of charge. Furthermore, the notice must contain information on creditors' right to object to the transfer (Sec. 10(2) SE Act).[13]

---

[10] If the transfer proposal is not published in its entirety, the notice must state where the proposal is available for consultation.

[11] Prop. 2003/04:112, 56.

[12] At present, employees and others with claims for wages, other forms of compensation or pension benefits, all of which have priority pursuant to the Priority Rights Act (*Förmånsrättslagen (1973:1152)*), are considered 'creditors' for this purpose. However, as from 8 October 2005, employees will be entitled to receive guaranteed salary ('*lönegaranti*') in the Member State where they are employed in accordance with an amendment to Directive 80/987/EEC by Directive 2002/74/EC of 23 September 2002. Once this right has been transposed into Swedish law, the legislature intends to exclude employees from the definition of creditors, as is currently the case for mergers in Sweden (Prop. 2003/04:112, 60).

[13] Special rules apply to the transfer of the registered office of an SE that conducts banking or insurance business or certain other financial services. If such an SE wishes to transfer its registered office from Sweden to another Member State, it must, in accordance with the Banking and Financial Services Act (Chap. 10, Secs. 33–35 and Chap. 11, Sec. 1) and the Insurance Business Act (Chap. 1a), apply to the FSA or, if the matter is of particular interest, the Swedish government. The creditors of the SE are not notified. Rather, the FSA shall verify (i) whether the SE's creditors have received satisfactory security, to the extent such protection is necessary taking into account the SE's financial position, and (ii) whether the SE's finances in other respects are such that the transfer is compatible with the interests of depositors/policy holders and other creditors. The SE must also apply in advance for a permit to conduct the business in question in the new Member State. Likewise, an SE with its registered office in another Member State engaged in banking or insurance business, or any other business requiring authorisation,

9. An SE must apply to the Companies Registration Office for approval of the decision to transfer its registered office. The application must be submitted within one month following approval of the transfer proposal by the general meeting (Sec. 11 SE Act). The Companies Registration Office will then request the SE's creditors to notify it in writing within a specified period of time if they oppose the transfer. The notice shall be published in the official gazette (Sec. 12 SE Act).[14] If a creditor expresses its opposition to the transfer within the specified time limit, the matter shall be referred to the district court of the place where the SE's registered office is located.[15] If no creditor opposes the transfer, it shall be approved (Sec. 13 SE Act). If a matter regarding the transfer of an SE's registered office has been referred to the district court, the transfer will only be approved if the SE can demonstrate that those creditors who oppose the transfer have received full payment or satisfactory security for claims that arose prior to expiry of the time period specified by the Companies Registration Office.[16] Otherwise, the court shall not allow the transfer to go through (Sec. 14 SE Act).

The Companies Registration Office will issue a certificate attesting to the completion of the requisite pre-transfer acts and formalities once the transfer has been approved and this decision has attained force of law (Sec. 15 SE Act; Art. 8(8) Reg.). An SE cannot be registered in another Member State until this certificate has been submitted and evidence provided that the formalities required for registration in that Member State have been completed (Art. 8(9) Reg.). The transfer of an SE's registered office and the subsequent amendment to its articles shall take effect on the date the SE is recorded in the new register (Art. 8(10) Reg.). For a description of the registration process, please refer to Chap. 2, no. 84 of this book. A notice of the transfer must also be published in the *Official Journal of the European Communities* (Art. 14(2) Reg.). With respect to the effects of a transfer on third parties, please refer to Chap. 2, no. 86 of this book.

10. An SE subject to proceedings for winding up, liquidation, insolvency, cessation of payments or other similar proceedings may not transfer its registered office (Art. 8(15) Reg.).[17] As regards any cause of action that arose prior to the transfer, an SE will be considered as having its registered office in the Member

---

that wishes to transfer its registered office to Sweden must apply for a permit to conduct the business in question prior to the transfer (Prop. 2003/04:112, 65–67).

[14] The Companies Registration Office will also forward the notice to the Swedish tax authorities and to the debt enforcement authority ('*Kronofogdemyndigheten*') of the county where the SE's registered office is located.

[15] Only creditors whose claims arose prior to expiry of the specified period may oppose the transfer (Prop. 2003/04:112, 126).

[16] Creditors bear the burden of proving that a claim has arisen, while the SE must prove that a claim has been settled or satisfactory security provided (Prop. 2003/04:112, 126).

[17] The Swedish translation of Article 8(15) of the Regulation states that a company that has been subject to proceedings for winding up, liquidation, insolvency or cessation of payments or

State where it was registered when the claim arose (Art. 8(16) Reg.). This shall be the case even if the SE is sued after the transfer takes effect. See also Chap. 2, no. 86 of this book in this respect.

The FSA will be able to oppose the transfer of the registered office of an SE subject to its supervision. In order to ensure effective tax control, the Swedish tax authorities will also be able to object to the transfer of an SE's registered office.[18]

D   Corporate purpose

11. The Swedish rules on corporate purpose apply equally to SEs. This implies that an SE's corporate purpose should be clearly defined and that an SE may only engage in acts that fall within or are incidental to its corporate purpose as set forth in its articles of association. However, an SE can act contrary to its corporate purpose if all shareholders so agree.[19]

E   Capital

(i) **General remarks**

12. The share capital of an SE registered in Sweden shall be expressed in euros (Art. 4(1) Reg.). The share capital of an SE may not be expressed in SEK.[20] An SE must have share capital of at least €120,000 (Art. 4(2) Reg.). The capital is represented by shares (Art. 1(2) Reg.). The nominal value of the shares shall also be expressed in euros (Chap. 1, Sec. 3(5) Companies Act).

2   Different means of formation

A   Formation by merger

(i) **Procedure and publication requirements**

13. A Swedish public limited-liability company can participate in the formation of an SE by merger with public limited-liability companies from other Member States even if its accounts are not denominated in euros or if the resulting SE will have its registered office in a Member State other than Sweden (Sec. 5 SE Act). The merger can be organised as either an acquisition or as the formation of a new company (Art. 17 Reg.). For a description of these two methods,

---

    other similar proceedings may not transfer its registered office. The Swedish government has initiated proceedings to correct the Swedish translation in order to clarify that only a company subject to *ongoing* proceedings of this kind may not transfer its registered office (Prop. 2003/04:112, 58).

[18] No such rules are currently in force. However, the Swedish legislature is expected to draft rules in this respect (Prop. 2003/04:112, 70-73).

[19] Rodhe, K. 'Aktiebolagsrätt', *Nordstedts Juridik* AB, 2002, 243.

[20] Prop. 2003/04:112, 110-111.

please refer to Chap. 2, no. 23 of this book. In Sweden, the consideration to be paid in a merger may take the form of cash (Chap. 14, Sec. 1(1) Companies Act).

The formation of an SE by merger is initiated by the board of directors or (with respect to the two-tier system) the management board of each merging company, which prepares draft terms of merger (Art. 20 Reg.).[21] For the content of these terms, please refer to Chap. 2, no. 25 of this book. The board of directors or the management board of each merging company also prepares a detailed report explaining the legal and economic grounds for the merger, in particular how the consideration has been determined and any special valuation difficulties that may have arisen in connection with preparation of the draft terms (Chap. 14, Sec. 6 Companies Act). The annual accounts of each merging company for the past three financial years must be enclosed with the draft terms. If the last annual accounts of a merging company relate to a financial year that ended more than six months prior to the date of the draft terms of merger, that company must prepare an accounting statement to reflect its financial situation no earlier than the first day of the third month preceding the date of the draft terms (Chap. 14, Sec. 4, last paragraph, Companies Act).[22]

It should also be noted that for mergers between listed companies the Swedish Securities Council (i.e. the regulatory body responsible for overseeing good practice on the Swedish stock market) sets certain requirements with respect to (i) how consideration in a merger should be determined in order for the valuation to be deemed objective and (ii) the information that must be provided to shareholders in the draft terms of merger.[23]

14. The draft terms of merger must be examined by one or more auditors.[24] The auditors shall prepare a report on the draft terms of each merging company[25]

---

[21] With respect to companies engaged in banking or insurance business or certain other financial services, special rules apply to the formation of an SE by merger (see Chap. 15a of the Insurance Business Act and Chap. 10, Secs. 20–27 and 31 and Chap. 11, Sec. 1 of the Banking and Financial Services Act).

[22] If an SE formed by merger will have its registered office outside Sweden, the participating Swedish company will be required to prepare a special accounting statement. The Swedish legislature is expected to adopt rules in this respect (Prop. 2003/04:112, 110).

[23] Statements 2004:02 and 2005:02 of the Swedish Securities Council.

[24] According to Chapter 14, Section 7(4) of the Companies Act, the draft terms of merger must be examined by one or more auditors appointed by the general meeting of the participating Swedish company or, if no such appointment is made, by the participating Swedish company's auditors. Alternatively, one or more independent experts appointed at the joint request of the companies by a judicial or administrative authority in the Member State of one of them or of the proposed SE may examine the draft terms and prepare a single report for all shareholders (Art. 22(1) Reg.).

[25] The statement must, among other things, indicate whether the consideration to be paid in the merger and the principles for its distribution have been determined in an objective and fair

and are entitled to request from each merging company any information they consider necessary to enable them to perform their duties (Art. 22(2) Reg.). The auditors' report must be appended to the draft terms of merger (Chap. 14, Sec. 7 Companies Act).

Within one month following preparation of the draft terms of merger, the participating Swedish company must file them with the Companies Registration Office. A notice of the registration, including certain information about the merger and the merging companies (see Chap. 2, no. 28 of this book), must also be published in the official gazette by the Companies Registration Office without delay (Chap. 14, Secs. 9 Companies Act; Art. 21 Reg.).[26] The draft terms shall be submitted to the general meeting of each merging company for approval (Art. 23(1) Reg.). The general meeting may be held at the earliest one month following publication of the notice in the official gazette.[27] With respect to a participating Swedish company, the draft terms of merger must usually be approved by two-thirds of the votes cast and shares represented at a general meeting. The Swedish legislature has not adopted the option contained in Article 24(2) of the Regulation to enact further protection for minority shareholders that oppose a merger.[28] The draft terms must be approved in their entirety or the merger cannot go through (Chap. 14, Secs. 10–11 Companies Act).

Following approval of the draft terms of merger, the participating Swedish company must notify its known creditors in writing.[29] The notice must mention that the company intends to apply for an authorisation to execute the draft terms of merger, as well as information regarding creditors' right to oppose the merger. If the participating Swedish company is the acquiring company, its creditors need not be notified of the merger if the auditors stated in their report that they are of the opinion that the merger will not pose any risk to the company's creditors (Chap. 14, Sec. 13 Companies Act).

15. The participating Swedish company must apply for an authorisation to execute the draft terms of merger with the Companies Registration Office within one month following approval of the terms by the merging companies and in any

manner. The statement must also set forth the method(s) used to value the companies' assets and liabilities, the results of these valuation methods, and the appropriateness of each method and its significance in the overall appraisal of each company. Any special valuation difficulties should also be mentioned.

[26] If the draft terms of merger are not published in their entirety, the notice must state where they are available for inspection.

[27] Before the general meeting can vote on the merger, the draft terms of merger must be made available to shareholders for inspection at least one month following publication of the notice in the official gazette and a copy should be promptly sent to any shareholder who so requests free of charge.

[28] Prop. 2003/04:112, 78–80.

[29] It is not necessary to notify creditors with claims for wages and other forms of compensation or pension benefits, all of which have priority pursuant to the Priority Rights Act.

event no later than two years following publication of the notice of registration in the official gazette (Chap. 14, Sec. 14 Companies Act). If the Companies Registration Office determines that there are no obstacles to approving the application, it shall notify the participating Swedish company's creditors.[30] If the participating Swedish company is the acquiring company, the Companies Registration Office need not notify its creditors if the auditors stated in their report on the draft terms that they are of the opinion that the merger will not pose any risk to these creditors. The notice to creditors must mention that anyone who opposes the merger must file a written objection by a specified date or will be deemed to have consented. The Companies Registration Office shall cause this notice to be published promptly in the official gazette (Chap. 14, Sec. 16 Companies Act).[31]

If a creditor who has been notified of a proposed merger files an objection to the merger within the specified period of time, the Companies Registration Office shall refer the matter to the district court of the county where the participating Swedish company's registered office is located. If there are no objections to an application, the Companies Registration Office shall authorise the company to carry out the merger (Chap. 14, Sec. 17 Companies Act). Where a matter regarding authorisation of a merger has been referred to the courts, the authorisation shall be granted if it is demonstrated that those creditors who objected to the merger have received full payment or satisfactory security for their claims. Otherwise, the application shall be rejected (Chap. 14, Sec. 18 Companies Act).

Pursuant to Article 25(2) of the Regulation, the Companies Registration Office shall issue a certificate conclusively attesting to the completion of all pre-merger acts and formalities once it has authorised the participating Swedish company to carry out the merger and the decision has attained force of law (Sec. 6 SE Act).

If the proposed registered office of an SE is to be located in a Member State other than Sweden, the participating Swedish company shall submit the aforementioned certificate to the competent authority in that Member State, which shall then proceed to scrutinise the legality of the merger as regards the part of the procedure concerning completion of the merger and formation of the SE (Art. 26 Reg.).

If the proposed registered office of an SE is to be located in Sweden, the board of directors of the participating Swedish company must file an application to register the merger with the Companies Registration Office within two months

---

[30] The Companies Registration Office shall not notify creditors with claims for wages and other forms of compensation or pension benefits, all of which have priority pursuant to the Priority Rights Act.

[31] The Companies Registration Office shall also notify the debt enforcement authority in the county where the company's registered office is located.

once the authorisation to execute the merger has attained force of law. The application shall include a statement from an auditor that the acquired company's assets have been transferred to the acquiring company (Chap. 14, Sec. 19 Companies Act; Art. 26(1) Reg.). Each participating company (apart from the Swedish company) must provide the Companies Registration Office with a certificate issued by the competent authority in its Member State attesting to the completion of all pre-merger acts and formalities (Art. 26(2) Reg.).[32] The merger and simultaneous formation of the SE shall take effect upon recordation of the SE in the SE register (Arts. 27(1) and 12 Reg.; see also Section 3.4 *Registration and publication*). With respect to the consequences upon completion of a merger (by acquisition or by formation of a new company), see Chap. 2, nos. 32 and 33 of this book.

(ii) **Right to object to a company participating in a merger**
16. It will be possible for the FSA to oppose participation by companies subject to its supervision in the formation of an SE by merger. In order to ensure effective tax control, it will also be possible for the national tax authorities to object to participation by a given company in the formation of an SE by merger.[33]

(iii) **Minority shareholders**
17. The Member States are free to adopt appropriate provisions to protect minority shareholders who oppose the formation of an SE by merger. Sweden has not adopted any specific rules in this respect.

Swedish law does not provide for a procedure to scrutinise and amend the share-exchange ratio or proceedings to compensate minority shareholders. If the laws of the Member States of the other merging companies contain such provisions, these provisions shall apply only if expressly approved by the shareholders of the participating Swedish company along with the draft terms of merger (Art. 25(3) Reg.).

(iv) **Rights of creditors**
18. This discussed in no. 15 of this report.

(v) **Acquisition of a wholly owned subsidiary**
19. The acquisition by a parent company of a wholly owned subsidiary in Sweden is subject to a simplified merger procedure (Chap. 14, Secs. 22–29 Companies Act; Art. 31(1) Reg.).[34] For example, it is not necessary to submit the draft terms of merger to the subsidiary's general meeting for approval.

---

[32] Sec. 5, last paragraph, Swedish SE Regulation.
[33] No such rules are yet in force, although the Swedish government is expected to prepare rules in this respect (Prop. 2003/04:112, 76–78).
[34] There is no simplified procedure in Sweden where a parent company holds at least 90% but less than 100% of the shares in a subsidiary (Prop. 2003/04:112, 80).

Furthermore, since no consideration changes hands in this type of merger, there is no need for an auditors' report on the consideration and the principles for its distribution. Finally, the subsidiary is dissolved once the Companies Registration Office approves the application to execute the terms of merger, so a separate application to register the merger is not required.

(vi) **Avoidance of a merger**

20. The Companies Act does not contain any provisions for the courts to declare a merger null and void. Once it has been recorded by the Companies Registration Office, the merger and simultaneous formation of an SE are effective and cannot be avoided (see also Art. 30 Reg.).

B Formation of a holding SE

(i) **Procedure and publication requirements**

21. Swedish public or private limited-liability companies may participate in the formation of a holding SE, in which case shareholders of the participating companies contribute their shares to the SE in exchange for shares in the latter and the SE becomes the parent company of the participating companies.

The formation of a holding SE is initiated by the board of directors or, with respect to the two-tier system, the management board of each participating company, which prepares draft terms of formation (Art. 32(2) Reg.). For the content of these draft terms, see Chap. 2, no. 37 of this book. A report by an independent expert must be commissioned in which the expert gives an opinion on the draft terms to shareholders. For the content of such a report, see Chap. 2, no. 38 of this book. The shares contributed by the shareholders of each participating company must represent more than 50% of the voting rights.

The draft terms of formation for the holding SE must be submitted to the Companies Registration Office for recordation and published no later than one month prior to the general meeting of the participating Swedish company scheduled to vote on formation of the holding SE (Sec. 8 SE Act; Art. 32(3) Reg.). The Companies Registration Office shall publish a notice of registration without delay (Sec. 8 SE Act).[35]

The draft terms of formation must be approved by the general meeting of the participating Swedish company by a simple majority of votes cast. The Swedish legislature has not adopted the option contained in Article 34 of the Regulation to enact further protection for minority shareholders that oppose the formation of a holding SE.[36] The shareholders of the participating companies shall have a period of three months in which to decide whether to contribute

---

[35] If the draft terms of formation are not published in their entirety, the notice must mention where they are available for inspection.
[36] Prop. 2003/04:112, 81–82.

their shares to the holding SE (Art. 33(1) Reg.). If the conditions for formation of the holding SE are fulfilled, the participating Swedish company shall inform the Companies Registration Office accordingly (Art. 33(3) Reg.; Sec. 8 SE Act). The Companies Registration Office will publish the notice of registration without delay (Sec. 8 SE Act). Shareholders who have not indicated whether they intend to contribute their shares shall have an additional month in which to decide (Art. 33(3) Reg.).

Shareholders that contribute their shares to a holding SE shall receive shares in the latter (Art. 33(4) Reg.).[37] A holding SE shall be registered in the Member State where its registered office is located (see Section 3.4 *Registration and publication*).

(ii) **Minority shareholders**

22. Sweden has not enacted specific provisions to protect minority shareholders who oppose the formation of a holding SE.

C   Formation of a subsidiary SE

23. The rules on formation of a Swedish limited-liability company apply to the formation of a subsidiary SE with its registered office in Sweden. The Companies Act permits the shares in a subsidiary SE to be held by a sole shareholder.

D   Conversion into an SE

24. A Swedish public limited-liability company may be converted into an SE (Art. 2(4) Reg.). The conversion of a public limited-liability company into an SE will not result in the dissolution of the company or in the creation of a new legal person (Art. 37(2) Reg.).

The process to convert a Swedish limited-liability company into an SE is initiated by its board of directors, which prepares draft terms of conversion and a report explaining and justifying the legal and economic consequences of the conversion and the implications for shareholders and employees (Art. 37(4) Reg.).

The draft terms of conversion must be submitted to the Companies Registration Office for recordation. The Companies Registration Office shall publish a notice of registration without delay (Sec. 8 SE Act).[38] The draft terms of

---

[37] If the participating Swedish companies are banks, insurance companies or certain other financial institutions, the holding SE must apply to the FSA for approval to acquire their shares (see e.g., Chap. 3, Arts 2–2a of the Insurance Business Act and Chap. 14 of the Banking and Financial Services Act).

[38] If the draft terms of conversion are not published in their entirety, the notice must state where they are available for inspection.

conversion must be published at least one month prior to the general meeting scheduled to vote on the conversion (Art. 37(5) Reg.). The draft terms must be reviewed by independent experts who shall certify that the company has net assets at least equivalent to its capital plus non-distributable reserves (Art. 37(6) Reg.).

The conversion, which also requires an amendment to the company's articles, must be approved by two-thirds of the votes cast and shares represented at a general meeting. The Swedish legislature has not adopted the option contained in Article 37(8) of the Regulation to condition a conversion on a favourable vote of a qualified majority or unanimity in the organ within which employee participation is organised (i.e. the board of directors).[39] The resolution to convert the company into an SE together with the new articles of association must be recorded with the Companies Registration Office. Upon registration, the company is effectively converted into an SE (see Part III, Section 4 of this report).

A company may not transfer its registered office to another Member State while undergoing a conversion into an SE (Art. 37(3) Reg.).

An SE may be converted into a public limited-liability company governed by the laws of the Member State in which its registered office is situated. For further information in this respect, please refer to Chap. 2, no. 90 of this book.

3 Acts committed on behalf of an SE in formation

25. If acts have been performed in the name of an SE prior to its registration and the SE does not assume the obligations arising out of such acts afterwards, the legal entities that performed the acts shall be jointly and severally liable for them, without limitation, in the absence of an agreement to the contrary (Art. 16(2) Reg.). For further information in this respect, please refer to Chap. 2, no. 55 of this book.

4 Registration and publication

26. An SE with its registered office in Sweden will be recorded in an SE register (the 'SE register') and will be provided with a company identification number.[40] The SE register is kept by the Companies Registration Office (Sec. 7 SE Act). Registration is required for a newly formed SE to acquire legal personality (Art. 16(1) Reg.) and in order to complete a merger or a conversion into an SE. An

---

[39] Prop. 2003/04: 112, 82–83.
[40] There are no uniform rules in the European Union with regard to company identification numbers. Therefore, an SE that transfers its registered office from Sweden to another Member State will normally have to change its company number (Prop. 2003/04:112, 105).

SE only exists once it has been registered. The date of registration is therefore the date of formation of an SE.

An SE may not be registered unless and until the requirements of the Directive have been fulfilled (Art. 12(2) Reg.; see also Part V of this report). The Companies Registration Office shall verify that the requirements of the Regulation are satisfied and that the SE has complied with the rules of national law applicable to public limited-liability companies and shall publish a notice of registration (Chap. 18, Sec. 2 Companies Act).[41] Any registration of an SE or deletion of a registration shall be published in the *Official Journal* (Art. 14 Reg.).

Furthermore, the board of directors or (with respect to the two-tier system) the management board shall notify the Companies Registration Office of, among other things, the appointment of new directors, deputy directors and auditors; the election of a new chairman and managing director; who is authorised to sign for an SE; and any amendments to an SE's articles or changes to its share capital.[42] This information must also be published in the official gazette.

5 Acquisition of legal personality

27. An SE formed as a holding SE, a subsidiary SE or by merger through formation of a new company and with its a registered office in Sweden acquires legal personality upon recordation in the SE register (Art. 16(1) Reg.). An SE formed by conversion of a public limited-liability company officially becomes an SE upon recordation in the SE register but remains the same legal person (Art. 37(2) Reg.). The same should also hold true with respect to an SE formed by a merger through acquisition.

IV Organisation and management

1 General remarks

28. The organisation of an SE largely complies with existing Swedish rules applicable to public limited-liability companies. In Sweden, the decision-making power in a public limited-liability company is divided between the general meeting of shareholders and the board of directors. Prior to implementation of the Regulation, Sweden recognised only a one-tier system of management. However, since the Regulation allows an SE to choose between a two-tier and a one-tier management structure (Art. 38(b) Reg.), the Swedish legislature introduced new rules in the SE Act to accommodate two-tier SEs.

---

[41] Prop. 2003/04:112, 105.   [42] See Chap. 8, Sec. 36 Companies Act.

2 General meeting

A Decision-making process

29. An annual general meeting must be held within six months following the close of an SE's financial year.[43] The annual general meeting must pass certain resolutions, in particular with respect to approval of an SE's annual accounts, disposition of its profit or losses, and the discharge from liability of members of its board of directors or (with respect to a two-tier SE) management board[44] and managing directors (Chap. 9, Sec. 7 Companies Act). An extraordinary general meeting may be held whenever the board of directors, management board or supervisory board sees fit. Such a meeting must be held when so requested for a specified purpose by an auditor or the holders of at least 10% of the SE's share capital (Arts. 54(2) and 55(1) Reg. and Chap. 9, Sec. 8 Companies Act).[45]

Any shareholder in an SE has a right to request that one or more items be placed on the agenda at a general meeting. The request must be made in writing to the board of directors or (with respect to a two-tier SE) the management board. An item shall be added to the agenda provided the request is received by the board of directors or the management board (i) no later than one week prior to the earliest date on which the notice of the general meeting may be sent (i.e. six weeks with respect to an annual general meeting and two weeks with respect to an extraordinary general meeting) or (ii) after the time specified above but in time for the item to be included in the notice of the general meeting (Sec. 27 SE Act).

Resolutions at a general meeting are normally passed by a simple majority of votes cast and, in the event of a tie, the chair casts the deciding vote. A shareholder may vote all shares held, unless the articles of association provide otherwise. However, in order to protect minority shareholders, certain resolutions, such as amendments to an SE's articles, must normally be approved by two-thirds of the votes cast and shares represented at a general meeting; a greater majority may be required for certain substantive amendments (Chap. 9, Secs. 5, 28–33 Companies Act). The articles may also stipulate a larger majority or increase the quorum required by law with respect to certain or all decisions.

---

[43] The first general meeting may be held at any time during the first 18 months following incorporation of an SE (Chap. 3, Sec. 3 Bookkeeping Act (*Bokföringslag 1999:1078*)).
[44] The supervisory board is not subject to oversight by the SE's auditor and therefore is not released from liability by the general meeting (Prop. 2004/04:112, 92–93).
[45] If a general meeting is not convened in accordance with the requirements of law or the company's articles of association, the County Administrative Board (*Länsstyrelsen*) of the place where the SE's registered office is located shall immediately convene a general meeting at the request of any shareholder (Sec. 28 SE Act).

B   Rights and obligations of shareholders

30. In principle, the majority of shareholders control an SE. However, the Companies Act contains several provisions to protect minority shareholders. For example, shareholders holding less than 10% of the shares and voting rights of an SE have the right to have their shares redeemed by the parent company, and shareholders holding 10% or more of the shares in an SE have the right to request dividend distributions and the appointment of a special assessor or additional auditor to examine the company's management and accounts.

Shareholders also have a general obligation to treat one another fairly and equally. For example, the general meeting may not pass resolutions liable to give an unfair advantage to a particular shareholder or to another party to the detriment of the SE or other shareholders (Chap. 9, Sec. 37 Companies Act). Violation of this rule or any other provisions of the Companies Act, the Annual Accounts Act or the company's articles of association may result in liability for damages or an obligation to redeem the shares of the injured shareholders (Chap. 15, Secs. 3–4 Companies Act). Furthermore, any shareholder, irrespective of the number of shares held, may challenge in court resolutions taken by the general meeting (Chap. 9, Sec. 39 Companies Act).

3   Management and supervision

A   Two-tier system/one-tier system

(i) General remarks

31. The founders of an SE must select either a one-tier or a two-tier system of management. In the former, management is entrusted to a board of directors. In the two-tier system, management is entrusted to a management board, which is overseen by a supervisory board.

Legal entities may not serve as members of the board of directors, the management board or the supervisory board (Chap. 8, Sec. 9 Companies Act).

(ii) One-tier system

32. In an SE with a one-tier system, the board of directors is responsible for managing the company. The board of directors is supervised by the general meeting. The rules contained in the Companies Act and other national legislation applicable to boards of directors shall apply to the board of directors of an SE, unless the Regulation provides otherwise.[46] The board of directors must have at least three members (Sec. 23 SE Act).

---

[46] The Swedish law on employee representation on boards shall not apply to the board of directors of an SE. Rather, the law on employee involvement in an SE is applicable (Sec. 22 SE Act).

(iii) **Two-tier system**

33. The management board shall consist of at least three members (Sec. 23 SE Act). The supervisory board shall have at least five members (Sec. 23 SE Act). No person may sit simultaneously on both the management board and the supervisory board. However, the supervisory board may nominate one of its members to sit on the management board in the event of a vacancy on the latter body. During this period of time, which may not exceed two months, the duties of that member on the supervisory board shall be suspended (Sec. 19 SE Act; Art. 39(3) Reg.).

The management board is responsible for managing the company (Art. 39(1) Reg.) and is overseen by a supervisory board, which does not have any managerial authority (Art. 40(1) Reg.). The supervisory board may in certain cases convene the general meeting (Art. 54(2) Reg.). The supervisory board also directly oversees the managing directors (Sec. 25 SE Act).

With respect to the management board, the rules contained in the Companies Act regarding boards of directors shall apply unless the Regulation provides otherwise (Sec. 16(2) SE Act).[47] Certain provisions shall also apply to members of the supervisory board, such as those regarding (i) residence requirements and disqualification, (ii) conflicts of interest, (iii) minutes of meetings, (iv) the prohibition on extending financial assistance, and (v) liability for damages. A full list of the provisions of the Companies Act applicable to members of an SE's supervisory board can be found in Section 16(3) of the SE Act.[48]

34. For the quorum and decision-making rules applicable to the supervisory and management boards, please refer to Chap. 2, no. 68 of this book. Sweden has not adopted the option contained in Article 50(3) of the Regulation to make the supervisory board's quorum and decision-making subject to the rules applicable to national public limited-liability companies.

The supervisory board can make certain categories of decisions taken by the management board or the managing director subject to its approval. The supervisory board shall submit any such resolutions to the Companies Registration Office for recordation. The decision enters into effect upon recordation (Sec. 17(1) SE Act). An SE's articles may also provide that certain categories of decisions require the approval of the supervisory board.[49] The rights of the

---

[47] The Swedish law on employee representation on boards shall not apply to the management board of an SE. Rather, the Swedish law on employee involvement in an SE is applicable (Sec. 16(2) SE Act).

[48] With respect to an SE that conducts insurance business, the provisions of the Insurance Business Act with respect to boards of directors and their members shall apply to the supervisory board and its members. With respect to an SE engaged in insurance business, banking or certain other financial services that require authorisation, specific provisions with respect to boards of directors and their members shall apply to the supervisory board and its members, such as those regarding the qualifications and remuneration of officers and directors (Prop. 2003/04:112, 95).

[49] Prop. 2003/04:112, 90–91.

supervisory board may not be used to alter the separation of powers between the management board and the supervisory board. Examples of decisions that may require the authorisation of the supervisory board are a decision to sell shares in a subsidiary or to spin off or close down a certain business.[50]

35. Each member of the supervisory board may request from the management board and the managing director any information necessary to properly oversee them pursuant to Article 40(1) of the Regulation (Secs. 20 and 25 SE Act).

B   Appointment and removal

36. Members of the board of directors are appointed by the general meeting for a period stated in the company's articles of association, which may not exceed six years (Arts. 43(3) and 46(1) Reg.). They can be reappointed one or more times, unless the articles provide otherwise (Art. 46(2) Reg.). An SE's articles may stipulate that less than half the members of its board of directors can be appointed by means of an alternate procedure. The right to elect a member of the board of directors cannot be delegated to the board itself or to its members (Chap. 8, Sec. 6 Companies Act). Members of the board of directors can be removed prior to expiry of their term of office by the general meeting (or other body that appointed the member in question) (Chap. 8, Sec. 11 Companies Act).

37. Members of the supervisory board are appointed by the general meeting for a period stated in the articles of association, which may not exceed six years (Arts. 40(2) and 46(1) Reg.). They can be reappointed one or more times, unless the articles provide otherwise (Art. 46(2) Reg.). Members of the management board are appointed by the supervisory board for a period stated in the articles of association, which may not exceed six years (Arts. 39(2) and 46(1) Reg.). They can be reappointed one or more times, unless the articles provide otherwise (Art. 46(2) Reg.). Members of the management board can be removed prior to expiry of their term of office by the supervisory board or other body which appointed them (Chap. 8, Sec. 11 Companies Act).

C   Managing director

38. An SE shall have a managing director responsible for the day-to-day running of the company as in a Swedish public limited-liability company (Sec. 24(1) SE Act). The provisions of the Companies Act regarding the managing directors of Swedish public limited-liability companies shall also apply to the managing director of an SE.[51] The managing director must be a resident of the EEA (Chap. 8, Sec. 26 Companies Act).

In a two-tier SE, the managing director is appointed by the management board and may not be a member of the supervisory board (Sec. 24(2) SE Act). The

[50] *Ibid.*, 130.   [51] *Ibid.*, 133.

managing director shall be subject to oversight by both the management board and the supervisory board (Sec. 25(1) SE Act). In a one-tier SE, the managing director shall be appointed and supervised by the board of directors (Secs. 24(3) and 26 SE Act).

D Representation

39. The board of directors or (in a two-tier SE) the management board represents the SE and signs for it collectively (Sec. 16 SE Act; Chap. 8, Sec. 29 Companies Act). A managing director is always authorised to represent an SE and to sign on its behalf with regard to measures related to the day-to-day management of the company (Chap. 8, Sec. 30 Companies Act).

The board of directors or (in a two-tier SE) the management board may decide that the right to represent the SE and sign on its behalf can be exercised only by two or more persons acting jointly. No other limitations may be recorded by the Companies Registration Office (Chap. 8, Sec. 31 Companies Act). The board of directors or (in a two-tier SE) the management board may authorise one or more of its members, the managing director or another person to represent the SE and sign on its behalf, unless such delegation of authority is prohibited by the company's articles of association (Chap. 8, Sec. 31 Companies Act).

E Liability

40. Liability of members of the board of directors, the management board and the supervisory board is determined by the rules applicable to Swedish public limited-liability companies. Due to the supervisory board's special duties, the case law on liability for damages of directors of a Swedish limited-liability company is not applicable *per se* to its members.[52]

V Employee involvement

41. Sweden has transposed the Directive into national law by the Act on Employee Involvement in an SE (the 'Employee Involvement Act') (*Lag (2004:559) om arbetstagarinflytande i europabolag*). Activities of a religious, scientific, artistic or other not-for-profit character, activities with co-operative, political or other opinion-shaping aims and union-related activities are excluded from the scope of the Act.[53] Sweden has not adopted the option contained in Article 13(4) of the Directive, which allows the Member States to take measures to guarantee that employee representation structures in participating companies which will cease to exist as separate legal entities are maintained after registration of an SE.

[52] *Ibid.*, 129.   [53] Option for exemption derived from Article 8(3) of the Directive.

Since the provisions of the Employee Involvement Act are very similar to those of the Directive, the following section is limited to a discussion of aspects specific to Swedish law.

1 Formation of a special negotiating body

42. Seats on the special negotiating body (SNB) allocated to employees in Sweden shall be distributed among the participating companies and, provided seats are still available, to concerned subsidiaries and establishments with one seat each by decreasing order of the number of employees they employ until all seats are allocated. Local trade unions may, however, agree on a different allocation of seats. Such an agreement shall guarantee, insofar as possible, that employees in each participating company are allocated one seat (Secs. 11–12 Employee Involvement Act).

The Swedish members of the SNB shall be elected by local trade unions which are party to a collective bargaining agreement with a participating company, concerned subsidiary or establishment in Sweden. If only one member is to be elected and the local unions cannot reach agreement, the union that represents the most employees shall elect that member. If several members are to be elected, the selection shall be carried out in accordance with Section 8(2) and (3) of the Board Representation (Private Sector Employees) Act (*Lag (1987:1245) om styrelserepresentation för de privatanställda*), i.e. the two unions representing the most employees shall elect the members. If four members are to be elected, each union shall elect two; if five members are to be elected, the largest union shall elect three members and the second largest two, etc. If none of the participating companies, concerned subsidiaries or establishments in Sweden is party to a collective bargaining agreement, the Swedish members shall be elected by the local trade union that represents the most employees, unless the unions agree otherwise (Secs. 16–17 Employee Involvement Act).

Sweden has not adopted the option contained in Article 3(2)(b) of the Directive, which provides that trade unions representatives can serve as SNB members regardless of whether they are employees of a participating company, concerned subsidiary or establishment.[54] Nor does the Employee Involvement Act contain budgetary rules regarding the operation of the SNB or a limitation on funding to cover one expert only (Art. 3(7) Dir.).[55]

2 Standard rules

43. Sweden has not adopted the option to exempt application of the standard rules when an SE is formed by merger.[56]

---

[54] Prop. 2003/2004:122, 50.
[55] Prop. 2003/2004:122, 59–60.
[56] Prop. 2003/2004:122, 65.

3 Employee participation on the board of directors or supervisory board

44. If the SNB does not take a decision as to which form of employee participation within the various participating companies shall continue in the SE and there is more than one form of participation in the various participating companies, the latter shall decide which form of participation to apply to the SE (Secs. 33 and 35 Employee Involvement Act; Art. 7(3) Dir.).[57]

Seats on the board of directors or (with respect to a two-tier SE) the supervisory board allocated to Swedish employee representatives shall be filled by the local trade unions following the same procedure as applicable to Swedish members of the SNB.[58] The unions may, however, decide to transfer this right to the employee council (the employees' representative body established in accordance with the standard rules) (Sec. 59 Employee Involvement Act).

Even though employee representatives on the board of directors or supervisory board shall have the same rights and obligations as shareholder representatives, they may not participate in discussions regarding collective bargaining agreements or strikes or any other matters in which the employees or trade unions have a substantial interest contrary to the SE's. One employee representative may be present at and participate in discussions if a topic to be decided by an SE's board of directors or supervisory board at a later date has been prepared by members of the company's administrative or supervisory board or by officers especially appointed for this purpose (Secs. 62–63 Employee Involvement Act).

4 Protection of employee representatives; jurisdiction; confidentiality; damages

45. Employee representatives who usually perform their duties in Sweden are protected by Sections 3(1), 4 and 6 through 8 of the Trade Union Representatives (Status in the Workplace) Act (*Lag (1974:358) om facklig förtroendemans ställning på arbetsplatsen*). This means, among other things, that employee representatives may not be prevented from performing their duties or discriminated against as a result of their appointment and shall be entitled to time off to perform their duties whilst retaining all employment benefits. They shall also be given priority with regard to continued employment in the event of a shortage of work or redundancies if it is of special importance for their activities in the workplace. Any dismissal contrary to the foregoing shall be deemed invalid (Sec. 65 Employee Involvement Act). Claims regarding application of the Employee Involvement Act must be brought before the labour courts (Sec. 69 Employee Involvement Act).

The Employee Involvement Act does not stipulate specific cases in which the supervisory or administrative organ of an SE or of a participating company

---

[57] Prop. 2003/2004:122, 66.   [58] See no. 37 of this report.

is not obliged to transmit information (Art. 8(2) Dir.) as Swedish law already permits a refusal to inform and negotiate in certain exceptional cases.[59]

Violation of the Employee Involvement Act, an agreement concluded in accordance with this act or the duty of confidentiality shall result in liability for damages in accordance with selected provisions of the Employment (Codetermination in the Workplace) Act (*Lag (1976:580) om medbestämmande i arbetslivet*). No employee or trade union, however, shall be entitled to damages from another employee or union (Sec. 68 Employee Involvement Act).

VI Annual accounts and consolidated accounts

1 Accounting principles

46. An SE with its registered office in Sweden is required to prepare its annual accounts (and consolidated accounts, where applicable) in accordance with the Annual Accounts Act (*Årsredovisningslag (1995:1554*).[60] Accounting standards and interpretations thereof are promulgated by the Swedish Financial Accounting Standards Council. These guidelines are not legally binding but are highly authoritative nonetheless. As from 2005, listed SEs must prepare their annual accounts in accordance with International Financial Reporting Standards (IFRS). An SE must denominate its annual accounts (and consolidated accounts, where applicable) in euros.[61]

An SE's annual accounts must be prepared by its board of directors or, with respect to a two-tier SE, by its management board and approved by the general meeting of shareholders within six months following the close of its financial year (Chap. 9, Sec. 7 Companies Act). The accounts must be filed with the Companies Registration Office no later than seven months following the close of the financial year (Chap. 8, Sec. 6 Annual Accounts Act). Subject to certain exceptions, a parent company is required to prepare consolidated accounts for its group (Chap. 7, Secs. 1–2 Annual Accounts Act). Consolidated accounts must also be approved by the general meeting of shareholders (Chap. 9, Sec. 7 Companies Act).

47. In a two-tier SE, the supervisory board must submit an opinion on the annual accounts, as well as on the management board's and the managing director's administration, to the annual general meeting at which the SE's income statement and balance sheet will be adopted (Sec. 17(2) SE Act). The opinion must be submitted at least two weeks prior to the annual general

---

[59] Prop. 2003/2004:122, 85.
[60] Special accounting rules apply with respect to SEs that conduct banking or insurance business or that engage in certain other financial services (Art. 62 Reg.; Prop. 2003/04:112, 47).
[61] Prop. 2003/04:112, 110–111.

meeting and made available for shareholders to inspect at the SE's offices. A copy of the opinion must be sent immediately to any shareholder who so requests (Sec. 17(2) SE Act; Chap. 9, Sec. 16 Companies Act). It is not necessary to publish the opinion together with the annual accounts as the opinion constitutes an internal document whose purpose is to allow shareholders to form a basis for taking decisions in connection with the general meeting.[62]

2 Auditors

48. An SE must have at least one auditor and may appoint one or more deputy auditors (Chap. 10, Secs. 1–2 Companies Act). The auditors are elected by the general meeting for a term of four years (Chap. 10, Sec. 20 Companies Act).[63] Depending on the size of the SE and other factors, the auditor must normally be a certified public or chartered accountant (Chap. 10, Secs. 12–13 Companies Act). An accounting firm may serve as an SE's auditor (Chap. 10, Sec. 18 Companies Act).

An SE's auditor is, among other things, responsible for examining the annual accounts and the administration of the board of directors or, with respect to a two-tier SE, the management board and the managing director. If the SE is a parent company, the auditor shall also examine the consolidated accounts and the relationships between companies in the group. At the end of each financial year, the auditor shall submit an audit report to the SE's general meeting and, where applicable, a group audit report (Chap. 10, Secs. 3 and 5 Companies Act).

VII Supervision by the national authorities

49. The Companies Registration Office is the competent authority with respect to registration matters for SEs registered in Sweden. This office is also responsible for duties delegated by the Regulation to the 'competent authority in each Member State', which include matters pertaining to the transfer of an SE's registered office, the formation of an SE by merger and violations of Article 7 of the Regulation.[64] An SE registered in Sweden that conducts banking or insurance business or engages in certain other financial services is subject to supervision by the FSA.

---

[62] *Ibid.*, 89.
[63] Where several auditors are to be appointed, the articles of association may provide that one or more, but not all, may be appointed by an alternate procedure, i.e. other than by the general meeting (Chap. 10, Sec. 8 Companies Act).
[64] Prop. 2003/04:112, 104–105.

VIII Dissolution

1 Liquidation and winding up

50. The general meeting can resolve to place an SE in voluntary liquidation (winding up) by a simple majority of votes cast, unless the company's articles provide otherwise (Chap. 13, Secs. 1 and 6 Companies Act). In order to voluntarily liquidate, an SE must have sufficient assets to repay its debts and cover the costs of liquidation. The liquidation can take effect immediately or at a specified date (Chap. 13, Sec. 8 Companies Act).

Under Swedish law, a company may also be involuntarily liquidated pursuant to an order of the Companies Registration Office. The Companies Registration Office shall order an SE to liquidate where, for example, the company has failed to file the names of its directors etc. (appointed pursuant to the Companies Act) or its annual report and auditors' report within 11 months following the close of its financial year (Chap. 13, Sec. 10 Companies Act). Involuntary liquidation may also occur if an SE's equity falls below less than half its registered share capital (Chap. 13, Secs. 12–16 Companies Act) or at the request of shareholders holding more than 10% of the company's share capital if a shareholder abuses its influence over the SE in violation of the Companies Act, the Annual Accounts Act or the company's articles of association (Chap. 13, Sec. 20 Companies Act).[65]

2 Insolvency

51. An SE that is deemed insolvent can be declared bankrupt. A company shall be deemed insolvent if it is unable to pay its debts as they fall due and such inability is not merely temporary (Chap. 1, Sec. 2 Insolvency Act). Proceedings are commenced by filing a petition in bankruptcy with the relevant district court. Any creditor is entitled to do so, although it must prove to the court that the debtor is indeed insolvent. In addition, an SE can also petition the court to be declared bankrupt.

Once the district court has rendered an adjudication in bankruptcy, it shall appoint one or more trustees in bankruptcy to administer the bankruptcy estate. After having been declared bankrupt, a debtor has no authority to take any decisions or incur any commitments whatsoever.

Distribution of proceeds shall take place as soon as all available property has been realised. At that time, the trustee in bankruptcy shall draw up a distribution proposal to be ratified by the court. Thereafter, the proceedings shall be terminated. Upon distribution of the bankruptcy proceeds, the trustee shall render a final account.

---

[65] Rather than involuntary liquidation, the court may, at the company's request, order it to redeem the plaintiff's shares (Chap. 13, Sec. 21 Companies Act).

3   Cessation of payments

52. Cessation of payments is not regulated under Swedish law but rather is effected by notifying an SE's creditors. A cessation of payments may be followed by specific proceedings to reorganise an SE's business, such as restructuring in accordance with the Corporate Restructuring Act (*Lag (1996:764) om företagsrekonstruktion*), the purpose of which is to facilitate restructuring by companies that are estimated to have good business prospects even if they are not currently profitable.

IX   Applicable law

53. An SE with its registered office in Sweden is governed primarily by the Regulation and by its articles of association, where expressly authorised by the Regulation. For matters not addressed by the Regulation or addressed only in part, an SE is governed by the SE Act and the Swedish SE Regulation. For matters not regulated by the latter legislation, an SE is governed by the provisions of national law applicable to Swedish public limited-liability companies. Finally, an SE is governed by its articles of association in the same way as Swedish limited-liability companies (Art. 9(1) Reg.). An SE's articles of association may not conflict with the arrangements for employee involvement concluded pursuant to the Directive (Art. 12(4) Reg.). Specific provisions with respect to certain sectors (such as insurance, banking and certain other financial services) shall apply in full to an SE that conducts such business (Art. 9(3) Reg.).

X   Tax treatment

1   Income tax

54. Under Swedish law, an SE incorporated and having its registered office in Sweden shall be treated as a Swedish limited-liability company, while an SE registered outside Sweden shall be treated as a foreign company. An SE with its registered office in Sweden is taxed the same way as a Swedish limited-liability company. Consequently, an SE with its registered office in Sweden that conducts cross-border business through a permanent establishment (as opposed to a subsidiary) shall be taxed in Sweden on its worldwide income. Double taxation is generally avoided due to the application of tax treaties. An SE registered outside Sweden shall be taxed in Sweden on its income from business conducted in Sweden at a rate of 28%.

Shareholdings in an SE shall be treated the same way as shareholdings in national companies, so shares in an SE with its registered office in Sweden shall be treated as shares in a Swedish company while shares in an SE with its registered office outside Sweden shall be treated as shares in a foreign company.

2 Tax issues when forming an SE

55. As long as a permanent establishment or assets remain in Sweden, the formation of an SE will not normally have any adverse tax consequences in Sweden. If the assets are transferred out of Sweden, however, exit tax will generally be levied, i.e. the assets will be deemed to have been sold at their fair market value.

The formation of an SE may have tax consequences for shareholders resident in Sweden. However, since Sweden has transposed Council Directive 90/434/EEC of 23 July 1990 on the common system of taxation applicable to mergers, divisions, transfers of assets and exchanges of shares concerning companies of different Member States (the 'Merger Directive'), which will be amended to include SEs, any adverse tax consequences can usually be avoided under the directive's provisions on roll over relief or deferral of taxation on share exchanges.

A Formation by merger

56. Mergers between Swedish public limited-liability companies and public limited-liability companies from other Member States will not normally trigger any corporate tax liability in Sweden provided the rules on *qualifying mergers*[66] apply. If assets are transferred out of Sweden pursuant to a merger, however, exit tax will be levied, i.e., the assets will be deemed to have been sold at their fair market value. If the assets remain subject to tax in Sweden, i.e. in a Swedish permanent establishment, there is no exit tax.

Chapter 20a of the Income Tax Act governs the acquisition of assets and liabilities entering Sweden when a limited-liability company from another Member State is acquired by a Swedish limited-liability company. Normally, the acquiring company assumes the target company's acquisition costs. It should be noted that when a Swedish company acquires a company from another Member State, losses carried forward by the foreign company prior to the merger cannot be utilised in Sweden when aggregating the income from the permanent establishment.

The formation of an SE by merger entails tax consequences for shareholders. If the shareholders are Swedish residents, they shall be taxed as if they had sold their shares in the Swedish company for cash or exchanged them for shares in the SE. Since Sweden has transposed the Merger Directive, the adverse tax consequences of a share exchange can often be avoided under the directive's provisions on roll-over relief or deferral of taxation on share exchanges. Sweden does not impose withholding tax on Swedish shares exchanged for shares in another company pursuant to a merger, although it does levy withholding tax on any cash consideration received.

[66] See Chapter 37 of the Income Tax Act (*Inkomstskattelagen (1999:1229)*).

B   Formation of a holding SE

57. Formation of a holding SE does not trigger taxation of the Swedish public or private limited-liability companies whose shares are contributed to the SE.

The formation of a holding SE can have adverse tax consequences for shareholders. If the shareholders are residents of Sweden, they will be taxed as if they had sold their shares in the Swedish company for cash or exchanged them for shares in the SE. However, since Sweden has transposed the Merger Directive, the tax consequences of a share exchange can often be avoided under the directive's provisions on roll-over relief or deferral of taxation on share exchanges.

C   Formation of a subsidiary SE

58. No stamp duty or other transfer taxes will be levied on the establishment of a subsidiary SE in Sweden.

D   Conversion into an SE

59. When converting a Swedish limited-liability company into an SE or vice versa, the company undergoing conversion maintains its legal personality and, therefore, the conversion does not trigger any adverse tax consequences in Sweden.

E   Transfer of registered office and head office

60. An SE may transfer its registered office to another Member State while maintaining legal personality. Provided no assets are transferred out of Sweden, the transfer shall have no adverse tax consequences. However, it should be borne in mind that assets that are not tied to a business in Sweden shall be transferred from Sweden when the office is transferred and thus subject to exit tax. Shares in subsidiaries and any transfer of employees are not generally subject to tax in Sweden.

3   Value added tax

61. The formation of an SE, as such, is not subject to Swedish VAT. Operating a permanent establishment rather than a subsidiary may at present be favourable for VAT purposes for certain categories of companies, such as Swedish banks.

An SE will be subject to Swedish VAT at the same conditions as Swedish limited-liability companies.

4   Other taxes

61. Dividends distributed by an SE and capital gains arising from the sale of shares in an SE shall be subject to tax in Sweden (unless they are exempt under

the Swedish participation exemption rules).[67] Dividends distributed by an SE with its registered office in Sweden to shareholders that are not residents of Sweden shall be subject to withholding tax under the same conditions as shares in Swedish limited-liability companies. The same holds true for certain other payments made by an SE as a result of a share redemption, a reduction in its share capital or a share buy-back. The current rate of withholding tax is 30%. However, Swedish law provides that shares that would have been deemed held for business purposes had the owners been Swedish residents shall be exempt from withholding tax.[68] In addition, under most tax treaties, dividend withholding tax is reduced or eliminated altogether.

Pursuant to certain tax provisions (including applicable tax treaties), individual taxpayers who once resided in Sweden shall continue to be subject to tax in Sweden on any capital gains arising from the sale of shares and certain other securities in an SE with its registered office in Sweden for up to ten years after having left Sweden. However, if an SE transfers its registered office and permanent establishment out of Sweden, individuals holding shares in the SE shall be subject to tax on their capital gains for only five years following the transfer.

XI   Conclusion

62. In our opinion, the SE will be an interesting alternative for corporate groups with European-wide operations. Above all, we believe that for certain sectors the SE could be an interesting vehicle to streamline existing corporate groups, such as banks. The Nordic banking group Nordea has made public its intention to restructure under an SE with its registered office in Sweden as from 2006. In addition, Alfred Berg, a Nordic investment firm, has announced its intention to become an SE in September 2005, by turning its subsidiaries in Denmark, Finland and Norway into branches of an SE with its registered office in Sweden. Use of an SE could also be interesting for other sectors that wish to obtain a legal framework for their operations. We believe the SE will be an interesting and viable alternative in connection with cross-border acquisitions within the European Union, particularly cross-border mergers, at least until the Council

---

[67] Shares held for business purposes are exempt from tax.
[68] Unlisted shares are generally deemed to be held for business purposes if they constitute a capital asset for the holder. Shares in listed companies shall be deemed to be held for business purposes if, among other things, the shareholding is a capital asset for the holder and represents at least 10% of the voting rights in the company or is connected to the holding company's business (or the business of an affiliate). For dividends on listed shares to be tax exempt for Swedish resident shareholders, the shares must not be sold for one year following the date on which they were deemed to have been acquired for business purposes. For dividends on listed shares to be tax exempt for shareholders residing outside Sweden, the shares must have been held for at least one year at the time of the dividend distribution.

directive on cross-border mergers of public limited-liability companies is transposed into national law. Another advantage of the SE is that it can transfer its registered office from one Member State to another with relative ease.

In this context it should be mentioned that the Swedish legislature is currently investigating whether to introduce a right for shareholders in national mergers to have the share-exchange ratio scrutinised by an arbitral panel (similar to the compulsory redemption procedure in Sweden today) or to require a higher majority (i.e. more than two-thirds) to approve such a merger. In our opinion, such provisions could have a negative effect on Swedish business, although it is unlikely they will be extended to cover cross-border mergers used to form an SE in the absence of the express approval of the shareholders of the other participating companies (see also Art. 25(3) Reg.).

It should also be mentioned that an updated Companies Act is expected to enter into force on 1 January 2006. The proposal contains a complete linguistic and systematic modernisation of the current Companies Act, which dates back to the 1970s. Some noteworthy material changes in this respect are: (i) non-CSD companies may impose transfer restrictions on their shares by including a pre-emptive right, a right of first refusal or a consent clause in their articles of association (currently, only a pre-emptive right is permitted); (ii) greater possibilities for shareholders to participate in meetings at a distance; (iii) the introduction of a new instrument for restructuring, namely the demerger or split of one company into two or more new companies; and (iv) confirmation of the possibility to take decisions regarding dividend distributions at an extraordinary general meeting by a simple majority.

Another recent development in Sweden is the new corporate governance code (the 'Code'), which applies to companies listed on the Stockholm Stock Exchange, including SEs. Currently, the Code applies only to companies on the A list and to larger companies on the O list, which must implement its provisions as soon as possible after 1 July 2005, and in any event no later than their 2006 annual general meeting. In a few years' time, however, the Code is expected to apply to all companies listed on the Stockholm Stock Exchange.

17

United Kingdom

NIGEL BOARDMAN
Slaughter and May

I   Introduction   457
II   Formation   458
    1   General remarks   458
        A   Founding parties   458
        B   Name   458
        C   Registered office and transfer   458
            (i)   Registered office   458
            (ii)   Transfer   459
        D   Corporate purpose   461
        E   Capital   461
    2   Different means of formation   461
        A   General remarks   461
        B   Formation by merger   462
        C   Formation of a holding SE   464
        D   Formation of a subsidiary SE   465
        E   Conversion into an SE   465
    3   Acts committed on behalf of an SE in formation   466
    4   Registration and publication   467
    5   Acquisition of legal personality   467
III   Organisation and management   467
    1   General remarks   467
    2   Shareholders   468
        A   General meeting   468
            (i)   Decision-making process   468
        B   Rights and obligations of shareholders   469
    3   Management and supervision   469
        A   One-tier system/two-tier system   469
            (i)   General remarks   469
            (ii)   Supervisory organ: the two-tier system   470
        B   Appointment and removal   471
        C   Liability   472
IV   Employee involvement   472
    1   Special negotiating body ('SNB')   472
    2   Participation rights   473
    3   Protection of employee representatives   473
    4   Complaints procedure   473

         5 Information and confidentiality   474
         6 Exiting employee involvement rights   474
    V   Annual accounts and consolidated accounts   474
         1 Accounting principles   474
            A General remarks   474
            B Annual accounts   475
            C Consolidated accounts   475
         2 Auditors   476
    VI   Supervision by the national authorities   477
    VII Dissolution   477
         1 General remarks   477
         2 Composition with creditors   477
         3 Administration   477
         4 Administrative receivership   477
         5 Liquidation   478
            A Voluntary liquidation   478
            B Involuntary liquidation   478
    VIII Tax treatment   479
         1 Introduction   479
         2 Income tax   479
         3 Value added tax   480
         4 Other taxes   480
    IX   Recent developments regarding the implementation of
         Community Directives in the UK   481
    X   Conclusion   482

I **Introduction**

1. The Regulation and the Directive have been implemented in Great Britain partly by means of a new statutory instrument, the European Public Limited-Liability Company Regulations 2004 (the 'ECRs').[1] The ECRs are supplemented by the law applicable to public limited companies, found mainly in the Companies Act 1985 ('CA'), together with the Insolvency Act 1986 ('IA') and the common law.

This report focuses on implementation of the Regulation and transposition of the Directive in Great Britain, and in particular on the options provided in the Regulation which Great Britain has chosen to adopt. It should be noted that the ECRs and the CA apply only in Great Britain, while a separate consultation process has been carried out in Northern Ireland.

---

[1] Further information on the UK's views can be found in the consultative document published by the Department for Trade and Industry, Implementation of the European Company Statute: The European Public Limited-Liability Company Regulations 2004 (October 2003).

References to 'Britain' in this report should be deemed to refer to 'Great Britain', which comprises England and Wales and the separate jurisdiction of Scotland.

II Formation

1 General remarks

A Founding parties

2. British law defers to the provisions of the Regulation with respect to the requirements with which an SE's founders must comply.

3. Britain has chosen to allow a company whose head office is not in a Member State to participate in the formation of an SE if that company's registered office is located in a Member State and the company has a real and continuous link with the economy of a Member State (Art. 2(5) Reg.).[2]

B Name

4. Under the Regulation, the name of an SE must be preceded or followed by the abbreviation 'SE', and only SEs may include this abbreviation in their names. Under the ECRs, if a legal entity or natural person fails to comply with this provision, that entity or person shall be liable on summary conviction for a fine of one fifth of the statutory maximum.[3] The statutory maximum on summary conviction is currently £5,000.

The CA contains detailed provisions prohibiting the registration of certain names, and the Secretary of State for Trade and Industry (the 'Secretary of State') has the power[4] to require a company to abandon a misleading name. Using a name which is deceptively similar to that of another company, so that actual damage occurs or is likely to occur, also amounts to the tort of passing off and may be restrained by an injunction.

C Registered office and transfer

(i) Registered office

5. The memorandum of an SE registered with the Registrar of Companies (the 'Registrar') in England and Wales must state that its registered office is to be situated in England or Wales, and the memorandum of an SE registered with the Registrar in Scotland must state that its registered office is to be situated in Scotland.[5] The memorandum thus fixes the country where the SE is registered while the location of an SE's registered office establishes its domicile.

---

[2] Reg. 55 ECRs. [3] *Ibid.*, Reg. 84. [4] Sec. 32 CA. [5] *Ibid.*, Sec. 10.

The provision allowing Member States to require that the registered office and head office of an SE be in the same place (Art. 7 Reg.) has not been adopted in Britain on the grounds that there is no such requirement for British companies.

(ii) **Transfer**

6. Where it is proposed to transfer the registered office of an SE to England, Wales or Scotland from another Member State, a transfer proposal must be drawn up by the management or administrative organ in accordance with Article 8 of the Regulation. This proposal must be filed at Companies House[6] (using form SE68). If the SE is currently registered in Britain, the Registrar will file the proposal with the company's other documents and will flag it so that an examination of the company's records will reveal the SE's intention to transfer its registered office.[7]

Publication of the transfer proposal is effected by filing the proposal at Companies House and publishing it in the relevant gazette.[8] The same publication requirements apply to the new registration in Britain of an SE transferred from another Member State.

7. The transfer of an SE's registered office will necessitate an amendment to its articles (Art. 59(1) Reg.). An SE that is proposed to be transferred out of Britain will be governed by British law as far as the amendment of its articles is concerned, and, therefore, the transfer must be approved by 75% of the SE's shareholders in order to go ahead.[9]

An SE must notify its shareholders and creditors at least one month prior to the general meeting scheduled to vote on the transfer that they have the right to examine the transfer proposal and to obtain, free of charge, a copy of the proposal and of the management report.[10]

In addition, mention of the transfer proposal must be made in all letters, documents, invoices etc. that the SE issues following publication of the proposal.[11] If these requirements are not met, the SE could be fined one-fifth of the statutory maximum.[12]

8. Before the competent authority can issue a certificate attesting to the completion of the acts and formalities necessary for the transfer, the SE must satisfy it that, in respect of any liabilities that arose prior to publication of the transfer proposal, the interests of creditors and the holders of other rights have been adequately protected in accordance with the requirements prescribed by

---

[6] The filing must be effected at Companies House in Cardiff, if the SE is to be transferred to England or Wales, or in Edinburgh, if the SE is to be transferred to Scotland.
[7] Reg. 68 ECRs.
[8] The *London*, *Edinburgh* and *Belfast Gazettes* are the official newspapers of record in the UK.
[9] Under Section 9 CA, a special resolution is required to amend a company's articles of association.
[10] Reg. 56(1) ECRs.   [11] *Ibid.*, Reg. 56(2).   [12] *Ibid.*, Reg. 56(3).

the Member State where the SE's registered office was located prior to the transfer (Art. 8(7) Reg.). In Great Britain, the SE must furnish a statement of solvency using form SE72(6). If the company has a one-tier management system, this statement must be made by all members of the administrative organ. If the SE has a two-tier system, the statement must be made by all members of the management organ (authorised by the supervisory organ). The statement must provide that all members of the relevant organ are of the opinion that:

- as regards the financial situation of the SE immediately after the transfer, there will be no grounds on which the SE will be unable to pay its debts; and
- as regards the prospects of the SE for the year following the transfer date, the SE will be able to conduct business as a going concern (and thus will be able to pay its debts as they fall due throughout that year), having regard to the projected management of the SE's business during that year and the amount and character of the financial resources which will likely be available to the SE during that year.[13]
- Any member of an administrative or management organ who makes a statement of solvency without having reasonable grounds for the opinion expressed therein can be imprisoned for up to two years or fined the statutory maximum or both.[14]

The option to extend the definition of liabilities to include those arising subsequent to publication of the transfer proposal but prior to the transfer itself (Art. 8(7) Reg.) has been enacted so as to ensure that any creditors whose claims arise during the 'post-proposal' period are afforded similar protection to those with outstanding claims at the time of publication of the transfer proposal.[15]

10. A form SE10 must be filed with the Registrar, together with a copy of the SE's articles and a copy of the certificate issued by the former competent authority attesting to the completion of the requisite pre-transfer acts and formalities.[16] A separate form (form SE11) is required to transfer the registered office of an SE from Great Britain.[17] This form must be filed together with a copy of the resolution approving the transfer, a statement of solvency, and a report explaining and justifying the legal and economic aspects of the transfer and the implications of the transfer for creditors, shareholders and employees (Art. 8(3) Reg.).

11. The right of Member States to oppose transfer applications (Art. 8(14) Reg.) is prescribed under the ECRs in order to protect the public interest.[18]

[13] *Ibid.*, Reg. 72. [14] *Ibid.*, Reg. 72(7). [15] *Ibid.*, Reg. 57. [16] *Ibid.*, Reg. 10.
[17] *Ibid.*, Reg. 11. [18] *Ibid.*, Reg. 58.

The competent authority for this purpose is the Secretary of State. Other public authorities, such as the Inland Revenue and the police, can notify the Secretary of State if they have concerns about a proposed transfer. A decision to oppose a transfer is subject to judicial review.

12. UK company law already provides remedies to protect minority shareholders and, therefore, no further protection has been implemented pursuant to Article 8(5) of the Regulation.

D   Corporate purpose

13. The corporate purpose (or objects) of an SE registered in Great Britain must be clearly defined, as a company may only do what is within or incidental to the objects stated in its memorandum. The memorandum must delimit and identify the corporate purpose in such a way that the reader can identify the field of industry within which the company's activities are to be confined.[19]

E   Capital

14. Section 118 of the CA requires public limited companies to denominate their share capital, up to at least $50,000, in sterling. Share capital in excess of this amount may be denominated in any currency, including sterling. Such companies may prepare their accounts in any currency they choose, including sterling. It has therefore been deemed necessary to take advantage of the option, whilst the UK remains outside the EMU, of allowing the capital of an SE to be expressed in sterling[20] (Art. 67(1) Reg.). Under Article 4 of the Regulation, the subscribed capital of an SE must not be less than £120,000.

Britain has not adopted the option provided in Article 67(2) of the Regulation (which would allow the accounts of an SE to be expressed in sterling): it was felt that the adoption of Article 67(1) alone would suffice to allow the accounts of SEs registered in Great Britain to be prepared and published in *any* currency, as is the case with public limited companies registered in Great Britain. Conversely, it could be argued that adopting the option contained in Article 67(2) would *require* SEs to draw up their accounts in sterling.

2   Different means of formation

A   General remarks

15. In respect of each method of formation outlined below which requires the approval of the shareholders of the participating companies, the general meeting

---

[19] However, under Section 35A CA, in favour of a person dealing with a company in good faith, the power of the board to bind the company or to authorise others to do so shall be deemed free of any limitation under the company's constitution.
[20] Reg. 67 ECRs.

of a British company participating in the formation of an SE must approve the proposal by a 75% majority of those shareholders present and voting or, if there are different classes of shares, 75% of each class of shareholders whose rights will be affected must approve the decision. Such action amounts to an amendment to the company's articles under Section 9 CA and therefore requires the approval of the general meeting by a special resolution.

B Formation by merger

16. Public limited companies established in at least two Member States can form an SE by merger. Those UK companies that qualify as public limited companies for this purpose are (i) public companies limited by shares and (ii) public companies limited by guarantee and having share capital.

Pursuant to the Regulation, the management or administrative organs of the merging companies must draw up draft terms of merger.[21] In addition to the information referred to in Chap. 2, no. 25 of this book, the draft terms should include the following information with respect to UK companies participating in a merger: (i) whether such companies are limited by shares or by guarantee and their share capital; and (ii) any rights or restrictions attached to shares or other securities to be allotted under the terms of merger to the holders of shares (or other securities) to which any rights or restrictions attach or the measures concerning them.[22]

The company's directors must also prepare a report explaining the effects of the merger and stating if they have any material interests (whether as directors, shareholders, creditors or otherwise) and the effects of the merger on their interests, insofar as these are liable to be affected differently from like interests of other people. The report must also explain the legal and economic grounds for the draft terms of merger, in particular the share exchange ratio, and must specify any valuation difficulties.

17. An expert's report must also be prepared. The court may, pursuant to a joint petition filed by the participating companies, approve the appointment of a single expert to prepare one report on behalf of all companies involved. The expert must be independent of all participating companies, that is a person qualified at the time of the report to be appointed, or to continue to serve as, an auditor of any of the companies. The expert's report must contain at least the information set out under Chap. 2, no. 27 of this book. Under the CA, the expert's report must also describe any special valuation difficulties which have arisen and, in the case of a valuation made by a person other than the expert, must state whether it appeared reasonable to arrange for or accept such a valuation. The experts have the right to access all relevant documents of the

---

[21] See Chap. 2, no. 25 of this book for further details.   [22] Sched. 15B para. 2(2) CA.

company and to request from the company's officers any information deemed necessary to draft their report.[23]

18. The draft terms of merger must be filed by the company with the Registrar, who in turn will publish a notice of receipt of the draft terms in the relevant gazette.[24] This notice must be published at least one month prior to the date of the general meeting scheduled to approve the terms. The information required under Article 21 of the Regulation should also be published in the relevant gazette.[25]

The draft terms of merger, the reports described above, and the company's annual accounts, together with the relevant directors' report and the auditors' report for the last three financial years, should be made available to shareholders at the company's registered office for at least one month prior to the general meeting scheduled to approve the draft terms. If the latest annual accounts relate to a financial year that ended more than six months before the date of the draft terms of merger, an accounting statement must also be made available. This statement should consist of (i) a balance sheet indicating the company's financial position as at a date no later than three months prior to adoption of the draft terms by the directors, and (ii) where the company is required to prepare consolidated accounts if that date was the last day of a financial year, a consolidated balance sheet indicating the state of affairs of the company and of its subsidiary undertakings as of that date.[26]

19. The notice to convene the general meeting to vote on the merger must contain a statement explaining the effect of the merger, as described above with reference to the directors' report.[27]

The draft terms of merger must be approved by the general meeting of each merging company (Art. 23(1) Reg.). As explained above, the relevant majority for any participating British company is 75% of those shareholders present and voting. The draft articles of association of the SE must also be approved by a simple majority of the participating British company's shareholders (an ordinary resolution).[28]

20. The competent authority must issue a certificate attesting to the completion of the pre-merger acts and formalities (Art. 25(2) Reg.). The competent authority in Great Britain is either the High Court for England and Wales or the Court of Session for Scotland (see Part VI of this report). These courts are also the

---

[23] *Ibid.*, para. 5.
[24] The *London, Edinburgh* and *Belfast Gazettes* are the official newspapers of record in the UK.
[25] Sched. 15B, para. 3 CA.   [26] *Ibid.*, para. 6.   [27] *Ibid.*, Sec. 426.
[28] *Ibid.*, Sched. 15B, para. 3(f) CA.

competent authorities for the purpose of scrutinising the merger pursuant to Article 26(1) of the Regulation.[29]

A notice of completion of the merger must be published in the relevant gazette[30] and a form SE5 filed with the Registrar.[31] The articles of the proposed SE and an office copy of the court order confirming that Article 26 of the Regulation has been complied with must also be filed along with form SE5.

Where a merger by acquisition is carried out by a company holding at least 90% (but not all) of the shares and other voting securities of another company, Article 31(2) of the Regulation states that the directors' and the expert's report and the documents necessary for scrutiny are required 'only to the extent that the national law governing either the acquiring company or the company being acquired so requires'. Although there is an option to make this requirement compulsory, it is irrelevant in Britain as there are no relevant provisions under domestic company law allowing derogation from the requirement to make reports available.

21. The option contained in the Regulation to allow the Member States to oppose the formation of an SE by merger in order to protect the public interest (Art. 19 Reg.) has been adopted in the ECRs.[32] The competent authority in Britain for this purpose is the Secretary of State. Other public authorities may notify the Secretary of State of any concerns they have about the proposed formation of an SE by merger. A decision by the Secretary of State to oppose a merger is subject to judicial review.[33]

22. Britain has not enacted any provisions pursuant to Article 24(2) of the Regulation to protect the interests of minority shareholders who oppose the formation of an SE by merger or of creditors or employees, over and above those already applicable under existing British company law.

C   Formation of a holding SE

23. In the UK, public and private limited companies may participate in the creation of a holding SE. The management or administrative organ of each promoting company must prepare draft terms of formation (Art. 32(2) Reg.).

An expert's report, similar to that described above for the formation of an SE by merger, must be provided by an independent expert. This report should contain the information set out in Chapter 2, no. 38 of this book. In addition, the draft terms must be approved by the general meeting of each company involved and subsequently filed at Companies House on form SE68(2)(a). The Registrar must ensure that these terms are published in the relevant gazette.[34] If all conditions for the formation of a holding SE have been fulfilled, a document to this effect

---

[29] Reg. 75, ECRs.   [30] *Ibid.*, Reg. 69.   [31] *Ibid.*, Reg. 5.   [32] *Ibid.*, Reg. 60.
[33] *Ibid.*, Reg. 74.   [34] *Ibid.*, Reg. 68.

must also be filed at Companies House within 14 days, and the Registrar must ensure publication of this information in the relevant gazette (Art. 33(3) Reg.). If the company fails to comply with these publication requirements, it shall be liable for a fine of one fifth of the statutory maximum.[35]

24. A form SE6 must also be filed with the Registrar[36] along with the SE's articles, the independent expert's report, and copies of the resolutions of the promoting companies approving the draft terms of formation of the holding SE. If applicable, copies of the resolutions of the promoting companies expressly ratifying the arrangements for employee involvement should also be filed, although this is only required in the case of reserved rights under Article 32(6) of the Regulation.

25. Britain has not enacted any provisions pursuant to Article 34 of the Regulation beyond those already applicable under existing company law to protect the rights of either creditors and employees or minority shareholders who oppose the formation of a holding SE.

D   Formation of a subsidiary SE

26. Companies involved in the formation of a subsidiary SE in the UK are subject to the same rules as those governing the formation of a subsidiary of a regular public limited company.

There is one exception, however. Single-member SEs can be created only as wholly owned subsidiaries of another SE. In such circumstances, the provisions of the Companies (Single Private Limited Companies) Regulations 1992, which provide for single-member companies, shall apply.

Where it is proposed to register a subsidiary SE in accordance with Article 2(3) of the Regulation, a form SE7 must be filed with the Registrar, along with a declaration on employee involvement, also on form SE7.[37]

Where it is proposed to register an SE formed as the subsidiary of another SE in accordance with Article 3(2) of the Regulation, a form SE9(1) must be filed with the Registrar, together with a declaration on employee involvement, also on form SE9(1).[38] Reference to an SE whose subsidiary is to be registered in accordance with this paragraph includes an SE with its registered office in another Member State.

E   Conversion into an SE

27. A British public limited company can be converted into an SE. Draft terms of conversion (analogous to those required for the formation of a holding SE or of an SE by merger) must be drawn up (Art. 37(2) Reg.) and an independent

---

[35] *Ibid.*, Reg. 70.   [36] *Ibid.*, Reg. 6.   [37] *Ibid.*, Reg. 7.   [38] *Ibid.*, Reg. 9.

expert's report prepared. The expert must certify that the company has net assets at least equivalent to its capital increased by those reserves which cannot be distributed by law or pursuant to the company's articles.

The draft terms of conversion must be approved by the general meeting of shareholders. For a British company, the requisite majority to approve the terms is 75% of those shareholders present in person or by proxy and voting.[39] The option afforded the Member States to require that the conversion of a public limited company into an SE be subject to a favourable vote of a qualified majority or unanimity in the organ of the company within which employee participation is organised (Art. 37(8) Reg.) has not been adopted in Britain on the ground that UK public limited companies do not provide for formal employee participation on the board.

28. A form SE8 must be filed with the Registrar, together with the SE's articles, the resolution approving the draft terms, the independent expert's report and the report explaining and justifying the legal and economic aspects of the conversion pursuant to Article 37(4) of the Regulation.[40] A declaration on employee involvement must also be signed.

3 Acts committed on behalf of an SE in formation

29. The Regulation reflects UK common law, according to which a contract purportedly made by or on behalf of a company in formation shall be given the same effect, subject to any agreement to the contrary, as one made with the persons purporting to act on behalf of the company or as its agent, who shall be jointly and severally liable on the contract unless the company assumes the obligations arising out of such acts.[41]

Under the Company Directors Disqualification Act 1986 (the 'CDDA'), the courts can issue a disqualification order against a person convicted of an indictable offence, whether on indictment or summarily, in connection with the promotion, formation or management of a company, so as to prohibit that person from serving as a director of any company. The effect of Article 9(1)(c)(ii) of the Regulation appears to be that the provisions of the CDDA also apply to directors of an SE, thus ensuring that any person convicted of an indictable offence in connection with the promotion, formation or management of an SE will be disqualified from serving as a director of another SE or of any other company.

If the disqualification order is issued by a court of summary jurisdiction, the maximum period of disqualification that can be imposed under these provisions is five years; in other cases, the maximum period is 15 years.[42]

---

[39] Subject to any quorum requirements expressed in the company's articles of association.
[40] Reg. 8 ECRs.   [41] Sec. 36(1) CA.   [42] See the CDDA.

4 Registration and publication

30. An SE formed in or transferred to England or Wales must be registered at Companies House in Cardiff. An SE formed in or transferred to Scotland must be registered at Companies House in Edinburgh.[43] In order to register an SE at Companies House, a declaration on employee involvement must be completed (unless the SE has been formed by merger or is transferring its registered office to Great Britain), indicating the arrangements for employee involvement that will apply to the SE. In most cases, an authorised member of the special negotiating body and a member of the management or administrative organ of the proposed SE must sign the declaration. Where the standard rules on employee involvement are to be applied, only an authorised member of the management or administrative organ of the proposed SE need sign the declaration. Other documents may also be required, as outlined above.

Under Regulation 81 of the ECRs, notice of an SE's registration (or of a change to its registered office) must be published in the relevant gazette.[44]

5 Acquisition of legal personality

31. An SE acquires legal personality on the date on which it is registered by the Registrar of Companies, once the latter is satisfied that the requirements of the ECRs and the Regulation with respect to formation, transformation or transfer of the SE's registered office, as the case may be, have been met. The main consequence of acquiring legal personality under UK law is that the subscribers of the memorandum, together with any other such persons as may from time to time become shareholders in the company, become a body corporate under the name contained in the memorandum. A body corporate is separate and distinct from its individual shareholders and is capable of exercising all the functions of an incorporated entity, but with a duty on the part of its members (absent limited liability) to contribute to its capital if it is wound up. The ECRs provide that references to a 'body corporate' in domestic law shall apply equally to SEs.[45]

III Organisation and management

1 General remarks

32. The organisational and management structure of an SE, as set out in the Regulation, largely mirrors the relevant provisions of British company law, in that British public limited companies divide decision-making power between the general meeting of shareholders and the board of directors in much the same

---

[43] Reg. 12 ECRs.
[44] The *London, Edinburgh* and *Belfast Gazettes* are the official newspapers of record in the UK.
[45] Reg. 81 ECRs.

way as does an SE. However, the two-tier system of management described in the Regulation is not common within British companies. Britain has therefore taken a flexible approach to these provisions so as to ensure that, insofar as possible, the legal framework for the SE is not prescriptive but rather provides a maximum degree of flexibility in the way an SE is structured.

2 Shareholders

A General meeting

(i) Decision-making process

33. Subject to the rules on general meetings set out in the Regulation, the rules applicable to the convening and conduct of general meetings of an SE are those prescribed by the CA.

Under UK law, the board of directors has authority to call a general meeting. Under the ECRs, the first general meeting may be held at any time during the first 18 months following the formation of an SE (Art. 54(1) Reg.).[46]

34. Shareholders representing 10% of the issued share capital may request that the SE convene a general meeting (Art. 55(1) Reg.). Shareholders representing 5% of the SE's issued share capital may require that items be added to the agenda of a general meeting.[47] These provisions reflect those of the CA with respect to UK companies.

The Secretary of State has the power to convene the general meeting of an SE if the company itself fails to do so (Arts. 54 and 55 Reg.).

35. British companies can pass two types of resolutions at a general meeting – ordinary resolutions and extraordinary or special resolutions. Under the CA, ordinary resolutions must be approved by a simple majority of votes cast. Therefore, ordinary resolutions of an SE may be passed in accordance with the provisions of Article 57 of the Regulation (which stipulates a majority of votes validly cast, unless the law of the Member State in which the SE's registered office is situated specifies otherwise). However, the CA also sets out separate provisions with respect to extraordinary and special resolutions, which must be approved by 75% of shareholders in attendance and voting at a general meeting. Accordingly, resolutions that would require a 75% majority under domestic law will also require a 75% majority if the company is an SE.

36. The CA provides that a company's memorandum and articles of association can only be amended by a special resolution, which must be approved by 75% of those shareholders in attendance and voting at a general meeting.[48] This majority also applies to proposed changes to an SE's articles, as Great

[46] *Ibid.*, Reg. 65.   [47] *Ibid.*, Reg. 66.   [48] Secs. 4 and 9 CA.

Britain has chosen not to adopt the option contained in the Regulation allowing the Member States to provide that where at least half of an SE's subscribed capital is represented at a meeting, a simple majority is sufficient (Art. 59(2) Reg.).

Article 12(4) of the Regulation allows the Member States to provide that if the articles of an SE need to be amended due to a conflict with the new arrangements for employee involvement required by the Directive, the management or administrative organ of the SE is entitled to do so without the approval of the general meeting. This option was adopted in the ECRs in order to encourage flexibility and avoid imposing an unnecessary burden on SEs.[49] The Secretary of State can enforce compliance with this provision through the courts in circumstances where the management or administrative organ has failed to amend the SE's articles.[50]

Amendments to the articles of an SE must be published in the relevant gazette.

B   Rights and obligations of shareholders

37. The rights and obligations of shareholders, as provided by law, must be stated in an SE's articles of association.

The provisions of the CA and the IA, which apply equally to SEs, provide that certain decisions regarding a company's affairs may only be taken by its shareholders. Such decisions include, for example, amending the company's objects (i.e. its corporate purpose) or articles of association, changing its name, ratifying the actions of directors that fall outside the company's corporate purpose, and changes to the company's share capital. The CA also grants shareholders specific rights, such as the right to remove directors by a simple majority of votes cast. The company's articles, however, may provide further rights.

Shareholders are also bound by certain statutory obligations under domestic law. For example, the shareholders of a public company have a duty to disclose certain acquisitions or disposals of shares in that company.

3   Management and supervision

A   One-tier system/two-tier system

(i)   **General remarks**

38. An SE may choose between a one-tier and a two-tier system of management, as described in Chapter 2, no. 68 of this book.

Article 47(1) of the Regulation (which allows companies and other legal entities to sit on an SE's management organs provided the law applicable to public

---

[49] Reg. 59 ECRs.   [50] *Ibid.*, Reg. 76.

limited companies in the Member State concerned so allows) is applicable in Great Britain. 'Corporate' directors are permitted under British law and accordingly, an SE's articles can provide that companies and other legal entities may sit on its management organ. However, this provision should be viewed in light of planned changes to British company law. In its White Paper published in March 2005,[51] the government proposed to require that a company have at least one director who is a natural person. If this proposal is enacted into law, it will also apply to SEs registered in Britain. The ECRs stipulate that the management organ, supervisory organ and administrative organ must have at least two members (Arts. 39(4), 40(3) and 43(2) Reg.).[52]

39. Articles 39(1) and 43(1) of the Regulation (regarding the two-tier system and one-tier system, respectively) state that the Member States may provide that one or more managing directors shall be responsible for the day-to-day management of an SE under the same conditions applicable to public limited companies registered within that Member State. However, there is no provision under British law requiring British public limited companies to have a certain number of managing directors. Nor does Britain wish to change the law applicable to public limited companies in this regard. Consequently, SEs registered in Britain may choose to have one or more (or even no) managing directors. Article 50 of the Regulation sets out the internal rules relating to quorums and decision-taking in SE organs. As employee participation is not recognised under British law, the derogation permitted by Article 50(3) is not relevant in Britain.

(ii) **Supervisory organ: the two-tier system**
40. The Regulation imposes a structural framework for SEs under which the power to represent, manage and determine the company's affairs is divided between its organs by law. However, British company law does not recognise two-tier boards. Consequently, Great Britain has taken advantage of the option provided in Article 39(5) of the Regulation to adopt appropriate measures for SEs with two-tier boards. These measures do not purport to provide a comprehensive guide to regulation of the two-tier system.

Any references to directors in the CA and other legislation applied by the Regulation should be deemed to refer to members of both the supervisory board and the management board of an SE with a two-tier system. The relevant legislation is applied by the Regulation based on either:

- Article 9(1)(c)(ii), which requires application of the provisions of national law applicable to public limited companies formed in accordance with the laws of the Member State in which the SE's registered office is located; or
- articles that specifically invoke the laws of a Member State.

[51] 'Company Law Reform', Cm. 6456 March 2005. [52] Regs. 61, 62 and 64 ECRs.

41. However, if an SE has a two-tier system, any functions relating to the management of the SE (which cannot be carried out by the supervisory organ) may not be undertaken by the supervisory board.[53] This restriction limits, to a certain extent, the requirement that members of each organ be treated as directors. For example, the CA provides that any director who has an interest in a contract with the company must declare this interest at a meeting of the company's directors. In the case of a proposed contract, this information must be disclosed at the meeting during which the question of entering into the contract is first deliberated. In an SE with a two-tier system, this provision will apply differently to members of its management organ and of its supervisory organ. As the former can enter into contracts on behalf of the SE, the provision will apply in full as regards both contracts and proposed contracts. However, since members of the supervisory organ cannot represent the company or enter into contracts on its behalf, the portions relating to proposed contracts will not apply.

42. The ECRs provide that where any transaction or function carried out by the management organ requires the authorisation of the supervisory organ (either by virtue of the Regulation or pursuant to the SE's articles), nothing in the ECRs can affect or dispense with such a requirement.[54]

Britain has opted to extend the scope of the supervisory organ's powers (pursuant to Art. 41(3) Reg.) so as to allow each member to request from the management organ any information necessary to perform its duties.[55]

Britain has not enacted the options contained in Article 48(1) and (2) of the Regulation, pursuant to which a Member State may provide that (i) the supervisory organ in an SE with a two-tier system can make certain categories of decisions subject to its approval and (ii) certain categories of transactions must be indicated in the articles of SEs registered within the territory of that Member State.

B Appointment and removal

43. Under UK law, directors are appointed by a company's general meeting of shareholders. The same holds true for SEs. However, if the SE has a two-tier board, only members of the supervisory board will be appointed by the general meeting.

The ECRs do not stipulate that an SE's articles may permit or require members of its management organ to be appointed or removed by the general meeting under the same conditions as those applicable to public limited liability companies (Art. 39(2) Reg.). UK law does not provide explicitly for two-tier boards for public limited companies so the 'same conditions' could not be applied to SEs registered in Great Britain. Members of the management organ may therefore only be appointed or removed by the supervisory organ.

---

[53] *Ibid.*, Reg. 78(5).   [54] *Ibid.*, Reg. 78(6).   [55] *Ibid.*, Reg. 63.

Britain has not chosen to stipulate a maximum period of time during which a member of the supervisory board can fill a vacancy on the management board (Art. 39(3) Reg.). In any event, the member concerned will not be able to exercise both functions simultaneously and shall thus cease to serve on the supervisory organ.

44. Under the CA, directors may be removed by an ordinary shareholder resolution prior to the end of their term.

C   Liability

45. The liability of directors is governed by the provisions of the CA applicable to directors of UK companies.

As explained at Part II.4 of this report, the CDDA also applies to directors of an SE, thus ensuring that misconduct in relation to the running or insolvency of an SE will result in disqualification of the director in question from acting in such a capacity for another company or SE.

IV   Employee involvement

46. The Directive has also been transposed into national law through the ECRs. Although a detailed explanation of the relevant provisions is unfortunately outside the scope of this report, the following section describes certain key points relevant to transposition of the Directive in Britain.

1   Special negotiating body ('SNB')

47. An SNB must be elected to agree a level of employee involvement in the SE. The allocation of SNB members is by Member State. Therefore, where the employees of the participating companies are based in both Great Britain and Northern Ireland, ballots must be cast on a UK basis. The UK members of the SNB must be elected by the company's UK employees (as set out in the ECRs) or appointed by a consultative committee where such a committee exists.[56] The voting arrangements in the ECRs are modelled on those contained in the Transnational Information and Consultation of Employees (TICE) Regulations of 1999, which transposed the Community Works Council Directive (94/45/EC).

Trade union representatives who are not employees are able to stand for election or be appointed if the management of the participating companies so agrees (Art. 3(2)(b) Dir.).

---

[56] *Ibid.*, Regs. 21 and 23.

2 Participation rights

48. UK law does not currently recognise the right of employees to participate in the corporate decision-making process or to sit on the board (although they are not prevented from serving as directors). Thus, if formal negotiations for arrangements on employee involvement via the SNB (as set forth in the Directive) fail, then under the standard rules contained in the ECRs, an SE formed by a UK company need only guarantee employee participation to the extent such participation exists in the other companies forming the SE.[57] Where the standard rules on employee participation apply and if more than one form of participation exists in the participating companies, the SNB shall determine which form should be continued in the SE.

Britain has not made further provision for amending the rules applicable in the absence of any decision on the matter, as permitted by Article 7(2) of the Directive.

Britain has not opted to lay down budgetary rules for the operation of the SNB, as permitted by Article 3(7) of the Directive; nor has Britain opted to take advantage of the derogation provided in Article 7(3) of the Directive.

3 Protection of employee representatives[58]

49. Members of the SNB are protected under the ECRs (Art. 10 Reg.). They are entitled to reasonable paid time-off to perform their duties and are protected against unfair dismissal or harassment by an employer when acting as employee representatives under the law, standing as candidates for such a position, seeking to enjoy rights conferred by the law, and in certain other situations. A claim for unfair dismissal or a complaint of harassment can be brought before the employment tribunals.

4 Complaints procedure[59]

50. Complaints regarding the provisions on employee involvement must be brought before the Central Arbitration Committee ('CAC') in Britain. Complaints may be brought in respect of decisions of the SNB, disputes regarding the implementation of an arrangement for employee involvement or of the standard rules on employee involvement, misuse of an SE for the purpose of depriving employees of their participation rights, and breach of the duty of confidentiality. An order issued by the CAC may be enforced by means of an application to the Employment Appeals Tribunal, which can enforce the order as it considers just and equitable under the circumstances.

---

[57] *Ibid.*, Sched. 3.   [58] *Ibid.*, Part 3 Chap. 7.   [59] Ibid., Regs. 44–46.

If the CAC is of the opinion that an application or complaint is reasonably likely to be settled by mediation, it will refer the complaint to the Advisory, Conciliation and Arbitration Service ('ACAS'), which will seek to promote a settlement of the matter. If attempts at reconciliation fail, the matter will be referred back to the CAC which will then proceed to hear and rule on the application or complaint.

5 Information and confidentiality

51. The competent organ of a British participating company for an SE to be registered in Britain is not required to disclose any information or document if the nature of such information or document is such that disclosure would seriously harm the functioning of, or be prejudicial to, the SE, a participating company or any concerned subsidiary or establishment, judging by objective criteria. Britain has not opted to make this dispensation subject to prior administrative or judicial authorisation (Art. 8(2) Dir.). However, where there is a dispute between the competent organ and a recipient as to whether the information should be disclosed, either party may petition the CAC for a declaration as to whether the information should be deemed confidential.[60]

Britain has not laid down provisions that aim to provide ideological guidance with respect to information and the expression of opinions pursuant to Article 8(3) of the Directive.

6 Exiting employee involvement rights

52. As permitted under Article 13(4) of the Directive, Britain has provided that, except in relation to participation rights, nothing in the ECRs shall affect the involvement rights of employees of an SE, its subsidiaries or establishments provided by law or practice in the Member State in which they were employed immediately prior to registration of the SE.[61]

V Annual accounts and consolidated accounts

1 Accounting principles

A General remarks

53. The rules governing public limited companies in Britain also apply to SEs registered in Britain as regards the preparation, auditing and publication of their annual (and, where applicable, consolidated) accounts (Art. 61 Reg.).

---

[60] *Ibid.*, Reg. 35.   [61] *Ibid.*, Reg. 50.

B Annual accounts

54. The directors of a British company must prepare an annual balance sheet for the last day of the financial year and an income statement. The accounts must give a true and fair overview of the company's state of affairs and must comply with the provisions of the CA as to their form and content and any additional information provided by way of notes. Where compliance with the statutory provisions as to matters to be included in the individual accounts would be insufficient to give a true and fair view of the company's financial situation, additional information must be provided. If compliance with any of the provisions would be inconsistent with the requirement of providing a true and fair view of the company's financial situation, the directors must derogate from these provisions to the extent necessary. The particulars of such a derogation, the reasons for doing so, and its effects must be provided in a note to the accounts.[62] The SE's accounts must be approved by its shareholders and filed with the Registrar. The period allowed for approving and filing the annual accounts is ten months following the end of the relevant accounting period for private companies and seven months for public companies.

55. The UK listing rules[63] require UK-listed companies to issue an annual report and accounts prepared in accordance with the company's national laws and accounting standards or IAS. In addition, these documents must be independently audited in accordance with UK, US or international auditing standards. If the company has subsidiary undertakings, it must prepare consolidated accounts, unless the UK Listing Authority agrees otherwise. Such accounts must provide additional information if they do not give a true and fair view of the group's financial situation, profit and loss, and cash flow. The accounts must be published as soon as possible after approval, and in any event within six months following the end of the financial period to which they relate (unless the UK Listing Authority grants an extension).

56. In addition, new regulations[64] amending the CA will require public companies and larger private companies to carry out an annual operating and financial review, covering business strategies and objectives, key risk factors and developments over the course of the year, etc. The aim of this review is to increase shareholder awareness. Companies will be required to comply with these new regulations for financial years beginning on or after 1 January 2005.

C Consolidated accounts

57. Subject to certain exceptions, consolidated accounts must be prepared if the company in question is the parent company of a group of companies (so SEs

---

[62] Sec. 226 CA.   [63] As amended in July 2005.
[64] The Companies Act 1985 (Operating and Financial Review and Directors' Report etc) Regulations 2005.

formed as subsidiaries will not need to do so). Consolidated accounts comprise a consolidated balance sheet detailing the state of affairs of the parent company and its subsidiary undertakings and a consolidated income statement of the profit and loss of each company in the group. Consolidated accounts are required to give a true and fair view of the group's state of affairs at the end of the financial year and the profit or loss for the financial year recorded by each undertaking included in the consolidation. Subject to certain exceptions, all subsidiary undertakings of a parent company must be included in the consolidation. Consolidated accounts must comply with the provisions of the CA as to their form and content and any additional information provided by way of notes.[65]

Special rules apply to banks and insurance companies. Article 62 of the Regulation states that these rules shall also apply to SEs.

2 Auditors

58. An SE must appoint auditors unless (i) its turnover for the year in question does not exceed £5.6 million and (ii) its balance sheet total for that year is not more than £2.8 million.[66]

The SE's auditors are required to prepare a report on its annual accounts. A copy of this report must be provided to shareholders at the annual general meeting. The report must state whether, in the auditors' opinion, the annual accounts have been prepared properly in accordance with the CA and, in particular, whether they provide a true and fair overview of the SE's state of affairs at the end of the financial year and its profit and loss for that year.[67]

In preparing their report, the auditors must carry out investigations in order to enable them to form an opinion as to whether the company has kept proper accounting records, whether they have received proper and adequate returns from branches not visited, and whether the individual accounts conform to the accounting records and returns. The auditors must also determine whether the information provided in the management report for the financial year in question is consistent with the accounts for that year. If they find that it is not, they must make a statement to this effect in their report.[68] In addition, if the auditors find that any of the foregoing requirements have not been met, they must make a statement to this effect in their report and indicate if they failed to obtain any information and explanations they considered necessary in order to perform their audit. If this is the case, or where the auditors disagree with certain items, disclosures or treatment in the accounts, and the matter in question is material, they must include a reservation to this effect in their report if they are unable to resolve the issue.

[65] Sec. 227 CA.   [66] *Ibid.*, Sec. 388A.   [67] *Ibid.*, Sec. 235.
[68] *Ibid.*, Sec. 237.

VI Supervision by the national authorities

59. The competent authorities in Great Britain, for the purposes of Article 68(2) of the Regulation, are:

- the Secretary of State (for Articles 8, 55 and 64); and
- the courts (for Articles 25 and 26). Where the proposed location of the registered office of an SE is in England or Wales, the relevant court will be the High Court; where the proposed location is in Scotland, the relevant court will be the Court of Session.[69]

VII Dissolution

1 General remarks

60. Pursuant to Article 63 of the Regulation, the Insolvency Act 1988 ('IA') applies to SEs registered in Great Britain.

2 Composition with creditors

61. In a composition with creditors, 75% of a company's unsecured creditors voting at a creditors' meeting can impose on all unsecured creditors a plan or arrangement proposed by the company's directors, a liquidator or an administrator and approved by its shareholders. A composition with creditors is an insolvency procedure, usually invoked for insolvent companies. Compositions are largely governed by Sections 1 to 7 of the IA. A composition with creditors can only be initiated by court order.

3 Administration

62. An administrator may be appointed by the court at the request of the company or one of its creditors. The company's directors can also petition the court to appoint an administrator. The administrator is asked to formulate, if possible, a plan to restructure the company other than by liquidation. The administrator's proposals must be submitted to the company's unsecured creditors for approval within three months following his or her appointment. Administration is only an option for a company that is, or is likely to become, insolvent. This area is largely governed by Sections 8 to 27 of the IA.

4 Administrative receivership

63. An administrative receiver takes control of all (or most) of a company's assets for the purpose of paying a creditor secured by a floating charge (or

---

[69] Reg. 75 ECRs.

occasionally a group of creditors who have common security in the form of a floating charge). No other groups are involved. Administrative receivership arises from the security agreement between the company and one or more of its creditors: by agreeing to a security arrangement with this type of creditor, the company grants preference to a particular creditor over others. Administrative receivership is usually invoked for insolvent companies. Except in rare cases, the involvement of the court is not required to commence or confirm the use of this procedure. The law on this topic is governed by Sections 42 to 49 of the IA.

5 Liquidation

64. The winding up of a company pursuant to Part IV of the IA may be either voluntary or involuntary. Upon winding up, every former and current shareholder must contribute to the company's assets an amount sufficient to enable the company to pay its debts and cover its liquidation expenses and to adjust their rights amongst themselves.

A Voluntary liquidation

65. Voluntary liquidation is initiated by the company itself. The general meeting must pass a resolution to this effect. If the company is solvent and the directors make a declaration of solvency, the liquidation is referred to as a 'members' voluntary liquidation'. If no such declaration is provided, or if it later transpires that the company is unable to meet its liabilities in full within the period specified in the declaration, the liquidation is termed a 'creditors' voluntary liquidation'.

The company's assets in voluntary liquidation are applied to satisfy its liabilities *pari passu* (or without preference) and, unless the company's articles provide otherwise, the proceeds are distributed amongst the shareholders in accordance with their rights and stake in the company.

B Involuntary liquidation

66. Either the company or any of its shareholders or creditors, its liquidator, temporary administrator or a justice's chief executive (if the company has failed to pay a fine) or all or any of these parties, jointly or severally, can petition the court to order the involuntary dissolution of the company. The Secretary of State can also petition the court to wind up the company in the public interest.

The following grounds for involuntary liquidation by court order are relevant to SEs:

- The company has passed a special resolution to be wound up by the court.
- The company does not commence business within a year following incorporation or suspends its activities for an entire year.
- The number of shareholders falls below two.

- The company is unable to pay its debts (as described in the IA).
- A moratorium instituted pursuant to the IA has come to an end and there is no composition with creditors in effect.
- The court is of the opinion that it is just and equitable for the company to be wound up.

The job of the liquidator of a company in involuntary liquidation is to ensure that the company's assets are realised and the proceeds distributed to the company's creditors and, if there is a surplus, to any other parties entitled to receive them.

VIII Tax treatment

1 Introduction

67. For most purposes, it is envisaged that SEs will be able to operate within the UK under existing tax law. A brief overview of the current tax rules applicable to UK companies is set out below.

However, some changes to UK tax law will be necessary. The Inland Revenue have published draft legislation designed to give effect to the amendments to Directive 90/434/EEC (generally known as the 'Merger Directive') which have been made to cover the formation of an SE by merger (either a merger by acquisition or a merger that results in the formation of a new company). The principal effect of the legislation (if implemented in its current form) is that, provided the relevant assets remain within the charge to UK tax after the merger, it will operate to postpone the tax charge that might otherwise arise (i) on transfers of assets by companies involved in such a merger until the eventual disposal of the assets by the SE resulting from the merger and (ii) on an exchange of shares by shareholders in the existing companies for shares in the new company until a disposal of those new shares. The other significant effect of the draft legislation is that it provides that an SE which transfers its registered office into the UK will be treated in the same way as a company incorporated in the UK for the purposes of tax residence and stamp duty reserve tax. Although the legislation has yet to be formally enacted, it is nevertheless intended to apply with effect from 1 April 2005.

2 Income tax

68. Companies resident in the UK for tax purposes do not pay income tax or capital gains tax. Rather, they are liable for corporation tax on their worldwide profits, including both income and capital gains (Section 6 of the Income and Corporation Taxes Act 1988 ('ICTA')) for the accounting period in question. Chargeable profits include income, assessed under various headings known as 'schedules' (Secs. 15–20 ICTA), plus chargeable capital gains

(calculated in accordance with the relevant rules contained in the Taxation of Chargeable Gains Act 1992), less charges on income and certain other deductions. A company which carries on a trade in the UK through a permanent establishment in the UK is liable for corporation tax on the income and gains that are attributable to that permanent establishment.

The current standard rate of corporation tax rate is 30%. However, companies with taxable profits of less than £1,500,000, in certain circumstances, pay tax at a reduced rate with the amount of the reduction depending on the taxable profits in the relevant accounting period. Corporation tax is normally due and payable nine months and one day following the end of the relevant accounting period. However, large companies must pay the tax in quarterly instalments.

3 Value added tax

69. Supplies are divided into four main categories for VAT purposes – standard-rated (currently 17.5%), reduced-rated (currently 5%), zero-rated (0%) and exempt. In principle, the tax rate (or exemption) is determined by reference to the nature of the goods or services supplied. Subject to a few exceptions, VAT on any supply is a liability for the supplier, who must account to HM Customs and Excise for the VAT, even though the tax is generally borne ultimately by the recipient in the form of increased consideration for the relevant supply. The additional amount paid by the recipient in respect of VAT may, however, be recoverable as input tax.

Zero-rated supplies include a number of socially beneficial items such as medicines, children's clothing, books and newspapers. Exempt supplies include financial services and certain transactions in land and buildings. Neither zero-rated nor exempt suppliers are required to account for VAT; however, whereas a maker of zero-rated supplies can recover in full the input tax incurred in order to make the supplies, a maker of exempt supplies cannot recover input tax.

4 Other taxes

70. Stamp taxes include stamp duty, stamp duty reserve tax ('SDRT') and stamp duty land tax ('SDLT'). Stamp duty, or transfer duty, is a tax on documents and is still governed primarily by the Stamp Act 1891. Since 1 December 2003, stamp duty only applies to transfers of stock or marketable securities and certain partnership interests. The rate for the former is generally 0.5%, rounded up to the nearest multiple of £5, whilst there is a sliding scale of rates governing the latter (from nil to 4% depending on the relevant consideration). With rare exceptions, there is no obligation to pay stamp duty. However, neither the Registrar of Companies nor HM Land Registry will act upon an unstamped document, and such a document is inadmissible as evidence in civil proceedings in the UK.

SDRT was introduced by the Finance Act 1986. SDRT is payable by an accountable person on agreements to transfer chargeable securities where no stamped document evidencing a transfer of legal title has been executed. If a stamped document is subsequently produced, this franks the obligation to pay SDRT on the agreement, so there is no double taxation. SDRT is usually charged at a rate of 0.5% of the consideration and, unlike stamp duty, is directly enforceable against the accountable person – usually the purchaser. The tax arises on the date the agreement is made and is generally payable seven days following the end of the month in which the charge arises. In practice, SDRT is usually collected and paid by intermediaries in the securities market or, if relevant, by CRESTCo.

71. Part 4 of the Finance Act 2003 brought SDLT into being on 1 December 2003. This tax is designed to accommodate the move to e-conveyancing as well as to clamp down on avoidance of stamp duty in the real property sector. Unlike stamp duty, which is a tax on documents, SDLT is chargeable on 'land transactions', widely defined to include transactions in freehold and leasehold interests and legal and equitable interests. The limited number of exempt interests includes licences and franchises. There is a sliding scale of rates for SDLT, from nil where the relevant consideration is £150,000 or less (for transactions relating to non-residential mixed-use property or residential property located in a designated disadvantaged area) or £120,000 or less where the transaction relates to residential property located in a non-disadvantaged area to 4% where the relevant consideration exceeds £500,000. SDLT is directly enforceable and must be paid by the purchaser within 30 days of the relevant transaction.

IX Recent developments regarding the implementation of Community Directives in the UK

72. Section 2(2) of the European Companies Act 1972 (the 'ECA') grants the British government the power to make regulations for the purpose of implementing any Community obligations in the UK or 'for the purpose of dealing with matters arising out of or related to any such obligation or right'. There is a dispute as to what extent, if any, regulations made pursuant to the ECA may make changes to UK law beyond what is strictly required by the directive in question. If such regulations purport to change the law beyond what is allowed by the ECA, they will be null and void.

In a recent judgment (*Oakley v Animal*),[70] the High Court held that regulations implementing Community obligations cannot be used to exercise an option given by a directive 'by way of derogation' from its mandatory requirements

---

[70] High Court Chancery Division (Patents Court), 17 February 2005, England and Wales High Court, 210.

in order to preserve certain aspects of existing national law. The effect of the judgment is that regulations issued pursuant to the ECA cannot be used as a policy-making tool. Rather, such regulations should be viewed as a technical means of bringing in laws which the UK has no choice but to enact due to its EU membership. While the specific decision in the case at hand (namely, that ECA regulations cannot be used to make an election concerning a derogation permitted by a directive) may be overturned on appeal, the general analysis by the High Court (that the ECA does not permit the implementation of regulations that yields a substantive result beyond what is required by the directive) may very likely survive.

This issue is not relevant in respect of the Regulation, which has direct effect in the UK. However, it is worth bearing in mind with respect to transposition of the Directive into national law. While the provisions of the ECRs do not appear to go beyond what is required by the Directive or to derogate from Britain's obligations under the Directive, it is now a distinct possibility that any UK regulations which purport to transpose Community directives could be challenged on such grounds in the future.

X Conclusion

73. Implementation of the Regulation and transposition of the Directive in Britain may yield a number of potential advantages:

   (a) UK company law previously contained no explicit provisions for cross-border mergers in the form set out in the Regulation. Once the relevant tax legislation is in place, it will be possible to carry out a cross-border merger with no additional tax liability as long as the acquiring company (in the case of a merger by acquisition) or the new company (in the case of a merger by formation) is an SE.
   (b) It was not previously possible for a UK company to have a two-tier board. The new legislation will allow SEs formed in Britain to opt for separate management and supervisory boards, if they wish.
   (c) An SE can transfer its registered office to another Member State with relative ease. A UK company cannot do so without first winding up its operations in the UK and re-registering in the other Member State. Companies operating on a pan-European basis may find that the use of an SE provides greater flexibility and relieves the administrative and financial burdens of operating a network of subsidiaries.
   (d) Companies that engage in cross-border transactions, such as international joint ventures, may find the SE a useful vehicle, possibly even more so where there are sensitive issues between the nationalities involved, as the SE could be perceived as more neutral. Nevertheless, because an SE can have its registered office in only one country, it is still not truly neutral in all respects.

(e) As long as an SE is registered in the UK, it will be eligible for inclusion in the FTSE indices, which means it will not be at a disadvantage compared to other UK-listed companies.

74. However, potential disadvantages can also be identified:

(a) UK law does not currently provide for high levels of employee involvement on company boards. UK boards may not wish to go through the long consultation process with their employees required by the Directive and risk damaging labour-management relations if the employees' views on information, consultation and participation are rejected by the directors.

(b) Should an SE opt for a two-tier board, the UK approach to implementation of the Regulation requires the company to define in its corporate charter the duties and responsibilities of each board. This requirement may make the choice of the two-tier model unpalatable in the UK.

(c) The procedure for transferring the registered office of an SE is complex and subject to various safeguards to protect the interests of creditors. The scope of the public interest exception in the Regulation is uncertain. In addition, due to the required amendments to the SE's charter to reflect changes to national company law, substantial costs may be incurred.

75. Time will tell how successful the SE will prove in practice in Great Britain. As much of the detailed regulation governing the functioning of the SE has been left to the Member States, there are currently a number of areas of uncertainty regarding some features of the SE, particularly those which are unfamiliar to British company law. However, if these uncertainties are remedied, the attractiveness of the SE as a pan-European corporate vehicle may well increase.

National reports for EEA Member States

18
Iceland

THORUNN GUDMUNDSDOTTIR
Thorunn Gudmundsdottir Lex Law Office

I   Introduction   488
II   Reasons to opt for an SE   489
III   Formation   489
     1   General remarks   489
         A   Founding parties   489
         B   Name   490
         C   Registered office   490
         D   Corporate purpose   492
         E   Capital   492
     2   Different means of formation   492
         A   Formation by merger   492
         B   Formation of a holding SE and a subsidiary SE; formation of an SE by conversion   493
     3   Acts committed on behalf of an SE in formation.   493
     4   Registration and publication   493
     5   Acquisition of legal personality   494
IV   Organisation and management   494
     1   General remarks   494
     2   General meeting   494
         A   Decision-making process   494
         B   Rights and obligations of shareholders   495
     3   Management and supervision   497
         A   Two-tier system/one-tier system   497
         B   Appointment, removal and representation   498
         C   Liability   498
V   Employee involvement   498
VI   Annual accounts and consolidated accounts   499
     1   Accounting principles   499
     2   Auditors   499
VII   Supervision by the national authorities   499
VIII   Dissolution   500
     1   General remarks   500
     2   Winding up   500
     3   Liquidation, insolvency and cessation of payments   501
IX   Applicable law   501
X   Tax treatment   501

            1   General remarks   501
            2   Income tax   502
            3   Value added tax   502
            4   Other taxes   502
    XI   Conclusion   503

I   **Introduction**

1. Over the decade or so that Iceland has been a member of the European Economic Area (EEA),[1] Icelandic company law has been amended on numerous occasions to bring it into line with Community law.

In the explanatory memorandum to a bill amending Icelandic company law, later adopted by the Althing[2] as Act No. 2/1995 on public limited companies,[3] reference was made to a proposal for a Community regulation on a European company as well as to a proposed directive on employee involvement in such a company. The proposed regulation was intended to simplify and make possible the merger and establishment of holding companies and joint ventures by companies from different Member States. The proposed directive outlined three different ways to guarantee employee involvement in the new European company. The explanatory memorandum stated that although Icelandic law did not (yet) contain any provisions on employee involvement, Iceland should be able to choose one of the three methods described in the proposed directive, if the other EFTA countries and the EU Member States were able to do so. Many organisations and entities were asked to comment on the bill and their comments were submitted to the Althing. However, no particular questions were raised regarding the Statute for a European company (SE).

2. Pursuant to a resolution dated 13 December 2002, the Althing authorised the government to adopt two EEA joint committee decisions integrating into the EEA Agreement Council Regulation (EC) No. 2157/2001 of 8 October 2001 on the Statute for a European company (SE) (the 'Regulation') and Council Directive 2001/86/EC of 8 October 2001 supplementing the Statute for a European company with regard to the involvement of employees (the 'Directive').[4]

---

[1] The Agreement on the European Economic Area (EEA) introduced a single internal market for the 25 EU Member States and the three EFTA countries (Iceland, Liechtenstein and Norway). The EEA Agreement was signed on 2 May 1992 and entered into force on 1 January 1994. It was subsequently amended on 1 May 2004 following the most recent enlargement of the European Union.
[2] The Althing is the national legislative assembly in Iceland.
[3] Hereinafter referred to as Act No. 2/1995.
[4] Joint Committee Decision No. 93/2002 of 25 June 2002, amending Annex XXII (Company Law) of the EEA Agreement, and Decision No. 89/2002 of 25 June 2002, amending Annex XVIII (Health and Safety at Work, Labour Law and Equal Treatment of Men and Women), respectively.

Accordingly, the Icelandic minister of trade and commerce introduced a bill on the European company into the Althing in October 2003 to implement the Regulation under national law. The bill was enacted on 16 April 2004 as Act No. 26/2004[5] and entered into force on 8 October 2004. Another bill to transpose the Directive into national law was also enacted on 16 April 2004 and entered into force on 8 October 2004 as Act No. 27/2004. [6]

According to Article 1 of Act No. 26/2004, the provisions of the Regulation shall have the force of law in Iceland in conformity with Protocol 1 of the EEA Agreement.

3. Act No. 26/2004 contains important references to Act No. 2/1995 and should be read in conjunction with the latter. When interpreting Act No. 26/2004 with regard to the regulation of an SE in Iceland, references to Act No. 2/1995 should thus be taken into account.

II   Reasons to opt for an SE

4. The main advantage of the SE is its European character. However, since Iceland is not a Member State of the EU, Icelandic companies are not particularly prone to express a 'European' identity in any way. However, in the unlikely event the SE becomes popular in Iceland, such popularity will undoubtedly be due to its advantages over national corporate forms, mainly the relative ease with which the registered office of an SE can be transferred from one Member State to another and the fact that an SE can be formed by means of a cross-border merger.

III   Formation

1   General remarks

A   Founding parties

5. The types of companies that may form an SE in Iceland are specified in Article 2(1) through (4) of the Regulation (see also Chap. 2, no. 19 *et seq.* of this book). Iceland has adopted the option contained in Article 2(5) of the Regulation by providing that a public or private limited company having its head office in a state outside the EEA can take part in the formation of an SE in Iceland if the company is formed under the laws of an EEA member country, has its registered office in that country and has a real and continuous link with the economy of an EEA country (Art. 5 Act No. 26/2004).

---

[5] Hereinafter referred to as Act No. 26/2004.
[6] Hereinafter referred to as Act No. 27/2004.

The above applies not only to public and private limited companies but also to legal bodies, within the meaning of Article 2(3) of the Regulation, in relation to the formation of a subsidiary SE.

B Name

6. An SE must include the abbreviation 'SE' in its name. In addition, the company may include the words 'European company' or the abbreviation 'EF', which stands for *Evrópufélag* or European company in Icelandic. The name of an SE should be clearly distinguishable from that of other companies registered with the Icelandic Registry of Limited Companies, which means an SE is entitled to take legal action and seek an injunction against a legal identity that uses a name deceptively similar or identical to its own (Art. 3 Act No. 26/2004; Art. 11 Reg.).

C Registered office

7. An SE registered in Iceland must have its registered office in that country (Art. 12 Reg.). The registered office of an SE may nevertheless be transferred to another EEA country or to an EU Member State (Art. 8 Reg.; see also Chap. 2, no. 81 of this book). Act No. 26/2004 does not require that the head office of an SE also be located in Iceland. An SE subject to supervision by the Icelandic Financial Supervisory Authority (FSA) may not transfer its registered office from Iceland if the FSA objects to the transfer within two months following publication of the transfer proposal in the relevant national gazette, the *Legal Gazette* (Art. 10 Act No. 26/2004; Art. 8(6) Reg.). The company should submit an application to the FSA for review no later than two weeks following publication of the transfer proposal in the *Legal Gazette* (Art. 8(14) Reg.). The FSA can only oppose the transfer on grounds of public interest. The Act does not define what constitutes the public interest, but the prevention of organised crime and money laundering come to mind. If the FSA encounters irregularities in the course of its review, it will give the company an opportunity to be heard within a certain period of time or to rectify its situation. If the company fails to do so, the application to transfer its registered office shall be rejected. Act No. 26/2004 does not contain provisions designed to protect minority shareholders that oppose a transfer (Art. 8.5 Reg.).

8. If the general meeting of an SE approves the transfer (Art. 8 Reg.) of its registered office to another EEA country, the company shall notify all known creditors to this effect in writing. The notice should contain information about the right of creditors (Art. 8(4) Reg.) to examine the transfer proposal and the management report (prepared pursuant to Art. 8(3) Reg.) at least one month before the general meeting scheduled to vote on the transfer and to oppose the transfer (Art. 11 Act No. 26/2004).

9. An SE must apply to the Registry of Limited Companies (the 'Registry') for a permit to transfer its registered office to another EEA country. The application must be submitted within one month following the resolution of the general meeting approving the transfer. The following documents must be attached to the application (Art. 11 Act No. 26/2004):

(1) two copies of the minutes of the meeting at which the resolution on the transfer was passed;
(2) a copy of the transfer proposal;
(3) a copy of the management report (drafted pursuant to Art. 8(3) Reg.);
(4) a certificate from the management organ (if the SE has a two-tier system) or the administrative organ or manager (if the SE has a one-tier system) attesting that all known creditors of the company have been informed of the transfer; and
(5) confirmation from the FSA as regards companies subject to its supervision that it has examined the application and does not oppose the transfer.

If the SE has not enclosed these documents with its application or if review of the transfer application reveals other irregularities, the Registry shall give the company an opportunity to be heard within a certain period of time and to rectify its situation. If the company fails to do so, the Registry shall reject the application.

10. Upon commencement of its review of a transfer application, the Registry shall notify the creditors of the SE. This notice should state that any creditor who opposes the transfer of the SE's registered office must inform the Registry to this effect in writing within two weeks following publication of the transfer proposal in the *Legal Gazette*. The Registry shall also send a special notice to the competent court in the judicial district where the SE's registered office is located.

If a creditor opposes the transfer within the specified time limit, the Registry shall inform the district court in the judicial district where the SE's registered office is located. If no creditors object to the transfer, the Registry shall issue the requested transfer permit (Art. 14 Act No. 26/2004).

If an application to transfer the registered office of an SE to another EEA country has been referred to the district court, that court shall be competent to issue the transfer permit, provided the company can prove that the claims of its creditors have been paid in full or that satisfactory security has been provided as regards claims that arose in the two weeks following publication of the transfer proposal in the *Legal Gazette*. If the company cannot furnish such proof, the court shall reject its application. Upon conclusion of the transfer proceedings, the court shall inform the Registry accordingly (Art. 15 Act No. 26/2004).

11. Once all formalities and acts required for the transfer have been completed, the district court or the Registry shall issue a certificate attesting to this fact

(Art. 8(8) Reg.). Iceland has not adopted the options contained in Article 8(7) and (14) of the Regulation.

D Corporate purpose

12. The corporate purpose of an SE registered in Iceland must be stated in its articles of association (Art. 9 Act No. 2/1995). There are no restrictions on the corporate purpose of an SE, other than that it must be lawful.

E Capital

13. An SE must have share capital of at least €120,000. This requirement is not stated specifically in Act No. 26/2004; however, Article 4 of the Regulation applies. Iceland is not an EMU member as it is not an EU Member State. However, it should be kept in mind that according to Article 10A of Accounting Act No. 145/1994[7] and Articles 11 and 11A of Annual Accounts Act No. 144/1994,[8] a company's accounts may be denominated in a foreign currency. An SE registered in Iceland may therefore express its capital in the national currency, euros or another foreign currency, although it must seek permission to express its capital in a foreign currency (Art. 67 Reg.).

2 Different means of formation

A Formation by merger

14. An SE can be formed in Iceland by means of a merger in accordance with Section 2 of the Regulation (see also Chap. 2, no. 22 of this book). As stated above, Iceland has adopted the option contained in Article 2(5) of the Regulation by providing that a public or private limited company having its head office in a state outside the EEA can take part in the formation of an SE by merger (Art. 5 Act No. 26/2004). Iceland has also enacted the option expressed in Article 19 of the Regulation by not allowing a company subject to oversight by the FSA to take part in the formation of an SE by merger if the FSA, upon review of the merger proposal, opposes the merger on grounds of public interest, provided the FSA declares its objection prior to issuance of the certificate referred to under Article 25(2) of the Regulation (attesting to the completion of the requisite pre-merger acts and formalities). The company must submit an application to the FSA for review. If the FSA encounters any irregularities in the course of its review, it will give the company an opportunity to be heard within a certain period of time or to rectify its situation. If the company fails to do so, its application shall be rejected (Art. 6 Act No. 26/2004). Iceland has not enacted the options contained in Articles 24(2) and 31(2) of the Regulation.

---

[7] Hereinafter referred to as Act No. 145/1994.   [8] Hereinafter referred to as Act No. 144/1994.

The Registry shall reject an application if the FSA has not reviewed it or if the FSA opposes the merger after review. If the Registry cannot approve an application due to the fact that a review by the FSA is currently under way, approval can take up to six months.

15. The Registry shall issue a certificate pursuant to Article 25(2) of the Regulation attesting to the completion of all requisite pre-merger acts and formalities if it has previously issued a permit to the public limited company to implement either a shareholder resolution to participate in the formation of an SE by merger (Art. 124 Act No. 2/1995) or a board decision on the same (Arts. 124 and 129 Act No. 2/1995; Art. 7 Act No. 26/2004).

B   Formation of a holding SE and a subsidiary SE; formation of an SE by conversion

16. There are no specific provisions in Act No. 26/2004 regarding the formation of a holding SE or a subsidiary SE or the formation of an SE by conversion (*see* Chap. 2, no. 12 *et seq.* of this book).

3   Acts committed on behalf of an SE in formation

17. Article 16 of the Regulation applies to acts committed on behalf of an SE in formation (see Chap. 2, no. 55 of this book).

4   Registration and publication

18. It is not expected that many SEs will be registered in Iceland. Therefore, a special SE registry has not been formed and there are no plans to do so. The Registry of Limited Companies, run by the Internal Revenue Service, shall serve as the registry for SEs. Registration of an SE with the Registry is subject to the provisions of Act No. 2/1995 and other applicable statutory provisions, including those regarding the denomination of capital (Arts. 4 and 67(1) Reg.). Along with its application for registration, an SE must submit the minutes of its first general meeting and its memorandum and articles of association, containing information such as the name of the SE, its address, corporate purpose, share capital, the voting rights attached to its shares, etc. As far as registration is concerned, an SE engaged in financial activities is subject to the applicable laws in that area and other appropriate statutory provisions.

19. The provisions of Additional State Revenue Act No. 88/1991 on public limited companies apply to the registration fees of an SE and to additional notifications, etc. The minister of finance may issue regulations containing additional provisions regarding the formation of an SE (including the organization of registration, operation of and access to the Registry, the collection of fees for *inter alia* the issuance of certificates and the provision of information

kept in electronic form, etc.) to supplement the general provisions applicable to public limited companies. To date, the minister has yet to issue any such regulations. The Registry collects fees for publication in the *Legal Gazette* in accordance with the applicable laws and regulations as well as for publication of information regarding registration and deregistration of an SE in the *Official Journal of the European Communities* (Art. 14 Reg.).

20. The management organ of an SE with a two-tier system or the administrative organ of an SE with a one-tier system must submit to the Registry a transfer proposal (Art. 8(2) Reg.), draft terms for the formation of a holding SE (Art. 32(2) Reg.), draft terms of conversion of an existing public limited company into an SE (Art. 37(4) Reg.), or draft terms of conversion of an SE into a public limited company (Art. 66(3) Reg.)

Information on the registration of an SE shall be published in the *Legal Gazette* without delay, the cost being borne by the notifying party. If a proposal is not published in its entirety, a mention should be made of the place where it is available for review (Art. 9 Act No. 26/2004).

5 Acquisition of legal personality

21. An SE acquires legal personality on the date on which it is registered with the Registry (Art. 15 Act No. 2/1995; Art. 16 Reg.), at which time it will also receive a registration number.

IV Organisation and management

1 General remarks

22. Act No. 26/2004 provides for either a two-tier or a one-tier system of management for SEs. However, it is expected that most SEs registered in Iceland will have a one-tier system, as there is no two-tier system of management under Icelandic law for public limited companies.

2 General meeting

A Decision-making process

23. The general meeting of shareholders is the company's highest authority (Art. 80 Act No. 2/1995). Thus, the general meeting wields the ultimate authority in an SE. There is no quorum required for a general meeting; the only requirement is that the meeting be convened lawfully. In general, a simple majority of votes cast is sufficient to pass resolutions at a general meeting, unless otherwise provided by law or the company's articles. In the event of a tie, lots will be drawn to decide the issue, unless the company's articles provide otherwise (Art. 92 of

Act No. 2/1995). In some instances, a qualified majority of two-thirds of the votes cast or share capital represented at the meeting may be required. This is the case for amendments to the company's articles of association.

Unanimity is required for particularly burdensome or sensitive matters, including certain amendments to a company's articles such as (i) the placement of restrictions on shareholders' rights to dividends or other allocations by the company to third parties and (ii) the increase of shareholder liability vis-à-vis the company.

A decision to amend the articles that restricts the right of shareholders to receive dividends or other payments out of corporate assets which is not passed unanimously can still be valid if approved by those shareholders controlling at least nine-tenths of the share capital present at the general meeting.

A decision to amend a company's articles which undermines the legal relationship between shareholders will be valid only if approved by the affected shareholders (Art. 94 Act No. 2/1995).

B Rights and obligations of shareholders

24. Shareholders have a fundamental right to attend general meetings and to be heard and vote at those meetings. Without regard to their shareholdings, shareholders have the right to demand that items be placed on the agenda of a general meeting (Art. 24 Act No. 26/2004). A shareholder who wishes to have a matter taken up at a general meeting should submit a request in writing to the management organ (of an SE with a two-tier system) or to the administrative organ (of an SE with a one-tier system). The item will be added to the agenda of the next general meeting if the request was received at least five weeks in advance or early enough to include in the notice of the meeting.

If the general meeting of an SE is not called in accordance with the provisions of the Regulation, the company's articles or a shareholder resolution, an appropriate authority can convene the meeting (Art. 87 Act No. 2/1995) if a request to do so has been received from a member of the management or supervisory organ (of an SE with a two-tier system), a member of the administrative organ (of an SE with a one-tier system) or a managing director, auditor, inspector or shareholder (Art. 25 Act No. 26/2004).

25. At a meeting where the matter is on the agenda, shareholders have the right to submit a proposal to conduct an investigation into the formation of the company, specific items related to its activities or certain aspects of its bookkeeping and annual accounts. If the proposal is approved by at least one-quarter of the share capital present or represented, the shareholders may request the minister of commerce to appoint investigators within one month following the meeting (Art. 97 Act No. 2/1995).

26. In certain cases, an individual shareholder can be disqualified from voting at a meeting if that shareholder has a direct or indirect conflict of interest with the company. For instance, a shareholder is not permitted to vote on matters involving legal proceedings initiated against that shareholder or the liability of that shareholder to the company. The same holds true for proceedings against other shareholders or regarding the liability of another shareholder if that shareholder has a considerable interest to safeguard that could conflict with the company's interests (Art. 82(4) Act No. 2/1995).

27. As members of the general meeting, shareholders wield the collective power to take decisions on behalf of the company. A shareholder may be held liable for any losses sustained by the company, other shareholders or third parties attributable to misuse or abuse of this power (Art. 134 Act No. 2/1995).

28. An important right of shareholders is described in Article 91 of Act No. 2/1995. Shareholders have the right to request certain information if the board of directors feels that this information can be released without harm to the company. The board and the company's manager(s) shall submit to the general meeting information about matters relevant to assess the company's annual accounts and financial situation or that is liable to influence the opinion of shareholders with regard to items on the agenda at a general meeting. This duty to inform also applies to other companies within the same group. If requested or required information is not made available at the general meeting, shareholders have 14 days within which to request the information in writing. A copy of the request should also be sent to any shareholder who so desires.

29. The general meeting may not take a decision that is obviously geared to acquiring an improper interest for specific shareholders or other parties at the expense of the remaining shareholders or of the company (Art. 95 Act No. 2/1995).

30. A shareholder, director or manager can file a lawsuit if a decision is taken by the general meeting in an unlawful manner or in violation of Act No. 2/1995 or of the company's articles (Art. 96 Act No. 2/1995). Proceedings must be commenced within three months following the decision or it will be accorded force of law. This rule does not apply if: (i) a decision is unlawful, even if approved by all shareholders; (ii) the approval of all or specific shareholders is required in order for the decision to enter into force and such approval was not obtained; (iii) the general meeting was not properly convened or the rules applicable to calling a general meeting were not followed to a considerable extent; (iv) the shareholders commenced proceedings after expiry of the three-month period but within two years following the date of the decision, there was a justifiable reason for the delay and adherence to the three-month deadline would be manifestly unreasonable.

If the court finds that a decision taken by the general meeting is invalid, the decision shall be declared null and void or amended accordingly. However, the general meeting can only amend a decision if amendment is explicitly requested and it is within the court's authority to determine the proper outcome of the decision. Any such ruling shall be binding on all shareholders, even those who were not privy to the proceedings.

3 Management and supervision

A Two-tier system/one-tier system

31. According to Article 17 of Act No. 26/2004, the following provisions shall apply to an SE with a two-tier system pursuant to Articles 39 through 42 of the Regulation:

(1) Unless otherwise provided in the Regulation, statutory provisions applicable to public limited companies, and, where appropriate, to boards of directors or board members, shall also apply to the management organs of an SE and the members of these organs as well as to the supervisory organs and members thereof, where appropriate.

(2) In addition to the obligations set forth in the Regulation, the supervisory organ shall submit a report to the annual general meeting on issues relevant to evaluating the company's annual accounts and auditor's report. The modalities of this report shall be governed by Article 88(4) of Act No. 2/1995.

32. Unless otherwise provided by the Regulation, the statutory provisions applicable to public limited companies, and, where appropriate, to boards of directors and board members, shall also apply to the administrative organs of an SE with a one-tier system and to members of these organs pursuant to Articles 43 through 45 of the Regulation (Art. 19 Act No. 26/2004; see also Chap. 2, no. 67 of this book).

33. In an SE with a two-tier system, both the supervisory organ and the management organ oversee the managing director(s) (Art. 22 Act No. 26/2004; Arts 39–42 Reg.). The provisions of Articles 40 and 41 of the Regulation regarding oversight of the management organ by the supervisory organ shall also apply to each individual managing director. Members of the supervisory organ can request from the management organ and the managing director(s) any information necessary to enable them properly to perform their duties in this regard (Art. 40(1) Reg.). Members of the management organ have the right to request from the managing director(s) any information necessary to enable them to supervise the latter.

The provisions of Article 22 of Act No. 26/2004 on supervision by the management organ of the managing director(s) in an SE with a two-tier system and the right of the management organ to request information from the managing director(s) shall also apply to supervision by the administrative organ of the managing director(s) in an SE with a one-tier system (Arts. 43–45 Reg.).

B   Appointment, removal and representation

34. The members of the administrative, management and supervisory organs are appointed for a term stated in the company's articles of association which may not exceed six years (Art. 46(1) Reg.). Appointment for a one-year term is common in Iceland.

35. An SE shall have a managing director (Art. 21 Act No. 26/2004). If an SE has a two-tier system, the management organ shall appoint and remove the managing director(s), if need be. The managing director(s) cannot sit on the supervisory organ. If an SE has a one-tier system, the administrative organ shall appoint and remove the managing director(s). In the one-tier system, the managing director(s) can serve on the administrative organ but not as chair (Art. 70 Act No. 2/1995). The managing director(s) are also subject to the provisions of Act No. 2/1995 regarding the role and obligations of managers (see also Chap. 2, no. 67 of this book).

36. While the board of directors, as the highest management organ, has general authority to act on behalf of an SE with a one-tier system (which is expected to be the norm in Iceland), the managing director(s) usually represent the SE in daily matters. Representation, such as the authority to commit an SE or to bind it by contract, shall be governed by the rules for acting on behalf of an SE.

C   Liability

37. Management is bound to make good any loss caused the company through wilful misconduct or negligence on its part. The same holds true for any loss sustained by shareholders or others attributable to violation of the provisions of Act No. 26/2004, Act No. 2/1995 or the company's articles of association (Art. 134 Act No. 2/1995).

V   **Employee involvement**

38. As stated in Part I of this report, the Althing passed Act No. 27/2004 on employee involvement in the European company on 16 April 2004. The Act entered into force on 8 October 2004.

Act No. 27/2004 directly reflects the provisions of the Directive. Iceland, however, has not enacted the options contained in Articles 3(2)(b) and 8(3) of the Directive. The purpose of the Act is to ensure and govern employee involvement in an SE. Since the direct involvement of employees is not common in Iceland, it is not expected that transposition of the Directive will lead to lesser rights for employees. On the contrary, in some instances the formation of an SE will result in increased employee involvement in corporate affairs, which could result in a certain reluctance to form SEs in Iceland.

VI Annual accounts and consolidated accounts

1 Accounting principles

39. A pubic limited company is obliged to keep accounts. Therefore, an SE registered in Iceland must keep its books and prepare its annual accounts in accordance with Act No. 144/1994 and Act No. 145/1994 (Art. 61 Reg.). An SE may receive authorisation from the Registry of Annual Accounts to keep its books in a foreign currency, in accordance with the statutory provisions on bookkeeping, and prepare and disclose its annual accounts in this currency pursuant to Act No. 144/1994. If an SE with its registered office in another EEA country or EU Member State carries out activities in the form of a branch in Iceland, the books and annual accounts of the branch must conform to Act No. 144/1994 and Act No. 145/1994.

40. An SE shall use double-entry accounting. Each financial year, the supervisory and/or administrative organ (the directors) and the managers shall prepare the annual accounts, including the income statement, balance sheet, statement of cash flow and notes to the accounts. The directors shall also draw up a report on the previous year. The annual accounts constitute an integrated whole. The annual accounts and, if appropriate, the consolidated accounts must be signed by the directors and manager(s). If a director or manager is of the opinion that the annual or consolidated accounts should not be approved or has objections to the accounts which should be brought to the attention of shareholders, these objections should be mentioned in the management report. The annual accounts, signed by the directors, and the auditor's report must be presented to shareholders at least a week before the annual general meeting.

2 Auditors

41. An SE is required to appoint an auditor (Art. 9 Act No. 2/1995; Art. 32 Act No. 145/1994). The auditor is usually appointed by the annual general meeting. The auditor remains independent of the company's organs and has a purely supervisory role. Independence is important as an auditor not only performs internal functions within the SE but must also act in the public interest. With regard to the internal functioning of the company, the auditor works *with* management but *for* the general meeting.

VII Supervision by the national authorities

42. As stated in Part III, Section 4 of this report, there is no special registry for SEs in Iceland. The official supervisory authority for SEs is thus the Registry of

Limited Companies. An SE registered in Iceland is subject to the same degree of supervision by the national authorities as other public limited companies engaged in the same business. For instance, an SE is potentially subject to oversight by the tax authorities, the FSA (if it is engaged in an area of activity subject to supervision by this body), the national competition authority, or the Agency for Health and Safety at Work.

43. Article 28 of Act No. 26/2004 contains a penalty clause, which provides that the provisions of Chapter XVIII of Act No. 2/1995 on penalties (including penalties for failure to provide information in a timely manner to the Registry) shall apply in the same manner to the management of an SE registered in Iceland.

VIII Dissolution

1 General remarks

44. When it comes to winding up, liquidation, insolvency, cessation of payments and similar procedures, an SE registered in Iceland shall be governed by the statutory provisions applicable to national public limited liability companies (Art. 63 Reg.).

2 Winding up

45. An SE registered in Iceland can be voluntarily wound up by a decision of two-thirds of the share capital present or represented at a general meeting. An SE can also be liquidated involuntarily on the ground of insolvency and must be wound up if it lacks sufficient means to carry on business, fails to satisfy the minimum capital requirements, does not have proper management, has failed to file its annual accounts, etc.

46. Those shareholders who control one-fifth or more of the company's share capital may petition the court to dissolve the SE on the ground that certain shareholders have deliberately abused their position within the company or violated the provisions of Act No. 26/2004, Act No. 2/1995 or the company's articles of association. Rather than force the company to wind up, however, the court can order it to redeem the shares of those shareholders seeking to have it dissolved.

Involuntary dissolution is a measure of last resort and should only be contemplated if the behaviour in question is illegal and expected to continue.

47. By means of a proportional vote, a winding-up committee shall be elected composed of two to five members. Shareholders holding at least one-third of the share capital have the right to appoint a representative to the committee. The members of the committee shall be jointly and severally liable. An audit of

the company's accounts shall also be conducted. Insofar as possible, the company shall cease doing business, and the winding-up committee shall convert the company's assets into cash and ensure payment of the company's debts. Creditors of the SE shall be informed accordingly. Once creditors have been paid, any surplus can be distributed to shareholders and the final report sent to the Registry. The SE's registration is then deleted from the Registry and the company ceases to exist.

3 Liquidation, insolvency and cessation of payments

48. An SE's board of directors must make the company's assets available for the bankruptcy estate as stipulated in Act No. 21/1991 on bankruptcy administration etc. Any proceeds remaining once the company's assets have been placed in bankruptcy and all creditors' claims have been satisfied shall be divided amongst shareholders in proportion to their shareholdings, unless the company's articles stipulate an alternative arrangement. The general meeting of shareholders, however, may decide to continue operating the company, provided the conditions required by law to do so have been met.

IX Applicable law

49. The formation of an SE in Iceland shall be governed first and foremost by Act No. 26/2004 as well as by Act No. 2/1995 (Art. 9 Reg.). The business of an SE registered in Iceland is therefore governed by the Regulation, Act No. 2/1995, Act No. 144/1994 and Act No. 145/1994.

X Tax treatment

1 General remarks

50. The tax treatment of an SE is not dealt with in Act No. 26/2004 and there have not been any amendments to Icelandic tax law in connection with implementation of the Regulation. The Internal Revenue Service is currently monitoring the steps being taken in other Nordic countries in connection with the SE, but so far no decision has been taken in Iceland regarding the taxation of an SE. Therefore, national rules of tax law applicable to public limited companies shall apply. An SE shall thus be considered a resident of Iceland for tax purposes if it is registered with the Registry (Art. 2 Income and Property Tax Act No. 90/2003).[9] An SE is liable for national income tax and, until 31 December 2005, net worth tax. Municipal taxes are not levied on corporate profits.

---

[9] Hereinafter referred to as Act No. 90/2003.

2 Income tax

51. The corporate tax rate on an SE's worldwide income currently stands at 18% (Art. 71 Act No. 90/2003). Corporate profits are taxed regardless of whether they are distributed. The tax base is the company's net income, i.e. after deduction of business expenses and certain allowances provided by law. Economic double taxation between companies is avoided by exempting dividends received from taxable income. The net operating losses of a company may be carried forward ten years. Losses may not be carried back.

52. Dividends and interest payments received by an SE are subject to withholding tax at a rate of 10% (Art. 1 Act No. 94/1996 on financial income). Taxes withheld are credited against the company's tax liability.

3 Value added tax

53. According to Act No. 50/1988 on value added tax, Iceland levies VAT on the supply of food and services. The standard rate is 24.5%. Companies are subject to VAT. All taxable persons are required to register with the Internal Revenue Service, which occurs automatically upon registration with the Registry. Taxable transactions include the supply in Iceland of goods and services for consideration and the import of goods to Iceland. The taxable amount is the actual sales price (excluding VAT) of the goods and services. VAT paid on an undertaking's own purchases may be deducted. The most important exemptions, without credit for input tax, include insurance and insurance services, health care services, and certain financial services, including banking. The most important exemption with credit for input tax (zero rated) is the export of goods and services.

4 Other taxes

54. Companies are not subject to payroll taxes. Social security contributions are due on all remuneration for dependent personal services. These contributions are used to fund a portion of the social security system. The general rate is currently 5.64%.

55. A net wealth tax is assessed on the net wealth of companies and other taxable entities at the end of each calendar year. Immovable property is assessed at the real estate assessment value effective at the end of each year. The current rate of net wealth tax is 0.6%. This tax will be repealed on 31 December 2005, pursuant to an amendment to Act No. 90/2003 passed by the Althing on 10 December 2004.

56. Municipalities levy property tax on the estimated value of real property. The tax rate varies, depending on the municipality.

XI Conclusion

57. Act No. 26/2004 passed through the Althing without much discussion or delay. It has not generated much interest amongst lawyers or company directors so far. The general feeling is that the SE will not be a popular vehicle in Iceland. Moreover, those SEs that do register in Iceland will most likely opt for the one-tier system, as this is the only system available to public limited companies under national law. Only time will tell whether the SE will gain in popularity in Iceland.

PART III
Annexes

Annex Ia

I

(Acts whose publication is obligatory)

COUNCIL REGULATION (EC) No 2157/2001

of 8 October 2001

on the Statute for a European company (SE)

THE COUNCIL OF THE EUROPEAN UNION,

Having regard to the Treaty establishing the European Community, and in particular Article 308 thereof,

Having regard to the proposal from the Commission [1],

Having regard to the opinion of the European Parliament [2],

Having regard to the opinion of the Economic and Social Committee [3],

Whereas:

(1) The completion of the internal market and the improvement it brings about in the economic and social situation throughout the Community mean not only that barriers to trade must be removed, but also that the structures of production must be adapted to the Community dimension. For that purpose it is essential that companies the business of which is not limited to satisfying purely local needs should be able to plan and carry out the reorganisation of their business on a Community scale.

(2) Such reorganisation presupposes that existing companies from different Member States are given the option of combining their potential by means of mergers. Such operations can be carried out only with due regard to the rules of competition laid down in the Treaty.

(3) Restructuring and cooperation operations involving companies from different Member States give rise to legal and psychological difficulties and tax problems. The approximation of Member States' company law by means of Directives based on Article 44 of the Treaty can overcome some of those difficulties. Such approximation does not, however, release companies governed by different legal systems from the obligation to choose a form of company governed by a particular national law.

(4) The legal framework within which business must be carried on in the Community is still based largely on national laws and therefore no longer corresponds to the economic framework within which it must develop if the objectives set out in Article 18 of the Treaty are to be achieved. That situation forms a considerable obstacle to the creation of groups of companies from different Member States.

(5) Member States are obliged to ensure that the provisions applicable to European companies under this Regulation do not result either in discrimination arising out of unjustified different treatment of European companies compared with public limited-liability companies or in disproportionate restrictions on the formation of a European company or on the transfer of its registered office.

(6) It is essential to ensure as far as possible that the economic unit and the legal unit of business in the Community coincide. For that purpose, provision should be made for the creation, side by side with companies governed by a particular national law, of companies formed and carrying on business under the law created by a Community Regulation directly applicable in all Member States.

(7) The provisions of such a Regulation will permit the creation and management of companies with a European dimension, free from the obstacles arising from the disparity and the limited territorial application of national company law.

---

[1] OJ C 263, 16.10.1989, p. 41 and OJ C 176, 8.7.1991, p. 1.
[2] Opinion of 4 September 2001 (not yet published in the Official Journal).
[3] OJ C 124, 21.5.1990, p. 34.

(8) The Statute for a European public limited-liability company (hereafter referred to as 'SE') is among the measures to be adopted by the Council before 1992 listed in the Commission's White Paper on completing the internal market, approved by the European Council that met in Milan in June 1985. The European Council that met in Brussels in 1987 expressed the wish to see such a Statute created swiftly.

(9) Since the Commission's submission in 1970 of a proposal for a Regulation on the Statute for a European public limited-liability company, amended in 1975, work on the approximation of national company law has made substantial progress, so that on those points where the functioning of an SE does not need uniform Community rules reference may be made to the law governing public limited-liability companies in the Member State where it has its registered office.

(10) Without prejudice to any economic needs that may arise in the future, if the essential objective of legal rules governing SEs is to be attained, it must be possible at least to create such a company as a means both of enabling companies from different Member States to merge or to create a holding company and of enabling companies and other legal persons carrying on economic activities and governed by the laws of different Member States to form joint subsidiaries.

(11) In the same context it should be possible for a public limited-liability company with a registered office and head office within the Community to transform itself into an SE without going into liquidation, provided it has a subsidiary in a Member State other than that of its registered office.

(12) National provisions applying to public limited-liability companies that offer their securities to the public and to securities transactions should also apply where an SE is formed by means of an offer of securities to the public and to SEs wishing to utilise such financial instruments.

(13) The SE itself must take the form of a company with share capital, that being the form most suited, in terms of both financing and management, to the needs of a company carrying on business on a European scale. In order to ensure that such companies are of reasonable size, a minimum amount of capital should be set so that they have sufficient assets without making it difficult for small and medium-sized undertakings to form SEs.

(14) An SE must be efficiently managed and properly supervised. It must be borne in mind that there are at present in the Community two different systems for the administration of public limited-liability companies. Although an SE should be allowed to choose between the two systems, the respective responsibilities of those responsible for management and those responsible for supervision should be clearly defined.

(15) Under the rules and general principles of private international law, where one undertaking controls another governed by a different legal system, its ensuing rights and obligations as regards the protection of minority shareholders and third parties are governed by the law governing the controlled undertaking, without prejudice to the obligations imposed on the controlling undertaking by its own law, for example the requirement to prepare consolidated accounts.

(16) Without prejudice to the consequences of any subsequent coordination of the laws of the Member States, specific rules for SEs are not at present required in this field. The rules and general principles of private international law should therefore be applied both where an SE exercises control and where it is the controlled company.

(17) The rule thus applicable where an SE is controlled by another undertaking should be specified, and for this purpose reference should be made to the law governing public limited-liability companies in the Member State in which the SE has its registered office.

(18) Each Member State must be required to apply the sanctions applicable to public limited-liability companies governed by its law in respect of infringements of this Regulation.

(19) The rules on the involvement of employees in the European company are laid down in Directive 2001/86/EC [1], and those provisions thus form an indissociable complement to this Regulation and must be applied concomitantly.

___

[1] See p. 22 of this Official Journal.

(20) This Regulation does not cover other areas of law such as taxation, competition, intellectual property or insolvency. The provisions of the Member States' law and of Community law are therefore applicable in the above areas and in other areas not covered by this Regulation.

(21) Directive 2001/86/EC is designed to ensure that employees have a right of involvement in issues and decisions affecting the life of their SE. Other social and labour legislation questions, in particular the right of employees to information and consultation as regulated in the Member States, are governed by the national provisions applicable, under the same conditions, to public limited-liability companies.

(22) The entry into force of this Regulation must be deferred so that each Member State may incorporate into its national law the provisions of Directive 2001/86/EC and set up in advance the necessary machinery for the formation and operation of SEs with registered offices within its territory, so that the Regulation and the Directive may be applied concomitantly.

(23) A company the head office of which is not in the Community should be allowed to participate in the formation of an SE provided that company is formed under the law of a Member State, has its registered office in that Member State and has a real and continuous link with a Member State's economy according to the principles established in the 1962 General Programme for the abolition of restrictions on freedom of establishment. Such a link exists in particular if a company has an establishment in that Member State and conducts operations therefrom.

(24) The SE should be enabled to transfer its registered office to another Member State. Adequate protection of the interests of minority shareholders who oppose the transfer, of creditors and of holders of other rights should be proportionate. Such transfer should not affect the rights originating before the transfer.

(25) This Regulation is without prejudice to any provision which may be inserted in the 1968 Brussels Convention or in any text adopted by Member States or by the Council to replace such Convention, relating to the rules of jurisdiction applicable in the case of transfer of the registered offices of a public limited-liability company from one Member State to another.

(26) Activities by financial institutions are regulated by specific directives and the national law implementing those directives and additional national rules regulating those activities apply in full to an SE.

(27) In view of the specific Community character of an SE, the 'real seat' arrangement adopted by this Regulation in respect of SEs is without prejudice to Member States' laws and does not pre-empt any choices to be made for other Community texts on company law.

(28) The Treaty does not provide, for the adoption of this Regulation, powers of action other than those of Article 308 thereof.

(29) Since the objectives of the intended action, as outlined above, cannot be adequately attained by the Member States in as much as a European public limited-liability company is being established at European level and can therefore, because of the scale and impact of such company, be better attained at Community level, the Community may take measures in accordance with the principle of subsidiarity enshrined in Article 5 of the Treaty. In accordance with the principle of proportionality as set out in the said Article, this Regulation does not go beyond what is necessary to attain these objectives,

HAS ADOPTED THIS REGULATION:

TITLE I

GENERAL PROVISIONS

Article 1

1. A company may be set up within the territory of the Community in the form of a European public limited-liability company (*Societas Europaea* or SE) on the conditions and in the manner laid down in this Regulation.

2. The capital of an SE shall be divided into shares. No shareholder shall be liable for more than the amount he has subscribed.

3. An SE shall have legal personality.

4. Employee involvement in an SE shall be governed by the provisions of Directive 2001/86/EC.

Article 2

1. Public limited-liability companies such as referred to in Annex I, formed under the law of a Member State, with registered offices and head offices within the Community may form an SE by means of a merger provided that at least two of them are governed by the law of different Member States.

2. Public and private limited-liability companies such as referred to in Annex II, formed under the law of a Member State, with registered offices and head offices within the Community may promote the formation of a holding SE provided that each of at least two of them:

(a) is governed by the law of a different Member State, or

(b) has for at least two years had a subsidiary company governed by the law of another Member State or a branch situated in another Member State.

3. Companies and firms within the meaning of the second paragraph of Article 48 of the Treaty and other legal bodies governed by public or private law, formed under the law of a Member State, with registered offices and head offices within the Community may form a subsidiary SE by subscribing for its shares, provided that each of at least two of them:

(a) is governed by the law of a different Member State, or

(b) has for at least two years had a subsidiary company governed by the law of another Member State or a branch situated in another Member State.

4. A public limited-liability company, formed under the law of a Member State, which has its registered office and head office within the Community may be transformed into an SE if for at least two years it has had a subsidiary company governed by the law of another Member State.

5. A Member State may provide that a company the head office of which is not in the Community may participate in the formation of an SE provided that company is formed under the law of a Member State, has its registered office in that Member State and has a real and continuous link with a Member State's economy.

Article 3

1. For the purposes of Article 2(1), (2) and (3), an SE shall be regarded as a public limited-liability company governed by the law of the Member State in which it has its registered office.

2. An SE may itself set up one or more subsidiaries in the form of SEs. The provisions of the law of the Member State in which a subsidiary SE has its registered office that require a public limited-liability company to have more than one shareholder shall not apply in the case of the subsidiary SE. The provisions of national law implementing the twelfth Council Company Law Directive (89/667/EEC) of 21 December 1989 on single-member private limited-liability companies ([1]) shall apply to SEs *mutatis mutandis*.

Article 4

1. The capital of an SE shall be expressed in euro.

2. The subscribed capital shall not be less than EUR 120 000.

3. The laws of a Member State requiring a greater subscribed capital for companies carrying on certain types of activity shall apply to SEs with registered offices in that Member State.

Article 5

Subject to Article 4(1) and (2), the capital of an SE, its maintenance and changes thereto, together with its shares, bonds and other similar securities shall be governed by the provisions which would apply to a public limited-liability company with a registered office in the Member State in which the SE is registered.

Article 6

For the purposes of this Regulation, 'the statutes of the SE' shall mean both the instrument of incorporation and, where they are the subject of a separate document, the statutes of the SE.

Article 7

The registered office of an SE shall be located within the Community, in the same Member State as its head office. A Member State may in addition impose on SEs registered in its territory the obligation of locating their head office and their registered office in the same place.

Article 8

1. The registered office of an SE may be transferred to another Member State in accordance with paragraphs 2 to 13. Such a transfer shall not result in the winding up of the SE or in the creation of a new legal person.

([1]) OJ L 395, 30.12.1989, p. 40. Directive as last amended by the 1994 Act of Accession.

2. The management or administrative organ shall draw up a transfer proposal and publicise it in accordance with Article 13, without prejudice to any additional forms of publication provided for by the Member State of the registered office. That proposal shall state the current name, registered office and number of the SE and shall cover:

(a) the proposed registered office of the SE;

(b) the proposed statutes of the SE including, where appropriate, its new name;

(c) any implication the transfer may have on employees' involvement;

(d) the proposed transfer timetable;

(e) any rights provided for the protection of shareholders and/or creditors.

3. The management or administrative organ shall draw up a report explaining and justifying the legal and economic aspects of the transfer and explaining the implications of the transfer for shareholders, creditors and employees.

4. An SE's shareholders and creditors shall be entitled, at least one month before the general meeting called upon to decide on the transfer, to examine at the SE's registered office the transfer proposal and the report drawn up pursuant to paragraph 3 and, on request, to obtain copies of those documents free of charge.

5. A Member State may, in the case of SEs registered within its territory, adopt provisions designed to ensure appropriate protection for minority shareholders who oppose a transfer.

6. No decision to transfer may be taken for two months after publication of the proposal. Such a decision shall be taken as laid down in Article 59.

7. Before the competent authority issues the certificate mentioned in paragraph 8, the SE shall satisfy it that, in respect of any liabilities arising prior to the publication of the transfer proposal, the interests of creditors and holders of other rights in respect of the SE (including those of public bodies) have been adequately protected in accordance with requirements laid down by the Member State where the SE has its registered office prior to the transfer.

A Member State may extend the application of the first subparagraph to liabilities that arise (or may arise) prior to the transfer.

The first and second subparagraphs shall be without prejudice to the application to SEs of the national legislation of Member States concerning the satisfaction or securing of payments to public bodies.

8. In the Member State in which an SE has its registered office the court, notary or other competent authority shall issue a certificate attesting to the completion of the acts and formalities to be accomplished before the transfer.

9. The new registration may not be effected until the certificate referred to in paragraph 8 has been submitted, and evidence produced that the formalities required for registration in the country of the new registered office have been completed.

10. The transfer of an SE's registered office and the consequent amendment of its statutes shall take effect on the date on which the SE is registered, in accordance with Article 12, in the register for its new registered office.

11. When the SE's new registration has been effected, the registry for its new registration shall notify the registry for its old registration. Deletion of the old registration shall be effected on receipt of that notification, but not before.

12. The new registration and the deletion of the old registration shall be publicised in the Member States concerned in accordance with Article 13.

13. On publication of an SE's new registration, the new registered office may be relied on as against third parties. However, as long as the deletion of the SE's registration from the register for its previous registered office has not been publicised, third parties may continue to rely on the previous registered office unless the SE proves that such third parties were aware of the new registered office.

14. The laws of a Member State may provide that, as regards SEs registered in that Member State, the transfer of a registered office which would result in a change of the law applicable shall not take effect if any of that Member State's competent authorities opposes it within the two-month period referred to in paragraph 6. Such opposition may be based only on grounds of public interest.

Where an SE is supervised by a national financial supervisory authority according to Community directives the right to oppose the change of registered office applies to this authority as well.

Review by a judicial authority shall be possible.

15. An SE may not transfer its registered office if proceedings for winding up, liquidation, insolvency or suspension of payments or other similar proceedings have been brought against it.

16. An SE which has transferred its registered office to another Member State shall be considered, in respect of any cause of action arising prior to the transfer as determined in paragraph 10, as having its registered office in the Member States where the SE was registered prior to the transfer, even if the SE is sued after the transfer.

Article 9

1. An SE shall be governed:

(a) by this Regulation,

(b) where expressly authorised by this Regulation, by the provisions of its statutes

or

(c) in the case of matters not regulated by this Regulation or, where matters are partly regulated by it, of those aspects not covered by it, by:

   (i) the provisions of laws adopted by Member States in implementation of Community measures relating specifically to SEs;

   (ii) the provisions of Member States' laws which would apply to a public limited-liability company formed in accordance with the law of the Member State in which the SE has its registered office;

   (iii) the provisions of its statutes, in the same way as for a public limited-liability company formed in accordance with the law of the Member State in which the SE has its registered office.

2. The provisions of laws adopted by Member States specifically for the SE must be in accordance with Directives applicable to public limited-liability companies referred to in Annex I.

3. If the nature of the business carried out by an SE is regulated by specific provisions of national laws, those laws shall apply in full to the SE.

Article 10

Subject to this Regulation, an SE shall be treated in every Member State as if it were a public limited-liability company formed in accordance with the law of the Member State in which it has its registered office.

Article 11

1. The name of an SE shall be preceded or followed by the abbreviation SE.

2. Only SEs may include the abbreviation SE in their name.

3. Nevertheless, companies, firms and other legal entities registered in a Member State before the date of entry into force of this Regulation in the names of which the abbreviation SE appears shall not be required to alter their names.

Article 12

1. Every SE shall be registered in the Member State in which it has its registered office in a register designated by the law of that Member State in accordance with Article 3 of the first Council Directive (68/151/EEC) of 9 March 1968 on coordination of safeguards which, for the protection of the interests of members and others, are required by Member States of companies within the meaning of the second paragraph of Article 58 of the Treaty, with a view to making such safeguards equivalent throughout the Community ([1]).

2. An SE may not be registered unless an agreement on arrangements for employee involvement pursuant to Article 4 of Directive 2001/86/EC has been concluded, or a decision pursuant to Article 3(6) of the Directive has been taken, or the period for negotiations pursuant to Article 5 of the Directive has expired without an agreement having been concluded.

3. In order for an SE to be registered in a Member State which has made use of the option referred to in Article 7(3) of Directive 2001/86/EC, either an agreement pursuant to Article 4 of the Directive must have been concluded on the arrangements for employee involvement, including participation, or none of the participating companies must have been governed by participation rules prior to the registration of the SE.

4. The statutes of the SE must not conflict at any time with the arrangements for employee involvement which have been so determined. Where new such arrangements determined pursuant to the Directive conflict with the existing statutes, the statutes shall to the extent necessary be amended.

In this case, a Member State may provide that the management organ or the administrative organ of the SE shall be entitled to proceed to amend the statutes without any further decision from the general shareholders meeting.

([1]) OJ L 65, 14.3.1968, p. 8. Directive as last amended by the 1994 Act of Accession.

Article 13

Publication of the documents and particulars concerning an SE which must be publicised under this Regulation shall be effected in the manner laid down in the laws of the Member State in which the SE has its registered office in accordance with Directive 68/151/EEC.

Article 14

1. Notice of an SE's registration and of the deletion of such a registration shall be published for information purposes in the *Official Journal of the European Communities* after publication in accordance with Article 13. That notice shall state the name, number, date and place of registration of the SE, the date and place of publication and the title of publication, the registered office of the SE and its sector of activity.

2. Where the registered office of an SE is transferred in accordance with Article 8, notice shall be published giving the information provided for in paragraph 1, together with that relating to the new registration.

3. The particulars referred to in paragraph 1 shall be forwarded to the Office for Official Publications of the European Communities within one month of the publication referred to in Article 13.

TITLE II

FORMATION

Section 1

General

Article 15

1. Subject to this Regulation, the formation of an SE shall be governed by the law applicable to public limited-liability companies in the Member State in which the SE establishes its registered office.

2. The registration of an SE shall be publicised in accordance with Article 13.

Article 16

1. An SE shall acquire legal personality on the date on which it is registered in the register referred to in Article 12.

2. If acts have been performed in an SE's name before its registration in accordance with Article 12 and the SE does not assume the obligations arising out of such acts after its registration, the natural persons, companies, firms or other legal entities which performed those acts shall be jointly and severally liable therefor, without limit, in the absence of agreement to the contrary.

Section 2

Formation by merger

Article 17

1. An SE may be formed by means of a merger in accordance with Article 2(1).

2. Such a merger may be carried out in accordance with:

(a) the procedure for merger by acquisition laid down in Article 3(1) of the third Council Directive (78/855/EEC) of 9 October 1978 based on Article 54(3)(g) of the Treaty concerning mergers of public limited-liability companies [1] or

(b) the procedure for merger by the formation of a new company laid down in Article 4(1) of the said Directive.

In the case of a merger by acquisition, the acquiring company shall take the form of an SE when the merger takes place. In the case of a merger by the formation of a new company, the SE shall be the newly formed company.

Article 18

For matters not covered by this section or, where a matter is partly covered by it, for aspects not covered by it, each company involved in the formation of an SE by merger shall be governed by the provisions of the law of the Member State to which it is subject that apply to mergers of public limited-liability companies in accordance with Directive 78/855/EEC.

Article 19

The laws of a Member State may provide that a company governed by the law of that Member State may not take part in the formation of an SE by merger if any of that Member State's competent authorities opposes it before the issue of the certificate referred to in Article 25(2).

---

[1] OJ L 295, 20.10.1978, p. 36. Directive as last amended by the 1994 Act of Accession.

Such opposition may be based only on grounds of public interest. Review by a judicial authority shall be possible.

Article 20

1. The management or administrative organs of merging companies shall draw up draft terms of merger. The draft terms of merger shall include the following particulars:

(a) the name and registered office of each of the merging companies together with those proposed for the SE;

(b) the share-exchange ratio and the amount of any compensation;

(c) the terms for the allotment of shares in the SE;

(d) the date from which the holding of shares in the SE will entitle the holders to share in profits and any special conditions affecting that entitlement;

(e) the date from which the transactions of the merging companies will be treated for accounting purposes as being those of the SE;

(f) the rights conferred by the SE on the holders of shares to which special rights are attached and on the holders of securities other than shares, or the measures proposed concerning them;

(g) any special advantage granted to the experts who examine the draft terms of merger or to members of the administrative, management, supervisory or controlling organs of the merging companies;

(h) the statutes of the SE;

(i) information on the procedures by which arrangements for employee involvement are determined pursuant to Directive 2001/86/EC.

2. The merging companies may include further items in the draft terms of merger.

Article 21

For each of the merging companies and subject to the additional requirements imposed by the Member State to which the company concerned is subject, the following particulars shall be published in the national gazette of that Member State:

(a) the type, name and registered office of every merging company;

(b) the register in which the documents referred to in Article 3(2) of Directive 68/151/EEC are filed in respect of each merging company, and the number of the entry in that register;

(c) an indication of the arrangements made in accordance with Article 24 for the exercise of the rights of the creditors of the company in question and the address at which complete information on those arrangements may be obtained free of charge;

(d) an indication of the arrangements made in accordance with Article 24 for the exercise of the rights of minority shareholders of the company in question and the address at which complete information on those arrangements may be obtained free of charge;

(e) the name and registered office proposed for the SE.

Article 22

As an alternative to experts operating on behalf of each of the merging companies, one or more independent experts as defined in Article 10 of Directive 78/855/EEC, appointed for those purposes at the joint request of the companies by a judicial or administrative authority in the Member State of one of the merging companies or of the proposed SE, may examine the draft terms of merger and draw up a single report to all the shareholders.

The experts shall have the right to request from each of the merging companies any information they consider necessary to enable them to complete their function.

Article 23

1. The general meeting of each of the merging companies shall approve the draft terms of merger.

2. Employee involvement in the SE shall be decided pursuant to Directive 2001/86/EC. The general meetings of each of the merging companies may reserve the right to make registration of the SE conditional upon its express ratification of the arrangements so decided.

Article 24

1. The law of the Member State governing each merging company shall apply as in the case of a merger of public limited-liability companies, taking into account the cross-border nature of the merger, with regard to the protection of the interests of:

(a) creditors of the merging companies;

(b) holders of bonds of the merging companies;

(c) holders of securities, other than shares, which carry special rights in the merging companies.

2. A Member State may, in the case of the merging companies governed by its law, adopt provisions designed to ensure appropriate protection for minority shareholders who have opposed the merger.

Article 25

1. The legality of a merger shall be scrutinised, as regards the part of the procedure concerning each merging company, in accordance with the law on mergers of public limited-liability companies of the Member State to which the merging company is subject.

2. In each Member State concerned the court, notary or other competent authority shall issue a certificate conclusively attesting to the completion of the pre-merger acts and formalities.

3. If the law of a Member State to which a merging company is subject provides for a procedure to scrutinise and amend the share-exchange ratio, or a procedure to compensate minority shareholders, without preventing the registration of the merger, such procedures shall only apply if the other merging companies situated in Member States which do not provide for such procedure explicitly accept, when approving the draft terms of the merger in accordance with Article 23(1), the possibility for the shareholders of that merging company to have recourse to such procedure. In such cases, the court, notary or other competent authorities may issue the certificate referred to in paragraph 2 even if such a procedure has been commenced. The certificate must, however, indicate that the procedure is pending. The decision in the procedure shall be binding on the acquiring company and all its shareholders.

Article 26

1. The legality of a merger shall be scrutinised, as regards the part of the procedure concerning the completion of the merger and the formation of the SE, by the court, notary or other authority competent in the Member State of the proposed registered office of the SE to scrutinise that aspect of the legality of mergers of public limited-liability companies.

2. To that end each merging company shall submit to the competent authority the certificate referred to in Article 25(2) within six months of its issue together with a copy of the draft terms of merger approved by that company.

3. The authority referred to in paragraph 1 shall in particular ensure that the merging companies have approved draft terms of merger in the same terms and that arrangements for employee involvement have been determined pursuant to Directive 2001/86/EC.

4. That authority shall also satisfy itself that the SE has been formed in accordance with the requirements of the law of the Member State in which it has its registered office in accordance with Article 15.

Article 27

1. A merger and the simultaneous formation of an SE shall take effect on the date on which the SE is registered in accordance with Article 12.

2. The SE may not be registered until the formalities provided for in Articles 25 and 26 have been completed.

Article 28

For each of the merging companies the completion of the merger shall be publicised as laid down by the law of each Member State in accordance with Article 3 of Directive 68/151/EEC.

Article 29

1. A merger carried out as laid down in Article 17(2)(a) shall have the following consequences *ipso jure* and simultaneously:

(a) all the assets and liabilities of each company being acquired are transferred to the acquiring company;

(b) the shareholders of the company being acquired become shareholders of the acquiring company;

(c) the company being acquired ceases to exist;

(d) the acquiring company adopts the form of an SE.

2. A merger carried out as laid down in Article 17(2)(b) shall have the following consequences *ipso jure* and simultaneously:

(a) all the assets and liabilities of the merging companies are transferred to the SE;

(b) the shareholders of the merging companies become shareholders of the SE;

(c) the merging companies cease to exist.

3. Where, in the case of a merger of public limited-liability companies, the law of a Member State requires the completion of any special formalities before the transfer of certain assets, rights and obligations by the merging companies becomes effective against third parties, those formalities shall apply and shall be carried out either by the merging companies or by the SE following its registration.

4. The rights and obligations of the participating companies on terms and conditions of employment arising from national law, practice and individual employment contracts or employment relationships and existing at the date of the registration shall, by reason of such registration be transferred to the SE upon its registration.

Article 30

A merger as provided for in Article 2(1) may not be declared null and void once the SE has been registered.

The absence of scrutiny of the legality of the merger pursuant to Articles 25 and 26 may be included among the grounds for the winding-up of the SE.

Article 31

1. Where a merger within the meaning of Article 17(2)(a) is carried out by a company which holds all the shares and other securities conferring the right to vote at general meetings of another company, neither Article 20(1)(b), (c) and (d), Article 29(1)(b) nor Article 22 shall apply. National law governing each merging company and mergers of public limited-liability companies in accordance with Article 24 of Directive 78/855/EEC shall nevertheless apply.

2. Where a merger by acquisition is carried out by a company which holds 90 % or more but not all of the shares and other securities conferring the right to vote at general meetings of another company, reports by the management or administrative body, reports by an independent expert or experts and the documents necessary for scrutiny shall be required only to the extent that the national law governing either the acquiring company or the company being acquired so requires.

Member States may, however, provide that this paragraph may apply where a company holds shares conferring 90 % or more but not all of the voting rights.

Section 3

Formation of a holding SE

Article 32

1. A holding SE may be formed in accordance with Article 2(2).

A company promoting the formation of a holding SE in accordance with Article 2(2) shall continue to exist.

2. The management or administrative organs of the companies which promote such an operation shall draw up, in the same terms, draft terms for the formation of the holding SE. The draft terms shall include a report explaining and justifying the legal and economic aspects of the formation and indicating the implications for the shareholders and for the employees of the adoption of the form of a holding SE. The draft terms shall also set out the particulars provided for in Article 20(1)(a), (b), (c), (f), (g), (h) and (i) and shall fix the minimum proportion of the shares in each of the companies promoting the operation which the shareholders must contribute to the formation of the holding SE. That proportion shall be shares conferring more than 50 % of the permanent voting rights.

3. For each of the companies promoting the operation, the draft terms for the formation of the holding SE shall be publicised in the manner laid down in each Member State's national law in accordance with Article 3 of Directive 68/151/EEC at least one month before the date of the general meeting called to decide thereon.

4. One or more experts independent of the companies promoting the operation, appointed or approved by a judicial or administrative authority in the Member State to which each company is subject in accordance with national provisions adopted in implementation of Directive 78/855/EEC, shall examine the draft terms of formation drawn up in accordance with paragraph 2 and draw up a written report for the shareholders of each company. By agreement between the companies promoting the operation, a single written report may be drawn up for the shareholders of all the companies by one or more independent experts, appointed or approved by a judicial or administrative authority in the Member State to which one of the companies promoting the operation or the proposed SE is subject in accordance with national provisions adopted in implementation of Directive 78/855/EEC.

5. The report shall indicate any particular difficulties of valuation and state whether the proposed share-exchange ratio is fair and reasonable, indicating the methods used to arrive at it and whether such methods are adequate in the case in question.

6. The general meeting of each company promoting the operation shall approve the draft terms of formation of the holding SE.

Employee involvement in the holding SE shall be decided pursuant to Directive 2001/86/EC. The general meetings of each company promoting the operation may reserve the right to make registration of the holding SE conditional upon its express ratification of the arrangements so decided.

7. These provisions shall apply *mutatis mutandis* to private limited-liability companies.

Article 33

1. The shareholders of the companies promoting such an operation shall have a period of three months in which to inform the promoting companies whether they intend to contribute their shares to the formation of the holding SE. That period shall begin on the date upon which the terms for the formation of the holding SE have been finally determined in accordance with Article 32.

2. The holding SE shall be formed only if, within the period referred to in paragraph 1, the shareholders of the companies promoting the operation have assigned the minimum proportion of shares in each company in accordance with the draft terms of formation and if all the other conditions are fulfilled.

3. If the conditions for the formation of the holding SE are all fulfilled in accordance with paragraph 2, that fact shall, in respect of each of the promoting companies, be publicised in the manner laid down in the national law governing each of those companies adopted in implementation of Article 3 of Directive 68/151/EEC.

Shareholders of the companies promoting the operation who have not indicated whether they intend to make their shares available to the promoting companies for the purpose of forming the holding SE within the period referred to in paragraph 1 shall have a further month in which to do so.

4. Shareholders who have contributed their securities to the formation of the SE shall receive shares in the holding SE.

5. The holding SE may not be registered until it is shown that the formalities referred to in Article 32 have been completed and that the conditions referred to in paragraph 2 have been fulfilled.

Article 34

A Member State may, in the case of companies promoting such an operation, adopt provisions designed to ensure protection for minority shareholders who oppose the operation, creditors and employees.

Section 4

Formation of a subsidiary SE

Article 35

An SE may be formed in accordance with Article 2(3).

Article 36

Companies, firms and other legal entities participating in such an operation shall be subject to the provisions governing their participation in the formation of a subsidiary in the form of a public limited-liability company under national law.

Section 5

Conversion of an existing public limited-liability company into an SE

Article 37

1. An SE may be formed in accordance with Article 2(4).

2. Without prejudice to Article 12 the conversion of a public limited-liability company into an SE shall not result in the winding up of the company or in the creation of a new legal person.

3. The registered office may not be transferred from one Member State to another pursuant to Article 8 at the same time as the conversion is effected.

4. The management or administrative organ of the company in question shall draw up draft terms of conversion and a report explaining and justifying the legal and economic aspects of the conversion and indicating the implications for the shareholders and for the employees of the adoption of the form of an SE.

5. The draft terms of conversion shall be publicised in the manner laid down in each Member State's law in accordance with Article 3 of Directive 68/151/EEC at least one month before the general meeting called upon to decide thereon.

6. Before the general meeting referred to in paragraph 7 one or more independent experts appointed or approved, in accordance with the national provisions adopted in implementation of Article 10 of Directive 78/855/EEC, by a judicial or administrative authority in the Member State to which the company being converted into an SE is subject shall certify in compliance with Directive 77/91/EEC [1] *mutatis mutandis* that the company has net assets at least equivalent to its capital plus those reserves which must not be distributed under the law or the Statutes.

7. The general meeting of the company in question shall approve the draft terms of conversion together with the statutes of the SE. The decision of the general meeting shall be passed as laid down in the provisions of national law adopted in implementation of Article 7 of Directive 78/855/EEC.

8. Member States may condition a conversion to a favourable vote of a qualified majority or unanimity in the organ of the company to be converted within which employee participation is organised.

9. The rights and obligations of the company to be converted on terms and conditions of employment arising from national law, practice and individual employment contracts or employment relationships and existing at the date of the registration shall, by reason of such registration be transferred to the SE.

TITLE III

STRUCTURE OF THE SE

Article 38

Under the conditions laid down by this Regulation an SE shall comprise:

(a) a general meeting of shareholders and

(b) either a supervisory organ and a management organ (two-tier system) or an administrative organ (one-tier system) depending on the form adopted in the statutes.

---

[1] Second Council Directive 77/91/EEC of 13 December 1976 on coordination of safeguards which, for the protection of the interests of members and others, are required by Member States of companies within the meaning of the second paragraph of Article 58 of the Treaty, in respect of the formation of public limited liability companies and the maintenance and alteration of their capital, with a view to making such safeguards equivalent (OJ L 26, 31.1.1977, p. 1). Directive as last amended by the 1994 Act of Accession.

Section 1

Two-tier system

Article 39

1. The management organ shall be responsible for managing the SE. A Member State may provide that a managing director or managing directors shall be responsible for the current management under the same conditions as for public limited-liability companies that have registered offices within that Member State's territory.

2. The member or members of the management organ shall be appointed and removed by the supervisory organ.

A Member State may, however, require or permit the statutes to provide that the member or members of the management organ shall be appointed and removed by the general meeting under the same conditions as for public limited-liability companies that have registered offices within its territory.

3. No person may at the same time be a member of both the management organ and the supervisory organ of the same SE. The supervisory organ may, however, nominate one of its members to act as a member of the management organ in the event of a vacancy. During such a period the functions of the person concerned as a member of the supervisory organ shall be suspended. A Member State may impose a time limit on such a period.

4. The number of members of the management organ or the rules for determining it shall be laid down in the SE's statutes. A Member State may, however, fix a minimum and/or a maximum number.

5. Where no provision is made for a two-tier system in relation to public limited-liability companies with registered offices within its territory, a Member State may adopt the appropriate measures in relation to SEs.

Article 40

1. The supervisory organ shall supervise the work of the management organ. It may not itself exercise the power to manage the SE.

2. The members of the supervisory organ shall be appointed by the general meeting. The members of the first supervisory organ may, however, be appointed by the statutes. This shall apply without prejudice to Article 47(4) or to any employee participation arrangements determined pursuant to Directive 2001/86/EC.

3. The number of members of the supervisory organ or the rules for determining it shall be laid down in the statutes. A Member State may, however, stipulate the number of members of the supervisory organ for SEs registered within its territory or a minimum and/or a maximum number.

Article 41

1. The management organ shall report to the supervisory organ at least once every three months on the progress and foreseeable development of the SE's business.

2. In addition to the regular information referred to in paragraph 1, the management organ shall promptly pass the supervisory organ any information on events likely to have an appreciable effect on the SE.

3. The supervisory organ may require the management organ to provide information of any kind which it needs to exercise supervision in accordance with Article 40(1). A Member State may provide that each member of the supervisory organ also be entitled to this facility.

4. The supervisory organ may undertake or arrange for any investigations necessary for the performance of its duties.

5. Each member of the supervisory organ shall be entitled to examine all information submitted to it.

Article 42

The supervisory organ shall elect a chairman from among its members. If half of the members are appointed by employees, only a member appointed by the general meeting of shareholders may be elected chairman.

Section 2

The one-tier system

Article 43

1. The administrative organ shall manage the SE. A Member State may provide that a managing director or managing directors shall be responsible for the day-to-day management under the same conditions as for public limited-liability companies that have registered offices within that Member State's territory.

2. The number of members of the administrative organ or the rules for determining it shall be laid down in the SE's statutes. A Member State may, however, set a minimum and, where necessary, a maximum number of members.

The administrative organ shall, however, consist of at least three members where employee participation is regulated in accordance with Directive 2001/86/EC.

3. The member or members of the administrative organ shall be appointed by the general meeting. The members of the first administrative organ may, however, be appointed by the statutes. This shall apply without prejudice to Article 47(4) or to any employee participation arrangements determined pursuant to Directive 2001/86/EC.

4. Where no provision is made for a one-tier system in relation to public limited-liability companies with registered offices within its territory, a Member State may adopt the appropriate measures in relation to SEs.

Article 44

1. The administrative organ shall meet at least once every three months at intervals laid down by the statutes to discuss the progress and foreseeable development of the SE's business.

2. Each member of the administrative organ shall be entitled to examine all information submitted to it.

Article 45

The administrative organ shall elect a chairman from among its members. If half of the members are appointed by employees, only a member appointed by the general meeting of shareholders may be elected chairman.

Section 3

Rules common to the one-tier and two-tier systems

Article 46

1. Members of company organs shall be appointed for a period laid down in the statutes not exceeding six years.

2. Subject to any restrictions laid down in the statutes, members may be reappointed once or more than once for the period determined in accordance with paragraph 1.

Article 47

1. An SE's statutes may permit a company or other legal entity to be a member of one of its organs, provided that the law applicable to public limited-liability companies in the Member State in which the SE's registered office is situated does not provide otherwise.

That company or other legal entity shall designate a natural person to exercise its functions on the organ in question.

2. No person may be a member of any SE organ or a representative of a member within the meaning of paragraph 1 who:

(a) is disqualified, under the law of the Member State in which the SE's registered office is situated, from serving on the corresponding organ of a public limited-liability company governed by the law of that Member State, or

(b) is disqualified from serving on the corresponding organ of a public limited-liability company governed by the law of a Member State owing to a judicial or administrative decision delivered in a Member State.

3. An SE's statutes may, in accordance with the law applicable to public limited-liability companies in the Member State in which the SE's registered office is situated, lay down special conditions of eligibility for members representing the shareholders.

4. This Regulation shall not affect national law permitting a minority of shareholders or other persons or authorities to appoint some of the members of a company organ.

Article 48

1. An SE's statutes shall list the categories of transactions which require authorisation of the management organ by the supervisory organ in the two-tier system or an express decision by the administrative organ in the one-tier system.

A Member State may, however, provide that in the two-tier system the supervisory organ may itself make certain categories of transactions subject to authorisation.

2. A Member State may determine the categories of transactions which must at least be indicated in the statutes of SEs registered within its territory.

Article 49

The members of an SE's organs shall be under a duty, even after they have ceased to hold office, not to divulge any information which they have concerning the SE the disclosure of which might be prejudicial to the company's interests, except where such disclosure is required or permitted under national law provisions applicable to public limited-liability companies or is in the public interest.

Article 50

1. Unless otherwise provided by this Regulation or the statutes, the internal rules relating to quorums and decision-taking in SE organs shall be as follows:

(a) quorum: at least half of the members must be present or represented;

(b) decision-taking: a majority of the members present or represented.

2. Where there is no relevant provision in the statutes, the chairman of each organ shall have a casting vote in the event of a tie. There shall be no provision to the contrary in the statutes, however, where half of the supervisory organ consists of employees' representatives.

3. Where employee participation is provided for in accordance with Directive 2001/86/EC, a Member State may provide that the supervisory organ's quorum and decision-making shall, by way of derogation from the provisions referred to in paragraphs 1 and 2, be subject to the rules applicable, under the same conditions, to public limited-liability companies governed by the law of the Member State concerned.

Article 51

Members of an SE's management, supervisory and administrative organs shall be liable, in accordance with the provisions applicable to public limited-liability companies in the Member State in which the SE's registered office is situated, for loss or damage sustained by the SE following any breach on their part of the legal, statutory or other obligations inherent in their duties.

Section 4

General meeting

Article 52

The general meeting shall decide on matters for which it is given sole responsibility by:

(a) this Regulation or

(b) the legislation of the Member State in which the SE's registered office is situated adopted in implementation of Directive 2001/86/EC.

Furthermore, the general meeting shall decide on matters for which responsibility is given to the general meeting of a public limited-liability company governed by the law of the Member State in which the SE's registered office is situated, either by the law of that Member State or by the SE's statutes in accordance with that law.

Article 53

Without prejudice to the rules laid down in this section, the organisation and conduct of general meetings together with voting procedures shall be governed by the law applicable to public limited-liability companies in the Member State in which the SE's registered office is situated.

Article 54

1. An SE shall hold a general meeting at least once each calendar year, within six months of the end of its financial year, unless the law of the Member State in which the SE's registered office is situated applicable to public limited-liability companies carrying on the same type of activity as the SE provides for more frequent meetings. A Member State may, however, provide that the first general meeting may be held at any time in the 18 months following an SE's incorporation.

2. General meetings may be convened at any time by the management organ, the administrative organ, the supervisory organ or any other organ or competent authority in accordance with the national law applicable to public limited-liability companies in the Member State in which the SE's registered office is situated.

Article 55

1. One or more shareholders who together hold at least 10 % of an SE's subscribed capital may request the SE to convene a general meeting and draw up the agenda therefor; the SE's statutes or national legislation may provide for a smaller proportion under the same conditions as those applicable to public limited-liability companies.

2. The request that a general meeting be convened shall state the items to be put on the agenda.

3. If, following a request made under paragraph 1, a general meeting is not held in due time and, in any event, within two months, the competent judicial or administrative authority within the jurisdiction of which the SE's registered office is situated may order that a general meeting be convened within a given period or authorise either the shareholders who have requested it or their representatives to convene a general meeting. This shall be without prejudice to any national provisions which allow the shareholders themselves to convene general meetings.

Article 56

One or more shareholders who together hold at least 10 % of an SE's subscribed capital may request that one or more additional items be put on the agenda of any general meeting. The procedures and time limits applicable to such requests shall be laid down by the national law of the Member State in which the SE's registered office is situated or, failing that, by the SE's statutes. The above proportion may be reduced by the statutes or by the law of the Member State in which the SE's registered office is situated under the same conditions as are applicable to public limited-liability companies.

Article 57

Save where this Regulation or, failing that, the law applicable to public limited-liability companies in the Member State in which an SE's registered office is situated requires a larger majority, the general meeting's decisions shall be taken by a majority of the votes validly cast.

Article 58

The votes cast shall not include votes attaching to shares in respect of which the shareholder has not taken part in the vote or has abstained or has returned a blank or spoilt ballot paper.

Article 59

1. Amendment of an SE's statutes shall require a decision by the general meeting taken by a majority which may not be less than two thirds of the votes cast, unless the law applicable to public limited-liability companies in the Member State in which an SE's registered office is situated requires or permits a larger majority.

2. A Member State may, however, provide that where at least half of an SE's subscribed capital is represented, a simple majority of the votes referred to in paragraph 1 shall suffice.

3. Amendments to an SE's statutes shall be publicised in accordance with Article 13.

Article 60

1. Where an SE has two or more classes of shares, every decision by the general meeting shall be subject to a separate vote by each class of shareholders whose class rights are affected thereby.

2. Where a decision by the general meeting requires the majority of votes specified in Article 59(1) or (2), that majority shall also be required for the separate vote by each class of shareholders whose class rights are affected by the decision.

TITLE IV

ANNUAL ACCOUNTS AND CONSOLIDATED ACCOUNTS

Article 61

Subject to Article 62 an SE shall be governed by the rules applicable to public limited-liability companies under the law of the Member State in which its registered office is situated as regards the preparation of its annual and, where appropriate, consolidated accounts including the accompanying annual report and the auditing and publication of those accounts.

Article 62

1. An SE which is a credit or financial institution shall be governed by the rules laid down in the national law of the Member State in which its registered office is situated in implementation of Directive 2000/12/EC of the European Parliament and of the Council of 20 March 2000 relating to the taking up and pursuit of the business of credit institutions ([1]) as regards the preparation of its annual and, where appropriate, consolidated accounts, including the accompanying annual report and the auditing and publication of those accounts.

2. An SE which is an insurance undertaking shall be governed by the rules laid down in the national law of the Member State in which its registered office is situated in implementation of Council Directive 91/674/EEC of 19 December 1991 on the annual accounts and consolidated accounts of insurance undertakings ([2]) as regards the preparation of its annual and, where appropriate, consolidated accounts including the accompanying annual report and the auditing and publication of those accounts.

([1]) OJ L 126, 26.5.2000, p. 1.
([2]) OJ L 374, 31.12.1991, p. 7.

TITLE V

WINDING UP, LIQUIDATION, INSOLVENCY AND CESSATION OF PAYMENTS

Article 63

As regards winding up, liquidation, insolvency, cessation of payments and similar procedures, an SE shall be governed by the legal provisions which would apply to a public limited-liability company formed in accordance with the law of the Member State in which its registered office is situated, including provisions relating to decision-making by the general meeting.

Article 64

1. When an SE no longer complies with the requirement laid down in Article 7, the Member State in which the SE's registered office is situated shall take appropriate measures to oblige the SE to regularise its position within a specified period either:

(a) by re-establishing its head office in the Member State in which its registered office is situated or

(b) by transferring the registered office by means of the procedure laid down in Article 8.

2. The Member State in which the SE's registered office is situated shall put in place the measures necessary to ensure that an SE which fails to regularise its position in accordance with paragraph 1 is liquidated.

3. The Member State in which the SE's registered office is situated shall set up a judicial remedy with regard to any established infringement of Article 7. That remedy shall have a suspensory effect on the procedures laid down in paragraphs 1 and 2.

4. Where it is established on the initiative of either the authorities or any interested party that an SE has its head office within the territory of a Member State in breach of Article 7, the authorities of that Member State shall immediately inform the Member State in which the SE's registered office is situated.

Article 65

Without prejudice to provisions of national law requiring additional publication, the initiation and termination of winding up, liquidation, insolvency or cessation of payment procedures and any decision to continue operating shall be publicised in accordance with Article 13.

Article 66

1. An SE may be converted into a public limited-liability company governed by the law of the Member State in which its registered office is situated. No decision on conversion may be taken before two years have elapsed since its registration or before the first two sets of annual accounts have been approved.

2. The conversion of an SE into a public limited-liability company shall not result in the winding up of the company or in the creation of a new legal person.

3. The management or administrative organ of the SE shall draw up draft terms of conversion and a report explaining and justifying the legal and economic aspects of the conversion and indicating the implications of the adoption of the public limited-liability company for the shareholders and for the employees.

4. The draft terms of conversion shall be publicised in the manner laid down in each Member State's law in accordance with Article 3 of Directive 68/151/EEC at least one month before the general meeting called to decide thereon.

5. Before the general meeting referred to in paragraph 6, one or more independent experts appointed or approved, in accordance with the national provisions adopted in implementation of Article 10 of Directive 78/855/EEC, by a judicial or administrative authority in the Member State to which the SE being converted into a public limited-liability company is subject shall certify that the company has assets at least equivalent to its capital.

6. The general meeting of the SE shall approve the draft terms of conversion together with the statutes of the public limited-liability company. The decision of the general meeting shall be passed as laid down in the provisions of national law adopted in implementation of Article 7 of Directive 78/855/EEC.

TITLE VI

ADDITIONAL AND TRANSITIONAL PROVISIONS

Article 67

1. If and so long as the third phase of economic and monetary union (EMU) does not apply to it each Member State may make SEs with registered offices within its territory subject to the same provisions as apply to public limited-liability companies covered by its legislation as regards the expression of their capital. An SE may, in any case, express its capital in euro as well. In that event the national currency/euro conversion rate shall be that for the last day of the month preceding that of the formation of the SE.

2. If and so long as the third phase of EMU does not apply to the Member State in which an SE has its registered office, the SE may, however, prepare and publish its annual and, where appropriate, consolidated accounts in euro. The Member State may require that the SE's annual and, where appropriate, consolidated accounts be prepared and published in the national currency under the same conditions as those laid down for public limited-liability companies governed by the law of that Member State. This shall not prejudge the additional possibility for an SE of publishing its annual and, where appropriate, consolidated accounts in euro in accordance with Council Directive 90/604/EEC of 8 November 1990 amending Directive 78/60/EEC on annual accounts and Directive 83/349/EEC on consolidated accounts as concerns the exemptions for small and medium-sized companies and the publication of accounts in ecu [1].

TITLE VII

FINAL PROVISIONS

Article 68

1. The Member States shall make such provision as is appropriate to ensure the effective application of this Regulation.

2. Each Member State shall designate the competent authorities within the meaning of Articles 8, 25, 26, 54, 55 and 64. It shall inform the Commission and the other Member States accordingly.

Article 69

Five years at the latest after the entry into force of this Regulation, the Commission shall forward to the Council and the European Parliament a report on the application of the Regulation and proposals for amendments, where appropriate. The report shall, in particular, analyse the appropriateness of:

(a) allowing the location of an SE's head office and registered office in different Member States;

(b) broadening the concept of merger in Article 17(2) in order to admit also other types of merger than those defined in Articles 3(1) and 4(1) of Directive 78/855/EEC;

---

[1] OJ L 317, 16.11.1990, p. 57.

(c) revising the jurisdiction clause in Article 8(16) in the light of any provision which may have been inserted in the 1968 Brussels Convention or in any text adopted by Member States or by the Council to replace such Convention;

(d) allowing provisions in the statutes of an SE adopted by a Member State in execution of authorisations given to the Member States by this Regulation or laws adopted to ensure the effective application of this Regulation in respect to the SE which deviate from or are complementary to these laws, even when such provisions would not be authorised in the statutes of a public limited-liability company having its registered office in the Member State.

Article 70

This Regulation shall enter into force on 8 October 2004.

This Regulation shall be binding in its entirety and directly applicable in all Member States.

Done at Luxembourg, 8 October 2001.

For the Council

The President

L. ONKELINX

Annex Ib
Public limited-liability companies referred to in Article 2(1) of the Regulation

EU Member states

BELGIUM:
la société anonyme/de naamloze vennootschap

CZECH REPUBLIC:
akciová společnost'

DENMARK:
aktieselskaber

GERMANY:
die Aktiengesellschaft

ESTONIA:
aktsiaselts

GREECE:
ανώνυμη εταιρία

SPAIN:
la sociedad anónima

FRANCE:
la société anonyme

IRELAND:
public companies limited by shares
public companies limited by guarantee having a share capital

ITALY:
società per azioni

CYPRUS:
Δημόσια Εταιρεία περιορισμένης ευθύνης με μετοχές, Δημόσια Εταιρεία περιορισμένης ευθύνης με εγγύηση

LATVIA:
akciju sabiedrība

LITHUANIA:
akcinės bendrovės
uždarosios akcinės bendrovės'

LUXEMBOURG:
la société anonyme

HUNGARY:
részvénytársaság,
korlátolt felelősségű társaság

MALTA:
kumpaniji pubbliċi / public limited liability companies
kumpaniji privati / private liability companies

NETHERLANDS:
de naamloze vennootschap

AUSTRIA:
die Aktiengesellschaft

POLAND:
spółka akcyjna,
spółka z ograniczona odpowiedzialnośía'

PORTUGAL:
a sociedade anónima de responsabilidade limitada

SLOVENIA:
delniška družba,
družba z omejeno odgovornostjo

SLOVAKIA:
akciová spoločnos',
spoločnost' s ručením obmedzeným'

FINLAND:
julkinen osakeyhtiö//publikt aktiebolag

SWEDEN:
publikt aktiebolag

UNITED KINGDOM:
public companies limited by shares
public companies limited by guarantee having a share capital

EEA MEMBER STATES

ICELAND:
Hlutafélag

LIECHTENSTEIN:
die Aktiengesellschaft
die Kommanditaktiengesellschaft;

NORWAY:
Allmennaksjeselskap.

Annex Ic
Public and private limited-liability companies referred to in Article 2(2) of the Regulation

EU Member States

BELGIUM:
la société anonyme/de naamloze vennootschap
la société privée à responsabilité limitée/besloten vennootschap met beperkte aansprakelijkheid

DENMARK:
aktieselskaber
anpartselskaber

GERMANY:
die Aktiengesellschaft
die Gesellschaft mit beschränkter Haftung

GREECE:
ανώνυμη εταιρία
εταιρία περιορισμένης ευθύνης

SPAIN:
la sociedad anónima
la sociedad de responsabilidad limitada

FRANCE:
la société anonyme
la société à responsabilité limitée

IRELAND:
public companies limited by shares
public companies limited by guarantee having a share capital
private companies limited by shares
private companies limited by guarantee having a share capital

ITALY:
società per azioni
società a responsabilità limitata

LUXEMBOURG:
la société anonyme
la société à responsabilité limitée

NETHERLANDS:
de naamloze vennootschap
de besloten vennootschap met beperkte aansprakelijkheid

AUSTRIA:
die Aktiengesellschaft
die Gesellschaft mit beschränkter Haftung

PORTUGAL:
a sociedade anónima de responsabilidade limitada
a sociedade por quotas de responsabilidade limitada

FINLAND:
osakeyhtiö
aktiebolag

SWEDEN:
Aktiebolag

UNITED KINGDOM:
public companies limited by shares
public companies limited by guarantee having a share capital
private companies limited by shares
private companies limited by guarantee having a share capital

EEA member states

ICELAND:
Hlutafélag
Einkahlutafélag

LIECHTENSTEIN:
die Aktiengesellschaft
die Kommanditaktiengesellschaft
die Gesellschaft mit beschränkter Haftung

NORWAY:
Allmennaksjeselskap
Aksjeselskap

Annex II

COUNCIL DIRECTIVE 2001/86/EC

of 8 October 2001

supplementing the Statute for a European company with regard to the involvement of employees

THE COUNCIL OF THE EUROPEAN UNION,

Having regard to the Treaty establishing the European Community, and in particular Article 308 thereof,

Having regard to the amended proposal from the Commission [1],

Having regard to the opinion of the European Parliament [2],

Having regard to the opinion of the Economic and Social Committee [3],

Whereas:

(1) In order to attain the objectives of the Treaty, Council Regulation (EC) No 2157/2001 [4] establishes a Statute for a European company (SE).

(2) That Regulation aims at creating a uniform legal framework within which companies from different Member States should be able to plan and carry out the reorganisation of their business on a Community scale.

(3) In order to promote the social objectives of the Community, special provisions have to be set, notably in the field of employee involvement, aimed at ensuring that the establishment of an SE does not entail the disappearance or reduction of practices of employee involvement existing within the companies participating in the establishment of an SE. This objective should be pursued through the establishment of a set of rules in this field, supplementing the provisions of the Regulation.

(4) Since the objectives of the proposed action, as outlined above, cannot be sufficiently achieved by the Member States, in that the object is to establish a set of rules on employee involvement applicable to the SE, and can therefore, by reason of the scale and impact of the proposed action, be better achieved at Community level, the Community may adopt measures, in accordance with the principle of subsidiarity as set out in Article 5 of the Treaty. In accordance with the principle of proportionality, as set out in that Article, this Directive does not go beyond what is necessary to achieve these objectives.

(5) The great diversity of rules and practices existing in the Member States as regards the manner in which employees' representatives are involved in decision-making within companies makes it inadvisable to set up a single European model of employee involvement applicable to the SE.

(6) Information and consultation procedures at transnational level should nevertheless be ensured in all cases of creation of an SE.

(7) If and when participation rights exist within one or more companies establishing an SE, they should be preserved through their transfer to the SE, once established, unless the parties decide otherwise.

(8) The concrete procedures of employee transnational information and consultation, as well as, if applicable, participation, to apply to each SE should be defined primarily by means of an agreement between the parties concerned or, in the absence thereof, through the application of a set of subsidiary rules.

(9) Member States should still have the option of not applying the standard rules relating to participation in the case of a merger, given the diversity of national systems for employee involvement. Existing systems and practices of participation where appropriate at the level of participating companies must in that case be maintained by adapting registration rules.

(10) The voting rules within the special body representing the employees for negotiation purposes, in particular when concluding agreements providing for a level of participation lower than the one existing within one or more of the participating companies, should be proportionate to the risk of disappearance or reduction of existing systems and practices of participation. That

---

[1] OJ C 138, 29.5.1991, p. 8.
[2] OJ C 342, 20.12.1993, p. 15.
[3] OJ C 124, 21.5.1990, p. 34.
[4] See page 1 of this Official Journal.

risk is greater in the case of an SE established by way of transformation or merger than by way of creating a holding company or a common subsidiary.

(11) In the absence of an agreement subsequent to the negotiation between employees' representatives and the competent organs of the participating companies, provision should be made for certain standard requirements to apply to the SE, once it is established. These standard requirements should ensure effective practices of transnational information and consultation of employees, as well as their participation in the relevant organs of the SE if and when such participation existed before its establishment within the participating companies.

(12) Provision should be made for the employees' representatives acting within the framework of the Directive to enjoy, when exercising their functions, protection and guarantees which are similar to those provided to employees' representatives by the legislation and/or practice of the country of employment. They should not be subject to any discrimination as a result of the lawful exercise of their activities and should enjoy adequate protection as regards dismissal and other sanctions.

(13) The confidentiality of sensitive information should be preserved even after the expiry of the employees' representatives terms of office and provision should be made to allow the competent organ of the SE to withhold information which would seriously harm, if subject to public disclosure, the functioning of the SE.

(14) Where an SE and its subsidiaries and establishments are subject to Council Directive 94/45/EC of 22 September 1994 on the establishment of a European Works Council or a procedure in Community-scale undertakings and Community-scale groups of undertakings for the purposes of informing and consulting employees ([1]), the provisions of that Directive and the provision transposing it into national legislation should not apply to it nor to its subsidiaries and establishments, unless the special negotiating body decides not to open negotiations or to terminate negotiations already opened.

(15) This Directive should not affect other existing rights regarding involvement and need not affect other existing representation structures, provided for by Community and national laws and practices.

(16) Member States should take appropriate measures in the event of failure to comply with the obligations laid down in this Directive.

(17) The Treaty has not provided the necessary powers for the Community to adopt the proposed Directive, other than those provided for in Article 308.

(18) It is a fundamental principle and stated aim of this Directive to secure employees' acquired rights as regards involvement in company decisions. Employee rights in force before the establishment of SEs should provide the basis for employee rights of involvement in the SE (the 'before and after' principle). Consequently, that approach should apply not only to the initial establishment of an SE but also to structural changes in an existing SE and to the companies affected by structural change processes.

(19) Member States should be able to provide that representatives of trade unions may be members of a special negotiating body regardless of whether they are employees of a company participating in the establishment of an SE. Member States should in this context in particular be able to introduce this right in cases where trade union representatives have the right to be members of, and to vote in, supervisory or administrative company organs in accordance with national legislation.

(20) In several Member States, employee involvement and other areas of industrial relations are based on both national legislation and practice which in this context is understood also to cover collective agreements at various national, sectoral and/or company levels,

HAS ADOPTED THIS DIRECTIVE:

SECTION I

GENERAL

Article 1

Objective

1. This Directive governs the involvement of employees in the affairs of European public limited-liability companies (*Societas Europaea*, hereinafter referred to as 'SE'), as referred to in Regulation (EC) No 2157/2001.

([1]) OJ L 254, 30.9.1994, p. 64. Directive as last amended by Directive 97/74/EC (OJ L 10, 16.1.1998, p. 22).

2. To this end, arrangements for the involvement of employees shall be established in every SE in accordance with the negotiating procedure referred to in Articles 3 to 6 or, under the circumstances specified in Article 7, in accordance with the Annex.

Article 2

Definitions

For the purposes of this Directive:

(a) 'SE' means any company established in accordance with Regulation (EC) No 2157/2001;

(b) 'participating companies' means the companies directly participating in the establishing of an SE;

(c) 'subsidiary' of a company means an undertaking over which that company exercises a dominant influence defined in accordance with Article 3(2) to (7) of Directive 94/45/EC;

(d) 'concerned subsidiary or establishment' means a subsidiary or establishment of a participating company which is proposed to become a subsidiary or establishment of the SE upon its formation;

(e) 'employees' representatives' means the employees' representatives provided for by national law and/or practice;

(f) 'representative body' means the body representative of the employees set up by the agreements referred to in Article 4 or in accordance with the provisions of the Annex, with the purpose of informing and consulting the employees of an SE and its subsidiaries and establishments situated in the Community and, where applicable, of exercising participation rights in relation to the SE;

(g) 'special negotiating body' means the body established in accordance with Article 3 to negotiate with the competent body of the participating companies regarding the establishment of arrangements for the involvement of employees within the SE;

(h) 'involvement of employees' means any mechanism, including information, consultation and participation, through which employees' representatives may exercise an influence on decisions to be taken within the company;

(i) 'information' means the informing of the body representative of the employees and/or employees' representatives by the competent organ of the SE on questions which concern the SE itself and any of its subsidiaries or establishments situated in another Member State or which exceed the powers of the decision-making organs in a single Member State at a time, in a manner and with a content which allows the employees' representatives to undertake an in-depth assessment of the possible impact and, where appropriate, prepare consultations with the competent organ of the SE;

(j) 'consultation' means the establishment of dialogue and exchange of views between the body representative of the employees and/or the employees' representatives and the competent organ of the SE, at a time, in a manner and with a content which allows the employees' representatives, on the basis of information provided, to express an opinion on measures envisaged by the competent organ which may be taken into account in the decision-making process within the SE;

(k) 'participation' means the influence of the body representative of the employees and/or the employees' representatives in the affairs of a company by way of:

— the right to elect or appoint some of the members of the company's supervisory or administrative organ, or

— the right to recommend and/or oppose the appointment of some or all of the members of the company's supervisory or administrative organ.

SECTION II

NEGOTIATING PROCEDURE

Article 3

Creation of a special negotiating body

1. Where the management or administrative organs of the participating companies draw up a plan for the establishment of an SE, they shall as soon as possible after publishing the draft terms of merger or creating a holding company or after agreeing a plan to form a subsidiary or to transform into an SE, take the necessary steps, including providing information about the identity of the participating companies, concerned subsidiaries or establishments, and the number of their employees, to start negotiations with the representatives of the companies' employees on arrangements for the involvement of employees in the SE.

2. For this purpose, a special negotiating body representative of the employees of the participating companies and concerned subsidiaries or establishments shall be created in accordance with the following provisions:

(a) in electing or appointing members of the special negotiating body, it must be ensured:

   (i) that these members are elected or appointed in proportion to the number of employees employed in each Member State by the participating companies and concerned subsidiaries or establishments, by allocating in respect of a Member State one seat per portion of employees employed in that Member State which equals 10 %, or a fraction thereof, of the number of employees employed by the participating companies and concerned subsidiaries or establishments in all the Member States taken together;

   (ii) that in the case of an SE formed by way of merger, there are such further additional members from each Member State as may be necessary in order to ensure that the special negotiating body includes at least one member representing each participating company which is registered and has employees in that Member State and which it is proposed will cease to exist as a separate legal entity following the registration of the SE, in so far as:

   — the number of such additional members does not exceed 20 % of the number of members designated by virtue of point (i), and

   — the composition of the special negotiating body does not entail a double representation of the employees concerned.

   If the number of such companies is higher than the number of additional seats available pursuant to the first subparagraph, these additional seats shall be allocated to companies in different Member States by decreasing order of the number of employees they employ;

(b) Member States shall determine the method to be used for the election or appointment of the members of the special negotiating body who are to be elected or appointed in their territories. They shall take the necessary measures to ensure that, as far as possible, such members shall include at least one member representing each participating company which has employees in the Member State concerned. Such measures must not increase the overall number of members.

Member States may provide that such members may include representatives of trade unions whether or not they are employees of a participating company or concerned subsidiary or establishment.

Without prejudice to national legislation and/or practice laying down thresholds for the establishing of a representative body, Member States shall provide that employees in undertakings or establishments in which there are no employees' representatives through no fault of their own have the right to elect or appoint members of the special negotiating body.

3. The special negotiating body and the competent organs of the participating companies shall determine, by written agreement, arrangements for the involvement of employees within the SE.

To this end, the competent organs of the participating companies shall inform the special negotiating body of the plan and the actual process of establishing the SE, up to its registration.

4. Subject to paragraph 6, the special negotiating body shall take decisions by an absolute majority of its members, provided that a majority also represents an absolute majority of the employees. Each member shall have one vote. However, should the result of the negotiations lead to a reduction of participation rights, the majority required for a decision to approve such an agreement shall be the votes of two thirds of the members of the special negotiating body representing at least two thirds of the employees, including the votes of members representing employees employed in at least two Member States,

— in the case of an SE to be established by way of merger, if participation covers at least 25 % of the overall number of employees of the participating companies, or

— in the case of an SE to be established by way of creating a holding company or forming a subsidiary, if participation covers at least 50 % of the overall number of employees of the participating companies.

Reduction of participation rights means a proportion of members of the organs of the SE within the meaning of Article 2(k), which is lower than the highest proportion existing within the participating companies.

5. For the purpose of the negotiations, the special negotiating body may request experts of its choice, for example representatives of appropriate Community level trade union organisations, to assist it with its work. Such experts may be present at negotiation meetings in an advisory capacity at the request of the special negotiating body, where appropriate to promote coherence and consistency at Community level. The special negotiating body may decide to inform the representatives of appropriate external organisations, including trade unions, of the start of the negotiations.

6. The special negotiating body may decide by the majority set out below not to open negotiations or to terminate negotiations already opened, and to rely on the rules on information and consultation of employees in force in the Member States where the SE has employees. Such a decision shall stop the procedure to conclude the agreement referred to in Article 4. Where such a decision has been taken, none of the provisions of the Annex shall apply.

The majority required to decide not to open or to terminate negotiations shall be the votes of two thirds of the members representing at least two thirds of the employees, including the votes of members representing employees employed in at least two Member States.

In the case of an SE established by way of transformation, this paragraph shall not apply if there is participation in the company to be transformed.

The special negotiating body shall be reconvened on the written request of at least 10 % of the employees of the SE, its subsidiaries and establishments, or their representatives, at the earliest two years after the abovementioned decision, unless the parties agree to negotiations being reopened sooner. If the special negotiating body decides to reopen negotiations with the management but no agreement is reached as a result of those negotiations, none of the provisions of the Annex shall apply.

7. Any expenses relating to the functioning of the special negotiating body and, in general, to negotiations shall be borne by the participating companies so as to enable the special negotiating body to carry out its task in an appropriate manner.

In compliance with this principle, Member States may lay down budgetary rules regarding the operation of the special negotiating body. They may in particular limit the funding to cover one expert only.

Article 4

Content of the agreement

1. The competent organs of the participating companies and the special negotiating body shall negotiate in a spirit of cooperation with a view to reaching an agreement on arrangements for the involvement of the employees within the SE.

2. Without prejudice to the autonomy of the parties, and subject to paragraph 4, the agreement referred to in paragraph 1 between the competent organs of the participating companies and the special negotiating body shall specify:

(a) the scope of the agreement;

(b) the composition, number of members and allocation of seats on the representative body which will be the discussion partner of the competent organ of the SE in connection with arrangements for the information and consultation of the employees of the SE and its subsidiaries and establishments;

(c) the functions and the procedure for the information and consultation of the representative body;

(d) the frequency of meetings of the representative body;

(e) the financial and material resources to be allocated to the representative body;

(f) if, during negotiations, the parties decide to establish one or more information and consultation procedures instead of a representative body, the arrangements for implementing those procedures;

(g) if, during negotiations, the parties decide to establish arrangements for participation, the substance of those arrangements including (if applicable) the number of members in the SE's administrative or supervisory body which the employees will be entitled to elect, appoint, recommend or oppose, the procedures as to how these members may be elected, appointed, recommended or opposed by the employees, and their rights;

(h) the date of entry into force of the agreement and its duration, cases where the agreement should be renegotiated and the procedure for its renegotiation.

3. The agreement shall not, unless provision is made otherwise therein, be subject to the standard rules referred to in the Annex.

4. Without prejudice to Article 13(3)(a), in the case of an SE established by means of transformation, the agreement shall provide for at least the same level of all elements of employee involvement as the ones existing within the company to be transformed into an SE.

Article 5

Duration of negotiations

1. Negotiations shall commence as soon as the special negotiating body is established and may continue for six months thereafter.

2. The parties may decide, by joint agreement, to extend negotiations beyond the period referred to in paragraph 1, up to a total of one year from the establishment of the special negotiating body.

Article 6

Legislation applicable to the negotiation procedure

Except where otherwise provided in this Directive, the legislation applicable to the negotiation procedure provided for in Articles 3 to 5 shall be the legislation of the Member State in which the registered office of the SE is to be situated.

Article 7

Standard rules

1. In order to achieve the objective described in Article 1, Member States shall, without prejudice to paragraph 3 below, lay down standard rules on employee involvement which must satisfy the provisions set out in the Annex.

The standard rules as laid down by the legislation of the Member State in which the registered office of the SE is to be situated shall apply from the date of the registration of the SE where either:

(a) the parties so agree; or

(b) by the deadline laid down in Article 5, no agreement has been concluded, and:

— the competent organ of each of the participating companies decides to accept the application of the standard rules in relation to the SE and so to continue with its registration of the SE, and

— the special negotiating body has not taken the decision provided in Article 3(6).

2. Moreover, the standard rules fixed by the national legislation of the Member State of registration in accordance with part 3 of the Annex shall apply only:

(a) in the case of an SE established by transformation, if the rules of a Member State relating to employee participation in the administrative or supervisory body applied to a company transformed into an SE;

(b) in the case of an SE established by merger:

— if, before registration of the SE, one or more forms of participation applied in one or more of the participating companies covering at least 25 % of the total number of employees in all the participating companies, or

— if, before registration of the SE, one or more forms of participation applied in one or more of the participating companies covering less than 25 % of the total number of employees in all the participating companies and if the special negotiating body so decides,

(c) in the case of an SE established by setting up a holding company or establishing a subsidiary:

— if, before registration of the SE, one or more forms of participation applied in one or more of the participating companies covering at least 50 % of the total number of employees in all the participating companies; or

— if, before registration of the SE, one or more forms of participation applied in one or more of the participating companies covering less than 50 % of the total number of employees in all the participating companies and if the special negotiating body so decides.

If there was more than one form of participation within the various participating companies, the special negotiating body shall decide which of those forms must be established in the SE. Member States may fix the rules which are applicable in the absence of any decision on the matter for an SE registered in their territory. The special negotiating body shall inform the competent organs of the participating companies of any decisions taken pursuant to this paragraph.

3. Member States may provide that the reference provisions in part 3 of the Annex shall not apply in the case provided for in point (b) of paragraph 2.

SECTION III

MISCELLANEOUS PROVISIONS

Article 8

Reservation and confidentiality

1. Member States shall provide that members of the special negotiating body or the representative body, and experts who assist them, are not authorised to reveal any information which has been given to them in confidence.

The same shall apply to employees' representatives in the context of an information and consultation procedure.

This obligation shall continue to apply, wherever the persons referred to may be, even after the expiry of their terms of office.

2. Each Member State shall provide, in specific cases and under the conditions and limits laid down by national legislation, that the supervisory or administrative organ of an SE or of a participating company established in its territory is not obliged to transmit information where its nature is such that, according to objective criteria, to do so would seriously harm the functioning of the SE (or, as the case may be, the participating company) or its subsidiaries and establishments or would be prejudicial to them.

A Member State may make such dispensation subject to prior administrative or judicial authorisation.

3. Each Member State may lay down particular provisions for SEs in its territory which pursue directly and essentially the aim of ideological guidance with respect to information and the expression of opinions, on condition that, on the date of adoption of this Directive, such provisions already exist in the national legislation.

4. In applying paragraphs 1, 2 and 3, Member States shall make provision for administrative or judicial appeal procedures which the employees' representatives may initiate when the supervisory or administrative organ of an SE or participating company demands confidentiality or does not give information.

Such procedures may include arrangements designed to protect the confidentiality of the information in question.

Article 9

Operation of the representative body and procedure for the information and consultation of employees

The competent organ of the SE and the representative body shall work together in a spirit of cooperation with due regard for their reciprocal rights and obligations.

The same shall apply to cooperation between the supervisory or administrative organ of the SE and the employees' representatives in conjunction with a procedure for the information and consultation of employees.

Article 10

Protection of employees' representatives

The members of the special negotiating body, the members of the representative body, any employees' representatives exercising functions under the information and consultation procedure and any employees' representatives in the supervisory or administrative organ of an SE who are employees of the SE, its subsidiaries or establishments or of a participating company shall, in the exercise of their functions, enjoy the same protection and guarantees provided for employees' representatives by the national legislation and/or practice in force in their country of employment.

This shall apply in particular to attendance at meetings of the special negotiating body or representative body, any other meeting under the agreement referred to in Article 4(2)(f) or any meeting of the administrative or supervisory organ, and to the payment of wages for members employed by a participating company or the SE or its subsidiaries or establishments during a period of absence necessary for the performance of their duties.

Article 11

Misuse of procedures

Member States shall take appropriate measures in conformity with Community law with a view to preventing the misuse of an SE for the purpose of depriving employees of rights to employee involvement or withholding such rights.

Article 12

Compliance with this Directive

1. Each Member State shall ensure that the management of establishments of an SE and the supervisory or administrative organs of subsidiaries and of participating companies which are situated within its territory and the employees' representatives or, as the case may be, the employees themselves abide by the obligations laid down by this Directive, regardless of whether or not the SE has its registered office within its territory.

2. Member States shall provide for appropriate measures in the event of failure to comply with this Directive; in particular they shall ensure that administrative or legal procedures are available to enable the obligations deriving from this Directive to be enforced.

Article 13

Link between this Directive and other provisions

1. Where an SE is a Community-scale undertaking or a controlling undertaking of a Community-scale group of undertakings within the meaning of Directive 94/45/EC or of Directive 97/74/EC [1] extending the said Directive to the United Kingdom, the provisions of these Directives and the provisions transposing them into national legislation shall not apply to them or to their subsidiaries.

However, where the special negotiating body decides in accordance with Article 3(6) not to open negotiations or to terminate negotiations already opened, Directive 94/45/EC or Directive 97/74/EC and the provisions transposing them into national legislation shall apply.

2. Provisions on the participation of employees in company bodies provided for by national legislation and/or practice, other than those implementing this Directive, shall not apply to companies established in accordance with Regulation (EC) No 2157/2001 and covered by this Directive.

3. This Directive shall not prejudice:

(a) the existing rights to involvement of employees provided for by national legislation and/or practice in the Member States as enjoyed by employees of the SE and its subsidiaries and establishments, other than participation in the bodies of the SE;

(b) the provisions on participation in the bodies laid down by national legislation and/or practice applicable to the subsidiaries of the SE.

4. In order to preserve the rights referred to in paragraph 3, Member States may take the necessary measures to guarantee that the structures of employee representation in participating companies which will cease to exist as separate legal entities are maintained after the registration of the SE.

Article 14

Final provisions

1. Member States shall adopt the laws, regulations and administrative provisions necessary to comply with this Directive no later than 8 October 2004, or shall ensure by that date at the latest that management and labour introduce the required provisions by way of agreement, the Member States being obliged to take all necessary steps enabling them at all times to guarantee the results imposed by this Directive. They shall forthwith inform the Commission thereof.

2. When Member States adopt these measures, they shall contain a reference to this Directive or shall be accompanied by such reference on the occasion of their official publication. The methods of making such reference shall be laid down by the Member States.

Article 15

Review by the Commission

No later than 8 October 2007, the Commission shall, in consultation with the Member States and with management and labour at Community level, review the procedures for applying this Directive, with a view to proposing suitable amendments to the Council where necessary.

Article 16

Entry into force

This Directive shall enter into force on the day of its publication in the *Official Journal of the European Communities*.

Article 17

Addressees

This Directive is addressed to the Member States.

Done at Luxembourg, 8 October 2001.

For the Council
The President
L. ONKELINX

---

[1] OJ L 10, 16.1.1998, p. 22.

ANNEX

STANDARD RULES

(referred to in Article 7)

Part 1: Composition of the body representative of the employees

In order to achieve the objective described in Article 1, and in the cases referred to in Article 7, a representative body shall be set up in accordance with the following rules.

(a) The representative body shall be composed of employees of the SE and its subsidiaries and establishments elected or appointed from their number by the employees' representatives or, in the absence thereof, by the entire body of employees.

(b) The election or appointment of members of the representative body shall be carried out in accordance with national legislation and/or practice.

Member States shall lay down rules to ensure that the number of members of, and allocation of seats on, the representative body shall be adapted to take account of changes occurring within the SE and its subsidiaries and establishments.

(c) Where its size so warrants, the representative body shall elect a select committee from among its members, comprising at most three members.

(d) The representative body shall adopt its rules of procedure.

(e) The members of the representative body are elected or appointed in proportion to the number of employees employed in each Member State by the participating companies and concerned subsidiaries or establishments, by allocating in respect of a Member State one seat per portion of employees employed in that Member State which equals 10 %, or a fraction thereof, of the number of employees employed by the participating companies and concerned subsidiaries or establishments in all the Member States taken together.

(f) The competent organ of the SE shall be informed of the composition of the representative body.

(g) Four years after the representative body is established, it shall examine whether to open negotiations for the conclusion of the agreement referred to in Articles 4 and 7 or to continue to apply the standard rules adopted in accordance with this Annex.

Articles 3(4) to (7) and 4 to 6 shall apply, *mutatis mutandis*, if a decision has been taken to negotiate an agreement according to Article 4, in which case the term 'special negotiating body' shall be replaced by 'representative body'. Where, by the deadline by which the negotiations come to an end, no agreement has been concluded, the arrangements initially adopted in accordance with the standard rules shall continue to apply.

Part 2: Standard rules for information and consultation

The competence and powers of the representative body set up in an SE shall be governed by the following rules.

(a) The competence of the representative body shall be limited to questions which concern the SE itself and any of its subsidiaries or establishments situated in another Member State or which exceed the powers of the decision-making organs in a single Member State.

(b) Without prejudice to meetings held pursuant to point (c), the representative body shall have the right to be informed and consulted and, for that purpose, to meet with the competent organ of the SE at least once a year, on the basis of regular reports drawn up by the competent organ, on the progress of the business of the SE and its prospects. The local managements shall be informed accordingly.

The competent organ of the SE shall provide the representative body with the agenda for meetings of the administrative, or, where appropriate, the management and supervisory organ, and with copies of all documents submitted to the general meeting of its shareholders.

The meeting shall relate in particular to the structure, economic and financial situation, the probable development of the business and of production and sales, the situation and probable trend of employment, investments, and substantial changes concerning organisation, introduction of new working methods or production processes, transfers of production, mergers, cut-backs or closures of undertakings, establishments or important parts thereof, and collective redundancies.

(c) Where there are exceptional circumstances affecting the employees' interests to a considerable extent, particularly in the event of relocations, transfers, the closure of establishments or undertakings or collective redundancies, the representative body shall have the right to be informed. The representative body or, where it so decides, in particular for reasons of urgency, the select committee, shall have the right to meet at its request the competent organ of the SE or any more appropriate level of management within the SE having its own powers of decision, so as to be informed and consulted on measures significantly affecting employees' interests.

Where the competent organ decides not to act in accordance with the opinion expressed by the representative body, this body shall have the right to a further meeting with the competent organ of the SE with a view to seeking agreement.

In the case of a meeting organised with the select committee, those members of the representative body who represent employees who are directly concerned by the measures in question shall also have the right to participate.

The meetings referred to above shall not affect the prerogatives of the competent organ.

(d) Member States may lay down rules on the chairing of information and consultation meetings.

Before any meeting with the competent organ of the SE, the representative body or the select committee, where necessary enlarged in accordance with the third subparagraph of paragraph (c), shall be entitled to meet without the representatives of the competent organ being present.

(e) Without prejudice to Article 8, the members of the representative body shall inform the representatives of the employees of the SE and of its subsidiaries and establishments of the content and outcome of the information and consultation procedures.

(f) The representative body or the select committee may be assisted by experts of its choice.

(g) In so far as this is necessary for the fulfilment of their tasks, the members of the representative body shall be entitled to time off for training without loss of wages.

(h) The costs of the representative body shall be borne by the SE, which shall provide the body's members with the financial and material resources needed to enable them to perform their duties in an appropriate manner.

In particular, the SE shall, unless otherwise agreed, bear the cost of organising meetings and providing interpretation facilities and the accommodation and travelling expenses of members of the representative body and the select committee.

In compliance with these principles, the Member States may lay down budgetary rules regarding the operation of the representative body. They may in particular limit funding to cover one expert only.

Part 3: Standard rules for participation

Employee participation in an SE shall be governed by the following provisions

(a) In the case of an SE established by transformation, if the rules of a Member State relating to employee participation in the administrative or supervisory body applied before registration, all aspects of employee participation shall continue to apply to the SE. Point (b) shall apply *mutatis mutandis* to that end.

(b) In other cases of the establishing of an SE, the employees of the SE, its subsidiaries and establishments and/or their representative body shall have the right to elect, appoint, recommend or oppose the appointment of a number of members of the administrative or supervisory body of the SE equal to the highest proportion in force in the participating companies concerned before registration of the SE.

If none of the participating companies was governed by participation rules before registration of the SE, the latter shall not be required to establish provisions for employee participation.

The representative body shall decide on the allocation of seats within the administrative or supervisory body among the members representing the employees from the various Member States or on the way in which the SE's employees may recommend or oppose the appointment of the members of these bodies according to the proportion of the SE's employees in each Member State. If the employees of one or more Member States are not covered by this proportional criterion, the representative body shall appoint a member from one of those Member States, in particular the Member State of the SE's registered office where that is appropriate. Each Member State may determine the allocation of the seats it is given within the administrative or supervisory body.

Every member of the administrative body or, where appropriate, the supervisory body of the SE who has been elected, appointed or recommended by the representative body or, depending on the circumstances, by the employees shall be a full member with the same rights and obligations as the members representing the shareholders, including the right to vote.

Annex III
List of national laws implementing the Regulation and the Directive

This Annex contains a list of the national legislation implementing the Regulation and the Directive in the various countries which have adapted their legislation, and where an SE can be incorporated.

Austria

Bundesgesetz, mit dem ein Bundesgesetz über das Statut der Europäischen Gesellschaft (Societas Europaea – SE) – (SE-Gesetz – SEG) erlassen wird sowie das Aktiengesetz, das Firmenbuchgesetz, das Rechtspflegergesetz, das Gerichtsgebührengesetz, das EWIV-Ausführungsgesetz, das Genossenschaftsrevisionsgesetz 1997 und das Versicherungsaufsichtsgesetz geändert werden (Gesellschaftsrechtsänderungsgesetz 2004 – GesRÄG 2004), *Bundesgesetzblatt für die Republik Österreich I 67/2004*, 24 June 2004.

Bundesgesetz, mit dem das Arbeitsverfassungsgesetz, das Bundesgesetz über die Post-Betriebsverfassung und das Arbeits – und Sozialgerichtsgesetz geändert werden, 8 October 2004, *Bundesgesetzblatt für die Republik Österreich I 82/2004*, 15 July 2004.

Belgium

Koninklijk besluit houdende tenuitvoerlegging van verordening (EG) nr. 2157/2001 van de Raad van 8 oktober 2001 betreffende het statuut van de Europese vennootschap / Arrêté royal portant exécution du règlement (CE) n° 2157/2001 du Conseil du 8 octobre 2001 relatif au statut de la Société européenne, 1 September 2004, *Belgisch Staatsblad / Moniteur Belge*, 9 September 2004.

Collectieve arbeidsovereenkomst nr 84 betreffende de rol van de werknemers in de europese vennootschap / Convention collective de travail n° 84 concernant l'implication des travailleurs dans la société européenne, 6 October 2004, algemeen bindend verklaard door Koninklijk besluit / rendue obligatoire par arrêté royal, 22 December 2004, *Belgisch Staatsblad / Moniteur belge*, 19 January 2005.

Denmark

Lov No 281 om medarbejderindflydelse i SE-selskaber, 26 April 2004, *Lovtidende*, 27 April 2004.

Lov No 363 om det europaeiski selskab, 19 May 2004, *Lovtidende*, 21 May 2004.

Lov No 364 om oendering af aktieselskabsloven mv, 19 May 2004, *Lovtidende*, 21 May 2004.

Estonia

Euroopa Liidu Nõukogu määruse (EÜ) nr. 2157/2001 'Euroopa äriühingu (SE) põhikirja kohta' rakendamise seadus, 10 November 2004, *Riigi Teataja*, 30 November 2004.

Üleühenduselise ettevõtja, üleühenduselise ettevõtjate grupi ja Euroopa äriühingu tegevusse töötajate kaasamise seadus, 12 January 2005, *Riigi Teataja*, 1 February 2005.

Finland

Eurooppayhtiölaki / Lag om europabolag 13.8.2004/742; 13 August 2004, *Suomen säädöskokoelma / Finlands författningssamling*, 18 August 2004.

Laki henkilöstöedustuksesta eurooppayhtiössä (SE) / Lag om arbetstagarinflytande i europabolag 13.8.2004/758, 13 August 2004, *Suomen säädöskokoelma / Finlands författningssamling*, 18 August 2004.

Germany

Gesetz zur Ausführung der Verordnung (EG) 2157/2001 des Rates vom 8 Oktober 2001 über das Statut der Europäischen Gesellschaft (SE) (SEAG), 22 December 2004, *BGBl. I 2004*, 28 December 2004.

Gesetz über die Beteiligung der Arbeitnehmer in einer Europäischen Gesellschaft (SEBG), 22 December 2004, *BGBl. I 2004*, 28 December 2004.

Hungary

2004. évi XLV törvény az európai részvénytársaságról, 28 May 2004, *Magyar Közlöny*, 28 May 2004.

Iceland

Lög nr. 26/2004 um Evrópufélög, 16 April 2004, *Stjórnartíðindi A-deild 2004*, 27 April 2004.

Lög nr. 27/2004 um aðild starfsmanna að Evrópufélögum, 16 April 2004, *Stjórnartíðindi A-deild 2004*, 27 April 2004.

Latvia

Eiropas komercsabiedrību likums, 24 March 2005, *Latvijas VÁstnesis*, 24 March 2005.

Lithuania

Lietuvos Respublikos Europos bendrovių įstatymas Nr. IX-2199, 29 April 2004, *Valstybės Žinios*, 11 May 2004.

Lietuvos Respublikos Vyriausybės nutarimas Nr. 185 'Dėl Lietuvos Respublikos Vyriausybės 2003 m. lapkričio 12 d. nutarimo Nr. 1407' Dėl Juridinių asmenų registro įsteigimo ir Juridinių asmenų registro nuostatų patvirtinimo 'pakeitimo', 17 February 2005, *Valstybės Žinios*, 22 February 2005.

Lietuvos Respublikos įstatymas dėl darbuotojų dalyvavimo priimant sprendimus Europos bendrovėse Nr. X-200, 12 May 2005, *Valstybės Žinios*, 28 May 2005.

Netherlands

Wet tot uitvoering van verordening (EG) Nr. 2157/2001 van de Raad van de Europese Unie van 8 oktober 2001 betreffende het statuut van de Europese vennootschap (SE), 17 March 2005, *Staatsblad 2005*, 24 March 2005.

Wet tot uitvoering van richtlijn nr. 2001/86/EG van de Raad van de Europese Unie van 8 oktober 2001 tot aanvulling van het statuut van de Europese vennootschap met betrekking tot de rol van de werknemers, 17 March 2005, *Staatsblad 2005*, 31 March 2005.

Norway

Lov nr. 14/2005 om europeiske selskaper ved gjennomføring av EØS-avtalen vedlegg XXII nr. 10a (rådsforordning (EF) nr 2157/2001) (SE-loven), 1 April 2005, *Norsk Lovtidend Avd. I*, 4 May 2005.

Forskrift nr. 273 om arbeidstakeres rett til innflytelse i europeiske selskaper, 1 April 2005, *Norsk Lovtidend Avd. I*, 4 May 2005.

Poland

Ustawa o europejskim zgrupowaniu interesów gospodarczych i spóce europejskiej, 4 March 2005, *Dziennik Ustaw*, 18 April 2005.

Slovakia

Zákon č. 562/2004 Z.z. o európskej spoločnosti a o zmene a doplnení niektorých zákonov, 9 September 2004, *Zbierka zákonov Slovenskej republiky*, 23 October 2004.

Sweden

Lag 2004:559 om arbetstagarinflytande i europabolag, *SFS 2004:559*, 10 June 2004.

Lag 2004:575 om europabolag, *SFS 2004:575*, 10 June 2004.

Förordning 2004:703 om europabolag, *SFS 2004:703*, 10 June 2004.

United Kingdom

The European Public Limited Liability Company Regulations 2004, 13 September 2004, *The Stationery Office*, 12 October 2004.

Index

accounting principles *see* annual accounts and consolidated accounts
accounting statement 40–41
acts committed on behalf of SE in formation 57
  Austria 128
  Belgium 159
  Denmark 187
  Estonia 312
  Finland 217–218
  Germany 248
  Hungary 337
  Iceland 493
  Lithuania 351
  Netherlands 276–277
  Poland 377
  Slovak Republic 408
  Sweden 439
  United Kingdom 466
administration
  United Kingdom 477
administrative receivership
  United Kingdom 477–478
annual accounts and consolidated accounts 42, 68, 522
  accounting principles
    Austria 141
    Belgium 167–168
    Denmark 196–197
    Estonia 322–323
    Finland 229
    Germany 255
    Hungary 342
    Iceland 499
    Lithuania 358–359
    Netherlands 288
    Poland 387–388
    Slovak Republic 416–417
    Sweden 448–449
    United Kingdom 474–476
auditors 68
  Austria 141
  Belgium 168
  Denmark 197–198
  Estonia 324
  Finland 230
  Germany 255
  Hungary 342–343
  Iceland 499
  Lithuania 359
  Netherlands 288
  Poland 388
  Slovak Republic 417–418
  Sweden 449
  United Kingdom 476
  Austria 141
  Belgium 167–168
  credit institutions 68, 522
  Denmark 196–198
  Estonia 322–324
  euros, in 68
  financial institutions 68, 522
  Finland 228–229
  Germany 255
  Hungary 342–343
  Iceland 499
  insurance undertakings, of 68, 522
  Lithuania 358–359
  national currency, in 68
  Netherlands 288
  Poland 387–388
  Slovak Republic 416–418
  Sweden 448–449
  United Kingdom 474–476

Index

applicable law 36–37, 45, 75
  Austria 142
  Belgium 171
  Denmark 201
  Estonia 328
  Finland 234
  Germany 256
  Hungary 343
  Iceland 501
  Lithuania 362–363
  Netherlands 291
  Poland 391
  shares 35
  Slovak Republic 422
  Sweden 451
  transfer of registered office and 12
articles 37, 58–59
  amendments 38, 42, 58, 61–62, 384
  conflicts 59
  employee involvement and 58
  memorandum or instrument of incorporation 37, 58
  permanent rules 37, 58
auditors *see* annual accounts and consolidated accounts
Austria
  acts committed on behalf of SE in formation 128
  annual accounts and consolidated accounts
    accounting principles 141
    auditors 141
  applicable law 142
  capital 124
  capital duty 144–145
  cessation of payments 142
  conversion, formation by 127–128
  corporate purpose 124
  employee involvement
    fines for non-compliance 141
    generally 134
    information and consultation 138
    protection of employee representatives 139–140, 141
    reservation and confidentiality 140
    special negotiating body 134–137
    standard rules 137–139
    transitional provisions 140
    works council 137–138
  employee participation 17, 138–139
  formation
    capital 124
    conversion, by 127–128
    corporate purpose 124
    founding parties 121
    holding SE, of 126
    merger, by 124–125
    name 121–122
    registered office 122–124
    subsidiary SE, of 126
  founding parties 121
  general meeting
    decision-making process 129–130
    generally 129
    shareholders' rights and obligations 131
  generally 120–121, 145
  holding SE, formation of 126
  income tax 142–144
  information and consultation of employees 138
  insolvency 142
  laws implementing the Regulation and the Directive 541
  legal personality 128–129
  liquidation 142
  management 131
    one-tier system 15, 129, 131–132
    two-tier system 129, 131, 132–133
  merger, formation by 124–125
  name 121–122
  private limited-liability companies, single-member 126
  publication 128
  reasons to opt for SE 121
  registered office 122–124
  registration 128
  special negotiating body
    appointments 135–136
    composition 135–136
    meetings and decisions 136–137
    members 136
    provision of information for creation 134–135

reconvention/reorganisations in event of
   substantial changes 137
subsidiary SE, formation of 126
supervision by national authorities 141
tax treatment 142–145
valued added tax 144
winding up 142

bankruptcy 32
see also insolvency; liquidation; winding up
banks
   annual accounts and consolidated accounts
      68, 522
   mergers and 38
Belgium
   acts committed on behalf of SE in
      formation 159
   annual accounts and consolidated accounts
      accounting principles 167–168
      auditors 168
   applicable law 171
   capital duty 173
   cessation of payments 170–171
   conversion, formation by 158–159
   corporate purpose 152
   creditors, protection of 156, 157
   employee involvement 165
      protection of employee representatives
         166
      special negotiating body 166
   employee participation 166
   formation
      acquisition by company holding 90or
         more of shares in another company 156
      avoidance of merger 156
      capital 152
      conversion, by 158–159
      corporate purpose 152
      founding parties 149
      holding SE, of 157
      merger, by 152–155
      name 149
      registered office 149–150
      subsidiary SE, of 158
      transfer of registered office 150–152
   founding parties 149
   general meeting
      decision-making process 160–162
      shareholders' rights and obligations 162
   generally 147, 173
   holding SE, formation of 157
   income tax 171–173
   insolvency 169–170
   laws implementing the Regulation and the
      Directive 541
   legal personality 160
   liability of members 165
   liquidation 169
   management 162
      appointment and removal 164–165
      liability 165
      one-tier system 162–163, 165
      representation 165
      two-tier system 163–164
   merger
      avoidance of 156
      formation by 152–155
      right to object to company participating
         in merger 155
   minority shareholders, protection of 156,
      157
   name 149
   publication 155, 157, 159
   reasons to opt for SE 147–148
   registered office 149–150
      transfer 150–152
   registration 159
   representation 165
   special negotiating body 166
   special purpose vehicles (SPVs) 148
   subsidiary SE, formation of 158
   supervision by national authorities 169
   supervisory board 163–164
   tax 171–173
   transfer of registered office 150–152
   value added tax 173
   winding up 169
bondholders
   protection of 39
bonds 35

capital 30, 34–35
   Austria 124
   Belgium 152

553

Index

capital (*cont.*)
  Denmark 180–183
  Estonia 305–306
  euros, expressed in 34
  Finland 210
  Germany 243
  Hungary 336
  Iceland 492
  Lithuania 348–349
  minimum share capital 31, 32, 35
  Netherlands 270
  Poland 373–374
  share capital 34
  Slovak Republic 402
  subscribed capital 35, 42
  subsidiary SE, of 51
  Sweden 432
  United Kingdom 461
capital contributions tax
  Netherlands 297
  Poland 396
capital duty
  Austria 144–145
  Belgium 173
central management 33
  see also head office; management
cessation of payments 73, 522–523
  Austria 142
  Belgium 170–171
  Denmark 200
  Finland 234
  formalities 73
  Germany 256
  Hungary 343
  Iceland 501
  Lithuania 362
  Netherlands 290–291
  Poland 389
  Slovak Republic 418, 421–422
  Sweden 431–432, 451
choice of law 36
  head office (*siège réel*) theory 36
  incorporation theory 36
Ciampi, Carlo 14
consolidated accounts *see* annual accounts and consolidated accounts
conversion

national company, into 73–74
SE formed by 12, 29, 35, 52–54, 517–518
  agreement for employee involvement 86
  Austria 127–128
  Belgium 158–159
  Denmark 186–187
  draft terms of conversion 53
  employee participation and 86, 94
  Estonia 311–312
  Finland 206, 217
  Germany 248
  Hungary 337
  Iceland 493
  Lithuania 350–351
  Netherlands 276
  procedure 12, 52–54
  publication 54
  recording in national registry 54
  Slovak Republic 407–408
  special negotiating body 80–81
  Sweden 438–439
  United Kingdom 465–466
corporate form 32–33
corporate identity 32–34
  see also name; registered office
corporate purpose
  Austria 124
  Belgium 152
  Denmark 180
  Estonia 305
  Finland 209–210
  Germany 243
  Hungary 336
  Iceland 492
  Netherlands 270
  Poland 373
  Slovak Republic 402
  Sweden 432
  United Kingdom 461
corporate tax 76
  Austria 142–144
  Belgium 171
  Estonia 328–329
  Hungary 343–344
  Lithuania 363–364
  Netherlands 291–295
  United Kingdom 479–480

Council Directive 2001/86/EC (the
    'Directive') 4, 16, 27, 79, 509,
    530–540
  application 28
  compliance 96, 536
  content of agreement 534
  duration of negotiations 535
  employee participation 91–94
  entry into force 79
  information and consultation of employees
    536
  laws implementing 28, 541–544
  misuse of procedures 536
  negotiation procedure 535
  protection of employee representatives 536
  reservation and confidentiality 535–536
  scope 79
  special negotiating body 532–534
  standard rules 19–20, 535, 538–540
  transposition 97
Council Regulation No 2157/2001 (the
    'Regulation') 4, 26–28, 507–524
  annual and consolidated accounts 522
  applicable law 75
  application 28
  capital 34–35
  conversion, holding SE, of 46–50
  creditors, protection of 10
  employee involvement 16, 509
  formation 7
    conversion, by 52–54, 517–518
    holding SE, of 12, 516–517
    merger, by 37–45, 513–516
    subsidiary SE, of 12, 50–52, 517
  general meeting 59–62, 520–522
  head office 7–8, 11, 509
  laws implementing 541–544
  legal personality and 16, 509
  minority shareholders, protection of 10
  name 32–33, 512
  one-tier system 519–520
  opposition to formation of SE 10
  registered office 7–8, 11, 33–34
  special negotiating body 16
  tax provisions, absence of 98–99
  transfer of registered office 11–13, 509,
    510–512
  two-tier system 518–520
  winding up, liquidation insolvency and
    cessation of payment 73, 522–523
credit institutions
  annual accounts and consolidated accounts
    68, 522
creditors
  protection of 10, 39, 47
    Belgium 156
    Estonia 309
    Germany 242, 246
    Hungary 335
    Netherlands 273, 275
    Slovak Republic 401, 405–406
  shareholders and 29–30
creditors, rights of
  Belgium 156
cross-border mergers
  national law, under 4–7
  Societas Europaea and 7–11

definition of *Societas Europaea* 28–29
Denmark
  acts committed on behalf of SE in
    formation 187
  annual accounts and consolidated accounts
    accounting principles 196–197
    auditors 197–198
  applicable law 201
  capital 180–183
  cessation of payments 200
  conversion, formation by 186–187
  corporate purpose 180
  employee involvement
    protection of employee representatives
      196
    special negotiating body 194–196
  employee participation 17,
    196
  formation
    capital 180–183
    conversion, by 186–187
    corporate purpose 180
    founding parties 176–177
    holding SE, of 185
    merger, by 183–185
    name 177–178

555

Index

Denmark (*cont.*)
    registered office 178–180
    subsidiary SE, of 185–186
  founding parties 176–177
  general meeting 189
    decision-making process 189–190
    shareholders' rights and obligations 190–191
  generally 175, 202
  holding SE, formation of 185
  income tax 201–202
  insolvency 199–200
  laws implementing the Regulation and the Directive 542
  legal personality 187–188
  liability of members 194
  liquidation 199
  management 188–189
    appointment and removal 192–193
    liability of members 194
    one-tier 188, 191–192
    representation 193
    two-tier 191–192
  merger, formation by 183–185
  name 177–178
  publication 187
  reasons to opt for SE 175–176
  registered office 178–180
  registration 187
  representation 193
  special negotiating body 194–196
  subsidiary SE, formation of 185–186
  supervision by national authorities 198
  tax treatment 201–202
  transfer of registered office 179–180
  value added tax 202
  winding up 198–199
Directive, the *see* Council Directive 2001/86/EC
dissolution 5
  see also cessation of payments; insolvency; liquidation; winding up
dividend withholding tax *see* withholding tax

employee involvement 16, 509
  acquired rights 22
  agreement 19, 85
    absence of agreement within negotiations period 16, 19, 86–87
    conclusion of 83, 85–87
    content and form 85–86, 534
    none reached, where 17, 19
    registration of SE and 35
    renegotiation 89
    SE formed by conversion and 86
    voting rules 86
  articles and 58
  Austria 134–141
  'before and after' principle 17–18, 21, 78–79
  Belgium 165–166
  companies without employees and 18, 35
  confidentiality 95–96, 535–536
    Austria 140
    Finland 228
    Sweden 448
    United Kingdom 474
  Denmark 194–196
  the Directive and 16, 27, 509, 530–540
    application 28
    compliance 96, 536
    confidentiality 535–536
    content of agreement 534
    duration of negotiations 535
    entry into force 79
    information and consultation of employees 536
    laws implementing 28, 541–544
    misuse of procedures 536
    negotiation procedure 535
    protection of employee representatives 536
    reservation and confidentiality 535–536
    scope 79
    special negotiating body 532–534
    standard rules 19–20, 535, 538–540
    transposition 97
  employee participation distinguished 17
  Estonia 322
  European works council 94–95
  exiting employee involvement rights, United Kingdom 474
  Finland 226–228
  generally 16–18, 78–79, 97

Germany 16–17, 253–255
Hungary 341–342
Iceland 498–499
information and consultation 17, 90–91, 536
  Austria 138
  EWC Directive and 17
  United Kingdom 474
judicial remedy, Hungary 342
legal personality and 16
Lithuania 356–358
misuse of procedure 96, 536
national rules 95
negotiation procedure 80–85, 535
  see also special negotiating body
Netherlands 284–287
Poland 385–387
post-formation 22–23
protection of employee representatives 96–97
  Austria 139–140
  Belgium 166
  Denmark 196
  the Directive and 536
  Estonia 322
  Finland 228
  Hungary 342
  Netherlands 287
  Poland 386–387
  Sweden 447
  United Kingdom 473
registration of SE and 16, 18, 19, 20, 21, 35, 39, 44
representative body 536
  appointment of members 88
  composition 88
  continued application of standard rules 89
  creation 87–91
  duty to cooperate 89
  funding 91
  information and consultation 88–89
  information provided to employee representatives 90–91
  internal measures 91
  meetings 89–90
  operation 89–91, 536
  renegotiation of agreements 89
  role 88–89
  standard rules 87–91
reservation and confidentiality 95–96, 535–536
  Austria 140
  Slovak Republic 415–416
special negotiating body *see* special negotiating body
standard rules 19–20, 87–94
  Austria 137–139
  continued application 89
  the Directive and 19, 535, 538–540
  employee participation 91–94
  Finland 227–228
  representative body, creation of 87–91
  Sweden 446
Sweden 445–448
United Kingdom 472–474, 483
works councils 94–95
  Austria 137–138
  Netherlands 284–285
employee participation 16–17, 26, 78, 91
  Austria 17, 138–139
  avoiding 18–24
  'before and after' principle 17–18, 21, 78–79
  Belgium 166
  companies without employees and 18, 35
  cross-border transfers and 5
  definition 16
  Denmark 17, 196
  employee involvement distinguished 17
  Estonia 322
  Finland 17
  formation of SEs
    conversion, by 94
    holding SE, as 93–94
    merger, by 4–5, 10, 93–94
    subsidiary SE, as 93–94
  Germany 16–17, 254
  Luxembourg 17
  Netherlands 17, 286–287
  Poland 17, 386
  registration of SE and 16, 18, 19, 20, 21, 35, 39, 44
  Slovak Republic 17, 415–416
  structure of company and 17

employee participation (*cont.*)
   Sweden 17, 447
   transfer of registered office and 5
   United Kingdom 473
   see also employee involvement; employee representatives; special negotiating body
employee representatives
   information provided to 90–91
   protection of 96–97, 536
      Austria 139–140, 141
      Belgium 166
      Denmark 196
      Estonia 322
      Finland 228
      Hungary 342
      Netherlands 287
      Poland 386–387
      Sweden 447
      United Kingdom 473
   supervisory board, membership of 62
   see also representative body; special negotiating body
employees, protection of 45, 47, 275
Estonia
   acts committed on behalf of SE in formation 312
   annual accounts and consolidated accounts
      accounting principles 322–323
      auditors 324
   applicable law 328
   capital 305–306
   conversion, formation by 311–312
   corporate income tax 328–329
   corporate purpose 305
   creditors, protection of 309
   employee involvement
      generally 322
      protection of employee representatives 322
      special negotiating body 322
   employee participation 322
   excise tax 329
   formation
      capital 305–306
      conversion, by 311–312
      corporate purpose 305

      founding parties 302
      holding SE, of 310–311
      merger, by *see* merger, formation by *below*
      name 302–303
      registered office 303
      subsidiary SE, of 311
      transfer of registered office 304–305
   founding parties 302
   general meeting
      decision-making process 315–317
      shareholders' rights and obligations 317
   generally 300–301, 329–330
   holding SE, formation of 310–311
   income tax 328–329
   insolvency 325–328
   laws implementing the Regulation and the Directive 542
   legal personality 314
   liability of members 320–321
   liquidation 325
   management
      appointment and removal 319
      generally 317
      liability of members 320–321
      one-tier system 15, 317–319
      representation 320
      two-tier system 15, 319, 320
   merger, formation by
      acquisition by company holding 90 or more of shares in another company 309
      avoidance of merger 310
      creditors' rights 309
      minority shareholders 308–309
      procedure and publication requirements 306–307
      publication 307
      right to object to participation 307–308
   minority shareholders, protection of 308–309, 311
   name 302–303
   publication 307, 310, 313–314
   reasons to opt for SE 302
   registered office 303
      transfer 304–305
   registration 313–314
   representation 320

special negotiating body 322
subsidiary SE, formation of 311
supervision by national authorities 324
tax treatment 328–329
transfer of registered office 304–305
value added tax 329
winding up 324–325
euro 34, 68
European Central Bank 34
European cooperative society (SCE) 27
European Economic Area (EEA) 27, 33
   tax treatment of SEs 107–108
   see also Iceland; Liechtenstein; Norway
European economic interest grouping (EEIG) 98
   allocation of profits and losses 31
   board of managers 31
   characteristics 30
   distribution of profits 31
   introduction 26–27
   joint and several liability 31
   management 31
   nationality requirements 32
   purpose 30, 31
   Societas Europaea compared 30–32
   tax treatment 31, 98
   unlimited liability 31
European Free Trade Association (EFTA) 27, 488
European works council 94–95
   see also works councils
euros
   annual accounts and consolidated accounts in 68
excise tax
   Estonia 329
   Finland 235
   Slovak Republic 423
exit tax 104–106
experts' report 41, 48

financial institutions
   annual accounts and consolidated accounts 68, 522
Finland
   acts committed on behalf of SE in formation 217–218

annual accounts and consolidated accounts 228–230
   accounting principles 229
   auditors 230
applicable law 234
capital 210
cessation of payments 234
conversion, formation by 206, 217
corporate purpose 209–210
debt restructuring 233
employee involvement 226–228
   confidentiality 228
   protection of employee representatives 228
   special negotiating body 226
   standard rules 227–228
employee participation 17
excise tax 235
formation
   capital 210
   conversion, by 206, 217
   corporate purpose 209–210
   founding parties 205–206
   generally 205
   holding SE, of 205, 215–216
   income tax and 235
   merger, by 205, 210–215
   name 206
   registered office 206–207
   subsidiary SE, of 205, 216–217
   transfer of registered office 207–209
founding parties 205–206
general meeting
   decision-making process 219–220
   shareholders' rights and obligations 220–221
generally 204, 235–236
holding SE, formation of 205, 215–216
income tax 234–235
insolvency 232–233
   debt restructuring 233
laws implementing the Regulation and the Directive 542
legal personality 218
liability of members 225
liquidation 231
   in bankruptcy 233

559

Finland (*cont.*)
  involuntary 232
  procedure 231
  voluntary 231
  management
    appointment and removal 223–224
    liability of members 225
    one-tier system 221–222
    representation 224–225
    two-tier system 221–222
  merger, formation by 205, 210–215
  name 206
  publication 218
  real estate tax 235
  reasons to opt for SE 204–205
  registered office 206–207
    transfer 207–209
  registration 218
  representation 224–225
  special negotiating body 226
  subsidiary SE, formation of 205, 216–217
  supervision by national authorities 230–231
  tax treatment 234–235
  transfer of registered office 207–209
    inbound 209
    outbound 207–208
  transfer tax 235
  value added tax 235
  winding up 231
formation *see* capital; conversion; corporate purpose; founding parties; head office; holding SE; merger; name; registered office; subsidiaries; transfer of head office; transfer of registered office
founding parties
  Austria 121
  Belgium 149
  Denmark 176–177
  Estonia 302
  Finland 205–206
  Germany 240
  Hungary 333
  Iceland 489–490
  Lithuania 347
  Netherlands 266
  Poland 372
  Slovak Republic 399–400

  Sweden 427–428
  United Kingdom 458
freedom of establishment 5, 10
freedom of movement 3–4

general meeting 59–62, 520–522
  agenda 15, 60
  amendments to articles of SE 61–62
  Austria 129–131
  authority to call 60
  Belgium 160–162
  conversion into national company, approval of 74
  decision-making process
    Austria 129–130
    Belgium 160–162
    Denmark 189–190
    Estonia 315–317
    Finland 219–220
    Germany 249
    Hungary 338–339
    Iceland 494–495
    Lithuania 353
    Poland 378–379
    Slovak Republic 410–411
    Sweden 441
    United Kingdom 468–469
  Denmark 189–191
  Estonia 315–317
  Finland 219–221
  formation of SE by merger, approval 39
  Germany 249–250
  Hungary 338–339
  Iceland 494–497
  Lithuania 352–354
  Netherlands 279–280
  organisation 60
  Poland 378–380
  powers 59–60
  quorum 61
  shareholders' rights and obligations
    agenda 15, 60
    Austria 131
    Belgium 162
    Denmark 190–191
    Estonia 317
    Finland 220–221

Index

Germany 250
Hungary 339
Iceland 495–497
Lithuania 353–354
Poland 379–380
Slovak Republic 411
Sweden 442
United Kingdom 469
Slovak Republic 410–411
Sweden 441–442
transfer of registered office, approval 69, 70–71
United Kingdom 468–469
voting 60, 61
   tie votes 62, 68
Germany
  acts committed on behalf of SE in formation 248
  annual accounts and consolidated accounts
    accounting principles 255
    auditors 255
  applicable law 256
  appraisal right 245–246
  capital 243
  cessation of payments 256
  conversion, formation by 248, 261
  corporate purpose 243
  creditors, protection of 242, 246
  employee involvement 253–255
  employee participation 16–17, 254
  employee representation (*Mitbestimmung*) 16–17
  formation
    capital 243
    conversion, by 248, 261
    corporate purpose 243
    founding parties 240
    holding SE, of 246–248, 261
    merger, by 243–246
    name 240
    registered office 240–242
    subsidiary SE, of 248, 261
  founding parties 240
  general meeting 249–250
    decision-making process 249–250
    shareholders' rights and obligations 250
  generally 238–239, 262

  holding SE
    formation 246–248, 261
    tax treatment 261
  insolvency 256
  laws implementing the Regulation and the Directive 542
  legal personality 249
  liability of members 253
  liquidation 255–256
  management
    appointment and removal 252–253
    liability of members 253
    one-tier system 15, 251–252
    representation 253
    two-tier supervision 15, 250–251
  merger, formation by 243–246
  minority shareholders, protection of 242, 244
  name 240
  publication 248–249
  reasons to opt for SE 239–240
  registered office 240–242
    transfer 241–242, 260
  registration 248–249
  representation 253
  review of share-exchange ratio 244–245
  special negotiating body 253–254
  subsidiary SE
    formation 248, 261
    tax treatment 261
  supervision by national authorities 255
  tax treatment
    conversion of public limited company into SE 261
    generally 256
    holding SE 261
    inbound mergers 257–258
    outbound mergers 258–260
    subsidiary SE 261
    transfer of registered office and place of effective management 260
  transfer of registered office 241–242, 260
  winding up 255

head office
  concept of 8–9
  definition 13, 33

561

head office (*cont.*)
  Denmark 178
  outside of European Union 36, 37, 50
  registered office and 33, 36, 37, 69, 510
    regularisation of location 33–34
  the Regulation and 7–8, 11, 509
  SE formed by merger, of 8
  situation 33
  transfer *see* transfer of head office
head office (*siège réel*) theory 36
holding SE, formation by incorporation as 12, 29, 35, 46–50, 516–517
  Austria 126
  Belgium 157
  Denmark 185
  draft terms for formation 47–48
  employee participation and 93–94
  Estonia 310–311
  experts' report 48
  Finland 205, 215–216
  Germany 246–248, 261
  Hungary 337
  Iceland 493
  legal personality 50
  Lithuania 350
  nationality requirements 32
  Netherlands 274–275
  Poland 375–376
  procedure 12, 46–50
  publication 50
  registration 50, 55
  share-exchange ratio 47
  Slovak Republic 406
  special negotiating body 80–81
  Sweden 437–438
  terms of formation 47–49
  United Kingdom 464–465
Hungary
  acts committed on behalf of SE in formation 337
  annual accounts and consolidated accounts
    accounting principles 342
    auditors 342–343
  applicable law 343
  capital 336
  cessation of payments 343
  conversion, formation by 337

corporate purpose 336
corporate tax
  adjustment of tax base 344
  carry forward of losses 344
creditors, protection of 335
employee involvement 341
  judicial remedy 342
  protection of employee representatives 342
  special negotiating body 341–342
formation
  capital 336
  conversion, by 337
  corporate purpose 336
  founding parties 333
  holding SE, of 337
  merger, by 337
  name 333
  registered office 333–334
  subsidiary SE, of 337
  transfer of registered office 334–336
founding parties 333
general meeting
  decision-making process 338–339
  shareholders' rights and obligations 339
generally 332, 345
holding SE, formation of 337
income tax 343–344
insolvency 343
laws implementing the Regulation and the Directive 542
legal personality 338
liquidation 343
local business tax 345
management
  appointment and removal 341
  one-tier system 339–340
  two-tier system 340–341
merger, formation by 337
minority shareholders, protection of 334–335
name 333
publication 337–338
registered office 333–334
registration 337–338
special negotiating body 341–342
subsidiary SE, formation of 337

Index

supervision by national authorities 343
tax treatment 343–345
transfer of registered office 334–336
  accounting 335–336
  creditors, protection of 335
  minority shareholders, protection of 334–335
value added tax 344
winding up 343

Iceland
  acts committed on behalf of SE in formation 493
  annual accounts and consolidated accounts
    accounting principles 499
    auditors 499
  applicable law 501
  capital 492
  cessation of payments 501
  conversion, formation by 493
  corporate purpose 492
  employee involvement 498–499
  formation
    capital 492
    conversion, by 493
    corporate purpose 492
    founding parties 489–490
    holding SE, of 493
    merger, by 492–493
    name 490
    registered office 490–492
    subsidiary SE, of 493
  founding parties 489–490
  general meeting
    decision-making process 494–495
    shareholders' rights and obligations 495–497
  generally 27, 488–489
  holding SE, formation of 493
  income tax 502
  insolvency 501
  laws implementing the Regulation and the Directive 543
  legal personality 494
  liability of members 498
  liquidation 501
  management
    appointment and removal 498
    liability of members 498
    one-tier system 497–498
    representation 498
    two-tier system 497–498
  merger, formation by 492–493
  name 490
  net wealth tax 502
  publication 493–494
  reasons to opt for SE 489
  registered office 490–492
  registration 493–494
  social security contributions 502
  subsidiary SE, formation of 493
  supervision by national authorities 499–500
  tax treatment 501–502
  transfer of registered office 13, 490–492
  value added tax 502
  winding up 500–501
income tax
  Austria 142–144
  Belgium 171–173
  corporate tax 76
    Austria 142–144
    Belgium 171
    Estonia 328–329
    Hungary 343–344
    Lithuania 363–364
    Netherlands 291–295
    United Kingdom 479–480
  Denmark 201–202
  Estonia 328–329
  Finland 234–235
  Hungary 343–344
  Iceland 502
  Netherlands 291–296
  Poland 391–395
  Slovak Republic 422
  United Kingdom 479–480
  withholding tax *see* withholding tax
incorporation theory 36
insolvency 73, 522–523
  Austria 142
  Belgium 169–170
  Denmark 199–200
  Estonia 325–328
  Finland 232–233

Index

insolvency (*cont.*)
  formalities 73
  Germany 256
  Hungary 343
  Iceland 501
  Netherlands 290
  Poland 389, 390–391
  Slovak Republic 418, 420–421
  Sweden 431–432, 450
  transfer of registered office and 68, 69
  United Kingdom 477–478
insurance companies
  annual accounts and consolidated accounts 68, 522
  mergers and 38

judicial review 38

land tax
  United Kingdom 480, 481
Latvia
  laws implementing the Regulation and the Directive 543
legal personality 16, 29–30, 50, 509
  Austria 128–129
  Belgium 160
  Denmark 187–188
  employee involvement and 16
  Estonia 314
  Finland 218
  Germany 249
  Hungary 338
  Iceland 494
  Lithuania 351–352
  loss of 5
  Netherlands 277
  Poland 377
  shareholder liability and 29–30
  Slovak Republic 409
  Sweden 440
  transfer of registered office and 5, 68
  United Kingdom 467
liability
  members, of 63–64
    Austria 134
    Belgium 165
    Denmark 194

EEIGs 31
Estonia 320–321
Finland 225
Germany 253
Lithuania 356
Netherlands 283–284
Poland 384–385
Sweden 445
shareholders, of 29–30, 31
Liechtenstein 27
transfer of registered office 13
limited-liability companies *see* public limited-liability company
liquidation 5, 73, 522–523
  Austria 142
  Belgium 169
  Denmark 199
  Estonia 325
  failure to regularise location of head office and registered office 34
  Finland 231–232
  formalities 73
  Germany 255–256
  Hungary 343
  Iceland 501
  Lithuania 361–362
  Netherlands 289–290
  Poland 389–390
  Slovak Republic 418, 419–420
  Sweden 431–432, 450
  transfer of registered office and 68
  United Kingdom 478–479
Lithuania
  acts committed on behalf of SE in formation 351
  annual accounts and consolidated accounts
    accounting principles 358–359
    auditors 359
  applicable law 362–363
  capital 348–349
  cessation of payments 362
  conversion, formation of SE by 350–351
  corporate form, change of 366
  corporate tax 363–364
  employee involvement 356–358
  formation
    capital 348–349

564

Index

conversion, by 350–351
founding parties 347
generally 347
holding SE, of 350
merger, by 349–350
name 348
registered office 348
subsidiary SE, of 350
transfer of registered office 348
founding parties 347
general meeting
   decision-making process 353
   generally 352–353
   shareholders' rights and obligations 353–354
generally 347, 367–368
head office, transfer 366
holding SE, formation of 350
land tax 365
laws implementing the Regulation and the Directive 543
legal personality 351–352
liquidation 361–362
management
   appointment and removal 355
   generally 352
   liability of members 356
   one-tier system 354–355
   representation 355–356
   two-tier system 354–355
merger, formation of SE by 349–350
name 348
property tax 365
publication 351–352
registered office 348
   transfer 348
registration 351–352
reorganisation of company 360–361
subsidiary SE, formation of 350
supervision by national authorities 359–360
tax treatment
   corporate form, change in 366
   corporate tax 363–364
   cross-border merger and 367
   generally 363
   land tax 365
   property tax 365

   subsidiary SE, establishment of 366
   tax framework for formation of SE 365–366
   tax-free merger, consequences of 366
   transfer of head office 366
   transfer of registered office 367
   value added tax 364–365
   withholding tax 364
transfer of head office 366
transfer of registered office 348
value added tax 364–365
winding up 360–362
withholding tax 364
local business tax
   Hungary 345
Luxembourg
   employee participation 17

management
   appointment and removal 21, 54–54, 63–64, 65
      Austria 133
      Belgium 164–165
      conditions of eligibility 64
      Denmark 192–193
      Estonia 319, 320
      Finland 223–224
      Germany 252–253
      Hungary 341
      Iceland 498
      Lithuania 355
      Netherlands 282–283
      Poland 383
      Slovak Republic 414
      Sweden 444
      United Kingdom 471–472
   Austria 15, 129–133
   Belgium 162–165
   central management 33
      see also head office
   conditions of eligibility 64
   conflicts of interest 66
   daily management, delegation of 65
      Belgium 162–163
      Denmark 191–194
      EEIGs, of 31–32
      Estonia 15, 317–321

management (*cont.*)
  Finland 221–225
  generally 15, 31
  Germany 15, 250–253
  Hungary 339–341
  Iceland 497–498
  liability 63–64
    Austria 134
    Belgium 165
    Denmark 194
    Finland 225
    Germany 253
    Iceland 498
    Lithuania 356
    Netherlands 283–284
    Poland 384–385
    Slovak Republic 414–415
    Sweden 445
    United Kingdom 472
  Lithuania 354–356
  Netherlands 15, 281–284
  one-tier system 15, 32, 59, 62–63, 67–68, 519–520
    Austria 15, 129, 131–132
    Belgium 162–163
    Denmark 191–192
    Estonia 317–319
    Finland 221–222
    Germany 251–252
    Hungary 339–340
    Iceland 497–498
    Lithuania 354–355
    Netherlands 282, 283, 284
    Poland 380–383, 384–385
    Slovak Republic 412–413
    Sweden 442
    United Kingdom 469–470
  Poland 380–385
  powers and functioning 62–63
  representation
    Belgium 165
    Denmark 193
    Estonia 320
    Finland 224–225
    Germany 253
    Iceland 498
    Lithuania 355–356
    Netherlands 283
    Poland 384
    Slovak Republic 414
    Sweden 445
  Slovak Republic 15, 411–415
  Sweden 442–445
  two-tier system 15, 32, 59, 62–67, 518–520
    Austria 15, 129, 131, 132–133
    Belgium 163–165
    Denmark 191–192
    Estonia 15, 319, 320
    Finland 221–222
    Germany 15, 250–251
    Hungary 340–341
    Iceland 497–498
    Lithuania 354–355
    Netherlands 15, 281, 282–283
    Poland 383–385
    Slovak Republic 15, 411–412
    Sweden 442, 443–444
    United Kingdom 470–471, 482, 483
  United Kingdom 469–472, 482, 483
management reports 42
managing director
  Sweden 444–445
merger
  acquisition, by 35–38
    definition 37–38
    see also wholly-owned subsidiary *below*
  avoidance 45
    Belgium 156
    Estonia 310
    Sweden 437
  banks and 38
  cross-border mergers 4–7
    national law, under 4–7
    Societas Europaea and 7–11
  double scrutiny of 9
  formation by merger through acquisition by parent company holding 90of share capital of subsidiary 35, 45–46
    Belgium 156
    Estonia 309
  formation of new company, by 37, 38
    definition 38
  formation of SE by 29, 35, 37–45, 513–516
    accounting statement 40–41

566

administrative oversight 43
approval 39
articles, amendments to 38, 42
assets and liabilities, ownership of 38, 45
Austria 124–125
Belgium 152–155
certificate of completion of pre-merger acts and formalities 9, 10, 38, 43–44, 71
company holding 90or more of shares in another company 156, 309
Denmark 183–185
draft terms of merger 18, 39–42, 43, 44, 80
employee participation and 4–5, 10, 93–94
employment rights and 45
Estonia 306–310
experts' report 41
Finland 205, 210–215
Germany 243–246
Hungary 337
Iceland 492–493
judicial oversight 43
Lithuania 349–350
nationality requirements 32
Netherlands 270–274
notary, role of 9, 43
opposition to 10, 13, 38, 272, 307
parent company holding 90of share capital of subsidiary 35, 45–46
Poland 374–375
procedure 38–45
publication 41–42
registration 44, 55
share-exchange ratio 41
Slovak Republic 403–406
special negotiating body 81–82
Sweden 432–437, 452
Third Company Law Directive 37, 38–39
United Kingdom 462–464
insurance companies and 38
subsidiary specially created for the purpose, with 13
tax treatment 6–7, 23, 110–113

wholly owned subsidiary, acquisition of 46
Belgium 156
Sweden 436–437
minority shareholders, protection of 10, 39, 43, 47
Belgium 156, 157
Estonia 308–309, 311
Germany 242, 244
Hungary 334–335
Netherlands 273, 275
Slovak Republic 401, 404–405, 406
Sweden 436, 438

name 32–33, 512
Austria 121–122
Belgium 149
Denmark 177–178
Estonia 302–303
Finland 206
Germany 240
holding out as SE 32
Hungary 333
Iceland 490
Lithuania 348
Netherlands 266
Poland 372
'SE', use of 32–33
Slovak Republic 400
Sweden 428
United Kingdom 458
national authorities
supervision by *see* supervision by national authorities
national company
conversion into 73–74
national company law 14, 15
cross-border mobility under 38–68
national official gazettes
publication in 41, 44, 50, 52, 54, 55, 72
Netherlands
acts committed on behalf of SE in formation 276–277
annual accounts and consolidated accounts
accounting principles 288
auditors 288
applicable law 291
capital 270

Netherlands (*cont.*)
  capital contributions tax 297
  cessation of payments 290–291
  conversion, formation by 276
  corporate purpose 270
  corporate tax
    Community directives 292–293
    conversion of NV into SE (and vice versa) 293
    double taxation 292
    investment institutions 292
    tax group 292
    tax residency 291–292
    transfer of registered office 293–295
  creditors, protection of 273, 275
  depositary receipts for shares 15
  dividend withholding tax 297–298
  employee involvement
    Employee Involvement Act 285–287
    European Works Council Act 285
    generally 284
    protection of employee representatives 287
    special negotiating body 285–286
    Works Council Act 284–285
  employee participation 17, 286–287
  formation
    capital 270
    conversion, by 276
    corporate purpose 270
    founding parties 266
    holding SE, of *see* holding SE, formation of *below*
    merger, by *see* merger, formation by *below*
    name 266
    registered office 266–270
    subsidiary SE, of 275–276
  founding parties 266
  general meeting
    decision-making process 279–280
    shareholders' rights and obligations 280
    generally 265
  head office 8
  holding SE, formation of
    creditors, protection of 275
    employees, protection of 275
    minority shareholders, protection of 275
    procedure and publication requirements 274–275
    prospectus and offer document 275
  income tax
    corporate tax 291–295
    personal income tax 295–296
  insolvency 290
  laws implementing the Regulation and the Directive 543
  legal personality 277
  liability of members 283–284
  liquidation 289–290
  management
    appointment and removal 282–283
    generally 281
    liability of members 283–284
    one-tier system 15, 282, 283
    representation 283
    two-tier system 15, 281, 282–283
  merger, formation by
    creditors, protection of 273
    holders of depository receipts 273–274
    intra-group mergers 273
    minority shareholders, protection of 273
    procedure 270–272
    public interest opposition 272
    publication 271
  minority shareholders, protection of 273, 275
  name 266
  personal income tax 295
    transfer of registered office 295–296
  publication 270–272, 274–275, 277
  reasonableness and fairness 278–279
  reasons to opt for SE 266
  registered office 266–270
  registration 272, 277
  representation 283
  special negotiating body 285–286
  structure regime 277–278
  supervision by national authorities 288–289
  tax treatment 291–298
  transfer of registered office 267–270, 293–297, 298
    capital contributions tax 297
    corporate tax 293–295
    dividend withholding tax 298

inbound 269–270, 294–295, 296, 298
outbound 267–269, 293–294, 295–296, 298
personal income tax 295–296
value added tax 296–297
value added tax 296
tax group 296
transfer of registered office 296–297
winding up 289
non-profit making organisations 51
Norway 27
laws implementing the Regulation and the Directive 543–544
transfer of registered office 13
notary, role of 9, 43, 44, 71

OECD model convention
tax treaties 106–107
Office for Official Publications 56
Official Journal of the European Communities 37, 44, 50, 52, 54, 72
official national gazettes 41, 44
one-tier management system *see* management
organisation *see* general meeting; management
Poland
accounts and consolidated accounts, auditors 388
acts committed on behalf of SE in formation 377
annual accounts and consolidated accounts, accounting principles 387–388
applicable law 391
capital 373–374
capital contributions tax 396
cessation of payments 389
conversion, formation by 376–377
corporate purpose 373
employee involvement 385
protection of employee representatives 386–387
special negotiating body 385–386
employee participation 17, 386
formation
capital 373–374
conversion, by 376–377
corporate purpose 373
founding parties 372

holding SE, of 375–376
merger, by 374–375
name 372
registered office 372–373
subsidiary SE, of 376
founding parties 372
general meeting
decision-making process 378–379
shareholders' rights and obligations 379–380
generally 370–371, 396
holding SE, formation of 375–376
income tax 391–395
insolvency 389, 390–391
laws implementing the Regulation and the Directive 544
legal personality 377
liability of members 384–385
liquidation 389–390
management 380
amendment of articles 384
liability of members 384–385
one-tier system 380–383, 384–385
representation 384
two-tier system 383–385
merger, formation by 374–375
name 372
publication 377
reasons to opt for SE 371–372
registered office 372–373
registration 377
special negotiating body 385–386
appointment of members 385–386
election of members 386
generally 385
subsidiary SE, formation of 376
supervision by national authorities 388–389
tax treatment 391–396
capital contributions tax 396
income tax 391–395
value added tax 395
value added tax 395
winding up 389

property tax
Iceland 502
Lithuania 365

569

Index

public financing 30
public limited-liability company
   SE as 29, 30, 75
publication 37, 44–45, 52, 55–56
   Austria 128
   Belgium 155, 157, 159
   conversion, formation of SE by 54
   conversion into national company 74
   date of 56
   deletion of registration, of 55
   Denmark 187
   effects 56
   Estonia 307, 310, 313–314
   Finland 218
   formalities 45
   Germany 248–249
   holding SE, formation by incorporation as 50
   Hungary 337–338
   Iceland 493–494
   Lithuania 351–352
   merger, formation of SE by 41–42
   national official gazettes, in 41, 44, 50, 52, 54, 55, 72
   Netherlands 271, 274–275, 277
   Office for Official Publications 56
   Official Journal of the European Communities, in 37, 44, 50, 52, 54, 55–56
   Poland 377
   Slovak Republic 408–409
   subsidiary, formation by incorporation as 52
   Sweden 432–436, 437–438, 439–440
   transfer of registered office, of 56, 72
   United Kingdom 467
   winding up, liquidation, insolvency or cessation of payment, initiation and termination of procedures 73

real estate tax
   Finland 235
   Slovak Republic 423
registered office 7–8, 11, 30, 33–34, 510
   Austria 122–124
   Belgium 149–150
   Denmark 178–180
   Estonia 303

   Finland 206–207
   Germany 240–242
   head office and 33, 36, 37, 69
      regularisation of location 33–34
   Hungary 333–334
   Iceland 490–492
   incorporation theory 36
   Lithuania 348
   Netherlands 266–270
   Poland 372–373
   publication and 37
   SE formed by merger, of 8
   situation 33
   Slovak Republic 400–402
   Sweden 428–429
   transfer *see* transfer of registered office
   United Kingdom 458–459
registration 37, 44, 45, 50, 54–55
   Austria 128
   Belgium 159
   changes to information on file 55
   conversion, SE formed by 54
   Denmark 187
   employee involvement and 16, 18, 19, 20, 21, 35, 39, 44
   Estonia 313–314
   Finland 218
   Germany 248–249
   holding SE, incorporation as 50, 55
   Hungary 337–338
   Iceland 493–494
   Lithuania 351–352
   merger, SE formed by 44, 55
   national registry 41, 49
   Netherlands 272, 277
   Poland 377
   procedure 54–55
   publication *see* publication
   Slovak Republic 408–409
   subsidiary, incorporation as 51–52
   Sweden 439–440
   transfer of registered office, of 71–72
   United Kingdom 467
Regulation, the *see* Council Regulation No 2157/2001
reorganisation of company
   Lithuania 360–361

Index

representation
  Belgium 165
  Denmark 193
  Estonia 320
  Finland 224–225
  Germany 253
  Netherlands 283
representative body
  appointment of members 88
  composition 88
  continued application of standard rules 89
  creation 87–91
  the Directive and 536
  duty to cooperate 89
  funding 91
  information and consultation 88–89
  information provided to employee representatives 90–91
  internal measures 91
  meetings 89–90
  operation 89–91, 536
  renegotiation of agreements 89
  role 88–89
  standard rules 87–91
  see also employee involvement; employee representatives
Republic of Estonia *see* Estonia
Republic of Hungary *see* Hungary
Republic of Lithuania *see* Lithuania

Sanders, Piet 16
seat 3
  indirect transfer 13
  transfer 5, 6, 7, 13
  see also head office; registered office
securities 35
shareholders
  creditors and 29–30
  experts' report 41, 48
  liability 29–30, 31
  protection of 11
  rights and obligations
    agenda 15, 60
    Austria 131
    Belgium 162
    Denmark 190–191
    Estonia 317

    Finland 220–221
    Germany 250
    Hungary 339
    Iceland 495–497
    Lithuania 353–354
    Poland 379–380
    Slovak Republic 411
    Sweden 442
    United Kingdom 469
  see also general meeting
shares
  applicable law 35
  depositary receipts for 15
  minimum share capital 31, 32, 35
  share capital 34, 35
  share-exchange ratio 47, 244–245
  stapled stock 4
siège réel theory 36
Slovak Republic
  acts committed on behalf of SE in formation 408
  annual accounts and consolidated accounts
    accounting principles 416–417
    auditors 417–418
  applicable law 422
  capital 402
  cessation of payments 418, 421–422
  conversion, formation by 407–408
  corporate purpose 402
  creditors, protection of 401, 405–406
  employee involvement 415–416
  employee participation 17, 415–416
  excise tax 423
  formation 399
    capital 402
    conversion, by 407–408
    corporate purpose 402
    founding parties 399–400
    holding SE, of 406
    merger, by 403–406
    name 400
    registered office 400–402
    subsidiary SE, of 406–407
  founding parties 399–400
  general meeting 410
    decision-making process 410–411
    shareholders' rights and obligations 411

Slovak Republic (*cont.*)
  generally 398, 423–424
  holding SE, formation of 406
  income tax 422
  insolvency 418, 420–421
  laws implementing the Regulation and the Directive 544
  legal personality 409
  liquidation 418, 419–420
  management
    appointment and removal 414
    liability of members 414–415
    one-tier system 412–413
    representation 414
    two-tier system 15, 411–412
  minority shareholders, protection of 401, 404–405, 406
  name 400
  publication 408–409
  real estate tax 423
  reasons to opt for SE 398–399
  registered office 400–401
    obligatory transfer 402
  registration 408–409
  special negotiating body 416
  subsidiary SE, formation of 406–407
  supervision by national authorities 418
  tax treatment 422–423
  transfer of registered office 402
  value added tax 422–423
  winding up 418–419
special negotiating body (SNB)
  agreement
    absence of agreement within negotiations period 16, 19, 86–87
    conclusion of 83, 85–87
    content and form 85–86, 534
    generally 19, 85
    none reached, where 17, 19
    registration of SE and 35
    renegotiation 89
    SE formed by conversion and 86
    voting rules 86
  appointment or election of members 82–83
  Austria 134–137
  Belgium 166
  composition 80–83
    conversion, SEs formed by 80–81
    creation of system for 18, 19, 85–87
    Denmark 194–196
    the Directive and 532–534
    election of members, Poland 386
    Estonia 322
    EWC Directive and 17
    expert assistance 84
    Finland 226
    functioning 84
      assistance of experts 84
      duration of negotiations 84
      duty to cooperate 84
      funding 84–85
      generally 50, 80
    Germany 253–254
    holding SEs 80–81
    Hungary 341–342
    merger, SEs formed by 81–82
    negotiations
      absence of agreement within negotiations period 16, 19, 20, 86–87
      absence or termination 19, 83–84
      applicable legislation 535
      assistance of experts 84
      decision not to open or to terminate 19, 87, 95
      duration 19, 535
      duty to cooperate 84
      funding 84–85
      generally 19
      procedure 80
    Netherlands 285–286
    Poland 385–386
    the Regulation and 16
    role
      absence or termination of negotiations 83–84
      conclusion of agreement 83
    Slovak Republic 416
    subsidiary SEs 80–81
    Sweden 446
    United Kingdom 472
    see also employee representatives
stamp duty
  United Kingdom 480
stamp duty land tax (SDLT)

Index

United Kingdom 480, 481
stamp duty reserve tax (SDRT)
   United Kingdom 480, 481
stapled stock 4
statutes *see* articles
subscribed capital 35, 42
subsidiaries 14–15
   formation by incorporation as subsidiary
      12, 13, 29, 50–52, 517
      applicable law 51, 52
      Austria 126
      Belgium 158
      Denmark 185–186
      employee participation and 93–94
      Estonia 311
      Finland 205, 216–217
      Germany 248, 261
      Hungary 337
      Iceland 493
      Lithuania 350
      nationality requirements 32
      Netherlands 275–276
      procedure 12, 50–52
      publication 52
      registration 51–52
      Slovak Republic 406–407
      special negotiating body 80–81
      Sweden 438
      United Kingdom 465
   formation by merger through acquisition by
      parent company holding 90of share
      capital of subsidiary 35, 45–46
      Belgium 156
      Estonia 309
   formation by merger through acquisition of
      wholly owned subsidiary 46
      Sweden 436–437
   merger with subsidiary specially created for
      the purpose 13
   subsidiary set up by SE 13, 57–58, 510
supervision by national authorities 43
   Austria 141
   Belgium 169
   Denmark 198
   Estonia 324
   Finland 230–231
   Germany 255

Hungary 343
Iceland 499–500
Lithuania 359–360
Netherlands 288–289
Poland 388–389
Slovak Republic 418
Sweden 449
United Kingdom 477
Sweden
   acts committed on behalf of SE in
      formation 439
   annual accounts and consolidated accounts
      accounting principles 448–449
      auditors 449
   applicable law 451
   capital 432
   cessation of payments 431–432, 451
   conversion, formation by 438–439, 453
   corporate purpose 432
   employee involvement 445–446
      confidentiality 448
      damages 448
      protection of employee representatives
         447
      special negotiating body 446
      standard rules 446
   employee participation 17, 447
   formation
      capital 432
      conversion, by 438–439, 453
      corporate purpose 432
      founding parties 427–428
      holding SE, of *see* holding SE, formation
         of *below*
      merger, by *see* merger, formation by
         below
      name 428
      registered office 428–429
      subsidiary SE, of 438, 453
      transfer of registered office 429–432
   founding parties 427–428
   general meeting
      decision-making process 441
      shareholders' rights and obligations 442
   generally 426–427, 454–455
   holding SE, formation of
      minority shareholders 438

Index

Sweden (cont.)
  procedure and publication requirements 437–438
  tax treatment 453
insolvency 431–432, 450
laws implementing the Regulation and the Directive 544
legal personality 440
liability of members 445
liquidation 431–432, 450
management
  appointment and removal 444
  liability of members 445
  managing director 444–445
  one-tier system 442
  representation 445
  two-tier system 442, 443–444
merger, formation by
  acquisition of wholly owned subsidiary 436–437
  avoidance of merger 437
  minority shareholders 436
  procedure and publication requirements 432–436
  right to object to company participating in merger 436
  tax treatment 452
minority shareholders, protection of 436, 438
name 428
publication 432–436, 437–438, 439–440
reasons to opt for SE 427
registered office 428–429
  transfer 429–432
registration 439–440
special negotiating body 446
subsidiary SE, formation of 438, 453
supervision by national authorities 449
tax treatment
  conversion into SE 453
  holding SE, formation of 453
  income tax 451
  merger, formation by 452
  subsidiary SE, formation of 453
  transfer of registered office and head office 453
  value added tax 453
  transfer of head office, tax issues 453
  transfer of registered office 429–432, 453
  tax issues 453
  value added tax 453
  winding up 431–432, 450

tax treatment 4, 13, 31, 98–102
  Austria 142–145
  Belgium 171–173
  capital contributions tax
    Netherlands 297
    Poland 396
  capital duty
    Austria 144–145
    Belgium 173
  corporate tax 76
    Austria 142–144
    Belgium 171
    Estonia 328–329
    Hungary 343–344
    Lithuania 363–364
    Netherlands 291–295
    United Kingdom 479–480
  Denmark 201–202
  directives
    Capital Directive 108
    generally 23, 107–109
    Interest and Royalties Directive 100, 107, 113–114
    Merger Directive 99, 106, 107, 110–113, 114, 256–260, 293
    Netherlands 292–293
    Parent-Subsidiary Directive 99, 107, 109–110, 111, 112, 113, 114, 201, 292
    Savings Directive 108–109
    VAT directives 109
  dividend withholding tax see withholding tax below
  EEA member countries, in 107–108
  EEIGs, of 31, 98
  Estonia 328–329
  excise tax
    Estonia 329
    Slovak Republic 423
  exit tax 104–106
  Finland 234–235
  Germany 256–261

Hungary 343–345
Iceland 501–502
income tax *see* income tax
interest and royalties payments 113–114
land tax
   Lithuania 365
   United Kingdom 480, 481
Lithuania 363–367
local business tax, Hungary 345
mergers 6–7, 23, 110–113
net wealth tax, Iceland 502
Netherlands 291–298
Poland 391–396
property tax
   Iceland 502
   Lithuania 365
real estate tax, Slovak Republic 423
residence 102–106
   Netherlands 291–292
Slovak Republic 422–423
stamp duty, United Kingdom 480
stamp duty land tax (SDLT), United Kingdom 480, 481
stamp duty reserve tax (SDRT), United Kingdom 480, 481
Sweden 451–454
tax treaties 102, 103, 106–107
transfer tax, Finland 235
United Kingdom 479–481
value added tax
   Austria 144
   Belgium 173
   Denmark 202
   Estonia 329
   Finland 235
   Hungary 344
   Iceland 502
   Lithuania 364–365
   Netherlands 296–297
   Poland 395
   United Kingdom 480
   VAT directives 109
withholding tax
   Hungary 343–344
   Lithuania 364
   Netherlands 297–298
   Poland 391

Sweden 454
termination 73
   see also cessation of payments; insolvency; liquidation; winding up
transfer of head office 5–6, 11, 69
   conversion and 52
   cross-border 5–6
   freedom of establishment 5
   Lithuania 366
   restrictions 6, 7
   Sweden 453
   tax rules 13
transfer of registered office 7, 11–13, 68–73, 509, 510–512
   applicable law and 12
   Belgium 150–152
   certificate of completion of requisite acts and formalities 71, 511
   conversion and 52
   Denmark 179–180
   employee participation and 5
   Estonia 304–305
   European Commission consultation document on 5
   Finland 207–209
   general meeting, approval of 69, 70–71
   Germany 241–242, 260
   head office, relocation of 69
   Hungary 334–336
   Iceland 13, 490–492
   insolvency and 68, 69
   legal personality and 5, 68
   Liechtenstein 13
   Lithuania 348
   Netherlands 267–270, 293–297, 298
   Norway 13
   Official Journal of the European Communities, mention in 72
   opposition 13, 69, 72
   procedure 12–13, 69–72
   publication 56, 72
   registration 71–72
   shareholder rights, changes to 70
   Slovak Republic 402
   Sweden 429–432, 453
   tax residency, change of 104
   transfer proposal 69–70

Index

transfer of registered office (*cont.*)
  transfer report 70
  United Kingdom 459–461, 482, 483
  winding up and 68, 69
transfer of seat 5, 6, 7, 13
transfer tax
  Finland 235
two-tier management system *see* management

United Kingdom
  acts committed on behalf of SE in formation 466
  administration 477
  administrative receivership 477–478
  annual accounts and consolidated accounts
    accounting principles 474–476
    auditors 476
  capital 461
  Community directives, implementation 481–482
  composition with creditors 477
  conversion, formation by 465–466
  corporate purpose 461
  corporate tax 479–480
  employee involvement
    complaints procedure 473–474
    confidentiality 474
    exiting employee involvement rights 474
    generally 472, 483
    information and confidentiality 474
    participation rights 473
    protection of employee representatives 473
    special negotiating body 472
  formation 461–462
    capital 461
    conversion, by 465–466
    corporate purpose 461
    founding parties 458
    holding SE, of 464–465
    merger, by 462–464
    name 458
    registered office 458–459
    subsidiary SE, of 465
    transfer of registered office 459–461
  founding parties 458
  general meeting
    decision-making process 468–469
    shareholders' rights and obligations 469
    generally 457–448, 482–483
    holding SE, formation of 464–465
  income tax 479–480
  insolvency 477–478
  laws implementing the Regulation and the Directive 544
  legal personality 467
  liquidation 478
    involuntary 478–479
    voluntary 478
  management
    appointment and removal 471–472
    generally 469–470
    liability of members 472
    two-tier system 470–471, 482, 483
  merger, formation by 462–464
  name 458
  publication 467
  registered office 458–459
  registration 467
  special negotiating body 472
  stamp duty 480
  stamp duty land tax (SDLT) 480, 481
  stamp duty reserve tax (SDRT) 480, 481
  subsidiary SE, formation of 465
  supervision by national authorities 477
  tax treatment 479–481
  transfer of registered office 459–461, 482, 483
  value added tax 480

value added tax
  Austria 144
  Belgium 173
  Denmark 202
  Estonia 329
  Finland 235
  Hungary 344
  Iceland 502
  Lithuania 364–365
  Netherlands 296–297
  Poland 395

576

Slovak Republic 422–423
United Kingdom 480
VAT directives 109

wholly owned subsidiary
  merger by acquisition of 46
    Belgium 156
    Sweden 436–437
winding up 73, 522–523
  Austria 142
  Belgium 169
  Denmark 198–199
  Estonia 324–325
  Finland 231
  formalities 73
  Germany 255
  grounds 44, 73
  Hungary 343

  Iceland 500–501
  Lithuania 360–362
  Netherlands 289
  Poland 389
  Slovak Republic 418–419
  Sweden 431–432, 450
  transfer of registered office and 68, 69
withholding tax
  Hungary 343–344
  Lithuania 364
  Netherlands 297–298
  Poland 391
  Sweden 454
worker participation *see* employee
    participation
works councils 94–95
  Austria 137–138
  Netherlands 284–285